A Grammar of Digo

SIL International®

Publications in Linguistics
Publication 154

Publications in Linguistics is published by SIL International®. The series is a venue for works covering a broad range of topics in linguistics, especially the analytical treatment of minority languages from all parts of the world. While most volumes are authored by members of SIL, suitable works by others also form part of the series.

Series Editor

Susan McQuay

Managing Editor

Eugene Burnham

Proofreader

Eric Kindberg

Production Staff

Priscilla Higby, Production Manager
Judy Benjamin, Compositor
Barbara Alber, Graphic Designer

A Grammar of Digo

A Bantu Language of Kenya and Tanzania

Revised Edition

Steve Nicolle

SIL International®
Dallas, Texas

© 2023 SIL International®
Library of Congress Control Number: 2022944473
ISBN: 978-1-55671-437-5 (pbk)
ISBN: 978-1-55671-492-4 (ePub)
ISSN: 1040-0850

First edition published 2013. First edition revised 2023.

All rights reserved

No part of this publication may be reproduced, stored in a retrieval system, or transmitted in any form or by any means—electronic, mechanical, photocopy, recording, or otherwise—without the express permission of SIL International®. However, short passages, generally understood to be within the limits of fair use, may be quoted without permission.

Data and materials collected by researchers in an era before documentation of permission was standardized may be included in this publication. SIL makes diligent efforts to identify and acknowledge sources and to obtain appropriate permissions wherever possible, acting in good faith and on the best information available at the time of publication.

Copies of this and other publications of SIL International® may be obtained through distributors such as Amazon, Barnes & Noble, other worldwide distributors and, for select volumes, publications.sil.org:

SIL International® Publications
7500 W. Camp Wisdom Road
Dallas, Texas 75236-5629 USA

General inquiry: publications_intl@sil.org
Pending order inquiry: sales@sil.org

Contents

Illustrations	xi
Preface	xiii
Acknowledgments	xv
1 Introduction	1
1.1 Linguistic classification and speech varieties	1
1.2 Geography and environment	4
1.3 Culture and history	4
1.4 Approach and methodology	5
1.5 Abbreviations and glossing conventions	7
1.5.1 Abbreviations	7
1.5.2 Glossing conventions	9
2 Phonology and Orthography	11
2.1 Orthography	11
2.2 Phonology	12
2.2.1 Consonants	12
2.2.2 Vowels	14
2.2.3 Syllable structure	15
2.2.4 Tone	15
3 Noun Phrases	17
3.1 Nominal morphology	17
3.1.1 Noun classes	17
3.1.2 Concord categories for nouns	21

3.1.3 Noun class agreement in conjoined NPs	23
3.1.4 Nominalizing derivational processes	23
3.1.5 Noun compounding	28
3.1.6 Denominalizing processes	29
3.2 Qualificatives	29
3.2.1 Overview	29
3.2.2 Possessives	31
3.2.3 Quantifiers	34
3.2.4 Numerals and *-ngaphi* 'how many/much'	39
3.2.5 Lexical adjectives	41
3.2.6 Phrasal adjectives	44
3.3 Pronouns	47
3.3.1 Scope and definitions	47
3.3.2 Independent pronouns	47
3.3.3 Exclusive pronouns	49
3.3.4 Vocative pronouns	53
3.3.5 Interrogative pronouns	53
3.4 Demonstratives	55
3.4.1 Definition	55
3.4.2 Classification and forms of demonstratives	57
3.4.3 Functions of demonstratives	60
3.4.4 Distribution of demonstrative forms	80
4 Verbal Morphology	**87**
4.1 Structure of the verb group	87
4.1.1 Initial slot	88
4.1.2 Subject concord	90
4.1.3 TAM and negation	92
4.1.4 Relative concord	95
4.1.5 Verb complement	95
4.1.6 Verb root	99
4.1.7 Verb stem	100
4.1.8 Extensions	101
4.1.9 Final slot	111
4.1.10 Postfinal slot	114
4.1.11 Clitics	119
4.2 Irregular and defective verbs	121
4.2.1 *edza* 'come to'	121
4.2.2 *la* 'come from'	122
4.2.3 *pha* 'give'	123
4.2.4 *phiya* 'go to'	123
4.3 Verbal derivation	124

4.3.1 Verb-forming derivational processes	124
4.3.2 Complex predicates and light verbs	124
5 Tense, Aspect, and Movement Markers	**129**
5.1 TAM categories	130
5.1.1 Tenses	131
5.1.2 Aspects	131
5.1.3 Status markers	131
5.1.4 Movement grams	132
5.1.5 Complex constructions	132
5.1.6 Format of examples	132
5.2 Tenses	132
5.2.1 Absolute tenses	132
5.2.2 Dependent tenses	135
5.2.3 Tenses in relative clauses	138
5.3 Aspects	141
5.3.1 Fully grammaticalized aspects	141
5.3.2 Less grammaticalized aspects	152
5.4 Status markers	158
5.4.1 Simple status markers	158
5.4.2 Complex conditional clauses with *kala*	162
5.5 Movement grams	164
5.5.1 Fully grammaticalized movement grams	165
5.5.2 Less grammaticalized movement grams	168
5.6 Complex constructions	171
5.6.1 Complex constructions with *kala*	171
5.6.2 Complex constructions with *che*	175
5.7 Different forms of *ka-*	176
5.7.1 Evidence from Northeast Coast Bantu languages	177
5.7.2 Historical development	179
6 Other Word Classes	**183**
6.1 Relational expressions	184
6.1.1 The comitative particle *na*	185
6.1.2 Forms preceding associative particle *-a* + noun	188
6.1.3 Expressions preceding comitative particle *na* + noun	191
6.1.4 Locative elements preceding nouns	193
6.1.5 Associative particle *-enye* + noun	194
6.1.6 Nonfinite verb forms	195
6.1.7 Agent phrases in passive sentences	195
6.2 Sentence adverbials and discourse markers	196
6.2.1 Definitions	196

6.2.2 Modal sentence adverbials	197
6.2.3 Question words	197
6.2.4 Markers of speaker attitude and interpersonal relations	198
6.2.5 Logical connectives	200
6.3 Additives	202
6.3.1 Simple additives	202
6.3.2 Referential additives	207
6.4 Adverbs and ideophones	213
6.4.1 Adverbs	214
6.4.2 Ideophones	217
7 Clause and Sentence Structure	**223**
7.1 Basic clause structure	224
7.1.1 Intransitive clauses	224
7.1.2 Transitive clauses	225
7.1.3 Ditransitive clauses	228
7.1.4 Interrogative clauses	229
7.2 Information structure	231
7.2.1 Basic concepts of information structure	231
7.2.2 Switch topics, continued topics, and right-dislocation	232
7.2.3 Topic-comment articulation and predicate focus	237
7.2.4 Identificational articulation and argument focus	238
7.2.5 Presentational articulation and sentence focus	239
7.2.6 The focus marker *che*	241
7.2.7 Text	243
7.3 Relative clauses	245
7.3.1 Introduction	245
7.3.2 Types of relative clause	245
7.3.3 Relativized heads and the NP accessibility hierarchy	252
7.3.4 Functions of relative clauses	258
7.3.5 Phonological variation	260
7.4 Complex sentences	261
7.4.1 Clause chaining	261
7.4.2 Complement clauses	266
7.5 Locative inversion—parameters of variation	271
7.5.1 Parameters of variation	274
8 Being and Having	**281**
8.1 Copula constructions: Forms	281
8.1.1 Invariable constructions	282
8.1.2 Constructions indicating noun class or person/number	284
8.1.3 Aspectual copulas	288

	8.1.4 Hypothetical clauses (if X had been Y)/(if X were Y)	289
	8.1.5 Copula constructions in relative clauses	289
8.2	Copula constructions: Functions	292
	8.2.1 Nominal predicates	292
	8.2.2 Focus predicates	294
	8.2.3 Adjectival predicates	295
	8.2.4 Locative predicates	296
	8.2.5 Existential predicates	298
8.3	Comparative constructions	301
	8.3.1 Superiority	301
	8.3.2 Equality	303
	8.3.3 Sufficiency	304
	8.3.4 Superlative	304
	8.3.5 Excessive	305
	8.3.6 Completive	305
8.4	'Having' or 'being with'	306
	8.4.1 'Having' in simple declarative clauses	306
	8.4.2 'Having' in relative clauses	308
8.5	Examples from a narrative text	309

Appendix A: Sample Texts — 313
- A.1 Narrative text 1: *Mhegi wa Mihambo* — 313
- A.2 Narrative text 2: *Mwiya Anatiwa Dibwani ni Mkaza Ise* — 327
- A.3 Hortatory text: Farewell advice to a son going to study abroad — 338
- A.4 Expository text: *Uvyazi* (Birth) — 346

Appendix B: Wordlist and Botanical Names — 353
- B.1 SIL Comparative African Wordlist — 353
  - 1 Man's physical being — 354
  - 2 Man's nonphysical being — 360
  - 3 Persons — 362
  - 4 Personal interaction — 365
  - 5 Human civilisation — 368
  - 6 Animals — 380
  - 7 Plants — 386
  - 8 Environment — 389
  - 9 Eevents and actions — 393
  - 10 Quality — 396
  - 11 Quantity — 398
  - 12 Grammatical items — 400
- B.2 Botanical names — 402

Appendix C: The Relationship Between Digo and Swahili   407
   C.1 Swahili influence on Digo vocabulary   408
   C.2 Possible Swahili influence on Digo grammar   409
   C.3 Possible Swahili influence on Digo pronunciation   411

Appendix D: Publications on Digo Language and Culture   413

References   415

Author Index   425

Language Index   429

Subject Index   431

Illustrations

Map
1.1 Coastal area of East Africa from Malindi, Kenya, to Tanga, Tanzania   4

Figure
3.1 Singular-plural noun class pairings   19

Tables
2.1 Phonemic consonant chart   13
2.2 Phonemic vowel chart   14
3.1 Noun class prefixes   17
3.2 Noun classes and their concords: adjectives   21
3.3 Noun classes and their concords: other modifiers   22
3.4 Regular morphophonological processes.   23
3.5 Deverbal nominalizations   24
3.6 Noun-to-noun correspondences   25
3.7 Noun-to-verb correspondences   29
3.8 Possessive concords with persons   31
3.9 Possessives with *mya* and *aya*   33
3.10 Selected monosyllabic adjectives   42
3.11 Independent pronouns   48
3.12 Exclusive personal pronoun constructions   50
3.13 Interrogative pronouns   54
3.14 Demonstratives   58

4.1 Template of the verb group	88
4.2 Person markers and noun class prefixes in the SC slot	90
4.3 Person markers in the VC slot	96
4.4 Verbal extensions	101
4.5 Examples of the causative extension -*iz*/-*ez*	103
4.6 Examples of the causative extension -*ish*/-*esh*	104
4.7 Causatives derived from Swahili adjectives and relational expressions	104
4.8 Causatives derived from Swahili nouns	105
4.9 Other causatives	105
4.10 Personal pronouns, referential makers, and relative markers	118
4.11 Forms of *edza*	121
4.12 Complex predicates involving *piga*	125
4.13 Complex predicates involving *kata*, *ika*, and *tsupha*	126
4.14 Complex predicates involving *henda*	127
5.1 Combinations of TAM markers in conditional clauses with *kala*	163
6.1 Referential additives	207
C.1 Swahili loans in Digo listed in Hinnebusch (1999) with attested Digo forms	408
C.2 Swahili and Digo demonstratives	409

Preface

Digo, or Chidigo (ISO 639-3 code [dig]), is a Bantu language spoken in the coastal region of Kenya and Tanzania, and is classified as E73 (Maho 2003).

The emphasis in this grammar of Digo is on the structure of words, clauses, and larger units of language, and on the meanings and functions of these segments. Phonology and tonology are dealt with only briefly. As far as possible, all examples are taken from collected texts. This emphasis on the use of the language in context means that special attention is paid to features of the language that have significant textual functions. For example, Digo has a large number of demonstrative forms which play an important role in distinguishing major and minor participants, indicating the start of the main event line, maintaining continuity across episode boundaries, etc. Because of this, the description of Digo demonstratives runs to over thirty pages, whereas many grammars of Bantu languages deal with demonstratives in just a few paragraphs. Similarly, a complete chapter is devoted to describing the forms and functions of markers of tense, aspect, and movement. The final two chapters describe clause structure, including information structure, and nonverbal predicates. Because of the importance attached to the use of language in context, this volume includes an appendix containing two narrative texts, one hortatory text, and one expository text.

The large number of Bantu languages and the many similarities that they share make the Bantu language sub-family a fruitful field of study for comparative linguistics. In light of this, common features such as the noun class system and verbal morphology have not been neglected. To aid comparative research I have also included as appendices the 1,700-item SIL Comparative African Wordlist (plus 113 botanical terms) and a discussion of the relation of Digo to Swahili (the language of wider communication spoken in the Digo area).

Field research was conducted in Kenya whilst I worked with the Digo Language and Literacy Project under Research Permit No. OP.13/001/17 C 180/20 issued by the Government of Kenya to BTL (Bible Translation and Literacy).

Steve Nicolle
Africa International University, Nairobi
February 2012

Acknowledgments

From November 1999 to January 2004 my family and I lived in the village of Chigato, between Kwale town and the coast in southern Kenya. Our Digo neighbours welcomed us into their community and taught us their language; they invited us to their weddings and their funerals; they watched out for my family when I took people to hospital at night; their children played with our children; many of them became our friends. This book would not have been possible without the patience and trust of our Digo friends and neighbours.

Particular thanks go to my colleagues in the Digo Language and Literacy Project: Maliki Garashi, Rodgers Maneno, Gideon M'mbetsa, Joseph Mwalonya, Juma Mwayani and Annah Ramtu. I am also grateful to Andy Clark, Martin de Groot and Robert Maneno, who preceded us in the Digo Language and Literacy Project, and to the staff of BTL (Kenya) who managed the project.

Various people read and commented on individual chapters and sections of this grammar; in particular, I would like to thank Michael J. Diercks, Helen Eaton, Oliver Kröger, Stephen Levinsohn, Lutz Marten, Oliver Stegen, Jenneke van der Wal, and Roger Van Otterloo. Constance Kutsch Lojenga read through the first draft of the entire manuscript and gave me many detailed and helpful suggestions for improvement.

At SIL International Publications, I especially want to thank George Huttar for his sharp editorial eye, which saved me from many embarrassing errors. All remaining errors are, of course, my own responsibility. Thanks also go to Lois Gourley and Mike Cahill, and to Dennis Felkner for dealing with the technicalities of styles and fonts.

I am grateful to Joan Russell, whose Swahili classes at the University of York kindled an interest in Bantu languages and linguistics that has grown ever since.

Finally, I want to thank my wife, Alison, not just for her editorial assistance, but for her companionship in many a journey, and for her steadfast encouragement to see this particular journey through to the end.

1

Introduction

1.1 Linguistic classification and speech varieties

Digo[1] is a Bantu language. Bantu languages are spoken throughout sub-Saharan Africa and constitute the largest sub-group of the Bantoid branch of the Benue-Congo group of the Niger-Congo language family. Digo [dig[2]] is classified as E73 (Guthrie 1967–1971) and is part of the Nyika-Taita Group (Maho 2003) or Northeast Coast, Sabaki (Nurse 1999). It is the southernmost language in the Mijikenda cluster. Nurse and Hinnebusch (1993:17) write: "Mijikenda can usefully be subdivided into Northern and Southern Mijikenda. On lexicostatistical grounds, Southern Mijikenda means Digo and Segeju,[3] Northern Mijikenda refers to the rest (Chonyi, Duruma, Jibana, Kambe, Kauma, Giryama, Rabai, Ribe). Phonologically, however, at least some of the innovations that characterize Digo and Segeju also show up in some lexical items in adjacent Northern

---

[1] Digo speakers refer to their language as 'Chidigo', *chi-* being the noun class prefix used to denote manner (e.g. of speaking). However, following the convention followed by most of the contributors in Nurse and Philippson (2003), I have used the name form without the prefix both for Digo and for other Bantu languages. The only exception to this practice occurs when a language is not well-known, and the major or only published sources use the prefix when referring to the language, e.g. 'Lucazi' where the *lu-* prefix is used in Fleisch (2000) which is the major published source on this language.
[2] This is the code assigned to Digo by the ISO 639-3 standard (ISO 2007) as used in *Ethnologue* (Lewis 2009).
[3] The Segeju language is spoken in Tanzania only (although some ethnic Segeju live in Kenya and speak either Digo or Swahili), and is linguistically close to Digo. The Segeju as a group are excluded from the Mijikenda cluster on cultural grounds.

Mijikenda (e.g. Duruma)." Walsh (2006:158) defines Northern Mijikenda as Giryama, Chonyi, Ribe, Kambe, Kauma, and Jibana, and Southern Mijikenda as Rabai, Duruma, and Digo. Spear (1981:12) notes that the six Northern Mijikenda "dialects" plus Rabai "are extremely similar to one another, while Digo differs more and Duruma exists midway between the two."

Any division of the languages (or speech varieties) that constitute the Mijikenda cluster will depend on the importance given to different factors. Nurse and Hinnebusch (1993) prioritized lexicostatistical data, but the Digo word list that was used for their analysis is based on the southern variety of Digo (see below) and contains many Swahili words which, although they are used by Digo speakers especially near the coast, have more common 'Mijikenda' synonyms which are used by other Digo speakers. Even using Nurse and Hinnebusch's (1993) Swahili-influenced word list for Digo, there is 74% lexical similarity between Digo and Duruma. Because of the phonological and cultural similarities between Digo and Duruma, Walsh's (2006) classification of Digo and Duruma (but probably not Rabai) as maximally distinct from the other varieties probably reflects the perception of most Digo and Duruma speakers of themselves in relation to the other speech communities that make up the Mijikenda cluster. Ultimately, however, a division of these speech varieties into 'Northern Mijikenda' and 'Southern Mijikenda', as well as being subjective, is potentially misleading, as it may suggest that there is a Mijikenda language, whereas in fact the reality is of a group of culturally related but distinct speech communities speaking closely related but distinct speech varieties.

Within Digo, different speech varieties (or dialects) can be distinguished, but different researchers have proposed different classifications of these. Walsh (2006:158-159) distinguishes (1) Chinondo (or 'Northern Digo'), spoken along the south Kenyan coast between Likoni, just south of Mombasa island, and Msambweni, approximately 50 km from the border with Tanzania (Hinnebusch 1973; Walsh 1986; de Groot 1988a); (2) Ungu (Lungu, or 'Southern Digo'), spoken in the coastal strip south of Msambweni into northern Tanzania as far as Tanga (Dammann 1938; 1944, Hinnebusch 1973); (3) Ts'imba (or Tsimba), "spoken in the Shimba Hills between Vuga in the east and Ng'onzini in the west (not described in the literature); and (4) Tsw'aka (Chw'aka), spoken in and around the village of the same name on the Shimoni peninsula (Lambert 1957; Möhlig 1992; Nurse and Walsh 1992)" (Walsh 2006:159). Regarding the last of these, Nurse and Hinnebusch (1993:10n) write: "Chwaka (Digo: Tswaka), spoken on the Shimoni peninsula in the Vumba area, is a further, very Swahili-ized form of Digo." It will not be discussed in this study.

According to Nurse and Hinnebusch (1993:17), "there are two variants of Digo, the division being at Gazi," Vumba being discussed separately and the Tsimba variety not at all. This division appears to correspond approximately to Walsh's Northern and Southern Digo (Gazi is located approximately 5 km north of Msambweni); Walsh mentions that his Digo informant described the Tsimba variety as being similar to the Chinondo variety, but with more

1.1 Linguistic classification and speech varieties

Duruma-like pronunciation. Judging by the word list provided for 'Digo' in Nurse and Hinnebusch (1993), most of their data comes from the Southern Digo variety. The division into northern and southern speech varieties of Digo is justified on the basis of pronunciation (there is a clear difference in accent between the two varieties, a notable distinction being that the southern variety often uses 'r' where the northern variety uses 'l') and lexical variation.[4]

Divisions of Digo beyond a northern and a southern variety appear to be subjective. In addition to 'Ts'imba' and 'Tsw'aka', Walsh (2006:159) mentions varieties of Digo spoken by "assimilated Segeju and Degere." The Segeju were formerly speakers of a Central Kenya Bantu (Thagicu) language who, according to Digo tradition, worked for the Digo as slaves. The Segeju had their origins in a pastoralist society that became allied to the ancestors of the northern Mijikenda tribes, whom they may have dominated politically and militarily (Walsh 2014); the Digo tradition that the Segeju were their slaves may either be incorrect or may reflect a later period of history by which time the Segeju had migrated to the southern end of the range occupied by the Mijikenda tribes and were no longer dominant. Regarding the current linguistic situation, Nurse and Hinnebusch (1993:539) comment: "Our data, based on a lengthy word list and a short interview, suggests that Tanzanian Segeju is similar, but not identical to, Digo. Some Digo expressed this differently—Segeju was a garbled form of their own language!" The Degere are former hunter-gatherers who appear to have once spoken an Eastern Cushitic language, possibly Waata according to Walsh (1990, 1992/93). Annah Ramtu (p.c. 5/6/03) comments: "As for specific Chidigo dialects, there is Chidegere (named after clan) which is spoken by the Adegere. Their dialect is closest to Duruma in their speech. Culturally, these people are not expected to intermarry with the Digos of other clans." She also mentions Tsimba, Pungu, and Tiwi as dialects.

The data for this study is from the northern variety of Digo (including Tsimba), mostly based on the speech of people from inland areas where the influence of Swahili is generally less than at the coast. Written, audio, and audio-visual materials in the northern variety have been presented to speakers of the southern variety (in both Kenya and Tanzania), and although these people recognized that the northern variety was being used, they generally had very few problems understanding what was said or written. When asked about different varieties of Digo, speakers of the southern variety (in Tanzania) occasionally commented that the northern variety was a "purer" form than their own speech, as it is less influenced by Swahili.

---

[4] The Digo-English-Swahili dictionary of Mwalonya et al. (2012) was based on the northern variety and indicated words that are found only in the southern variety with the abbreviation *Tz* for 'Tanzania' (where the majority of speakers of the southern variety live).

1.2 Geography and environment

Map 1.1 Coastal area of East Africa from Malindi, Kenya, to Tanga, Tanzania

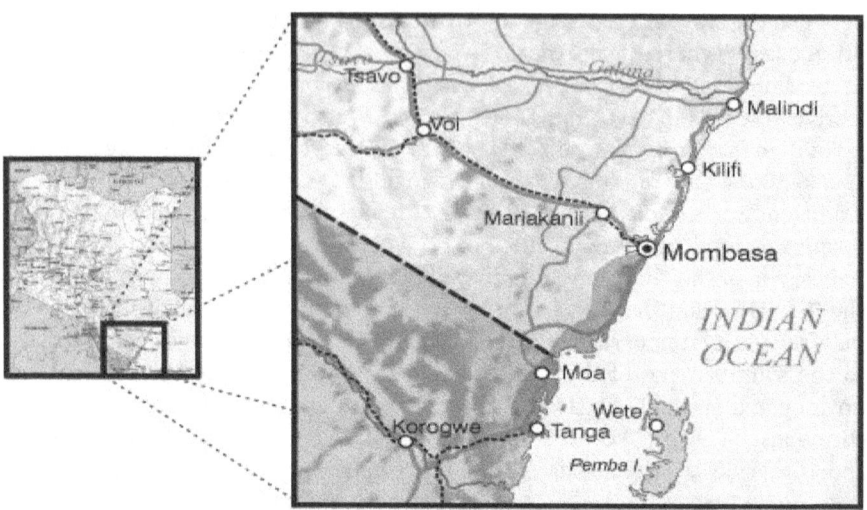

Source: Digo Language Development Project. Used with permission.

Altitude: Sea-level–400m
Longitude: 39° E
Latitude: 4–6° S
Ecosystem type: Tropical forest, coastal forest
Agriculture: Coconuts, cassava, maize, rice, beans
Geological type: Coastal
Climate: Tropical: hot and damp with the long rains in April–July and short rains in October–November

1.3 Culture and history

The Digo, along with the other tribes in the Mijikenda cluster plus the Pokomo, the Swahili, the Segeju,[5] and the (non-Bantu) Aweer (formerly known by the derogatory name Boni), all claim to have originated in the (possibly mythical) Shungwaya (or Singwaya) in what is now modern Somalia. However, some recent researchers have suggested that this tradition was adopted from the Segeju (Walsh 1992) or the Swahili (Willis 1993). Bergman (1988) states: "There

---

[5]The Segeju claim to have originated in central Kenya, and indeed the name Segeju and contemporary ethnonyms Sagidzu, Daiso and Daicho are variants of the name Thagicũ, which is widespread in the traditions of different members of the Central Kenya Bantu group of languages (Nurse 1982; Walsh 2014). However, some oral traditions place the Segeju in Shungwaya as part of their ancestral migration from central Kenya to the coast.

are ... no references to the Shungwaya myth in anything published before the colonial period; according to some sources, the Digo at least were in the area from as early as 1204 (Hollis 1900; see also Gerlach 1961 and Gillette 1978), when they first made contact with the Shirazi at Vumba Kuu .... Sharpe, the Kwale D.C. in the 1920's, held that the Digo had been in the area for over a millenium."

There is strong linguistic and cultural evidence to suggest that the Digo and Duruma can trace their origins, at least in part, to a migration from the south rather than from Shungwaya in the north. Before the colonial period, only the Digo and Duruma practised matrilineality, in contrast to the other speech communities in the Mijikenda cluster, who practised patrilineality (see Spear 1978). This is a characteristic which the Digo share with a number of Bantu-speaking groups in eastern Tanzania: the Zaramo, Kwere, Luguru, Kutu, Kaguru, Sagara, Vidunda, Ngulu, and Zigula (Beidelman 1967). Of these groups, the nearest to the Digo are the Zigula, who are also predominantly Muslim and who practise a similar form of traditional religion to the Digo. In addition, the northern Mijikenda groups traditionally practised an age-set system (possibly adopted from the Segeju) which is lacking in traditional Digo culture. Linguistically, there are some striking similarities between Digo and Duruma and the languages spoken south of the Usambara mountains in Tanzania. In addition to a number of cognate lexical items (see Nicolle 2006), the usual order of demonstrative and noun in Digo is Dem+N which is the case in the Tanzanian languages Shambala, Pare, and Rangi, and in the Nguni languages even further south, but different from most Bantu languages, including Swahili (see §3.4.4.1).

1.4 Approach and methodology

The approach that I have adopted is guided by the structure of Bantu languages and by the fact that numerous grammars of Bantu languages already exist. Since there is much structural similarity between many of the Eastern Bantu languages, I have tried to devote more space to features that are unique to Digo or at least less widespread among Bantu languages, such as the peculiarities of the demonstrative and TAM systems. At the same time, unless there was a compelling reason to use an unfamiliar term, I have adopted the categories that have been used in previous descriptions of Bantu languages in order to ensure that this grammar will be accessible to researchers interested in comparative studies. I have also attempted to answer, as far as I am able, some of the questions that Bantu grammarians are asking at the start of the 21st century (see for example, Marten et al. 2007). I can only hope that if anyone is reading this description in 50 or 100 years' time, it will not appear too dated as a result.

For the most part, the grammatical terms used in Bantu studies are the same as those used in general linguistics, and I have used these uncritically despite the considerable evidence that some grammatical categories are language-specific rather than universal (see for example, Croft 1990, 2001; Dryer 1997a). It would have been theoretically satisfying to have described the grammar of Digo in terms of "propositional act constructions" rather than word classes (parts of speech), and "argument linking constructions" instead of syntactic roles (Croft 2001:59), but to have done so would have made the grammar inaccessible to most readers and would have hindered its usefulness in comparative studies. However, in §6.1 'Relational expressions', I felt obliged to adopt a constructional approach, as the traditional grammatical categories 'preposition' and 'conjunction' proved hard to maintain in Digo.

One feature of my approach is an emphasis on the use of the language in context. In part, this is my small attempt to redress the balance in Bantu studies, since less has been written about discourse features of Bantu languages than about their phonology and morphology. But it also reflects a conviction that a description of a language that does not discuss how it is used does justice to neither the language nor the community that speaks it. As a result, the analysis presented in this book relies heavily on collected texts. These are for the most part recordings of people telling stories or giving speeches that have subsequently been transcribed. Some texts were used in their original, unedited form, whilst others have been edited and published. These texts were collected by my colleagues in the Digo Language and Literacy Project, Robert Maneno, Joseph Mwalonya, Rodgers Maneno and Maliki Garashi, from their friends and family members. I am most indebted to all of them. I also include data and observations based on my own conversations with people; whenever I encountered an interesting or unusual construction I would try to note it down as soon as I could and then discuss it with a Digo speaker. Most such conversations occurred in the course of day-to-day interactions with friends and neighbours in the village of Chigato, Matuga Division, where I lived from November 1999 to January 2004, and which I visited regularly until August 2007. (I often kept a notebook and pencil with me, and was sometimes quite rightly rebuked if I went out without them!)

In the interest of comprehensiveness, it was necessary to supplement this corpus of collected texts and opportunistic observations with other data. This came from two main sources. First, I was fortunate to have access to the Digo translation of the books of Genesis and Exodus and of the New Testament. All of this material was drafted by mother-tongue speakers of Digo and checked by a reviewers' committee consisting of between five and twenty Digo speakers—men and women—at any given meeting. The members of the committee came from a variety of locations in Kenya in order to ensure that the translated material was comprehensible and acceptable to as wide an audience as possible. I have as far as possible avoided using translated material for discourse level analysis, but have used it to illustrate grammatical structures not found in the nontranslated corpus, or where the examples from the nontranslated corpus contained extraneous material that would have made it less suitable as an illustrative example of a particular feature. The second source of data came from elicited material such as was obtained by asking Digo speakers to complete paradigms, by asking questions such as 'How would you say ...?', or by presenting sample sentences for evaluation. This was the method of last resort, but it did yield data that I would not otherwise have obtained (for example, in §7.5 on Locative Inversion).

Ideally, data would have been collected from monolingual speakers of Digo who have been minimally influenced by other languages. In practice, however, almost all adult speakers of Digo have some competence in Swahili (see appendix C) and are frequently exposed to Swahili (for example, through formal education, exposure to Kenyan and Tanzanian mass media, and direct contact with non-Digo speakers). Speakers from certain locations and from certain social groups exhibit greater Swahili influence in their speech than other speakers. That said, it has been my experience that most Digo speakers are proficient at keeping Digo and Swahili apart both in informal speech and when asked to reflect on the structure of their language.

1.5 Abbreviations and glossing conventions

As far as possible, I have followed the Leipzig Glossing Rules, which provide conventions and standard abbreviations for interlinear morpheme-by-morpheme glosses.

1.5.1 Abbreviations

1, 2, 3, 4 …	noun class concord
1PL	first person plural
1SG	first person singular
2PL	second person plural
2PL>-…-<2PL	discontinuous second person plural
2SG	second person singular
3PL	third person plural
3SG	third person singular
ADD	additive
ADV	adverb
ANT	anterior aspect marker
APPL	applicative extension
ASS	associative marker
CAUS	causative extension
COM	comitative marker
COMP	complementizer
COMPL	completive marker
COND	conditional status marker
CONS	consecutive tense marker
CONT	continuous aspect
COP	copula
DEG	degree adverb

DEM	demonstrative
DEM1	demonstrative series 1
DEM1_VAR	demonstrative series 1 short variant form
DEM1_VARIANT	demonstrative series 1 long variant form
DEM2	demonstrative series 2, etc.
DEM2_VAR	demonstrative series 2 short variant form, etc.
DEM2_VARIANT	demonstrative series 2 long variant form, etc.
DEP	dependent status marker
DIST	distal movement gram
DM	discourse marker
EMPH	emphatic (clitic in initial slot or aspect marker)
EXCL or EXCLAM	exclamation
FOC	focus marker
FUT	future tense marker
FV	final vowel
GEN	generic aspect marker
HAB	habitual aspect marker
HOD	hodiernal past tense marker
IDEO	ideophone
IMPFV	imperfective aspect marker
INC	inceptive aspect marker
INF	infinitive
INTR	intransitive
IT or ITIVE	itive movement marker
LOC	locative
n	noun
NEG	negative
PAS	passive extension
PERS	persistive aspect marker
PFV	perfective aspect marker
PL	plural
POS	possessive
POT	potential status marker
PST	past tense marker
Q	question marker
RECIP	reciprocal extension
REF	referential marker
REFL	reflexive verb complement marker
REL	relative marker
SC	subject concord
SEQ	sequential tense marker
SIM	simultaneous aspect marker
STAT	stative extension

1.5 Abbreviations and glossing conventions

SUB	subjunctive
TR	transitive
V	verb
VC	verb complement concord
VENT or VENTIVE	ventive movement marker
WELL	manner adverbial clitic

1.5.2 Glossing conventions

The following examples illustrate some of the glossing conventions used in this grammatical description.

Example (1) is taken from chapter 6:

(1) Uwe   m-gayi   **tsona**   m-chiya   wa   mwisho
    2SG   1-poor_person   ADD   1-poor_person   1.ASS   3.end
    u-na-tak-a   mwanangu!
    2SG-CONT-want-FV   1.child.1.1SG.POS

'You are a poor man <u>moreover</u> **a complete pauper,** (yet) you want to marry my daughter!'

The first line is the Digo text; the word *tsona* is underlined as this is the expression which is being discussed in the section the example is taken from, and *tsona mchiya wa mwisho* is in bold type as this is the relevant construction which is being described (an additive followed by a noun phrase).

The second line provides a morpheme-by-morpheme gloss. The word *mgayi* is glossed as 1-poor_person; 1 indicates the noun class and poor_person is written with an underscore as the two English words are together used to gloss a single Digo word. Small caps are used for technical terms and labels. The final word *mwanangu* is a compound form consisting of *mwana* 'child' and *angu* 'my' which is abbreviated from the noun class 1, 1st person singular possessive *wangu*. It is glossed as 1.child.1.1SG.POS which can be read as "noun class 1, meaning 'child', plus the noun class 1 form of the 1st person singular possessive." 1.child and 1.1SG.POS have been joined with a dot since there is no clear division between them (the second *a* belongs both to *mwana* and to *angu*), but where a clear division between morphemes can be made, the morphemes are separated with hyphens both in the Digo and in the gloss, as in *u-na-tak-a* and 2SG-CONT-want-FV.

The final line provides a free translation. Wherever possible, the translation corresponding to the constituent under discussion has been highlighted in the free translation in the same way as in the Digo text. In example (1), 'moreover' is underlined indicating that this is an idiomatic translation of *tsona*, and 'moreover a complete pauper' is in bold as this is a translation of *tsona mchiya wa mwisho* which is in bold in the Digo text. The word 'yet' is included in the free translation as it is required for the translation to read naturally in English, but the parentheses indicate that there is no corresponding word in the Digo text.

Some of the examples consist of a long stretch of Digo text and a free translation followed by part of the Digo text repeated with morpheme divisions indicated and a morpheme-by-morpheme gloss, as in example (2):

(2) *Hara baba na mayo akpwendamenya nyumba yao* **naye mwana wao ambaye ni liwali achendamenya yakpwe.**
 'That father and mother went and entered their house **and likewise their son who was governor went and entered his.**'

na=ye	*mwana*	*wao* ...	*a-chenda-meny-a*	*y-akpwe*
COM=1.REF	1.child	2.3PL.POS	3SG-CONS.IT-enter-FV	9-3SG.POS

This format is used when it is useful to show a particular expression or construction in context, but it is not practical to provide a morpheme-by-morpheme gloss of the whole text. In example (2), the expression being discussed is *naye* and so only *naye* plus the following clause has been glossed. The clause itself has been shortened by removing the relative clause *ambaye ni liwali* 'who was governor', and this elision has been indicated using three dots. The expression *naye* consists of two morphemes—*na* and *ye*—but these have been joined by the symbol = rather than by a hyphen. This indicates that one or more of the morphemes is a clitic rather than an affix. (A clitic typically combines with a variety of word classes or participates in a variety of constructions, whereas an affix typically combines with a particular word class or participates in a very restricted range of constructions.) In fact, the comitative marker *na* and the referential marker *ye* are both clitics.

2
Phonology and Orthography

This chapter provides a brief summary of the phonology of Digo, and of the transcription conventions used in this book.

2.1 Orthography

The transcription used is the one used in the orthography developed by the BTL Digo Language and Literacy Project in consultation with the Digo community and SIL orthography specialists. The symbols in the Digo orthography corresponding to certain sounds (shown by IPA symbols) are as follows:

IPA	Digo orthography	IPA	Digo orthography
ᵐb	mb	ⁿdʒ	nj
ⁿd	nd	β	ph
ᵑg	ng	ᵐβ	mph
k͡p	kpw	ᵐv	mv
g͡ɓ	gbw	ʃ	sh
ᵑg͡ɓ	ngbw	ɲ	ny
ⁿdz	ndz	ŋ	ng'
tʃ	ch	j	y
dʒ	j		

Apart from stem-internal examples, virtually all occurrences of *kpw*, *gbw* and *ngbw* are underlyingly [kw], [gw] and [ⁿgʷ] respectively. For example, *fung-* 'close' + *-wa* (passive plus final vowel) gives *fungbwa* 'closed' pronounced [fungba], and *ku-* (class 17 concord) + *-a* (associative marker) gives *kpwa* 'of' pronounced [kpa]. Note that *gbw* and *ngbw* are implosive; that is, (prenasalized) voiced labiovelar plosive with ingressive airflow. In actual pronunciation, a preceding [m] (shortened from [mu]) may cause a following [k_V] to be pronounced [kp_V] and a following [g_V] to be pronounced [gɓ_V]. This has been reflected in the spelling: *mkpwono* 'hand' (morphologically *m-kono*, plural *mikono*), *mgbwanga* 'traditional healer' (morphologically *m-ganga*, plural *aganga*). However, the alternative spellings *mkono*, *mganga* are also acceptable.

<m'> is used instead of <m> to distinguish syllabic nasals of noun classes 1 and 3 from nonsyllabic nasals of noun class 9/10 preceding /b/.

The prenasalized forms of both /dz/ and /z/ are written as <ndz>, for example, *ndziro* 'pot used for distributing liquor during a wedding ceremony' unsegmentable root, versus *ndziho* 'heavy' class 9/10 prefix *n-* plus root *-ziho* (not *nziho*).

<ph> is a voiced bilabial fricative (or occasionally approximant) and often corresponds to <p> in Swahili (e.g. *kpwapha* 'armpit' cf. Sw: *kwapa*). This is why the digraph <ph> was chosen rather than the cross-linguistically more common <b> or <bh> often used in languages in which [β] is derived from [b] or is cognate with [b] in related languages.

Palatization and labialization of consonants occur and are symbolized by a following /y/ and /w/ respectively: *fyokpwa* 'diarrhoea', *ryaka* 'quiver', *kufwa* 'to die'.

The following symbols are only found in loan words; *dh* and *th* are borrowed from Swahili (e.g. *dhikiri* 'an Islamic ritual for the appeasement or exorcism of spirits' and *theluji* 'snow'), and *zh* occurs in a very few words, probably of Giryama origin (e.g. *chitindizho* 'cattle pen'). These sounds are not included in the phoneme inventory.

IPA	Digo orthography
ð	dh
θ	th
ʒ	zh

2.2 Phonology

2.2.1 Consonants

There are 35 consonant phonemes in Digo, including prenasalized consonants:

2.2 Phonology

Table 2.1. Phonemic consonant chart

Manner of articulation	Bilabial		Alveolar		Palatal		Velar	
Stops	p		t				k	
	b	mb	d	nd			g	ng
							kpw	
							gbw	ngbw
Affricates			ts		ch			
			dz	ndz	j	nj		
Fricatives	f		s		sh		h	
	v	mv	z					
	ph	mph						
Nasals	m		n		ny		ng'	
Approximants			l		y		w	
Flaps/Taps			r					

An alphabetical list of words illustrating the consonant phonemes is provided below:

b	*bara*	to become used to	nd	*ndata*	walking stick
ch	*chala*	finger	ndz	*ndzala*	hunger
d	*dang'a*	young child	ng	*ngarawa*	outrigger canoe
dz	*dzana*	yesterday	ng'	*ng'ala*	to shine
f	*fanana*	to resemble	ngbw	*ngbwadu*	sour
g	*gana*	hundred	nj	*njasasa*	Lantana camara
gbw	*gbwanda*	sheet	ny	*nyanya*	tomato
h	*hala*	to take	p	*papa*	shark
j	*jaba*	be silly	ph	*phana*	to brand
k	*kala*	jackal	r	*raka*	voice
kpw	*kpwala*	to stumble	s	*sala*	to remain
l	*laga*	to promise	sh	*shaka*	disaster
m	*mamba*	crocodile	t	*tanya*	to divide
m'b	*m'bara*	jackal berry tree	ts	*tsaha*	louse
mb	*mbara*	appointment	v	*valavala*	red-headed agama
mph	*mphaka*	border	w	*wawa*	grandmother
mv	*mvarika*	young she-goat	y	*yaya*	to disappear
n	*namna*	kind, sort	z	*zama*	to bend over

A note on the phoneme /h/

The phoneme /h/ has three allophones: voiceless glottal fricative [h], lenis[1] voiced glottal fricative [ɦ], and nasalized voiced glottal fricative [ɦⁿ]. The nasalized allophone [ɦⁿ] only occurs in word-final syllables (where it causes the immediately adjacent vowels also to be nasalized), whilst the nonnasalized allophones only occur in non-word-final syllables. The voiceless glottal fricative [h] and the lenis voiced glottal fricative [ɦ] are in free variation in word-intitial position. [ɦ] is found consistently in the 1PL subject concord: *hu-* [ɦu] and in the initial /h/ of demonstratives such as *hipha* [ɦiβa] 'here', but elsewhere, there is variation between speakers, to the extent that /h/ can be realized as such a lenis sound (that is, pronounced with such a weak degree of muscular effort and breath force) that no glottal fricative articulation can be perceived.[2] As a result, *hadisi* 'story' can be realized as [hadisi], [ɦadisi], or [adisi], and *halafu* 'then' can be realized as [halafu], [ɦalafu], or [alafu].

2.2.2   Vowels

Digo has 5 phonemic short vowels and 5 phonemic long vowels; nasal vowels are conditioned by the presence of intervocalic /h/ (see above):

Table 2.2. Phonemic vowel chart

Height	**Front**		**Central**		**Back**	
Close	i	ii			u	uu
Mid	e	ee			o	oo
Open			a	aa		

---

[1] The term 'lenis' "refers to a sound made with a relatively weak degree of muscular effort and breath force, compared with some other sound" (Crystal 1991:197). The symbol ɦ (known as 'hook-top h') is defined by the International Phonetic Association (IPA) as representing a "voiced (or murmured, or whispery, or breathy-voiced) glottal fricative" (Pullum and Ladusaw 1996:75).

[2] This observation is in line with Pullum and Ladusaw's generalization that [ɦ] "is often described as a voiced glottal fricative, but there is no aspect of this description that is uncontroversial. First, it is a matter of debate among phoneticians whether [h]-like sounds are fricatives or approximants. And second, the glottis is not fully in a state of voicing during the production of [ɦ]; it is generally in the "murmur" or "breathy voice" state characteristic of the release of the breathy-voiced ("voiced aspirate") stops of Indic languages" (Pullum and Ladusaw 1996:75–76).

2.2 Phonology

An alphabetical list of words illustrating the vowel phonemes is provided below:

a	*cha*	to dawn	aa	*chaa*	animal enclosure
e	*akare*	ancestors	ee	*akaree*	his/her ancestors
i	*dina*	to continue	ii	*dii*	continually
o	*nyongo*	bile	oo	*nyongoo*	illness associated with childbirth
u	*munyu*	salt	uu	*muuyu*	baobab

2.2.3 Syllable structure

Digo has the following syllable types, where G represents the vowel glides /y/ and /w/, N represents a nasal consonant, and VV represents a long vowel:

> V
> CV   CGV
> CVV   CGVV
> NCV   NCGV
> NCVV

In addition, N can occur as a prefix.

2.2.4 Tone

The major studies of tone in Digo are Kisseberth's (1984) and Volk's (2011) comparative descriptions of tone in all nine of the Mijikenda varieties. According to Volk (2011:1), "Mijikenda has a complex tone system, which is rendered quite opaque by the interplay of several tonal processes, among which are the high mobility of high tones (a high tone is often heard on a different word than its word of origin), consonant-tone interaction (depressor consonants, unique to Mijikenda among Northeastern Bantu languages) and many cases of 'hidden tones'—tones that are not pronounced in certain phonological environments, and yet are evident through their interaction with other tones."

Nouns in Digo can be grouped into 6 tonal classes depending on whether they have an initial underlying high tone and a hidden high on the final or penultimate syllable. Verb stems either have an underlying high tone on the first mora or are toneless; some bisyllabic verb stems also have a hidden high tone on the penult. The lexical tone of the verb stem can be partially or completely overwritten in certain tenses, when a high tone starts on the second stem mora and shifts to the end of the stem or beyond (Volk 2008, 2011).

A notable feature of tone in Digo is high tone shift, in which an underlying high tone will be realized as a slight rise on the penult and a falling tone on the final vowel of the intonational phrase (Volk 2011:35). (In other Mijikenda varieties, a high tone will surface as a rising tone or as a level high tone on the penult only.) The intonational phrase can extend well beyond a single word, and so in some cases an underlying high tone may be manifest only on a following word. When a phrase has more than one high tone, each high will surface at or immediately before the underlying location of the next high tone. Underlying high tones can originate in noun or verb stems, certain tense markers, such as the past tense (Volk 2011:73–75), some subject concords and all verb complement (object) concords except the singular human prefixes, and certain other morphemes, such as the associative marker -a (Volk, 124–126).

High tone spread is also affected by the occurrence in an intonational phrase of voiced obstruents (but not prenasalized stops and [β]) which act as 'depressors'. If a depressor consonant occurs before the position where a high tone would be expected to surface, the high tone will instead occur before the depressor consonant.

Volk's data for Digo consisted of 15 hours of recordings of 5 speakers (both northern and southern dialects) made by Charles Kisseberth in the 1980s and 1990s. Volk notes (2011:2) that often speakers differ both tonologically and morphologically in their speech, which corresponds to my experience. In fact, many younger speakers failed to produce or to recognize many tonal distinctions, perhaps due to the influence of Swahili (see appendix C).

Despite its complexity, tone in Digo has a low functional load (in that it is rarely crucial to interpretation) and—apart from a very small number of lexical minimal pairs—is only marked in the orthography to distinguish between 1st person singular present and past tenses: *naphiya* 'I am going (present)' versus *náphiya* 'I went (past)'. Even though the actual high tone of the past tense is often pronounced on one or more of the syllables of the verb stem rather than on the tense marker (*á*) itself, it is indicated on the tense marker for consistency. The situation in Digo seems to be similar to that observed by Fleisch (2000:315) for the Bantu languages Lucazi and Cokwe in which "tone is intertwined with stress[3] and the latter tends to play an increasingly large role."

---

[3]Stress is manifested as lengthening, frequently with higher amplitude.

3

Noun Phrases

3.1 Nominal morphology

3.1.1 Noun classes

A noun stem in Digo consists of a nominal root and its noun class prefix. (There is no augment in Digo.) Noun classes are (very) loosely semantically defined classes; each noun is in some class, and each class controls its own agreement markers for verbs, qualificatives, demonstratives, etc. The noun class prefixes are lexically defined and change according to the number specification. Table 3.1 lists the noun class prefixes which occur on nouns (markers on verbs, qualificatives, demonstratives, etc., are listed in the sections dealing with those word classes).

Table 3.1. Noun class prefixes

Class	Prefix	Examples	Morphophonological processes
1	m/mu/ mw	*mutu* 'person', *mwana* 'child', *mjeni* 'guest, stranger', *mwenehu* 'my/our sibling'	glide formation, vowel elision
2	a	*atu* 'people', *ana* 'children', *ajeni* 'guests, strangers'	
1a	Ø	*baba* 'father', *sowe* 'your father', *ise* 'his/her father', *simba* 'lion'	

Table 3.1, continued

Class	Prefix	Examples	Morphophonological processes
2a	Ø (ano)	*ano baba* 'fathers', *simba* 'lions'	
3	m/mu/ mw	*muhi* 'tree, wild plant', *mwezi* 'moon, month', *moyo* 'heart', *munda* 'field' (but *mndani* 'in the field')	glide formation, vowel elision, semivowel epenthesis
4	mi	*mihi* 'trees, wild plants', *miezi* 'moons, months', *mioyo* 'hearts', *minda* 'fields' (*mindani* 'in the fields')	
5	dz/ dzi/Ø	*dzina* 'name', *dziwe* 'stone', *bofulo* 'bread roll'	
6	ma	*madzina* 'names', *mawe* 'stones', *mabofulo* 'bread rolls', *makongo* 'illnesses'	
7	chi/ch	*chitsulu* 'anthill', *chala* 'finger'	vowel elision
8	vi/vy	*vitsulu* 'anthills', *vyala* 'fingers'	
9	N/Ø	*nyumba* 'house', *tsi* 'country'	nasal consonant assimilation
10	N/Ø	*nyumba* 'houses', *tsi* 'countries', *mbiga* 'clay bowls', *pazi* 'ladles'	
11	li	*liga* 'clay bowl', *liphazi* 'ladle', *lichigo* 'fence'	
14	u/w	*usiku* 'night', *uchigo* 'fence', *uchiya* 'poverty', *ukongo* 'illness', *wivi* 'theft'	
15	ku/ kpw	*kufwitsa* 'hiding, to hide', *kpwedza* 'coming, to come' (infinitive)	[ku+V] > [kp]
16	pha	*phahali, phatu* 'place'	
17	ku/ kpw	*kpwahali* 'place', *kpwereru* 'outside'	[ku+V] > [kp]
18	mu/m/ mw	*mwahali* 'inside place'	

3.1.1.1 Singular-plural pairings of noun classes

In Digo, as in other Bantu languages, one of the functions of noun classes is to indicate number (one or more). Although most classes can be grouped into singular/plural pairings, not all nouns conform to this system. There is not necessarily a one-to-one mapping of singular to plural; classes 9 and 11 each have two plural forms, and classes 6 and 10 each function as the plural forms for three singular forms. Figure 3.1 shows the singular-plural noun class pairings plus those classes which also contain noncount nouns (with examples). Class 15 (containing verbal infinitives) and classes 16, 17, and 18 (containing locatives) have been excluded.

3.1 Nominal morphology

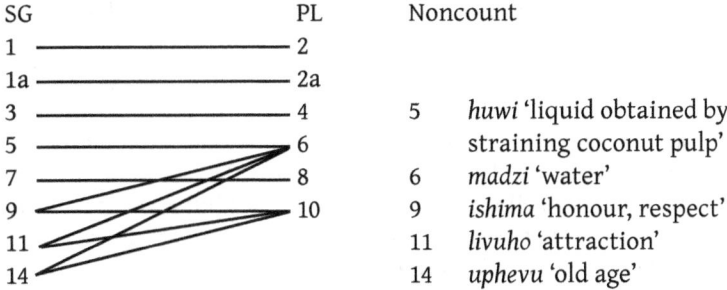

Figure 3.1. Singular-plural noun class pairings.

3.1.1.2 Discussion of individual noun classes

1/2
These classes refer to animate entities, particularly humans.

1a/2a
These classes contain kinship terms and names of certain animals. They take the same agreement markers (concords) as classes 1 and 2, and refer to animate entities, but they lack the nominal prefixes m-/a- of classes 1 and 2. The word *manga* 'cassava' also takes class 1/2 agreement, although cassava is not an animate entity:

(3) *Manga   a-ka-huluk-a;   ka-ri-k-a.*
     1a.cassava 1-ANT-be_undercooked-FV NEG.1-eat-STAT-FV
     'The cassava is undercooked; it is inedible.'

2a *ano*
The plural of kinship terms is marked by the word *ano* preceding the noun, as in *ano baba* 'fathers, men, menfolk' and *ano mayo* 'mothers, women, womenfolk'. *Ano* can be prefixed to the name of an adult to refer to the family of which they are part or their household as a whole, or to the name of a clan to refer to all the members of the clan or the clan collectively, and so is perhaps better characterized as a collective marker than simply as a plural marker.[1] The general word for sibling, *mwenehu*, has a regular plural form, *enehu*, but it is possible to refer to all the siblings in a particular family by using *ano* before the name of any one of the siblings e.g. *ano Nasiri* 'Nasiri and his siblings'. *Ano* can also precede more than one name as in *kaya pha ano Fatumu na Maryamu* 'Fatuma and Maryamu's home/household'. *Ano* is also used before the interrogative pronoun

---
[1] *Ano* fits the description of the associative plural marker, as defined by Daniel and Moravcsik (2013): "Associative plural constructions consist of a noun X (typically of human reference, usually a person's name or a kin term) and some other material, most often an affix, a clitic, or a word. The meaning of the construction is 'X and other people associated with X'." It will be glossed throughout as 'pl'.

ani in questions: *Ni ano ani hano?* 'Who are these people?' (lit: 'They are collective who-plural these?')

3/4
Classes 3 and 4 contain many plants and also many extended and round objects. There is also one word in class 3/4 *mtume/mitume* 'messenger/s, apostle/s' (both Muslim and Christian) which is borrowed from Swahili and which behaves like a noun of class 1a/2a in that it takes class 1/2 agreements, e.g. *mitume anjina* 'apostles some-cl.2' (not **mitume minjina* 'apostles some-cl.4').

5/6
These classes include some terms for humans when described by occupation or status (*fundi* 'craftsman'; *nabii* 'prophet'). In the singular (class 5) these nouns take class 1 agreements: *fundi* **wa** (not **ra*) *mbao* 'carpenter'; *fundi* **mmwenga** (not **mwenga*) 'one craftsman'; *fundi* **mzuri** (not **zuri*) 'a good craftsman'. However, in the plural (class 6) they take class 6 agreements with the 'associative' -*a* and possessives: *mafundi* **ga** (not **a*) *kudzenga* 'builders'; *mafundi***ge** (not **mafundie*) 'his craftsmen', but class 2 agreements elsewhere: *mafundi* **osi** (not **gosi*) 'all the craftsmen'; *Hinyo* **mafundi** *ariphosikira hivyo, atsukirwa sana* (not **gariphosikira ... gatsukirwa*) 'When those craftsmen heard this, they became very angry'. Classes 5 and 6 are also used for augmentatives of nouns intrinsically in other noun classes. Note that there are two alternative noun class prefixes for augmentatives: *dzi-* (*dz-*) and *dzidz-* (e.g. *dude* 'thing' > **dzi**dude 'big thing', *nyoka* 'snake' > **dz**oka or **dzidz**oka 'big snake'). See §3.1.4.3.1 for details.

7/8
As well as words which belong intrinsically to classes 7 and 8 (typically inanimate objects and some illnesses in class 7), these classes are also used for diminutives. Note that there are two alternative noun class prefixes for diminutives: *chi-* (*ch-*) or *chidzi-* (e.g. *gogo* 'log' > **chi**gogo 'small log', *muhi* 'tree, wild plant' > **chidzi**hi 'small tree'). See §3.1.4.3.1 for details.

9/10
These classes contain words for various objects, and are common classes for loan words. The usual class for plurals of class 9 is class 10, e.g. *siku mwenga* 'one day'; *siku mbiri* 'two days', but plurals can also be made in class 6 where the emphasis is on quantity rather than individuation, e.g. *masiku* '(many) days'.

11
Class 11 contains many words for long thin objects. It takes its plurals in either class 6 or class 10. Most nouns in class 11 take a class 10 plural: *liga* 'clay bowl' > **mbiga**; *linyasi* 'grass' > *nyasi*; *lifusi* 'species of grass' > *fusi*; *ling'ongo* 'length of cord or fibre' > *ng'ongo*. Other words in class 11 take class 6 plurals in which the *li-* prefix is either retained: *liphazi* 'ladle' > **maliphazi**, or omitted: *liphungo* 'twig,

3.1 Nominal morphology

cutting' > *maphungo*. (Note that the class 11 concords are identical to those of class 5; see table 3.2.) A few words, e.g. *liphazi* 'ladle' have attested plural forms in both classes: *maliphazi* (class 6) and *pazi* (class 10). When the noun stem begins with *ph* ([β] a voiced bilabial fricative) as in *liphazi* 'ladle' and the plural form is in class 10, the root of the plural usually begins with *p* as in *pazi* 'ladles'. However, there are exceptions, e.g. *liphyero* 'broom' which has two attested class 10 plural forms: *pyero* and *phyero* (both meaning 'brooms').

14

Class 14 contains nouns describing many abstract concepts, e.g. *ufwa* 'inheritance' and *utsai* 'witchcraft'. Some words in class 11 take alternate class 14 prefixes (*lichigo* vs. *uchigo* 'fence'), perhaps under the influence of Swahili in which these two classes have merged into one. Plurals of class 14 nouns are in class 10 and class 6 (as are plurals of class 11).

15

This class contains infinitive forms of verbs, used as nominals.

16/17/18

These are the locative classes: 16 specific locations, 17 approximate locations, and 18 interior locations.

3.1.2 Concord categories for nouns

In Digo, as in other Bantu languages, the head noun of a noun phrase exhibits morphological connections with its modifiers using noun class prefixes; this is the system of noun concord. This is distinct from agreement, which links the head of a verb phrase—a verb—with its arguments, that is, the subject and direct object of the verb phrase. Adjectives, including numerals, and *-nji*[2] 'many' take the same prefixes as nouns, and are summarized in table 3.2. Note that augmentatives in class 5 differ from words that are inherently in class 5 where adjectival agreement is concerned: *dziwe kulu* 'large stone' (inherent) vs. *dzinyama dzikulu* 'large animal/huge beast' (augmentative).

Table 3.2. Noun classes and their concords: adjectives

Class	#-C -*zuri*, -*nono* 'good', -*nji* 'many'	#-V -*iru* 'black' -*embamba* 'thin'
1	mzuri, mnono	mwiru, mwembamba
2	azuri, anono, anji	aru, embamba
3	mzuri, mnono	mwiru, mwembamba
4	mizuri, minono, minji	miru, miembamba
5	zuri, nono	dziru, dzembamba

---

[2] A hyphen before a form indicates that it is a suffix or that it requires a prefix, in this case a noun class prefix.

Table 3.2, continued

Class	#-C -zuri, -nono 'good', -nji 'many'	#-V -iru 'black' -embamba 'thin'
6	mazuri, manono, manji	maru, membamba
7	chizuri, chinono	chiru, chembamba
8	vizuri, vinono, vinji	viru, vyembamba
9	ndzuri, nono	nyiru, nyembamba
10	ndzuri, nono, nyinji	nyiru, nyembamba
11	zuri, nono	dziru, dzembamba
14	mzuri, mnono	mwiru, mwembamba
15	kuzuri, kunono	—
16	phazuri, phanono	—
17	kuzuri, kunono	—
18	mzuri, mnono	—

Other modifiers (including associative -a, possessives, relative markers, the quantifiers -osi 'all' and -anjina 'some', and '[an]other') take different concords, as summarized in table 3.3. Classes 1 and 2 are somewhat irregular. For verbal agreements with the subject concord, see §4.1.2, and for demonstrative agreements see §3.4.

Table 3.3. Noun classes and their concords: other modifiers

Class	Associative -a 'of'	Possessive -angu 'my'	=phi 'which'	Relative -osi 'all/any'	-anjina 'some/other' -enye 'self'
1	wa	wangu	yuphi	ye, yesi	wanjina, mwenye
2	a	angu	aphi	o, osi	anjina, enye
3	wa	wangu	uphi	wo, wosi	wanjina, wenye
4	ya	yangu	iphi	yo, yosi	yanjina, yenye
5	ra	rangu	riphi	ro, rosi	ranjina, renye
6	ga	gangu	gaphi	go, gosi	ganjina, genye
7	cha	changu	chiphi	cho, chosi	chanjina, chenye
8	vya	vyangu	viphi	vyo, vyosi	vyanjina, vyenye
9	ya	yangu	iphi	yo, yosi	yanjina, yenye
10	za	zangu	ziphi	zo, zosi	zanjina, zenye
11	ra	rangu	riphi	ro, rosi	ranjina, renye
14	wa	wangu	uphi	wo, wosi	wanjina, wenye
15	kpwa	kpwangu	—	ko, kosi	kpwanjina, kpwenye
16	pha	phangu	phaphi	pho, phosi	phanjina, phenye
17	kpwa	kpwangu	kuphi	ko, kosi	kpwanjina, kpwenye
18	mwa	—	—	mo, mosi	mwenye

3.1 Nominal morphology

Some of the agreement markers listed above can be predicted on the basis of the regular morphophonological processes described in table 3.4.

Table 3.4. Regular morphophonological processes

Class	Process	Examples
1, 3, 14	(m)u + V > (m)wV	wa, wangu, mwembamba, mwiru
2, 6	(m)a + a > a	angu, (m)anji, (m)aru
2, 6	(m)a + e > (m)e	(m)embamba
2	a + o > o	o, osi
4	mi + i > (m)i	minji, miru
4, 9	i + a/e/o > ya/ye/yo	yanjina, yenye, yosi
7	chi + V > chV	cha, chenye, chiru, chosi
8	vi + i > vi	vinji
8	vi + a/e/o > vya/vye/vyo	vya, vyenye, vyosi
15	ku + a > kpwa [kpa]	kpwangu
9, 10	N + C > assimilation	mbaya, mfupi (*except voiceless stops*)

3.1.3 Noun class agreement in conjoined NPs

When two or more nouns from different noun classes are conjoined in a single phrase, there are two ways in which agreement marking works:

1. The agreement markers of the plural form of the last mentioned noun are used, e.g. the plural of class 5 is class 6:

(4) sindano na bomba amba-**go** ta-**ga**-ka-chem-sh-w-a
    9.needle COM 5.syringe REL-6.REL NEG-6-ANT-boil-CAUS-PAS-FV
    'needle and syringe which have not been sterilized'

2. The class 10 agreement marker is used, e.g.:

(5) sindano na bomba amba-**zo** ta-**zi**-ka-chem-sh-w-a
    9.needle COM 5.syringe REL-10.REL neg-10-ANT-boil-CAUS-PAS-FV
    'needle and syringe which have not been sterilized'

3.1.4 Nominalizing derivational processes

Digo exhibits many of the nominalizing devices typically found in Bantu languages. These are classified below according to the source category (verb, adjective, or noun).

3.1.4.1 Verb to noun

The infinitive form of a verb exhibits many of the characteristics of a noun, and for that reason the infinitive prefix (*ku-*) is simultaneously characterized as the prefix for noun class 15. In addition, nouns of other noun classes can be formed from verbs. Deverbal nominalization involves the addition of a noun class prefix (sometimes modified) and a suffix to a verb stem (which consists of a root plus any extensions). The most common and productive nominalization processes are summarized in table 3.5. Note that although there are multiple processes, they affect different noun classes; in all cases, however, the noun class marker is prefixed to the verb stem and a specific final vowel is suffixed to the verb stem.

Table 3.5. Deverbal nominalizations

Class	Prefix	Suffix	Example	Source (verb stem)
1/2	m(u)-/a-	-a	m*risa* 'herdsman'	*ris* 'feed, take to graze'
1/2	m(u)-/a-	-i	m*uiki* 'keeper'	*ik* 'keep, place'
1/2	m(u)-/a-	-adzi	m*semuriradzi* 'narrator, storyteller'	*semurir* 'narrate, tell a story'
1/2	mwana-/ana-	-i	*mwanafundzi* 'student'	*fundz* 'teach'
1a/2a	chi-/vi-	-i	*chimanyi* 'expert'	*many* 'know'
3/4	m(u)-/mi-	-o	*muhego* 'trap'	*heg* 'trap'
5/6	—/ma-	-o	*sikiro* 'ear'	*sikir* 'hear'
			mafundzo 'teachings'	*fundz* 'teach'
5/6	—/ma-	-a	*makosa* 'fault, error'	*kos* 'fail, wrong s.o.'
			maisha 'life'	*ish* 'live'
7/8	chi-/vi-	-e	*chiumbe* 'creature'	*umb* 'create'
7/8	chi-/vi-	-o	*chitseko* 'laughter'	*tsek* 'laugh'
9/10	N-/N-	-o	*ngurumo* 'loud noise, thunder, roar'	*ngurum* 'roar'
11	li-	-o	*liphyero* 'broom'	*phyer* 'sweep'
14	u- (w-)	-a	*windza* 'hunting'	*indz* 'hunt'
14	u-	-i	*ushindi* 'victory'	*shind* 'vanquish, win'

There is no consistent correlation between form (noun class prefix and suffix) and function (agent, patient, instrument, etc.), as shown by *fundzo* 'teaching' class 5 + -*o* patient vs. *sikiro* 'ear' class 5 + -*o* instrument, and *mrisa* 'herdsman' -*a* suffix versus *muiki* 'keeper' -*i* suffix, both agent.

Some cases of nominalization exhibit the phonological effect of spirantization whereby /d/ > /dz/ and /h/, /l/ > /z/, e.g.:

3.1 Nominal morphology

rinda 'guard, protect' > *mrindzi* 'guard'
shuha 'fart' > *ushuzi* 'fart'
lóla 'marry' > *ulozi* 'marriage negotiation'

There is one other (unproductive) nominalization process which involves the prefix *mwam-* (class 3): *mwamdzifwitso* 'hiding place' < *dzifwitsa* 'hide oneself'.

3.1.4.2 Adjective to noun

Nouns can be formed from adjectives using the noun class 14 prefix *u-*:

-nono 'good' > *unono* 'goodness'
-phya 'new' > *uphya* 'newness'
sawa 'same' > *usawa* 'equality'

The same process creates the noun *unji* 'large quantity, amount' from the quantifier *-nji* 'many, much' as in example (6):

(6) Maisha   ga   mutu   ta-ga-kal-a   kamili   ku-a
    6.life   6.ASS   1.person   NEG-6-become-FV   complete   17-ASS

    unji   wa   mali   a-ri=zo   na=zo.
    14.amount   14.ASS   10.wealth   3SG-COP=10.REF   COM=10.REF

'A person's life does not consist of the amount of wealth which he has.'

3.1.4.3 Noun-to-noun

With the exception of augmentatives and diminutives (see below), it is often not possible to state with any certainty which is the source noun and which is the derived noun in cases of noun-to-noun derivation. I will therefore talk of noun-to-noun correspondences. The following are some of the regular noun-to-noun correspondences in Digo:

Table 3.6. Noun-to-noun correspondences

Country	Nationality/ ethnic group	Language/culture	English gloss
Digo (proper noun)	*Mdigo* (cl. 1/2)	*Chidigo* (cl. 7)	Digo
Ujerumani (cl. 14)	*Mjerumani* (cl. 1/2)	*Chijerumani* (cl. 7)	German
Plant name	**Fruit**	**English gloss**	
muuyu (cl. 3/4)	*uyu* (cl. 5/6)	baobab	
mwembe (cl. 3/4)	*embe* (cl. 5/6)	mango	

Table 3.6, continued

Occupation	Quality	English gloss	
mrindzi (cl. 1/2) < *rinda* 'protect'	*urindzi* (cl. 14)	guard	protection
mganga (cl. 1/2)	*uganga* (cl. 14)	traditional healer	traditional medicine

3.1.4.3.1 Augmentatives and diminutives

A noun of any class[3] can be 'augmented' by inclusion in class 5/6. That is, a noun can be described as being a large example of its kind by replacing the regular noun class prefix with a class 5/6 prefix. The noun class prefix on nouns is either *dzi-* (*dz-*) or *dzidz-* (e.g. **dzi**dude 'large object, big thing' < *dude* 'thing' cl.9, **dz**oka or **dzidz**oka < *nyoka* 'snake' cl.1a). Concords, except those on adjectives (see §3.1.2), are the regular class 5/6 concords; this holds for both inanimate and animate referents. In example (7), the class 5/6 concords have been highlighted:

(7) Wa-aon-a   **dzi**-dude   avi   ni   **dzi**-kabati   **dzi**-kulu
    3SG.PST-see-FV 5AUG-thing   like COP   5AUG-cupboard   5AUG-big

    ra-sukum-w-a   ni   madzi.
    5.PST-push-PAS-FV by   6.water

'He saw something large like a big cupboard being pushed by the water.'

Class 7/8 is used for diminutives and there are two alternative noun class prefixes for nouns: *chi-* (*ch-*) or *chidzi-*, and the corresponding plurals: *vi-* (*vy-*) or *vidzi-*. The *chi-/vi-* prefixes occur with nouns which belong intrinsically to some other noun class and whose stems have two or more syllables (e.g. **chi**dibwa < *dibwa* 'hole' cl.5). The *chidzi-/vidzi-* prefixes are used with nouns which belong intrinsically to class 7/8 (e.g. **chidzi**tambo 'a little while ago' < *chitambo* 'a while/long time ago' cl.7; **vidzi**tabu 'booklets' < *vitabu* 'books' cl.8) and nouns with monosyllabic stems (**chidzi**dzi 'village, hamlet' < *mudzi* 'town, location' cl.3; **vidzi**hi 'shrub, herb' < *mihi* 'trees, wild plants', cl.4). An exception is the diminutive of the prefix *mwana-* used to describe baby animals (see §3.1.5), e.g. **vidzi**ana-kuku 'small chicks' < *ana-kuku* 'chicks'. The noun class concords used with diminutives are those of class 7/8 for all parts of speech.

In the same way that changing the noun class of a noun can create a diminutive or augmentative form, diminutive and augmentative noun class prefixes can be attached to appropriate adjectives. Note that the form of the diminutive prefix is *chidzi-* even when the adjective stem is disyllabic:

---

[3] There are no recorded instances of nouns which belong intrinsically to class 5/6 being augmented in this way.

3.1 Nominal morphology

-dide	'small'	>	***chidzidide***	'tiny, minute'
-baha	'large' (rare)	>	***dzibaha***	'huge'

3.1.4.3.2 Noun to locative noun

Locative nouns are formed through the addition of the suffix *-ni*[4] to the whole noun (including the noun class prefix if there is one). The result of this process is a noun in one of the locative noun classes (16, 17, and 18) rather than a prepositional phrase (which glosses in English and other languages might suggest). Although the resulting locative noun does not itself take one of the locative noun class prefixes, all demonstratives, qualificatives, verbs, etc. which modify the locative noun do. The three locative noun classes are illustrated in the following examples; the locative elements are in bold type and the locative suffix has been underlined:

munda 'field' (class 3)   >   *mndani*

(note *mu-* is reduced to *m-* as the penultimate syllable is accented)

(8)   Machero   phiy-a   **phara**   **ph**-ako   **mnda-<u>ni</u>**   **pha**=na   mkuyu
     tomorrow   go-FV   16.DEM2   16-2SG.POS   field-LOC   16=COM   3.fig_tree
     'Tomorrow go **there** to **your field where there** is a fig tree'

chumba 'room' (class 7)   >   *chumbani*

(9)   Ngoma ya gbwagbwara kala n'kpwandza kuvumbwa **ko chumbani kpwa** mufwa.
     'The "gbwagbwara" dance was the first to be danced **there at/in the room of** the deceased person.'

ko	***chumba-<u>ni</u>***	*ku-a*	*mu-fwa*
17.DEM3_VAR	room-LOC	17-ASS	1-dead_person

mikono 'hands' (class 4)   >   *mikononi*

(10)   Kulengana na utamaduni wa mdigo, ulongozi wowosi kala u **mikononi mwa mlume** na hata vivi sambi mambo ga chere gago.
      'According to Digo custom, any leadership was **in the hands of a man** and even nowadays things are still like that.'

mikono-<u>ni</u>	*mw-a*	*m-lume*
hands-LOC	18-ASS	1-man

---

[4] This is a reflex of the locative suffix *-ini* which is found only in Eastern Bantu languages (Guthrie's zones E, G, P, S) (Schadeberg 2003:82).

3.1.4.4 Other nominalizing derivations: adverb to noun

The prefix *chi-* is used to indicate manner in adverbials, e.g. *chihivyo* 'thus', *chifalume* 'royally', *chilume* 'bravely, boldly'. In certain words, this *chi-* prefix has been reanalysed as the class 7 prefix with the result that the entire form is nominalized, e.g. *chilume* 'bravery, boldness' as in (11):

(11) Chilume-**che** rero **chi**-ka-many-ikan-a.
 7.brave-3SG.7.pos today 7-HOD-know-STAT-FV
 'His bravery has become known today.'

3.1.5 Noun compounding

There are three kinds of agent nominalization in which the derived noun describes an agent but is composed of a compound of the agent plus a patient. The first construction is formed with the suffix *-adzi* on the agent followed by the patient, and the spelling convention is to hyphenate the two nouns:

mhendadzi-kazi 'worker' (lit: 'doer-work')
mlavyadzi-sadaka 'offerer of offerings' (i.e. priest, lit: 'offerer-offering')

In the second construction, the suffix on the derived noun is the regular final vowel *-a*, and the convention is to write the two nouns as separate words, reflecting the fact that this construction is arguably a syntactic phrase (albeit without an associative marker linking the two nouns).

mtema kuni 'woodcutter' (lit: 'cutter wood')

Some plant names which describe a property of the plant have a similar structure:

chivuma-nyuchi 'Agathisanthemum bojeri' (lit: 'buzzing-bees')
mdzenga-tsongo 'Antidesma venosum' (lit: 'builder-weaverbird')

In the final construction, the suffix on the derived agent noun is *-i* and the patient noun is part of a syntactic phrase headed by the class 1 associative marker *wa* 'of' since the agent noun is in class 1 and is the head of the noun phrase:

mhegi wa mihambo 'setter of traps' (i.e. trapper)

Another kind of noun compounding derives the names of young animals by prefixing *mwana-* 'child' to the name of the animal. In the plural the prefix is *ana-* and the name of the animal remains in the singular form.

mwana-diya 'puppy' cf. *diya* 'dog'
ana-diya 'puppies' cf. *madiya* 'dogs'

The prefix *mwana* is also found in the nouns *mwanachetu* 'woman', *mwanachiya* 'orphan', *mwanadamu* 'person', *mwanafundzi* 'student', *mwanajeshi* 'soldier', *mwanalume* 'man, husband', *mwanamadzi* 'assistant to a traditional healer', and *mwanatsi* 'citizen'.

3.1.6 Denominalizing processes

A noun can be made into a verb by the addition of the causative extension and a final vowel (for a more detailed discussion, see §4.3.1.2). However, this appears not to be a productive process in Digo, as it applies only to a few nouns of Swahili origin:

Table 3.7. Noun-to-verb correspondences

Noun	Verb
hakika 'certainty' (cl.9)	*hakikisha* 'confirm, make certain'
kodi 'tax' (cl.9)	*kodisha* 'rent'
shughuli 'business' (cl.9)	*shugulisha* 'occupy'

3.2 Qualificatives

3.2.1 Overview

Qualificatives are words or expressions which provide more information about noun phrases. All of the qualificatives in Digo can function both attributively (where the qualificative modifies a noun phrase) and predicatively (where the qualificative functions as a noun phrase in a similar way to a pronoun). With the exception of *chila* 'each, every', all qualificatives in Digo follow the noun which they modify. The usual order[5] of qualificatives following a noun is:

possessive > quantifier[6] > numeral > lexical adjective > phrasal adjective

For example:

(12) noun   quantifier   numeral   phrasal adjective
      ng'ombe *z-anjina*   *sabaa*   *za*   *ku-nona*
      10.cows   10-others   seven   10.ASS   INF-be_fat
      'seven other fat cows'

---

[5]There are occasional exceptions to this order, such as *mwaka mzima wosi* (year whole all i.e. 'the whole year') which violates the order of quantifier > adjective, but these are rare.
[6]The relative order of quantifiers is described in §3.2.3.2.

(13) noun   numeral   lexical adjective   phrasal adjective
     punga   sabaa   nyembamba   za   ku-nyala
     10.ears   seven   10.thin   10.ASS   INF-be_withered
     'seven thin withered ears of corn'

(14) noun   possessive   quantifier   phrasal adjective
     vitu   vyehu   vyosi   vya   gali
     8.things   8.1PL.POS   8.all   8.ASS   expensive
     'all our expensive things'

Qualificatives in Digo can be divided into two main types on the basis of their noun class concords. Lexical adjectives, numerals, and -nji 'many, much' take the same prefixes as the nouns they modify (although classes 11 and 14 are irregular), subject to the following assimilation rules:

mu + e > mwe	a + e > e	Ci + e > Cye	N + e > nye
mu + i > mwi	a + i > a	Ci + i > Ci	N + i > nyi

The associative marker -a, possessives, relative markers, and the quantifiers -osi 'all' and -anjina 'some, (an)other' take the same prefixes as the subject agreement markers on verbs (except for noun class 1 which is irregular in this respect), subject to the following assimilation rules (C can be /w/ class 1, 3 or 14, /r/ class 5 or 11, /g/ class 6, /ch/ class 7, /z/ class 10, or /ph/ class 16):

a + a > a	a + e > e	a + o > o
(v)i + a > (v)ya	(v)i + e > (v)ye	(v)i + o > (v)yo
Ci + a > Ca	Ci + e > Ce	Ci + o > Co
u + a > wa	u + e > we	u + o > wo
ku + a > kpwa	ku + e > kpwe	ku + o > ko

The concord sets are summarized in tables 3.2 and 3.3 above. In the rest of this section, possessives, quantifiers, numerals and adjectives will be discussed in the same order in which they occur in a noun phrase.

A note on demonstratives

Traditional grammars group possessives and demonstratives together as classifiers; since possessives are classified here as qualificatives it would be reasonable to expect that demonstratives would also be treated as qualificatives. However, I have decided to treat demonstratives in Digo as a separate word class for the following two reasons. First, there is little evidence for the category

3.2 Qualificatives

'classifier' in Digo. In English and other European languages there is only one classifier per noun phrase, and this is one of the distinctive characteristics of classifiers, but in most (all?) Bantu languages, possessives and demonstratives can co-occur (as in the examples below), which casts doubt on the existence of a category 'classifier' in Bantu languages.

(15) **hira**   nyumba-**ye**
     9.DEM2   9.house-9.3SG.POS
     'that house of hers' (lit: 'that her house')

(16) **yuya**   mwana   w-**ao**   m-mwenga
     1.DEM2   1.child   1-3PL.POS   1-one
     'that one child of theirs'

Second, possessives pattern with the associative marker -a, relative markers, and the quantifiers -osi 'all' and -anjina 'some, (an)other' with regard to the form of the noun class concords with which they are prefixed, and they occur in a fixed order relative to nouns and other qualificatives. Demonstratives, on the other hand, do not follow either of the patterns of noun class concords exhibited by the qualificatives, nor do they occur in a fixed order relative to nouns (the position of demonstratives in the noun phrase is discussed in §3.4.4.1). For this reason I have decided not to treat demonstratives as a kind of qualificative.

3.2.2 Possessives

Possessives in Digo always occur immediately following the head noun or demonstrative, if there is one. Adnominal possessives (modifying a noun) and pronominal possessives (self-standing) have the same form, except for the monosyllabic 2nd and 3rd person singular adnominal possessives which are suffixed to the noun. All of the other forms occur as separate words (with a noun class prefix) except where the first person singular possessive modifies most kinship terms, in which case they are suffixed to the noun they modify: akazangu < a-kaza-angu 'my wives', muwangu < mu-wa-wangu 'my niece/nephew', etc. The possessive forms are listed in table 3.8; for details of the agreement patterns with all noun classes, refer to table 3.3.

Table 3.8. Possessive concords with persons

Psn	Suffix	Psn	Suffix
1SG	'my, mine' -angu	1PL	'our, ours' -ehu
2SG	'your, yours' -o, -ako	2PL	'your, yours' -enu
3SG	'his, her, its' -e, -akpwe	3PL	'their, theirs' -ao

Examples:

(17) chakurya-ch-e   /   vyakurya-vy-e
     7.food-7-3SG.POS   8.food-8-3SG.POS
     'her/his food'

(18) chakurya   ch-osi   ni   ch-akpwe
     7.food   7-all   COP   7-3SG.POS

     vyakurya   vy-osi   ni   vy-akpwe
     8.food   8-all   COP   8-3SG.POS

     'all the food is hers/his'

(19) nyumba y-angu   nyumba-y-o   nyumba-y-e
     9.house 9-1SG.POS   9.house-9-2SG.POS   9.house-9-3SG.POS
     'my house'   'your (sg) house'   'her/his house'

     nyumba y-ehu   nyumba y-enu   nyumba y-ao
     9.house 9-1PL.POS   9.house 9-2PL.POS   9.house 9-3PL.POS
     'our house'   'your (pl) house'   'their house'

Kinship terms:

(20) mkpwazangu   mcheo   mchewe
     m-kaza-w-angu   mche-o   mche-we
     1-wife-1-1SG.POS   1.wife-1.2SG.POS   1.wife-1.3SG.POS
     'my wife'   'your (sg) wife'   'his wife'

(21) mwanangu   mwanao   mwanawe
     mwana-w-angu   mwana-o   mwana-w-e
     1.child-1-1SG.POS   1.child-1.2SG.POS   1.child-1-3SG.POS
     'my child'   'your (sg) child'   'her/his child'

(22) mwana w-ehu   mwana w-enu   mwana w-ao
     1child 1-1PL.POS   1.child 1-2PL.POS   1.child 1-3PL.POS
     'our child'   'your (pl) child'   'their child'

but

(23) m-lume w-angu   m-lume-o   m-lume-w-e
     1-man 1-1SG.POS   1-man-1.2SG.POS   1-man-1-3SG.POS
     'my husband'   'your (sg) husband' 'her husband'

3.2 Qualificatives

(24) m-tsedza w-angu   m-tsedza-o   m-tsedza-w-e
1-in_law 1-1SG.POS   1-in_law-1.2SG.POS   1-in_law-1-3SG.POS
'my in-law'   'your (sg) in-law'   'his in-law'

The morpheme *mya-* (plural *aya-*), which expresses the idea of one of the same kind, only ever occurs in conjunction with a possessive,[7] which is suffixed to the noun as in the case of kinship terms. Note that even with the plural *aya-* the plural possessive forms begin with /w/: *ayawehu* 'our companions'[8] as opposed to *asena ehu* 'our friends'.

Table 3.9. Possessives with *mya* and *aya*

Psn	*mya*	*aya*
1SG	myangu (< mya-wangu)	ayangu (< aya-wangu)
1PL	mya-wehu	aya-wehu
2SG	mya-o	aya-o
2PL	mya-wenu	aya-wenu
3SG	mya-we	aya-e
3PL	mya-wao	aya-wao

Forms of *mya-* (*aya-*) occur in vocative, attributive, and predicative (nominal) constructions:

(25) Ayangu   ku-redz-a   ma-adui!
2.fellows.2.1SG.POS   17-come-FV   6-enemy
'My companions, enemies are coming!'

(26) A-digo   aya-wao
2-Digos   2.fellows-2.3PL.POS
'Their fellow Digos'

(27) Ka ni   aya-wehu.
PST COP 2.fellows-2.1PL.POS
'They were our fellows.'

Like other noun phrases, forms containing *mya-* and *aya-* can be modified by other qualificatives, e.g. *ayangu anjina* 'my other companions' or 'others of my companions', *ayawao osi* 'all their companions'.

---

[7] The same situation occurs in Makua (P30, spoken in Mozambique) where the noun *mukhwa* 'companion' occurs only with possessives: *mukhwaaka* 'my companion', *mukhwiihu* 'our companion', *mukhwaawo* 'your (sg.) companion', *mukhwiinyu* 'your (pl.) companion', *mukhwaawe* 'his/her companion', *mukhwaaya* 'their companion' (Oliver Kröger, p.c. 2007). Similarly, possessives are often suffixed to the Swahili noun *mwenzi* 'friend, companion'.

[8] There is, however, one occurrence of *ayehu* 'our companions' in the database.

3.2.3 Quantifiers

As noted above, the quantifier *-nji* 'many, much' takes the nominal prefixes that occur on nouns, adjectives and numerals, whereas the quantifiers *-osi* 'all' and *-anjina* 'some, (an)other' take the same prefixes as the subject concords which occur (subject to assimilation rules) on verbs and which also occur on the associative marker *-a*, possessives, and relative markers:

(28) nyumba   nyinji
     10.houses 10.many
     'many houses'

(29) nyumba   z-anjina
     10.houses 10-other
     'other houses' or 'some houses'

(30) nyumba   z-osi
     10.houses 10-all
     'all the houses'

When *-osi* quantifies a singular noun it has the meaning 'whole, entire':

(31) ziya   r-osi
     5.lake 5-all
     'the whole lake'

Uniquely among the quantifiers, *-osi* can be prefixed by the 1PL, 2PL, and 3PL subject concords to express 'we all', 'you all' and 'they all':

hu + osi	>	hosi 'we all'
mu + osi	>	mosi 'you all'
a + osi	>	osi 'they all'

All of the quantifiers can function both attributively and predicatively. Attributive uses (where the quantifier modifies a noun) have been illustrated above. Examples of predicative use (where the quantifier replaces a noun phrase, much like a pronoun) are given below:

(32) Anjina   enu   a-na-hend-a   ngulu.
     2.other 2.2PL.POS 2-CONT-do-FV 9.pride
     'Some of you are boasting.'

3.2 Qualificatives

(33) Osi   a-chi-gomb-a   chilimwenga.
2.all   2-CON-speak-FV   together
'They all spoke in unison.'

(34) Fujo   ra-kal-a   dzi-nji.
5.trouble   5.PST-become-FV   5-much
'The trouble became great.'

When the 3rd person singular possessive is suffixed to -anjina it expresses 'some of them':

(35) anjina-e   piya   rero   phano   ta-a=pho
2.other-2.3SG.POS   also   today   16.DEM4   NEG-3PL=16.REF
'some of them also are not here today'

3.2.3.1 Other quantifiers

3.2.3.1.1 Any

The derivative quantifier 'any' is based on the quantifier 'all' with the first syllable being reduplicated (alternatively, this can be thought of as a combination of the relative marker and the quantifier 'all'): *yeyesi* (cl.1), *o osi* (cl.2), *wowosi* (cl.3/11/14), *yoyosi* (cl.4/9), *rorosi* (cl.5), *gogosi* (cl.6), *chochosi* (cl.7), *vyovyosi* (cl.8), *zozosi* (cl.10), *phophosi* (cl.16), *kokosi* (cl.17).[9] The quantifier 'any' can occur both attributively and predicatively, and can be modified by adjectives:

(36) chochosi   chi-i
7.any   7-evil
'anything evil'

(37) chakurya   chochosi
7.food   7.any
'any food'

3.2.3.1.2 Et cetera and so forth

Another derivative quantifier can be translated as 'et cetera, likewise'. This is formed from the quantifier -anjina 'some, (an)other' plus a 3rd person singular possessive suffix with the same concord:

---

[9] In the standardized orthography, these are written unhyphenated (*wowosi* 'etc.') as one word, except for *o osi* which is written as two words to avoid the potentially confusing sequence /oo/. The class 18 form *momosi* is theoretically possible but not attested in the database.

(38) ma-pango-ni   na   mw-anjina-mwe
     6-cave-LOC   COM   18-other-18.3SG.POS
     'caves, etc.' or 'caves and similar places'

In the following examples, the quantifier and the noun to which it refers are both highlighted:

(39) Mfwano wa **ma-dzina** ga fuko ni Nchandze, Ndzombo, N'gomba, N'gandi, Mwagandi, Mwakuriya, na Mkuriya **na g-anjina-ge**.

   ma-dzina ...   na   g-anjina-ge.
   6-names ...   COM   6-other-6.3SG.POS

   'Examples of the names of matrilineal clans are Nchandze ... and so forth.'

(40) **vitu**   kama   nazi,   ma-embe,   ngorosho
     8.things   like   10.coconuts,   6-mangoes,   10.cashews
     na   **vy-anjina-vye**
     COM   8-OTHER-8.3SG.POS

   '**things** like coconuts, mangoes, cashews, **etc**.'

(41) Adigo kala achisherehekea arusi kpwa kuvwina **ngoma** kama chimungbwe, marimba, chikpwarya, tsikitsi, madzumbano ama **zanjinaze**.

   'Digos used to celebrate weddings by performing **dances** like chimungbwe, marimba, chikpwarya, tsikitsi, madzumbano, or **similar ones**.'

   ngoma ...   z-anjina-ze
   10.dances ...   10-other-10.3SG.POS

The class 8 form *vyanjinavye* can form the basis of an adverb by the addition of the class 7 prefix *chi-*:

(42) Hinya   samaki   a-na-zuru   **ku-a**   **ku-a-ry-a**
     2.DEM1   2a.fish   2-CONT-harm   15-ASS   INF-2-eat-FV
     na   **chi-vy-anjina-vye**.
     COM   7-8-OTHER-8.3SG.POS

   'These fish can harm (a person) **by being eaten** (lit: eating them), **and so forth**.'

3.2.3.1.3 One of a group

One individual can be singled out from among a group of similar individuals using a quantifier which consists of the numeral *mwenga* 'one' with the appropriate noun class prefix followed by the associative form with the appropriate

3.2 Qualificatives

concord and the class 16 referential marker[10] *pho* within a single word. This expression is then followed immediately by the same form of the associative particle as a separate word:

(43) m-mwenga-wa=pho   wa   hara   a-falume
     1-one-1.ASS=16.REF 1.ASS   2.DEM2   2-kings
     'one of those kings'

(44) mwango   m-mwenga-wa=pho   wa   miango
     3.mountain   3-one-3.ASS=16.REF   3.ASS   4.mountains
     'one of the mountains'

(45) mbari   mwenga-ya=pho   ya   kabila
     9.clan   9.one-9.ASS=16.REF 9.ASS   5.tribe
     'one of the clans of the tribe'

This quantifier can be used clause finally (i.e. without the following associative phrase) when the group of individuals is identifiable (for example, because it is physically present):

(46) ruwa   mwenga-ra=pho
     5.flower   5.one-5.ASS=16.REF
     'one of (these) flowers'

3.2.3.1.4 Chila 'each, every'

The quantifier *chila* 'each, every' is invariable (it does not take noun class concords) and is the only qualificative to precede the noun when it occurs attributively:

(47) **Chila**   **pepho**   a-na   ma-wira-ge   amba-go
     every   spirit   3SG=COM   6-song-6.2SG.POS   REL-6.REL

     m-ganga   ni   a-kal-e   a-na-ga-many-a.
     1-healer   COP   3SG-be-SUB   3SG-CONT-6-know-FV

'Every spirit has its own songs which a traditional healer must know.'

Chila can also be used predicatively, in which case it often, but not always, stands for *chila wakati* or *chila mara* 'every time, whenever':

---

[10] See §4.1.10.2 for a discussion of referential markers.

(48) **Chila** a-chi-fika nyama a-ka-gbwir-w-a.
every 3SG-DEP-arrive 1a.animal 1-ANT-catch-PAS-FV
'**Every time** he arrived (at the trap) an animal had been caught.'

In other predicative (nominal) uses of *chila*, the 'understood' noun (in the following example *mutu* 'person' determines the noun concord on the following verb):

(49) Ichifika ligundzu atu anakutana na **chila ariyekala achedza** hipho kurimani njira kala achedza na mbeyu.
'When morning arrived the people came together and **every (person) who had come** there to farm the road would come with seeds.'
chila a-ri-ye-kal-a a-chedz-a
every 3SG-PST.REL-3SG.REL-be-FV 3SG-CONS.come-FV

3.2.3.1.5 Kamili *'complete'*

Another invariable quantifier is *kamili* 'complete' which can be used both attributively as in (50) and predicatively, as in (51):

(50) bei **kamili**
9.price complete
'the **full** price'

(51) maisha ga mutu ta-ga-kal-a **kamili** ku-a
6.life 6.ASS 1.person NEG-6-become-FV complete 17-ASS
unji wa mali a-ri=zo na=zo.
14.amount 14.ASS 10.wealth 3SG-COP=10.REF COM=10.REF

'A person's life does not become **complete** through the amount of wealth he has.'

3.2.3.2 *Relative order of quantifiers*

When a noun is modified by a quantifier, the resulting noun phrase can in turn be modified by another quantifier; that is, the 'outermost' quantifier (the one furthest from the noun) has scope over any quantifiers to its left. The following are the attested orders.

(52) -*anjina* 'some, (an)other' > -*nji* 'many, much'
mambo ganjina manji (matters other many) 'many other matters'
atu anjina anji (people other many) 'many other people'

3.2 Qualificatives

(53) *-anjina* 'some, (an)other' > *-osi* 'all'
 atu anjina osi (people other all) 'all other people'

(54) *o osi* 'any' > *-anjina* 'some, (an)other'
 chochosi chanjina (anything other) 'anything else'
 sababu yoyosi yanjina (reason any other) 'any other reason'

There are, however, exceptions to these orders, although these are rare (the order *-osi* > *-anjina* below only occurs once in the corpus):

(55) *atu osi anjina* (people all others) 'all other people'

(56) *mutu wanjina yeyesi* (person other any) 'any other person'

3.2.4 Numerals and *-ngaphi* 'how many/much'

3.2.4.1 Cardinal numbers

The cardinal numbers 1–10 are listed below. A preceding hyphen indicates that the form takes a noun class prefix, and forms in parentheses are the forms used in isolation where these differ from the form with noun class agreement.

1	*-mwenga*	2	*-iri (mbiri)*
3	*-hahu (tahu)*	4	*-ne (nne)*
5	*-tsano*	6	*sita*
7	*sabaa*	8	*nane*
9	*tisiya*	10	*kumi/-rongo (mrongo)*

There are also archaic forms *-handahu (tandahu)* 'six', *fungahe* 'seven' and *chenda* 'nine' which are rarely used now in Digo but which are still used in some related languages including Duruma and Giryama.

The common forms for units of ten are listed below; they are all invariable:

20	*ishirini*	30	*salasini*
40	*arubaini*	50	*hamsini*
60	*sitini*	70	*sabini*
80	*themanini/samanini*	90	*tisini*

One of the terms for 10 (*-rongo*) functions simultaneously as a qualificative and a noun (*mrongo* in noun class 3). It can modify noun phrases but can also be modified by other numerals; the numerals 20, 30, etc. can be made using *mirongo* (class 4) the plural of *mrongo*, although invariable forms borrowed from Swahili, e.g. *ishirini* (20), *salasini* (30), are more commonly used.

(57) A-na   nyumba   mi-rongo   mi-iri.
    3SG-COM   10.house   4-ten   4-two
    'He has twenty houses.'

The words for 100 (*mia* and *gana*), 1,000 (*elufu* and *chikwi*), and 100,000 (*laki*) also function simultaneously as qualificatives and nouns. The words *mia*, *elufu* and *laki* have been borrowed from Swahili and, being invariable, all take class 9/10 concords; *gana* is in class 5 and takes its plural in class 6: *magana*. They can modify noun phrases but can also be modified by other numerals: *mia mwenga* (100), *mia mbiri* (200), *gana mwenga* (100), *magana mairi* (200), *elufu mwenga* (1,000), *elufu mbiri* (2,000), *laki mwenga* (100,000), *laki mbiri* (200,000), etc.

Numerals can modify quantifiers when they are used predicatively (in place of a noun phrase) or attributively (modifying a noun phrase):

(58) osi   a-iri
    2.all   2-two
    'both of them, them both'

(59) atu   anjina   a-iri
    2.people   2.other   2-two
    'two other people'

3.2.4.2 Ordinal numbers

The ordinal numbers from 4 to 10 are the same as the cardinal numbers. However, the ordinal forms for 'first', 'second' and 'third' are *kpwandza* 'first' formed from the infinitive form of the verb *andza* 'begin', *phiri* 'second' which is derived from the stem *-iri* although *ph* is not analysable as a prefix, and *hahu* 'third'. Ordinal numbers are preceded by the associative marker *-a* and function like phrasal adjectives: *safari yangu ya kpwandza* 'my first journey', *mwezi wa phiri* 'the second month', *mara ya hahu* 'the third time', *siku ya nne* 'the fourth day', etc.

3.2.4.3 -ngaphi 'how many/much'

When the number or quantity of something is not known, this information can be requested using *-ngaphi*.[11] The position of *-ngaphi* within the noun phrase is not fixed; it occurs after possessives and quantifiers but has a variable position relative to lexical and phrasal adjectives:

---

[11] Fleisch (2000:97) calls the equivalent form in Lucazi *-ngáhì* a 'quantitative interrogative pronoun' but both *-ngáhì* and *-ngaphi* behave morphologically as qualificatives, taking the same noun class prefixes that occur on nouns, adjectives, and numerals.

(60) Vitabu   vy-angu   **vi-ngaphi?**
     8.books   8-1SG.POS   8-how_many
     'How many books of mine?' 'How many of my books?'

(61) Mihi   y-anjina   **mi-ngaphi?**
     4.trees 4-other   4-how_many
     'How many other trees?'

(62) Kaphu   **ngaphi**   nono?
     10.baskets 10.how_many 10.good
     'How many good baskets?'

(63) Mihi   mi-kulu   **mi-ngaphi?**
     4.trees 4-big   4-how_many
     'How many big trees?'

(64) Kaphu   **ngaphi**   za   ku-tsukul-a?
     10.baskets 10.how_many 10.ASS   INF-carry-FV
     'How many baskets for carrying?'

(65) Vitabu   vy-a   kare   **vi-ngaphi?**
     8.books 8-ASS   long_ago   8-how_many
     'How many old books?'

3.2.5 Lexical adjectives

Digo has invariable lexical adjectives (many of Arabic origin, most likely borrowed from Swahili) and lexical adjectives which agree with the noun being modified (see table 3.2);[12] both are exemplified below:

(66) Chitabu **rahisi** chi   dzulu   ya   meza   **rahisi.**
     7.book   cheap   7SC   on_top   9.ASS   9.table   cheap
     'The **cheap** book is on the **cheap** table.'

(67) Chitabu **chi-ziho** chi   dzulu   ya   meza   **n-ziho.**
     7.book   7-heavy   7SC   on_top   9.ASS   9.table   9-heavy
     'The **heavy** book is on the **heavy** table.'

---

[12] In the citation forms of the Digo dictionary (Mwalonya et al. 2012), lexical adjectives which agree with the noun being modified are written with a preceding hyphen: -ziho, whereas invariable lexical adjectives are written without a hyphen: rahisi.

3.2.5.1 Monosyllabic adjectives

The monosyllabic adjectives such as *-i* 'evil', *-re* 'long, tall', *-phya* 'new',[13] and *-dzo* 'good' agree with the noun which they modify, taking the same prefixes as vowel-initial adjectives as listed in table 3.2, with the exceptions listed in table 3.10.

In class 9/10, the *nyi-* prefix is obligatory with *-re* and strongly preferred with *-phya* (*nyire*, *nyiphya*), whilst the *mbi-* prefix is obligatory with *-i* and *-dzo* (*mbii*, *mbidzo*):

(68) Bada   ya   chakurya hwa-kal-a   na   **ng'andzi**   **mbidzo.**
     after 9.ASS 7.food   1PL.PST-be-FV COM   9.conversation   9.good
     'After the meal we had **a good conversation**.'

In class 14, the *mu-* prefix occurs when the adjective modifies a concrete noun, e.g. *wira muphya* 'a new song' and the *u-* prefix occurs when the adjective expresses an abstract quality, e.g. modifying an abstract noun: *utu ui* 'an evil thing', or functioning as an adverb: *nidzenge uphya* 'let me build anew'.

Table 3.10. Selected monosyllabic adjectives

Class	-phya 'new'	-i 'evil'	Class	-phya 'new'	-i 'evil'
1	muphya	mui	7	chiphya	chii
2	aphya	ai	8	viphya	vii
3	muphya	mui	9	nyiphya (mbiphya)	mbii
4	miphya	mii	10	nyiphya (mbiphya)	mbii
5	dziphya	dzii or iyi	11	dziphya	dzii
6	maphya	mai	14	muphya or uphya	mui or ui

3.2.5.2 Reduplicated adjectives

A number of adjectives are formed through reduplication, e.g. *tsini-tsini* 'low', *jolo-jolo* 'extraordinarily tall', *tsifwi-tsifwi* 'fine' (of flour or grains). In some cases the unreduplicated form is a meaningful unit (e.g. *tsini* 'underneath, below') but in others the unreduplicated form has been lost from the language, if it ever existed. In the case of adjectives which take noun class prefixes, such as *adzo-adzo*, the reduplicated form includes the noun class prefix *a-*:

(69) Nyumba   iratu   i-na   atu   **a-dzo-a-dzo.**
     9.house   9.DEM2_VARIANT 9-COM   2.people 2-good-2-good
     'That family (lit: house) has **kind-hearted** people.'

---

[13] In southern (Tanzanian) Digo 'new' is *-piamu*.

3.2 Qualificatives

3.2.5.3 Adjectives functioning as adverbs and quantifiers

Some adjectives can become adverbs through the addition of a class 8 or 11 prefix:

-nono 'good'   >   vinono 'well'
-phya 'new'   >   uphya 'anew'

Other expressions can function both as adjectives and as adverbs without any change of form:

(70) Wa-hend-a   kazi   **maruru.**
     3SG.PST-do-FV 9.work   hasty/hastily
     'He did **hasty** work.'

(71) A-ka-hend-a   kazi-ye   **maruru.**
     3SG-HOD-do-FV 9.work-6.3SG.POS   hasty/hastily
     'He did his work **hastily**.'

(72) Kamba   i   **reje-reje;**   i-ka-fung-w-a   **reje-reje.**
     9.rope 9SC loose/loosely   9-ANT-tie-PAS-FV   loose/loosely
     'The rope is **loose**; it has been tied **loosely**.'

The noun *ndulu* 'heap' can function both as an adverb and as an adjective. Note that *ndulu* remains a noun syntactically in that it can be modified by the adjective *ndzima* 'whole' which takes the class 9 agreement prefix:

(73) Vitu   vya-tsam-iz-w-a   ni   atu   **ndulu.**
     8.things   8.PST-move-CAUS-PAS-FV   by   2.people   9.heap
     'The things were moved by people (into) **a heap**.'

(74) Kumbavi   ta-m-many-a   rorosi,
     EXCL   NEG-2PL-know-FV   5.anything

     m=na   ma-shaka   **ndulu   ndzima!**
     2PL=COM   6-trouble   9.heap   9.whole

     'Good heavens you don't know anything, you have **a whole heap of trouble!**'

In example (74), *-zima* 'whole' functions more like a quantifier than an adjective. Similarly, the adjective *-huphu* 'empty' can function as a quantifier expressing completeness:

(75) Na-gomb-a   u-kpweli   **mu-huphu**.
     1SG.CONT-speak-FV 14-truth   14-empty
     'I am speaking the **complete** truth.'

(76) Mudzi   m-zima   ni   fujo   **huphu**.
     3.town   3-whole   COP 5.uproar   5.empty
     'The whole town was in **complete** uproar.'

(77) Ka-ya-kut-a   chochosi   ela   ma-kodza   **ma-huphu**.
     3SG.NEG-PST-find-FV   7.anything   but   6-leaves   6-empty
     'He found nothing but leaves.'

3.2.5.4 Colours

The three 'basic' colours—black, white and red—are expressed by colour terms which are lexical rather than phrasal adjectives (-*iru* 'black', -*ereru* 'white', *kundu* 'red'). They also have corresponding ideophones (see §6.4.2.6). The adjective -*ereru* 'white' can also mean 'open':

(78) Mkpwaphi   nku-vwal-a   shuka   za   **kundu**.
     1.Maasai   HAB-wear-FV 10.robes   10.ASS red
     'A Maasai usually wears **red** clothes.'

(79) Mwezi   u-chi-kal-a   **kundu** **do-do-do**   dza   mlatso.
     3.moon   3-CONS-become-FV   red   IDEO   like   3.blood
     'The moon became **bright red** like blood.'

(80) A-ka-rich-a   mi-fugo-ye   kondze   **ku-ereru**.
     3SG-HOD-leave-FV   4-livestock-4.3SG.POS outside   17-white
     'He has left his livestock outside **in the open**.'

Other colours are derived from nouns:

ivu 'ash'	>	-*ivu-ivu* 'grey'
chiphanga 'black kite'	>	-*a chiphanga-chiphanga* 'grey (only for birds)'
dongo 'soil'	>	*rangi ya dongo* 'brown'
ini 'liver'	>	*rangi ya ini* 'dark brown'
linyasi liitsi 'young grass'	>	*rangi ya linyasi liitsi* 'green'
mandano 'turmeric'	>	*rangi ya mandano* 'yellow'

3.2.6 Phrasal adjectives

Phrasal adjectives are defined here as syntactic phrases of various kinds which function as adjectives. In Digo, phrasal adjectives can be formed in two main

3.2 Qualificatives

ways: as relative clauses, and using the two associative particles -*a* and -*enye*. Relative clauses are discussed elsewhere (§7.3) and so only the use of the associative particles will be described here. In phrasal adjectives with the associative particle -*a*, the associative particle can be followed by a noun, an adjective, or an infinitive form of a verb. These constructions can express a range of meanings which can be variously translated into English using adjectives, adverbial phrases, prepositional phrases, possessives and quantifiers; however, formally there is no difference between them in Digo, and so they are all classed as phrasal adjectives. The following examples illustrate a range of phrasal adjectives consisting of the associative particle followed by a noun.

(81) nyumba   ishirini   za   simiti
     10.house twenty   10.ASS 9.cement
     'twenty cement houses'

(82) pembe   za   ndzovu
     10.horn 10.ASS 2a.elephant
     'elephants' tusks'

(83) mafuha ga   taa
     6.oil   6.ASS 9.lamp
     'lamp oil (kerosene)'

(84) madzi   ga   pwani
     6.water 6.ASS 16.coast
     'sea water'

Phrasal adjectives consisting of an associative particle and the infinitive form of a verb can likewise express a range of meanings:

(85) ng'ombe za   ku-ond-a
     10.cow   10.ASS INF-become_thin-FV
     'thin cows'

(86) ng'ombe za   ku-rim-a
     10.cow   10.ASS INF-farm-FV
     'cows to plough with'

(87) madzi   ga   ku-tosh-a
     6.water 6.ASS INF-suffice-FV
     'enough water'

(88) ruwiya za ku-tish-a
10.vision 10.ASS INF-frighten-FV
'frightening visions'

(89) sherehe ya ku-vyal-w-a mwana
9.party 9.ASS INF-bear-PAS-FV 1.child
'a celebration for the birth of a child'

In example (90), the noun *nyama* 'meat' is modified by two phrasal adjectives, the first consisting of the associative particle followed by the locative noun *sokoni* 'market' and the second consisting of an associative particle and the infinitive form of the verb *gula* 'buy' with the emphatic 'modal' marker *henda*:

(90) Mkpwazangu karya sima, arya **nyama za sokoni za kuhendagula.**
 'My wife does not eat maize flour, she eats **meat from the market which has to be bought.**'
 nyama za soko-ni za ku-henda-gul-a
 10.meat 10.ASS market-LOC 10.ASS INF-EMPH-buy-FV

The following examples illustrate the combination of the associative particle and lexical adjectives.[14] There are, of course, fewer phrasal adjectives which incorporate lexical adjectives (since there are very few lexical adjectives in Digo).

(91) tsi za kure
10.country 10.ASS distant
'distant countries'

(92) vitu vya gali
8.things 8.ASS expensive
'expensive things'

(93) madzi ga ngó
6.water 6.ASS cold
'cold water'

(94) chitabu cha kare
7.book 7.ASS old
'an old book'

---

[14] Syntactically, there is a strong case for regarding these as nouns rather than adjectives, since the associative particle typically conjoins nouns. However, since these expressions only ever occur elsewhere as adjectives (e.g. *ni kure* 'it is far', *ni gali* 'it is expensive') and never as nouns, they are treated as adjectives in this analysis.

Phrasal adjectives with the associative particle *-enye* are far less frequent. The following examples illustrate attributive and predicative (nominal) uses of this construction respectively (see also §6.1.5).

(95) mutu   mw-enye   haki
     1.person 1-ASS   9.right
     'a just/righteous person'

(96) mw-enye   dambi
     1-ASS   10.sin
     'a sinner'

3.3 Pronouns

3.3.1 Scope and definitions

This section deals with only a subset of the forms that are termed 'pronouns' in some other grammatical descriptions. For example, what Fleisch (2000:97–98) calls 'indefinite pronouns' and glosses as 'a different', 'another', 'all' and 'any, each' are treated as quantifiers here (cf. §3.2.3). The same applies to 'quantitative interrogative pronouns' (Fleisch 2000:97) expressing 'how much' or 'how many' (cf. §3.2.4.3). Similarly, what Fleisch (2000:86–88) calls 'possessive pronouns' can, in Digo, function both predicatively (that is, in place of a noun phrase like English 'mine', 'yours', etc.) and attributively (that is, modifying a noun phrase like English 'my', 'your', etc.). Rather than label the same form as both a pronoun and a qualificative, depending on whether it is used predicatively or attributively, possessives are treated uniquely as qualificatives here (cf. §3.2.2), since most qualificatives in Digo can also be used predicatively as well as attributively. On the other hand, I have kept 'emphatic pronouns' here (§3.2.3), even though they function more like adverbs (they modify verb phrases) than like pronouns (they don't replace noun phrases). Finally, the system of demonstratives in Digo is so complex and plays such an important role in the organization of Digo discourse that it is discussed separately from pronouns (see §3.4).

3.3.2 Independent pronouns

Independent personal pronouns are words that (in their complete forms) consist of two syllables, are free morphemes, and function as a nominal constituent (that is, they behave syntactically as noun phrases). There are no distinct forms used for, e.g. children or elderly (respected) people in Digo, nor is there any difference in form when independent pronouns function syntactically as subjects, objects, or obliques.

Independent pronouns occur in both complete and reduced forms. The reduced forms consist (with one exception discussed below) of the final syllable of the primary complete form (listed first) and are identical to the referential markers which occur in copula constructions *ndimi* 'it is me', *siswi* 'we are not', etc. (see §4.1.10.2 and §8.1.2.1) and which follow the comitative particle *na* to create 'referential additives' *nami*, *naswi*, etc. (see §6.3.2). The independent pronouns are listed in table 3.11.

Table 3.11. Independent pronouns

	1st person	2nd person	3rd person
Singular	mimi, mino	uwe	iye
	mi	we	ye
Plural	swiswi, sisi, sino	mwimwi, mwino	aho
	swi	mwi	o (nyo)

From table 3.11 it is clear that there are differences between the independent pronouns attested for each person/number in terms of both the number of pronouns and their morphological forms:

- 1SG, 1PL and 2PL all have alternative forms ending in *-no*. These have a very similar distribution to the metarepresentational demonstratives (see §3.4.3.1.4) which also end in *-no* (and for this reason I call them 'metarepresentational pronouns').
- In addition to the metarepresentational pronoun *sino*, there are two additional 1PL pronouns: the primary form *swiswi* and another form *sisi*. *Sisi* is identical with the Swahili 1PL pronoun and is almost certainly a borrowed form; *swiswi* is probably the original Digo pronoun, as this is the form which is reduced to *swi* and which occurs in the negative copula construction *siswi* 'we are not' (see §7.6.1.2.1) and the 'referential additive' *naswi* (see §6.3.2).
- The reduced form of the 3PL pronoun *aho* could be expected to be *ho*, but due to phonological elision of [h] which intervocalically is realized phonetically only by nasalization of the adjacent vowels, the attested form is *o*. However, *o* is rare, perhaps because it is not always phonologically distinct in speech, and often *nyo* is found where *aho* or *o* would be expected. The form *nyo* is identical to the reduced form of the demonstrative *hinyo*, and this is almost certainly its origin.

As mentioned above, Digo also has a set of demonstratives. There are two main distributional differences between independent pronouns and demonstratives in Digo. First, unlike some other Bantu languages, such as Kitalinga (Paluku 1998:189–192), independent pronouns are restricted to referents within the person and number set (of which third person singular and plural correspond to noun classes 1 and 2, respectively), whereas demonstratives occur with every noun class but not with first and second person referents. It follows that independent pronouns are invariable, i.e. they do not take noun class concords, and refer to animate entities only. Second, demonstratives in Digo can occur either predicatively, that is, in place of a noun phrase, or attributively,

3.3 Pronouns

that is, modifying a coreferential noun phrase, whereas independent pronouns always occur predicatively.

Since the subject and object of a clause with a verbal predicate are indicated by means of the subject concord and verb complement concord (or 'object marker') in each verb group, independent pronouns are often redundant as indicators of participant reference, apart from their use as obliques and in certain referential predicates:

(97) Ni **aho** a-iri tu, mutu na ndugu-ye.
COP 3PL 2-two IDEO 1.person COM 9.brother-9.3SG.POS
'It was just **them** two, the person and his brother'

Instead, independent pronouns are commonly used for emphasis, often—but not always—contrastive. Independent pronouns can be coreferential with the subject concord or the verb complement concord, and can occur before or after the verb group in which either of these occurs, and occasionally, as in example (98), both before and after the verb group:

(98) Hiyo kulu ya aphu-yo, **we** u-na-i-hal-a **uwe**,
9.DEM3 9.big 9.ASS 9.uncle-9.2SG.POS 2SG 2SG-CONT-9-take-FV 2SG
sababu?
9.reason
'This large (plate) is for your uncle, **you** are taking it **you**, why?'

3.3.3 Exclusive pronouns

Exclusive pronouns indicate that a particular referent and no other is being referred to; that is, the referent is mentioned to the exclusion of other potential referents, either because the referent is taken to be acting or acted upon alone 'by herself', or because mention of other potential referents is not relevant 'she herself'. In (99) below, the addressees are told "Go and look for it yourselves", that is, without help from anyone else (including the speaker). In (100), the point is that the addressee knew how the speaker worked for him; whether anyone else also knew this is irrelevant.[15]

(99) M-ka-endz-e **enye**.
2PL-IT-search-SUB 2.EXCLUSIVE
'Go and search (for it) **yourselves**.'

---

[15]Exclusive pronouns in Digo correspond to what in Bentley and Kulemeka (2001:16–17) and Cammenga (2004:212–213) are called 'reflexive pronouns' or simply 'reflexives'. The use of the term 'reflexive' reflects the fact that such expressions are usually translated in English by 'yourself', 'ourselves', 'herself', etc., which share the form of the reflexive pronoun in English (compare the exclusive 'I saw her myself' and the reflexive 'I shaved myself'). True reflexives are expressed in Digo by means of the reflexive marker *dzi-* in the verb complement concord slot within the verb group (§4.1.5).

(100) **Uwe** **mw-enye** *u-na-many-a* *vyo-ku-hend-er-a* *kazi.*
2SG 1-EXCLUSIVE 2SG-CONT-know-FV 8.REL-2SG-do-APPL-FV 9.work
'**You yourself** know how I worked for you.'

Exclusive pronouns are based on the root *-enye* preceded by the same nominal prefix which occurs on nouns, adjectives, numerals, and some quantifiers. In its exclusive pronoun use, *-enye* functions morphologically as a lexical adjective, as noted by Cammenga (2004:212) in respect of the Kuria 'reflexive' *-enɛ*. The same root behaves morphologically as an associative particle when it coordinates two noun phrases; in this case it functions either as a phrasal adjective (§3.2.6) or as a relational expression (§6.1.5). Historically, it is likely that all of these functions of *-enye* derive from a lexical expression meaning 'owner' or 'own', which is still current:

(101) *Ng'ombe* *i-olag-w-a* *ni* *chala* *cha* **mwenye.**
9.cow 9-kill-PAS-FV by 7.finger 7.ASS 1.owner
'A cow is killed by the finger of its **owner**.'

(102) *Muoza* *nyama* *ni* **mwenye** *muhambo.*
1.rot 9.meat COP 1.owner 3.trap
'The one who lets the meat rot is the **owner** of the trap.'

(103) *A-kal-e* *na* *nyama-e* **mw-enye.**
3SG-COP-SUB COM 2a.animals-2.3SG.POS 1-own
'Let him keep (lit: be/remain with) his **own** animals.'

As an exclusive pronoun, *-enye* can occur either alone or preceded by an independent pronoun or a noun phrase. The meaning of *-enye* in all of these constructions is essentially the same. In addition to the construction NP + *-enye* which expresses 'the NP itself', constructions consisting of an independent pronoun and *-enye* also occur. These are listed in table 3.12.

Table 3.12. Exclusive personal pronoun constructions

	1st person	2nd person	3rd person
Singular	mimi mwenye	uwe mwenye	iye mwenye
	mi mwenye	we mwenye	ye mwenye
	mwenye	mwenye	mwenye
Plural	sisi enye	mwimwi enye	aho enye
	si enye	mwi enye	o enye
	swi enye[a]	enye	nyo enye
	enye		enye

[a] Digo speakers have informed me that *swiswi enye* is possible but archaic, and I have never heard or seen it used.

3.3 Pronouns

Examples of *-enye* with complete and reduced forms of the 2SG independent pronouns are provided below:

(104) Ela **uwe mw-enye** u-nda-kal-a m-tumiya na
but 2SG 1-EXCLUSIVE 2SG-FUT-become-FV 1-old_person COM
u-nda-fw-a=to.
2SG-FUT-die-FV=WELL

'But **you yourself** will be an old man and you will die well.'

(105) Hebu lol-a **we mw-enye,** vira maisha ga-phiy-a-vyo,
EXCL look-FV 2SG 1-EXCLUSIVE 8.DEM2 6.life 6-go-FV-8.REL
m-chetu, anache na **we mw-enye** u-na-tak-a
1-woman 2.children COM 2SG 1-EXCLUSIVE 2SG-CONT-want-FV
chakurya na ta-pha=na.
7.food COM NEG-16=COM

'Now look **(you) yourself** how life is going, your wife, children and **you yourself** want food and there is none.'

Examples are provided below of *-enye* without an independent pronoun referring respectively to 1SG and 2SG referents:

(106) Mafuha ni g-angu, ná-ga-lavy-a **mw-enye.**
6.oil COP 6-1SG.POS 1SG.PST-6-give-FV 1-EXCLUSIVE

'The oil is mine, I gave it **myself** (i.e. of my own accord).'

(107) Ni-ph-a atu, lakini mali hal-a **mw-enye.**
1SG-give-FV 2.people but 9.wealth take-FV 1-EXCLUSIVE

'Give me the people, but the plunder take it **yourself.**'

The combination NP + *-enye* expresses 'the NP itself' or 'the actual NP':

(108) **Uchaguzi w-enye** wa-andz-a na mtsudzo
14.election 11-EXCLUSIVE 11.PST-begin-FV COM 3.nomination
wa KANU.
3.ASS PROPER_NAME

'**The election itself** started with the nominations for KANU.'

(109) Phahi,   yuya   m-sichana   wa-kpwenda-hal-a
      so   1.DEM2   1-girl   3SG.PST-ITIVE-fetch-FV
      nine   **mw-enye**   wa   yuya   mwana.
      1a.mother   1-EXCLUSIVE   1.ASS   1.DEM2   1.child

'So, the girl went and fetched **the real mother** (lit: the mother herself) of the child.'

(110) *Namba ya mafuko ga mdigo ni kumi na sita na mbari zao piya ni kumi na sita, na **mafuko genye** ndigo higa ...*

'The number of matrilineal clans is sixteen and the patrilineal clans are also sixteen, and **the matrilineal clans themselves** are the following ...'

ma-fuko   **g-enye**   ndi=go   higa ...
6-matrilineal_clan   6-EXCLUSIVE   COP=6.REF   6.DEM1

When *-enye* follows a verb group, the emphasis is on the agency of the event described, hence in the example below the author is stating not that the gate itself opened (in contrast to some part of the gate or some other opening) but the the gate opened by itself, that is, without any other agent being involved:

(111) Hiro   ryango   ra-vuguk-a   **r-enye**   na   a-chi-tsap-a.
      5.DEM3   5.gate   5.PST-open-FV   5-EXCLUSIVE   COM   3PL-CONS-pass-FV

'The gate opened **by itself** and they passed through.'

There are also some idiomatic uses of *-enye*. The expression *enye kpwa enye* (also *o enye kpwa enye*) expresses 'among themselves':

(112) A-bish-a   o   enye   ku-a   enye.
      3PL.PST-speak-FV   3PL   2.EXCLUSIVE   17-ASS   2.EXCLUSIVE

'They spoke **among themselves**.'

(113) *Mihi yanjina taidzengerwa. Mihi hino Adigo anaamini kukala inahendesa atu kuheha makaya au kukosana **enye kpwa enye**.*

'Other trees were not used for building. These trees Digos believed that they make people fight at home or quarrel **among themselves**.'

ku-kosan-a   enye   ku-a   enye
INF-quarrel-FV   2.EXCLUSIVE   17-ASS   2.EXCLUSIVE

The construction NP-possessive + *-enye* expresses 'one's very own':

3.3 Pronouns

(114) mwana-o **mw-enye** m-lume
 1.son-1.2SG.POS 1-EXCLUSIVE 1-male
 'your **very own** son'

The reduplicated construction *-enye -enye* means 'genuine, real':

(115) M-digo mw-enye mw-enye
 1-Digo 1-EXCLUSIVE 1-EXCLUSIVE
 'a real Digo'

3.3.4 Vocative pronouns

The vocative forms of the 2nd person pronouns (like English *Hey, you!*) are *wee* (singular, sometimes shortened to *we*) and *mwi* (plural). These can co-occur with coreferential noun phrases, e.g.:

(116) **Wee** bwana ndzoo!
 2SG 1a.sir come.IMP
 '**You** sir come here!'

(117) **Mwi** ayangu, ni-godz-a-ni phapha!
 2PL 2.fellows.2.1SG.POS 1SG-wait-FV-PL 16.DEM1_VARIANT
 '**You** my companions, wait for me there!'

Vocative forms can also be used, particularly in questions, for emphasis:

(118) "Amba ni handzo, ku-on-ere jahazi **wee**?
 DM COP 9.lie 2SG.NEG-see-PFV 9.dhow 2SG
 Mo ndani ku-on-ere mwanachetu **wee**?"
 18.DEM3_VAR 18.inside 2SG.NEG-see-PFV 1-woman 2SG

"So it's a lie, you didn't see the dhow (did) **you**? There inside you didn't see the woman (did) **you**?"

3.3.5 Interrogative pronouns

Interrogative pronouns consist (with the exception of noun class 1) of the subject concord prefixed to the clitics *ani* or *phi*. When *ni* (possibly a reduced form of *ani*) and *phi* are attached to verbs they express 'what' and 'where' respectively (see §4.1.11.1), but *ani* and *phi* attached to subject concords function as more general question markers. Apart from distributional differences (*ani* is more restricted in terms of the noun classes with which it can occur than *phi*), the two forms have similar if not identical meanings. Compare (119) with *ani* and (120) with *phi*:

(119) Ni   maneno   g=**ani**   gano   u-chi-go-hend-a?
      COP   6.words   6=Q   6.DEM4   2SG-DEP-6.REL-do-FV
      'What is this you have done?'

(120) Ni   mambo   ga=**phi** gano   u-hend-a-go?
      COP   6.matters 6=Q   6.DEM4   2SG-do-FV-6.REL
      'What is this you are doing?'

Table 3.13 lists the forms of the interrogative pronouns.

Table 3.13. Interrogative pronouns

Class	Who?/which? *ani* form	Who?/which? *phi* form
1	ani *or* wani	yuphi
2	ano ani	aphi
3	wani	uphi
4	yani	iphi
5	rani	riphi
6	gani	gaphi
7	chani	chiphi
8	vyani	viphi
9	yani	iphi
10	zani	ziphi
11	rani	riphi
14	wani	uphi
16/17/18		kuphi

There are three interrogative pronouns listed for noun class 1: one consists of the subject concord *a-* plus *ani* giving *ani* 'who, whom'; another consists of the prefix *wa-* (which is used with the associative marker *-a*, the possessive, and the quantifier 'another') plus *ani* giving *wani* 'which'; the final form consists of the prefix *yu-* (found in copula constructions) plus *phi* giving *yuphi* 'who, whom, which'. The forms *ani* and *yuphi* are very similar in meaning (compare *U ani we?* with *We u yuphi?* both meaning 'Who are you?') but *ani* is statistically far more frequent than *yuphi* in the available corpus.

The forms *ani* and *wani* differ in that *ani* is used predicatively (i.e. without an accompanying coreferential NP) whereas *wani* is used attributively (i.e. with an accompanying coreferential NP); the following examples illustrate the difference:

(121) M-na-endz-a   **ani?**
      2PL-CONT-search-FV   3SG.Q
      'You looking for whom?'

3.4 Demonstratives

(122) Yuya   m-chetu   a-nda-kal-a   m-kaza   **ani**?
      1.DEM2 1-woman   3SG-FUT-become-FV   1-wife   3SG.Q
      'That woman will become the wife of whom?'

(123) Yuno   ni   **nyama   wani**?
      1.DEM4   COP   1a.animal 1.Q
      'Which animal is/was that?'

1SG and 2SG interrogative pronouns correspond to the forms for noun class 1, and 1PL and 2PL interrogative pronouns correspond to the forms for noun class 2 (although naturally 1st person interrogative pronouns are extremely rare). The following two examples[16] illustrate the use of interrogative pronouns which are coreferential with 2nd person subjects.

(124) We   kpwani   ndi=we   **ani**?
      2SG   why.EXCL   COP=2SG   3SG.Q
      'Who are you?' ('Who on earth are you?')

(125) Mwino   mu   **ano   ani**?
      2PL   2PL.COP   PL   3PL.Q
      'Who are you?'

A final point of note is the relation between the two interrogative markers *ani* and *ni*. The clitic *ani* occurs as a bound morpheme attached to subject concords, as illustrated above; *ni* occurs both as a bound morpheme attached to verbs and in the question words *nini* 'what' and *rini* 'when' and as a free morpheme in clause-final position (note the homophonous copula preceding the question marker):

(126) Kazi   y-enu   ni   **ni**?
      9.work   9-2PL.POS   COP   Q
      'What is your work?'

3.4 Demonstratives

3.4.1 Definition

Demonstratives can be classified in various ways, each of which highlights a valid feature of the distribution or function of demonstratives within the system of reference of a given language. Perhaps the most common classification

---

[16]Note that in (124), *kpwani* is an emphatic expression which occurs only in interrogative clauses or in other clauses used as questions where there is an element of surprise. It probably derives historically either from *kpwa nini* 'why' or from the class 15 or 17 SC plus *ni*. The usual expression for 'why?' in Digo is *kpwa utu wani*? (lit: 'for thing what').

is to treat demonstratives as a kind of pronoun; many grammars of Bantu languages, from Cole (1955:129–134) and Doke ([1930] 1990:90–93) to Cammenga (2004:218–220) and Fleisch (2000:88–93) use the term 'demonstrative pronoun'. Doke ([1930] 1990:88) defines a pronoun as "a word which signifies anything concrete or abstract without being its name." However, this definition entails that adjectives, used predicatively (in place of a noun phrase) can be classified as pronouns—an approach which none of the grammars listed above takes. Since demonstratives, like adjectives but unlike the independent pronouns discussed in §3.3.2, can occur both attributively and predicatively (that is, they can modify as well as replace a noun phrase), they are not treated as pronouns here. In addition, demonstratives are not restricted to referents within the person and number set, whereas independent pronouns are.

Alternatively, the term 'demonstrative' has been used as an inclusive term covering a range of indexical expressions such as personal pronouns, 'now', 'yesterday', 'here', and 'this'. I have avoided this use of the term 'demonstrative', which is characteristic of the philosophical (notably Fregean) as opposed to linguistic literature (see, for example, Yourgrau 1990), as it is too broad for the purposes of describing linguistic forms and functions in detail. That said, a number of indexical expressions referring to time 'now', 'whilst' and manner 'thus', 'in this way' are clearly demonstratives in Digo according to morphological criteria, and their distribution resembles that of demonstrative forms used to refer to physical entities.

A more logical way to categorize demonstratives is to classify them as a subcategory of qualificatives, as do Zimmermann and Hasheela (1998:85–87). According to this approach, demonstratives are viewed as classifiers or specifiers. In languages like English, demonstratives and other classifiers are restricted to one per noun and occur in a fixed position relative to the noun. In Digo, however, demonstratives can co-occur with possessives and even with other demonstratives, and can occur both before and after the noun which they modify. However I have decided against treating demonstratives under the heading 'qualificatives' not because of these differences, but for the following two reasons.

First, demonstratives are treated separately from qualificatives or any other word class because of the complex and pervasive nature of the Digo demonstrative system. Each noun class has at least five demonstratives, most of which can be used predicatively (that is, standing alone) and attributively (that is, modifying a noun phrase), and can occur both before a noun (Dem+N) and after a noun (N+Dem). For example, noun class 6 has the following demonstrative forms listed in order of frequency in my database, with the most common first (the English glosses are only approximate): *higa* 'these', *higo* 'these/those previously referred to', *gara* 'those', *gano* 'these' (almost always used in information questions), *gago* 'those, those same, such', *garatu* 'those very same' and *gaga* 'these'. There is also a short form *go* 'those'. Most of these demonstrative forms can occur alone, preceding a noun, or following a noun, but whereas *higa* usually follows a noun (N+*higa*), *gara* almost always precedes a noun (*gara*+N) and on the rare occasions when it follows a noun this is often in the construction 'N *garatu gara*' 'those very same N' in which two demonstratives co-occur.

3.4 Demonstratives

Second, demonstratives in Digo can be used as both spatial-deictic expressions, referring to an entity within the interlocutors' physical environment, and as discourse-deictic expressions, referring to an entity within a stretch of discourse, such as a story. At the level of discourse, demonstratives play an important role in keeping track of participants (that is, characters in a story) as they 'enter', 'leave', and 're-enter' the story as the narrative progresses. They also play a role in identifying participants as either 'major' (important characters which play an active role throughout) and 'minor' (less important characters which may only appear for a short time or which do not play an active role). Demonstratives in classes 8 and 17 may also function as 'manner-deictic' expressions (Güldemann 2002:278) expressing similarity in relation to events in respect of manner 'thus' and time of occurrence 'now', 'whilst'. Manner deictics in Digo include a range of meanings expressing the notions of 'that way already referred to', 'this way which is about to be described', and 'that very same way'.[17]

3.4.2 Classification and forms of demonstratives

Many Bantu languages have at least three kinds of demonstratives, which are often described as 'proximal' (near to the speaker, e.g. Swahili *huyu*), 'distal' (far from the speaker or the addressee, e.g. Swahili *yule*) and 'nonproximal' (near to the addressee, e.g. Swahili *huyo*, but also used when the speaker can't identify the referent specifically).[18] Often, each kind of demonstrative has a variant form which differs from the 'basic' form distributionally as well as structurally. Demonstratives with these three basic functions are found in Digo also, although the use of the nonproximal form is not as clear-cut as the characterization above suggests. In addition, Digo has a further kind of demonstrative (lacking a variant form) which consists of a noun class prefix and the invariable ending *-no*. The *-no* ending also occurs in variant forms of the 1SG, 1PL and 2PL independent personal pronouns (see §3.3.2) which have a similar distribution to these demonstratives. Demonstratives with a root consisting of a *-no* suffix occur in various other Bantu languages, as part of a system of either three or four kinds of demonstrative. In most of these languages the *-no* form indicates the closest degree of proximity to the speaker, but in Digo, the *-no* demonstrative does not enter into a contrastive system based on degrees of spatial distance from the speaker, as will be illustrated below.

The complete list of all four kinds of demonstratives in Digo is given in table 3.14. The basic form together with both long and short variant forms of each kind of demonstrative will be referred to as a series.[19] Series 1 demonstratives

---

[17] The following discussion of demonstratives is a substantially enlarged version of Nicolle (2007c). I am grateful to Alison Nicolle for finding and classifying much of the data on demonstratives.

[18] One of the earliest authors to notice this fact was Torrend (1891).

[19] The term 'series' is common in descriptions of Bantu languages, although 'position' (Doke [1930] 1990; 1935), 'grade' (Givón 1970) and 'type' (Harjula 2004) are also used. There is no set correspondence between the demonstrative forms and the series numbers; in languages where the *-no* form indicates close proximity, this is usually the first series (e.g. Devos 2008:168; Fleisch 2000:89) but the same form was Doke's 'third position'.

are proximal, series 2 demonstratives are distal, series 3 demonstratives are nonproximal, and series 4 demonstratives are metarepresentational (the label metarepresentational is explained below).

Table 3.14. Demonstratives

Noun class	Series 1	Series 2	Series 3	Series 4
1	hiyu	yuya, huya	hiye	yuno
variant	yuyu, yu	yuyatu	ye	
2	hinya	hara (hawa)	hinyo (aho)	hano
variant	aha	(h)aratu	nyo, o	
3	hinyu	hura	hinyo	huno
variant		(h)uratu	nyo	
4	hii	hira	hiyo	hino
variant		(h)iratu	yo	
5	hiri	rira	hiro	rino
variant	riri	riratu	riro, ro	
6	higa	gara	higo	gano
variant	gaga	garatu	gago, go	
7	hichi	chira	hicho	chino
variant	chichi, chi	chiratu	chicho, cho	
8	hivi	vira	hivyo	vino
variant	vivi, vi	viratu	vivyo, vyo	
9	hii	hira	hiyo	hino
variant		(h)iratu	yo	
10	hizi	zira	hizo	zino
variant	zizi	ziratu	zizo, zo	
11	hiri	rira	hiro	rino
variant	riri	riratu	riro, ro	
14	hinyu	hura	hinyo	huno
variant		(h)uratu	nyo, o	
16	hipha	phara	hipho	phano
variant	phapha, pha	pharatu	phapho, pho	
17	hiku	kura	hiko	kuno
variant	kuku, ku	kuratu	kuko, ko	
18	himu	mura	himo	muno
variant	mumu, mu	muratu	mumo, mo	

The four series of demonstratives each contain a demonstrative root, which is invariable, and a noun class concord, which is specific to each noun class. These are described below.

3.4 Demonstratives

3.4.2.1 The form of series 1 demonstratives

In series 1 demonstratives, the demonstrative root is *hi-* for all noun classes, and the noun class concord is a suffix with the same form as the verbal subject concord for all noun classes except 1, 2, 3, and 14. The variant form is simply a reduplicated noun class concord for most classes; the lack of variant forms in noun classes 4 and 9 appears to be phonologically motivated (*hii* being hard to distinguish from *ii* since the /h/ is lenis, i.e. pronounced with very little friction), but the lack of variant forms of series 1 demonstratives in noun classes 3 and 14 may be related to the fact that the noun class concord is not the regular subject concord *u* but *nyu*.

3.4.2.2 The form of series 2 demonstratives

In series 2 demonstratives, the demonstrative root is *-ra* for all noun classes except noun class 1 in which it is *-ya*. The noun class concord is identical to the verbal subject concord for all noun classes except noun class 1 which has two irregular forms, *yuya* and *huya*, and the noun classes in which the subject concord begins with a vowel (2 *a*, 3 *u*, 4 *i*, 14 *u*), in which the subject concord is preceded by *h*. Noun class 1 has two alternative forms; the form of the demonstrative root in both forms is *-ya* and the noun class concords are *yu-* and *hu-*. In the variant form, the root takes the form *-ratu* (*-yatu* in class 1) and is preceded by the noun class concord (*yu-* in class 1). An irregular form *hawa* is occasionally heard for class 2.

3.4.2.3 The form of series 3 demonstratives

In series 3 demonstratives, the demonstrative root is *hi-* (the same as in series 1) for all noun classes, and the noun class concord is a suffix with the same form as the noun class concord for series 1 demonstratives (for all noun classes except classes 1 and 2, which are irregular), except that the final vowel changes to *o* (and in class 8 *vi* becomes *vyo*). The variant has a long and a short form in most noun classes: there is no long form for classes 1 and 2; for all other noun classes, the long variant form is the same as the variant form of the series 1 demonstrative except that the final vowel changes to *o*. (For classes 3, 4, 9 and 14, which do not have series 1 variants, there is, naturally, no long form of the series 3 variant.) The short variant form is simply the series 3 demonstrative noun class concord, except for classes 2 and 14 which have a short variant based on the noun class concord *nyo* and an alternative form *o*.[20]

---

[20] Note that the form *nyo* in noun class 2 is also found as a variant form of the noun class 2 relative marker and referential marker (see §7.3.5 for examples and discussion).

3.4.2.4 The form of series 4 demonstratives

In series 4 demonstratives, the demonstrative root is *-no* for all noun classes, and the noun class concord has the same form as the noun class concord used with series 2 demonstratives, that is, it is identical to the verbal subject concord for all noun classes, except noun class 1 (in which the form is *yu-*) and the noun classes in which the subject concord begins with a vowel (2 *a*, 3 *u*, 4 *i*, 14 *u*) in which the subject concord is preceded by *h*.

3.4.3 Functions of demonstratives

When an entity which is being referred to with a demonstrative is physically copresent with the speaker and the hearer, the factors which influence the speaker's choice of a particular demonstrative in preference to the others are primarily concerned with physical proximity, as mentioned above. That is, it is the physical location of the mentioned entity relative to the interlocutors which influences which demonstrative is appropriate. The exception is series 4 demonstratives which profile the psychological salience of a mental representation of the entity being referred to rather than spatial deixis. Series 4 demonstratives will be described in greater detail below.

It is a more challenging matter to account for the choices that speakers make in situations in which the entities referred to using demonstratives are not physically copresent with the interlocutors. I will discuss two kinds of situation in which physical proximity to the interlocutors is not the primary factor influencing the speaker's choice of demonstrative. First, in narratives, demonstratives may be used presentationally (or 'discourse-deictically') to introduce or reintroduce an entity into a discourse, or anaphorically to maintain the addressee's attention on an already salient entity. Second, in both conversations and narratives, demonstratives can be used to refer to abstract qualities such as time and manner; in Digo this primarily involves demonstratives in class 8.

The following paragraph from part way through a Digo narrative text illustrates the variety of different demonstratives which can occur in a short fragment of text. There are five distinct 3rd person singular (noun class 1) demonstratives referring to three referents: an antelope (*kulungu*), a corpse (*maiti*) also referred to as 'the woman' (*mchetu*) in the last clause, and a (live) woman (*mchetu*). The noun class 1 demonstratives and coreferential NPs have been highlighted in bold text. There are also three noun class 16 (locative) demonstratives (underlined). Prior to the events described in the example below, the hyena and the man had met each other by the man's trap in the forest; the hyena was dragging the corpse of a woman who had been buried at the man's village the day before and was sure that the man would tell the other villagers about this.

3.4 Demonstratives

(127) *Phahi, fisi rauka fuli richendahala **yuya kulungu** richiricha **yuya maiti** <u>pharatu</u>. Kikiri kikiri ya madzi kuhekpwa hata kuganya miyo yao, ndipho "Haya huphiye," anafika <u>hipho</u> kulungu taphana, ariyepho ni **yuyatu maiti**. **Yuyu mchetu** ndipho anauza, "Amba we ukaamba kala **yuno maiti** ukamuona na fisi, nawe ukagbwira kulungu, mbona **ye mchetu** ndiye ariye <u>phapha</u> na **ye kulungu** kapho?"*

'So, the hyena left quickly and went and fetched **the antelope** leaving **the corpse** <u>right there</u> (i.e. in its place). By the time water had been fetched and they (the man and his wife) had decided who would carry what, then "Okay, let's go," but when they arrived <u>there</u> (where the antelope was) there was no antelope, what was there was **the corpse**. **The woman** asked, "I thought you told me that **this corpse**, you saw it with the hyena, whilst you had caught an antelope, so why is it **the woman** who is here and **the antelope** is not here?"'

This paragraph raises a number of questions concerning the narrator's motivation for his choice of demonstratives. Why does the first mention of the antelope and the corpse in this text fragment use the series 2 (distal) demonstrative *yuya* whilst the first mention of the woman uses the variant series 1 (proximal) demonstrative *yuyu*? Why does the second mention of the antelope have no demonstrative while the second mention of the corpse uses the variant series 2 (distal) demonstrative *yuyatu*? Why does the woman's speech contain different demonstratives again, both referring to the same entity: *yuno maiti* (series 4: metarepresentational) and *ye mchetu* (variant series 3: nonproximal)?

In the rest of this section I will attempt to begin to provide answers to questions such as these. I will begin by describing the use of all four series of demonstrative to express spatial deixis. I will then describe the functions of each series of demonstratives in narrative texts, focusing primarily on demonstratives in noun class 1, and attempt to relate these functions to the spatial-deictic uses. Finally, I will describe the use of demonstratives in class 8 to refer to time and manner.

3.4.3.1 Spatial-deictic uses of demonstratives

Spatial-deictic uses of Digo demonstratives can be clearly seen in the use of the locative noun classes. The following examples provide representative illustrations of spatial deixis involving demonstratives in classes 16 (specific location), 17 (less precise or external location) and 18 (interior location).

3.4.3.1.1 Series 1: Proximal (close to speaker)

Hipha (class 16) designates a location near to the speaker; usually the speaker is at the location she is referring to. It occurs most frequently of the series 1 locative demonstratives, either alone (most often) or preceding another element which it modifies, usually a noun or a relational expression; each syntactic possibility is illustrated below:

(128) Sagal-a **hipha** we m-chetu, ...
sit-FV 16.DEM1 2SG 1-woman
'Sit **here** you woman, ...'

(129) Ná-tazami-a atu a-gbwir-an-e **hipha** kaya.
1SG.PST-expect-FV 2.people 3PL-hold-RECIP-SUB 16.DEM1 9.home
'I expected people to stick together **here** at home.'

(130) Edz-e u-hal-e hiyu mutu a-ri-ye **hipha**
come-SUB 2SG-fetch-SUB 1.DEM1 1.person 3SG-COP-1.REL 16.DEM1
dzulu ya muhi.
up 9.ASS 3.tree
'Come and fetch this man who is **here** up the tree.' (the speaker is at the base of the tree)

Most occurrences of *hiku* (class 17) occur in the expression *hiku na hiku* which means 'here and there within a specified place'. There are no examples of *hiku*+N in the available corpus, but *hiku* can occur alone.

(131) Ná-lol-a **hiku** na **hiku**.
1SG.PST-look-FV 17.DEM1 COM 17.DEM1
'I looked **here** and **there** (right around me)'

(132) N-ka-fik-a **hiku** ná-kpwedza-kal-a liwali.
1SG-SEQ-arrive-FV 17.DEM1 1SG.PST-VENT-become-FV governor
'When I got to **here** I became governor.'

Himu (class 18) is used when the speaker is inside or very close to the location being referred to. *Himu* occurs either alone or preceding the expression which it modifies.

(133) Bada n-ka-mu-on-a ka-dzangbwe ku-tuluk-a
after 1SG-ANT-3SG-see-FV 3SG.NEG-INC INF-come_out-FV
himu tsaka-ni.
18.DEM1 5.BUSH-LOC
'Afterwards I saw that he hadn't yet left **this** wood (which we are all in).'

(134) Ela hiyu kala a-ka-ni-tiy-a **himu** ili ni-fw-e.
but 1.DEM1 PST 3SG-ANT-1SG-put_in-FV 18.DEM1 so_that 1SG-die-SUB
'But he put me **here** (in this well which we are all standing next to) so that I would die.'

3.4 Demonstratives

The long variant forms of series 1 locative demonstratives are less common than the forms described above. In class 16, *phapha* expresses a precise location 'right here'; it usually occurs alone or occasionally preceding a relational expression, but does not co-occur with bare nouns.

(135) Ni-godz-a-ni **phapha.**
 1SG-wait-FV-PL 16.DEM1_VARIANT
 'Wait for me **right here**.'

(136) Mimi ni **phapha** kanda-kanda ya madzi.
 1SG COP 16.DEM1_VARIANT beside 9.ASS 6.water
 'I am (right) **here** at the water's edge.'

The long variant forms *kuku* (class 17) and *mumu* (class 18) are relatively rare (only 4 examples were found in the available corpus) and imply an intense closeness; *mumu* is only used when the speaker is inside an object. The short variant forms *pha/ku/mu* are also rare and will not be illustrated here.

(137) A-na-amb-w-a, "Jumamosi, ndzo ligundzu **kuku** ..."
 3SG-CONT-tell-PAS-FV Saturday come morning 17.DEM1_VARIANT
 'He was told, "Come **right here** on Saturday morning ..."'

(138) Ko ku-heg-a n'=kpweli, ela amba
 17.DEM3_VAR INF-trap-FV COP=true but DM
 mumu tsaka-ni mu=na mwenye.
 18.DEM1-VARIANT 5.bush-LOC 18=COM 1.owner
 'This is a good place to trap, but say **here in this forest** (where I am) there must be an owner.'

3.4.3.1.2 Series 2: Distal (far from speaker and hearer)

Phara (class 16), *kura* (class 17) and *mura* (class 18) occur either alone or preceding a noun or relational expression to indicate a specific location at a distance. Often the location is out of sight of both interlocutors, as in (139), but it need not be, as in (140).

(139) Machero phiy-a **phara** pha-ko mnda-ni
 tomorrow go-FV 16.DEM2 16-2SG.POS 3.field-LOC
 'Tomorrow go **there** to your field'

(140) Tsamiz-a-ni vitu vi-phiy-e **kura** meli-ni.
 move-FV-PL 8.things 8-go-SUB 17.DEM2 9.boat-LOC
 'Move the things and put them **in that** boat (over there).'

Series 2 locative demonstratives can also be used to refer to locations which have not previously been mentioned but whose existence can be inferred from the context. In (141), the grave (pit) has not specifically been mentioned before, but the audience has been told that a woman had died and was buried, and so the existence of the pit can be inferred. In (142), the narrator has recounted how when he was a hospital orderly he took a patient to Nairobi for treatment; the specific place has not been mentioned but its existence can be inferred and so the class 17 demonstrative *kura* is appropriate.

(141) *fisi   ra-kpwenda-m-fukul-a   **mura**   dibwa-ni* ...
      5.hyena   5.PST-IT-3SG-unearth-FV   18.DEM2   5.pit-LOC
      'the hyena went and dug her **out of that pit** ...'

(142) ... *ili   a-m-hal-e   yuya   m-kongo   na*
          so_that   3SG-3SG-fetch-SUB   1.DEM2   1-sick_person   COM

      *a-m-phirik-e   **kura**   amba-ko   a-ya-lagul-w-a.*
      3SG-3SG-take-SUB   17.DEM2   REL-17.REL   3SG-FUT.IT-treat-PAS-FV

      '... so that he could fetch the sick man and take him **there where he was going to be treated**.'

The variant forms *pharatu*, *kuratu*, and *muratu* indicate locations which have just been mentioned or are otherwise accessible to the listener (for example, by identification with an already known location). The main function of the variant series 2 demonstratives is to indicate the 'sameness' of the place, that is, that the place referred to is precisely the same as some salient location (e.g. the current deictic centre or a previously mentioned location). The locations referred to can be near to the speaker or the deictic centre of the narrative, as in (143) and (144), or far from the speaker or the deictic centre of the narrative, as in the final examples:

(143) *Kumbavi   **pharatu**   pha=na   mamba.*
      EXCL   16.DEM2_VARIANT   16=COM   1a.crocodile
      'Well, **at that very place** (where the man was standing) there was a crocodile.'

(144) *kumbavi   a-ka-unuk-a   **kuratu**   na   a-chi-m-sukum-a*
      EXCL   3SG-ANT-arise-FV   17.DEM2_VARIANT   COM   3SG-CONS-3SG-push-FV

      myawe   mo   chisima-ni.
      1.fellow.1.3SG.POS   18.DEM3-VAR   7.well-LOC

      'suddenly he got up from **that same place** and pushed his friend into the well.'

3.4 Demonstratives

(145) | hu-ka-ri-tsopoz-e-ni | ***pharatu*** | a-bish-a-pho |
| --- | --- | --- |
| 1PL-ITIVE-5-drop-SUB-PL | 16.DEM2_VARIANT | 3SG-chat-FV-16.REL |
| na | m-chewe | na | ana-e. |
| COM | 1.wife-1.3SG.POS | COM | 2.children-2.3SG.POS |

'let's throw it **right there** where he is talking with his wife and children.'

(146) | Chimiri-miri | ku-ka-lavi-w-a | atu | kare |
| --- | --- | --- | --- |
| 7.dawn | 17-ANT-offer-PAS-FV | 2.people | ANT |
| ***kuratu*** | ku-a | ye | Mwarabu. |
| 17.DEM2_variant | 17-ASS | 1.DEM3_VAR | 1.Arab |

'Just after dawn people were already **right there** at the Arab's (i.e. at that same house where the Arab lived).'

(147) | N-ya-meny-a | ***muratu*** | chisima-ni |
| --- | --- | --- |
| 1SG-FUT.IT-enter-FV | 18.DEM2_VARIANT | 7.well-LOC |
| na=mi | n-ka-hal-e | w-angu. |
| COM=1SG | 1SG-IT-fetch-SUB | 14-1SG.POS |

'I am going to enter **inside that same** well and get my [reward].'

3.4.3.1.3 Series 3: Nonproximal (place or thing just mentioned)

Occasionally, the series 3 locative demonstratives *hipho*, *hiko* and *himo* are used to refer to a location close to the addressee or which the speaker cannot identify with precision, as in the following example:

(148) | We, | phiy-a | ***hipho***, | pha=na | mbuzi | zi-ka-angam-ik-a. |
| --- | --- | --- | --- | --- | --- |
| 2SG | go-FV | 16.DEM3 | 16=COM | 10.goats | 10-ANT-lose-STAT-FV |

'You, go to **a certain place**, there are goats which are lost.'

Note that *hipho* also occurs in the phrases *hipho kare* 'long ago' and *adisi na ngano ikasira na hipho* 'the story and fable has ended with that', which are respectively the formulaic beginning and ending of fictional narratives.

Hiko (as well as the short form *ko*) often occurs before a named place:

(149) | Ela | u-na-phiy-a | u-ka-og-e | hiko | Mambasa |
| --- | --- | --- | --- | --- |
| but | 2SG-CONT-go-FV | 2SG-IT-swim-SUB | 17.DEM3 | Mombasa |
| madzi | ga | pwani |
| 6.water | 6.ASS | 9.coast |

'But you are going to swim in the sea **there at Mombasa**'

More frequently, however, series 3 demonstratives are used to refer to previously mentioned locations. Series 3 demonstratives referring to entities rather than locations appear to be used exclusively to refer to previously mentioned entities, both in conversations and in narratives (see below for a discussion of the narrative functions of demonstratives). The long variant forms *phapho*, *kuko* and *mumo* usually refer to a previously mentioned location, which is often a long way from the speaker or is out of sight.

(150) Nyuma   simba   wa-fw-a   ***phapho.***
       behind   1a.lion   3SG.PST-die-FV   16.DEM3_VARIANT
       'Behind them the lion died **in that place** (where the previous action had occurred).'

(151) ***Phapho***   u-ri-pho   mwandzo ...
       16.DEM3_VARIANT   2SG-PST-16.REL   first
       '**There** where you were at first ...' [the addressee is now a long way from the place referred to using the series 3 demonstrative]

(152) ... a-ka-ni-gbwarur-a   a-ka-ni-rich-a   ***phapho***   au a-ka-ni-ry-a.
       3SG-SEQ-1SG-maul-FV   3SG-SEQ-1SG-leave-FV   16.DEM3_VARIANT   or 3SG-SEQ-1SG-eat-FV
       '[The lion] could have mauled me and left me **there** [the previously mentioned location at which the speaker encountered the lion] or he could have eaten me.'

If the location has not been explicitly mentioned, it should at least be inferable by means of a bridging implicature, as is the case with *phapho phao laloni* 'there at their village'. The second mention of the location in the example below uses the basic series 3 demonstrative *hipho*.

(153) *Hipho kare kpwakala na atu ambao kala anakuluphira windza kpwa chakurya chao. Phachikala na mjeni **phapho** phao laloni. Mjeni hiye kala kamanywa arivyo lakini achikala anahenda kazi sawa na ayae osi a **hipho** laloni.*

'Long ago there were people who depended on hunting for their food. Now there was a stranger **there** at their village. This stranger he was not known how he was, but he worked just as hard as all his companions of **there** in the village.'

phapho	*phao*	*lalo-ni*		
16.DEM3_VARIANT	16.3PL.POS	5.village-LOC		
aya-e	*osi*	*a*	***hipho***	*lalo-ni*
2.fellows-2.3SG.POS	2.all	2.ASS	16.DEM3	5.village-LOC

The short variant forms *pho, ko,* and *mo* are far more common than the long variant forms, and even than the base forms *hipho, hiko,* and *himo*. They serve primarily to emphasize the location being referred to.

3.4 Demonstratives

(154) **Pho**   *munda*   *n-ka-u-hend-a*   *m-kulu.*
16.DEM3_VAR   3.field   1SG-HOD-3-make-FV   3-big
'**That field** I've made it big.'

(155) ... *a-ch-enda-beben-w-a*   **ko**   *ma-tsaka-ni.*
3SG-CONS-IT-chew-PAS-FV   17.DEM3_VAR   6-bush-LOC
'... and he was chewed up **out there in the bush**.'

The short variant forms of series 3 locative demonstratives often precede expressions containing a relative, possessive or locative suffix (underlined in the examples below). For further discussion of the short variant forms, see §3.4.4.3.

(156) **pho**   *pha-ri-pho*   *ye*   *mlungu*
16.DEM3_VAR   16-COP.PST-16.REL   1.DEM3_var   1a.god
'**there** where the god was'

(157) **ko**   *a-phiy-a-ko*
17.DEM3_VAR   3PL-go-FV-17.REL
'**there** where they were going'

(158) **ko**   *nyuma-ze*
17.DEM3_VAR   10.behind-10.3SG.POS
'**there** behind him'

(159) *Hu-phiy-e-ni*   *na=ro*   *hata*   **pho**   *pha-kpwe ...*
1PL-go-SUB-PL   COM=5.REF   even   16.DEM3_VAR   16-3SG.POS
'Let's go with [the box] **there** to his place ...' ['his place' has been previously mentioned and is far from the place where the speaker currently is]

Pho has another time-deictic usage as a discourse marker 'now', often introducing a thought of a character:

(160) **Pho**   *mino*   *n-chi-chelew-a*   *phapha ...*
16.DEM3_VAR   1SG   1SG-DEP-delay-FV   16.DEM1_VARIANT
'**Now** if I delay myself here ...'

The co-occurrence restrictions and functions of the short variant forms of demonstratives from all noun classes are discussed in greater detail in §3.4.4.3.

3.4.3.1.4 Series 4: Metarepresentational

Series 4 demonstratives occur primarily in speech and reported thoughts, especially questions, rhetorical usage, exhortations, commands, and for emphasis.

When series 4 demonstratives occur in questions, the speaker almost invariably uses the question to express shock, surprise or disbelief. It is not necessarily the location (in the case of series 4 demonstratives in locative noun classes) or the referent modified by a series 4 demonstrative which is the object of the question or otherwise emphasized over other elements of the clause; often some other element of the clause or the clause as a whole is in question or otherwise emphasized. Nonetheless, series 4 demonstratives occur almost exclusively in such contexts,[21] which are termed 'metarepresentational' (see §3.4.3.2.3).

(161) *We   bwana,   u-si-ni-chelew-esh-e   **phano**!*
       2SG   1a.sir   2SG-NEG-1SG-delay-CAUS-SUB   16.DEM4
       'Hey you, don't make me wait **here**!'

(162) *Mi-shahara   y-ao   **phano**   ph-ako   u-riph-a*
       4-wages   4-3PL.POS   16.DEM4   16-2SG.POS   2SG-pay-FV
       pesa   ngaphi?
       10.money   10.how_much
       'Their wages **there** at your place how much money do you pay?'

The referent of a series 4 demonstrative may or may not be within sight of the speaker and the addressee; the one necessary condition for it to be used is that its referent must be accessible to the hearer (that is, the hearer must be capable of accessing a mental representation of the entity). Example (163) was addressed to the author by a Digo man after the author had asked him if he knew what had caused a power cut. The utterance was accompanied by the speaker looking in the direction of the smouldering body of a colobus monkey on an electrical transformer about ten metres away. The location was neither very distant nor very close to the interlocutors, nor had it been previously mentioned, but it was accessible in that the speaker believed that the addressee should have been able to identify it.

(163) *Lol-a   mbega   **phano**.*
       look-FV   1.colobus   16.DEM4
       'Look at the colobus monkey **there**.'

Series 4 demonstratives do not exclusively refer to entities or locations which are physically present, however, as the following example illustrates. The context was a conversation about the Christmas party that the addressee had hosted the previous year during which he had given the speaker a hat. The hat, along with everything else associated with the previous year's Christmas party, was therefore accessible to the addressee, even if only weakly, and so the

---

[21] By this I mean both that series 4 demonstratives hardly ever occur elsewhere, and also that other demonstratives rarely occur in such contexts. When other demonstratives occur in questions, these are simply requests for information, without any overtones of shock, surprise or disbelief (Nicolle 2007b:133).

3.4 Demonstratives

speaker was able to refer to the hat using the series 4 demonstrative *hino* even though the hat had not been previously mentioned nor was it physically present. The conditions under which series 4 demonstratives are used depend on the speaker's assessment that a mental representation of an entity or location is accessible to the addressee, rather than on physical proximity or previous mention, as is the case with the other three series of demonstratives.

(164) U-na-tambukir-a **hino** **kofiya?** N'-chere na=yo.
2SG-CONT-remember-FV 9.DEM4 9.hat 1SG-PERS COM=9.REF
'Do you remember **that hat**? I still have it.'

3.4.3.2 Narrative functions of demonstratives

In addition to the spatial-deictic uses described above, demonstratives in Digo exhibit a range of narrative or discourse-deictic uses. In this section, I will describe the narrative functions of the four demonstrative series.

3.4.3.2.1 Series 1 (proximal) demonstratives

The first time a major participant is mentioned after the introduction, it is usually referred to by a noun followed by a series 1 (proximal) demonstrative (*Asichana hinya* 'These girls'); this is often the point at which the participant starts to play an active role in the story and the point at which the event line begins. This is illustrated in example (165).

(165) Hipho kare, ku-a-kal-a na a-sichana a-iri, Mbodze na Matsozi.
Long ago 17-PST-be-FV PST 2-girls 2-two NAME COM NAME
A-sichana hinya a-phiy-a ku-enda-nyendek-a.
2-girls 2.DEM1 3PL.PST-go-FV INF-ITIVE-walk-FV

'Long ago there were two girls, Mbodze and Matsozi. **These girls** went for a walk.'

In the following example, a series 1 demonstrative (*yuyu*) and a coreferential NP are used to refer to an already salient referent, even when there has been no change of subject. The effect is to maintain the salience of the referent and hence the continuity of the events so that the two sentences are represented as being part of the same informational or thematic unit. In this example, the noun follows the demonstrative.

(166) *Waphiya **yuya bwana** hiko tsakani, akafika waona nyama akavyoga-vyoga, anaamba, "Nchihega phano nyama achedza mino ni nimgbwire kare." Lakini achidzikanya **yuyu bwana,** achiamba, "Ko kuhega n'kpweli, ela amba mumu tsakani muna mwenye ...."*

'**That man** [series 2] went into the forest, and when he arrived he saw animals wandering around, [so] he said, "If I set traps here animals will come along and I will catch them easily." But he warned himself **that man** [series 1, variant], saying, "Setting traps is all very well, but surely here in the forest there is an owner ...."'

3.4.3.2.2 Series 2 (distal) and series 3 (nonproximal) demonstratives

In the orientation sections of narratives series 2 demonstratives are typically used to refer to minor participants and series 3 demonstratives are typically used to refer to major participants.

Example (167) is taken from the beginning of a fictional narrative and introduces the cast of participants. The first paragraph introduces a boy called Mwiya (the 'antagonist' in the story[22]), his father, Mwazewe (who is a minor participant in the story), the father's second wife (who is a very minor participant, as she dies in the first clause of the third paragraph), and the second wife's son, also called Mwiya (who becomes a major participant, albeit less important than his older half brother).

The second paragraph sets the scene for the rest of the story. Here, the senior wife is mentioned for the first time (she becomes the 'protagonist' in the story). She is not formally introduced because her existence can be inferred from the fact that for Mwiya's father to have married a second wife, he must have already had a first wife. Also mentioned is the family's wealth; again, this has not previously been mentioned using this term, but it obviously refers to the father's cattle and crops which are mentioned in the first paragraph.

In this passage, only demonstratives of series 2 (distal) and series 3 (nonproximal) are used. These demonstratives and their coreferential NPs have been highlighted in the text and in the following free translation, and will be discussed below.

---

[22] The 'antagonist' is the primary character who reacts to the 'protagonist', the character who initiates the main chain of events.

3.4 Demonstratives

(167) *Zamani za kare kpwakala na mvulana mmwenga yeihwa Mwiya. Mwiya wavyalwa ni ise tajiri, na ambaye kala ana ng'ombe nyinji sana, na kala achirima kpwakpwe mindani kala achitsenga vyakurya vinji: matsere, muhama, ngano, mphunga, na vyakurya vyanjina vinji. Kama vyokala desturi ya atu hipho kare, mutu ka achikala tajiri ka n'lazima alole achetu anji. Phahi, mzee Mwazewe, ambaye kala ni ise wa Mwiya, naye piya walóla mchetu wa phiri.* **Huya mchetu** *ariphogbwira mimba, wavyala mwana wa chilume achimuiha Mwiya.*

Hiye mchetu mvyere ariphoona mchetu myawe naye akavyala mwana wa chilume, wamanya **hira mali** *indaganywa, kpwa hivyo achiona baha amuolage* **yuya mchetu mdide** *phamwenga na* **hiye mwanawe** *na utsai.*

'Long ago there lived a boy who was called Mwiya. Mwiya was born to a rich father, who had very many cattle, and when he cultivated his fields he used to harvest a lot of food: maize, millet, wheat, rice, and many other foods. As was the custom of people long ago, if a person was rich he had to marry many wives. So, elder Mwazewe, who was the father of Mwiya, he too married a second wife. **That woman** [series 2] when she became pregnant, she gave birth to a boy and called him Mwiya.

That senior wife [series 3] when she saw that her cowife had also given birth to a son, she knew that **that wealth** [series 2] would be divided, therefore she thought it better to kill **that junior wife** [series 2] together with **that child of hers** [series 1] by witchcraft.'

Huya mchetu 'That woman' at the end of the first paragraph uses a series 2 (distal) demonstrative because the junior wife is a minor participant. The same applies to *hira mali* 'that wealth' which uses a noun class 9 series 2 demonstrative. *Huya* (series 2) is fairly rare; the form *yuya* (series 2) is far more common, being the default way of referring to major and minor participants after they have been introduced until the 'peak' is reached, as in *yuya mchetu mdide* 'that junior wife' in the second paragraph.

Series 3 (nonproximal) demonstratives are used to refer to the major participants in the orientation section. The protagonist (the senior wife) is referred to as *Hiye mchetu mvyere* 'That senior wife' and the antagonist (the junior wife's child) is referred to as *hiye mwanawe* 'that child of hers', both using a series 3 (nonproximal) demonstrative followed by a noun phrase. All subsequent references to the senior wife, and to both of the boys called Mwiya and their father, use the series 2 variant demonstrative *yuya*. *Hiye*+N only occurs again near the end of the story to refer to the senior wife when she is discovered and punished:

(168) **Hiye mchetu** *ariyemtiya yuya mwanache dibwani, wagbwirwa ni mchecheta achigbwa.*

'**The woman who had put the small child in the pit** was gripped by panic and fell down.'

Hiye	*m-chetu*	*a-ri-ye-m-tiy-a ...*	*dibwa-ni*
1.DEM3	1-woman	3SG-PST-1.REL-3SG-put-FV	5.pit-LOC

Once the main event line has begun, series 2 demonstratives are used to maintain reference to both minor and major participants. A typical construction in which to find series 3 demonstratives is 'tail-head linkage', where the information in one clause is repeated, using a different construction, in the immediately following clause. In example (169), tail-head linkage creates continuity despite a change of location in the narrative. All of the demonstratives in this example have been highlighted. Most are of series 2 (distal): *yuya* in class 1 is the default reference on the event line for participants which are already salient, *phara* is a series 2 class 16 demonstrative which indicates that the location was far away from the deictic centre of the narrative, and *kuratu* and *pharatu* are variant series 2 demonstratives in noun classes 17 and 16, respectively, which identify the locations referred to as being the same as some known locations. There is one variant series 3 demonstrative, *ye*, without an accompanying NP, which appears to function as a marker of emphasis. Immediately after the change of location, the series 3 demonstrative *hipho* is used to refer to the location mentioned in the previous clause, thereby helping to create continuity between the events at the two different locations.

(169) *Wauya kaya **yuya mutu**, akafika **phara kaya** wasagala **ye** hata saa mbiri, achiuka achiphiya **kuratu pangoni**. Ariphofika **hipho**, wakpwera dzulu ya muhi kulola **pharatu** phatulukirapho fisi.*

'He returned home **that man** (series 2), he arrived **there** (series 2) **at home** he remained **this one** (series 3, variant) until eight o'clock, then he left and went to **that same cave** (series 2, variant). When he arrived **there** (series 3), he climbed to the top of a tree to observe **that same place** (series 2, variant) from which the hyena had emerged.'

3.4.3.2.3 Series 4 (metarepresentational) demonstratives

As noted above, in conversational use series 4 demonstratives profile the accessibility of mental representations of their referents, rather than properties pertaining to spatial deixis. In narratives, metarepresentational demonstratives most frequently occur in quoted direct speech and thoughts, often in information questions, commands, exhortations, and exclamations. The following example illustrates some of these uses as well as various forms already discussed.

3.4 Demonstratives

(170) **Yuya mutu** waangalala sana mwakpwe rohoni, "Nimuambedze **yuno mkpwazangu**? Na mino che n'namanya kala kulungu ndiye wangu na ndiye chemreha **hipha** nkamuika **hipha**; nkalunga mkpwazangu, ela **vino** kulungu kapho, **ye maiti** nchiyemuona na fisi ndiye achiyeikpwa **hipha**! **Yu kulungu** akahalwa ni **yuyu fisi**, lakini taphana neno."

'The man [series 2] was amazed. "What can I say to **that wife of mine** [series 4]? Now I know that the antelope was mine and it was me who brought it **here** [series 1] and I put it **here** [series 1]; I fetched my wife, but **now** [series 4] the antelope is not here, **that corpse** [series 3, variant] which I saw with the hyena has been put **here** [series 1]! **The antelope** [series 1, variant, short form] has been taken by **the hyena** [series 1, variant], but there is nothing I can say (lit: there is no word).'"

The first demonstrative *yuya* is the default series 2 demonstrative used to refer to participants on the main event line. The series 4 demonstrative *yuno* occurs in an interrogative clause; rather than being a genuine information question, this has the force of a rhetorical question, "What can I say to my wife?" The speaker is representing the thought 'I can say something to my wife' to himself for the purpose of considering and rejecting it. This is a case of metarepresentation, that is, the representation of a representation. For this reason, in Nicolle (2007b), series 4 demonstratives were described as metarepresentational demonstratives. The three occurrences of the noun class 16 series 1 demonstrative *hipha* are straightforward proximal demonstratives referring to a location very near to the speaker. The class 8 metarepresentational demonstrative *vino* functions as a time adverbial 'now'. The use of class 8 to describe time and manner adverbials will be discussed below, but for the moment it suffices to note that the speaker (or rather, the narrator through the speaker) has chosen to use *vino* in this exclamative context rather than any of the alternative expressions indicating 'now' (*hivi, vivi, vi, sambi*, and various combinations of these). The short form of the series 3 nonproximal demonstrative *ye* has been used to refer to the corpse which the speaker had previously seen with the hyena. Finally *Yu kulungu* 'That antelope' and *yuyu fisi* 'that hyena' contain series 1 demonstratives. The entities to which these expressions refer, the antelope and the hyena, are both highly salient, having been mentioned in the previous sentence.

Most of the remaining series 4 demonstratives found in narrative texts involve emphasis or culmination (for example, at the peak or conclusion of a story) as in the following example which is the final sentence of a story about how the sea became salty.

(171) **Chino chuma** chinataka mutu chiambirwe chiriche kusaga, na **higa madzi** galago mihoni na ga mvula ichinya, **gano madzi ga bahari** ganaweza kukala ga pepho.

'**That iron** [series 4] wants to be told by someone to stop grinding, and (when) **the water** [series 1] that comes from the rivers and the rain comes, **that sea water** [series 4] will be able to become fresh.'

The contexts in which series 4 demonstratives occur in narrative texts (reported speech and thoughts, information questions, expressions of surprise, exhortations and commands, and for emphasis) are all examples of metarepresentational use; that is, the speaker (or narrator) represents another thought, such as a thought attributed to someone else, a thought which is surprising, or a thought that is a representation of an incomplete proposition (a question which requires an answer). It seems that series 4 demonstratives do not merely refer to specific entities, but present the entire proposition of which they are a part as being metarepresentational in nature, hence their frequent occurrence in exclamative and interrogative sentences.

A rhetorical feature of Digo storytelling is to highlight important or surprising events in a narrative by having one of the major participants express them verbally, and this may explain the fact that so many series 4 demonstratives occur in reported speech (89 percent of sentences containing one or more series 4 demonstrative was a reported direct speech or thought). Thus, although the surface-syntactic scope of all demonstratives is the noun phrase which they determine, the logical-semantic scope of series 4 demonstratives is propositional, in that the whole proposition, and not merely the referent, is being metarepresented. This, incidentally, explains why series 4 demonstratives are not used metalinguistically, that is, to represent the form (including the pronunciation) as opposed to the content of an utterance. Series 4 demonstratives thus help the addressee to identify the speaker's attitude towards the proposition expressed.

3.4.3.3 *Time and manner deictics using class 8 demonstratives*

Class 8 demonstratives can refer to entities in that noun class in the same way as all other classes. Thus, in the following example, the series 3 demonstrative *hivyo* refers to a kind of food (*vyakurya*) mentioned in the previous clause. The demonstrative and the coreferential expression have both been highlighted.

(172) **hivyo**   ndi=vyo   **vyakurya** vyo-mu-enjerez-a   mamba.
8.DEM3 COP=8.REF 8.food [1SG.PST]8.REL-3SG-add-FV 1a.crocodile
'**this** is **the food** that I have provided (lit: added) for the crocodile.'

However, class 8 demonstratives also function as time and manner adverbials, with different meanings being encoded by the four series of demonstrative and the variant forms.

3.4.3.3.1 Series 1 'proximal'—manner and time

The class 8 series 1 demonstrative *hivi* is used as a manner adverbial referring to actions which are about to happen, whilst the variant form *vivi* refers to actions which are ongoing:

(173) Phahi   yuya   bwana   wa-hend-a   **hivi:** ...
      so   1.DEM2   1a.man   3SG.PST-do-FV   8.DEM1
      'So the man did **this**:' (a description of the action follows)

(174) U-na-kos-a   miko   **vivi.**
      2SG-CONT-miss-FV   4.custom   8.DEM1_VARIANT
      'You are breaking with custom by doing **this**.'

(175) Phahi,   yuya   bwana   wa-kal-a   na   yuya
      so   1.DEM2   1a.man   3SG.PAST-be-FV   COM   1.DEM2

      mjeni-we   **vivi**   hata   a-chi-ih-w-a.
      1.guest-1.3SG.POS   8.DEM1_VARIANT   until   3PL-CONS-call-PAS-FV

      'So, the man remained with his guest **in this way** until they were called.'

Both *hivi* and *vivi* can function as adverbials of time indicating simultaneity with a temporal reference point; *hivi* is used to refer to a time given by the context which need not be coreferential with the speech time, whilst *vivi* is used to refer to the speech time itself, and hence is more frequent in conversations.

(176) Dza   **hivi**   ná-on-a   dzi-nyama   dzi-kulu   sana.
      as   8.DEM1   1SG.PST-see-FV   5-animal   5-big   DEG
      'Right **then** I saw a huge animal.'

(177) hata   **vivi**   rero
      even   8.DEM1_VARIANT   today
      'even to this day (lit: even now today)'

3.4.3.3.2 Series 2 'distal'—manner

The class 8 series 2 demonstratives can be used as manner adverbials but not as time adverbials. In contrast to series 1 demonstratives which refer to events which are ongoing or about to occur, the class 8 series 2 demonstrative *vira* refers to events which have already occurred or which have been occurring for an extended period of time, usually followed by a verbal complex containing the class 8 relative marker *-vyo*. This demonstrative also occurs in the expression *kpwa vira* 'since, because' referring to an established or inferable fact.

(178) Yuya   mwanache   wa-elez-a   **vira**   a-ri-vyo-ti-w-a
      1.DEM2 1.child   3SG.PST-explain-FV 8.DEM2   3SG-PST-8.REL-put-PAS-FV
      mura   dibwa-ni.
      18.DEM2   5.pit-LOC

'The child explained **how** he had been put into that pit.'

(179) Lakini si-elew-a   **vira**   a-zi-lavy-a-**vyo**.
      but   1SG.NEG-understand-FV 8.DEM2   3SG-10-give-FV-8.REL
      'But I don't understand **how** he has been spending it (referring to money).'

(180) **ku-a** **vira**   pha=na   lichigo   li-kulu   sana
      17-ASS   8.DEM2   16=COM   11.fence   11-big   DEG
      'because there was a very big fence'

The variant series 2 demonstrative *viratu* occurs in the construction *dza viratu* which indicates that two qualities or actions are comparable or of equal value.

(181) m-kulu   **dza**   **viratu**   Mambasa
      3-big   as   8.DEM2_VARIANT   PLACE_NAME
      '**just as** big **as** Mombasa'

(182) Wa-phiy-a   hiku   na   hiku   **dza**   **viratu**
      3SG.PST-go-FV   17.DEM1   COM   17.DEM1   as   8.DEM2_VARIANT
      dzina-re   kala   ndi=ye   Njira   Nyinji.
      5.name-5.3SG.POS   PST   COP=1.REF   10.paths   10.many

'He went this way and that way **just as** his name was Many Paths.'

3.4.3.3.3 *Series 3 'nonproximal'—action*

The series 3 demonstrative *hivyo* refers to an action or event which occurred previously. Whereas the series 2 demonstrative *vira* refers to the manner in which an action occurred, *hivyo* refers back to the action itself.

(183) Bada   ya   ku-hend-a   **hivyo**   a-chi-yay-a.
      after   9.ASS INF-do-FV   8.DEM3   3SG-CONS-disappear-FV
      'After doing **that** she disappeared.'

3.4 Demonstratives

(184) Yuya   Mwiya m-vyere   a-ri-pho-sikir-a   **hivyo** ...
      1.DEM2   Mwiya 1-elder   3SG-PST-16.REL-hear-FV   8.DEM3
      'When the elder Mwiya heard **this** ...'

(185) Phahi **hivyo** ndi=vyo   safari   y-angu   Ø-vyo-kal-a.
      so   8.DEM3   COP=8.REF 9.journey   9-1SG.POS (9-PST-)8.REL-be-FV
      'So **that** was how my journey was.'

The expression *kpwa hivyo* 'therefore' refers back to what has happened before.

(186) Kumbavi   na=o   a-ka-zi-reh-a   **ku-a**   **hivyo**
      EXCL   COM=2.REF   3PL-HOD-10-bring-FV   17-ASS   8.DEM3
      na=hu-ry-e   pesa   phahi.
      EMPH=1PL-eat-SUB   10.money   so
      'Amazingly they have brought it (the money) **therefore** let us spend (lit: eat) money then.'

The variant series 3 demonstrative *vivyo* refers more generically to a kind of action or situation which must have already been explicitly mentioned.

(187) ... chisha   we   u-nda-hend-a   pesa   **vivyo**.
          then   2SG   2SG-FUT-do-FV   10.money   8.DEM3_VARIANT
      '... then you will make money **thus** (in the way just described).'

(188) A-na-amb-a,   "Ni   **vivyo**."
      3SG-CONT-say-FV   COP   8.DEM3_VARIANT
      'He said, "It is **so**."'

The short form *vyo* can refer to either time or manner. Like *vira* it often co-occurs with the class 8 relative marker *-vyo*.

(189) Lakini   **vyo**   amba-**vyo**   a-na-lumban-a
      but   8.DEM3_VAR   REL-8.REL   3PL-CONT-argue-FV
      pho   chi-phephi   ka   pha=na   tsungula.
      8.DEM3_VAR   7-near   PST   16=COM   9.hare
      'But **as/whilst** they were arguing there nearby was a hare.'

(190) ni-onyes-a   **vyo**   a-chi-**vyo**-gbwir-w-a   hiyu   m-chetu.
      1SG-show-FV   8.DEM3_VAR   3SG-CONS-8.REL-seize-PAS-FV   1.DEM1   1-woman
      'show me **how** this woman was caught.'

3.4.3.3.4 Series 4 'metarepresentational'

The class 8 series 4 demonstrative *vino* indicates time 'now', but always with an implied comment on the proposition (e.g. surprise, disapproval) or with emphatic usage, in line with the metarepresentational characterization discussed above, and often in combination with other series 4 demonstratives.

(191) **Yuno**   bwana   ná-m-tiy-a   chisima-ni,
      1.DEM4   1a.man   1SG.PST-put-FV   7.well-LOC
      vino   wa-zembul-a   utajiri!
      8.DEM4   3SG.PST-discover-FV   14.wealth

'**That man** I put him in the well, and **now** he has suddenly become rich!'

(192) ... haya   ***vino***   mbona   u-na-ni-cheng-a?
      EXCL   8.DEM4   why.EXCL   2SG-CONT-1SG-deceive-FV

'... but **now** why are you deceiving me?'

(193) Atu   a-lal-a   na   ndzala   na
      2.people   3PL.PST-sleep-FV   COM   9.hunger   COM
      vino a-nda-sind-a   na=yo!
      8.DEM4   3PL-FUT-spend_day-FV   COM=9.REF

'People slept with hunger and **now** they will spend the day with it!'

One other use of *vino* (shared with class 17 *kuno*) is to indicate simultaneity with other events.

(194) A-ka-kal-a   a-ka-vuk-a   rira   lichigo
      3SG-SEQ-be-FV   3SG-ANT-cross-FV   11.DEM2   11.fence
      vino   a-na-phiy-a.
      8.DEM4   3SG-CONT-go-FV

'She had crossed that trap **while** she was walking.'

3.4.3.3.5 Dialect variation

In the northern dialect of Digo, the class 8 demonstratives *vivi* and *vino* are used as temporal adverbials meaning 'now', similar to *sambi*. In the southern (Tanzanian) variety, none of these forms is reported as occurring; instead the Swahili loanword *sasa* 'now' is used.

The series 4 class 17 and class 8 demonstratives *kuno* and *vino* can be used with the sense of 'while' in the northern variety of Digo, whereas in the southern (Tanzanian) variety they are not used in this way. In Tanzania, the 'simultaneous' TAM marker *chopho* is used for 'while' (see §5.3.1.8).

3.4 Demonstratives

3.4.3.4 Correspondences between spatial-deictic, discourse-deictic, and time- and manner-deictic uses of demonstratives

The ways in which different class 8 demonstratives express time and manner corresponds to a large extent to the functions of those demonstratives as indicators of spatial deixis and when referring to entities in narratives (discourse-deictic functions).

3.4.3.4.1 Series 1 demonstratives

Series 1 demonstratives indicate spatial proximity and function in narratives to introduce participants onto the main event line and to refer to them at dramatic peaks. Series 1 demonstratives in class 8 function as manner adverbials referring to actions which are about to happen and as time adverbials indicating simultaneity with a temporal reference point. In all these uses, the demonstrative serves to increase the conceptual salience of the coreferential entity (what is near is more salient than what is far), and in both narrative (discourse-deictic) and adverbial (manner- and time-deictic) uses, this additionally involves the anticipation of what is about to occur.

3.4.3.4.2 Series 2 demonstratives

Series 2 demonstratives indicate spatial distance and are used in narratives to refer to minor participants and as the default means of identifying all participants whose salience has already been established (i.e. those which are continuing to feature on the main event line). Series 2 demonstratives in class 8 function as manner adverbials referring to events which have already occurred or which have been occurring for an extended period of time. In both the narrative and the adverbial uses, the salience of the referent is either already established or is not important, and series 2 demonstratives are used in situations where continuity is being maintained. The variant form indicates the sameness of its referent (e.g. 'those same caves', 'that same place'), and the corresponding class 8 adverbial indicates that two qualities or actions are comparable or of equal value (i.e. the same).

3.4.3.4.3 Series 3 demonstratives

Series 3 demonstratives refer to entities which are already highly salient by virtue of having been recently mentioned, and serve to maintain a high level of salience in situations in which the salience of the entity being referred to might decrease (for example, if the referent has not been mentioned for a while). Series 3 demonstratives maintain continuity in discourses in which a discontinuity (for example, of time, place, or purpose) might otherwise be perceived. As class 8 adverbials, *hivyo* refers to actions and events which have already occurred and *vivyo* refers generically to kinds of actions or situations which have already been described.

3.4.3.4.4 Series 4 demonstratives

Series 4 demonstratives are used in contexts in which a speaker expresses a thought in order to question it, challenge it, draw attention to it, or otherwise comment on it; that is, in metarepresentational contexts. The class 8 temporal adverbial *vino* 'now' occurs in many of the same contexts as the other metarepresentational demonstratives, such as questions and reported thoughts. This demonstrative series is formally and distributionally related to the 1SG, 1PL and 2PL 'metarepresentational pronouns': *mino*, *sino* and *mwino* (see §3.3.2).

3.4.4 Distribution of demonstrative forms

In this final section, we will discuss the distribution of various demonstrative forms, focusing on the relative orders of demonstrative and noun within a NP (or demonstrative phrase), double demonstrative constructions in which two demonstratives co-occur or modify the same noun, and the distribution of short variant forms.

3.4.4.1 *Relative orders of demonstrative and noun*

All possible orders of demonstrative and noun are recorded in Digo: demonstratives can precede the noun (Dem+N) or follow it (N+Dem), and very occasionally two demonstratives may occur either side of a noun (Dem+N+Dem); demonstratives can also stand alone (functioning predicatively).

For most noun classes, each demonstrative series exhibits all possible word orders, but there is often a preferred order within each combination of demonstrative series and noun class. For example, all of the class 6 demonstratives can occur alone, preceding a noun, or following a noun, but whereas *higa* (series 1) usually follows a noun, *gara* (series 2) almost always precedes a noun, and on the rare occasions when it follows a noun, this is often in the construction 'N *garatu gara*' 'those very same N'. However, all demonstratives in the locative classes 16-18 and the short variant forms of all noun classes (i.e. *ye*, *zo*, etc.) always precede the noun which they modify, as do the series 2 demonstratives *yuya* (class 1) and *hara* (class 2).

Overall, the preferred order is Dem+N, and this applies to all demonstrative series.[23] In this respect, Digo patterns with Shambala, Pare, Rangi and the Nguni languages which all have the preferred order Dem+N, rather than with

---

[23]The preference for Dem+N is particularly strong in series 2, whilst in series 1, 3, and 4 there is a slight preference for Dem+N even excluding the effect of the locative noun classes, in which the order Dem+N is obligatory. However, in series 3, once the short forms have been discounted, there is a slight preference for the order N+Dem.

3.4 Demonstratives

most other Bantu languages, including Swahili, Makhuwa, and Kikuyu, which have the preferred order N+Dem (Riedel 2006). Excluding the frequent occurrences of *yuya* N in narrative texts and the obligatory Dem+N order with locative noun classes, Dem+N occurs more than twice as often as N+Dem in a corpus of untranslated Digo texts.

Given that Dem+N is the preferred order in Digo, it is instructive to look at examples of the N+Dem order to see if any patterns of usage emerge.[24] There appear to be both discourse-related and non-discourse-related reasons why certain demonstratives are postnominal.

3.4.4.1.1 Ease of articulation

Series 1 and 3 demonstratives which modify nouns in class 7 beginning with *chi* are almost always postnominal. This may be because most nouns in class 7 begin with *chi* and it is difficult to articulate two unstressed '*chi*' in succession: *chitabu hichi* may be easier to pronounce than *hichi chitabu*.

3.4.4.1.2 Influence of Swahili

Swahili is probably an influence in some instances, as Swahili demonstratives tend to follow the noun. When a word is the same in Swahili and Digo, the demonstrative is more likely to follow the noun, especially in common collocations such as time expressions (in fact the expression *saa iyo iyo* 'at that very moment' has been borrowed directly from Swahili, together with the use of doubled demonstratives and the lack of initial [h] in the demonstratives). In example (195), a series 2 demonstrative (unusually) follows the noun *siku* 'day' which is the same in Swahili.

(195) kala si-dzangbwe ku-tayarish-a ma-somo ga **siku hira.**
PST 1SG.NEG-INC INF-prepare-FV 6-lessons 6.ASS 9.day 9.DEM2
'I had not yet prepared my lessons for **that day**.'

3.4.4.1.3 Avoidance of scopal ambiguity

Postnominal demonstratives are also found when the order Dem+N might otherwise have an unclear referent. In (196), the demonstrative *hinya* unambiguously modifies *ajeni* 'visitors', whereas if it had preceded the noun it could have modified either *ajeni* alone or the conjoined NP *ajeni airi na aphuye* 'two visitors and his uncle':

(196) **Ajeni hinya** a-iri na aphu-ye a-tsolok-a.
2.visitors 2.DEM1 2-two COM 9.uncle-9.3SG.POS 3PL.PST-arrive-FV
'**These** two **visitors** and his uncle arrived.'

---

[24]Patterns do emerge, and I am grateful to Alison Nicolle for identifying them.

3.4.4.1.4 Discourse-related reasons for N+Dem order

Other occurrences of N+Dem are related to discourse. As mentioned above, at the point in a narrative where a major participant performs his or her first action on the event line (the 'point of departure' for that participant) it is usually referred to using a noun followed by a series 1 demonstrative:

(197) Siku   mwenga, **mutu**   **hiyu**   wa-gbwir-a   kulungu ...
      9.day   9.one   1.person   1.DEM1   3SG.PST-catch-FV   1a.antelope
      'One day, **this man** caught an antelope ...'

(198) **A-sichana hinya**   a-phiy-a   ku-enda-nyendek-a ...
      2-girls   2.DEM1   3PL.PST-go-FV   INF-ITIVE-walk-FV
      '**These girls** went for a walk ...'

When a demonstrative occurs immediately before the end of a thematic unit (e.g. a paragraph break or the end of a narrative) it is often postnominal:

(199) yuya   mwana   m-gayi   kala   a-chi-imb-a   **wira**   **huno:**
      1.DEM2   1.child 1-poor   PST   3SG-DEP-sing-FV   14.song   14.DEM4
      'that poor child was singing **this song**.' (song follows)

(200) ama   n-nge-kal-a   ná-olag-w-a   ni   **simba**   **hiye**.
      or   1SG-COND-be-FV   1SG.PST-kill-PAS-FV   by   1a.lion   1.DEM3
      'or I could have been killed by **that lion**.' (end of story)

3.4.4.1.5 Emphasis

In speech, postnominal demonstratives tend to be stressed, which suggests that they have an emphatic function. Postnominal demonstratives (often of series 4) also occur frequently in emphatic contexts in narratives. The question in (201) is asked by a character in a story who cannot believe that a person who was previously very poor now has enough money to pay two hundred workers at ten times the going rate (note that although the first demonstrative *yuno* is postnominal, the second *zino* occurs in the more usual prenominal position). Example (202) is the third of a sequence of questions in which the speaker refers to a woman who in fact is his mother, although she hasn't recognized him. Finally, example (203) occurs at the climax of a story—the participants, including the speaker, discover that they have eaten the bird which had been laying money for them while it stayed in their house.

(201) **Mutu**   **yuno**   zino   pesa   a-zi-phah-a=phi?
      1.person   1.DEM4   10.DEM4   10.money   3SG.PST-10-get-FV=Q
      'Where did **that man** (of all people) get that (much) money from?'

3.4 Demonstratives

(202) **M-chetu**   **yuno**   si=ye   ye-ni-vyal-a   mimi?
 1-woman   1.DEM4   NEG=1.REF   1.REL-1SG-bear-FV   1SG
 '**This woman** is it not she who gave birth to me?'

(203) **Nyama**   **hiyu**   ni   ye   a-ri-ye   mo   chumba-ni.
 1.animal   1.DEM1   COP   1.DEM3_VAR   3SG-PST-1.REL   18.DEM3_VAR   7.room-LOC
 '**This animal** is the one which was in the room.'

3.4.4.1.6 Events which are contrary to expectation

The order N+Dem also often occurs in the description of an event which is contrary to expectation. In (204) the animal has been caught in a trap even though the trap had only just been set, and in (205) the speaker is a son addressing his parents, and it is unusual for a son to leave an inheritance to his parents.

(204) Wee   bwana   ndzoo,   **nyama**   **hiyu**   a-ka-gbwir-w-a
 2SG   1a.sir   come   1a.animal   1.DEM1   3SG-HOD-catch-PAS-FV
 nyuma-zo.
 behind-10.2SG.POS
 'You sir come, **that animal** has been caught behind you.'

(205) ela   n-chi-fw-a   mimi   utajiri   **hinyu**   u-nda-kal-a   w-enu
 but   1SG-DEP-die-FV   1SG   14.wealth   14.DEM1   14-FUT-be-FV   14-2PL.POS
 'but if I myself die, **this wealth** will be yours'

3.4.4.1.7 Procedural usage: sequential events

In procedural texts, it is common to find a sequence of events being described, e.g. A is made into B, B+Dem is made into C, C+Dem is made into D, etc. The following extract from a description of how to cook *jora* 'cassava meal' illustrates this usage; the repeated nouns and their associated demonstratives have been highlighted:

(206) *Jora ni* **chakurya** *cha Adigo.* **Chakurya hichi** *chinavugbwa kpwa kutsanganya unga wa makopa na madzi.... Makopa nkukunwa kuusa uchafu halafu gakavundwa-vundwa* **viphande** *vidide vidide.* **Viphande hivi** *nkutiwa chinuni. Chisha mutu akahala mutsi akabunduga na gara makopa nkutika-tika gakakala* **unga**. **Unga hinyo** *nkutiwa lungoni na nkutsungbwa .... Madzi gachiira, unga mchache unatiwa halafu unafwidza na chifwidzo mpaka utsanganyike na madzi vinono na badaye ukale* **uji**. **Uji hinyo** *nkurichwa ukaokoha kpwa muda mchache ....*

'Jora is **food** of the Digo people. **This food** [N+DEM1] is prepared by mixing dried cassava flour with water .... The dried cassava is scraped to remove dirt and then it is broken up into very small **pieces**. **These pieces** [N+DEM1] are put in a wooden mortar. Then you (lit: person) take the pestle and pound them and that dried cassava is crushed and becomes **flour**. **This flour** [N+DEM3] is put into a winnowing basket and sifted .... When the water starts to boil, a little flour is put in then stirred with a whisk until it mixes well with the water and then it will become **porridge**. **This porridge** [N+DEM3] is left to boil for a little while ....'

3.4.4.2 Double demonstrative constructions

Constructions involving two demonstratives are too rare for generalizations to be drawn about their function, although the referents would appear to be left-dislocated (fronted) discourse topics. Where two demonstratives co-occur, both must be of the same noun class (since they refer to the same referent, which is usually overtly represented) but need not belong to the same series. Where there is an overt noun this usually occurs between the two demonstratives. There appear to be no co-occurrence restrictions or restrictions on the permitted order of demonstratives (demonstratives of different series and the same series can co-occur, long and short forms can co-occur, and short variant forms can occupy both the first and second positions). The following examples illustrate some of the possible combinations of demonstratives.

(207) **Hiyu**   mutu   **ye**   hata   a-ka-chimbir-a
      1.DEM1   1.person   1.DEM3_VAR   even   3SG-POT-flee-FV
      n'=kazi   ya   bure.
      COP=9.work   9.ASS   pointless

   '**That** person even if he runs away it will be futile.'

(208) **Yuya**   bwana   **ye**   wa-zam-a
      1.DEM2   1a.man   1.DEM3_VAR   3SG.PST-bend_over-FV
      '**That** man he bent over'

(209) **Zo**   nguwo   **zo**   na-wez-a
      10.DEM3_VAR   10.clothes 10.DEM3_VAR   1SG.CONT-be_able-FV
      ku-gomb-a   na=zo.
      INF-speak-FV COM=10.REF

   '**Those** clothes I am able to talk with them.'

3.4.4.3 Short variant forms

The short variant forms of Digo demonstratives exhibit three quite different patterns of distribution from the basic and long variant forms.

3.4 Demonstratives

1. Short variant forms almost always occur prenominally (i.e. Dem+N). Out of a total of 129 short variant forms in a corpus of nontranslated texts, only one instance of N+Dem order was recorded, not including double demonstrative constructions where a short variant form is preceded by both a demonstrative and a noun, such as the two instances of a short variant form co-occurring with a long form (e.g. *yuya bwana ye wazama* 'that man he bent over').

2. Short variant forms often co-occur in relative clauses (although they rarely, if ever, precede *amba*-relative constructions) or as part of a possessive noun phrase. Out of a total of 60 short variant forms (excluding locatives), 6 occurred in relative clauses and 12 occurred in possessive noun phrases; that is, almost a third of the occurrences of short variant forms were in combination with a coreferential relative or possessive particle (highlighted along with the demonstratives in the examples below):

(210) **Ye**   mwanachetu   a-si-**ye**-gomb-a
      1.DEM3_VAR   1-woman   3SG-NEG-1.REL-speak-FV
      '**That** woman who does not speak'

(211) **go**   a-chi-**go**-hend-a   mche-o
      6.DEM3_VAR   3SG-CONS-6.REL-do-FV   1.wife-1.2SG.POS
      '**the things** which your wife did'

(212) **Zo**   tembe-**zo**   mbiri
      10.DEM3_VAR   10.seeds-10.2SG.POS   10.two
      'Your two seeds' or '**Those** two seeds of yours'

(213) **nyo**   a-tumishi-**e**
      2.DEM3_VAR   2-servants-2.3SG.POS
      'his servants' or '**those** servants of his'

3. The short variant forms of the locative noun classes in series 3, *pho, ko,* and *mo,* are far more common than both the series 3 base forms and long variant forms. Over half of the short variant forms (69 out of 129) in a corpus of nontranslated texts were locatives.

4

Verbal Morphology

Verbal morphology in Bantu languages is typically complex and Digo is no exception. Apart from singular imperative forms, the verb root always occurs with a number of affixes which occur in fixed positions both before the verb root (prefixes) and following the verb root (suffixes). The following description of Digo verbal morphology is dominated by a description of the various affixes which can modify a verb root, including some clitics which occur at the end of the verb group, and concludes with a description of irregular and defective verbs, and verbal derivation.

4.1 Structure of the verb group

What I will call the 'verb group' (following Besha 1989) consists of the verb root plus a variable number of inflectional and derivational morphemes. A verb group can include markers for the person or noun class of both a grammatical subject and an object, instrument or location; it can also include markers of verbal negation, tense-aspect-movement, a passive marker, and one or more derivational markers. Each marker occurs in a specific position or 'slot' relative to the verb root and to the other markers in the verb group. The canonical structure of a lexical verb group in Digo is shown (slightly simplified) in table 4.1.

Table 4.1. Template of the verb group

1	2	3a and 3b	4	5	6	7	8	9
Initial	Subject concord	Tense-aspect-movement	Verb complement	ROOT	Extensions	Final vowel	Post-final	Clitics
	SC	TAM	VC	VS (verb stem)		FV	post	

Note that table 4.1 does not include the relative concords, which occur between the TAM marker and the (optional) verb complement concord, and in the postfinal slot. Relative clauses are discussed in §7.3.

4.1.1 Initial slot

This slot contains the following morphemes: Negative and 'Emphatic' subjunctive.

4.1.1.1 Negative

The form of the negative prefix in declarative clauses is *ta* for all noun classes (except class 1) and for first, second and third person plural subjects:

(214) ***ta**-hu-many-a*
NEG-2PL-know-FV
'we do not know'

(215) *matunda-ge*   ***ta**-ga-ri-k-a*
6.fruit-6.3SG.POS   NEG-6-eat-STAT-FV
'its fruit is not edible'

With 2nd and 3rd person singular subjects the form of the negative morpheme is *k*:

(216) a. ***k**-u-many-a*   b. ***k**-a-many-a*
NEG-2SG-know-FV   NEG-3SG-know-FV
'you do not know'   's/he does not know'

With 1st person singular subjects, the negative prefix combines with the subject marker to form the portmanteau form *si*:

(217) ***si**-many-a*
1SG.NEG-know-FV
'I do not know'

This form is widespread in Eastern Bantu languages, occurring, for example, in Daiso (Nurse 2000:46), Mbugwe (Mous 2004:9), Shambala (Besha 1989:70) and Swahili, and so is almost certainly an inherited form rather than an innovation in Digo. The first person singular negative *si* should be distinguished from the *si* negative marker which occurs in subjunctive clauses in slot 3a.

4.1.1.2 'Emphatic' subjunctive

In subjunctive clauses, the initial slot can also contain the clitic *na*:

(218) Hu-som-e-ni   vs.   **Na**=hu-som-e-ni
       2PL-read-SUB-PL   EMPH=2PL-read-SUB-PL[1]
       'Let's read/we should read'   'Let us read!'

(219) Mlungu a-togol-w-e.   vs.   Mlungu **na**=a-togol-w-e!
       God   3SG-praise-PAS-SUB   God   EMPH=3SG-praise-PAS-SUB
       'God should be praised.'   'Let God be praised!'

The clitic *na* may be an instantiation of the comitative marker *na* (which indicates an association between entities), but its function is distinct. Amidu (2001:66–67) claims that in the parallel construction in Swahili, *na* can be separated from the verb group (for example, by being placed before an independent pronoun), with no change in meaning, as follows:

(220) a. *Sasa sisi na[2] tuwatazame wanaoalika mikutano.*   (Swahili)

       and

       b. *Sasa na sisi tuwatazame wanaoalika mikutano.*   (Swahili)

       both mean: 'And now let us look at those who invite people to gatherings.'

In Digo, however, placing *na* before an independent (or cliticized) pronoun changes the meaning; when used as an emphatic marker, *na* can only occur attached to the verb group—in other positions, *na* functions as a comitative marker:

(221) Sambi sisi **na**=hu-som-e-ni   Chidigo.
       now   1PL   EMPH=2PL-read-SUB-PL   7.Digo_language
       'Now let us read the Digo language!'

---

[1] The plural addressee suffix *-ni* in the postfinal slot indicates more than 2 people.
[2] In Swahili *na* in this use is written as a separate word, whereas in Digo it is written as part of the verb group. Amidu (2001:67) notes that the first example is preferred by most speakers, and that *na* in the second example can also be interpreted as a conjunction.

(222) a. Sambi **na** sisi hu-som-e-ni Chidigo.
      now COM 1PL 2PL-read-SUB-PL 7.Digo_language

  b. Sambi **na**=swi hu-som-e-ni Chidigo.
      now COM=1PL 2PL-read-SUB-PL 7.Digo_language

  both mean either 'Now let us also read the Digo language.'
  or 'Now we also should read the Digo language.'

4.1.2 Subject concord

This slot contains the subject concord (SC) for the different persons and noun classes, as described in table 4.2.

Table 4.2. Person markers and noun class prefixes in the SC slot

Person+no./ noun class	Form	Comments
1SG	ni/n	n always occurs before vowels and in fast speech before consonants; with the continuous aspect marker na, the following morphosyntactic change occurs: n + na > na
1PL	hu	the initial h is a very lenis (weak) voiced glottal fricative; it may be perceived as 'breathy voice' and some speakers do not pronounce it at all; hu > hw before a
2SG	u	the regular morphophonological change u > w occurs before a and e
2PL	mu/m	mu occurs in stressed syllables (i.e. in monosyllabic verbs) and mu > mw before a, i and e; m occurs elsewhere
3SG (class 1)	a/w	w occurs before a (past tense marker); evidence from the related language Duruma suggests that the 3SG subject marker may once have had the form u (which became w following the regular u > w pattern)
3PL (class 2)	a	a + á (past tense marker) > a
3	u	u > w before a and e
4	i	i > y before a and e
5	ri	ri > r before a and e
6	ga	
7	chi	chi > ch before a and e
8	vi	vi > vy before a and e
9	i	i > y before a and e
10	zi	zi > z before a and e

4.1 Structure of the verb group

Table 4.2, continued

Person+no./ noun class	Form	Comments
11	ri	ri > r before a and e
14	u	u > w before a and e
15	ku	ku > kpw [kp] before a and e
16	pha	
17	ku	ku > kpw [kp] before a and e
18	mu/ m	mu occurs in stressed syllables (i.e. in monosyllabic verbs) and mu > mw before a and e

Morimoto (2006) suggests that there are languages that have 'salience-based agreement' in which the verb agrees with the topic, and languages that have 'role-based agreement' in which the verb agrees with the logical subject (for example, the most agent-like argument of a transitive verb). There is a grammaticalization cline in which languages change from salience-based agreement to role-based agreement and many (probably most) Bantu languages are somewhere along that cline, showing features of both. Digo generally exhibits role-based agreement in that the grammatical subject (that is, the NP which determines the noun class of the SC) is almost always also the logical or thematic subject (for example, the agent in an active verb phrase).[3]

There are few tonal distinctions discernible as a result of subject marking. The 3SG subject marker has an underlying high tone, however, not all speakers recognize or produce a high tone with 3SG subjects, and tone is not marked in this environment in the standard orthography.

The class 15 SC needs to be distinguished from the homophonous noun class prefix, which also functions as the infinitive marker. In example (223), *kulapha* 'swearing an oath' functions as the subject of the following verb group *kunaonyesa* 'shows', and so *ku* in *kulapha* is the class 15 noun class prefix and has been glossed as INF, whereas *ku* in *kunaonyesa* is the class 15 SC.

(223) **kulapha kunaonyesa** *gara gachigogombwa ni ga kpweli.*

'swearing an oath shows that those [words] that have been spoken are true.'

ku-laph-a   ku-na-onyes-a
INF-swear-FV   15-CONT-show-FV

In imperatives, there is no subject marking in the subject concord slot, but a 2nd person plural subject is marked by the suffix -ni in the postfinal slot (see §4.1.10). In subjunctive clauses, a plural/dual distinction is made in the

---

[3] It is also possible for the SC to be in one of the locative noun classes (16 pha, 17 ku, and 18 mu) whilst the logical subject is an NP from another noun class which follows the verb. This is known as locative inversion and is discussed in greater detail in §7.5.

1st person which is marked by the presence or absence of the suffix *-ni* in the postfinal slot:

(224) **hu**-phiy-e   vs.   **hu**-phiy-e-**ni**
       1PL-go-SUB   1PL-go-SUB-PL
       'let us both go'   'let us all (more than two) go'

4.1.3 TAM and negation

Slot 3 contains most of the tense-aspect-movement and "status" (TAM) morphemes[4] and the negative markers *si* and *sa*. Slot 3 must be divided into two sub-slots, as a limited number of TAM markers and the negative *sa* can follow other TAM morphemes in the same verb group.

4.1.3.1 Slot 3a

What I have called slot 3a is the location in the verb group for most of the TAM markers and the negative marker *si* (not the homophonous 1SG negative marker, which occurs in the initial slot).

4.1.3.1.1 TAM markers

Listed below are the TAM morphemes which occur in slot 3a in the verb group. For details, see chapter 5.

General (can occur in both affirmative and negative clauses)

conditional	nge
future	nda
hodiernal past	ka
inceptive	dzangbwe
potential	ka
sequential	ka

Affirmative (do not occur with negative markers)

consecutive	chi	a preceding past tense marker establishes temporal reference
continuous	na	also occurs in tensed relative clauses
dependent	chi	used in dependent clauses
distal	cha	dependent on previous verb for temporal reference

---

[4]Other TAM morphemes occur in the final slot. The complete TAM system is described in chapter 5.

4.1 Structure of the verb group

future + movement	ya	
generic	∅	only possible with passive verbs
habitual	ku/nku	ku is only preceded by 1st and 2nd person SCs, otherwise nku is used for all classes
imperfective	chi	always preceded by a past tense auxiliary
itive + subjunctive	ka + e	e occurs in the final slot
remote past (past)	a	+ floating high tone realized on following verb stem
anterior	ka	
persistive	chere	
simultaneous	chopho	no preceding subject concord; only used in the southern (Tanzanian) dialect

Negative (only occur with negative markers)

general negative	∅
negative past	ya

Relative (only occur in tensed relative clauses)

relative past	ri	
relative anterior	chi	
relative future	ndi	no preceding subject concord

4.1.3.1.2 Negative marker si

In addition to the TAM markers listed above, slot 3a can also be filled by the negative marker *si* in subjunctive clauses and preceding the conditional marker *nge*:

(225) a-*si*-many-e
  3SG-NEG-know-SUB
  's/he should not know'

(226) A-*si*-nge-hend-a
  3PL-NEG-COND-do-FV
  'If they had not done'

The conditional *nge-* can also be negated using the negative prefixes that occur in the initial slot. The fact that the conditional marker ends in *e*, which is characteristic of subjunctive verb forms, may indicate that the *si-nge-* negative form may have originated as a negative subjunctive construction.

4.1.3.2 Slot 3b

What I have called slot 3b is the location in the verb group for three TAM markers which appear to be less grammaticalized than the rest, and for the negative marker *sa*.

4.1.3.2.1 TAM markers

The following TAM morphemes occur in slot 3b in the verb group:

emphatic	*henda*
itive	*kpwenda (enda)*
ventive	*kpwedza (edza)*

These three TAM markers have been placed in slot 3b because they must all be preceded by another TAM marker, or by the infinitive prefix *ku-*:

(227) a. ná-**henda**-on-a
1SG.PST-EMPH-see-FV
'I saw' (emphatic)

b. ku-**henda**-och-w-a
INF-EMPH-burn-PAS-FV
'to be burnt/being burnt'

(228) a. ná-**kpwenda**-mu-ih-a
1SG.PST-IT-3SG-call-FV
'I went and called him'

b. ku-**enda**-mu-ih-a
INF-IT-3SG-call-FV
'to go and call him'

(229) Ligundzu a-chetu a-k-**edza**-hek-a madzi.
morning 2-women 3PL-HOD-VENT-draw-FV 6.water
'In the morning the women came and drew water.'

4.1.3.2.2 Negative marker *sa*

The negative marker *sa* is used to negate the infinitive marker *ku-*, the sequential TAM marker *ka-*, and the (possibly related) potential TAM marker *ka-*:

(230) **ku**-**sa**-many-a[5]
INF-NEG-know-FV
'not to know', 'not knowing'

(231) a-**ka**-**sa**-hend-a
3SG-SEQ-NEG-do-FV
'and he does not do'

---

[5] The form *kuso-* is also heard occasionally; this may be the result of partial borrowing from Swahili, in which the corresponding form is *kuto-*.

4.1 Structure of the verb group

(232) *n-**ka**-**sa**-kpwedz-a ...*
1SG-POT-NEG-come-FV
'if I don't come ...'

4.1.4 Relative concord

In tensed relative clauses, a relative concord marker occurs immediately after the TAM slot and can itself be followed immediately by a verb complement marker ('object marker'). The same forms are used for both subject and object relatives:

1	2	3	4	5	6	7	8	9	10	11	14	15	16	17	18
ye	o	wo	yo	ro	go	cho	vyo	yo	zo	ro	wo	ko	pho	ko	mo

Examples (233) and (234) illustrate subject and object relatives, respectively; the relativized subject or object and the coreferential concords are in bold type, and the relative concord is underlined:

(233) **hiye**   **m-chetu**   *a-ri-ye-m-tiy-a*   *yuya*
1.DEM3   1-woman   3SG-REL.PST-1.REL-3SG-put-FV   1.DEM2
mwanache   *dibwa-ni*
1.child   5.hole-LOC
'the woman who had put the small child in the pit'

(234) **rorosi**   *m-ndi-ro-voy-a*
5.whatever   2PL-FUT-5.REL-ask-FV
'whatever you ask'

The same forms can occur in the postfinal slot (see §4.1.10.2). For a description of relative clauses, see §7.3.

4.1.5 Verb complement

Although many Bantu grammars refer to this slot in the verbal complex as the 'object' slot (and the element which occurs in this slot as the 'object marker' or 'object concord'), it does not always contain objects. Rather, it contains incorporated arguments, of which objects are one kind; others include instruments and locations. For the reasons given below, I prefer to follow Thwala (2006) and use the term 'Verb Complement concord' (abbreviated to VC) to describe the relationship between morphemes in this slot and the verb complements which control them.

Objects are typically defined as nominals that occur as internal arguments of the verb (that is, as verb complements). Various diagnostic tests have been proposed to identify syntactic objects in Bantu languages, notably verb-adjacency (the noun phrase which occurs immediately after the verb is an object), object concord (a noun phrase that is coreferential with the so-called 'object marker' is an object), and possibility to become the subject of a passive construction. However, these diagnostics cannot be applied consistently. Thwala (2006) notes a number of problems, the most important of which are the following:

- In some languages, the position immediately after the verb is reserved for whichever internal argument of the verb is highest in an animacy hierarchy, regardless of grammatical role.
- The nominal immediately after the verb does not necessarily corefer with the 'object marker'; in fact, the noun phrase that is coreferential with the 'object marker' typically exhibits free word order, suggesting that it is a topic rather than a syntactic object (in which case, if there is a syntactic object, it must be the 'object marker' itself).
- The nominal that corefers with the 'object marker' does not necessarily become the subject of a passive construction.
- Prepositional phrases (PPs), both locatives and instrumentals, can pass all of the diagnostic tests in some languages, including Digo, yet PPs are not usually considered to be objects.[6]

All noun classes are represented, including classes 16, 17 and 18 (locatives) and the reflexive marker. The form of the VC is the same as that of the SC in each class except for classes 1 and 2. The VCs for persons and the reflexive are given in table 4.3 (details of the 2nd person plural form can be found in §4.1.10.1).

Table 4.3. Person markers in the VC slot

Person/number	VC (slot 4)
1SG	*ni*
1PL	*hu*, or *w* with verb roots beginning with *u*; the [h] is often silent
2SG	*ku*
2PL	*ku* plus *ni* in the postfinal slot (slot 8)
3SG (= class 1)	*m* or *mu/mw* before verb roots beginning with a vowel
3PL (= class 2)	*a*
Reflexive	*dzi*

Digo allows only one Verb Complement to be marked in the VC slot per verb.[7] Digo allows VC concord not only with coreferential object nominals (e.g. *nine* in example [235]) but also with nominals that are not grammatical objects (e.g.

---

[6]This can also be used as an argument against the existence of PPs in Bantu languages; for further discussion, see §6.1 'Relational expressions'. For more detailed arguments against the notion of syntactic objects in Bantu see Thwala (2006).
[7]It is what Bearth (2003:124) calls an OM-1 language. In this respect, Digo patterns with Swahili and the other Northeast Coast languages, as well as Chewa, Herero, Lozi, Swati, and Xhosa, which also have a single VC slot; it differs from languages including Bemba, Chaga, Haya, Rwanda, Runyambo, and Tswana, which allow more than one VC to be marked on the verb.

4.1 Structure of the verb group

Juma in example [236] which is part of the grammatical subject [*mwana hiyu wa Juma*]), and with reflexives (237):

(235) Mwana   hiyu   wa   Juma   a-na-**mu**-ig-a   **nine.**
1.child   1.DEM1   1.ASS   NAME   3SG-CONT-3SG-resemble-FV   1a.mother
'This child of Juma's resembles his mother (i.e. resembles his own mother).'

(236) Mwana   hiyu   wa   **Juma**   a-na-**mu**-ig-a.
1.child   1.DEM1   1.ASS   NAME   3SG-CONT-3SG-resemble-FV
'This child of Juma's resembles him (i.e. resembles Juma).'

(237) Punde   **a**-ka-**dzi**-uz-a,   "Ano atu   a-phiy-a=phi?"
immediately   3SG-SEQ-REFL-ask-FV   PL   2.people   3PL-go-FV=Q
'Immediately he asked himself, "Where did those people go?"'

When there are two or more lexical Verb Complements, the VC concord can only be coreferential with a fronted (topicalized) Verb Complement, in which case it is also obligatory. In the following examples with an animate beneficiary and an inanimate patient, either the beneficiary or the patient may be fronted, but in each case a coreferential VC is obligatory.

(238) **Anafundzi,**   mwalimu   a-ka-**a**-som-er-a   vitabu.
2.students   1.teacher   3SG-HOD-2-read-APPL-FV   8.books
'The teacher read the students some books (today).'

*Mwalimu   a-ka-a-som-er-a   anafundzi   vitabu.
1.teacher   3SG-HOD-2-read-APPL-FV   2.students   8.books

(239) **Vitabu,**   mwalimu   a-ka-**vi**-som-er-a   anafundzi.
8.books   1.teacher   3SG-HOD-8-read-APPL-FV   2.students
'The teacher read the books to some students (today).'

*Mwalimu   a-ka-vi-som-er-a   anafundzi   vitabu.
1.teacher   3SG-HOD-8-read-APPL-FV   2.students   8.books

The same principle applies with other Verb Complements, including goal and location; example (240) contains a fronted 'goal', while example (241) contains a fronted location. (The locative suffix -*ni* causes *nyumbani* to function in a locative noun class, hence the coreferential VC concord is the locative class 17 concord *ku*-.)

(240) **Mboga**   n-ka-**zi**-enjerez-a   munyu.
10.vegetables   1SG-HOD-10-increase-FV   9.salt
'I added salt to the vegetables (rather than to the rice, etc.).'

```
*N-ka-zi-enjerez-a      mboga            munyu
1SG-HOD-10-increase-FV  10.vegetables    9.salt
```

(241) **Nyumba-ni** mayo   a-ka-**ku**-jit-ir-a   sima.
      house-LOC   1a.mother 3SG-HOD-17-cook-APPL-FV 9.maize_meal

      'Mother cooked maize meal in the house (rather than somewhere else).'

```
*Mayo       a-ka-i/ku-jit-ir-a        sima          nyumba-ni.
1a.mother   3SG-HOD-9/17-cook-APPL-FV 9.maize_meal  house-LOC
```

In object relatives, the VC concord is optional. The first two examples below illustrate inflected relative clauses; in (242) the class 14 VC *u-* is present in *ariouimba* but in (243) the class 6 VC *ga-* does not occur in *hurigobisha* (the relative clauses are enclosed in square brackets):

(242) wira   wenye   [a-ri-o-**u**-imb-a]
      14.song   14.ASS   3SG-PST-14.REL-14-sing-FV

      'the song itself [which he sang (it)]'

(243) gara   [hu-ri-go-bish-a   dzuzi]
      6.DEM2   1PL-PST-6.REL-discuss-FV   day_before_yesterday

      'those (matters) [which we discussed two days ago]'

Similarly, in the relative clauses formed with the *amba-* relativizer below, the class 10 VC *zi-* is present in *akaziphaha* in (244) but the class 7 VC *chi-* does not occur in *undarya* in (245):

(244) mali   z-osi   [amba-zo   kala   a-ka-**zi**-phah-a]
      10.wealth   10-all   REL-10.REL PST   3SG-ANT-10-get-FV

      'all the wealth [which he had got (it)]'

(245) chakurya-cho   [amba-cho   u-nda-ry-a]
      7.food-7.2SG.POS   REL-7.REL   2SG-FUT-eat-FV

      'your food [which you will eat]'

The VC concord is also optional in uninflected relative clauses. In the following examples, the class 10 VC *zi-* is present in *nizimanyazo* in (246) but the class 7 VC *chi-* does not occur in *asomacho* in (247):

(246) koma   z-osi   [ni-**zi**-many-a-zo]
      10.ancestral_spirits 10-all   1SG-10-know-FV-10.REL

      'all the ancestral spirits [which I know (them)]'

(247) chitabu   [a-som-a-cho]
      7.book   3SG-read-FV-7.REL

      'the book [which she reads]'

4.1 Structure of the verb group

The Verb Complement concord properties are summarized below:[8]

Can the VC concord and the coreferential noun phrase co-occur?	Yes, unless there is more than one Verb Complement, neither of which has been fronted.
Is the co-occurrence of the VC and the coreferential NP required in some contexts?	Yes, when the VC concord is coreferential with a fronted (topicalized) Verb Complement.
Are there locative VC concords?	Yes, for all three locative noun classes.
Is only one VC concord allowed per verb?	Yes.
Can either Verb Complement (e.g. direct and indirect object) be expressed by a VC concord?	Yes, if and only if either a) it is not overtly expressed as a noun phrase, or b) the Verb Complement has been fronted.
Is a VC concord required, disallowed, or optional in object relatives?	A VC concord is optional in object relatives.

4.1.6 Verb root

The verb root typically has the syllable structure CVC (e.g. *jit*), although the citation form includes the final vowel *-a* (e.g. *jita* 'cook') since no closed syllables occur in actual speech. In principle, either C can consist of a prenasalized consonant; that is, a prenasalized consonant is treated as a single C in syllable structure since the nasal element is never syllabic. However, verb roots beginning with a prenasalized consonant are rare; some examples are: *ndzirita* and *ngirita* 'tie tightly', *ngorota* 'snore', and *nguryusa* 'gulp'. There are, however, many verbs with vowel-initial roots; the following is just a small selection: *ata* 'trim', 'extract' or 'divorce', *eza* 'clean', *imba* 'sing', *ola* 'rot', and *usa* 'remove' or 'celebrate a ceremony'.

Digo also has a few verbs which are monosyllabic, even with the final vowel (that is, the root itself is not syllabic); these are listed below:

cha	'dawn' or 'stop raining' or 'revere'	*nywa*	'dry up *intr*'
dai	'claim, be owed'	*pha*	'give'
fwa	'die'	*phya*	'burn *intr*'
gbwa	'fall'[9]	*pwa*	'ebb, fall (tide)'
hwa	'pound, husk'	*rya*	'eat' or 'be sharp'
kaa	'be late'	*tii*	'obey'
la	'come from'	*tswa*	'set (sun)'
nwa	'drink'	*twa*	'spit'
nya	'rain' or 'excrete'	*tya*	'have had enough'

---

[8] The following summary is based on parameters used in Marten et al. (2007).
[9] This verb is also used of the sun setting, sediment settling, and aeroplanes landing.

Although these roots do not take any compensatory syllables, most of them contain either long vowels, glides, or diphthongs (the exception being *la*) and the passive forms of those verbs that can be passivized contain syllabic verb roots (with the structure CV). This suggests that historically, these verb roots had a CV structure:

(248) *a-nda-**ry**-a*   passive: *a-nda-**ri**-w-a*
       3SG-FUT-eat-FV   3SG-FUT-eat-PAS-FV
       's/he will eat'   's/he will be eaten'

(249) *a-**nw**-a*   *madzi*   passive: *madzi*   *ga-**nwe**-w-a*
       3SG.PST-drink-FV 6.water   6.water   6.PST-drink-PAS-FV
       's/he drank water'   'water was drunk'

4.1.7 Verb stem

I will refer to the verb root plus any extensions and/or the final vowel as the 'verb stem'. This is the vowel harmony domain. Extensions beginning with a vowel which alternates between *e* and *i* select one or the other on the basis of the height of the final vowel of the verb root. This is also true of the negative perfective marker *-ire/-ere* which occurs in the final slot. Verb roots whose last vowel is *a*, *i*, or *u* are followed by *i* and verb roots whose last vowel is *e* or *o* are followed by *e*:

(250) *wa-**jit**-a*   >   *ka-**jit**-**ire***
       3SG.PST-cook-FV   3SG.NEG-cook-PFV
       's/he cooked'   's/he did not cook'

(251) *wa-**som**-a*   >   *ka-**som**-**ere***
       3SG.PST-read-FV   3SG.NEG-read-PFV
       's/he read'   's/he did not read'

The verb stem is also the part of the verbal group which is involved in reduplication; extensions (if there are any) and the final vowel are involved in reduplication. The following examples illustrate this; in the first, the final vowel is involved in reduplication, hence **suk-suka*:

(252) *suka* 'shake'   >   *suka-suka* 'shake repeatedly'

The passive extension is involved in reduplication (k + w results in a double plosive [kp] written as /kpw/), hence **tika-tikpwa* and **tikpwa-tika*:

(253) *tika-tika*   >   *tikpwa-tikpwa ni magulu*
       'crumble'   'to go weak at the knees'

4.1 Structure of the verb group

The verb *uyira* derives from *uya* 'return' plus the applicative suffix; the applicative suffix is involved in reduplication, hence **uya-uyira* and **uyira-uya*:

(254)   *uyira* 'repeat'   >   *uyira-uyira* 'to carry on repeating'

None of the verbal prefixes is involved in reduplication; for example, the reflexive verb complement concord *dzi-* in slot 3 occurs only once in the reduplicated form *dziliya-liya* 'to prepare oneself' (**dziliya-dziliya*).

4.1.8 Extensions

The verbal extensions which occur in Digo are listed in table 4.4, along with the Proto-Bantu form from which they are believed to derive.

Table 4.4. Verbal extensions

Proto-Bantu > Digo form	Label	Digo example	Gloss
Productive			
*ik or **ek*[10] > ik/ek	stative (neuter)	mwag-**ik**-a on-**ek**-a	'be spilt' 'be visible/be seen'
*í/*íc > Vsh/Vz (vowel harmony/ spirantization)	causative	tayar-**ish**-a uy-**iz**-a og-**esh**-a el-**ez**-a pho-**z**-a	'prepare (cause to be ready)' 'return *tr*' 'wash *tr*' 'explain (cause to understand)' 'heal *tr*' < *phola* 'get well'
*id or **ed* > ir/er	applicative (prepositional)	jit-**ir**-a gomb-**er**-a	'cook for (someone)'/'at (place)'/'with' 'rebuke (speak against someone)'
*an > an	reciprocal	gbwir-**an**-a	'join together *intr*'
*ú > w	passive	gbwir-**w**-a	'be held'
No longer productive			
*am > am	static	kak-**am**-a	'tremble'
*ud > ul	reversive (transitive)	fum-**ul**-a	'unpick a hem or seam' < *fuma* 'knit'
*uk > uk	reversive (intransitive)	lam-**uk**-a tsats-am-**uk**-a	'awake' < *lala* 'sleep' 'melt *intr*'

In the rest of this subsection the five productive extensions—stative (also called 'neuter'), causative, applicative, reciprocal, and passive—will be illustrated, together with the relative order of extensions within a single verb phrase.

---

[10] The symbol * before a form indicates that this is a reconstruction. The reconstructions here are based on those proposed by Meeussen (1967). The reconstructed forms **ek* and **ed* for the stative and applicative respectively are proposed in Hyman (1999:273).

4.1.8.1 Stative (neuter)

The form of the stative is either *-ik* or *-ek* as determined by vowel height harmony rules. If the preceding vowel (the final vowel of the verb stem) is either *a, i,* or *u*, the form of the stative is *-ik*, but if the preceding vowel is *e* or *o* the form of the stative is *-ek*. In a number of verbs, the form of the stative is *-ikan/-ekan: manyikana* 'be known'; *onekana* 'be visible' (varies with *oneka*); *phahikana* 'be available'; etc.

The stative makes the object of a nonstative verb (specifically, the 'patient') into the subject of a corresponding stative verb. The agent (usually the subject of the corresponding nonstative verb) cannot be overtly mentioned (even by an agentive adjunct phrase); that is, it decreases the valence of the verb stem by 1. A stative verb indicates that its subject will enter, is entering or has entered into a certain state.

(255) a. *Omari a-na-mwag-a madzi*
Omari 3SG-CONT-spill-FV 6.water
'Omari is spilling water'

b. *Madzi ga-na-mwag-**ik**-a*
6.water 6-CONT-spill-STAT-FV
'Water is being spilt'

Because the object of a nonstative verb becomes the subject of a stative verb, and the agent cannot be mentioned, stative verbs often exhibit behaviour typical of intransitive verbs. However, it is nonetheless possible for a verb complement concord (i.e. an 'object marker') to occur with stative verbs. The verb *angamika* 'be lost' is a fossilized form but this behaviour is characteristic of most stative verbs:

(256) a. *Pehe ya Maryamu i-ka-**mu**-angamik-a.*
9.ring 9.ASS Maryamu 9-ANT-3SG-be_lost-FV
'Maryamu's ring is lost/has got lost.'

b. *Pehe i-ka-**mu**-angamik-a Maryamu.*
9.ring 9-ANT-3SG-be_lost-FV Maryamu
'Maryamu has lost her ring'/'Maryamu's ring has got lost.'

4.1.8.2 Causative

The main effect of the causative extension is to turn an intransitive verb into a transitive verb, or a transitive verb into a ditransitive verb; that is, it increases the valence of the verb stem by 1. When the causative is used in this way, the grammatical subject is the instigator, or causer of the action described by the verb, and the grammatical object is the agent of the action (i.e. the person or

4.1 Structure of the verb group

thing doing the action). The causative extension can also turn certain adjectives and nouns into verbs.

The form of the causative is either *-iz/-ez* or *-ish/-esh* (occasionally varying with *-is/-es*), the initial vowel being determined by the same vowel height harmony rules as for the stative. The suffix is added to the final consonant of the verb root unless the verb root ends in *r* or *l*, in which case this consonant is replaced by *z*, for example:

hurira 'be still'	>	*huriza* 'appease, calm'
lala 'sleep'	>	*laza* 'put to sleep'
mera 'grow'	>	*meza* 'make something grow'

The *-iz/-ez* form of the causative is the more common allomorph when the causative form of a verb is derived from a recognizable root form which corresponds to a verb in current usage in Digo (table 4.5):

Table 4.5. Examples of the causative extension *-iz/-ez*

-iz/-ez	Source
angamiza 'destroy'	cf. *angamika* 'be lost, perish' (stative)
apiza 'insult, curse'	*apa* 'swear'
aziza 'discourage'	*aza* 'desire' (possibly)
elekeza 'point, show, guide'	*elekea* 'face, go towards' (n.b. *kuelekeza* = towards)
eleza 'explain'	cf. *elewa* 'understand'
eneza 'spread *tr*'	*enea* 'spread'
fukiza 'burn *intr*'	*fuka* 'to rise up (of smoke), evaporate'
galuza 'turn, change *tr*'	cf. *galuka* 'turn, change *intr*' (stative)
gbwiza 'cause to hold'	*gbwira*, e.g. *undamgbwiza haya* 'you will make him be ashamed'
gombekeza 'answer'	stative form of *gomba* 'speak' (archaic?)
goteza 'spread *tr*'	*gota* 'spread'
gutiza 'cause to touch'	*guta* 'touch'
huriza 'appease, calm'	*hurira* 'be still'
injiza 'escort inside'	*injira* 'enter'
laphiza 'insult, curse'	*lapha* 'swear'
laza 'put to sleep'	*lala* 'sleep' (also 'admit to hospital')
lumiza 'harm, hurt'	*luma* 'be in pain'
meza 'cause to grow'	*mera* 'grow'
pandiza 'load, place upon'	*panda* 'climb'
reyeza 'anger *tr*'	*reya* 'be angry'
riphiza 'repay'	*ripha* 'pay'
riza 'make s.o. cry'	*rira* 'cry'
sikiza 'hear, obey'	synonymous with *sikira*

Table 4.5, continued

-iz/-ez	Source
tambukiza 'remind'	tambukira 'remember'
tanguliza 'pass s.th. on ahead'	tanguliya 'go ahead'
tikanyiza 'stretch out e.g. hand'	tikanya 'cross e.g. road'
timiza 'fulfil'	timiya 'fulfil, obey'
tsamiza 'move things or people to/from place'	tsama 'move house'
tsapiza 'agree, pass a motion'	tsapa 'pass'
tsatsamusa 'melt tr'	tsatsamuka 'melt' [note k > s]
tsereza 'melt tr'	tserera 'descend'
tsopoza 'drop tr'	tsopoka 'fall down' (stative)
tsukiza 'offend'	offend (cf. tsukirwa 'be angry')
uyiza 'return tr'	uya 'come back'

The *-ish/-esh* allomorph is less frequent, as table 4.6 illustrates:

Table 4.6. Examples of the causative extension *-ish/-esh*

-ish/-esh	Source
andikisha 'cause to write'	andika 'write'
chelewesha 'delay'	chelewa 'be late'
fananisha 'compare'	fanana 'resemble'
ogesha (alt: ogesa) 'wash tr'	oga 'wash intr'
patanisha 'reconcile'	patana 'agree' (Swahili)
pimisha 'compare'	pima 'test'
risa 'feed'	rya 'eat'
shibisha 'satisfy, fill'	shiba 'be full' (Swahili)
unganisha 'unite, join tr'	ungana 'unify, join together'
wezesha 'enable'	weza 'be able'
zamisha 'bend s.th.'	zama 'bend over' (alternative form: zamisa)
zidisha 'increase tr'	zidi 'increase intr'

In verbs for which the root form is either unknown or is of Swahili origin, the *-ish/-esh* form of the causative extension is the most common allomorph. In many cases, Digo has borrowed Swahili causative verb forms without having borrowed the corresponding verb root in isolation. Forms (all of which contain *-ish/-esh*) for which there is a current source construction in another word class (adjective, relational expression, or 'preposition', and noun) are listed below. All of these words (causatives and their sources) are also found in Swahili and so it is not possible to say whether Digo borrowed the source alone or both the source and the corresponding causative.

4.1 Structure of the verb group

Table 4.7. Causatives from Swahili adjectives and relational expressions

Causatives	Source
halalisha 'ritually cleanse'	halali 'ritually clean'
kamilisha 'complete'	kamili 'completely'
karibisha 'welcome, bring near'	karibu 'near'
lazimisha 'force, compel'	lazima 'necessary'
safisha 'cleanse'	safi 'clean'
shurutisha 'force, compel'	sharti 'necessary'
starehesha 'give pleasure'	starehe 'comfortable'
tajirisha 'make s.o. wealthy'	tajiri 'wealthy'
tayarisha 'prepare'	tayari 'ready'

Table 4.8. Causatives derived from Swahili nouns

Causatives	Source
hakikisha 'confirm, make certain'	hakika 'certainty' (cl.9)
kodisha 'rent'	kodi 'tax' (cl.9)
shugulisha 'occupy'	shughuli 'business' (cl.9)

Table 4.9 lists other nonproductive causatives for which there is no current source construction or which are borrowed from Swahili; these may contain either -ish/-esh or -iz/-ez.

Table 4.9. Other causatives

-ish/-esh	-iz/-ez
angaisha 'disturb'	enjereza 'increase'
badilisha 'change'	hindimiza 'hit with a fist'
fundisha 'teach' (from Swahili; alt. Digo form: fundza)	himiza 'urge'
furahisha 'gladden' < furaha 'be glad' (Swahli)	miza 'swallow' (possibly not a causative because monosyllabic roots are rare)
hangaisha 'trouble'	
komesha alt: komesa 'bring to a stop'	sisitiza 'urge'
kopesha 'lend' (a form kopa with the same meaning also exists but is rare)	tengeza 'make, construct, repair' (Swahili = tengeneza)
linganisha 'compare' (a borrowing from Swahili, although kulengana na 'according to' occurs in Digo)	teza 'amaze' (this may not be a causative, because monosyllabic roots are rare; also the verb tezeka 'wonder' with a stative extension exists, and it is unusual for the stative to follow the causative; see §4.1.8.6)
tisha 'fear' (possibly not a causative, because monosyllabic roots are rare)	
wakilisha 'represent'	

4.1.8.3 Applicative (prepositional)

The applicative suffix increases the valence of the verb stem by 1; the additional argument can then be incorporated into the verbal complex in the form of a prefix in the VC slot. In traditional terminology, the applicative suffix makes an intransitive verb transitive, and a transitive verb ditransitive by adding an argument that (generally) is a beneficiary, recipient, location, instrument, goal or location.[11] Unlike when the causative is used, the subject of a verb with the applicative extension remains the agent.

The form of the applicative is either *-ir* or *-er* (the initial vowel being determined by the same vowel height harmony rules as for the causative and stative). When the verb stem ends in *ir*, the form of the applicative suffix is *-iy*, hence *fikira* 'think' > *fikiriya* 'think of/about'. If the verb stem ends in *l*, this changes to *r* before the applicative suffix:

(257) a-tsambul-a   >   a-dzi-tsambur-**ir**-a
      3PL.PST-choose-FV   3PL.PST-REFL-choose-APPL-FV
      'they chose'   'they chose for themselves'

With monosyllabic verbs, the applicative extension is reduplicated (it appears twice consecutively). In these cases there is no difference in meaning from the use of a single applicative extension with a disyllabic verb stem:

(258) A-chi-humir-a   mboko   ku-nw-**erer**-a   uchi.
      3SG-NARR-use-FV 9.gourd   INF-drink-APPL-FV   14.palm_wine
      'And he used a gourd to drink palm wine from.' (*nwerera* < *nwa*)

(259) Ná-jez-a   ku-humir-a   uma   ku-r-**irir**-a   mtele.
      1SG.PST-try-FV   INF-use-FV   11.fork   INF-eat-APPL-FV   3.rice
      'I tried to use a fork to eat rice.' (*ririra* < *rya*)

The following example illustrates how an intransitive verb *fwa* 'die' becomes transitive by the addition of the applicative suffix. (Because the verb *fwa* is monosyllabic, the applicative suffix is reduplicated.) The beneficiary of the verb *fwa* can be mentioned in a separate phrase headed by *kpwa* 'for', but the addition of the applicative suffix allows the beneficiary to function as the object of the verb (as illustrated by the occurrence of the 1PL VC *hu*):

(260) Jesu   w-a-hu-fw-**erer**-a.
      Jesus   3SG-PST-1PL-die-APPL-FV
      'Jesus died for us.'

---

[11] But see, for example, Whiteley (1968), Whiteley and Mganga (1969), Amidu (2001), and Thwala (2006:209–210) for discussions of the difficulties there are distinguishing intransitive and transitive clauses in Bantu languages.

4.1 Structure of the verb group

The object of an applicative-marked verb can be a 'maleficiary' as well as a beneficiary, that is, a person who suffers as a result of the action described by the verb:

(261) A-iziraeli a-m-nung'unik-**ir**-a Musa.
2-Israelites 3PL.PST-3SG-grumble-APPL-FV Moses
'The Israelites grumbled against Moses.'

The applicative can also introduce a location into the verb phrase; in example (262), *ko* is the relative pronoun for class 17 (locative):

(262) Alafu Yakobo waphiya Misiri, **ambako ndiko kofwerera**[12] na anae.
'Then Jacob went to Egypt, which is where he died with/among his children.'

amba-ko ndi=ko ko-fw-**erer**-a
REL-17.REL COP-17.REF 17.REL-die-APPL-FV

The applicative can be used to make an instrument part of the verb phrase (e.g. *mihi* 'trees' in the examples below); note that the negative construction requires the use of a relative clause and the passive suffix:

(263) a. mihi ya ku-dzeng-**er**-a (nyumba)
4.trees 9.ASS INF-build-APPL-FV (10.houses)
'trees for building (houses) with'

b. mihi amba-yo ta-i-dzeng-**er-w**-a
4.trees REL-4.REL NEG-9-build-APPL-PASS-FV
'trees which are not for building with'

The following examples illustrate how a transitive verb *jita* 'cook' becomes ditransitive by the addition of the applicative suffix. The additional argument can function as a beneficiary or recipient:

(264) a. Mayo a-na-jit-a sima ku-a anache.
1a.mother 3SG-CONT-cook-FV 9.maize_meal 17-ASS 2.children
'Mother is cooking maize meal for the children.'

b. Mayo a-na-jit-**ir**-a anache sima.
1a.mother 3SG-CONT-cook-APPL-FV 2.children 9.maize_meal
'Mother is cooking maize meal for the children.'

c. Mayo a-na-a-jit-**ir**-a sima.
1a.mother 3SG-CONT-3PL-cook-APPL-FV 9.maize_meal
'Mother is cooking maize meal for them.'

---

[12] The verb group *kofwerera* is an abbreviation of *arikofwerera* 'where he died', with the SC *a-* and relative past tense marker omitted (see §7.3 for further examples and discussion).

The additional argument can also function as instrument (265) and location (266):

(265) a. Mayo   a-nda-jita   na   kuni.
         1a.mother   3SG-FUT-cook   COM   9.firewood
         'Mother will cook with firewood.'

   b. A-nda-zi-jit-**ir**-a.
      3SG-FUT-10-cook-APPL-FV
      'She will cook with it.'

(266) a. Mayo   a-nda-jit-a   sima   mnda-ni.
         1a.mother   3SG-FUT-cook-FV   9.maize_meal   field-LOC
         'Mother will cook maize meal in the field.'

   b. A-nda-**ku**-jit-**ir**-a.
      3SG-FUT-17-cook-APPL-FV
      'She will cook there.'

In addition to indicating action at a location, the applicative can also indicate direction towards or away from a location or object, as in *galukira* 'turn towards' < *galuka* 'turn'.

Unlike some other Bantu languages, Digo does not use the applicative to indicate reason or purpose, so the starred examples below are unacceptable as paraphrases of the unstarred examples:

(267) w-a-fw-a   na /ku-a   sababu   ya   maleria
      3SG-PST-die-FV   COM/17-ASS   9.reason   9.ASS   9.malaria
      's/he died from/because of malaria'
      *w-a-fw-erer-a maleria

(268) a-na-jit-a   sima   ku-a   sababu   ya   ndzala
      3SG-CONT-cook-FV   9.maize_meal   17-ASS   9.reason   9.ASS   9.hunger
      'she is cooking maize meal because of hunger'
      *a-na-jit-ir-a sima ndzala

4.1.8.4 Reciprocal

The reciprocal is used when two or more individuals are both the agents and the patients or beneficiaries of the same action. In the most frequent construction, two or more individuals are identified as a joint subject:

4.1 Structure of the verb group

(269) *Mayo   na   anache   a-hek-ir-**an**-a   madzi.*
1a.mother   COM   2.children   3PL.PST-draw-APPL-RECIP-FV   6.water
'Mother and the children drew water for one another.'

Two other agreement patterns are also found with the reciprocal. In the first, one individual (or group) is identified as the grammatical subject of a verb containing a reciprocal, and the other individual (or group) is indicated periphrastically (introduced by the comitative *na* 'with, and'):

(270) *Mayo   wa-hek-ir-**an**-a   madzi   na   anache.*
1a.mother   3SG.PST-draw-APPL-RECIP-FV   6.water   COM   2.children
'Mother and the children drew water for one another.'

In the second agreement pattern, the grammatical subject is plural (indicating both participants), but one of them is also indicated periphrastically:

(271) *A-nyol-**an**-a   na   aphu-ye.*
3PL.PST-shave-RECIP-FV   COM   9.uncle-9.3SG.POS
'He and his uncle shaved each other.' (lit: 'They shaved each other with his uncle.')

4.1.8.5 Passive

The passive extension makes the object of an active clause into the subject, and the subject of an active clause into an optional oblique, expressed as the complement of the particle *ni* 'by' (cognate with the copula particle *ni*). The object which is made into the subject of the passive clause can be either primary or secondary (see §7.1.3), but does not include locative and instrumental arguments. In the examples below, the corresponding active sentence precedes each example for comparison:

(272) a. *Mayo   a-na-jit-a   sima.*
1a.mother   3SG-CONT-cook-FV   9.maize_meal
'Mother is cooking maize meal.'

b. *Sima   i-na-jit-**w**-a   ni   mayo.*
9.maize_meal   9-CONT-cook-PAS-FV   by   1a.mother
'Maize meal is being cooked by mother.'

(273) a. *Mayo   a-na-jit-ir-a   anache   sima.*
1a.mother   3SG-CONT-cook-APPL-FV   2.children   9.maize_meal
'Mother is cooking the children maize meal.'

b. *Anache   a-na-jit-ir-**w**-a   sima   ni   mayo.*
   2.children   3PL-CONT-cook-APPL-PAS-FV   9.maize_meal   by   1a.mother
   'The children are being cooked maize meal by mother.'

The presence of the passive suffix allows a 'zero' TAM marker to occur in verb phrases describing generic or habitual action; this construction is only possible with the passive extension (see §5.3.1.3 for details):

(274) *Dzambo   hiri   ri-Ø-hend-**w**-a   ni   A-digo*
      5.thing   5.DEM1   5-GEN-do-PAS-FV   COP   2-Digos
      'This thing is (always) done by Digos.'
      *Dzambo hiri ri-Ø-hend-ek-a

4.1.8.6 Order of extensions

If more than one extension occurs in a single verb phrase, the preferred order in which these occur is stative > causative > applicative > reciprocal/passive.[13] Example (273b) illustrates the order applicative > passive; the following examples illustrate various other combinations of extensions:

stative > causative > passive:

(275) *mutu   amba-ye   ka-gomb-**ek**-**ez**-**w**-a*
      1.person   REL-3SG.REL   3SG.NEG-speak-STAT-CAUS-PAS-FV
      'a person who is not spoken about'

stative > applicative:

(276) *A-na-shugul-**ik**-**ir**-a   mambo   g-ao   g-enye.*
      3PL-CONT-busy-STAT-APPL-FV   6.matter   6-3PL.POS   6-own
      'They deal with their own concerns.'

stative > reciprocal:

(277) *a-ka-tsangany-**ik**-**an**-a   phamwenga*
      3PL-ANT-mix-STAT-RECIP-FV   together
      'they got mixed up together'

---

[13] The reciprocal and the passive do not co-occur for semantic reasons. In Chewa and Xhosa the causative and applicative (in that order) precede the other extensions, and Mchombo (2004:125) claims that this may reflect a thematic hierarchy, since the causative and applicative are argument-increasing morphemes whereas the stative, reciprocal and passive are argument-reducing morphemes. However, Mchombo (2004:126) does note that the stative can precede the applicative in Chewa but only if the applicative is associated with a locative, circumstantial, or malefactive reading; this is a constraint which does not apply in Digo.

4.1 Structure of the verb group

causative > applicative:

(278) N'-nda-ku-uy-**iz**-**ir**-a   pesa-zo.
      1SG-FUT-2SG-return-CAUS-APPL-FV   10.money-10.2SG.POS
      'I will give you back your money.'

causative > applicative > passive:

(279) A-nda-uy-**iz**-**ir**-**w**-a   pesa-ze.
      3SG-FUT-return-CAUS-APPL-PAS-FV   10.money-10.3SG.POS
      'He will be given back his money.'

causative > reciprocal:

(280) ku-elek-**ez**-**an**-a   na   urefu   wa   mufwa
      INF-face-CAUS-RECIP-FV   COM   14.length 14.ASS 1.deceased_person
      'aligned with the corpse' i.e. lengthways alongside or under the corpse

applicative > reciprocal:

(281) Ano   mayo   a-na-hek-**ir**-**an**-a   madzi.
      PL   1a.mother 3PL-CONT-draw-APPL-RECIP-FV   6.water
      'The women are drawing water for one another.'

4.1.9   Final slot

The term 'final slot' follows traditional terminology but although it is often the last slot to be filled when a Digo verb is used, there is the possibility of a further slot being filled, which is traditionally termed the 'postfinal slot'. Morphemes which may occur in the final slot incude: (a) -*a* neutral suffix (final vowel), (b) -*e* subjunctive suffix, (c) -*ire/-ere* 'perfective'.

4.1.9.1   *neutral suffix (final vowel)* -*a*

The neutral suffix (or final vowel, glossed 'FV') -*a* is the default vowel which ensures that the verb stem is an open syllable. It is not itself part of the verb root or stem since it can be separated from the root by various extensions and can be replaced by the subjunctive suffix -*e* and perfective suffix -*ire/-ere*. However, because verb stems never occur in speech as closed syllables, the final vowel is included in the citation form of verb stems and roots.

The neutral suffix occurs with most tenses and the infinitive and also in affirmative imperative verb forms (negative imperatives are formed using the subjunctive suffix, as described below):

(282) *Phiy-a*
 go-FV
 'Go!'

Unlike some other Bantu languages, such as Swahili, Digo has no general or habitual negative suffix *-i*, but uses the neutral suffix instead:

(283) *si-many-a*
 1SG.NEG-know-FV
 'I do not know'

(284) *ta-a-som-a*
 NEG-3PL-study-FV
 'they do not study'

However, two verbs are irregular with respect to the form of the final vowel with the general or habitual negative tense: *mendza* 'like' which takes the suffix *-e* and *taka* 'want' which is borrowed from Swahili and takes the Swahili present tense negative suffix *-i*:

(285) *ta-hu-mendz-e*
 NEG-1PL-like-FV(e)
 'we do not like'

(286) *ka-tak-i*
 3SG.NEG-want-FV(i)
 's/he does not want'

4.1.9.2 subjunctive suffix -e

Subjunctive clauses are characterized by the suffix *-e* and the lack of tense/aspect marking.

(287) *ni-phiy-e*
 1SG-go-SUB
 'let me go/I should go'

(288) *u-si-phiy-e*
 2SG-NEG-go-SUB
 'you should not go/don't go'

4.1 Structure of the verb group

The subjunctive is used in complement clauses in which the subject of the complement is different from the subject of the matrix clause (see §7.4.2) and to express purpose, sometimes preceded by the connective *ili* 'so that' (see §7.4.1.2).

(289) *Mvulana hipho kare kala akagbwira msichana* **akale ngudziwe***.*

'A young man long ago used to seize a young woman **to be his go-between.**'

a-kal-e	*ngudzi-we.*
3SG-be-SUB	1a.mediator-1.3SG.POS

(290)

hiyu	*kala*	*a-ka-ni-tiy-a*	*himu*	***ili***	***ni-fw-e***
1.DEM1	PST	3SG-ANT-1SG-put_in-FV	18.DEM1	so_that	1SG-die-SUB

'this one had put me in here **so that I would die**'

The suffix *-e* also occurs as part of the itive TAM marker *ka- + -e*, which combines the subjunctive with the added meaning of movement away from the deictic centre (see §5.5.1.3). Whether *-e* in this context should be distinguished from the subjunctive is open to debate, but I have glossed it as 'subjunctive' for the sake of consistency.

(291) *u-ka-som-**e***
2SG-ITIVE-study-SUB
'you should go and study'

(292) *Na=a-phiy-e* *a-ka-lól-w-**e**.*
EMPH=3SG-go-SUB 3SG-ITIVE-marry-PAS-SUB
'Let her go and be married.' Or: 'Let her go so that she might be married.'

There are a number of verbs[14] (most of Arabic origin, probably borrowed from Swahili), where the final vowel in indicative clauses is not *a* and does not change to *e* in the subjunctive form:

(293)

M-si-zarau	*hinya*	*a-dide.*
2PL-NEG-despise	2.DEM1	2-small

'Do not despise these small ones.'

---

[14] Including *abudu* 'worship', *ahidi* 'promise', *amini* 'belive', *baki* 'remain', *balehe* 'mature', *buni* 'establish', *busu* 'kiss', *dai* 'claim', *dumu* 'endure', *dzidai* 'boast', *dzihendere* 'do for oneself', *dzuphi* 'feel paranoid', *fikiri* 'think', *furahi* 'be happy', *fwaidi* 'benefit', *garimu* 'cost', *hitaji* 'require', *hubiri* 'preach', *hukumu* 'judge', *husu* 'concern', *isabu* 'count', *ishi* 'live', *ishimu* 'honour', *jaribu* 'try', *jibu* 'reply', *kabidhi* 'transfer', *kubali* 'agree', *kufuru* 'blaspheme', *lani* 'curse', *laumu* 'blame', *risi* 'inherit', *ruhusu* 'permit', *safari* 'travel', *samehe* 'forgive', *shauri* 'advise', *shiriki* 'share', *shitaki* 'accuse', *shukuru* 'thank', *sitiri* 'cover', *stahili* 'desire', *tabiri* 'prophesy', *tafasiri* 'translate', *taili* 'assess', *tamani* 'desire', *tii* 'obey', *tubu* 'repent', *tumaini* 'hope', *zamiri* 'intend', *zarau* 'scorn', *zidi* 'increase', *zini* 'commit adultery', and *zulumu* 'oppress'.

4.1.9.3 perfective suffix -ire/-ere

The -*ire*/-*ere* suffix is a reflex of the Proto-Bantu suffix *-i̧le which marks verbs as perfective (that is completed) in many Eastern Bantu languages. For this reason, I will gloss it as PFV ('perfective') throughout, even though in Digo it has two uses. In affirmative clauses the suffix -*ere* functions as a resultative TAM marker. It occurs with a limited number of verbs of state, including *sagala* 'sit', *lala* 'sleep', *ima* 'stand', and *nyamala* 'keep silent'—often with changes to the verb stem—to indicate a resultant state. The initial vowel of the suffix is determined by vowel harmony rules (if the last vowel of the verb stem is *a*, *i*, or *u*, -*ire* is used; if it is *e* or *o*, -*ere* is used):

(294) a-seg-**ere**   <   *sagala* 'sit'
       3SG-sit-PFV
       's/he is seated'

(295) a-im-**ire**   <   *ima* 'stand'
       3SG-stand-PFV
       's/he is standing'

In negative past clauses, where the specific time range (today or before today) is not in focus, the -*ire*/-*ere* suffix is used. The initial vowel of the suffix is determined by the same vowel harmony rules:

(296) k-edz-**ere**
       3SG.NEG-come-PFV
       's/he did not come', 's/he has not come'

(297) si-many-**ire**
       1SG.NEG-know-PFV
       'I did not know'

The -*ire*/-*ere* perfective suffix can follow extensions (such as the causative) and can be followed by clitics (e.g. *to* 'well'), but it never co-occurs with a TAM prefix:

(298) ka-mw-og-es-**ere**=to
       3SG.NEG-3SG-wash-CAUS-PFV=WELL
       's/he did not wash her/him well'

4.1.10 Postfinal slot

The postfinal slot contains the plural addressee suffix -*ni* and relative concord markers.

4.1.10.1 Plural addressee

Digo is one of a number of Bantu languages[15] with a suffix -*ni* in the postfinal slot which indicates plurality of the addressee (see Schadeberg 1977). The plural addressee suffix -*ni* occurs in imperatives (to indicate that the agent of the verb is 2nd person plural), subjunctive clauses (to distinguish plural from dual in the 1st person), and as part of the 2nd person plural verb complement. These uses are illustrated in turn below:

(299) *Dzi-many-irir-e-**ni***   equivalent to: *M-dzi-many-irir-e*
REFL-know-APPL-SUB-PL   2PL-REFL-know-APPL-SUB
'Take care!' 'Watch out for yourselves!'

(300) *hu-phiy-e-**ni***   vs.   *hu-phiy-e*
1PL-go-SUB-PL   1PL-go-SUB
'let us all go'   'let us both go'

(301) *Na-ku-lag-a-**ni***.
1SG.CONT-2PL-leave-FV-PL
'I am leaving you all/both.'

Whether it occurs in an imperative clause, a subjunctive clause, or as part of a 2nd person plural verb complement, the plural suffix -*ni* always precedes relative concords, wh-question markers, and *to* 'well', indicating that it is a suffix and not a clitic:

(302) *sikiz-a-**ni**=to*
listen-FV-PL=WELL
'listen carefully'

(303) *m-lol-e-**ni**=to*
2PL-look-SUB-PL=WELL
'you all should look carefully'

(304) *m-na-mendz-a*   *a-ku-mendz-a-**ni**-o*
2PL-CONT-love-FV   3PL-2PL-love-FV-PL-3PL.REL
'you love those who love you'

(305) *n'-nda-fikir-iy-a*   *ni-ku-hend-e-**ni**=dze.*
1SG-FUT-think-APPL-FV   1SG-2PL-do-SUB-PL=Q
'I will think about what I should do with you.'

---

[15] And other Benue-Congo languages, such as Igboid languages and Bantoid languages (e.g. Tikar, Güldemann 2003:186).

4.1.10.2 Relative concords (and referential markers)

The relative concord markers that occur between the TAM marker and the verb complement slot can also occur in postfinal position in tenseless relative clauses, but a single verb group cannot contain a relative concord in both slots simultaneously. The following examples illustrate relative concord markers (glossed as REL) corresponding to subject, object, manner, and location, respectively. (Note that when the subject is 1SG or 2SG, the coreferential relative concord marker is that of class 1, and when it is 1PL or 2PL, the concord marker is that of class 2.)

(306) Mimi   ni-gomb-a-**ye**   ndi=ye.
      1SG   1SG-speak-FV-1.REL   COP=1.REF
      'I who am speaking am he.'

(307) maneno   a-gomb-a-**go**
      6.words   3SG-speak-FV-6.REL
      'words which s/he speaks'

(308) a-gomb-a-**vyo**
      3SG-speak-FV-8.REL
      'how s/he speaks'

(309) ko   a-heg-a-**ko**   mi-hambo
      17.DEM3_VAR   3SG-set-FV-17.REL   4-traps
      'there where he sets his traps'

Note that in (306), the form *ye* also occurs as part of the copula construction *ndiye* 'I am he'. This has been glossed as REF, which stands for referential marker, and the connecting symbol '=' indicates that the referential marker is a clitic. It has been analysed as a clitic because clitics typically combine with a variety of word classes or participate in a variety of constructions, whereas affixes combine with a particular word class or participate in a very restricted range of constructions. The following examples illustrate how referential markers can occur in different copula constructions.[16]

In example (310), *cho* is attached to the comitative marker *na* in a possessive construction; *cho* functions as an anaphoric pronoun referring back to *cha kukuphani* 'anything to give you'.

---

[16]Referential markers are discussed here, rather than in the following section on clitics, as they resemble relative concord markers and can be easily confused with them.

4.1 Structure of the verb group

(310) Mino   si-na   cha[17]   ku-ku-ph-a-ni,
      1SG   1SG.NEG-COM   7.ASS   INF-2PL-**give**-FV-PL

      ela   kala   n'-na=**cho**   nku-ku-ph-a-ni.
      but   if   1SG-COM=7.REF   1SG.HAB-2PL-give-FV-PL

      'As for me I don't have anything to give you, but if I did have anything I would give it to you.'

In (311), *mo* and *pho* refer to places (*nyumbani* 'inside the house' and *mryangoni* 'at the door/in the doorway' respectively); while *mo* is attached to a verb, *pho* is attached directly to the class 7 subject concord (agreeing with *chitswa* 'head'). In (312), *ko* likewise refers to a place (*kaya* 'home') and serves to specify the location in much the same way as a demonstrative pronoun. Although *mo* in (311) and *ko* in (312) are attached to verb groups just as relative concord markers are, these verb groups are finite and do not form part of relative clauses, whereas relative concord markers occur in tenseless relative clauses.

(311) Mwanyika   wa-odzal-a=**mo**   nyumba-ni,
      NAME   3SG.PST-fill-FV=18.REF   house-LOC

      hata   chitswa   chi=**pho**   mryango-ni.
      even   7.head   7=16.REF   3.door-LOC

      'Mwanyika filled the house, even its head was in the doorway.'

(312) Hu-chi-fik-a=**ko**   kaya
      1PL-DEP-arrive-FV=17.REF   9.home

      'When we reach home'

It is tempting to combine relative concord markers and referential markers into a single category, as Amidu (2001) does,[18] but two facts suggest that relative and referential markers should be kept distinct. The first is that there are distinctive 1st and 2nd person forms of the referential markers which are used with the copula particles *ndi* and *si*, and with the comitative marker *na* (to form referential additives, see §6.3.2), but not with tenseless relative clauses and *amba* relative clauses. These forms may be derived from, or otherwise related to, the free personal pronouns, although the forms of the 3rd person singular and plural are also identical to the class 1 and 2 relative concord markers. However, the situation is complicated by the fact that the class 2 relative concord marker is

---

[17] The class 7 associative marker agrees with an understood (elided) *chitu* 'thing'.

[18] Amidu (2001) combines relative concord markers and referential markers into a single class which he refers to variously as 'O' topicalized concords, topicalized agreement markers, and topicalized affixes, although he glosses these forms as OM, ORM, and SRM depending on the morphosyntactic context in which they occur. According to Amidu's analysis, copulas, as well as *amba* and the comitative marker *na*, are verbs, and so within his framework these forms are affixes rather than clitics.

used obligatorily with the *ndi* copula particle and optionally with the *si* negative copula particle instead of the regular form of the 1st person plural referential marker. This suggests that the distinction between relative concord markers and referential markers is not absolute. The various forms under discussion are listed in table 4.10:

Table 4.10. Personal pronouns, referential markers, and relative markers

Person/ number	Personal pronoun	Referential additive	Affirmative copula	Negative copula	*amba* relative
1SG	mimi	nami	ndimi	simi	ambaye
1PL	sisi	nasi	ndio	sio	ambao
	or swiswi	*or* naswi		*or* siswi	
2SG	uwe	nawe	ndiwe	siwe	ambaye
2PL	mwimwi	namwi	ndimwi	simwi	ambao
3SG	iye	naye	ndiye	siye	ambaye
3PL	aho	nao	ndio	sio	ambao

The second argument for keeping relative concord markers and referential markers distinct is that the relative copula *ri* can occur with a relative concord marker followed immediately by a referential marker, as in example (313):

(313) a-na-fik-a   hipho   kulungu   ta-pha=na,
3SG-CONT-arrive-FV   16.DEM3   1a.antelope   NEG-16=COM

a-ri-ye=pho   ni   yuyatu   maiti
3SG-COP-1.REL=16.REF   COP   1.DEM2_VARIANT   1a.corpse

'on arriving at that place there was no antelope, **what was there** was the very same corpse (that he had seen earlier)'

In (313), *ye* is a subject relative concord marker whilst *pho* is a locative referential marker. If *ye* and *pho* were both instances of the same morphological class, as proposed by Amidu (2001), then this situation would be unique[19] as Digo does not otherwise allow more than one SC, VC, or relative concord marker to occur in a single predicate. However, if two distinct categories are recognized, there is nothing unusual about the behaviour of either; *ye* occurs, as expected, immediately after the tenseless relative copula *ri*, and *pho*, being a clitic, can occur in a variety of positions. An alternative analysis would be to interpret *pho* as a reduced form of the class 16 demonstrative[20] *hipho* which occurs earlier in the exam-

---

[19] Amidu (2001:116) notes that the cognate relative copula *li* "is the only predicate in Kiswahili capable of taking two 'O' topicalized concords one immediately after the other" in his framework.
[20] The similarity in form between referential markers, relative markers, and demonstrative pro-

ple. However, phonologically *ariyepho* is a single word (stress/pitch accent, which falls on the penultimate syllable in Digo falls on *ye* in *ariyepho*), which makes it more likely that *pho* should be analysed as a clitic.

One consequence of this analysis is that in order to be consistent, all **non-subject** expressions occurring after *ri* must also be analysed as referential markers. In examples (314) and (315), *pho* and *ko* are not coreferential with the subjects of the clauses (2SG and 3SG, respectively) and are therefore referential markers, whereas in example (316) *o* is coreferential with the subject (2PL) and is therefore a relative concord marker:

(314) *Phapho   u-ri=**pho**   mwandzo*
       16.DEM3_VARIANT 2SG-PST.COP=16.REF first
       'There where you were at first'

(315) *Si-m-many-a   a-ri=**ko**.*
       1SG.NEG-3SG-know-FV   3SG-COP=17.REF
       'I do not know where he is.'

(316) *Mwimwi   m-osi   m-ri-o   hipha*
       2PL   2PL-all 2PL-REL.COP-2.REL   16.DEM1
       'You all who are here'

4.1.11 Clitics

The following clitics can be attached to the end of the verb group: the wh-question markers *dze* 'how', *ni* 'what', and *phi* 'where', and the manner adverbial *to* 'well'. In addition, these elements can be found attached to other parts of speech, such as subject concords, copulas, and relative markers. Although there are no clear boundaries between the categories 'clitic' and 'affix', or between 'clitic' and 'word', it is true to say that low selectivity of adjacent items is a characteristic of clitics but not of affixes, and so these expressions are characterized as clitics rather than as affixes.

4.1.11.1 Wh-*question markers*

The *wh*-question markers *dze* 'what, how', *ni* 'what', and *phi* 'where' occur after the postfinal slot; they are illustrated in turn:

---

nouns is almost certainly not coincidental and there is probably a historical connection between these forms. It is possible that at one time the situation in Digo and Swahili resembled the current situation in Lucazi. In Lucazi, there are no relative pronouns, but Fleisch (2000:202) suggests that demonstratives, which are often used with noun phrases specified by a relative clause, may be developing into relative pronouns.

(317) U-na-on-a=**dze**?
 2SG-CONT-see-FV=Q
 'What do you think?' (lit: 'How do you see?')

(318) Ni-m-riph-e=**ni**?
 1SG-3SG-pay-SUB=Q
 'What shall I give him?'

(319) U-na-phiy-a=**phi**?
 2SG-CONT-go-FV=Q
 'Where are you going?'

These question markers are best characterized as clitics rather than affixes. *Dze* and *ni* also occur as independent words (free morphemes capable of taking stress), and *ni* and *phi* can be attached to parts of speech other than verbs (see §3.3.5). When *dze* occurs as a word, its usual position is before the clause which is being questioned (320). It can also be affixed to a verb in the same clause for emphasis (321); note also the emphatic personal pronoun *mwino*. In neither case is word order affected; the same declarative word order can be retained with interrogative intonation in order to express a question:

(320) **Dze,** mambo gano m-na-ga-elew-a?
 Q 6.matters 6.DEM4 2PL-CONT-6-understand-FV
 'Do you understand these things?'

(321) **Dze** mwino m-na-amba=**dze**?
 Q 2PL.EMPH 2PL-CONT-say=Q
 'Well what do YOU think?'

4.1.11.2 to 'well'

The clitic *to* can be suffixed to most verbs, including those in which the extension, final, or postfinal slot has been filled. It has the meaning of 'to do something well or completely':

(322) m-lol-e-ni=**to**
 2PL-look-SUB-PL=WELL
 'look carefully'

(323) w-a-hend-a=**to**
 2SG-PST-do-FV=WELL
 'you did well'

4.2 Irregular and defective verbs

Occasional irregularities in other verb forms are dealt with elsewhere (for example, irregular forms of *mendza* 'like' in §4.1.9.1, and stem changes in the resultative forms of *lala* 'sleep', *sagala* 'sit, stay', and *nyamala* 'keep silent' in §4.1.9.3 and §5.3.1.10). This section describes four verbs in particular: *edza* 'come to', *la* 'come from', *pha* 'give', and *phiya* 'go to', as these are systemically irregular or defective.

4.2.1   *edza* 'come to'

The verb *edza* is irregular in a number of ways. First, in two tenses, past and future (affirmative and negative), the *ku-* infinitive prefix forms part of the verb stem (*ku* + *edza* = *kpwedza*). Second, in the continuous aspect/present tense *na-* + V > *r*V (where V is an elided vowel, probably /a/). Third, *edza* is unusual in that the verb root begins with a vowel; this means that the vowel of the hodiernal past tense marker *ka-* is elided (*ka* + *edza* = *kedza*) following the regular vowel assimilation rule *a* + *e* > *e*. Fourth, in the (affirmative) imperative, the form is completely irregular: *ndzoo*.

Table 4.11. Forms of *edza*

Tense/Aspect	Affirmative	
	Singular	Plural
present/continuous	n-redz-a	hu-redz-a
	u-redz-a	m-redz-a
	a-redz-a	a-redz-a
hodiernal past	n-k-edz-a	hu-k-edz-a
	u-k-edz-a	m-k-edz-a
	a-k-edz-a	a-k-edz-a
past	ná-kpwedz-a	hwa-kpwedz-a
	wa-kpwedz-a	mwa-kpwedz-a
	wa-kpwedz-a	a-kpwedz-a
consecutive	n-ch-edz-a	hu-ch-edz-a
	u-ch-edz-a	m-ch-edz-a
	a-ch-edz-a	a-ch-edz-a
future	n'-nda-kpwedz-a	hu-nda-kpwedz-a
	u-nda-kpwedz-a	m-nda-kpwedz-a
	a-nda-kpwedez-a	a-nda-kpwedz-a
imperative	ndzoo	ndzoo-ni
subjunctive	w-edz-e	mw-edz-e

Table 4.11, continued

	Negative	
Tense/Aspect	Singular	Plural
present/continuous	s-edz-a	ta-hu-edz-a
	kpw-edz-a	ta-mw-edz-a
	k-edz-a	ta-a-edz-a
hodiernal past	si-k-edz-a	ta-hu-k-edz-a
	ku-k-edz-a	ta-m-k-edz-a
	ka-k-edz-a	ta-a-k-edz-a
past	si-ya-kpwedz-a	ta-hu-ya-kpwedz-a
	ku-ya-kpedz-a	ta-m-ya-kpwedz-a
	ka-ya-kpwedz-a	ta-a-ya-kpwedz-a
general past negative	s-edz-ere	ta-hu-edz-ere (*pronounced* tawedzere)
	kpw-edz-ere	ta-mw-edz-ere
	k-edz-ere	ta-a(y)-edz-ere
future	si-nda-kpwedz-a	ta-hu-nda-kpwedz-a
	ku-nda-kpwedz-a	ta-m-nda-kpwedz-a
	ka-nda-kpwedz-a	ta-a-nda-kpwedz-a
imperative	u-s-edz-e	m-s-edz-e
subjunctive	u-s-edz-e	m-s-edz-e

4.2.2 *la* 'come from'

The verb *la* (*ra* in the southern dialect of Digo) is a 'defective' verb in the present tense only, in which it does not occur with the present tense marker *na-*:

(324) a. *U-l-a-phi?*
  2SG-come_from-FV-Q
  'Where are you from?'/'Where have you come from?'

  b. *Ni-l-a   Ukunda.*
  1SG-come_from-FV   PLACE_NAME
  'I am from Ukunda.'/'I have come from Ukunda.'

In other tenses and aspects, *la* behaves like a regular verb:

(325) *Tsawe   wa-l-a   Tiwi.*
  1a.grandfather 3SG.PST-come_from-FV PLACE
  'Grandfather came from Tiwi.'

(326) *A-ka-ni-l-a*
  3SG-HOD-1SG-come_from-FV
  'He has left me' (i.e. 'I do not want to associate with him any more')

(327) U-nda-**l**-a Nairobi.
2SG-FUT-come_from-FV PLACE
'You will come from Nairobi.' (future)

4.2.3 pha 'give'

The verb *pha* takes an irregular passive form: *hewa*. Rather than being a phonological variant of *pha*, the root *he* (which is followed by the passive suffix *-w*) may come from a different source. Whereas *pha* is cognate with *pa* 'give' in Swahili, Shona, and other languages, *he* is probably cognate with *he* 'give' in Gĩkũyũ.

(328) N-ka-mu-**ph**-a   pesa.
1SG-HOD-3SG-give-FV 10.money
'I gave him/her money.'

(329) Wa-**hew**-a   pesa.
3SG.PST-give.PAS-FV 10.money
'S/He was given money.'

4.2.4 phiya 'go to'

The verb *phiya* 'go to' is cognate with Swahili *pita* 'pass'. Its current meaning is probably a relatively recent innovation, given that 'go to' in Swahili and other Mijikenda and Sabaki languages is *enda*, and the form *enda* is retained in Digo as an itive marker (with characteristics of both a TAM marker and an auxiliary verb; see §5.5.2.1); *enda* is also the probable source of the future tense marker *nda-*. In Digo words with Swahili cognates, there are regular sound correspondences Swahili [p] > Digo [β] and Swahili [t] > Digo [h], and intervocalic /h/ is realized as nasalization of both vowels. Given that a palatal glide [j] occurs intervocalically between [i] and [a], one would expect [pita] > [βĩjã]. In actual fact, however, nasalization is entirely or largely absent and the verb is pronounced [βija] and written *phiya*. In the negative perfective form of the verb, however, the [h] is retained in pronunciation, and the verb form is written *kaphihire*. The following example illustrates this:

(330) Hira Jumane ambayo kala akaambwa **aphiye, kaphihire, achiphiya** Alamisi.
'That Wednesday on which he had been told **he should go, he did not go, he went on Thursday.**'

a-phiy-e, ka-phih-ire, a-chi-phiy-a Alamisi.
3SG-go-SUB 3SG.NEG-go-PFV 3SG-CONS-go-FV Thursday

4.3 Verbal derivation

4.3.1 Verb-forming derivational processes

Verbal derivation is discussed in relation to the causative extension (see §4.1.8.2), but is repeated here for the sake of continuity.

4.3.1.1 From adjective to verb

The causative extension can turn an adjective into a verb:

halali	'ritually clean'	>	halalisha	'ritually cleanse'
kamili	'completely'	>	kamilisha	'complete'
karibu	'near'	>	karibisha	'welcome', 'bring near'
lazima	'necessary'	>	lazimisha	'force', 'compel'
safi	'clean'	>	safisha	'cleanse'
starehe	'comfortable'	>	starehesha	'give pleasure'
tajiri	'wealthy'	>	tajirisha	'make s.o. wealthy'
tayari	'ready'	>	tayarisha	'prepare tr'

4.3.1.2 From noun to verb

The causative extension can turn a noun into a verb. However this appears not to be a productive process in Digo, as it applies only to a few nouns of Swahili origin suggesting that the corresponding verbs may also have been borrowed from Swahili:

hakika	'certainty'	>	hakikisha	'confirm', 'make certain'
kodi	'tax'	>	kodisha	'rent'
shughuli	'business'	>	shugulisha	'occupy'

4.3.2 Complex predicates and light verbs

Complex predicates[21] are defined by Schultze-Berndt (2006:361–362) as "monoclausal constructions involving two predicative elements which jointly contribute to the valency of the complex predicate." When this definition is applied to Digo, complex predicates are clauses containing a verb and its complement which receive an intransitive interpretation. It is the complement and not the verb which carries the main semantic weight, hence the complement (be it a nominal, adverb, etc.) functions not as an object but as a predicator. The verbs in such constructions are termed "light verbs". Light verbs—also called "function verbs" (Schultze-Berndt 2006) and "secondary verbs" (Dixon 1991:88)—are defined as "independent verbs which can be used both as regular simple predicates and as parts of complex predicates"

---
[21] Not to be confused with complex sentences discussed in §7.4.

4.3 Verbal derivation

(Schultze-Berndt 2006:360). When a light verb combines with a complement to form a complex predicate, it takes the same range of verbal inflections as it does when functioning as a simple predicate.

Complex predicates behave syntactically like intransitive verbs and inherit all the morphological properties of the light verb component, but most of the semantic content of complex predicates is derived from the complement (usually a nominal). Complex predicates can therefore be viewed as a mechanism by which new semantic verbs are formed from pre-existing verbal and nonverbal elements.

The most common and most productive light verb in Digo is *piga* 'hit'. Table 4.12 illustrates some of the complex predicates which contain *piga* functioning as a light verb.

Table 4.12. Complex predicates involving *piga*

Complex predicate	Meaning (intr)	Meaning of complement (noun class)
piga bako	curse	*bako*: curse (5)
piga chimiya	to fish with a net	*chimiya*: fishing net (7)
piga hanga	start a funeral	*hanga*: mourning, funeral (5)
piga kululu	shout	*kululu*: noise (5)
piga kura	cast lots; vote	*kura*: lot; vote (9)
piga magoti	kneel	*magoti*: knees (6)
piga mbiru	blow a horn	*mbiru*: horn (9)
piga milozi	whistle	*milozi*: whistle (9)—sound rather than instrument
piga msuwaki	brush one's teeth	*msuwaki*: toothbrush (3)
piga myasa	sneeze	*myasa*: sneeze (9)
piga myayu	yawn	*myayu*: yawn (9)
piga myono	snore	*myono*: snore (9)
piga ngari	swim on one's back	*ngari*: face-up (adv)
piga ngoto	rap on something	*ngoto*: knuckle (9)
piga njere-njere	ululate	*njere-njere*: ululation (9)
piga pasi	iron clothes	*pasi*: iron (9)
piga pindu	turn a somersault	*pindu*: somersault (5)
piga simu	make a phone call	*simu*: telephone (9)
piga tsogo	make a noise	*tsogo*: noise (9)

The complex predicate *piga kululu* 'shout' is virtually synonymous with *tiya likululu* (from *tiya* 'put in' plus *likululu* 'noise' class 11) and *kota likululu* (from *kota* 'hammer' plus *likululu* 'noise' class 11) indicating that the complement (usually a noun) contributes most of the semantic content to the complex predicate. However, the light verb is more than simply a grammatical place-holder; the last example in table 4.12 (*piga tsogo* 'make a noise' contrasts with *richa tsogo* 'stop making a noise', indicating that *piga* contributes some semantic content to the resulting complex predicate.

Schultze-Berndt (2006:362) states that light verbs must be both productive, in that they must be able to form complex predicates with members of an open lexical category (verb, nominal, ideophone, etc.), and also subject to collocational restrictions. This means that light verbs (or more specifically verbs functioning as light verbs) are distinct from verbs used in idiomatic constructions (where the meaning of the idiom is not derived directly from the meaning of the main predicate) and from lexical verbs (which are not subject to collocational restrictions). Thus, neither *piga tsi* 'urinate', from *tsi* 'land, earth' nor *piga ngoma* 'beat a drum' are complex predicates: *piga tsi* is an idiomatic construction (the meaning 'urinate' cannot be derived directly from 'earth') and *piga ngoma* is a transitive verb plus complement (*ngoma* could be replaced by any number of nouns that designate objects capable of being beaten).

The distinction between a verb used as a light verb and the same verb used either in an idiomatic construction or as a lexical verb can be harder to make with other (potential) light verbs. Consider the following constructions containing *kata* 'cut', *ika* 'keep, put', and *tsupha* 'throw':

Table 4.13. Complex predicates involving *kata*, *ika*, and *tsupha*

Predicate	Meaning	Meaning of complement (noun class)
kata mairo	run quickly	*mairo*: high speed (6)
kata ng'andzi	chat, discuss	*ng'andzi*: conversation, discussion (9)
kata roho	die (used euphemistically)	*roho*: spirit (9)
kata tamaa	despair	*tamaa*: desire, hope (9)
ika ahadi	make a promise, keep a promise	*ahadi*: promise (9)
ika nafwasi	leave a space	*nafwasi*: space (9)
ika siku	fix a day (set a date)	*siku*: day (9)
ika uphya	renew	*uphya*: newness (14)
ika usalama	make secure (e.g. from attack)	*usalama*: security (14)
tsupha kumbi	raise eyebrows (to signal agreement)	*kumbi*: eyebrows (10)
tsupha lago	kick	*lago*: upper leg[22] (5)
tsupha nyuswi	wink	*nyuswi*: eyelids (10)

Whilst *kata mairo* and *kata ng'andzi* are almost certainly complex predicates, *kata roho* and *kata tamaa* are arguably idioms which make use of a metaphorical extension of 'cut' to yield a meaning close to 'be separated from something'. This

---

[22] *Lago* is the singular form of *mago* 'lap' from which we get the adjective *magogbwe*: the opposite of bow-legged; the state of having thighs which rub or slap against each other whilst one is walking.

4.3 Verbal derivation

analysis is supported by the fact that Digo already has the lexical verbs *fwa* 'die' and *luhukpwa* 'despair' and that these are concepts which are often expressed euphemistically cross-linguistically (compare English *pass away* and *lose hope*). It could also be argued that the various constructions containing *ika* 'keep, put' involve metaphorical extension from the physical domain to the abstract domain (even a space is an abstract concept), and that the constructions involving *tsupha* involve a generalization from throwing, which involves rapid movement of the hand and arm, to rapid movement of any part of the body.

Note also that English glosses may give the impression that certain constructions are complex predicates when in fact they are not. Once we recognize that the verb *ona* 'see' is also used to describe how people experience nonvisual stimuli (including emotions), expressions such as *ona ajabu* 'be amazed' (from *ajabu* 'wonder'), *ona haya* 'be shy' (from *haya* 'shame, shyness') and *ona ndzala* 'feel hungry' (from *ndzala* 'hunger') can be analysed as regular lexical verb plus complement constructions.

Finally, Schultze-Berndt (2006:363) notes that when a light verb with a general action meaning 'do' is used, "it is more difficult to speak of collocational restrictions" between the light verb and the complement, since the light verb is not in semantic opposition to other light verbs (in other words, a light verb with a very general meaning is more nearly semantically empty). However, even *henda* 'do' can contrast with other light verbs, as in *henda wasi-wasi* 'be afraid, worry' (from the noun *wasi-wasi* 'worry') as opposed to *usa wasi-wasi* 'reassure' (from *usa* 'remove' plus *wasi-wasi* 'worry'). Conversely, *henda mimba* 'become pregnant' is virtually synonymous with *gbwira mimba* (from *gbwira* 'take, hold' and *mimba* 'pregnancy'). Other complex predicates involving *henda*[23] are listed below (the list is far from complete):

Table 4.14. Complex predicates involving *henda*

Predicate	Meaning	Meaning of complement
henda aphasa	buy on credit	*aphasa*: lend *tr*
henda chinyume	undermine (someone)	*chinyume*: opposite, against (adv)
henda kani	be stubborn	*kani*: stubbornness (9)
henda ngata	administer first aid	*ngata*: first aid treatment (9)
henda ngulu	boast, brag, be proud	*ngulu*: pride (9)
henda choyo	be jealous	*choyo*: selfishness (9)

---

[23] Complex predicates involving *henda* and a bare verbal complement are syntactically and semantically distinct from the use of the *henda* 'emphatic' aspect marker (see §5.3.2.4).

5

Tense, Aspect, and Movement Markers

In §4.1.3 TAM morphemes occurring in the TAM/Negation slot (slot 3) in the verb group were listed according to the structural criteria of whether they occur in both affirmative and negative clauses, affirmative clauses only, negative clauses only, relative clauses only, or as auxiliaries (in slot 3b). In the current chapter, these morphemes, together with the *-ire/-ere* perfective suffix discussed in §4.1.9.3, are categorized according to semantic criteria.

The terms 'tense', 'aspect', 'mood' (or 'modality'), and 'evidentiality' have traditionally been used to label grammaticalized forms which provide information about events and situations and speaker's perspectives on these. *Tenses* provide information concerning the relation between the time at which an event occurs or during which a situation holds and some other time, either the moment of speech or some predefined temporal reference point. *Aspects* describe the internal structure of events: whether or not they are completed, ongoing at the temporal reference point, of long duration, or repeated punctual events, for example. *Moods* describe the speaker's perspective on an event: whether she can verify that an event has actually occurred, the degree of certainty she has that an event might have occurred, or whether she is describing an event as hypothetical or as on a condition, etc. *Evidentials* describe the kind of evidence that a speaker has for an assertion.

The terms 'mood' and 'modality' are problematic and will not be used here. Rose et al. (2002:52) note that for some Bantuists, these terms are synonymous, whereas for others 'mood' is used for the binary contrast marked by *-a* or *-e* in the final slot and 'modality' is used to refer to categories such as ability, desire, intention, obligation, permission, probability, possibility, conditional, itive, and ventive, none of which (apart from conditional, itive, and ventive) are usually expressed inflectionally in Bantu languages. Digo is no exception to this generalization: dynamic, deontic, and epistemic modality (that is, ability, desire, intention, obligation, permission, probability, and possibility) are expressed through verbs such as *weza* 'be able', *londa* 'want', *londwa* 'be required', and adverbials such as *lazima* 'necessarily', *hakika* 'certainly', *chahi, labuda, mendzerepho,* and *pengine* 'maybe, perhaps, (etc.)'. The remaining 'modal' categories that are expressed by means of grammaticalized morphemes in the verb group are restricted to a potential marker, a dependent marker and some conditionals which I have grouped together under the general label of 'status markers'.[1]

Digo also has number of morphemes which describe events not in relation to a reference time, such as the moment of speaking, but in relation to a reference location, such as the location of the speaker, or the location in a story of the central character. These have been grouped together under the general label of 'movement grams'. These forms share many of the structural characteristics of tense and aspect markers and play similar roles in the construction of coherent discourse (such as indicating continuity or discontinuity with previous clauses and establishing reference points), and so I have chosen to describe them here. The abbreviation 'TAM' therefore stands for 'tense-aspect-movement' rather than 'tense-aspect-mood' when used in relation to Digo.

5.1 TAM categories

Each language contains a unique system of TAM markers and the meaning of any single TAM marker depends on the total system, as it contrasts in specific ways with other members of the system. Because no two systems are identical, it follows that it is highly unlikely that individual TAM markers in different languages will express exactly the same meanings. Nevertheless, certain distinctions (such as between past, present and future time reference, and between completed and noncompleted events) are represented in many languages, and it is convenient to reuse labels for TAM markers which express similar meanings in other languages. As far as possible, I have used only terms which are included in Rose et al. (2002) and have endeavoured to use these terms in accordance with the definitions that Rose et al. provide.[2] However, when a familiar label is used to describe a TAM marker in Digo, it should be understood that the label is simply a convenient shorthand, and that the meaning and distribution of the TAM marker depends on its role in the system as a whole.

The TAM markers of Digo are listed below in the order in which they will be discussed. A hyphen following a form indicates that it is a prefix, a hyphen preceding a form indicates that it is a suffix, whilst the absence of a hyphen

---

[1] This label reflects the fact that these markers, along with epistemic modals and sentence negation, are what in Role and Reference Grammar are termed 'status operators' (Van Valin 2005:9–11), which relate the proposition expressed to realis-irrealis continua.
[2] The exceptions are the term 'resultative', which is used following Nedjalkov (1988) but is not found in Rose et al. (2002), and 'emphatic'.

indicates that the morpheme is (in at least some constructions) an auxiliary or a sentence adverbial. (A list of the TAM markers classified according to whether they can occur with or without negation is provided in §4.1.3.1.1.) Complex constructions, in which a finite[3] verb form is combined with a finite form of the verb *kala* 'be' or the hodiernal past marker *che*, are discussed separately, in §5.6. Finally, four of the TAM markers share the same form: *ka-*, so in §5.7 the different uses of the *ka-* forms and the possible historical relations between them are discussed in detail.

5.1.1 Tenses

Absolute tenses:
a-	remote past	*ya-*	negative past
ka-	hodiernal past	*na-*	present
nda-	future		

Dependent tenses:
chi-	consecutive	*ka-*	sequential

Tenses in relative clauses:
ri-	past	*ndi-*	future

5.1.2 Aspects

Fully grammaticalized aspects:
na-	continuous	*ku-/nku-*	habitual
Ø	generic	Ø	general negative
chi-	relative anterior	*chi-*	imperfective
ka-	anterior	*chopho-*	simultaneous
-ire/-ere	negative perfective	*-ere/-ire*	resultative

Less grammaticalized aspects:
kare	completive	*dzangbwe*	(negative) inceptive
chere	persistive	*henda*	emphatic

5.1.3 Status markers

Simple status markers:
ka-	potential	*chi-*	dependent
nge-	conditional		

Complex conditional constructions involving *kala*

---

[3] The term 'finite' is used here to refer to any verb form that contains a TAM marker, regardless of whether this is a tense, an aspect, a status marker, or a movement gram.

5.1.4 Movement grams

Fully grammaticalized movement grams:
  cha-   distal   *ya-*   future + itive
  ka- + -e itive + subjunctive
Less grammaticalized movement grams:
  kpwenda itive   *kpwedza* ventive

5.1.5 Complex constructions

Complex constructions with *kala*
Complex constructions with *che*

5.1.6 Format of examples

In the detailed description of each TAM marker in sections 5.2 through 5.7, its form and position in the verbal complex will be described first, followed by an example with a morpheme-by-morpheme gloss, and a description of the meaning and functions of the TAM marker together with illustrative examples. The following abbreviations are used:

  SC   Subject Concord
  NEG Negative marker
  VC   Verb Complement (Object) marker
  VS   Verb Stem
  REL Relative concord
  #   word boundary (end of word)

In each example, the TAM marker is the highlighted element within the verb group.

5.2 Tenses

Tenses describe events and situations in relation to a reference time; they can be absolute (time reference is defined in relation to the moment of speaking) or dependent (time reference is defined in relation to some temporal reference point which is established through the use of another TAM marker). In addition there are two tense forms in Digo which are restricted to use in relative clauses.

5.2.1 Absolute tenses

Absolute tenses indicate the time at which an event occurs in relation to the moment of speaking. Most of these TAM markers can also be used to indicate the time at which an event occurs in relation to a temporal reference point other than the moment of speaking. For example, an utterance of '*Andakpwedza*' 'She will come' means that the subject will come at some time after the moment of speaking, but an utterance of *'Akaniambira kala andakpwedza'* 'She told me that she would come' means that the subject will come at some time after the time when she told the speaker that she would come. However, this is seen as a secondary use as it occurs in a complex sentence involving two clauses, and so the label 'absolute tenses' will be retained.

5.2.1.1 Remote past ("past")

SC ***a*** (VC) VS *a* + floating high tone on following verb stem[4]

(331) 1st person: **ná**-gul-a — hw-**a**-gul-a
 1SG.PST-buy-FV — 1PL.PST-buy-FV
 'I bought' — 'we bought'
 2nd person: **wa**-gul-a — mw-**a**-gul-a
 2SG.PST-buy-FV — 2PL.PST-buy-FV
 'you(sg) bought' — 'you(pl) bought'
 3rd person: **wa**-gul-a — **a**-gul-a
 3SG.PST-buy-FV — 3PL.PST-buy-FV
 's/he bought' — 'they bought'

This tense is used to refer to events that occurred prior to the day of the utterance. It can also be used when the reference time is located in the future:

(332) n'-nda-kala ná-yal-w-a
 1SG-FUT-be 1SG.PST-forget-PAS-FV
 'I would/will have been forgotten'

5.2.1.2 Negative past

NEG SC ***ya*** (VC) VS *a*
(333) ka-**ya**-fik-a
 3SG.NEG-NEG.PST-arrive-FV
 's/he did not arrive'

The negative past indicates that an event did not take place at a time earlier than the day of the utterance (if a speaker wishes to specify that an event did not occur on the day of the utterance, the hodiernal past *ka*- must be used).

---

[4]In the Digo orthography the high tone is only indicated with 1SG subjects where there is the possibility of confusion with the 1SG form of the continuous aspect (both are portmanteau forms). Tone is marked on the tense morpheme but at the surface level the high tone spreads to the subsequent two syllables of the verbal complex rather than being manifested on the past tense marker itself. In this respect, Digo differs from Giryama, in which "whatever type the stem, the past tense will have two surface High tones, one on the fused subject prefix/tense marker and another on the penult" (Volk 2007:31). The form of the 3SG SC is also irregular (it is a fossilized form of the archaic 3SG SC *u*-) and so the complete paradigm has been provided.

(334) Phahi yuya   bwana   hura   wari   **ka-ya̠-u-ry-a**.
      so   1.DEM2 1a.man   14.DEM2 14.ugali 3SG.NEG-NEG.PST-11-eat-FV
      'So that man **did not eat** that ugali.'

5.2.1.3 Hodiernal past

    SC ***ka*** (VC) VS *a*   Negative: NEG SC ***ka*** (VC) VS *a*
(335) *a-**ka**-reh-a*   *k-a-**ka**-reh-a*
      3SG-HOD-take-FV   NEG-3SG-HOD-take-FV
      's/he took/has taken (today)'   's/he did not take (today)'

The hodiernal past tense indicates events which occurred on the day of the utterance. If the event occurred earlier than the day of the utterance then the past tense must be used instead. This function of *ka-* is very similar to that of the Haya *á(á)-* 'near past'. Hewson, Nurse, and Muzale characterize this as a 'Memorial Present', which is "a representation of the time that is coeval with the retentive memory (the memory of the stream of consciousness that is being recorded), or the working memory of consciousness" (2000:47). They (Hewson et al., 48) continue: "The conventions of the Ruhaya tense system are that this memory of the immediate past extends all the way back to the last sleep of the community, i.e. to the point where consciousness is interrupted by sleep. The referential scope of the Memorial Present is therefore 'earlier today'." The same convention holds in Digo, such that if an event took place within the day of the utterance, whether or not it has current relevance or gave rise to a resultant state, *ka-* must be used.

5.2.1.4 Present

    SC ***na*** (VC) VS *a*
(336) *a-**na**-gul-a*
      3SG/PL-CONT-buy-FV
      's/he or they are buying'

Note: In the first person singular, *na* coalesces with the 1SG SC *ni*: *ni+na > na*.

(337) ***na**-gul-a*
      1SG.CONT-buy-FV
      'I am buying'

Strictly speaking there is no present tense in Digo, in the sense that there is no TAM marker whose sole function is to indicate that the event time is the same as the speech time. However, when the continuous aspect marker *na-*, which is used to indicate that the event time overlaps with the reference time, is used in contexts where the reference time is the same as the speech time (for example, in the absence of a past or future tense marker), *na-* is typically interpreted as indicating present time reference. For this reason, *na-* is always glossed as CONT, even when its function is to indicate present time reference. The use of *na-* in this way does not entail that the event being described is actually ongoing at the moment of speech, so an utterance such as *Nahenda kazi Kwale* 'I work in Kwale' could either mean that the speaker is in the process of working in Kwale at the moment of speech, or that the speaker usually works in Kwale; the intended meaning is contextually determined.

5.2.1.5 Future

SC ***nda***[5] (VC) VS *a*

(338) *a-**nda**-reh-a*   *n'-**nda**-reh-a*
3SG-FUT-take-FV   1SG-FUT-take-FV
's/he will take'   'I will take'

NEG SC ***nda*** (VC) VS *a*

(339) *ka-**nda**-reh-a*   *si-**nda**-reh-a*
3SG.NEG-FUT-take-FV   1SG.NEG-FUT-take-FV
's/he will not take'   'I will not take'

The future tense indicates that the associated event occurs after the reference time, be it the moment of speaking or some other contextually determined time. In example (340), the event referred to by the verb group *hundariwa* 'we would be eaten' is situated after the time at which the subjects arrived at the ghost's house.

(340) *A-ri-pho-fik-a*   *hiko*   *nyumba-ni*   *ku-a*   *zimu*
3PL-PST-16.REL-reach-FV   17.DEM3   9.house-LOC   17-ASS   5.ghost
a-many-a   *kukala*   *sisi*   ***hu-nda-ri-w-a.***
3PL.PST-know-FV   COMP   1PL   1PL-FUT-eat-PAS-FV

'When they reached the ghost's house they knew that they would be eaten.' (lit: '... that us **we will be eaten**.')

In addition to occurring on the main verb to indicate the event time, the future tense can also occur in complex tense constructions on the verb *kala* 'be' to establish the reference time, as in example (332).

5.2.2 Dependent tenses

Dependent tenses can only indicate time reference in relation to some temporal reference point which must be specified independently using some other TAM

---

[5] The *nda-* form of the future, which is also found in other Mijikenda speech varieties and in the Nungwi dialect of Swahili (Riedel 2002:25, cited in Kipacha 2006:92), almost certainly derives from *enda* 'go to'.

marker and which may be different from the time of speaking. However, they are not syntactically dependent; that is, although they are semantically dependent on a previous verb form for their temporal interpretation, they occur in finite clauses with no overt dependency marking.

5.2.2.1 Consecutive

SC ***chi*** (VC) VS *a*
(341) n-***chi***-a-ambir-a
1SG-CONS-3PL-tell-FV
'I told them'

This tense is dependent on the previous verb for (nonhodiernal) past temporal reference; therefore, it only occurs following a past tense marker or as part of a series of consecutive tense markers, the first of which must be preceded by a past tense marker. The subject of a verb marked by the consecutive may be, but need not be, the same as the subject of the previous verb:

(342) Ná-fik-a   sukuli   **n-*chi*-a-*ambir*-a**   alimu   ayangu ...
      1SG.PST-arrive-FV 9.school   1SG-CONS-3PL-tell-FV   2.teachers   2.my_fellows
      'I arrived at school **and told** my fellow teachers ...'

The term 'consecutive' has been chosen for this tense in line with the following distinction between consecutive and narrative tenses suggested by Longacre (1990:109):

> A narrative tense ... is a special form which carries the primary event line of a story and is neither dependent on a special initial form in some span nor is rank-shifted in sequence with non-storyline initials. By contrast, a consecutive tense, which also carries the primary storyline, is either dependent on a special initial form in some span and/or is rank-shifted in sequence with non-storyline initials.

The consecutive does not have a negative form; to express the idea that something did not occur sequentially, the negative form of the sequential, *kasa-* (see below), must be used.

5.2.2.2 Sequential

SC ***ka*** (VC) VS *a*   Negative: SC ***ka sa*** (VC) VS *a*
(343) a-***ka***-vun-a   a-***ka-sa***-vun-a
      3SG-SEQ-reap-FV   3SG-SEQ-NEG-reap-FV
      'he reaps (afterwards)'   'she does not reap'

5.2 Tenses

Like the consecutive, this tense is dependent on a preceding verb form to establish temporal reference, and the subject of a verb marked by the sequential may be, but need not be, the same as the subject of the previous verb:

(344) M-mwenga nku-phand-a na wanjina a-<u>ka</u>-vun-a.
1-one HAB-plant-FV COM 3SG.other 3SG-SEQ-reap-FV
'One plants and (then) another **reaps**.'

The preceding verb form can contain any tense, aspect or movement marker except the past tense marker a- (and the associated consecutive tense chi-) or the future tense marker nda-. In the following examples, the sequential tense is dependent on the hodiernal past (ka-), the infinitive (ku-), a tenseless relative (with the suffix -ye), the habitual (nku-), and the distal marker cha- respectively. These have been underlined along with the verb containing the sequential. Note that the English free translations use various forms to translate the sequential, reflecting the variety of forms on which the sequential is dependent.

(345) Mlungu a-<u>ka</u>-sikir-a ma-voyo g-angu
1a.God 3SG-HOD-hear-FV 6-prayer 6-1SG.POS

na a-<u>ka</u>-ni-ph-a mwana m-lume.
COM 3SG-SEQ-1SG-give-FV 1.child 1-male
'God **has heard** my prayers and **he has given me** a son.'

(346) Mu-ogoph-e-ni Mlungu, amba-ye a=na uwezo wa
2PL-fear-SUB-PL 1a.God REL-1.REL 3SG=COM 14.power 14.ASS

<u>ku</u>-olag-a mutu na badaye a-<u>ka</u>-m-tsuph-a moho-ni.
INF-kill-FV 1.person COM afterwards 3SG-SEQ-3SG-throw-FV hell-LOC
'Fear God, who has power **to kill** a person and afterwards **throw him** into hell.'

(347) Mbeyu iriyogbwa mbararani ni mfwano wa mutu **asikiraye** neno na mara mwenga **akariphokera** na raha.
'The seed which fell among weeds is an example of a person **who hears** the word and immediately **receives it** with joy.'

mutu a-sikir-a-<u>ye</u> neno na mara mwenga
1.person 3SG-hear-FV-3SG.REL 5.word COM 9.time 9.one

a-<u>ka</u>-ri-phoker-a na raha.
3SG-SEQ-5-receive-FV COM 9.joy

(348) Mana mtsanga **nkuhenda** mbeyu **ikamera, ikatuluza** chikodza kpwandza, alafuye **ikakula, ikatuluza** suche, chisha mwisho suche **rikahenda** tembe.

'For the soil **makes** the seed **sprout, produce** buds first, then **grow,** and **produce** ears, then finally the ears **make** grains.'

Mana	mtsanga	**nku-**hend-a	mbeyu	i-**ka**-mer-a ...
for	3.soil	HAB-make-FV	9.seed	9-SEQ-sprout-FV

(349) Sambi yuya mchiya kala achiphiya kpwa nduguye **achavoya** chakurya; **akahewa** na **akedzarya** na mchewe na anae.

'Now that poor man had gone to his brother and **begged (there) for** food; **he was given** (some) and **he came and ate** with his wife and children.'

a-**cha**-voy-a	chakurya;	a-**ka**-he-w-a	na	a-**k**-edza-ry-a
3SG-DIST-beg-FV	7.food	3SG-SEQ-give-PAS-FV	COM	3SG-SEQ-VENT-eat-FV

The negative form of the sequential is formed using the negative marker *sa* which occurs AFTER the sequential TAM marker. The *sa* negative prefix is also used to negate the potential marker *ka-* and to form the negative infinitive (e.g. *kusahenda* 'not to do'). As in affirmative clauses, the negative form of the sequential is dependent on the previous verb form to establish temporal reference and may occur with the same or a different subject. In the following example, the controlling form in the first clause is a tenseless relative *Asikizaye* 'He who hears':

(350)
A-sikiz-a-ye	neno	na	a-**ka-sa**-hend-a	vira	ri-amba-vyo ...
3SG-hear-FV-3SG.REL	5.word	COM	3SG-SEQ-NEG-do-FV	8.DEM2	5-say-8.REL

'He who hears the word and **does not do** what it says ...'

5.2.3 Tenses in relative clauses

The following tenses are used exclusively to express time reference in relative clauses. In addition, the general negative tense (with no overt TAM marker), the relative anterior aspect marker *chi-* and the continuous aspect marker *na-*, all of which occur in matrix clauses, also occur in relative clauses. These are discussed with the other tense and aspect markers.

5.2.3.1 Relative past

SC *ri* REL (VC) VS *a*

(351) a-*ri*-pho-uk-a
3SG-PST-16.REL-leave-FV
'when s/he left'

5.2 Tenses

Optionally, both the past tense marker and the subject concord can be elided, leaving just the relative marker and the verb stem. This is particularly common when the head of the relative clause is the subject, but can also be the case when a nonsubject is relativized. The following examples illustrate the reduced forms of the past relative construction, with a relativized subject (352) and with a relativized nonsubject (353):

(352) *Sambi yuno mutu **yehenda** dzambo rino kala ni ani?*
   'Now who was that person **who did** this thing?'

mutu	ye-hend-a	dzambo	rino
1.person	3SG.REL-do-FV	5.thing	5.DEM4

   Equivalent to:
mutu	a-**ri**-ye-hend-a ...
1.person	3SG-PST-1.REL-do-FV

(353) *hiye ndi=ye **ye**-ku-ambir-a-ni*
   1.DEM3 COP=1.REF 1.REL-2-tell-FV-PL
   'this is the one I told you about/about whom I told you'

   Equivalent to:
   *hiye ndi=ye ni-**ri**-ye-ku-ambir-a-ni*
   1.DEM3 COP=1.REF 1SG-PST-1.REL-2-tell-FV-PL

This TAM marker indicates past temporal reference in relative clauses, whether the event in question occurred on the day of the utterance or earlier; it therefore corresponds either to the remote past or to the hodiernal past in matrix clauses.

The corresponding negative form is usually the *amba-* relativizer plus a negative verb form; however, the general negative can also be used if it is clear from the context that a past time reference is intended, or the relative past tense form of the copula *kala* followed by the negative form of the main verb can be used, as in example (354):

(354) *Hipho kare, kpwahenda mchetu **yekala karya** sima, arya nyama bahi.*
   'Long ago, there was a woman **who didn't eat** ugali, she only ate meat.'

m-chetu	**ye**-kala	**ka**-ry-a	sima
1-woman	1.REL-PST.COP	3SG.NEG-eat-FV	9.maize_meal

5.2.3.2 Relative future

(SC)* ***ndi*** REL (VC) VS *a* (*No subject marker except in 2PL)

(355) ***ndi**-ko-phiy-a*
   FUT-17.REL-go-FV
   'where I/you(sg)/they/, etc. will go'

(356) hali   yoyosi   **ndi**-yo-m-fik-a
9.state   9.any   FUT-9.REL-3SG-arrive-FV
'whatever will happen to him/her'

(357) rorosi   m-**ndi**-ro-voy-a
5.any   2PL-FUT-5.REL-ask-FV
'whatever you ask'

Just as the future tense marker indicates that an event described by a verb in the matrix clause occurs after the reference time, so the relative future tense marker indicates that the event described by a verb in a relative clause occurs after the reference time, be it the moment of speaking or some other contextually determined time.

ndi- is a 'defective' TAM marker in that it only occurs with an overt 2nd person plural subject concord marker, as in example (358) contrasted with a 2nd person singular subject in example (359):

(358) si   mwimwi   m-**ndi**-o-gomb-a
NEG.COP   2PL   2PL-FUT-2.REL-speak-FV
'it is not you(pl) who will speak'

(359) wakati   Ø-**ndi**-pho-kal-a   m-tumiya
14.time   (2SG)-FUT-16.REL-become-FV   1-old_person
'when you become an old man'

Occasionally, even the 2nd person plural subject marker is omitted, as in the following example:

(360) m-sagal-e   na=ye   hadi   Ø-**ndi**-pho-uk-a
2PL-stay-SUB   COM=1.REF   until   (2PL)-FUT-16.REL-leave-FV
'stay with him until you(pl) leave'

For some speakers, however, *ndi-* has been replaced with the Swahili relative future tense marker *taka-* which occurs with subject markers for all persons and noun classes.[6] Whether this is a result of the defective nature of *ndi-* causing it to fall into disuse, or whether *ndi-* has become defective as a result of a shift towards *taka-* is uncertain, although the former is more likely as there is no obvious independent motivation for a shift towards *taka-*.

---

[6] I first heard this form used by a male speaker who was raised and still lives in Vyongwani near Kwale, and have written evidence of it from a female speaker originally from Lunga-lunga on the Kenyan side of the Kenya-Tanzania border, both in their early 30s. I subsequently heard it used by other speakers from various locations and of various ages.

5.3 Aspects

Aspects indicate the nature of an event without reference to a specific time. The continuous, habitual, generic, persistive, and simultaneous are all concerned with duration over time, and the relative anterior, imperfective, anterior, negative perfective, resultative, completive, and the negative inceptive deal with whether or not events have occurred and the implications of this. I have included in this section another TAM marker which is not strictly speaking an aspect, namely the 'emphatic' auxiliary which emphasizes agency in an action.

The TAM markers in this section are divided into two groups. The first group consists of fully grammaticalized aspects, that is, TAM markers which occur as affixes on the verb and express typical aspectual meanings. The second group consists of less grammaticalized aspects, which include a sentence adverbial and auxiliaries.

5.3.1 Fully grammaticalized aspects

5.3.1.1 Continuous

SC **na** (VC) VS *a*
(361) a-**na**-gul-a
3SG/PL-CONT-buy-FV
's/he or they are buying'

In the first person singular, *na* coalesces with the 1sg SC *ni*: *ni+na* > *na*.

(362) **na**-gul-a
1SG.CONT-buy-FV
'I am buying'

When the continuous marker is used in relative clauses it occurs in the same position as tenses in relative clauses, i.e. between the subject prefix and the relative marker:

SC **na** REL (VC) VS *a*
(363) a-**na**-o-ku-zir-a-ni
3PL-CONT-2.REL-2PL>-hate-FV-<2PL
'those who hate you(pl)'

The continuous aspect marker indicates that the event time overlaps with the reference time. In contexts where the reference time is the same as the speech time, *na*- is typically interpreted as indicating present time reference (see §5.2.1.4). When it is used in complex tenses in which the reference time is nonpresent, it indicates the ongoing nature of the event or situation described in the main verb.

The continuous aspect marker can also occur in narratives at the peak or critical point of a story, even when the event described is not ongoing. The effect is to increase tension. In the example (364), *na-* is used at the moment when the hero of the story finally realizes that he has been dealing with spirits rather than with human beings. Other indicators of dramatic tension in this example are the combination of the anterior aspect marker *ka-* and the completive adverbial *kare* 'already' which together indicate immediacy, and the repetition of the focus particle *che*.

(364) *Ndipho naye **anatambukira** gara achigoambirwa phara usiku, akagagbwira kare. Mana hara atu achiomuambira, che sio atu che ni shetani.*

'Then **he remembered** those things that he had been told in the night, and he understood immediately. For those people who had told him, they were not really people they were actually spirits.'

a-**na**-tambukir-a   gara   a-chi-go-ambir-w-a
3SG-CONT-remember-FV   6.DEM2   3SG-CONS-6-tell-PAS-FV

5.3.1.2 Habitual

SC ***ku*** (VC) VS *a* (1st and 2nd persons)
(365) m-***ku***-lamuk-a   mapema
2PL-HAB-awake-FV   early

'you (pl) usually wake up early'

nku (VC) VS *a* (3rd person and all other noun classes)
(366) ***nku***-lamuk-a   mapema
HAB-awake-FV   early

'they usually wake up early' *or* 's/he usually wakes up early'

(367) *mikahe*   *mi-hahu*   ***nku**-fa-a*
4.loaves   4-three   HAB-be_suitable-FV

'Three loaves are usually enough.' (de Groot 1988b:5)

De Groot (1988b:3) notes that the form of the habitual in the neighbouring Duruma language (Guthrie's E.72d) is invariably *nikú-*, and suggests that this may originally have been the case in Digo also. He proposes that the initial *ni* (or syllabic *n*) became reinterpreted as a 1SG SC resulting in the habitual aspect marker being reinterpreted as *ku-*. Following this, the 1PL, 2SG and 2PL SCs may have been added to the new *ku-* habitual aspect marker, replacing the original *ni*. This regularization included replacing the underlying high tone with the low tone associated with 1st and 2nd person SCs. However, for some reason, this process of regularization has not been completed, and the *nku-* form of the habitual aspect marker (in which the /n/ is syllabic) has been retained for all

5.3.1.3 Generic

    SC Ø (VC) VS+**PAS** *a* (only possible with passive verbs)
(368) *Dzambo   hiri   ri-Ø-hend-w-a   ni   A-digo.*
     5.thing   5.DEM1   5-GEN-do-PAS-FV   COP   2-Digos
     'This thing is usually done by Digos.'

(369) *Dzambo   hiri   ta-ri-Ø-hend-w-a   ni   A-digo.*
     5.thing   5.DEM1   NEG-5-GEN-do-PAS-FV   COP   2-Digos
     'This thing is not usually done by Digos.'

This aspect resembles the general negative in having no overt TAM marker before the verb but, as the examples above illustrate, it can occur in both affirmative and negative constructions whereas the general negative obviously only occurs in negative constructions. Semantically, rather than being merely the passive counterpart to the active form of the general negative, this construction receives an obligatory generic interpretation, that is, it describes situations which hold for all time in the past, present, and future. The generic in Digo conforms to the tendency for generics to be unmarked in Bantu languages (Rose et al. 2002:35) even though it is restricted to passive verb forms.

The generic can occur with the verb *remwa* 'be/become tired' which although historically a passive no longer has a root form *rema* (the transitive counterpart of *remwa* is *remweza* 'to tire'). The following example also illustrates the use of this form in proverbs and sayings, where it is common.

(370) *M-kala   ka-Ø-remw-a,   a-chi-remw-a   a-na-och-a.*
     1-hunter   3SG.NEG-GEN-be_tired-FV   3SG-DEP-be_tired-FV   3SG-CONT-roast-FV
     'A hunter doesn't get tired, if/when he gets tired he roasts (what he has caught).'

5.3.1.4 General negative

    NEG SC* Ø (VC) *a*   (*1SG.NEG is a portmanteau form)
(371) **ta**-*u-Ø-uy-a*   *si-Ø-many-a*
     NEG-11-GEN-return-FV   1SG.NEG-GEN-know-FV
     'it does not return'   'I do not know'

The general negative usually indicates that an event is not happening or does not happen, or that a situation does not hold either at the moment of speech or in general. Whether a general negative verb form refers to the moment of speech or more generally must be inferred contextually; thus, *Simanya* 'I do not know' uttered in answer to a question refers to the speaker's state of mind at the moment of speech, whereas a saying such as (372) describes a universal truth.

(372) *Ujana   ni   mosi   u-chi-phiy-a   ta-u-uy-a.*
       14.youth   cop   9.smoke 14-DEP-go-FV   NEG-14-return-FV
       'Youth is (like) smoke, once it has gone it does not return.'

The general negative can also be used in hypothetical contexts where it describes what will not happen if some precondition is met:

(373) *a-chedz-a   si-mu-ph-a*
       3SG-DEP.come-FV   1SG.NEG-3SG-give-FV
       'if he comes I will not give him (anything)'

Two verbs are irregular with the general negative: *mendza* 'like' in which the final vowel becomes *-e*, and *taka* 'want' in which the final vowel becomes *-i* (see §4.1.9.1).

5.3.1.5 Relative anterior

(SC) ***chi*** REL (VC) VS *a*

(374) *a-**chi**-go-ambir-w-a*
       3SG-ANT-6.REL-tell-PAS-FV
       '(those things) that he had been told'

(375) *a-**chi**-o-mu-ambir-a*
       3PL-ANT-2.REL-3SG-tell-FV
       'those who had told him'

che (VC) VS *a* (3SG subjects only: *a+chi+ye > che*)

(376) ***che**-gbwir-w-a*
       3SG.ANT.1.REL-catch-PAS-FV
       'who was/had been caught'

A 3SG SC is usually omitted when the subject is relativized, and with other persons and noun classes the SC is optional in such environments. (Unlike the relative past tense, but like the relative future tense, the relative anterior marker itself cannot be omitted.)

(377) *gara   ga-**chi**-go-gomb-w-a*
       6.DEM2   6-ANT-6.REL-speak-PAS-FV
       'that which has been spoken'

(378) rira   Ø-***chi***-ro-angamik-a
    5.DEM2 (5)-ANT-5.REL-be_lost-FV
    'that which has been lost'

This aspect marker is used exclusively in relative clauses. Although its form is the same as that of the consecutive tense, imperfective aspect, and dependent marker, it is semantically distinct from each of these. The relative anterior indicates that the event in question was completed <u>before</u> the actions described in the accompanying main clause(s) and that the event in question is relevant to the situation at the referent time. In example (379), the man's wife is still caught in a trap when he arrives:

(379) *Yuya bwana wakpwedza, akatsoloka, wakuta ni mchewe **chegbwirwa ni muhambo**.*
    'That man came, he arrived, and he met with his wife **who had been caught in a trap**.'

    ni   mche-we   *che*-gbwir-w-a   ni   mu-hambo.
    COP   1.wife-1.3SG.POS 3SG.ANT.1.REL-catch-PAS-FV   COP   3-trap

(380) *Ndipho naye anatambukira gara **achigoambirwa** phara usiku, akagagbwira kare. Mana hara atu **achiomuambira**, che sio atu che ni shetani.*
    'Then he remembered those things **that he had been told** in the night, and he understood immediately. For those people **who had told him**, they were not people they were spirits.'

    Ndi=pho   na=ye   a-na-tambukir-a   gara   a-*chi*-go-ambir-w-a ....
    COP=16.REF   COM=1.REF   3SG-CONT-remember-FV   6.DEM2   3SG-ANT-6-tell-PAS-FV

    hara   atu   a-*chi*-o-mu-ambir-a
    2.DEM2 2.people   3PL-ANT-2.REL-3SG-tell-FV

5.3.1.6 Imperfective

         past copula SC ***chi*** (VC) VS *a*
(381) *kala*   *a*-***chi***-*phiy*-*a*
      PST   3SG-IMPFV-go-FV
    '(she) would go/used to go'

The imperfective aspect marker is used in complex constructions following the past copula or past tense form of *kala* 'be' to describe states that used to hold in the past[7] (see §5.6.1.1). The following examples are taken from an

---

[7] The imperfective *chi-* aspect marker in Digo is almost certainly cognate with the 'past imperfective' high-tone SC *ki-* in Mwani (a sub-Sabaki language spoken on the coast of Mozambique). According to Floor (2002), this TAM marker indicates background information with past time reference, which may be either stative or progressive. In Mwani, past time reference is indicated through the high tone on the SC (which spreads to the following *ki-* TAM marker), and so both past

account of Digo history and traditions, and refer to situations which have past time reference but which are viewed as being temporally unbounded (only one clause of example (383) has been glossed, as the structure of all the past imperfective verb phrases is the same).

(382) Mtumiya mmwenga wa Chiajemi **yekala a<u>ch</u>iihwa** Kalindi, warusa msichana wa Chigala.

'One elder from the Ajemi clan **who was called** Kalindi, seduced a young Gala woman.'

ye-kal-a   a-**chi**-ih-w-a
PST.3SG.REL-be-FV 3SG-IMPFV-call-PAS-FV

(383) Mchetu **kala a<u>ch</u>ilorerwa** achetu ayae, naye kpwakpwe kala ni sawa. Hinya achetu **kala a<u>ch</u>iganyirwa** minda yao ambayo **kala i<u>ch</u>iihwa** makoho. Mlume naye kala ana wakpwe munda ambao **kala u<u>ch</u>iihwa** dzumbe, ambao **kala u<u>ch</u>irimwa** ni achee osi phamwenga na ana ao.

'A woman **would be watched over** by her fellow wives and she would do the same for them. These wives **would be/were allocated** their own plots which **were called** 'makoho'. The husband would also have his own plot which **was called** 'dzumbe', which **would be/was farmed** by all his wives together with their children.'

Hinya   a-chetu   kala a-**chi**-gany-ir-w-a   minda   y-ao
2.DEM1   2-women   PST   3PL-IMPFV-divide-APPL-PAS-FV 4.fields 4-3PL.POS

5.3.1.7 Anterior

	SC **ka** (VC) VS a	Negative:	NEG SC **ka** (VC) VS a
(384)	u-**ka**-rim-a		ta-m-**ka**-fwih-a
	2SG-ANT-farm-FV		NEG-2PL-ANT-dance-FV
	'you have farmed/you farmed'		'you have not danced'

The anterior indicates that an event that was ongoing has been completed. However, unlike the past and hodiernal past tense markers it is not used to situate events temporally in the past, and unlike the sequential tense marker the anterior is not dependent on a previous verb phrase. Example (385) illustrates the typical function of the anterior.

---

tense and imperfective aspect are encoded in a single verb group; but in the Digo case past time reference is encoded on the copula whilst the verb group containing chi- expresses just imperfective aspect.

(385) Tsaka   u-**ka**-rim-a   kura   amba-ko   ku-na-tish-a
5.forest 2SG-ANT-farm-FV 17.DEM2 REL-17.REL 17-CONT-frighten-FV
ku-**ka**-sir-a.
17-ANT-finish-FV

'Where the forest has been cultivated is no longer a frightening place.' (lit: 'The forest **you have farmed** there where it is frightening **has finished**.')

The anterior can also be used to indicate the culmination of a series of events; de Groot (1988a:23) notes that *ka-* "is also used to express that an action or state is a result or consequence of something previously mentioned." The following example is taken from de Groot (1988a:23):

(386) Ku-wez-a   ku-tsuph-a   dziwe   kure   ku-a   tero
2SG.NEG-be_able-FV INF-throw-FV 5.stone far 17-ASS 9.sling

ri-**ka**-fik-a   mphaka   wa   munda.
5-ANT-reach-FV 3.boundary 3.ASS 3.field

'You cannot sling a stone so far **that it reaches** the boundary of the field.'

This use resembles the use of *ka-* in example (387) to indicate the culmination of a process; this is a perfective meaning in that it indicates the completion of an event, but the event as a whole is described not just by the verb which is marked by *ka-* (*fika* 'arrive') but also by the previous verbs (all *edza* 'come') which culminate in the subject's arrival.

(387) Phahi   mamba   wa-kpwedz-a,   a-ch-edz-a
so 1a.crocodile 3SG.PST-come-FV 3SG-CONS-come-FV

a-ch-edz-a   hata   a-**ka**-fik-a   kahi-kahi   ya   madzi.
3SG-CONS-come-FV until 3SG-ANT-arrive-FV middle 9.ASS 6.water

'So the crocodile kept on going (coming) until **he arrived** in the middle of the lake.'

Similarly, example (388) indicates the culmination of different stages in a complex event; repeating a verb using *ka-* in the second occurrence indicates the completion of one stage and the transition to the next. The final verb (*mala* 'finish') is not repeated but is marked by *ka-* and indicates the culmination of the whole event:

(388) Wasagala, vichache yuya Wa Livoyo **achedza, akedza** wajitirwa sima, anamanywa ana ndzala, wahewa dzogolo achitsindza, **achirya, akarya akamala.**

'He sat for a while that person Wa Livoyo and **came, having come** he was cooked maize meal, it being known that he was hungry, he was given a cockerel and he slaughtered it and **ate, having eaten he finished.**'

a-ch-edz-a,	a-**k**-edz-a ...	
3SG-CONS-come-FV	3SG-ANT-come-FV	

a-chi-ry-a,	a-**ka**-ry-a	a-**ka**-mal-a
3SG-CONS-eat-FV	3SG-ANT-eat-FV	3SG-ANT-finish-FV

The function of the anterior marker of indicating completed events is similar to the function of the completive aspect marker *kare*, and the two forms are often found together:

(389) *Yuya muwangbwa wahala riratu sahani kulu. Yu mwanachetu anaamba, "Hiyo kulu ya aphuyo, we unaihala uwe, sababu?"* **Iye akahala kare.**

'His nephew took that large plate. The woman said, "That big one is your uncle's, why are you taking it?" **He had already taken it.**'

Iye	a-**ka**-hal-a	kare.
3SG	3SG-ANT-take-FV	COMPL

The anterior can also be used in conjunction with another clause, which I will call the 'controlling clause', to indicate an action that began prior to or at the same time as the action described in the controlling clause and which continues throughout the period during which the action described in the controlling clause occurs. In this use, the verb containing the anterior marker must be preceded by an explicit marker of simultaneity (e.g. *kuno* 'whilst'), except examples which are also stative. It is possible that the occurrence of an explicit indicator of simultaneity licenses a stative interpretation of the associated action.

(390)
a-chi-rir-a	kuno	a-**ka**-m-kumbatir-a
3SG-CONS-cry-FV	whilst	3SG-ANT-3SG-embrace-FV

'he cried whilst **embracing him**'

(391) *ichikala mwana ni mchetu,* **kala nkutuluzwa kondze kuno akafungirwa** *chihiha cha kuni*

'if the child was a girl, **she was brought outside with a small bundle of firewood tied to her** (lit: whilst she has been tied to with a small bundle of firewood)'

kala	nku-tuluz-w-a	kondze	kuno	a-**ka**-fung-ir-w-a
PST	HAB-bring_out-PAS-FV	outside	whilst	3SG-ANT-tie-APPL-PAS-FV

5.3 Aspects

The anterior aspect marker can also express a resultant state without an explicit indicator of simultaneity when describing 'bodily' states such as being tired, wearing clothes, holding something, and—in the case of trees—bearing fruit. In this use, the anterior functions more like a resultative perfect (Hopper 1982 uses the term 'resultative perfect' for constructions which express both past actions with current relevance and present states resulting from past actions):

(392) Mwana   a-**ka**-remw-a.
 1.child   3SG-ANT-be_tired-FV
 'The child **is tired**.'

(393) Maliki   a-**ka**-vwal-a   kofiya.
 Maliki   3SG-ANT-wear-FV   9.hat
 'Maliki **is wearing** a hat.'

(394) Mw-akpwe m-kono-ni   kala   a-**ka**-gbwir-a   chikombe
 18-3SG.POS 3-hand-LOC   PST   3SG-ANT-grasp-FV   7.cup

 chi-**ka**-odzal-a   uchi.
 7-ANT-fill-FV   14.palm_wine
 'In his hand he **was holding** a cup (that was) **filled** (with) palm wine.'

(395) Mdzangbweona chikpwata **chika̲vyala** machungbwa, hebu mngololi **uka̲vyala** tende?
 'Have you ever seen a 'wait-a-bit' tree **bearing** oranges, or a thorn tree **bearing** dates?'

 chi-**ka**-vyal-a   ma-chungbwa ... u-**ka**-vyal-a   tende
 7-ANT-bear-FV   6-oranges   3-ANT-bear-FV   10.dates

Resultant states are often evident soon after the action which precedes them, and this can give the impression that *ka-* functions as a resultative marker in other cases too. However, when a resultant state other than a bodily state comes into being earlier than the day of the utterance, the past tense must be used, which indicates that *ka-* in example (396) in fact indicates hodiernal past tense and not anterior aspect.

(396) Chigongo   chi-ka-vundz-ik-a.
 7.stick   7-HOD-break-STAT-FV
 'The stick is broken.' (It was broken today.)

(397) Chigongo   cha-vundz-ik-a.
 7.stick   7-PST-break-STAT-FV
 'The stick is broken.' (It was broken earlier than today.)

Apart from the resultative suffix described below, which has a very restricted use, Digo does not have a regular verbal marker for the resultative (to express present states resulting from past actions). For this reason, a verb inflected with *ka-* cannot be used to translate the English sentence 'He has worked here for three years' meaning that the subject began working here three years ago and is still working here. Instead, a construction such as the following must be used:

(398) *Hinyu ni mwakawe wa hahu wa kuhenda kazi hipha.*
'This is his third year of working here.'

Like the hodiernal marker *ka-* but unlike the homophonous sequential and potential markers, the anterior is negated in the same way as most other TAM markers, using a negative prefix which precedes the SC:

(399) *Pho munda nkauhenda mkpwulu na **sikaphaha hata tsere mwenga**, kpwani nini?*
'The field I made it big but **I have not got even one cob of corn**, why ever not?'

si-ka-phah-a   hata   tsere   mwenga
1SG.NEG-ANT-get-FV   even   5.corn_cob   5.one

5.3.1.8 Simultaneous

chopho (VC) VS *a*

(400) *chopho-jit-a*
SIM-cook-FV
'whilst cooking'

This is a dependent TAM marker which indicates that the action described by the verb to which it is prefixed is ongoing during the period in which the action described by the independent verb phrase takes place. It has only been recorded in the southern dialect of Digo, as spoken in Tanzania; in the northern dialect a particle such as *kuno* or a construction such as *wakati wa* + infinitive, both of which express 'whilst', would be used instead. No SC is possible with the simultaneous marker:

(401) **Chopho**-*jit-a*   manga,   dze   *u-ka-tiy-a*   nazi?
SIM-cook-FV   1a.cassava   Q   3SG-ANT-put_in-FV   9.coconut
'Whilst cooking the cassava, did you add coconut?'

5.3.1.9 Negative perfective

NEG SC (VC) VS *ere/ire*

(402) *si-mu-on-ere*
1SG.NEG-3SG-see-PFV
'I did not see/have not seen him/her'

(403) **ka-fik-ire**
 3SG.NEG-arrive-PFV
 's/he did not arrive/has not arrived'

The negative perfective is so named because it is a reflex of the Bantu 'perfective' suffix *-ile* which marks verbs as completed in many Eastern Bantu languages. However, in Digo it is now only productive in negative clauses, where it indicates that an event did not happen at any time in the past. When the negative perfective is used with an auxiliary, such as the ventive TAM marker *kpwedza* 'come from', preceding a main verb, it is suffixed to the auxiliary rather than to the main verb:

(404) Kala s-edz-**ere**-gomb-a na=o
 if 1SG.NEG-come-PFV-speak-FV COM=2.REF
 'If I had not come and spoken with them ...'

5.3.1.10 Resultative

SC VS **ere/ire** (with verb stem modification)
(405) a-seg-**ere**   a-r-**ere**   a-im-**ire**
 3SG-sit-PFV   3SG-sleep-PFV   3SG-stand-PFV
 's/he is seated'   's/he is asleep'   's/he is standing'

The resultative is a fossilized form which is historically cognate with, but now distinct from, the negative perfective suffix *-ire/-ere*. For the sake of convenience, it is also glossed as PFV. It occurs with a limited number of verbs of state, including *sagala* 'sit', *lala* 'sleep', *ima* 'stand', and *nyamala* 'keep silent', and indicates a state arising from a previous action. Although the previous action (sitting down, falling asleep, etc.) is understood to have happened before the moment of speech, the resultative construction is used exclusively to describe a resultant state which obtains at the moment of speaking. This is the only true 'resultative' construction in Digo (i.e. a form which is used exclusively to indicate a state arising from a previous action, without reference to the action itself).

(406) Sino hu-ka-ona mutu **a-im-ire** mo chisima-ni.
 1PL.PRO 1PL-HOD-see 1.person 3SG-stand-PFV 18.DEM3_VAR 7.well-LOC
 'We saw a person **standing** inside the well.'

(407) ... ye a-**nyemere** tu gbwii, hata tse.
 1.DEM3_VAR 3SG-keep_silent.PFV IDEO IDEO even IDEO
 '... he **remained** totally **silent**, absolutely so.'

In the historical development of the resultative from the Proto-Bantu perfective suffix, and the use of the anterior prefix *ka-* as a 'resultative perfect' to describe bodily states, Digo provides a further corroboration of Hewson et al.'s observation that "Perfective and Retrospective [i.e. resultative] are very similar ..., hence their tendency to fall together historically, or for one form to be used in both functions" (2000:49).

5.3.2 Less grammaticalized aspects

5.3.2.1 Completive

kare

(408) n-ka-ry-a   kare
 1SG-ANT-eat-FV   COMPL
 'I have already eaten'

The sentence adverbial *kare*[8] can be used to mean 'long ago', as in the formulaic opening of traditional stories *Hipho kare*, and can be modified to give idiomatic expressions such as *kare chidide* 'some time ago' and *kare na kare* 'forever'. Postverbally, *kare* indicates that an event has been completed at the moment of speaking. It usually follows a verb in the anterior (perfect) aspect as in (409) and (410) or (less frequently) a verb with present time reference, as in (411) and (412), or past time reference, as in (413) and (414):

(409) N-**ka**-ry-a   **kare**   uphande   w-angu
 1SG-ANT-eat-FV   COMPL   14.side   14-1SG.POS

 n-ka-ku-saz-ir-a   w-ako.
 1SG-ANT-3SG-set_aside-APPL-FV   14-3SG.POS

 '**I have already eaten** my side and I have put aside yours.'

(410) Bada **nkatuluka kare** hiri tsaka na simba iye akaphiya vyakpwe, richa njeze kuphiya pore pore ...

 'Since **I have already left** the forest and this lion has gone away, let me try to go on slowly ...'

 Bada   n-**ka**-tuluk-a   **kare**   hiri   tsaka
 since 1SG-ANT-come_out-FV   COMPL   5.DEM1 5.forest

---

[8]Bastin and Schadeberg's (2003) database of Bantu Reconstructions lists *kàdé*[LH] 'olden times' (noun class 12, although this could be noun class 24), and this is a likely source for Digo *kare*. Identical forms are found in other Mijikenda languages, and similar forms with similar meanings are found in some other Eastern Bantu languages, e.g. Runyambo *kare* 'long ago, early' (Rugemalira 2002:70), Swahili *kale* 'long ago', Ma'a/Mbugu *kaé* (class 9) 'long ago, past' (Mous 2003), Mbugwe *kalei* (LHL) 'past' (Mous 2004).

5.3 Aspects

(411) Bwana, iye a-**na**=zo **kare** pesa dza zizo
1a.sir 3SG 3SG-COM=10.REF COMPL 10.money like 10.DEM3_VARIANT
mara kumi
10.times 10.ten
'Sir, **he already has** ten times this amount of money!'

(412) M-**na**-many-a=to **kare** mambo gaga
2PL-CONT-know-FV=WELL COMPL 6.things 6.DEM1_VARIANT
'**You already know** these things perfectly well.'

(413) Wahuguza na mali ariyoriphiwa **waihumira kare** yosi.
'He sold us and the money which he was paid **he has already used it** all.'
mali a-ri-yo-riphi-w-a wa-i-humir-a **kare** yosi.
9.wealth 3SG-REL.PST-9.REL-pay-PAS-FV 3SG.PST-9-use-FV COMPL 9.all

(414) Kala ni dziloni **kare**.
PST COP evening COMPL
'It was **already** evening.'

In other contexts, *kare* expresses a sense of immediacy.[9] In example (415), *akagagbwira kare* is literally 'he had already grasped/caught' but the intended meaning is 'he understood immediately'. In example (416), *kare* and the particle *tu* emphasize the fact that the reward will be given immediately and automatically, that is, with no delay and no questions asked.

(415) Ndipho naye anatambukira gara achigoambirwa phara usiku, **akagagbwira kare**.
'Then he remembered those things that he had been told in the night, and **he understood immediately**.'

a-ka-ga-gbwir-a **kare**
3SG-ANT-6-catch-FV COMPL

(416) Anaamba tu akaolaga Mwanyika hinya, mana waambwa, "Ndiyeolaga Mwanyika, mchetu ni wake **kare tu**."
'He was just saying that he had killed this Mwanyika (a serpent), for he had been told, "Whoever kills Mwanyika, the woman will be his **straight away**."'

m-chetu ni w-ake **kare** tu
1-woman COP 1-3SG.POS COMPL IDEO

According to Heine and Kuteva (2002:18) the completive aspect "indicates that something is done thoroughly and to completion." In Digo this feature

---
[9] Statistically, this is a less frequent use of *kare* in Digo, but in the closely related languages Giryama and Duruma this is by far the most common use of *kare*.

of the completive is evident in contexts in which *kare* indicates the ease with which an action can be accomplished:

(417) *Waphiya yuya bwana hiko tsakani, akafika waona nyama akavyoga-vyoga, anaamba, "Nchihega phano nyama achedza mino ni **nimgbwire kare**."*

'That man went into the forest, and when he got there he saw animals wandering around, and he said, "If I set my traps here, when an animal comes **I should be able to catch it easily**."'

N-chi-heg-a	*phano*	*nyama*	*a-ch-edz-a*
1SG-DEP-trap-FV	16.DEM4	1a.animal	3SG-DEP-come-FV

mino	*ni*	*ni-m-gbwir-e*	***kare.***
1SG	COP	1SG-3SG-catch-SUB	COMPL

(418) *Wamuamba Sulutani, "Mkpwongo nkamuona mino, ela niphahira minyau sabaa." Yo minyau hipho pha Sulutani ni minji hata taina kazi, **ichiphahikana kare**.*

'He said to the Sultan, "I have seen the patient, but bring me seven cats." There were many cats in the Sultan's [palace] so it was no work [to find them], **they were easily obtained**.'

i-chi-phahikan-a	***kare***
4-DEP-be_available-FV	COMPL

5.3.2.2 (Negative) inceptive

	SC NEG ***dzangbwe*** (VC) VS *a*	or	SC NEG ***dzangbwe*** #
(419)	*ta-ri-**dzangbwe**-dung-a*		*si-**dzangbwe***
	NEG-5-INC-pierce-FV		1SG.NEG-INC
	'it has not yet pierced'		'I have not yet'

The (negative) inceptive[10] in conjunction with a negative prefix indicates that an event has not occurred prior to and including the reference time. There is usually an implicature that the event may occur at some time after the reference time:

(420)
Dzuwa	*ta-ri-**dzangbwe**-dung-a*	*sawa sawa.*
5.sun	NEG-5-INC-pierce-FV	completely

'The sun is not yet shining through.'

---

[10]The term '(negative) inceptive' reflects the fact that although *dzangbwe* usually occurs as part of a negative construction, under specific conditions it can occur without a negative prefix. Other labels which have been used for similar markers in other languages include 'negative anterior' and 'yet' (Kozinskij 1988:523). The Digo (negative) inceptive is similar to what Comrie (1985:54) refers to as the 'not-yet tense', which is an absolute tense that asserts the nonoccurrence of an event at and before the moment of the utterance.

5.3 Aspects

Structurally, *dzangbwe* is a highly grammaticalized auxiliary; it usually occurs prefixed to the following verb root (or the verb complement if there is one) like fully grammaticalized TAM markers, but it can also occur word finally. Unlike the itive and ventive markers *kpwenda* and *kpwedza*, but like the persistive aspect marker *chere*, *dzangbwe* can not be preceded by any other TAM marker. However, like *kpwenda* and *kpwedza*, but unlike *chere*, *dzangbwe* can precede the infinitive form of a main verb:

SC NEG ***dzangbwe*** # INF (VC) VS a

(421) Kala si-***dzangbwe*** ku-tayarish-a ma-somo.
PST 1SG.NEG-INC INF-prepare-FV 6-lessons
'I had not yet prepared the lessons.'

The time reference of clauses containing *dzangbwe* must either be inferred from the context or indicated by a preceding tense marker, such as the past tense copula *kala* in example (421), or the anterior aspect marker *ka-* in (422):

(422) bada n-**ka**-mu-on-a ka-***dzangbwe*** ku-tuluk-a himu tsaka-ni
since 1SG-ANT-3SG-see-FV 3SG.NEG-INC INF-leave-FV 18.DEM1 forest-LOC
'since I saw that **he had not yet** left the forest ...'

When *dzangbwe* occurs clause finally (i.e. not preceding a main verb) it functions as a copula (see §8.1.3):

(423) Wakati w-angu ta-u-***dzangbwe***.
14.time 14-1SG.POS NEG-14-INC
'My time **is not yet**.' (i.e. 'My time has not yet come.')

It can also occur in relative clauses, still prefixed to the main verb:

(424) m-chetu a-si-ye-***dzangbwe***-lól-w-a
1-woman 3SG-NEG-REL-INC-marry-PAS-FV
'a woman who **has not yet** been married'

Very infrequently *dzangbwe* can occur without a negative prefix, but only in contexts with what is called 'negative polarity', such as questions:

(425) M***dzangbwe***ona muhi wa miya ukavyala zabibu, hebu mngololi ukavyala tende? Ng'o!
'**Have you ever seen** a thorn tree bear grapes, or a 'wait-a-bit' tree bear dates? Of course not!' (Matthew 7:16)

m-***dzangbwe***-on-a muhi wa miya
2PL-INC-see-FV 3.tree 3.ASS 4.thorns

5.3.2.3 Persistive

SC ***chere*** (VC) VS *a*

(426) *a-**chere**-tambukir-a*
3PL-PERS-remember-FV
'they still remember'

SC ***chere*** #

(427) a. *a-**chere*** *moyo*   b. *m-**chere*** *ku-heh-a*
    3SG-PERS heart   2PL-PERS INF-argue-FV
    's/he is still alive'   'you are still arguing'

The persistive[11] indicates that an event that began before the reference time continues throughout the reference time or that a situation that held before the reference time still holds at the reference time. The persistive can either occur as a prefix on the verb root (or preceding the verb complement if there is one) or it can precede a nonfinite verb or a nonverbal predicate such as *moyo* 'alive', in which case it functions as part of a copula or possessive construction (see §8.1.3). When *chere* occurs with a nonfinite verb or a nonverbal predicate, the convention is that these are written as separate words.

The Swahili translation equivalent of *chere* (and sometimes of the negative inceptive *dzangbwe*, described above) in most contexts is *bado*, and occasionally the same form, *bado*, precedes *chere* in Digo:

(428) *anjina kala bado a-**chere**-kpwedz-a.*
   2.others PST still 3PL-PERS-come-FV
   'others were still coming'

Digo *chere* may well be cognate with *chéri* in Mbugu and the Shona persistive *chiri*, which Güldemann (2003:192) analyses as a combination of *chi* (a reflex of the proposed Proto-Bantu persistive marker **ki-*[12]) plus the copula *ri*, which also occurs in the same form in Digo relative clauses. In Digo, the reflex of persistive **ki-* is *che* (as in Mbugu), and if *re* is derived from the relative copula **ri* then the assumption must be that vowel harmony resulted in a change from **ri* to *re*. The analysis of *re* as being historically a copula is reinforced by the fact that *chere* functions as part

---

[11] This term is taken from Hewson et al. (2000:50): "the Persistive is a representation of an event that is still incomplete or ongoing." This seems preferable to Mous' (2003:122) term 'unfinished' for the cognate form *chéri* in Mbugu since there is no requirement for the event in question to have an end point.

[12] Similarly, Fuliiru has a persistive 'aspectual copula' *ki* which always occurs with the copula *li* forming *kili*; Van Otterloo and Van Otterloo (2008) propose that the reason *ki* combines with *li*, unlike the other 'aspectual copulas' *kola* 'is now, but was not' and *shuba* 'was, but is not now' is to ensure that the final form is disyllabic; but the fact that Digo, Mbugu, Shona, and (presumably) other Bantu languages have a similar disyllabic form suggests that in fact the form of the Fuliiru persistive marker may be inherited rather than phonologically motivated.

of a copula or possessive construction when it precedes nonverbal predicates. An alternative analysis of Digo *chere* is that it is a combination of *chi* (a reflex of *ki* as Güldemann proposed) plus the suffix *-ere* which occurs in Digo in the resultative and negative perfective aspects but which can be safely assumed to have been more productive in the past, given the wide attestation of this form among Bantu languages. A similar form is attested in Kuria which Cammenga (2004:287) calls the 'current present persistive', in which a lexical verb is preceded by a persistive prefix *ke-* and followed by a perfective suffix *-ere*: /ne-βa-**ke**-søm-**ere**/ (focus-SC-PRES-read-PFV) 'they are still reading'. If this second scenario for the development of Digo *chere* is correct, *chi* would have functioned as an auxiliary verb rather than as an aspectual prefix.

5.3.2.4 Emphatic

SC TAM **henda** (VC) VS *a*
(429) ná-**henda**-on-a
1SG.PST-EMPH-see-FV
'I saw'

INF **henda** (VC) VS *a*
(430) ku-**henda**-och-w-a
INF-EMPH-burn-PAS-FV
'to be burnt/being burnt'

The emphatic marker is almost certainly derived historically from the lexical verb *henda* 'do, make'. When *henda* is the only verb in a verb group it functions as the main verb, but when *henda* precedes another verb root (optionally preceded by a verb complement marker) within a single word, it functions as an auxiliary or TAM marker.[13] In this use, *henda* must be preceded by either another TAM marker or the infinitive prefix *ku-* (the itive *kpwenda* and ventive *kpwedza* share this characteristic), which suggests that it has an intermediate status between being a verb (it inflects) and a TAM marker (it precedes and modifies a lexical verb). It can occur in both main clauses (431) and *amba-* relative clauses (432), and can precede a verb complement marker (e.g. *chi*):

(431) si=yo   ku-a   ku-**henda**-lazimish-w-a
NEG=9.REF   15-ASS   INF-EMPH-force-PAS-FV
'not (at all) by being forced'

(432) chitu   amba-cho   a-**henda**-chi-tengez-a
7.thing   REL-7.REL   3PL.PST-EMPH-7-make-FV
'a thing which they (actually) made'

---

[13] In this respect it differs from the similar construction in Swahili involving the verb *fanya* 'do', in that *fanya* is always followed by the infinitive form of the main verb rather than by the verb root as part of a single word.

The emphatic is a kind of focus marker, which emphasizes the importance or reality of the action described by the main verb, and in particular the notion of agency. It is relatively rare; there are 15 occurrences in a translated corpus of over 17,000 sentences and only one occurrence in a nontranslated corpus of approximately 900 sentences. However, 9 of these 16 occurrences are with passive verb forms, as in example (431), which may reflect a historical origin in passive constructions with subsequent generalization to active constructions. When used with a passive verb, the emphatic auxiliary emphasizes the role of the agent, even if the agent is not explicitly mentioned, as illustrated in the following example:

(433) "Aa,   mbavi gano   mafisi   ga-**henda**-lagiz-w-a
EXCL   really 6.DEM4 6.hyena 6.PST-EMPH-order-PAS-FV

ga-chi-kal-a   ga-na-phiy-a   ga-ka-tsum-e!"
6-CONS-be-FV   6-CONT-go-FV   6-IT-gather-SUB

'He was astonished, "Ah, those hyenas (really) **were given orders** and they went to gather."'

5.4 Status markers

The class of status markers in Digo includes the potential, dependent, conditional, and negative conditional markers (all of which are simple forms involving a single verb), and complex conditional constructions involving *(ichi)kala* and a following verb. All these constructions indicate the contingent nature of events, that is, they indicate that an event has or had the potential to occur but that it did not or has not yet occurred.

5.4.1 Simple status markers

5.4.1.1 Potential

         SC **ka** (VC) VS *a*   Negative: SC **ka sa** (VC) VS *a*
(434) n-**ka**-fw-a   n-**ka**-**sa**-kpwedz-a ...
         1SG-POT-die-FV   1SG-POT-NEG-come-FV
         'if I should die'   'if I don't come'

The potential TAM marker is used when referring to events which have not yet occurred, but which are potential. Typically, a verb marked by *ka-* follows a negative command/subjunctive or *-sedze* with the meaning "lest something happen" (or in more modern English usage "so that something won't happen") as in example (435). In addition to indicating a potential consequence, the potential can indicate a potential condition, as in example (436).

5.4 Status markers

(435) A-fikiriy-a   ra   ku-hend-a   ili   a-sedze   a-**ka**-ri-w-a
       3PL-think.APPL-FV 5.ASS INF-do-FV   so_that   3PL-lest   3PL-POT-eat-PAS-FV

   ni   rira   zimu.
   COP   5.DEM2   5.ghost
   'They thought about what to do so that they would not be eaten by that ghost.'

(436) Hata   n-**ka**-fw-a   dza   sambi,   ni   sawa.
       even   1SG-POT-die-FV   right   now   COP   fine
       'Even if I should die right now, that's alright.'

Like the *ka-* sequential marker, the negative of the potential is formed using the negative prefix *sa-* which occurs after *ka-* (in contrast to the *ka-* hodiernal and anterior markers which are negated using prefixes which occur before the SC):

(437) Phahi   n-k-edz-a,   n-**ka**-**sa**-kpwedz-a ...
       so   1SG-POT-come-FV   1SG-POT-NEG-come-FV
       'So if I come or if I don't come ...'

5.4.1.2 Dependent

   SC ***chi*** (VC) VS *a*
(438) u-***chi***-rim-a
       3SG-DEP-arrive-FV
       'when/if you farm'

All verb forms which occur in subordinate clauses are syntactically dependent on some other clause, but the label 'dependent' has been used for this TAM marker to reflect the use of the term "in discourse analysis to refer to verbs that contain backgrounded material" (Rose et al. 2002:25), as this is the primary function of this TAM marker.

The form of the dependent is identical to the consecutive tense marker,[14] but whereas the consecutive tense refers to past events and occurs in syntactically independent clauses (even though it is semantically dependent on there being a past tense marker in another clause to establish temporal reference), the dependent refers to nonpast events and occurs in syntactically dependent clauses. In the following examples, the clauses containing a dependent marker are syntactically dependent on independent clauses containing a

---

[14] The dependent is almost certainly cognate with the low-tone *ki-* 'situative aspect' marker in Mwani (a sub-Sabaki language spoken on the coast of Mozambique), which indicates a simultaneous action or state which is backgrounded in comparison with the main verb which it is dependent on (Floor 2002). Unlike the dependent in Digo, however, the Mwani situative marker can be used with past time reference (the main verb on which the Mwani situative is dependent can have past or perfect TAM markers as well as nonpast).

general negative (*tauuya* 'it does not return'), an emphatic subjunctive (*ni auye* 'he should return'), a negative imperative (*usiphiye* 'do not go'), and a future tense (*undarya* 'you will eat') respectively.

(439) *Ujana   ni   mosi   u-**chi**-phiy-a   ta-u-uy-a.*
      14.youth   COP   9.smoke   14-DEP-go-FV   NEG-14-return-FV
      'Youth is like smoke, **once it has gone** it does not return.'

(440) *A-phiya-ye   ukala-ni   a-**chi**-uy-a   ni   a-uy-e*
      3SG-go-1.REL   14.hunting-LOC   3SG-DEP-return-FV   COP   3SG-return-SUB

      na   nyama   phano.
      COM   9.meat   16.DEM4
      'The one who goes hunting **when he returns** he should return with meat.'

(441) *"U-**chi**-fik-a   kaya   u-si-phiy-e   u-cha-mu-ambir-a   mche-o ..."*
      2SG-DEP-arrive-FV   9.home   2SG-NEG-go-SUB   2SG-DIST-3SG-tell-FV   1.wife-2SG.POS
      '"**When you arrive** home do not go and tell your wife ..."'

(442) *Adigo nkuamba, "U**chirima** 'go', undarya 'go', lakini u**chirima** dii, undarya dii."*
      'The Digos say, "**If you cultivate** little you will eat little, but **if you cultivate** all day long you will eat all day long."'

      *u-**chi**-rim-a*
      3SG-DEP-arrive-FV

The meaning of the dependent marker in the above examples is invariably irrealis, in that the events described in the dependent clause do not refer to specific situations that have occurred. However, the conditions under which these events might be realized vary. In examples (439) and (440), *uchiphiya* and *achiuya* refer to generic situations that are true at all times but without referring to a specific instance; in example (441), *uchifika kaya* refers to a specific event that is anticipated to happen at some time in the future; and in (442), *uchirima* refers to a hypothetical event that could potentially occur but need not. For this reason, the English free translations use 'once', 'when', and 'if' to convey the idea expressed by the dependent.[15]

More than one clause with a dependent marker can depend on a single independent clause, as in example (443) in which all of the dependent clauses depend

---
[15]Following the mental spaces approach of Fauconnier (1994) and Dancygier and Sweetser (2005), clauses marked with the dependent set up a mental space against which the following independent clause is to be understood. The speaker's stance towards the mental space—whether it is likely or unlikely to occur, or is purely hypothetical—is not encoded by *chi*, which makes it less specific than the English translations 'if', 'once' and 'when'.

5.4 Status markers

on the final subjunctive *uambe* 'you should say'. Note that the final vowel of *chi* is elided when it precedes the vowel-initial verb root *edza*: *chi* + *edza* > *chedza*.[16]

(443) U-**ch**-edz-a   mwanangu   u-**chi**-ni-kut-a   ni   m-zima,
       2SG-DEP-come-FV   1.child.1.1SG.POS   2SG-DEP-1SG-meet-FV   COP 1-whole

n-**chi**-ku-guz-a,   "Tandzi   baba?"   **u-amb-e**,   "Ni   nyama
1SG-DEP-2SG-ask-FV   9.trap   1a.father   2SG-say-SUB   COP   9.meat

mwanangu."
1.child.1.1SG.POS

'**When you come** my child, **when you meet me** [and] I am well, **when I ask you**, "What have you trapped, father?" **you should say**, "It is meat, my child."'

There is no negative form of the dependent; instead, the negative form of the potential *kasa-* can be used (see e.g. §5.4.1.1).

5.4.1.3 Conditional

SC **nge** (VC) a
(444) u-**nge**-fik-a
       2SG-COND-arrive-FV

'you would arrive/would have arrived'

The conditional indicates that an event has potential to occur, but that it is unlikely to occur, or, in a past time context, that it had potential to occur but did not occur. Conditional clauses consist of two parts, the protasis which indicates the condition, and the apodosis which indicates the consequence. In English these sometimes correspond to *If...* and *then...*, respectively. The conditional *nge-* almost always occurs in the apodosis, and almost always in conditional clauses in which the protasis begins with the conditional particle *kala* (described below). Further examples are provided below in the discussion of conditional clauses with *kala*.

There are two ways in which the conditional can be negated, with no discernible difference in meaning between them.

1. The SC can be preceded by a negative prefix:

(445) Kala   Mlungu   ka-hend-ere   hivyo,   **ta**-ku-**nge**-sal-a   mutu.
       if   1a.God   3SG.NEG-do-PFV   thus   NEG-17-COND-remain-FV   1.person

'If God had not done this, no one would have remained.'

---

[16]Note also the reversal of roles when the father addresses his son (who will have returned from studies in Nairobi) as *baba* 'father' and the son addresses his father as *mwanangu* 'my child'.

(446) Kalapho   si-ya-ga-on-a   higa,   si-nge-ga-many-a.
      unless   1SG.NEG-PST-6-see-FV 6.DEM1   1SG.NEG-COND-6-know-FV
      'If I had not seen these things, I would not have known them.'

2. The conditional marker can be preceded by the negative prefix *si* which occurs after the SC, as in subjunctive clauses. This negation strategy, together with the fact that the conditional marker itself ends in *e* suggests that the conditional may have originated in a subjunctive verb form.

(447) A-**si-nge**-hend-a   hivyo,   a-nge-kal-a   a-on-a   na   matso.
      3PL-NEG-COND-do-FV   8.DEM3   3PL-COND-be-FV   3PL.PST-see-FV COM   6.eyes
      'If they had not done this, they would have seen with their eyes.'

(448) Kala   si   Shariya,   mimi   ni-**si-nge**-many-a   dambi   ni
      if   NEG   9.law   1SG   1SG-NEG-COND-know-FV   9.sin   COP

      utu   wani.
      14.thing   14.which
      'If it were not for the Law, I would not know what sin is.'

Both negative forms of the conditional indicate that an event had the potential not to occur but did in fact occur, and both can occur in either the protasis or the apodosis of conditional clauses.

5.4.2 Complex conditional clauses with *kala*

The form *kala* has a number of meanings, which can cause confusion when sentences are presented without their original context. When it is prefixed by a SC and a TAM marker *kala* functions as the verb 'be'; as a free morpheme (a 'stand alone' word) it can function as the singular imperative form of 'be', as the past tense copula, the past tense marker in a complex verb form, the complementizer 'that' (being a short form of *kukala*), and as a conditional marker. The use of *kala* as a copula is discussed in §8.1.2.3 and its use as a past tense marker in complex verb forms is discussed in §5.6.1; this section is concerned with the use of *kala* as a conditional marker.

Conditional *kala* is a reduced form of *ichikala* 'if it is (the case that)' and the reduced and the complete forms can be used interchangeably. Where *kala* cannot be replaced by *ichikala*, it is not functioning as a conditional. In table 5.1, which expands on unpublished work done by Martien de Groot, each of the examples begins with *kala* or *ichikala*, except for the first example, which is included to show the contrast in meaning between constructions involving *kala* and the *chi-* dependent marker. The type of condition is listed in the first column; TAM markers used in the protasis and the apodosis are listed in the

5.4 Status markers

second and third columns. Note that this does not constitute an exhaustive list of possible combinations of TAM markers in the protasis and apodosis.

Table 5.1. Combinations of TAM markers in conditional clauses with *kala*

Realizable – more likely	Protasis	Apodosis
U**chi**funika nyungu, madzi ga**nda**chemuka upesi. If you cover the pot, the water will boil quickly.	*chi* dependent	*nda* future

Realizable – less likely	Protasis	Apodosis
*Kala una*ripha, u**nge**phaha tikiti. If you paid, you would get a ticket.	*kala + na* continuous	*nge* conditional
(Ichi)kala basi rindauka kabla ya saa tsano, *u**nge**phaha feri.* If the bus leaves before 11:00, you would get the ferry.	*kala + nda* future	*nge* conditional

Unrealizable – contrary to fact	Protasis	Apodosis
*Kala chakurya chi**nge**phahikana, hu**nger**ya zaidi.* If the food were available, we would eat more.	*(kala) + nge* conditional	*nge* conditional
*Kala m**na**manya mana ga Maandiko higa, "Nilon-* *dacho ni atu akale na mbazi wala si kunipha* *sadaka bahi", m**singe**ahukumu asio na makosa.* But if you had known what this means, "I desire mercy and not sacrifice," you would not have condemned the guiltless.	*kala + na* continuous	*singe* negative conditional
Zo tembezo mbiri za chilume kala wazirerato, *zi**nge**kuokola, lakini gaphaphi?* Those two male progeny of yours, if you had raised them well they could have saved you, but where are they?	*kala + a* past	*nge* conditional
*Kala mutu hiyu ka**ya**kata pili kpwa Kaisari, a**ng-*** *erichirwa.* If this man had not appealed to the emperor, he would have been set free.	*kala + ya* negative past	*nge* conditional
*Kala Mlungu kahen**d**ere hivyo, taku**nge**sala mutu.* If God had not done this, nobody would remain.	*kala + ere* negative perfective	*nge* conditional
*(Ichi)kala chakurya chi**ka**phahikana, **kala*** *hu**ka**rya zaidi.* If the food had been available, we would have eaten more.	*kala + ka* hodiernal past	*kala* past *ka* hodiernal past

Table 5.1, continued

Unrealizable – contrary to fact	Protasis	Apodosis
(Ichi)kala chakurya chikaphahikana, hu**nge**rya zaidi. If the food had been available, we would have eaten more.	kala + ka hodiernal past	nge conditional
Kala **n**'chijana dza vivyo uwe mwanangu nami nk**a**amba ... If I were young like you, my child, I would have said ...	kala + ni copula	ka potential
Kala ak**a**ona pesa yuya **nge**kala akazihala. If he had seen money, that man would have taken it.	kala + ka anterior	nge conditional ka anterior
Kala **ka** inawezekana mn**ge**sokola matso genu mk**a**nipha. Had it been possible, you would have torn out your eyes and given them to me.	kala + ka anterior	nge conditional ka sequential
Kala n**chere**londa kufurahisha anadamu, phahi sin**ge**kala mtumishi wa Jesu. If I were still trying to please people, then I would not be a servant of Jesus.	kala + chere persistive	singe negative conditional

5.5 Movement grams

Movement grams are morphemes which indicate movement either towards or away from the deictic centre (that is, the notional location of the speaker or narrator), sometimes together with time reference. I include in this category a distal marker which expresses action at a distance from the deictic centre, implying prior movement on the part of the subject, although the movement itself is not part of the meaning of this morpheme.

The term 'movement grams' is an inclusive label under which to categorize a variety of morphemes. Morphemes which indicate movement away from or towards a point of reference are called 'itive' and 'ventive' markers, respectively.[17] A narrow definition of itive and ventive markers states that they must be accompanied by a motion verb such as 'jump', 'move', 'throw', or 'drive' (Heine et al. 1993:103–108), whereas the definitions and examples given for *itive* and *ventive* in Rose et al. (2002:48, 90) allow itive and ventive morphemes to modify nonmotion verbs such as 'pay'. Movement grams, as the term is used here, encode both direction and movement and can co-occur with both motion and nonmotion

---

[17]These are the terms employed in, for example, Dimmendaal (1983) and Bourdin (2000). The terms 'andative' and 'allative' are sometimes used for 'itive', and 'venitive' for 'ventive' (cf. Bourdin 1992 for a discussion). I prefer 'movement' to Meeussen's (1967:109) 'motional', as motion verbs describe both 'stationary motion' in which motion occurs in a single location (e.g. jumping on the spot) and 'change of location' in which an entity moves from one place to another (Miller and Johnson-Laird 1976), whereas movement verbs describe a change of location.

5.5 Movement grams

verbs, and so correspond more closely to Rose et al.'s broader definition of itive and ventive morphemes.[18]

The occurrence of a movement gram in Digo does not mean that a lexical verb such as 'go' or 'come' cannot also occur in the same clause. On the contrary, movement grams often occur in conjunction with lexical verbs of movement. For example, in the Digo New Testament, Genesis, and Exodus, which consists of over 17,000 sentences, there are 329 instances of the verb *phiya*[19] 'go' occurring as a main verb followed in the same sentence by another main verb with the same subject. Of these, the second main verb was marked by a movement gram in 290 cases (88%): on 191 occasions the movement gram was *enda-* (itive), on 43 occasions it was *edza-* (ventive), and on 56 occasions it was *ka-* + *-e* (itive + subjunctive). On a further 9 occasions the second main verb was marked by the distal marker *cha-*, and on 8 occasions the second verb was another movement verb e.g. *fika* 'arrive', leaving only 22 cases (7% of the total) in which the second verb was not marked for movement or deixis in some way. That is, in a clause containing a lexical movement verb followed by another verb, the second verb group almost always contains a movement gram. The high proportion of movement grams following explicit lexical indicators of movement (such as the verb *phiya*) shows that, although redundant from a purely propositional perspective, movement grams are very nearly obligatory when the verb group they are part of is preceded by a lexical movement verb. Conversely, the translated corpus contains 424 occurrences of the itive movement gram *enda*, many of which occurred following other lexical verbs of motion (e.g. *zola* 'run', *uya* 'return'), and 146 occurrences of the ventive movement gram *edza*, which indicate that for these movement grams, approximately one-third of their occurrences were in clauses which already contained a preceding lexical movement verb.

Further information about various features of movement grams, including their historical development and comparison with similar markers in other Bantu languages, can be found in Nicolle (2002b, 2003, 2007a).

5.5.1 Fully grammaticalized movement grams

5.5.1.1 Distal

SC ***cha*** (VC) VS *a*

(449) u-***cha***-mu-amb-ir-a
2SG-DIST-3SG-tell-APPL-FV
'you tell her (over there)'

---

[18] Having said that, Rose et al. (2002:48) state: "Itive is a dependent category, marked by reflexes of *-ka-*." Although Digo does have such a reflex it also has other itive morphemes which means that Rose et al.'s definition is also too restrictive, albeit in a different way from Heine et al. (1993).

[19] The verb stem *phiya* is cognate with Chewa *píta* 'go' and Swahili *pita* 'pass'. The regular sound changes [p] > [β] and [t] > [h] would have resulted in the form **phiha* [βīhā]; subsequently, nasalization and [h] was lost leaving just a glide between the vowels: *phiya* [βija]. Digo *phiya* is also probably cognate with Makhuwa *phíyá* 'arrive'.

The distal movement gram *cha-*[20] operates morphosyntactically as a typical TAM marker in that it occurs in the tense/aspect 'slot' in the verbal complex (immediately prior to the verb or verb complement if there is one) and cannot itself be preceded by another tense marker. It indicates that the action described by the verb phrase occurs at a distance from the deictic centre (the location of the speaker or the notional location of the narrator in a narrative) and is dependent on the TAM marker of the previous verb to establish temporal reference:

(450) "*U-chi-fik-a   kaya   u-si-phiy-e   u-**cha**-mu-ambir-a mche-o ...*"
      2SG-DEP-arrive-FV 9.home 2SG-NEG-go-SUB 2SG-DIST-3SG-tell-FV 1.wife-1.2SG.POS
      '"When you arrive home do not go and tell your wife ..."'

(451) *kala   a-chi-phirik-w-a   ku-a   mgbwanga   a-**cha**-lagul-w-a*
      PST   3SG-IMPFV-take-PAS-FV 17-ASS 1.healer   3SG-DIST-treat-PAS-FV
      '(s/he) would be taken to the healer and treated (there)'

See also examples (455) and (456).

5.5.1.2 Future + itive

   SC **ya** (VC) VS *a*
(452) *a-**ya**-mu-amb-ir-a*
      3SG-FUT.IT-3SG-tell-APPL-FV
      'he has gone to tell her' (he is on the way but has not yet arrived)

The movement gram *ya-*[21] also operates morphosyntactically as a typical TAM marker. The occurrence of *ya-* in the TAM slot before the verb indicates that the event described in the associated verb phrase will occur after the moment of speech and also that the location at which the event will occur is different from the location of the subject of the verb at the moment of speech. Furthermore, when the reference time is the moment of speech, *ya-* indicates that at the moment of speech the subject of the verb is in the process of moving towards the location at which the event occurs.

In the following two examples, the use of *ya-* is appropriate because the subject of the verb is moving towards the location at which the action of the verb

---

[20] The form *cha-* is also the future tense marker in the Makunduchi dialect of Swahili (Maganga 1990:228–229, cited in Kipacha 2006:90) and in the Vumba dialect of Swahili (Nurse and Hinnebusch 1993:420).

[21] The etymology of *ya-* is uncertain, but given that it is an itive marker, and also that cross-linguistically future markers often develop from verbs meaning 'go (to)', a source in a lexical verb meaning 'go (to)' is possible. A number of Bantu languages have a lexical verb 'go' with the form *ya* or *yá* (for example, Tembo J50, Lega D25, Xhosa S41, and Zulu S42) and Digo *ya-* may be a relic of such a verb. The Digo verb *phiya* 'go' is a less likely source as it has developed from *pita/*phiha (described above). A source in a verb meaning 'come', as is the case with the Yanzi ventive marker *yá-* (Rose et al. 2002:90), is also unlikely.

5.5 Movement grams

will take place. Example (453) was a question asked of the author while both he and the speaker were travelling towards Kwale in a car.

(453) U-**ya**-hend-a-dze   Kwale?
 2SG-FUT.IT-do-FV-Q   PLACE_NAME
 'What are you going to do in Kwale?'

In example (454) the clause *Huphiye kuko kaya* 'Let's go back home' indicates that the rest of the conversation takes place during the journey towards home. (The context is that the nephew knows that his uncle's food will have been poisoned, and he is beginning to explain his plan for the uncle to avoid eating the poisoned food without letting the poisoner know that she has been discovered.)

(454) *Wamwamba aphu, "Huphiye kuko kaya. Huchifikako kaya, **huyakuta sahani mbiri**, kulu na ndide. Yo ndide ni yangu mimi muwao, kulu ni yako. **Mino niyahenda choyo**, nihale yo kulu, we uhale yo ndide."*

'He told his uncle, "Let's go back home. When we reach home, **we are going to find two plates**, a big one and a small one. The small one is mine me your nephew, and the big one is yours. **As for me I am going to be selfish** (lit: I am going to do selfishness), and take the big one, and you should take the small one."'

hu-**ya**-kut-a   sahani   mbiri ...
1PL-FUT.IT-meet-FV   10.plates   10.two

Mino   ni-**ya**-hend-a   choyo ...
1SG   1SG-FUT.IT-do-FV   selfishness

In the following two examples, both of which illustrate the uses of *cha-* and *ya-*, the reference time is different from the moment of speech. Example (455) is direct speech in which the speaker informs the addressee that he knows all about his regular activities. The verb phrase *uchaguza* refers to the selling of firewood, and *cha-* indicates that this selling occurs at a different location from the deictic centre, i.e. the location of the speaker and addressee (in a forest). The verb phrase *uyagula chakurya* refers to the subsequent buying of food at yet another location; the reference time subsequent to which this action occurs is that implied by *uchaguza*.

(455) *"Kaziyo ni kutema hino mihi na kutsanga kuni **uchaguza**, uchiphaha pesa, **uyagula** chakurya."*

'"Your work is to chop down these trees and to cut firewood [which] **you sell** (distal), [and] if you get money, **you go and buy** food."'

u-**cha**-guz-a,   u-chi-phah-a   pesa,   u-**ya**-gul-a   chakurya
2SG-DIST-sell-FV   2SG-DEP-get-FV   10.money   2SG-FUT.IT-buy-FV   7.food

Example (456) describes the tradition of *kurima njra* 'farming the road'. In the first sentence, the graves (*vikurani*) are located at a distance from the deictic centre of the description which is the people's homestead, and so *cha-* is used. In the second sentence, the event described using *ya-* occurs subsequent to the time at which people were invited to attend that event, and also in a different location.

(456) *Atu kala achiona makongo gakazidi ama takuna mvula, phahi* **kala achiphiya vikurani a<u>cha</u>voya.** *Halafu kala achialikana kukala siku fulani atu a<u>ya</u>rima njira.*

'If people saw that sickness was increasing or that there wasn't any rain, then **they used to go to the graves and pray.** Then they used to spread the word (lit: invite one another) that on a certain day **people would go and farm** the road.'

kala	a-chi-phiy-a	vikura-ni	a-**cha**-voy-a.
PST	3PL-DEP-go-FV	8.graves-LOC	3PL-DIST-pray-FV
... atu	a-**ya**-rim-a	njira	
2.people	3PL-FUT.IT-farm-FV	9.road	

5.5.1.3 Itive + subjunctive

(SC) **ka** (VC) VS *e*

(457) n-**ka**-fundish-**e**   **Ka**-som-**e**
1SG-IT-teach-SUB   IT-read-SUB
'(that) I (might) go and teach'   'Go and study'

This is a construction consisting of *ka-* which indicates movement to a location and *-e* which is the subjunctive suffix (occurring in final position within the verb group). *Ka- + -e* can only occur in imperative and subjunctive clauses, in line with Botne's observation (1999:482) that itive *ka-* is most likely to occur in the subjunctive or imperative. This means that it occurs in complementary distribution with *enda-* (described below). Like *enda-*, *ka- + -e* indicates that the subject of the verb moves to a location which is not the deictic centre in order to perform the action described in the verb phrase.

5.5.2 Less grammaticalized movement grams

5.5.2.1 Itive 'go'

SC TAM **(kpw)enda** VS *a*

(458) ná-**kpwenda**-mu-ih-a
1SG.PST-IT-3SG-call-FV
'I went and called him'

(459) a-pig-a   mbiru   a-ch-**enda**-mu-endz-a
      3PL.PST-hit-FV   9.horn   3PL-CONS-IT-3SG-search-FV
      'they blew the horn and went and looked for him'

       INF **enda** (VC) VS a
(460) **ku-enda**-mu-ih-a
       INF-IT-3SG-call-FV
       'to go and call him'

       SC TAM (**kpw**)**enda** + SC TAM (VC) VS a
(461) a-ch-**end**-a   a-chi-vuw-a
       3SG-CONS-IT-FV   3SG-CONS-fish-FV
       'he went and fished'

Note that the SC and the TAM marker must be the same on both *enda* and the main verb. Like *edza* (and also the 'emphatic' marker *henda*), *enda* must be preceded by another TAM marker or the infinitive (class 15) prefix, and therefore never occurs in imperative or subjunctive clauses, which means that it is in complementary distribution with the *ka-* + *-e* construction (described above).

Enda indicates movement away from the deictic centre, that is, the location of the speaker or (in a narrative) the notional location of the narrator. In example (462), from an oral narrative, *enda* occurs in two sentences both of which also contain the main verb *phiya* 'go'; this is in line with the observation made at the beginning of this section, that lexical movement verbs typically occur in conjunction with movement grams. The first sentence illustrates the more grammaticalized construction with *enda-*, in which the movement gram immediately precedes the main verb in a single word; in the second sentence *enda* occurs in a less grammaticalized construction in which it behaves morphosyntactically like a verb since it occurs word finally (although there is no longer a lexical verb *enda* in Digo). Nonetheless the construction with *enda* in the second sentence is followed by the main verb with the same subject and TAM markers, and there is no difference in meaning between *achendavuwa* and *achenda achivuwa*, and so I treat *enda* in both constructions as TAM markers. In both cases, *enda* is glossed as 'IT' (for 'itive') since it is functioning as an itive movement gram.

(462) *Kukacha* **waphiya** *pwani ye mwanalume,* **ach<u>enda</u>vuwa**. *Achedza kukacha achiphiya ach<u>enda</u> achivuwa.*

'Early in the morning **he went to** the shore that man, and **he went and fished**. He came early in the morning and **he went and he went and fished**.'

wa-phiy-a   pwani   ye   mwanalume,   a-ch-**enda**-vuw-a ...
3SG.PST-go-FV   16.shore   1.DEM3_VAR 1-man   3SG-CONS-IT-fish-FV

a-chi-phiy-a   a-ch-**end**-a   a-chi-vuw-a.
3SG-CONS-go-FV   3SG-CONS-IT-FV   3SG-CONS-fish-FV

5.5.2.2 Ventive 'come'

	SC TAM (**kpw**)edza VS a, etc.	Negative perfective:
(463)	ná-**kpwedza**-reh-a	s-**edz**-ere-reh-a
	1SG.PST-VENT-bring-FV	1SG.NEG-VENT-PFV-bring-FV
	'I came to bring'	'I did not come to bring'

Edza, meaning 'come to', can occur as a lexical verb or as a movement gram. As a movement gram, it must be preceded by another TAM marker or the infinitive (class 15) prefix, and therefore never occurs in imperative or subjunctive clauses. It indicates movement towards a location, usually the deictic centre. In the following example, a water well is the deictic centre as this is the location at which the last action described in the narrative took place, and so *edza* is used:

(464) Ligundzu   a-chetu   a-k-**edza**-hek-a   madzi.
      morning   2-women   3PL-SEQ-VENT-draw-FV   6.water
      'In the morning the women came and drew water.'

In most clauses containing *edza*, the subject of the clause is the participant which moves towards the deictic centre (as in the examples above). However, it is possible for *edza* to be used in cases where it is a participant other than the subject of the clause which moves; in the following example a person who has died is the grammatical subject of a passive clause containing *edza* but the participants (hyenas) who actually move to the deictic centre (and away from it in the following clause) are the agents of the passive clause, referred to in an oblique noun phrase *ni mafisi* 'by hyenas':

(465) Siku   ya   nne   ya   tsano   yuya   mutu   wa-lum-w-a
      9.day   9.ASS 9.four 9.ASS 9.five 1.DEM2 1.person 3SG.PST-pain-PAS-FV

      n'=chitswa,   a-chi-fw-a   na   a-ch-**edza**-hal-w-a   ni
      COP=7.head   3SG-CONS-die-FV   COM   3SG-CONS-VENT-take-PAS-FV   by

      ma-fisi   a-ch-enda-beben-w-a   ko   ma-tsaka-ni.
      6-hyena   3SG-CONS-ITIVE-crunch-PAS-FV 17.DEM3_VAR 6-forest-LOC

      'On the fourth and fifth day that man had a headache, (then) he died and hyenas came and took him and went and crunched him up in the forest. (lit: **he came and was taken** by hyenas and went and was crunched up in the forest).'

5.6 Complex constructions

In complex constructions, a finite verb form is preceded by either a finite form of the verb *kala* 'be' or the hodiernal past marker *che*. The finite verb form and *kala/che* almost always occur adjacent to each other within a single clause; very occasionally another element, such as the adverb *ndipho* 'then' in the first example below, intervenes between *kala* or *che* and the main verb which follows it, but this is rare.

It has been claimed (for example, by Foley and Van Valin 1984 and Bybee 1985) that there is a relative order of TAM markers with respect to the clause nucleus (i.e. the main verb stem) which holds across languages such that where both tense and aspect are present, an aspect marker occurs closer to the verb stem than a tense marker. What in Role and Reference Grammar are termed status markers (which in Digo includes the dependent and the conditional) occur further from the verb than aspect markers where both are present, but tense and status markers "vary in their position relative to each other across languages" (Van Valin 2005:11). Similarly, movement grams (termed 'directionals' in Role and Reference Grammar) occur closer to the verb than status and tense markers. In Digo, this ordering is reflected in the fact that only status and tense markers occur with *kala* to constitute a finite form of the verb 'be' (*che* is inherently marked for tense). If *kala* is inflected for tense, the main verb which follows it cannot contain a status marker; if *kala* is inflected for status, the main verb must contain either an aspect marker, a movement gram, or a tense marker (which indicates that status markers occur outside of tense in Digo).

5.6.1 Complex constructions with *kala*

When *kala* 'be' functions as an auxiliary verb in complex constructions it can occur with various tenses and status markers. In this section, I will describe past tense forms of *kala* in complex constructions, then other tenses and status markers, and finally complex constructions with *kala* in relative clauses.

5.6.1.1 *Past tense forms of* kala

The most common tense with *kala* in complex constructions is the (remote) past tense. Sometimes *kala* in the past tense is formed with the subject concord and past tense marker, but usually the bare form *kala* is used. In example (466), the full form of *kala* in the past tense is followed by the main verb *rya* 'eat' in the continuous aspect. The unusual use of the full past tense form of *kala* in this example may have been occasioned by the insertion of the adverb *ndipho* 'then' between *wakala* and the main verb and by the fact that this example is the final sentence of a story before the formulaic ending *Hadisi na ngano ichisira hipho* 'The story and fable ends here'.

(466) Yuya mchetu **wakala ndipho anarya** sima na yuya mlume naye kayaphiya tsona mihamboni. Hadisi na ngano ichisira hipho.

'That woman **was then eating** ugali and the man likewise did not go trapping any more. The story and fable ends here.'

wa-kal-a	ndi=pho	a-na-ry-a
3SG.PST-be-FV	COP=16.REF	3SG-CONT-eat-FV

The bare form of *kala* is identical to the past tense copula, the only difference being that in copula constructions *kala* precedes nonverbal predicates whereas in complex constructions *kala* precedes verbal predicates. The following examples illustrate the reduced form of the past tense of *kala* followed by a main verb in the continuous, habitual, imperfective, and anterior aspect, respectively.

(467) **Kala** m-**na**-ni-endzer-a=ni?
PST   2PL-CONT-1SG-search-FV=Q

'Why were you searching for me?'

(468) mwana **kala** **nku**-tsul-w-a   na   mitsanga, badala ya sabuni
1.child   PST   HAB-wash-PAS-FV COM 4.soil instead 9.ASS 9.soap

'a (new-born) child used to be washed with soil, instead of soap'

(469) A-digo **kala** a-**chi**-ishi ndani ya hizi nganasa
2-Digos PST   3PL-IMPFV-live inside 9.ASS 10.DEM1 10.stockades

kama mw-ao   mafwitso-ni.
as   18-3PL.POS 6.hiding_places-LOC

'The Digos lived inside these stockades as their hiding places.'

(470) Ela hiyu **kala** a-**ka**-ni-tiy-a himu ili ni-fw-e
but 1.DEM1 PST 3SG-ANT-1SG-put_in-FV 18.DEM1 so_that 1SG-die-SUB

'But that one had put me in here so that I would die.'

Occasionally, an even more reduced form *ka* can be used in place of *kala*, as in example (471) (a translation of Matthew 11:7b–9 from the Digo New Testament). In the highlighted complex constructions, the reduced past tense forms of *kala* are followed by main verbs marked with the distal TAM marker *cha*.

5.6 Complex constructions

(471) *"Mriphophiya weruni kpwendamsikiza Johana, mwaona myaonani? Dze, mwakpwendalola nyasi zifwihavyo na phuto? Ichikala sio hivyo, sambi **ka mchalolani**? Hebu **ka mchalola** mutu wa kuvwala nguwo ndzuri? Hata! Atu avwalao nguwo nono akala madzumba ga chifalume. Haya niambirani, **kala mchalolani**? Kala mchalola nabii?"*

"'When you went to the desert to go and listen to John, what did you expect you were going to see? Did you go and see how grass is swayed by the wind? If not, then **what did you go and see**? Well **did you go and see** a person wearing beautiful clothes? Not at all! People who wear fine clothes live in royal palaces. So tell me, **what did you go and see? Did you go and see** a prophet?'"

ka   m-**cha**-lol-a=ni
PST   2PL-DIST-see-FV=Q

5.6.1.2 Other TAM forms of kala

The auxiliary verb *kala* can also occur with other TAM markers, followed by a variety of TAM forms on the main verb. The following examples are taken from both nontranslated and translated texts and illustrate some of the possible combinations. First, the future tense form of *kala* is illustrated with continuous, anterior, and past tense forms of the main verb, respectively:

(472) U-**nda**-kal-a   u-**na**-m-lagiz-a   ndi-go-gomb-a.
2SG-FUT-be-FV   2SG-CONT-3SG-command-FV   1SG.FUT-6.REL-speak-FV
'You **will be commanding** him what I tell you.'

(473) Vi-**nda**-kal-a   vi-**ka**-tengb-w-a   ku-a   Mlungu.
8-FUT-be-FV   8-ANT-separate.PAS-FV   17-ASS   1a.God
'They **will be set aside** for God.'

(474) Zo   hali   za   kare   zi-**nda**-kal-a   z-**a**-tsup-a.
10.DEM3_VAR   10.states   10.ASS   past   10-FUT-be-FV   10-PST-pass-FV
'The previous things **will have passed**.'

Second, the sequential tense form of *kala* is illustrated with continuous, anterior and general negative forms of the main verb respectively:

(475) N-**ka**-kal-a   **na**-vweh-a   madzi ...
1SG-SEQ-be-FV   1SG.CONT-draw-FV   6.water
'I **was drawing** water ...'

(476) a-**ka**-kal-a   a-**ka**-vuk-a   rira   lichigo   vino   a-na-phiy-a.
3SG-SEQ-be-FV   3SG-ANT-cross-FV   5.DEM2   5.fence   8.DEM4   3SG-CONT-go-FV
'she **had crossed** the fence and was now going.'

(477) mambo ga dunia, na tamaa za mali nkpwedzalinga-linga rira neno hata **rikakala tarivyala**.

'the cares of the world, and the desire of wealth come and choke the word until **it does not bear fruit**.'

ri-**ka**-kal-a   ta-ri-vyal-a.
5-SEQ-be-FV   NEG-5-bear-FV

Finally, the examples below illustrate *kala* inflected with status markers (the dependent and the conditional) followed by a main verb in either a tense or an aspect. The combinations are respectively dependent *kala* plus future tense on the main verb, conditional *kala* plus anterior aspect on the main verb, and conditional *kala* plus past tense on the main verb:

(478) "Mino che naamba, **uchikala undaphiya** hiko, ukalole rako, mwanangu."

"'I say this, **when you (will) go** there, you look out for yourself, my child.'"

u-**chi**-kal-a   u-**nda**-phiy-a   hiko
2SG-DEP-be-FV   2SG-FUT-go-FV   17.DEM3

(479) N'-**nge**-kal-a   n-**ka**-gbwarur-w-a-gbwarur-w-a ...
1SG-COND-be-FV   1SG-ANT-maul-PAS-FV-maul-PAS-FV

... n'-**nge**-kal-a   **ná**-olag-w-a   ni   simba   hiye.
1SG-COND-be-FV   1SG.PST-kill-PAS-FV   by   1a.lion   1.DEM3

'I could have been mauled ... I could have been killed by this lion.'

5.6.1.3 Relative clauses with **kala**

When complex tenses occur in relative clauses, the relative clause marker occurs on the auxiliary verb *kala* which is followed by the main verb. A short form of the relative clause containing *kala* can be used with the past tense (for example, *yekala* is typically used instead of *ariyekala*). The main verbs in the following examples contain the general negative and continuous aspect, respectively:

(480) Hipho kare, kpwahenda mchetu **yekala karya** sima, arya nyama bahi.

'Once upon a time there was a woman **who did not eat** ugali, she ate meat only.'

ye-kal-a   ka-ry-a
PST.3SG.REL-be-FV   3SG.NEG-eat-FV

5.6 Complex constructions

(481) *Hara ayae **ariphokala aredza**, mmwenga wagavyoga mavi.*

'[Those] his companions **when they were coming**, one of them stepped in the excrement.'

*a-**ri**-pho-kal-a a-**r**-edz-a*
3PL-PST-16.REL-be-FV 3PL-CONT-come-FV

Relative clauses with *kala* are also used to express resultative situations, that is, resultant states arising from an event. The following examples illustrate the resultative aspect and the resultative use of the anterior aspect, respectively:

(482) *yuya ye-kal-a a-seg-**ere** chihi*
1.DEM2 PST.3SG.REL-be-FV 3SG-be_seated-PFV 7.chair

'the one who **was seated** on the chair'

(483) *amreha mutu **yekala akaphola** mwiri mzima*

'they brought him a man **who was paralysed** in his whole body'

*ye-kal-a a-**ka**-phol-a mwiri m-zima*
PST.3SG.REL-be-FV 3SG-ANT-be_paralysed-FV 3.body 3-whole

In this final example, the *amba*-relative construction is used with *kala*:

(484) *hara amba-o m-**nda**-kal-a m-**ka**-a-tsambul-a*
2.DEM2 REL-3PL.REL 2PL-FUT-be-FV 2PL-ANT-3PL-choose-FV

'those whom **you will have chosen**'

5.6.2 Complex constructions with *che*

Complex constructions concerning events that happened earlier on the day of an utterance cannot be formed using *kala*; instead, the hodiernal past tense marker *che* must be used. *Che* is a free morpheme which does not inflect for tense, aspect or movement since it is inherently a hodiernal tense marker. In the following examples *che* is used in complex constructions followed in (485) by the continuous aspect and in (486) by the anterior aspect:

(485) *Hiyu **rero che anaganyirwa** utajiri ni nduguye, yuya liwali muphya.*

'This one **today he was being provided with** riches by his brother, the new governor.'

*rero che a-**na**-ganyir-w-a*
today HOD 3SG-CONT-provide-PAS-FV

(486) *Ng'ondzi rangu* **che rikaangamika** *na vino nkariphaha.*

'My sheep **was lost (earlier today)** and now it has been found.'

che	ri-**ka**-angamik-a
HOD	5-ANT-be_lost-FV

Che used as a hodiernal past tense marker is identical to the hodiernal copula, the only difference being that in copula constructions *che* precedes nonverbal predicates whereas in complex constructions *che* precedes verbal predicates. The following example illustrates the use of *che* in a negative existential copula construction:

(487) *Anaambwa ni mchewe, "Nyama hiyu ni ye ariye mo chumbani, mino* **che taphana mboga** *nkamtsindza."*

'He was told by his wife, "This animal is the one which was in the room, **there was no sauce** (food) so I slaughtered it."'

che	**ta**-pha-na	mboga
HOD	NEG-16-COM	9.sauce

Hodiernal *che* must be distinguished from the formally identical focus marker illustrated in example (488) (the focus marker *che* has been translated freely as 'for certain' but could equally well have been translated as 'honestly', 'really', or 'actually'):

(488) *Yuya mutu waangalala sana mwakpwe rohoni, "Nimuambedze yuno mkpwazangu, na mino* **che namanya** *kala kulungu ndiye wangu na ndiye chemreha hipha.*

'That man was astonished in his soul, "What shall I tell my wife, for **I know for certain** that the antelope was mine and it was me who brought it here."'

che	na-many-a
FOC	1SG.CONT-know-FV

5.7 Different forms of *ka*-

In this chapter, five TAM markers written as *ka*- have been described using the following labels: hodiernal past, sequential, anterior, potential, and itive + subjunctive. In this section we will look at evidence for treating the hodiernal past, sequential, anterior, and potential forms of *ka*- as distinct morphemes and suggest how they might be linked historically. The itive use of *ka*- is restricted to imperative and subjunctive clauses and will not be discussed further here.

In the closely related language Duruma, two *ka*- morphemes can be distinguished tonally, but in Digo any tonal distinctions have been lost.[22] However, in

---

[22] I recorded and interviewed Digo speakers from three locations in the Digo area; the only person

5.7 Different forms of ka-

Digo, as well as differences in meaning, there are differences of form between the four *ka-* markers in the way they form the negative:

sequential and potential: SC-*ka*-NEG-VS-*a* (where NEG = *sa*)
hodiernal and anterior: NEG-SC-*ka*-VS-*a*

The sequential and potential forms share a negation strategy with the infinitive but no other TAM markers. If there are historical links between the forms, the different negation strategies might suggest that the sequential tense and the potential status markers form one historical pairing, and the hodiernal tense and anterior aspect markers form another historical pairing.

In attempting to reconstruct the historical development of the various *ka-* TAM morphemes in Digo, we will be guided by the following principles:

1. Given a single form with a variety of functions, the more widely attested a function is cross-linguistically, the more likely it is to be inherited; conversely, the less widely attested a given function is cross-linguistically, the more likely it is to be an innovation.

2. If a historical change of the form X > Y has been widely documented for other languages, and a change of the form Y > X has been less widely or never documented, the relation between X and Y in Digo will be assumed to be X > Y and not Y > X. The development of Y need not entail the disappearance of X; as Lichtenberk (1991:37) notes, "one commonly finds the old and the new structure coexisting, often for a considerable period of time."

It is therefore necessary to look at the distribution of *ka-* forms in other related languages, and at cases of historical change in other languages involving the functional categories expressed by *ka-* in Digo.

5.7.1 Evidence from Northeast Coast Bantu languages

Wald (1976:272) observes that *ka-* is used as a consecutive or sequential marker following the hodiernal past in all the Mijikenda speech varieties (Duruma, Chonyi, Giryama, etc.), regardless of whether the marker of the hodiernal past in a given language is *ka-* or some other form. For example, Duruma and Giryama both have a hodiernal tense marker *dza-* which is probably an innovation deriving from the verb *dza* 'come' (Wald 1976:272; Sirya et al. 1993:18). The hodiernal past tense marker *dza-* is used if an event which occurred earlier on the same day is the first of a series of events or is described in isolation, and *ka-* is used for subsequent consecutive events. In a corpus of translated material (the New Testament) in Duruma and Giryama and in the closely related

---

who made any tonal distinction between different uses of /ka/ was a speaker whose mother was a Duruma and who was bilingual in Digo and Duruma, and even she had difficulty in deciding which was the appropriate tone in certain utterances. Nurse (2008:244), citing Nurse and Philippson (2006), notes that although itive and narrative (that is, sequential) *ka* forms in a number of Bantu languages are overwhelmingly low tone, when *ka* has developed into past or future tenses tonal data is inconclusive.

Northeast Coast language Pokomo, sequential *ka-* is found to follow not only the hodiernal past but also the infinitive, habitual aspect, present tense relative clauses, and tenseless relative clauses (but not the past and future). This strongly suggests that *ka-* functions as the sole sequential marker following all tenses and aspects except past and future in these languages as well as in Digo. This in turn suggests that the sequential use of *ka-* in Digo is an inherited function.

The use of *ka-* to indicate potential status is shared with other closely related languages. In Swahili, verbs following *-sije*, which is cognate with Digo *-sedze*, are marked with *ka-*[23]:

(489) *Kimbilieni milimani,* **msije** *m**ka**angamia.* (Swahili)
'Flee to the hills, lest you be destroyed.' (Genesis 19:17b)

(490) *Msinung'unikiane nyinyi kwa nyinyi* **msije** *m**ka**hukumiwa.* (Swahili)
'Do not grumble against one another lest you be judged.' (James 5:9a)

Ka- is also used as a potential marker in Giryama (following *sidze*) as illustrated by the Digo and Giryama translations of John 12:35:

(491) *Nyendekani mwangani* **msedze** *m**ka**gbwirwa ni jiza.* (Digo)
Tsemberani kahi za mulangaza, **sidze** *mu**ka**git'anirwa ni kiza.* (Giryama)
'Walk in the light lest you be caught by darkness.'

In Giryama, *ka-* is also used in the result clause of conditional sentences when these are not preceded by a negative command/subjunctive or *sedze*. In Digo and Swahili the forms *ngali* for past conditions and *nge* for present conditions are used in such cases.

(492) *Kala marima ma**ka**pata matsere.* (Giryama)
'If they had dug, they would have got maize.' (Sirya et al. 1993:50)

(493) *Kala nikuuka vivi kare ni**ka**fika mudzini saa ne.* (Giryama)
'If I left now, I would arrive home at 10 o'clock.' (Sirya et al., 51)

Giryama and Digo are very closely related, but Digo has borrowed from Swahili to a greater extent than Giryama which raises the possibility that the use of *ka-* to express potential may once have been more widespread in Digo than is currently the case. It seems more likely that potential *ka-* is an inherited feature of all three languages than that it is a borrowing into Digo from Swahili or an independent innovation in all three languages. In addition, in grammars of a number of other Eastern Bantu languages, *ka-* forms are glossed with labels such as 'if, when, conditional, participial', which seem to resemble the potential use of *ka-* in Digo. Nurse (2008:243) notes that these functions are most frequent

---

[23] The only other use of *ka-* in Swahili is as a consecutive/sequential marker.

in "a thin continuous strip of languages along the east coast and just inland, from Kenya through central and southern Tanzania, Malawi, Mozambique, and into northern South Africa." The potential use of *ka-* in Digo would therefore appear to be an inherited form.

Whilst the sequential and potential uses of *ka-* in Digo seem to be inherited features, only in Digo is *ka-* used as an anterior aspect marker and a hodiernal past tense marker, suggesting that these uses of *ka-* in Digo are innovations. These hypotheses correlate with the fact that the sequential and potential *ka-* forms are negated using SC-*ka-sa*-VS-*a* whilst the hodiernal and anterior *ka-* forms are negated using NEG-SC-*ka*-VS-*a*. Negation with *sa-* is only otherwise found in Digo in the negative infinitive construction and may be a relic of an early negation strategy which has elsewhere been replaced by the use of negative prefixes in the initial slot in the verb group. It is possible that, as *ka-* developed distinct anterior and hodiernal functions, it was negated using the more recent and productive NEG-SC-*ka*-VS-*a* strategy, whilst the inherited sequential and potential *ka-* forms retained the earlier, nonproductive SC-*ka-sa*-VS-*a* strategy.

5.7.2 Historical development

The sequential and potential uses of *ka-* are likely to be inherited forms, as noted above. They are conceptually related in that the sequential use of *ka-* describes an event as part of a temporal and/or causal sequence or as a culmination, whilst the potential use *ka-* describes an event as part of an as yet unrealized sequence of events. However, whether they are historically related will not concern us here, as we are assuming that Digo inherited both functions.

The questions that we will seek to answer are:
1. Are the hodiernal and anterior uses of *ka-* derived from the sequential and/or potential, or are they derived from an independent source which has an accidental similarity of form?
2. Is there a historical relationship between the hodiernal and anterior uses of *ka-* and if so which was the source construction?

5.7.2.1 *Sequential as a source category*

Cross-linguistically, sequential markers are a common source in various grammaticalization chains (contiguous stages in the development of, for example, a TAM maker). Sequential markers typically describe events which are discrete and bounded, and they are therefore common sources of perfectives,[24] as well

---

[24]For example, Hopper (1982:13) views the development of the Russian perfective as a grammaticalization of the function of indicating a sequence of events. This is not the only possible direction of change, however. Apparently, the opposite direction of change is happening in Lucazi (a Bantu

as anteriors ('perfects') and past tenses (Heine et al. 1991:240). However, in most Bantu languages in which a sequential with the form *ka-* has developed into a past tense, the resulting gram indicates far past rather than near or hodiernal past (Nurse 2008:305). This suggests that sequential *ka-* in Digo is more likely to have been the immediate source of the anterior than of the hodiernal past.

Although it is possible that the anterior use of *ka-* developed from an inherited sequential *ka-* form, it is also possible (given the different negative constructions) that the anterior use of *ka-* is historically independent of the sequential. However, even if this is the case, the similarity of meaning between the sequential and anterior, together with the similarity of form, may have resulted in the distinctions between these uses blurring over time, such that when events that are both sequential and completed are marked by *ka-*, it can be difficult to determine whether *ka-* is intended to mark sequential or anterior (or whether both uses coalesce in such cases).

5.7.2.2 Historical relations between anterior and hodiernal

Anterior and hodiernal *ka-* share the same negation strategy as most other TAM categories—the use of a negative prefix in the initial slot in the verb group—and are Digo innovations. It is possible that there is no historical relationship between them and that the hodiernal and anterior uses of *ka-* arose independently of each other. Alternatively, one could have developed from the other. Cross-linguistically, there is a tendency for anterior markers to develop into hodiernal past tense markers, rather than the reverse (Nicolle 2012). For example, Nurse (2008:266) observes that the Proto-Bantu anterior suffix **-ile* has developed into past tenses in a number of Bantu languages, and in the absence of an overt preverbal tense marker, these reflexes of **-ile* are more often markers of near past than of far pasts. Together with the likelihood of the anterior (but not the hodiernal) use of *ka-* having derived from the sequential use, the hodiernal use of *ka-* is probably a development from the anterior, rather than either being the source of the anterior or the two being unrelated.

The following two scenarios illustrate how the hodiernal past usage of *ka-* could have developed from the anterior use. In the first scenario, the hodiernal past usage developed from the resultative use of anterior *ka-* to describe bodily states (such as being tired, wearing clothes, holding something, etc.). Since bodily states tend to last no more than a day, the events leading up to them (becoming tired, putting on clothes, picking something up, etc.) usually occur on the same day and so *ka-* became reanalysed as a hodiernal past marker. In the other scenario, hodiernal *ka-* developed directly from the anterior use, without an intervening resultative stage. Anteriors indicate completed events without explicit temporal reference and therefore, in the absence of an explicit temporal marker (such as the past tense copula *kala*) indicating past

---

language spoken in Angola), where the perfective (in the form of a low-tone *a*) is used in narrative texts "in order to express a strictly consecutive order of actions or processes" (Fleisch 2000:161).

5.7 Different forms of ka-

time reference, verbs marked by the anterior will be viewed as being completed at or before the moment of speech. The default time frame in which such events are conceived is thus likely to coincide with what Hewson et al. (2000:47) call 'retentive memory' or 'the working memory of consciousness.' This, together with the fact that Digo already had a general past tense marker, *a-*, could have led to *ka-* developing into a hodiernal past marker.

In both of these scenarios, neither of which can be preferred with any certainty over the other, Digo already had an inherited past tense marker *a-*. Thus, when *ka-* developed into a hodiernal past (by whatever route) *a-* was restricted from being a general past tense to marking remote past reference.

6

Other Word Classes

So far, we have taken a semasiological (form-to-function) approach to the description of Digo. A particular form (say, an element occurring in a particular position within the verbal group, or a specific TAM marker) was chosen as the object of description, and the various functions associated with this form were described. In this chapter we will also at times adopt an onomasiological (function-to-form) approach in which we will take a particular function (or a related set of functions) and show how this function (or set of functions) is expressed in Digo.

We will first look at relational expressions, that is, expressions which relate elements within a clause to each other. These may be expressed by a variety of constructions which correspond to prepositions and conjunctions in Indo-European languages, although we will see that in Digo the distinction between prepositions and conjunctions cannot be systematically maintained, and indeed some 'prepositions' may be better characterized as noun phrases.[1]

The second section deals with sentence adverbials, discourse markers, and additives. These word classes help the addressee to interpret clauses and longer stretches of discourse in their contexts.

The third section discusses modal and degree adverbs and ideophones. The expressions discussed in this section cannot be coherently grouped together according to morphological or syntactic criteria, but they all describe or emphasize some quality of the expression which they modify; that is, they all share

---

[1] The term 'relational expression' is used in a similar way to the terms 'relational noun' and 'relational marker' in the Mayan languages, which also use possessed nouns to indicate a number of relations (location, agency, instrument, etc.) which are usually expressed by prepositions in Indo-European languages (Costello 2003).

a common set of functions. Similarly, the sentence adverbials and discourse markers discussed in the second section constitute a heterogeneous set morphologically, although syntactically they are adjuncts, but they share a common function of relating clauses or longer stretches of discourse to the wider context, including other parts of the text and the perspective of the speaker.

6.1 Relational expressions

This section deals with a number of expressions in Digo which occur before noun phrases and which describe relations between entities. Such expressions may indicate relative location (the relation between an entity and a place), but some can also be used to describe the relation between an entity and a beneficiary, between an action and a place, or between a time and an action. Other expressions of locality are discussed elsewhere and so will not be mentioned again here, such as locative noun classes and the locative suffix -*ni* (§3.1.4.3.2) and the applicative verbal extension (§4.1.8.3), which can be used to indicate a relation between an entity and a beneficiary or place.

Many of the expressions discussed in this section correspond to what are traditionally termed prepositions. However, I have avoided using the term 'preposition' since it is not easy to maintain a clear-cut distinction in Digo between prepositions and conjunctions on the one hand, and on the other hand between prepositions and nouns. In this, I follow Amidu (2001:283), who observes with respect to Swahili that, "perfectly common nouns like *juu* (upper part), *mbele* (the front), *nyuma* (the back), and even fossilized locatives like *chini* (on the ground), *ndani* (in at the interior) are often called prepositions by seasoned Bantu linguists when in fact the lexical words are nouns or nominal phrases." Evidence in favour of this view comes from the fact that the expressions in question often co-occur with the class 9 or 10 form of the associative particle (*ya* or *za*) and the possessive (*yake*, *zake*, etc.) in both Swahili and Digo. The resulting relational expressions behave like typical preposition phrases, however, which has caused some authors to refer to the associative particle as a preposition.

This section begins with a discussion of the comitative particle *na* (§6.1.1), followed by a discussion of the associative particle *-a* (§6.1.2). Cognate forms of both particles are found in many other Bantu languages. Schadeberg (2003:73) refers to the comitative particle *na* as a "clitic preposition" and other authors, e.g. Elderkin (2003:604-5) and Güldemann (2003:188), refer to both *na* and the associative particle *-a* as 'prepositions'. This reflects the fact that the distinction between 'prepositions' and 'conjunctions' is difficult to maintain in many Bantu languages, and so I will not try to impose this distinction on the Digo data, preferring simply to describe the various constructions involving *na* and *-a*. We will then consider locative expressions (§6.1.3 and 6.1.4), the associative particle *-enye* (§6.1.5), nonfinite verb forms with verbs of movement (§6.1.6), and finally the use of the copula *ni* to create agent phrases in passive sentences (§6.1.7).

6.1.1 The comitative particle *na*

The basic function of *na* is to indicate an association between two or more elements, but the elements themselves and the nature of the association between them are of various kinds. When the elements which *na* relates are of the same kind (clause, noun phrase, etc.) *na* functions grammatically as a coordinating conjunction. In other cases, the element which *na* precedes functions grammatically as an oblique and *na* functions as a preposition. Rather than say that there are two distinct forms of *na*: a coordinating conjunction and a preposition (which would make *na* polysemous), I maintain an analysis in which there is a single comitative particle *na* and will refer to conjunctive and prepositional uses of *na*.

6.1.1.1 *Conjunctive uses of* na

The following examples illustrate the function of *na* as a conjunction coordinating noun phrases and clauses respectively:

(494) mutu **na** mchewe
 1.person COM 1.wife-1.3SG.POS
 'a man **and** his wife' (coordinating conjunction)

(495) u-k-edza-tem-a mihi **na** ku-tsang-a kuni
 2SG-HOD-VENT-fell-FV 4.trees COM INF-chop-FV 9.firewood
 'you have come to fell trees **and** chop firewood' (coordinating conjunction)

If *na* precedes a noun phrase, it takes the form of a free morpheme (a separate word) but if it precedes a pronominal element it can optionally take the form of a clitic and be attached to either the short form of an independent personal pronoun or the referential marker (see §6.3.2 for further discussion). In example (496), the short form of the 3SG independent pronoun *ye* refers to the same referent as *mcheo* in the previous clause and has the grammatical role of subject; *na* functions as a conjunction and coordinates the two clauses.

(496) Mendz-a atu a mcheo **na=ye** a-nda-mendz-a
 like-FV 2.people 2.ASS 1.your_wife COM=1.REF 3SG-FUT-like-FV

 atu-o.
 2.people-2.2SG.POS
 'Like your wife's relatives **and she** will like your relatives.'

Conjunctive *na* can indicate an association between two locations represented by locative noun phrases. The collocation of *na* with *dza phapha* (*phapha* is the longer variant of the class 16, type 1 demonstrative) and the locative demonstrative *ko* (the shortened variant of the class 17, type 3 demonstrative) is an idiomatic expression meaning 'from here to there':

(497) a-chi-phiy-a   hadi   dza   phapha   **na**   ko   Golini
      3SG-CONS-go-FV   until   as   16.DEM1_VARIANT   COM   17.REF   PLACE_NAME
      'he went as far as from here to Golini'

6.1.1.2 Prepositional uses of *na*

With prepositional uses of *na*, the noun phrase which it precedes functions grammatically as an oblique. Examples (498) and (499) illustrate the use of *na* to introduce obliques of accompaniment.

(498) a-chi-nyamal-a   mutu   yuyu,   wala
      3SG-CONS-be_silent-FV 1.person   1.DEM1_VARIANT   nor
      ka-ya-gomb-a   **na**   **mutu**
      3SG.NEG-PST-speak-FV   COM   1.person
      'he became/remained silent that man, neither did he speak **to (with) anybody**'

(499) a-chi-kutan-a   **na**   **a-vuvi**   a-na-phiy-a   pwani
      3SG-CONS-meet-FV   COM   2-fishermen   3PL-CONT-go-FV   17.sea_shore
      'he met **with some fishermen** going to the sea-shore'

In example (500), *na* is attached as a clitic to the short form of the 3SG independent personal pronoun *ye* (which is identical to the noun class 1 referential marker), just as it was in example (496) where *na* functioned as a conjunction. This provides additional evidence for a unified analysis of *na*, In this example, *ye* refers to the person referred to by the 3SG verb complement concord ('object marker') *m* in the previous clause and has an oblique grammatical role.

(500) a-chi-m-tuluz-a   m-zima   a-chi-phiy-a   **na=ye**   kaya.
      3PL-CONS-3SG-remove-FV 1-whole   3PL-CONS-go-FV   COM=1.REF   5.home
      'they got him out alive and took him home (lit: and went **with him** home).'

In example (501), the second *na* introduces what is grammatically an oblique of accompaniment but what is semantically the agent of an action (despite the English gloss and the fact that the agent introduced by *na* is singular, the verb form *asionane* is reciprocal rather than passive). The first *na* indicates an association between a participant and a location (a locative oblique):

6.1 Relational expressions

(501) Wa-tserer-a,   a-chi-gbwir-a   **na**   **vuwe-ni**
      3SG.PST-descend-FV 3SG-CONS-catch-FV   COM   forest-LOC

  a-si-on-an-e   **na**   yuya   a-chi-ye-hum-w-a ...
  3SG-NEG-see-RECIP-SUB   COM   1.DEM2   3SG-ANT-1.REL-send-PAS-FV

  'He got down (out of the tree where he was hiding), and he fled **into the forest** (lit: he seized with forest-LOC) so that he wouldn't be seen **by the one who had been sent** (to look for him) ...'

A temporary state such as hunger, thirst or tiredness, can be attributed to a participant in a discourse when the noun in question functions as an oblique introduced by *na*:

(502) Wa-lal-a   **na**   ndzala   ku-ka-ch-a   ligundzu.
      3SG.PST-sleep-FV   COM   9.hunger   17-ANT-dawn-FV   11.morning

  'He went to sleep hungry (lit: He slept **with hunger**) until early in the morning.'

Another use of *na* is as part of a 'presentational construction'[2] introducing a major participant (especially the protagonist) into a narrative. Presentational contructions in which the SC is in class 17 and class 16 are illustrated in examples (503) and (504), respectively:

(503) Hipho kare,   ku-a-kal-a   **na**   mutu   m-mwenga ...
      long ago   17-PST-be-FV   COM   1.person   1-one

  'Long ago, there was a man ... (lit: there was with a man)'

(504) Chisha   pha-chi-kal-a   **na**   m-jeni   phapho
      then   16-CONS-be-FV   COM   1-stranger   16.DEM3_VARIANT

  pha-o   lalo-ni.
  16-3PL.POS   location-LOC

  'Now there was a stranger (lit: there was with a stranger) there at their place.'

Na is also used to specify the instrument used to perform a given action or the means by which an action occurs. In this use, *na* plus the noun phrase specifying the instrument together constitute an 'instrumental oblique'; four examples are provided below:

(505) u-na-fwidz-a   **na**   chifwidzo
      2SG-CONT-stir-FV   COM   7.whisk

  'you stir (it) **with a whisk**'

---

[2]The other most common presentational construction uses *kuahenda* (orthographically *kpwahenda*) literally: 'there did', without *na*.

(506) u-kat-e   milala   u-i-anik-e   **na**   dzuwa
     2SG-cut-SUB   4.raffia   2SG-4-put_out_to_dry-SUB   COM   5.sun
     'cut raffia and put it out to dry **in the sun**'

(507) a-chi-sikir-a   mutu   a-na-mu-ih-a,   tsona
     3SG-CONS-hear-FV   1.person   3SG-CONT-3SG-call-FV   moreover

     na   dzina-re
     COM   5.NAME-5.3SG.POS
     'he heard someone call him, moreover **by his name**'

(508) yuya   bwana   ye-kpwedz-a   **na**   meli
     1.DEM2   1a.man   3SG.REL-come-FV   COM   9.ship
     'that man who came **by ship**'

Na can also indicate the cause of an action; in example (509), 'fear' (*wasiwasi*) is the cause of the subject's shivering:

(509) Lakini   a-ri-pho-uk-a   n-chi-baki   pharatu
     but   3SG-PST-16.REL-return-FV   1SG-CONS-remain   16.DEM2_VARIANT

     na-kakam-a   **na**   wasiwasi.
     1SG.CONT-shiver-FV   COM   fear
     'But when it (a lion) left I stayed in the same place shivering **with fear**.'

Finally *na* occurs in constructions indicating possession (see also §7.6.4):

(510) A-si-ye   **na**   mwana   ka-many-a   utsungu-we.
     3SG-NEG-1.REL   COM   1.child   3SG.NEG-know-FV   14.pain-14.3SG.POS
     'Whoever does not **have a child** cannot know its pain.'

6.1.2   Forms preceding associative particle -*a* + noun

When two entities are involved and the relation between them is one of location, these can be described as the 'figure' (the thing that is located) and the 'ground' (the location):

(511) [*Hamisi* [figure]] *anasagala* [*ndani ya nyumba* [ground]].
     [Hamisi [*figure*]] is sitting [inside the house [*ground*]]
     'Hamisi is sitting in the house.'

It is also possible to talk about the 'path'[3] that a figure travels along:

---

[3] The terms 'figure', 'ground', and 'path' are well-established. Miller and Johnson-Laird (1976) and Talmy (1985) are two classic studies of how movement events are described. See also Thornell

(512) [Hamisi [figure]] anamenya [ndani ya nyumba [path]].
[Hamisi [*figure*]] is entering [inside the house [*path*]]
'Hamisi is going into the house.'

As examples (511) and (512) illustrate, there is no distinction between 'in' and 'into' in Digo. Typically in Bantu languages, the same expressions are used to refer to paths and grounds, although there are a few words like *kula* 'from' and *mpaka* 'up to, as far as' which, in combination with a noun phrase, can only express a path. The expression *ndani ya* 'inside' can be used to describe a static location, a goal (or a path culminating in a goal), or a source (or a path originating in a source) as the following examples, all from within a few lines of a single narrative, illustrate, respectively:

(513) u-chere **ndani ya** madzi
2SG-PERS inside 9.ASS 6.water
'you are still **in** the water' (ground – static location)

(514) u-chi-meny-a **ndani ya** madzi
2SG-DEP-enter-FV inside 9.ASS 6.water
'if you enter/go **into** the water' (goal)

(515) u-ka-tuluk-a **ndani ya** madzi
2SG-ANT-come_out-FV inside 9.ASS 6.water
'you have come **out of** the water' (source)

Most relational expressions in Digo precede the class 9 form of the associative particle, *ya*, consisting of the class 9 subject concord plus the associative marker (*i* + *a* > *ya*): *bada ya* 'after, in time', *dzulu ya* 'above, over', *kabla ya* 'before (in time)', *kanda-kanda ya* 'beside', *kahi ya* and *kahi-kahi ya* 'among', *ndani ya* 'inside, into, out of', *nyuma ya* 'behind/in back of', *mbere ya* 'in front of', *tsini ya* 'under, below, beneath'[4] and *bila ya* 'without'. Two of these, *mbere* and *kahi/kahi-kahi* also occur before the noun class 10 form of the associative particle, *za*, with *mbere za* being far more common than *mbere ya*, and one expression, *ndani-ndani za* 'in the midst/middle of' only occurs with *za*. (For more examples of the use of the associative particle, see §3.2.6 on phrasal adjectives.) All of these words can also occur without the associative particle, and for most this is by far the more common usage.

The following examples illustrate the use of *bada* 'after' both with and without the associative particle. The expression *bada ya* can precede a noun and an infinitive verb form (infinitives have many nominal qualities) whilst *bada* alone can only precede a tensed verb form:

(1997) and Nicolle (2007a). When the location is one to which the figure moves (for example *nyumba* 'house' in [512]), it is referred to as the 'goal' rather than the 'ground', and when the location is one from which the figure starts, it is referred to as the 'source'.

[4] *Tsini* derives from *tsi* 'earth, ground' (class 9) plus the locative suffix *-ni*. It can also mean 'on the ground', and this may well have been its original sense.

(516) **Bada** ya mi-ezi mi-iri
after 9.ASS 4-months 4-two
'**After** two months'

(517) **Bada** ya ku-hend-a hivyo a-chi-yay-a.
after 9.ASS INF-do-FV 8.DEM3 3SG-CON-disappear-FV
'**After** doing that she disappeared.'

(518) **Bada** n-ka-mu-on-a ka-dzangbwe-ku-tuluk-a himu tsaka-ni.
after 1SG-HOD-3SG-see-FV 3SG.NEG-INC-INF-leave-FV 8.DEM1 forest-LOC
'**After** I saw him he still hadn't left this forest.'

The expressions *bada* 'after', *dzulu* 'above, over', *ndani* 'inside, into, out of', *nyuma* 'behind/in back of', *mbere* 'in front of', and *tsini* 'under, below, beneath' can also occur with possessives as follows (*mbere* has been used as a representative form):

1SG	*mbere zangu*	in front of me
1PL	*mbere zehu*	in front of us
2SG	*mberezo*	in front of you
2PL	*mbere zenu*	in front of you
3SG	*mbereze*	in front of her/him
3PL	*mbere zao/mbere yao*	in front of them

The following example with *nyuma* 'behind/in back of' illustrates this kind of construction in context:

(519) Wee bwana ndzoo, nyama hiyu a-ka-gbwir-w-a **nyuma-zo.**
2SG 1a.sir come.IMP 1a.animal 1.DEM1 3SG-HOD-catch-PAS-FV behind-10.2SG.POS
'You sir come, this animal was caught behind you/after you had left.'

The locative suffix *-ni* can also be affixed to *mbere* with the sense of 'in the future', although this usage is far rarer than *mbere* used alone. In example (520), *mbereni* is preceded by the class 17 demonstrative *hiko*.

(520) Ye ndiyefwa n'ndamzika, ela nchifwa mimi, utajiri hinyu undakala wenu na **hiko mbereni** ichikala mmwenga naye akafwa, ye ndiyesala andahala utajiri.
'Whoever dies I will bury them, but if I die, this wealth will become yours (plural) and **in the future if one (of you) also dies,** the one who remains will inherit the wealth.'

hiko mbere-ni ichikala m-mwenga na=ye a-ka-fw-a
17.DEM3 in_front-LOC if 1-one COM-1.REF 3SG-ANT-die-FV

6.1 Relational expressions

The fact that *mbere* can take the locative suffix *-ni*, like many nouns, together with the fact that *ya* is the class 9 form of the associative marker, suggests that morphologically *mbere* is actually a noun. The same applies to the other expressions which combine with the associative particle and possessives to form relational expressions. However, these expressions can also be used without an associative particle to represent locations in either space or time, as illustrated below with *nyuma*. Each of these relational expressions can co-occur with different locative noun classes depending on the situation being described, rather than each expression being invariably associated with a specific locative noun class.

(521) **Kuratu**   *nyuma simba naye aredza alole yuya ambaye nkuika nyama.*
      17.DEM2   behind ...

'Right there behind the lion also came to see the person who trapped meat.'

(522) **Nyuma**   *yuyu*   *ndugu-ye*   *mwanachetu*
      behind   1.DEM1_VARIANT   9.sibling-9.3SG.POS   1-female
      wa-bwag-w-a   *ni*   *utsungu.*
      3SG.PST-fill-PAS-FV   by   14.labour_pains

'Afterwards his sister was seized by labour pains.'

6.1.3 Expressions preceding comitative particle *na* + noun

Three expressions which describe relative distance between objects or locations are obligatorily followed by the comitative particle *na* rather than by the associative particle *ya* when there is an overt 'ground' (i.e. a location or object relative to which distance is calculated); these are *kure na* 'far from', *kanda na* 'apart from', and *phephi na* 'near to':

(523) *a-ri-pho-kala*   *a*   **kure**   *chidide*   **na**   *yuya*   *mwana-we* ...
      1-PST-16.REL-be-FV   1SC   far   a_little   COM   1.DEM2   1.child-1.3SG.POS

'when he was **a little way** (lit: far a little) **from** the child ...'

(524) *A-sagal-a*   **kanda**   **na**   *vi-vyazi*   *vya*   *ana*   *anjina.*
      2.PST-live-FV   apart   COM   8-descendants   8.ASS   2.child   2.other

'They lived **apart from** the descendants of the other children.'

(525) *Zimu kala rina tabiya ya kuiha hara asichana wakati kala richifika*
      phephi   **na**   *hira*   *nyumba-ye*
      near   COM   9.DEM2   9.house-9.3SG.POS

'The ghost had a habit of calling out for those girls when it was coming **close to** its house.'

Time can also be treated metaphoricaly as a location with *phephi na*:

(526) *Saa   nane   i   **phephi   na**   ku-fik-a.*
      9.hour   9.eight   9SC   near   COM   INF-arrive-FV
      'It is almost 2 o'clock (lit: 2 o'clock is **near to** arriving).'

More frequently, however, *kure* and *phephi* occur without *na*, sometimes with the sense of 'far away, afar' (527) and (528) and 'nearby' (529):

(527) *a-chi-phiy-a,   a-chi-phiy-a   hata   ndi=pho   a   **kure**   kabisa*
      3SG-CONS-go-FV   3SG-CONS-go-FV   until   COP=16.REF   2.ASS   far   completely
      'he went and he carried on going until **he was really far away**'

(528) *We   bwana   u   m-jeni,   na   atu   a   **kure**   ndi=mwi*
      2SG   1a.sir   2SG   1-stranger   COM   2.people   2.ASS   far   COP=2PL
      a-ganga.
      2-healers
      'You sir are a foreigner, and you **people from afar** are great healers.'

(529) *Na   ná-many-a   ku-na   simba   anjina   **phephi***
      COM   1SG.PST-know-FV   17-COM   2a.lion   2.other   near
      'And I knew that there were other lions **nearby**'

Note also the following adjectival use of *phephi* with the class 7 noun class prefix *chi-*:

(530) *Ná-mu-on-a   **chi-phephi***
      1SG.PST-3SG-see-FV   7-near
      'I saw it (the lion) **close up**'

(531) *Lakini vyo ambavyo analumbana **pho chiphephi** ka phana tsungula.*
      pho   chi-phephi   ka   pha=na   tsungula
      16.DEM3_VAR   7-near   PST   16=COM   9.hare
      'But as they were arguing **there nearby** was a hare.'

An expression which is obligatorily followed by the comitative particle *na* but which does not describe distance is *kulengana na* 'according to':

(532) ***kulengana na***   *mila   za   A-digo*
      according   COM   10.customs   10.ASS   2-Digos
      'according to the customs of the Digo people'

6.1.4 Locative elements preceding nouns

The expressions *dzulu* 'above', *kure* 'far', *ndani* 'inside', *nyuma* 'behind/in back of', *mbere* 'in front of', *phephi* 'near', and *tsini* 'underneath', as well as noun phrases with the locative suffix *-ni*, represent locations and agree with the locative noun classes, but they do not themselves contain one of the locative noun class prefixes. As a result, the precise nature of the location is not always evident from the form of these expressions alone. However, they can be preceded by the reduced variant form of the series 3 (nonproximal) demonstratives (see §3.4.3.1.3) of the appropriate locative noun class.[5] The following examples (and also examples [497] and [520]) illustrate this construction with *kure* 'far' (533), *ndani* 'inside' (534), locative nouns (535) and (536), and a proper noun (537), which incidentally contains a fossilized locative suffix:

(533) A-chi-uk-a   tsona   a-chi-phiy-a   mpaka **ko**   **kure**   hiko.
      3SG-CONS-leave-FV again   3SG-CONS-go-FV   until 18.REF   far   17.DEM3
      'He left again and went as **far** as **over there** (a long way away).'

(534) A-chi-ri-tsuph-a   rira   dzidude   **pho**   **ndani**,
      3SG-CONS-5-throw-FV   5.DEM2   5.box   16.DEM3_VAR   inside
      ri-chi-gbw-a   'Gbwelee'   **ko**   **ndani**.
      5-CONS-fall-FV   'clang'   17.DEM3_VAR   inside
      'He threw that large box (there) **inside**, and it fell "Clang" (there) **inside**.'

(535) A-chi-m-phah-a   m-sichana   **pho**   chivuko-ni.
      3sg-CONS-3SG-get-FV 1-girl   16.DEM3_VAR   ferry-LOC
      'He met the girl (there) **at the ferry**.'

(536) A-meny-a   **mo**   **chisima-ni**   osi   airi.
      3PL.PST-enter-FV   18.DEM3_VAR   well-LOC   2.all 2.two
      'They both entered (there) **inside the well**.'

(537) u-ka-fik-a   **pho**   Rikoni.
      2SG-ANT-arrive-FV   16.DEM3_VAR   PLACE_NAME
      'you have arrived (there) **in Likoni**.'

This construction resembles the process, widespread across Bantu languages, whereby a locative noun class prefix is added to a whole noun (prefix plus stem) to create a locative noun, e.g. Chewa (N31) *ku-mudzi* 'at the village' (Bresnan and Kanerva 1989:2); Nyakyusa (M31) *mu-nyaanja* 'in the lake' (Schadeberg 2003:82);

---
[5] This construction is the likely origin of the fossilized forms *kondze* 'outside' and *photsi* 'below, on the ground' in which the reduced form of the demonstrative (*ko* and *pho*) has become affixed to what was originally a noun.

Rwanda (DJ61) *ku kíbáaho* 'on the blackboard' (Bearth 2003:137, following Kimenyi 1980). However, the Digo construction differs from this process in two important respects: (1) the preceding locative element is a reduced demonstrative *ko*, etc., rather than a noun class prefix *ku*, etc., and (2) the Digo construction is optional in the expression of locative nouns, the default process being the addition to a noun of the locative suffix *-ni*.

6.1.5 Associative particle *-enye* + noun

In addition to the general associative particle *-a*, Digo has another associative particle *-enye*.[6] Used alone or preceded by a noun or independent pronoun *-enye* functions as an emphatic marker, usually glossed as 'oneself', 'myself', 'yourself', itself', etc. (see §3.3.3). In these uses, *-enye* occurs in the final position of a noun phrase and behaves morphologically as an adjective. When preceded by a noun phrase and followed by a further noun phrase, on the other hand, it functions as an associative particle, coordinating two noun phrases into one. This is the function which will be described here.

N + *-enye* + N(possessive) expresses 'N having/with Y':

(538) m-lume **mw-enye** m-chetu na ana-e
 1-male 1-ASS 1-woman COM 2.child-2.3SG.POS
 'a man having/with a wife and children'

When *-enye* occurs with locative noun classes it expresses 'at' or 'in' a place; examples with the locative classes 16, 17, and 18 are illustrated below:

(539) **ph-enye** chivuri-vuri
 16-ASS 7.shade
 'in the shade'

(540) *Sherehe hino nkuhendwa* **kpwenye** *lalo ambaro rakosa mvula siku nyinji.*
 'This ceremony was performed **at a location** which had not had rain for many days.'

 ku-enye lalo
 17-ASS 5.location

---

[6] See also §3.2.6 for the use of this particle in phrasal adjectives and §3.3.3 for its use in emphatic pronouns.

(541) **Himo <u>mwenye</u> kaya** *kala muna mbira ambazo zazikpwa akare.*

'**There inside the homestead** there were graves (in) which had been buried the ancestors.'

Himo	mw-enye	kaya
18.DEM3	18-ASS	5.homestead

6.1.6 Nonfinite verb forms

Nonfinite forms of the verbs *kula* 'to come from', *kuandzira* 'to start from', *kutsapira* 'to pass along/through', and *kufikira* 'to arrive at' function as relational expressions. Note that in example (542), the invariable word *hadi* 'until, as far as' could be replaced by *kufikira* 'to arrive at' with little change of meaning:

(542) *Anaamba kukala waandza kuhumira Chiswahili* **kuandzira** *Port Said hiko ntsi ya Misiri,* **kutsapira** *pwani ya Afrika Mashariki* **hadi** *Durban na Cape Town hiko Afrika ya Kusini.*

'He says that he was able to use Swahili **(starting) from** Port Said in Egypt, **(passing) all along** the East African coast **until/as far as** Durban and Cape Town in South Africa.'

6.1.7 Agent phrases in passive sentences

In a passive sentence, the agent (i.e. the subject in a corresponding active sentence) can optionally be marked as an oblique argument following the passive verb phrase. Fleisch (2005) describes various ways in which Bantu languages express agents in passive sentences: in some Bantu languages (e.g. Swahili, Shona) the agent NP is preceded by a comitative marker; in others (e.g. Tonga, Ila, Luba) the agent is expressed as a locative; in others (e.g. Venda) the agent is marked in the same way as an instrument; in others (e.g. the Sotho-Tswana group, Xhosa and Zulu) the agent NP is preceded by a copula; and in yet others (e.g. Ganda, Haya) the agent NP occurs after the passive verb phrase without any morphological marker. Digo employs the strategy of using *ni*, which is a form identical to a copula particle (glossed as COP), to mark the agent NP:

(543)	yuya	m-chetu	wa-uz-w-a	**ni**	m-lume-we
	1.DEM2	1-woman	3SG.PST-ask-PAS-FV	COP	1-husband-1.3SG.POS

'the woman was asked **by** her husband'

The agent need not be animate, as example (544) illustrates; the trap is not being encoded as an instrument in this example, as instruments are preceded by the comitative particle *na* (see §6.1.1.2), as in example (545) which is provided to illustrate the contrast.

(544) yuya   m-chetu   a-chi-gbwir-w-a   **ni**   mu-hambo
      1.DEM2   1-woman   3SG-CONS-catch-PAS-FV   COP   3-trap
      'the woman was caught **by** (i.e. in) the trap'

(545) Nganasa   hizi   kala   zi-ka-dzeng-w-a   **na**   mikowa   ya
      10.stockades   10.DEM1   PST   10-ANT-build-PAS-FV   COM   4.ropes   4.ASS

      mbugu.
      10.vines

      'These stockades were built **with** ropes made from vines.'

When using the passive verb form *lumwa* 'be pained' to describe a part of the body which is hurting, the body-part NP is also preceded by the copula particle *ni*, which (here and in genuine agent phrases) can occur in a reduced form as a clitic attached to the following noun:

(546) yuya   mutu   wa-lum-w-a   **n'**=chitswa
      1.DEM2   1.person   3SG.PST-pain-PAS-FV   COP=7.head
      'the man had a headache'

6.2 Sentence adverbials and discourse markers

6.2.1 Definitions

Sentence adverbials and discourse markers are adjuncts which occur outside the clause or clauses which they modify (for example, they occur to the left or right of the verb and its arguments and are not represented in verbal morphology as concords). For the purposes of this section, sentence adverbials are taken to be expressions which relate to a single clause, specifying the mode of the predicate, or the attitude that the speaker holds in relation to the proposition, or providing clarification of the proposition expressed (for example, by introducing a reformulation). Discourse markers, on the other hand, relate to longer stretches of discourse and encode instructions to the addressee as to how to relate the associated stretch of discourse to the wider context. They can be thought of as instructing the addressee to interpret the associated stretch of discourse in a particular way: for example as being inferrable from the context (hence expressing an implicated conclusion), as reinforcing what has already been communicated, as contradicting an expectation set up by the preceding discourse or context, or as being independent of what has previously been communicated (hence indicating a new episode). Some discourse markers also indicate the speaker's attitude or degree of commitment towards the associated stretch of discourse.

Both sentence adverbials and discourse markers are (or consist of) invariable words. Note that: (a) the sentence adverbials and discourse markers described below constitute a representative rather than an exhaustive list, and (b) since

6.2.2 Modal sentence adverbials

Some words express epistemic modality, i.e. the speaker's opinion as to whether the clause is true or not. Modal adverbs follow verbs and are part of the clause headed by the verb (see §6.4.1.1) but modal sentence adverbials describing degrees of certainty (e.g. *hakika* 'certainly', *samba* 'surely', *chahi, labuda, mendzerepho, pengine* 'maybe, perhaps, possibly') are adjuncts occurring outside the clause, usually preceding it:

(547) **Samba** m-ka-sikir-a enye habari-ze.
surely 2PL-ANT-hear-FV yourselves 10.news-10.3SG.POS
'**Surely** you yourselves have heard about him.'

(548) **Labuda** ku-ya-phand-a vizuri.
perhaps 2SG.NEG-PST-plant-FV well
'**Maybe** you did not plant well.'

6.2.3 Question words

The clitic *dze* (§4.1.11.1) also occurs as a free morpheme preceding (or occasionally following) a clause.

(549) **Dze,** u-na-tak-a ku-rya go ama dii?
Q 2SG-CONT-want-FV INF-eat-FV a_little or all_day
"Well, do you want to eat little or all day long?'

Dze usually functions as a polar interrogative marker (that is, it signals a 'yes/no' question), but if another explicit interrogative marker is present in the clause which it modifies, *dze* is redundant as an interrogative marker and indicates instead the speaker's attitude of surprise, shock or disapproval. This function is very similar to that of the Swahili cognate *je* as described in Nicolle (2000). In this analysis, *je* indicates that the clause which it modifies should be interpreted as a representation of a thought from which the speaker wishes to dissociate herself. This function and that of marking clauses as interrogative are both cases of what in Relevance Theory is termed 'interpretive use' of language. In example (550), the clitic *dze* on the clause *andaphiyadze* 'how will she go' already marks the clause as interrogative; the preceding independent word *dze* contributes to the expression of surprise and disapproval on the part of the speaker, which is reinforced by the use of *lakini* 'but'—here connecting stretches of discourse rather than clauses—plus the adjunct *sambi* 'now', preceding *dze*, and the exclamative *mbavi*, which explicitly indicates surprise within the clause itself.

(550) **Lakini sambi <u>dze</u>, andaphiya<u>dze</u>** ichikala mbavi we ko kpwako ye ambaye ka anahusika alavye chitu kadzangbwelavya.

'But now, how will she go, if surprisingly you there in your place, the one who is required to offer something has not yet offered (it).'

Lakini	sambi	**dze,**	a-nda-phiy-a=**dze**
but	now	Q	3SG-FUT-go-FV=Q

Other question words express the speaker's attitude of surprise, shock, disapproval, etc., in addition to questioning the reason for a particular state of affairs. In this respect, the expressions below differ from the less emotionally charged expression *kpwa utu wani* 'why' which need not convey any particular attitude on the part of the speaker.

(551) Ichikala na-gomb-a kpweli, **kpwadze** ta-m-ni-amini?
if 1SG.CONT-speak-FV truly why NEG-2PL-1SG-believe

'If I am telling the truth, **why** don't you believe me?'

(552) **Mbona** mbeyu-zo zi-na-mer-a, z-angu ta-zi-mer-a?
why 10.seed-10.2SG.POS 10-CONT-sprout-FV 10-1SG.POS NEG-10-sprout-FV

'**Why** are your seeds growing and mine are not growing?'

(553) Pho **<u>kpwani</u> ni ani ndiyeaza** kukuhendani mai ichikala wakati wosi mna chadi cha kuhenda manono?

'**Now <u>why</u>, who will want** to harm you if you are always eager to do good?'

Pho	**kpwani**	ni	a=ni	ndi-ye-az-a
16.DEM3_VAR	why	COP	3SG=Q	COP-3SG.REL-desire-FV

6.2.4 Markers of speaker attitude and interpersonal relations

The hodiernal past copula *che* is also used as a discourse marker of deference, in particular signalling a polite way of beginning a request:

(554) **Che** na-tak-a hu-bish-e.
HOD 1SG.CONT-want-FV 1PL-discuss-SUB

'I wonder if we could talk.'

Che also functions as a focus marker (see §7.2.6), sometimes in combination with other discourse markers, such as *amba* 'really, certainly, possibly, approximately, as you know' as in example (555).

6.2 Sentence adverbials and discourse markers

(555) Lakini **amba** che a-na-many-a kukala a-chi-ry-a,
but DM FOC 3SG-CONT-know-FV COMP 3SG-DEP-eat-FV
ndugu-ye a-fw-e.
9.brother-9.3SG.POS 3SG-die-SUB
'But **really for sure** he knew that if he ate, his brother would die.'

The function of *amba* (which is derived from the verb *amba* 'tell, say') is to indicate that the speaker does not claim responsibility for the truth of her utterance, either because she is appealing to a higher authority (such as shared knowledge with the addressee, a universally held opinion, or cultural norms) or because the proposition expressed is an approximation or a case of hearsay. Various of these uses of *amba* are illustrated below (because it is not possible to give a consistent English gloss to every occurrence of *amba*, it has been glossed simply as DM in each example):

(556) **Amba** mi ná-phand-a uratu munyu amba-o wa-ni-amb-a!
DM 1SG 1SG.PST-plant-FV 14.DEM2_VARIANT 3.salt REL-3.REL 3SG.PST-1SG-tell-FV
'But **really** I planted that salt that you told me to!'

(557) Wa-phand-a munyu **amba**.
3SG.PST-plant-FV 3.salt DM
'He planted salt **you know**.'

(558) A-hend-a **amba** miezi mi-hahu pharatu.
3PL.PST-do-FV DM 4.months 4-three 16.DEM2_VARIANT
'They spent **about** three months right there.'

A similar discourse marker is *ati* which derives from a defective quotative verb *ti* (no longer attested in Digo); *ati* is used with a range of functions and can be glossed as 'supposedly', 'apparently', 'surely', 'even', etc.

(559) Mnaamba **ati** mu matajiri na muna chila chitu, hata tamuna mutsowacho!
'You say, **apparently**, that you are rich and you have everything, that you have no needs!'

(560) Kpwa utu wani yuno anagomba vino? Anakufuru Mlungu **ati**!
'Why is this fellow talking in this way? He is blaspheming **surely**!'

(561) Siyo vinono kunihendera kazi bure, **ati** kpwa sababu u muwangu.
'It is not good for you to work for me for nothing, **even** because you are my nephew.'

A more specific hearsay marker is *hangbwe* which indicates that the associated proposition is not one that the speaker has direct evidence for:

(562) Nasikira kukala mwenenu mvyere kasikirato, **hangbwe** ana kombereza.

'I hear that your elder brother does not feel well, **apparently** he has pneumonia.'

Another discourse marker with a specific meaning is *richa* 'let alone, not only' which derives from the verb *richa* 'leave':

(563) **Richa** uwe hata sowe achedza n'ndamwambira hivyo.

'**Not only** you, but your father, if he comes I will tell him the same thing.'

Other discourse markers derive from copula constructions, such as *pho* which is identical with the class 16 referential marker but probably derives from *ndipho* 'then' (*ndi* copula + *pho* class 16 referential marker) and *ndo* which may be a contraction of the copula construction *ndiyo* (*ndi* copula + *yo* class 9 referential marker):

(564) **Pho** yuno kanipha vitu, ananipha mafuha ga taa bahi, go mafuha ga taa **ndo** n'yarya?

'**Now** that one didn't give me anything, he just gave me kerosene, that kerosene am I **really** going to eat it?'

6.2.5 Logical connectives

Some connectives indicate relations between a proposition and some aspect of the nonlinguistic context of an utterance, or between stretches of discourse which are larger than a clause. A few of these are connectives which can also link clauses (in which case they function as conjunctions rather than as adjuncts). Connectives linking clauses are dealt with in §7.4.1 'Clause chaining'. Digo has a number of logical connectives, so rather than attempt to describe each one, in this section I shall describe two representative connectives, using examples from a text on Digo history and culture; one (*yani*) is a sentence adverbial and the other (*phahi*) is a discourse marker.

The sentence adverbial *yani* indicates that the clause which follows is a restatement of a previous clause or stretch of discourse:

(565) Lakini kala ni mchetu na mlumewe ambao kala taavyala, **yani** kala ni tasa.

'But they were a woman and her husband who had not had children, **that is** they were barren.'

(566) M'bora kala achifwa kala tapharirwa mpaka mabora ayae atsoloke. Achitsoloka, kala nkuphiya mpaka phara vifuduni pha yuya myawao achiyefwa. Vifudu ni vidzungu vyohewa madzina kulengana na mafuko ga akare ao, **yani** uphande wa kuchetu kpwa mufwa. Kala kuna madzina, mfwano kama M'bangawa, Ningare, N'zema.

'When a senior seer died there would be no crying until his fellow senior seers arrived. When they arrived, they would go to the 'vifudu' of their fellow (seer) who had died. 'Vifudu' are pots which are given different

6.2 Sentence adverbials and discourse markers

names according to the matrilineal clans of their ancestors, **that is** the maternal line of the deceased. They had names, such as M'bangawa, Ningare, N'zema.'

The discourse marker *phahi* indicates that the proposition or stretch of discourse which follows (or, less frequently, which precedes) should be understood as a consequence of a previously mentioned proposition or set of propositions, or as inferrable from some element of the context of an utterance, be it linguistic (a previous utterance) or nonlinguistic (some aspect of the interlocutors' shared environment). Rather than gloss the occurrences of *phahi* with an English expression such as 'so' or 'then' which may not be an accurate reflection of how *phahi* is interpreted in a given occurrence, I have used the term 'phahi' in the free translation.

(567) *Makabila ganjina gosi garigokala na nguvu na more gaenderera na charo chao. Makundi higa, kahi za charo chao, gafika seemu mwenga hiko Gariseni, mchetu mmwenga kala ana mimba komu.* **Phahi** *charo chamkarira chire achishindwa njirani.*

'All the other tribes who had strength and were in a hurry continued with their journey. This group, during their journey, they arrived in a part of Garsen, and there was a woman among them who was heavily pregnant. **Phahi** the journey became a problem for her and she could go no futher.'

(568) *Mwana hiyu kala ni mwanache wa chichetu,* **phahi***, mwanache wajibu achiamba, "Nataka nchikula na hadi nchikala mvyere, muda nchilólwa ni mlume na nchihenda mimba,* **phahi** *nedze niolagbwe ni mnyama wa pembe kulu."*

'The child was a girl, **phahi**, the child answered, "My wish is that I grow up and when I am an adult, and it is time to get married to a man and get pregnant, **phahi** I should be killed by an animal with a big horn."'

In the following example, *phahi* co-occurs with an explicit expression of reason 'because they felt bitter about being gossiped about':

(569) *Ariphofika phephi na pho shareheni, asikira kala anasengenywa ni hara ayawao ambao kala akaloka chimbere hadi ndipho kala nao akaremwa.* **Phahi** *kpwa sababu ya utsungu wa kusengenywa, ariphotsoloka hipho, ahula mizigo yao na bila ya kusagala, alaga na achiuka.*

'When they got close to where the party was to take place, they overheard themselves being gossiped about by their friends who had arrived before them and they felt rejected. **Phahi** because they felt bitter about being gossiped about, when they arrived at the place, they put down their bags and without even staying for a while, they said farewell and left.'

All the examples of *phahi* so far have illustrated it occurring before the clause which it modifies; the final example in this section illustrates the rarer use of *phahi* following the clause which it modifies:

(570) *Anamuamba mchewe, "Pesa hizi mkpwazangu náziona dzana kala niyaoga pwani, hata uwe uchinilaphiza ela mino siyajali. Lakini siyazihala mino náziricha nchilagiza avuvi, kumbavi nao akazireha kpwa hivyo nahurye pesa* **phahi.**"

'He said to his wife, "This money my wife I saw it yesterday (as) I was going to bathe in the sea, even though you insult me I don't care. But I didn't take it instead I left it and told the fishermen, and surprisingly they have brought it therefore let us spend (lit: eat) that money **phahi.**"'

6.3 Additives

Additives are expressions which indicate that an element (e.g. a predicate or one of its arguments) is to be processed as an addition to a previous element, usually of the same type. That is, an element which is modified by an additive is intended to be processed in parallel with a preceding element. Additives include expressions which can often be glossed in English as 'also, even, too, as well, moreover, likewise', etc. They show similarities with adverbs but are probably best analysed as connectives (Levinsohn 2002:171), although unlike coordinating conjunctions additives are never syntactically obligatory, and often more than one additive can co-occur within a single clause. It is possible to classify additives in Digo on the basis of their internal morphology into two kinds, which I will term simple additives and referential additives. Rather than produce an exhaustive (and tedious) list of all the conjunctions and related expressions in Digo, I have selected the most common additives and attempted to describe them in some detail.

6.3.1 Simple additives

Simple additives are invariable words which cannot be broken down into meaningful component parts. I will describe the three most common simple additives: *chisha*, *piya* and *tsona*.

6.3.1.1 Chisha

The basic function of *chisha* is to indicate that the clause which it introduces is dependent on a previous clause in some way and is to be processed in the light of that previous clause. The most common use of *chisha* is to indicate that the event described in the clause which it introduces follows another in a temporal sequence:

6.3 Additives

(571) Simba wa-on-a   mu-hambo, a-chi-ry-a   **chisha** a-chi-uy-a.
1a.lion 3SG.PST-see-FV 3-trap   3SG-CONS-eat-FV   ADD   3SG-CONS-return-FV

'The lion saw the trap, he ate **then** he returned.'

Chisha can be used to provide information which is additional to and of greater importance than the information contained in the previous clause. Example (572) is the introduction to a story about a hunting trip in which the stranger mentioned in the clause introduced by *chisha* becomes the protagonist (the primary character):

(572) Hipho kare kpwakala na atu ambao kala anakuluphira windza kpwa chakurya chao. **Chisha phachikala na mjeni phapho phao laloni.**

'Long ago there were people who depended on hunting for their food. **Now** there was a stranger there at their place.'

Chisha   pha-chi-kal-a   na   mjeni   phapho   pha-o
ADD   16-CONS-COP-FV   COM   1.stranger   16.DEM3_VARIANT   16-3PL.POS
lalo-ni.
5.location-LOC

Example (573) also illustrates the use of *chisha* to indicate that what follows is important additional information, but in this case the information introduced by *chisha* contrasts with that in the previous clause, and so can be interpreted as superseding it (the free English translation 'however' is meant to express this interpretation, not to suggest that *chisha* encodes the idea of contrast):

(573) Phofika usiku mkpwulu phakpwedza nyama wa mapha pho phondze, paaa, anang'ala dza taa. Achimuiha yuya bwana, "Fulani, fulani go achigohenda mcheo ukagaona?" Anaamba, "Ehee." Anaambwa, "Akadziyuga bure, **chisha we undahenda pesa vivyo**. Machero phiya phara phako mndani ..."

'In the middle of the night there came a bird outside, whoosh, shining like a lamp. It called that man, "So-and-so, those things which your wife did, did you see them?" He said, "Yes." He was told, "She has put herself out for nothing, **however you will make money in this way**. Tomorrow go there to your field ..."'

chisha   we   u-nda-hend-a   pesa   vivyo.
ADD   2SG   2SG-FUT-make-FV   9.money   8.DEM3_VARIANT

6.3.1.2 Piya

Piya indicates that the clause which it introduces is to be processed in parallel with the previous clause, and that the two clauses are of equal importance. In neither of the examples below is there any indication that the action described in the clause containing *piya* occurs in a temporal sequence after the action described in the preceding clause, nor that it is of greater importance.

(574) Mayo u-si-rim-e, hata na uwe baba **piya** u-si-rim-e.
1a.mother 2SG-NEG-farm-SUB even COM 2SG 1a.father ADD 2SG-NEG-farm-SUB

'Mother, do not farm, and even you father, do not farm **either**.'

(575) M-rich-e phapha mu-hambo-ni, hal-a mcheo
3SG-leave-FV 16.DEM1_VARIANT 3-trap-LOC take-FV 1.wife.1.3SG.POS
u-phiy-e kaya na=mi **piya** na-pha-uk-a.
2SG-go-SUB 9.home COM=1SG.REF ADD 1SG.CONT-16-depart-FV

'Leave him [= a lion] there in the trap, take your wife and go home and I will **also** leave here.'

6.3.1.3 Tsona

Tsona behaves syntactically both as a conjunction and as an adverb. When *tsona* precedes the element which it modifies, it behaves as a conjunction. The information in the clause or phrase which it introduces need not constitute additional information but it must serve to strengthen or clarify the information in the previous clause. The clause or phrase introduced by *tsona* is therefore intended to be processed in parallel with what precedes it and the basic function of *tsona* can be described as reinforcement.

In the following four examples, *tsona* modifies a noun phrase, an adverbial phrase (headed by the associative marker *-a*), a clause, and a phrase expressing an instrument (headed by the comitative marker *na*), respectively (all highlighted). In each case, the function of *tsona* is to reinforce the preceding information.

(576) Uwe m-gayi **tsona** m-chiya wa mwisho
2SG 1-poor_person ADD 1-poor_person 1.ASS 3.end
u-na-tak-a mwanangu!
2SG-CONT-want-FV 1.child.1.1SG.POS

'You are a poor man **moreover a complete pauper**, (yet) you want to marry my daughter!'

(577) Sisi hu-ka-ku-ph-a razi, na u-many-e razi
1PL 1PL-HOD-2SG-give-FV 9.blessing COM 2SG-know-SUB 9.blessing
ni chitu chi-kulu sana **tsona** cha mana.
COP 7.thing 7-big DEG ADD 7.ASS 9.worth

'We have given you a blessing, and you should know that a blessing is something very big, **moreover** (it is) **valuable**.'

6.3 Additives

(578) ná-mu-on-a chiphephi lakini nyama hiye hasa
1SG.PST-3SG-see-FV close but 1a.animal 1.DEM3 precisely
kala n'=simba **tsona** kala n'=simba m-chetu mana
PST COP=1a.lion ADD PST COP=1a.lion 1-female for
simba m-chetu ka-na cheru.
1a.lion 1-female 3SG.NEG-COM 7.beard

'I saw it close up and that animal was a lion, **moreover it was a female lion,** because female lions do not have a mane.'

(579) a-chi-sikir-a mutu a-na-mu-ih-a, **tsona na dzina-re.**
3SG-CONS-hear-FV 1.person 3SG-CONT-3SG-call-FV ADD COM 5.name-5.3SG.POS

'he heard someone calling him, **moreover by name.**'

Although the information in a clause or phrase introduced by *tsona* need not constitute additional information, it can do so so long as this information does not supersede or contradict the information in the previous clause. In example (580), the first sentence states that a man should not quarrel with or beat his wife, and the second sentence, introduced by *tsona*, reinforces this message whilst adding the information that fighting and quarrelling should not happen in front of children.

(580) Wakati mutu a-ka-lól-a n'=lazima a-sagal-e=to
14.time 1.person 3SG-ANT-marry-FV COP=necessary 3SG-sit-SUB=WELL
na mchewe, a-si-kal-e a-chi-m-pig-a ovyo ovyo.
COM 1.wife-1.3SG.POS 3SG-NEG-be-SUB 3SG-IMPFV-3SG-hit-FV carelessly
Tsona m-si-pig-an-e au ku-heh-a mbere za
ADD 2PL-NEG-hit-RECIP-SUB or INF-quarrel-FV 10.front 10.ASS
ana enu.
2.children 2.2PL.POS

'When a man is married he should get on well with his wife, he should not hit her for nothing. **Moreover** do not fight or quarrel in front of your children.'

The clause introduced by *tsona* in example (581) also contains new information. *Tsona* indicates that this information is to be processed in parallel with the information in the previous clause, with the result that the hearer understands that the subject could hear the bees buzzing but not see them. It would be possible to use *piya* here (but not *chisha*) in place of *tsona*, but if *piya* were used this would imply that the buzzing of the bees was no more important than the darkness, which is not the case, as the bees play an important role as the story develops.

(581) mu=na   giza   hata   ka-on-a   chitu,   **tsona**
      18=COM   9.darkness   even   3SG.NEG-see-FV 7.thing ADD
      m-na-vum-a   nyuchi.
      18-CONT-buzz-FV 10.bees

'it was so dark inside that he couldn't see a thing, **furthermore** there were bees buzzing in there.'

When *tsona* follows a verb (usually but not necessarily immediately), it functions as an adverb. With active verb phrases, it indicates repetition. The characterization of *tsona* as an additive still holds, however, as the repeated action presupposes a previous action with which a parallel is drawn (Stephen Levinsohn, p.c. 2008):

(582) u-heg-e   **tsona** nyo   mu-hambo.
      2SG-set-SUB   ADD   3.DEM3_VAR 3-trap

'set that trap **again**.'

(583) Ku-phiy-a   **tsona** mi-hambo-ni mino si-phiy-a.
      INF-go-FV   ADD   4-trap-LOC   1SG   1SG.NEG-go-FV

'As for going trapping **again** I won't go.'

In example (584), the first occurrence of *tsona* modifies the active verb phrase *wauya* 'he returned' and indicates repetition of the action, but the third occurrence of *tsona* modifies the stative verb phrase *takuna atu* 'there were no people'; because of the stative nature of the clause, *tsona* indicates not repetition but duration. (The second occurrence of *tsona* functions as a conjunction reinforcing the information in the previous clause and intended to be processed in parallel with it.) The context to the example is as follows: previously, the protagonist of the story had been given a magic machine which generates money and he had hired two hundred workers from an Arab merchant at ten times the usual wage. In (584), he goes to the merchant to request another two hundred workers whom he promises to pay at twenty times the usual wage.

6.3 Additives

(584) Yuya bwana **wauya** <u>tsona</u> **kpwa Mwarabu achendamuamba**, "Mino sindakubali kukala na hara atu mia mbiri bahi, <u>tsona</u> **niaphe pesa hizo**, ela nataka atu anjina mia mbiri akale miane. Chila mutu nndaripha elufu mbiri." Yuya Mwarabu **kpwakpwe ndipho takuna atu** <u>tsona</u> ...

'That man **he returned** <u>again</u> **to the Arab and said to him**, "I can't agree to have just those two hundred people, **and furthermore to pay them this money**, instead I want another two hundred people to make four hundred. To each person I will pay two thousand." Now that Arab **at his place there were** <u>no longer</u> **any people** ...'

wa-uy-a		**tsona**	ku-a	Mwarabu	a-chenda-mu-amb-a ...
3SG.PST-return-FV		ADD	17-ASS	1.Arab	3SG-CONS.IT-3SG-say-FV

tsona	ni-a-ph-e	pesa	hizo ...
ADD	1SG-3PL-give-SUB	10.money	10.DEM3

kw-akpwe	ndipho	ta-ku-na	atu	**tsona** ...
17-3SG.POS	then	NEG-17-COM	2.people	ADD

6.3.2 Referential additives

Referential additives consist of the comitative particle *na* (see §6.1.1) and a reduced form of an independent pronoun or a referential marker (see §4.1.10.2 for a discussion of referential markers, which are analysed as clitics). The complete list of referential additives is provided in table 6.1:

Table 6.1. Referential additives

Person/ number	Referential additive	Noun class	Referential additive	Noun class	Referential additive
1SG	nami	3	nao	11	naro
1PL	naswi	4	nayo	14	nao
2SG	nawe	5	naro	15	nako
2PL	namwi	6	nago	16	napho
3SG/ class 1	naye	7	nacho	17	nako
		8	navyo	18	namo
3PL/ class 2	nao	9	nayo		
		10	nazo		

Constructions with identical forms to referential additives occur as connectives within verb phrases. An example of the connective use of one these forms is provided in (585).

(585) zira   pesa   zo-ku-ph-a   wa-phiy-a   **na=zo**   Mambasa
      10.DEM2 10.money 10.REL-2SG-give-FV 2SG.PST-go-FV COM=10.REF PLACE_NAME
      'that money which he gave you you took it (lit: you went **with it**) to Mombasa'

Referential additives, on the other hand, indicate parallelism between some feature of the clause containing the referential additive and a preceding clause. The parallelism can take the form of parallel similarity or parallel contrast, but which is intended has to be inferred by the context and is not encoded by the referential additive. The same referential additive may be used to indicate parallelism between clauses with the same participant but a different predicate or between clauses with the same or similar predicate but different participants. (See Levinsohn 2002:176–178 for a discussion of languages in which these two kinds of parallelism are marked by different additive constructions.)

Parallelism involving the same participant but different predicates is common in hortatory texts, but is rare in narrative texts; that is, the use of referential additives in hortatory texts usually indicates parallelism between actions or states involving the same participant. Conversely, parallelism involving similar predicates but different participants is common in narrative texts but rare in hortatory texts; that is, the use of referential additives in narrative texts usually indicates parallelism between different participants involved in similar situations.

6.3.2.1 Same participant, different predicate

In example (586), the referential additive *naye* indicates parallelism between the various states experienced by the father of a girl following the initial state of becoming a father. In the previous clauses, the speaker had been referring to himself and his expectations as the father of a girl, so the first occurrence of *naye* sets up a parallelism between the speaker and fathers in general. In this example, each action or state follows from the previous and leads towards a culmination or fulfilment: fathering > desiring > knowing > being satisfied. Parallelism is reinforced through the repetition of the key verb forms *achivyala* 'if he fathers' and *anamanya* 'he knows', and the change to first person reference *n'ndalóza* 'I will marry (her) off' in direct speech.

6.3 Additives

(586) Ku-a   sababu   amba m-vyazi   **na=ye**   a-chi-vyal-a
      17-ASS   reason   DM   1-parent   COM=1.REF   1-DEP-bear-FV

   dza   viratu   **na=ye**   a=na   tamaa,   a-na-many-a,
   as   8.DEM2_VARIANT   COM-1.REF   1=COM   9.desire   3SG-CONT-know-FV

   a-chi-vyal-a   mwana   m-chetu   **na=ye**   a-na-many-a,
   1-DEP-bear-FV   1.child   1-female   COM=1.REF   3SG-CONT-know-FV

   "N'-nda-ló-z-a,   na   a-phah-e   chakpwe,"   **na=ye**
   1SG-FUT-marry-CAUS-FV   COM   3SG-get-SUB   7.3SG.POS   COM=1.REF

   a-sitiri   moyo-we.
   3SG-cover   3.heart-4.3SG.POS

   'Because really if a parent **also** bears a child in the same way **he also** hopes (to get dowry), he knows, if he produces a girl **he also** knows, "I will marry her off, and she should get her due," and he is satisfied (lit: **he also** can cover his heart).'

In example (587), the referential additive *naye* indicates that the two states of affairs concerning the same participant are intended to be processed in parallel. The participant in question is a wife whose dowry has not been paid and the speaker is her father. He is telling his son-in-law what will happen if the wife has to return to her parents' home: she will give the appearance of being happy, but in reality she will want to return to her husband. The material preceding *naye* describes the apparent state of the participant (that there is nothing the matter with her) and the material introduced by *naye* describes her actual state, betrayed by her words.

(587) A-nda-sagal-a,   a-nda-ry-a,   a-nda-og-a,   na   hali   yoyosi
      3SG-FUT-sit-FV   3SG-FUT-eat-FV   3SG-FUT-wash-FV   COM   9.state   9.any

   ndi-yo-m-fik-a   **na=ye**   a-chi-bish-a   mara
   FUT-9.REL-3SG-arrive-FV   COM=1.REF   3SG-DEP-speak-FV   immediately

   a-na-yal-a   a-na-amb-a,   "Na-tak-a   ku-angu."
   3SG-CONT-forget-FV   3SG-CONT-say-FV   1SG.CONT-want-FV   17-1SG.POS

   'She will stay, eat, wash, and no matter how things are for her when she speaks sometimes she will forget and say, "I want my own home."'

6.3.2.2 Similar predicate, different participants

When the predicates in two or more clauses are identical or similar, a referential additive in the final clause indicates parallelism with respect to the participant which is coreferential with the referential additive and a participant in the previous clause(s) with the same theta role (agent, patient, etc.). Parallelism may be indicated between any two (or more) participants regardless of discourse status (major or minor participants) and grammatical role (subject, object, etc.), so long as these participants have the same theta role (agent, patient, etc.).

In example (588), the predicate is *kufwa* 'to die' and the participants are the speaker and his brother. The referential additive *nami* indicates that the two clauses are to be processed in parallel:

(588) Pha   ndi-pho-kpwenda-fw-a   mwenehu,
      16.DEM1_VAR   FUT-16.REL-ITIVE-die-FV 1.my_sibling

      mimi **na=mi**   n-ya-fw-a   phapho.
      1SG   COM=1SG   1SG-FUT.IT-die-FV 16.DEM3_VARIANT

      'There where my brother is going to die, **I also** will go to die there.'

In example (589), a hunting party has killed an elephant and the protagonist has told his companions to take as much meat as they can carry. The subject (the stubborn man) refuses to do as the protagonist asks and insists on doing things differently from his companions. He first repeats the instruction of the protagonist (indicated with *naye*), but applies it only to his companions and not to himself, insisting that he would cut meat (again indicated with *naye*) after them. The use of the referential additive *naye* referring to the subject therefore indicates parallelism first between the actions of the subject and the protagonist and then between the actions of the subject and his companions. The example as a whole is understood as contrastive due in part to the use of *lakini* 'but' at the start of the sentence (Stephen Levinsohn, p.c. 2008).

(589) Lakini kahi ya hara atu kala phana mmwenga ambaye kala ana kani mana **naye** walagiza ayae akate nyama ndipho **naye** akate badaye.

'But among those people there was one who was stubborn because **he also** told his companions to cut meat and then **he also** would cut afterwards.'

na=ye   wa-lagiz-a   aya-e   a-kat-e
COM=1.REF   3SG.PST-order-FV   2.fellows-2.3SG.POS 3PL-cut-SUB

nyama   ndipho   **na=ye**   a-kat-e   badaye.
9.meat   then   COM=1.REF   3SG-cut-SUB   afterwards

Occasionally, a referential additive is followed by the connective *piya* 'also, too', as in the first occurrence of *naye* in example (590), but more often, a referential additive alone communicates parallelism, as in the second occurrence of *naye* in example (590). In the first occurrence of *naye*, the predicate is *kulóla* 'to marry' and the participants are *mzee Mwazewe* who is compared with a hypothetical rich person, and in the second occurrence of *naye*, the predicate is *kuvyala mwana wa chilume* 'to give birth to a male child' and the participants are the senior wife and her cowife.

6.3 Additives

(590) *Kama vyokala desturi ya atu hipho kare, mutu ka achikala tajiri ka n'lazima* **alóle** *achetu anji. Phahi,* **mzee Mwazewe, naye** *piya walóla mchetu wa phiri. Yuya mchetu ariphogbwira mimba, wavyala mwana wa chilume achimuiha Mwiya. Hiye mchetu mvyere ariphoona* **mchetu myawe naye akavyala mwana** *wa chilume, wamanya hira mali indaganywa.*

'As was the custom of the people long ago, if a person was rich it was necessary **that he marry** many wives. So, **elder Mwazewe, he too** he also married a second wife. When that woman became pregnant, she gave birth to a boy and called him Mwiya. The senior wife when she saw that **her cowife had also given birth to a son** (lit: child of male), she knew that the wealth would be shared.' (It is known that the first wife already has a son.)

a. m-zee   Mwazewe,   **na=ye**   piya   wa-lól-a ...
   1-elder   PROPER_NAME   COM=1.REF   ADD   3SG.PST-marry-FV

b. m-chetu   myawe   **na=ye**   a-ka-vyal-a   mwana
   1-woman   1.fellow.1.3SG.POS COM=1.REF   3SG-ANT-bear-FV   1.child

Parallelism involving different participants is rare in hortatory texts, but it does occur. In example (591), *naye* indicates that the younger son as well as the elder son is in a bad state. Note that in this example, although the referent of *naye* is the object of the following VP and the participant in the previous clause is a grammatical subject, both participants have the theta role of patient: the elder son was jailed and the younger son was not sent to school.

(591) *Haya lola sambi, mwanao mvyere wa chilume vi sambi, wafungbwa mana waiya matumbingbwa ga atu. Na yuno wanjina achiyesala* **naye kumphirika sukuli**.

'Now look what has become of your elder son recently, he was jailed because he stole someone's eggs. And the other one who remains (at home) **even him** you don't send him to school.'

na=ye   ku-m-phirik-a   sukuli
COM=1.REF   2SG.NEG-3SG-bring-FV   9.school

Parallelism between two or more participants is more common in hortatory texts if at least one of the participants is the speaker and/or the hearer(s), as in example (592).

(592) Mwanangu   na-ku-amb-a,   uwe   u-na-phiy-a   u-jeni-ni,
      1.child.1.1SG.POS 1SG.CONT-2SG-say-FV   2SG   2SG-CONT-go-FV   14-abroad-LOC

      ku-many-a   mutu   **na=o**   hiko   ta-a-ku-many-a.
      2SG.NEG-know-FV   1.person   COM=2.REF   17.DEM3   NEG-3PL-2SG-know-FV

'My child, I tell you, you are going to a strange place, you do not know anyone there and no one there knows you (lit: and they also they do not know you).'

6.3.2.3 Other functions of referential additives

The class 16 form of the referential additive, *napho*, which is very rarely used in a strictly locative sense, is used to express the idea of a condition which might or might not hold (hence the English gloss 'if'). Stephen Levinsohn (p.c. 2008) has pointed out that even this construction has the effect of adding a situation to what has been stated, and so could still be considered to be an additive use. The following examples are taken from a book on Digo culture and history; since the passages are quite long, only a free translation has been provided.

(593) *Huno kala ndio wakati ambapho mvulana ama msichana anafundzwa hali ya masagazige ili gakale manono kahi za maishage* **napho** *ni mvulana.* **Napho** *ni msichana kala akafundzwa hali ya masagazige ga kpwakpwe dzumbani na mlumewe.*

'This was the time when a young man or woman would be taught the traditional behaviour so that things would go well in his life **if** he were a youth. **In the case of** a young woman she would be taught about her behaviour in her household and with her husband.'

(594) *Ndipho vivyerengbwa akale andaambirwa mali ambayo andareha. [...]* **Napho** *hara vivyere ana nguvu, kala akaandza mahunda gao phapho kpwa phapho, lakini* **napho** *nguvu zao ni chache kala akaruhusiwa kulaga mbara.*

'Then the parents-in-law would be informed of the dowry they were to provide. [...] **If** the parents-in-law were able, they would begin to pay that money immediately, but **if** they weren't able they would be allowed to promise to pay later.'

(595) *Mwana wa kpwandza kala akazikpwa na gushe dziru pi-pi-pi na kala* **napho** *mufwa ni mdide, kala akatsukulwa na mikono hadi kpwakpwe mbirani, bila ya kuhumira chitanda. Chitanda mara nyinji kala chikahumirwa* **napho** *achiyefwa ni mutu mzima.*

'A firstborn child would be buried in a pitch black cotton cloth and **if** the deceased was small, he would be carried by hand to his grave, without using a bed. A bed would often be used **if** the person who had died was an adult.'

Finally, it is common not just in Digo but in many other languages for the final events in narratives to be packaged together using a connective (see Levinsohn 2000:73 on the use of Greek *kai* at the end of episodes such as Matt. 2:11–12). In Digo, a referential additive is often used, either as the sole connective or in conjunction with another connective such as the comitative particle *na* or *ndipho* 'then'. The events which are connected using a referential particle typically either describe the parting of the main participants (thereby bringing the story to an end) or state the situation at the end of the story (thereby providing a summary). Example (596) is taken from a first person factual narrative in which the narrator recounts a time when he worked as a hospital orderly and had to take a blind patient from Mombasa to Nairobi. The remaining examples are taken from a published collection of folktales.

(596) *Phahi yuya mkongo wahalwa achendalazwa kura kpwa akongo ayae a matso. Ndipho __nami__ nchiphiya nyumbani kpwa Dr. Maneno ambaye ni aphu.*

'So the patient was taken away to be admitted along with his fellow eye patients. **Then as for me I went to the home** of Dr. Maneno who is my uncle.'

Ndipho	***na=mi***	*n-chi-phiy-a*	*nyumba-ni*
then	COM=1SG.REF	1SG-CONS-go-FV	9.house-LOC

(597) *Ye mwanadamu kala akatsukulwa ni mamba, chisha mamba achiphiya vyakpwe na yuno mutu __naye__ achiphiya vyakpwe.*

'The man had been carried by the crocodile, then the crocodile went to his place **and that person also/for his part went to his place**.'

na	*yuno*	*mutu*	***na=ye***	*a-chi-phiy-a*	*vy-akpwe.*
COM	1.DEM4	1.person	COM=1.REF	3SG-CONS-go-FV	8-3SG.POS

(598) *Hara baba na mayo akpwendamenya nyumba yao __naye__ mwana wao ambaye ni liwali achendamenya yakpwe.*

'That father and mother went and entered their house **and likewise their son who was governor went and entered his**.'

na=ye	*mwana*	*wao ...*	*a-chenda-meny-a*	*y-akpwe*
COM=1.REF	1.child	2.3PL.POS	3SG-CONS.IT-enter-FV	9-3SG.POS

(599) *Yuya mchetu wakala ndipho anarya sima na yuya mlume __naye__ kayaphiya tsona mihamboni.*

'That woman was then eating maize meal **and that man for his part no longer went trapping**.'

na	*yuya*	*m-lume*	***na=ye***	*ka-ya-phiy-a*	*tsona*	*mi-hambo-ni*
COM	1.DEM2	1-man	COM=1.REF	3SG.NEG-PST-go-FV	ADD	4-trap-LOC

6.4 Adverbs and ideophones

Adverbs and ideophones, which will be defined below, are treated together in this section because they share the basic function of describing or emphasizing some quality of the expression which they modify, be it a predicate, a qualificative or an adverb. The motivation for distinguishing adverbs and ideophones from other parts of speech is, therefore, primarily functional rather than structural. It is not always easy to distinguish an adverb from an ideophone, but the following generalizations hold in Digo: (a) adverbs often derive from expressions in other word classes such as nouns or relational expressions, but ideophones are either onomatopoeic or etymologically obscure; (b) ideophones are usually monosyllabic or reduplicated forms of monosyllabic expressions; and (c) adverbs can be used to answer *wh*-questions (e.g. 'How did she work?' 'Quickly.'), but ideophones cannot.

6.4.1 Adverbs

Let us first establish what this section is not about. We will not be concerned here with expressions describing the time or location of an event ('temporal' and 'local' adverbs). Various words are used to specify the time frame or aspectual structure of an event (for example *ndipho* 'then', *badaye* and *halafu* 'afterwards', *chimarigizo* 'finally'). Similarly, we are not concerned here with modal sentence adverbials such as *hakika* 'certainly' and *chahi* 'maybe' which express degrees of certainty (§6.2.2). Syntactically, all of these adverbial expressions are obliques (in many functionally oriented approaches) or adjuncts (in generative syntax) which occur to the left or right of a verb clause nucleus, and many can also be classified as relational expressions (§6.1). This section is concerned only with expressions which describe how an action is performed (modal adverbs) or the degree or extent of an action or of a qualificative, etc. (degree adverbs), and this is the way in which the term "adverb" will be used henceforth.

6.4.1.1 Modal adverbs

Modal adverbs, as noted above, describe how an action is performed. In Digo, modal adverbs follow verbs. Many of them are derived from nouns or relational expressions, often prefixed with the class 7 agreement marker *chi*; for example, the relational adverb *chilimwenga* 'together' with class 7 agreement in example (600) derives from the (derived) class 11 noun *limwenga* 'one, unity' and both class prefixes co-occur on the adverb, and the adverb *chishariya* 'legally' with class 7 agreement in example (601) derives from the class 9 noun *shariya* 'law':

(600) Atu   osi   a-chi-jibu   **chi-li-mwenga.**
2.people 2.all 3PL-CONS-answer 7-11-one
'All the people answered **together.**'

(601) M-si-hend-e mambo amba-go **chi-shariya** ta-m-ruhus-iw-a
2PL-NEG-do-SUB 6.things REL-6.REL 7-9.law NEG-2PL-allow-PAS-FV
ku-ga-hend-a
INF-6-do-FV
'Do not do things which **legally** (according to the law) you are not allowed to do.'

Other modal adverbs are derived from adjectives prefixed with the class 8 agreement marker *vi*; for example, the evaluative adverbs *vibaya* 'badly' and *vinono* 'well' derive from the adjectives *baya* 'bad' and *nono* 'good' respectively through the addition of the class 8 prefix:

6.4 Adverbs and ideophones

(602) A-nda-pig-w-a   **vi-baya.**
      3SG-FUT-beat-PAS-FV 8-bad
      'He will be beaten **badly**.'

(603) Mtihani   wa-u-hend-a   **vi-nono.**
      3.exam   3SG.PST-3-do-FV   8-good
      'You did **well** in the exam.'

Some adverbs also exhibit stem reduplication. If the adverb is derived (such as *chikure-kure* which is derived from *kure* 'far'), the class 7 or 8 prefix is not reduplicated (see example 604), but in nonderived adverbs the whole stem is reduplicated (see examples 605 and 606):

(604) A-ka-im-a   **chi-kure-kure**   na   hipha.
      3SG-ANT-stand-FV   7-far-far   COM   16.DEM1
      'He stood at a distance from here.'

(605) Mvula   i-na-ny-a   **churu-churu.**
      9.rain   9-CONT-rain-FV   drizzling
      'It's drizzling.'

(606) Mwivi   wa-lung-w-a   **lunyo-lunyo.**
      1.thief 3SG.PST-follow-PAS-FV   closely
      'The thief was followed closely.'

Other adverbs are formed from the class 17 form of the associative marker followed by a noun or adjective, e.g. *kpwa bidii* 'with effort, i.e. diligently, conscientiously'.

6.4.1.2 Degree adverbs

Degree adverbs describe the degree or extent of the predicate, noun, or relational expression which they follow, or very occasionally precede, as in the case of the superlative degree adverb *hasa* in example (614):

(607) Phahi   ku-ri-pho-ch-a   **kabisa** ...
      so   17-PST-16.REL-dawn-FV   DEG
      'So when it had dawned completely ...'

(608) a-chi-phiy-a   hata   ndi=pho   a   kure   **kabisa.**
      3PL-CONS-go-FV   until   COP=16.REF   3PL   far   DEG
      'they went until they were very far away.'

(609) a-ri-pho-kal-a   a   kure   **chidide**   na   yuya   mwana-we ...
      3SG-PST-16.REL-be-FV   3SG   far   DEG   COM   1.DEM2 1.child-1.3SG.POS
      'when he was a little way from his child ...'

(610) Na   i-nda-kal-a   ma-kosa   **sana**   mwanangu   u-phiy-e   hiko ...
      COM   9-FUT-be-FV   6-mistake   DEG   1.child.1.1SG.POS 2SG-go-SUB 18.DEM3
      'And it would be a very big mistake, my child, to go that way ...'

(611) Muhi   huno   ni   m-kulu   **muno**.
      3.tree   3.DEM4   COP   3.big   DEG
      'This tree is very/too large.'

(612) Digbwa   ni   kali   **kamare**.
      9.vinegar   COP   sharp   DEG
      'Vinegar is extremely acidic.'

(613) Twiga   ni   nyama   m-refu   **hasa**   vuwe-ni.
      1a.giraffe   COP   1a.animal   1-long   DEG   bush-LOC
      'The giraffe is the tallest wild animal.'

(614) ná-mu-on-a   chi-phephi   lakini   nyama   hiye   **hasa**
      1SG.PST-3SG-see-FV   7-near   but   1a.animal   1.DEM3   DEG
      kala   n'=simba.
      PST   COP=1a.lion
      'I saw it close up and that animal was definitely a lion.'

(615) Pho   yuno   ka-ni-ph-a   vitu,   a-na-ni-ph-a
      16.REF   1.DEM4   3SG.NEG-1SG-give-FV 8.things   3SG-CONT-1SG-give-FV
      mafuha   ga   taa   **bahi** ...
      6.oil   6.ASS   9.lamp   DEG
      'Now that one didn't give me anything, he gave me kerosene (lamp oil) only ...'

Degree adverbs can often be reduplicated for emphasis:

(616) Siku   hizo   baba   a-chere   na   nguvu-ze
      10.days   10.DEM3   1a.father   3SG-PERS   COM   10.strength-10.3SG.POS
      kabisa   **kabisa**.
      DEG   DEG
      'In those days my father still had his full strength.'

6.4.2 Ideophones

6.4.2.1 Definition

Doke (1935:118) defines an ideophone as "[a] vivid representation of an idea in sound. A word, often onomatopoeic, which describes a predicate, qualificative or adverb in respect to manner, colour, sound, smell, action, state or intensity."[7] The segmental and suprasegmental characteristics of ideophones are often extra-normal, e.g. lengthening, nasalization of vowels, contour tones, and changed position of stress.

Doke includes the repetition of a verbal root as one kind of ideophone, e.g. Lamba: *ukusokola soko* 'to pull right out', *ukupama pame pame* 'to strike and strike' (Doke, 118). In Digo, a limited number of verb roots can be reduplicated as ideophones to express the completeness of the action, e.g. *rema* 'to refuse' > *remi-remi* (as opposed to reduplicating the verb stem within a verb group, e.g. *wa-m-rema* > *wa-m-rema-rema* which is also possible):

(617) Mwanache hiyu wa chi-chetu wa-m-rem-a **remi-remi**
1.child 1.DEM1 1.ASS 7-female 3SG.PST-3SG-refuse-FV IDEO
hiyu m-vulana.
1.DEM1 1-young_man
'This girl rejected the youth **completely**.'

Other ideophones in Digo will be described below, classified according to their segmental characteristics.

6.4.2.2 Monosyllabic ideophones

Some monosyllabic ideophones have very specific meanings or collocational restrictions, such as *pi* and *do* (relating to the colours black and red respectively, discussed in §6.4.2.6), *gbwii* 'completely silent' (see example 626), and *dii* 'all day':

(618) M-si-hend-er-e ana enu vibako ku-a
2PL-NEG-do-APPL-SUB 2.children 2.2PL.POS 8.provocation 17-ASS
ku-a-laumu **dii** yosi.
INF-3PL-criticise IDEO 9.all
'Do not provoke your children to anger by criticising them all **day long**.'

The ideophones *bii* and *bu* indicate completeness with negative and positive polarity respectively:

---
[7]Doke previously used the term 'radical' instead of 'ideophone'. He wrote, "*The Radical* may be defined as follows:—"A word, often onomatopoeic, which describes a predicate or qualificative in respect to manner, colour, sound, state or action." It must be remembered that the adverb describes in respect to "manner, place or time"'" (Doke 1931:221).

(619) M-kongo   kala   a=na   tabu   ya   matso,
      1-sick_person PST   3SG=COM 9.trouble   9.ASS 6.eyes
      kala ka-on-a   **bii.**
      PST   3SG.NEG-see-FV IDEO
      'The sick person had a problem with his eyes, he could not see **at all**.'

(620) Mendz-an-a-ni   na   m-kal-e   na   moyo   m-mwenga m-osi   **bu.**
      love-RECIP-FV-PL COM 2PL-be-SUB COM 3.heart 3-one   2PL-all IDEO
      'Love one another and be of one heart all of you **completely**.'

Other monosyllabic ideophones have more general meanings; *tu* expresses preciseness or limitation (in some cases there is no natural English gloss):

(621) Ni   aho   a-iri   **tu,** mutu   na   ndugu-ye.
      COP 2.DEM3 2-two   IDEO   1.person COM   9.brother-9.3SG.POS
      'It was **just** those two, the person and his brother.'

(622) Chi-li-mwenga **tu** a-uk-a,   a-uk-a,   a-uk-a.
      7-11-one   IDEO   3PL.PST-leave-FV 3PL.PST-leave-FV 3PL.PST-leave-FV
      'All together they left (and went away).'

(623) Ndi-ye-olag-a   Mwanyika,   m-chetu   ni   w-ake   kare **tu.**
      FUT-3SG.REL-kill-FV   PROPER_NAME 1-woman   COP 1-3SG.POS ANT   IDEO
      'Whoever kills Mwanyika (the Serpent), the woman is his right away/ without question.'

The ideophone *tse* expresses completeness or excess:

(624) Phahi chuma   ch-a-sag-a   hata   meli   i-chi-zam-a   **tse.**
      so   7.iron   7-PST-grind-FV until   9.ship 9-CONS-sink-FV   IDEO
      'So the iron ground until the ship sank **completely**.'

(625) ... yuya   m-kongo   ka=na   neno   **tse,** ni   m-zima.
      1.DEM2   1-sick_person   3SG.NEG=COM 5.word IDEO   COP 1-whole
      '... that sick person had absolutely nothing wrong with her, she was whole.'

It is not uncommon to find ideophones used in combination for emphasis:

6.4 Adverbs and ideophones

(626) *Vitu vyatsamizwa ni atu ndulu vichiphirikpwa melini magunia magunia ela yuya mutu na mchewe **ye anyemere tu gbwii, hata tse**.*

'The things were moved (by people) into a heap (then) they were taken onto the boat in sacks but that man and his wife **he just remained totally silent, absolutely so**.'

... ye	a-nyemere	tu	gbwii,	hata	tse.
1.DEM3_VAR	3SG-keep_silent.PFV	IDEO	IDEO	even	IDEO

6.4.2.3 Reduplication

Most monosyllabic ideophones (with the notable exception of *tu*) can be reduplicated, but they are always reduplicated twice, i.e. they occur three times in succession; stress can fall on the penultimate syllable or, more often, on the final syllable.

(627) | Baba | wa-phand-a | matsere | **ngi-ngi-ngi**. |
|---|---|---|---|
| 1a.father | 3SG.PST-plant-FV | 6.maize | IDEO |

'Father has planted the maize **very close together**.'

(628) | Ma-tone | ga | mvula | ga-na-mwag-ik-a | **dwe-dwe-dwe**. |
|---|---|---|---|---|
| 6-drops | 6.ASS | 9.rain | 6-CONT-pour-STAT-FV | IDEO |

'The raindrops are dripping **drip, drip, drip**.'

Reduplicated ideophones can co-occur with degree adverbs for emphasis:

(629) | Wa-mu-on-a | yuya | m-sichana | ni | mwereru | **tse-tse-tse** | **kabisa**. |
|---|---|---|---|---|---|---|
| 3SG.PST-3SG-see-FV | 1.DEM2 | 1-girl | COP | 1.white | IDEO | DEG |

'He saw that the girl was **absolutely completely** white.'

6.4.2.4 Disyllabic ideophones

Disyllabic ideophones are usually more specific in their meanings and collocational restrictions than monosyllabic ideophones, and they are always reduplicated:

(630) | Mvula | i-na-ny-a | **gbwaja-gbwaja**. |
|---|---|---|
| 9.rain | 9-CONT-rain-FV | IDEO |

'It is raining **torrentially**.'

(631) | Chitanda | hichi | chi-na-rir-a | **gbwenye-gbwenye**. |
|---|---|---|---|
| 7.bed | 7.DEM1 | 7-CONT-groan-FV | IDEO |

'This bed creaks **creak-creak**.'

(632) A-na-sikir-a   umande,   kpwa hivyo   a-ka-dzi-bwining-iz-a
      3SG-CONT-hear-FV   14.cold   therefore   3SG-HOD-REFL-cover-CAUS-FV
      nguwo   **kubu-kubu.**
      9.clothes   IDEO
      'He is feeling cold, so he has covered himself **from head to toe**.'

A number of disyllabic ideophones refer to the action or sound of water:

(633) Madzi   ga-na-okoh-a   **dzimwa-dzimwa.**
      6.water   6-CONT-boil-FV   IDEO
      'The water is boiling; it's bubbling nicely.'

(634) Madzi   ga   muho   ga-na-mwag-ik-a   **gubu-gubu.**
      6.water   6.ASS   3.river   6-CONT-pour-STAT-FV   IDEO
      'The river water is overflowing steadily.'

(635) Madzi   ga-na-mwag-ik-a   **puya-puya.**
      6.water   6-CONT-pour-STAT-FV   IDEO
      'The water is overflowing rapidly/gushing out.'

6.4.2.5 Onomatopoeic ideophones

Digo has other ideophones which are purely onomatopoeic; these typically occur as left- or right-dislocated elements outside the clause, and may be di- or trisyllabic:

(636) **Bugulu,**   a-chi-injir-a   ndani.
      IDEO   3SG-CONS-enter-FV   inside
      '**Kerplonk**, in he went.'

6.4.2.6 Ideophones describing colours

The three 'basic' colours (*kundu* 'red', *-ereru* 'white', and *-iru* 'black') can be modified by reduplicated ideophones which act as intensifiers but are specific to each colour:

(637) Mwezi   u-chi-kal-a   **kundu**   **do-do-do**   dza   mlatso.
      3.moon   3-CONS-become-FV   3.red   IDEO   like   3.blood
      'The moon became **bright red** like blood.'

(638) Kandzu   za-o   zi-chi-kal-a   **nyereru**   **tse-tse-tse.**
      10.gowns   10-3PL.POS   10-CONS-become-FV   10.white   IDEO
      'Their gowns became **brilliant white**.'

6.4 Adverbs and ideophones

(639) Ri-chi-galuk-a rangi ri-chi-kal-a **dz-iru** **pi-pi-pi**
5-CONS-change-FV 9.colour 5-CONS-become-FV 5-black IDEO

dza makala.
like 6.charcoal

'It changed colour and became **jet black** like charcoal.'

The ideophone *tse-tse-tse* can also mean 'completely, to a high degree' with reference to qualities other than the colour white, so only *pi-pi-pi* and *do-do-do* are uniquely colour ideophones.

7

Clause and Sentence Structure

This chapter is divided into five main sections:

§7.1 'Basic clause structure' looks at verbs and their arguments in clauses containing a single verb.
§7.2 'Information structure' describes (amongst other things) how variations in word order are used to indicate what a sentence is about (the topic) and what is "new information" (the focus).
§7.3 'Relative clauses' describes clauses which are embedded within a noun phrase and identify or provide information about the (actual or elided) head noun.
§7.4 'Complex sentences' looks at sequences of clauses in which one or more of the clauses is syntactically dependent on the first in the sequence. Clause chaining occurs when the clauses are semantically independent (in a coordinate relationship), whereas complement clauses function like complements of 'matrix' verbs such as 'persuade', 'appear', 'promise', and 'threaten'.
§7.5 'Locative inversion' describes clauses in which the subject concord on the verb agrees with one of the locative noun classes (16 *pha*, 17 *ku*, and 18 *mu*) whilst the logical or thematic subject is a noun phrase from another noun class which follows the verb.

Nonverbal predicates are dealt with separately, in chapter 8 'Being and Having'.

7.1 Basic clause structure

In this section we will look at the possible word orders in different clause types,[1] and the restrictions that the grammar imposes on word order variation. I will assume that Digo has a default canonical word order which can be overridden by grammatical agreement but which comes into play when agreement does not disambiguate syntactic roles.

7.1.1 Intransitive clauses

An intransitive clause, for our purposes, is a clause without a lexical object NP or a verb complement marker in the verbal group (locatives are treated as non-arguments of the verb). By far the most frequent order in intransitive clauses is SV(Loc):

(640) Simba   wa-fw-a.
      1a.lion 3SG.PST-die-FV
      'The lion died.'

(641) Yuya   bwana   wa-phiy-a   vy-akpwe   kaya.
      1.DEM2   1a.man   3SG.PST-go-FV   8-3SG.POS   9.home
      'That man went on his way home.'

The order VS(Loc) is also possible:

(642) A-chi-nyamal-a   yuno   bwana.
      3SG-CONS-fall_silent-FV   1.DEM4   1a.man
      'The man fell silent.' (lit: 'He fell silent that man.')

(643) Wa-phiy-a   yuya   bwana   hiko   tsaka-ni.
      3SG.PST-go-FV   1.DEM2   1a.man   17.DEM3 9.forest-LOC
      'The man went into the forest.' (lit: 'He went, that man, into the forest.')

The postverbal subject is in fact a right-dislocated topic (see §7.2.2), and therefore the grammatical subject is strictly speaking the SC and not the NP (*yuya bwana*). This is shown by the fact that a locative can also occur *before* a postverbal NP. Locatives are nonarguments of the predicate, and as such occur in the periphery of a clause, that is, outside the core which contains the predicate and its arguments. The fact that a locative can occur between the verb and the NP indicates that the NP is not part of the core, and therefore is not functioning syntactically as an argument:

---

[1] But see, for example, Whiteley (1968), Whiteley and Mganga (1969), Amidu (2001), and Thwala (2006:209–210) for discussions of the difficulties there are distinguishing intransitive and transitive clauses in Bantu languages.

7.1 Basic clause structure

(644) Wa-uy-a   kaya   yuya   mutu.
      3SG.PST-return-FV 9.home   1.DEM2   1.person
      'The man returned home.' (lit: 'He returned home, that person.')

This kind of construction is different from cases of locative inversion (see §7.5 for a fuller discussion). In locative inversion, illustrated in the following example, the SC agrees with one of the locative noun classes and so the logical or thematic subject which follows the verb is not the grammatical subject. Such sentences do not constitute either VS or (strictly speaking) VO order, since the NP is neither a grammatical subject nor a grammatical object.

(645) **Ku-a-tsap-a**   a-jema.
      17-PST-pass-FV   2-tapper
      'There passed palm wine tappers.' [No overt locative]

7.1.2 Transitive clauses

Transitive clauses are clauses containing verbal complements. Mchombo (2004:27–30) includes object NPs, infinitival constructions, and embedded sentences introduced by a complementizer as verbal complements. However, we will restrict our discussion here to clauses containing object NPs, since it is not always possible to categorize complement clauses as syntactic arguments such as direct object or oblique object; moreover prototypical transitive verbs (e.g. *make, build*) do not take complement clauses. Complement clauses are discussed separately in §7.4.2.

The canonical word order in transitive clauses is SVO:

(646) Yuya   bwana   wa-rim-a   munda.
      1.DEM2   1a.man   3SG.PST-cultivate-FV   3.field
      'That man cultivated a field.'

Dryer (1997b; 2007b:79) argues that if the traditional terms S, V, and O are used, they should be discussed in relation to two separate typologies: SV vs. VS and VO vs. OV. We have already seen how both SV and VS word orders are possible in intransitive clauses; in this section, we will look at VO and OV word orders in turn.

7.1.2.1 VO clauses

The majority of transitive clauses are VO without an overt subject NP. When the object NP occurs after the verb, it must be adjacent to the verb, so VOS is possible but not VSO. In speech, there is a pause before the subject NP in VOS clauses, indicating that 'S' is actually is a right-dislocated topic (see §7.2.3). As noted in the discussion of VS order in intransitive clauses, this means that, strictly speaking, the grammatical subject of the clause is the SC rather than the 'subject' NP, indicated by the parenthesis (S) in the examples below. (Note that 2nd person pronouns and demonstratives—as in the following examples— are inherently topical.)

(647) **Kuonere jahazi we** na mwanachetu kumuonere mumo.

'**You did not see the dhow** and you did not see the woman in it.'

Ku-on-ere	jahazi	we
2SG.NEG-see-PFV	9.dhow	2SG
V	O	(S)

(648)
Mwisho	wa-hend-a	mimba	yuyu.
finally	3SG.PST-do-FV	9.pregnancy	1.DEM1_VARIANT
	V	O	(S)

'Finally she became pregnant.' (lit: 'Finally she made pregnancy, that one.')

7.1.2.2 OV clauses

When the object NP precedes the verb, OSV and SOV word orders are possible. The following passage illustrates OSV and SOV word orders respectively. Note that in example (649b) with the order SOV, there is a verb complement concord (VC) which is, in fact, obligatory (*zi* in class 10 agreeing with *zino pesa*):

(649) Phahi wahewa hara atu, akafika atu auzwa, achiamba, "**Pesa sino hunahewa kpweli ni hiye Mwarabu.**" Ndipho yuya Mwarabu naye achidziuza, "**Mutu yuno zino pesa aziphahaphi?**"

'So he gave those people (money), (when) they arrived people were asked, and they said, "**Money we are given** truly by this Arab." Then that Arab likewise asked himself, "**That person that money where does he get it from?**"'

a.
Pesa	sino	hu-na-hew-a
10.money	1PL	1PL-CONT-give.PAS-FV
O	S	V

b.
Mutu	yuno	zino	pesa	a-zi-phah-a=phi?
1.person	1.DEM4	10.DEM4	10.money	3SG-10-get-FV=Q
[S	...]	[O	...]	V

With the order OSV, there may be no VC, as in the first part of the example above, in which *pesa* 'money' is indefinite, but when the object is definite (indicated, for example, by the presence of a demonstrative) a VC is required, as in the following example:

7.1 Basic clause structure

(650) labuda **zo pesa yuyu mlumewe azilavya** kuko hiko chumbani.
'perhaps **that money that husband of hers put it** there in the room.'

zo	pesa	yuyu	m-lume-we	a-zi-lavy-a
10.DEM3_VAR	10.money	1.DEM1_VARIANT	1-husband-1.3SG.POS	3SG-10-put-FV
[O	...]	[S	...]	V

The order OVS is also possible so long as there is a VC which agrees with the object NP. As with VOS clauses, there is a pause before the 'subject' NP indicating that this is a right-dislocated topic:

(651) M-kongo   n-ka-mu-on-a   mino.
      1-sick_person   1SG-HOD-3SG-see-FV   1SG
      O   V   (S)

'I have seen the sick person.' (lit: 'The sick person, I have seen her, me.')

With no overt subject NP, the order OV is possible so long as there is a VC coreferential with the object NP, as in the second clause of example (652), repeated below:

(652) Kuonere jahazi we na **mwanachetu kumuonere** mumo.
'You did not see the dhow and **you did not see the woman** in it.'

mwanachetu	ku-**mu**-on-ere	mumo.
1-woman	2SG.NEG-3SG-see-PFV	18.DEM3_VARIANT

(lit: 'the woman you did not see her in it')

In the two previous examples, where an 'object' NP immediately precedes the verb (with no intervening subject NP), the verb group contains a VC. In fact, whenever O immediately precedes V, a VC coreferential with O is obligatory. However, with the order OSV (where a subject NP intervenes between O and V), a VC is optional. This can be seen in example (649a), in which there is no VC, and example (649b) in which there is a VC (*zi* which is coreferential with *zino pesa*). The 'object' NP in an OV sentence can be either a topicalized NP or a left-dislocated constituent which has been moved out of the clause core and is therefore not the syntactic object. According to Foley and Van Valin (1984:132) left-dislocation "differs from topicalization structurally in that instead of a gap in the clause following the topic there is a resumptive pronoun," which functions structurally as the grammatical object. In Digo, the VC has the function of a resumptive pronoun in OV sentences. This means that the presence or absence of a coreferential VC indicates the grammatical status of the 'object' NP. Thus, when a VC is present, as in OV, SOV, and OVS sentences (where O immediately precedes V) and in some OSV sentences such as example (650), the presence of a VC indicates that the coreferential NP is a left-dislocated constituent rather than the grammatical object of the clause. When there is no VC, as in example (649a), the object NP is topicalized. Therefore, when there is a subject NP, it is the presence or absence of a VC which indicates the grammatical status of the 'object' NP, rather than which NP is adjacent to the verb.

The requirement to have a coreferential VC can be dropped in imperative clauses (which lack a SC and TAM marker):

(653) Mayo   ini   hiri   kalang-a u-ry-e.
      1a.mother 5.liver 5.DEM1 fry-FV   2SG-eat-SUB
      'Mother, this liver fry (and) eat (it).'

The order OV is obligatory when the logical object is 'possessed' by the grammatical object, as in the following example where the logical object *magombige* 'its dialect' is 'possessed' by the grammatical object *hichi chuma* 'this iron'—in the story, a magical machine which responds to spoken instructions. The grammatical object (coreferential with the class 7 VC marker *chi-*) is the topic, and the rest of the sentence is a comment on this topic:

(654) Hichi   chuma   si-**chi**-many-a   magombi-ge.
      7.DEM1 7.iron 1SG.NEG-7-know-FV 6.dialect-6.3SG.POS
      [O   ...   ] V
      'I don't know this iron's dialect.' (lit: 'This iron, I don't know it its dialect.')

7.1.3 Ditransitive clauses

Ditransitive clauses contain two objects. With the 3-place predicate 'give', in addition to the Agent (the giver) there are two nonsubject arguments: a Recipient (R) and a Theme (T) (something which undergoes a change of location or ownership). Languages differ as to whether R or T is marked in the same way as the single object of a transitive clause, which is typically a Patient (P). In languages in which T exhibits the same characteristics as P, T and P are grouped together as 'direct' objects while R is termed the 'indirect' object. In languages in which P and R exhibit the same characteristics, they are termed 'primary' objects while T is termed the 'secondary' object (Dryer 2007a:253–256).

The object of a transitive clause in Digo typically occurs immediately after the verb and can be indicated within the verbal group by a verb complement concord (VC). In a ditransitive clause, the recipient (in bold type in the example below) occurs immediately after the verb and is indicated within the verbal group by a VC, but the Theme cannot have these properties. Thus Digo has primary and secondary objects.

7.1 Basic clause structure

(655) Yuya   m-chetu   wa-**mu**-ph-a   **m-lume-we**   mtele na nyama.
    1.DEM2 1-woman 3SG.PST-3SG-give-FV 1-husband-1.3SG.POS 3.rice COM 9.meat
    'That woman gave **her husband** rice and meat.'

It is possible for either the primary object or the secondary object to be fronted, so long as the verbal group contains a VC coreferential with the primary object. In the following examples, the primary object and the coreferential VC are in bold type:

(656) **Chila   mutu**   n-nda-**m**-riph-a   elufu   mbiri.
    each   1.person 1SG-FUT-3SG-pay-FV 10.thousand 10.two
    '**Each person** I will pay **him** two thousand.'

(657) Hizi   pesa   na-**ku**-ph-a   **uwe**.
    10.DEM1 10.money 1SG.CONT-2SG-give-FV 2SG
    'This money I am giving (it) to **you**.'

7.1.4 Interrogative clauses

There is no distinctive syntax for polar interrogatives; declarative word order is used and the interrogative function is marked either by the question particle *dze* and/or by rising intonation.

7.1.4.1 Questioning subjects

Digo does not allow so-called *wh*-question words to occur in the preverbal position. This is because they are inherently focal (they are requests for information which is necessarily new information) and a focus NP must occur after the verb, or more accurately, after the predicator. To achieve this, the copula *ni* is introduced as the predicator immediately preceding the *wh*-question word, and the verb is placed in a relative clause. Usually the relative clause follows the copula and question word, but it can precede them. The relative clause may be any of the three types found in Digo: (1) those without a relativizer which are inflected for tense/aspect, (2) those without a relativizer which are not inflected for tense/aspect, and (3) those with a relativizer. Examples of all three constructions are provided below, with the copula and *wh*-question word in bold type:

(658) **Ni   a=ni**   Ø-ye-ku-hend-a[2]   m-tawala w-ehu   na   m-kanyi?
    COP 1=Q (3SG-PST-)1.REL-2SG-make-FV 1-ruler 1-1PL.POS COM 1-judge
    '**Who** made you our ruler and judge?' (lit: '**It is who** who made ...?')

---

[2]This is a shortened form of *a-ri-ye-ku-hend-a* in which the SC *a-* and the relative past tense marker *ri-* are elided.

(659) **Ni a=ni** a-m-hend-a-ye   mutu   a-kal-e   masito ama bubu?
      COP 1=Q 3SG-3SG-make-FV-1.REL 1.person 3SG-be-SUB deaf   or dumb
      '**Who** makes a person deaf or dumb?' (lit: '**It is who** who makes a person deaf or dumb?')

(660) Anjina   **ni** ano **a=ni** amba-o   a-nda-phiy-a na=mwi?
      2.others   COP   PL   2=Q   REL-2.REL 3PL-FUT-go-FV COM=2PL
      '**Which** others will go with you?' (lit: 'Others **are who** who will go with you?')

In equational sentences involving a copula, the *wh*-question word must occur after the copula, in the focus position:

(661) Mayo   **ni** **a=ni**? Na   enehu   **ni** **a=phi**?
      1a.mother COP   1=Q   COM 2.brothers COP   2=Q
      '**Who** is my mother? And **who** are my brothers?' (lit: 'My mother **is who**? And my brothers **are who**?')

7.1.4.2 *Questioning nonsubjects*

A complement of the verb can be questioned using a *wh*-question word *in situ*, since in the canonical SVO word order, verb complements occur after the verb, in the correct position for a focal element.

(662) Ni-gomb-e   **ga=phi**?
      1SG-speak-SUB   6=Q
      'What should I say?' (lit: 'I should say **what**?' Class 6 agrees with an understood *maneno* '6.words'.)

Other elements of the sentence, including nonarguments such as obliques (indicating time, location, instrument, accompaniment, manner, reason, etc.) and modifiers of the core arguments, are also questioned *in situ*:

(663) U-nda-zik-w-a   **ni** **a=ni** hano   a-chi-ku-chimbir-a?
      2SG-FUT-bury-PAS-FV   COP   1=Q   2.DEM4   3PL-DEP-2SG-run_away-FV
      'You will be buried **by whom** if these (people) desert you?'

(664) Yuya   mwanache a-l-a=**phi**?
      1.DEM2   1.child   3SG-come_from-FV=Q
      'Where does that child come from?' (lit: 'That child she comes from **where**?')

(665) Mino n-ka-hew-a   chakurya cha=**ni**?
      1SG   1SG-HOD-be_given-FV   7.food   7=Q
      'What food have I been given?' (lit: 'Me I have been given **what** food?')

(666) Ye   mwanachetu   a-si-ye-gomb-a   u-ya-gomb-a   na=ye   vi=**phi**?
      1.DEM3_VAR 1-woman   3SG-NEG-1.REL-   2SG-FUT.IT-   COM=3SG 8=Q
                               speak-FV   speak-FV
'The woman who doesn't speak, how are you going to speak with her?'
(lit: 'You are going to speak with her **how?**')

Nonsubjects can also be questioned using the interrogative clitics *dze* 'what, how', *ni* 'what', *phi* 'where' (see §4.1.11.1).

7.2 Information structure

This section picks up the issue of word order[3] variation which was introduced in §7.1. However, whereas §7.1 took as its starting point the various forms which sentences can take, this section looks at the functions of word order variation as it contributes to the pragmatic structuring of an utterance or text. The principles governing the relation of syntax (word order) to pragmatics (the expression of a communicator's intentions) are part of 'information structure', which concerns the ways in which communicators (speakers or writers) use linguistic resources to help addressees (hearers or readers) identify new information in an utterance or text and to combine it with information that they already have in order to arrive at a coherent interpretation. Information structure in Digo is primarily concerned with word order, but the use of pauses and the focus marker *che* (see §7.2.6) also play a role. In languages like English, intonation plays a prominent role.

7.2.1 Basic concepts of information structure

From the perspective of information structure, the basic 'building blocks' of a sentence are TOPIC and FOCUS; the ways in which these building blocks are assembled in particular sentences are known as SENTENCE ARTICULATIONS. In this section, topic and focus will be defined first of all, and then these notions will be related to the different sentence articulations. The sections that follow will describe information structure in Digo in greater detail.

A sentence typically provides information about something; that something is called the *topic*.[4] According to Lambrecht, "[t]he topic of a sentence is the thing which the proposition expressed by the sentence is *about*" (1994:118, original emphasis). The notion of 'aboutness' is intentionally broad: a sentence may provide additional information about the topic, it may be a request for information about

---

[3] Strictly speaking, what we will be concerned with here is 'constituent' order or phrase order; the order of words within a noun phrase is dealt with in chapter 3 (Noun Phrases). However, since the expression 'word order' is in common usage, we will use it here.
[4] Vallduví (1993) uses the term 'ground' rather than 'topic' but we will continue to use 'topic' since it is more widespread in the literature (e.g. Lambrecht 1994) and the term 'ground' is also used in a different sense in opposition to 'figure' as the background against which an object moves.

the topic (in the case of a question), or it may tell the addressee to do something about the topic (in the case of a command or request), and so on. It is possible for a sentence to contain more than one topic—although one topic will be the "main" topic (Erteschik-Shir 2007:22)—but it is also possible for an utterance to contain only new information (for example. at the beginning of a story), in which case there is no topic. Topics do not have to be definite, but they must be referential (Prince 1981).

Information "which cannot be taken for granted at the time of speech" (Lambrecht 1994:207), including information about the topic, is called the *focus*. Vallduví (1993:57–8) notes that the focus of a sentence is "the only nonelidable part of the sentence, since it is the only contribution to the hearer's knowledge store at the time of the utterance (or so the speaker assumes)." The focus may be encoded by an NP alone ('argument focus'), by a predicate and (optionally) its complements ('predicate focus', also called 'comment' when it occurs after the subject), or by a whole sentence ('sentence focus'). Predicate focus and sentence focus are together known as 'broad focus'. In Digo, a sentence need not contain a lexical subject since the SC indicates the subject; at the same time the SC is obligatory (with the exception of clauses containing certain TAM markers, described in chapter 5), and so there is often no formal difference between predicate focus and sentence focus in clauses without an overt lexical subject.

Topic and focus[5] can be represented in various ways within a sentence, following certain templates or generalized constructions known as sentence articulations. There are three primary sentence articulations: topic-comment, identificational, and presentational (Andrews 2007:148–51, Gundel 1988, Lambrecht 1994). Topic-comment articulation consists of a lexical (usually nominal) topic plus predicate focus; identificational articulation uses argument focus to identify a 'missing' argument in a proposition; presentational articulation uses sentence focus to introduce a new argument without reference to any existing topic or presupposed proposition. In the following sections, I will describe topics and various kinds of focus in Digo using the categories introduced above.

7.2.2   Switch topics, continued topics, and right-dislocation

Usually, a topic consists of established information which has been mentioned explicitly in a previous clause, but there are other ways in which something may be a topic. Situational topics are topics by virtue of being inherent in the speech situation; these include the speaker and the addressee (for example *mino* 'me' in example [667]):

---

[5]The terms 'topic' and 'focus' strictly speaking refer to components of information, "things" according to Lambrecht (1994:118), whilst the linguistic expressions which correspond to these components of information in a sentence are referred to as 'topic expressions' and 'focus expressions' respectively. However, following common usage, I will refer to both the components of information and their corresponding linguistic expressions as 'topic' and 'focus', as the contexts in which these terms are used make the intended referent clear.

7.2 Information structure

(667) "We bwana **mino** u-na-ni-many-a?"
2SG 1a.sir 1SG 2SG-CONT-1SG-know-FV
"'You sir, **me**, do you know me?'"

A referent may be a topic by virtue of being a member of a set of things which have been previously mentioned collectively:

(668) "... nataka atu anjina mia mbiri akale miane.
Chila   mutu   n-nda-m-riph-a   elufu   mbiri."
each   1.person   1SG-FUT-3SG-pay-FV   10.thousand   10.two
"'... I want another two hundred people to make four hundred. **Each person**, I will pay him two thousand.'"

A topic can also be implicit in the context but not overtly mentioned. Such an implied topic is a husband whose existence is presupposed by previous mention of a woman:

(669) Hipho kare, kpwahenda mchetu yekala karya sima, arya nyama bahi. Phahi **yuya mlume** waamba, "Mkpwazangu karya sima ..."

'Long ago, there was a woman who did not eat ugali, she only ate meat. So **that man (i.e. her husband)** said, "My wife does not eat ugali ..."'

As well as being subjects and objects, topics can be obliques (elements occurring outside of the clause core, typically expressing concepts such as time, location, instrument, accompaniment, manner, and comparison). In the following example, the topic zira pesa zokupha 'that money which he gave you' is an accompaniment:

(670) zira   pesa   Ø-zo-ku-ph-a
10.DEM2   10.money   (3SG-PST-)10.REL-2SG-give-FV
wa-phiy-a   na=zo   Mambasa
2SG.PST-go-FV   COM=10.REF   PLACE_NAME
'That money which he gave you, you went with it (to) Mombasa.'

There can be more than one topic in a sentence. In the following example, there are two topics: the man (yuya bwana) and the food which his wife has prepared (hura wari). Since both are topics, both are placed before the predicate giving a superficial SOV word order. This order is only possible with a verb complement (u- in this example) which agrees with the object (hura wari), which indicates that the object is left-dislocated (see §7.1.2.2). Since the subject occurs to the left of the object (and is separated from the object by a pause), this is also left-dislocated. In the story from which the example comes, the wife has just killed a magic bird which had been laying money for her husband ...

(671) *Anaambwa ni mchewe, "Nyama hiyu ni ye ariye mo chumbani, mino che taphana mboga nkamtsindza. Nkarya kare uphande wangu nkakusazira wako." Phahi* **yuya bwana hura wari kayaurya**, *mana ka anamanya iye ndiye nyama anyaye pesa. Yuya bwana walala na ndzala.*

'He was told by his wife, "This meat/animal is that (bird) which was in the room; (as for) me, well there was no sauce, and I slaughtered it. I have already eaten my portion and I have saved yours for you." So **that man, that food, he did not eat it**, for he knew that it was the animal which laid money. That man slept hungry.'

[yuya   bwana]   [hura   wari]   ka-ya-u-ry-a
1.DEM2   1a.man   14.DEM2   14.rice 3SG.NEG-PST-14-eat-FV
[(S)/Topic 1]   [(O)/Topic 2]   V

In a coherent discourse, the topic of one clause may continue to be the topic in the following clause, in which case it is called a continued topic. Alternatively, the topic may change and a new topic may be selected from the currently available referents, in which case it is called a switch topic (a topic in one clause which was not the topic of the previous clause). It is important to know whether a topic is a continued topic or a switch topic, as this can affect where it occurs in the sentence and the way it is referred to (with a 'bare' NP, with a Demonstrative Phrase containing a particular demonstrative, with zero reference, etc.). Typically, a continued topic receives minimal linguistic encoding whereas a switch topic is lexically encoded. In Digo, continued topics are almost always subjects referred to using a SC alone. The following example presents a sequence of continued topic followed by switch topic; the second clause (beginning *ananipha*) contains a continued topic referred to using a SC alone (*a-*) whereas the final clause contains a switch topic, *go mafuha ga taa* 'that lamp oil', which was the focus of the previous clause:

(672) *"Pho yuno kanipha vitu,* **a-na-ni-ph-a**   *mafuha   ga   taa*
                                 3SG-CONT-1SG-give-FV   6.oil   6.ASS 9.lamp

bahi,   **go**   **mafuha   ga   taa**   *ndo*   *n'-ya-ry-a?"*
only   6.DEM3_VAR   6.oil   6.ASS 9.lamp   EXCLAM   1SG-FUT.IT-eat-FV

"'So that one doesn't give me anything (lit: things), **he** gives me lamp oil only, **that lamp oil** can I eat (it)?'"

Switch topics always occur before the verb, whether they are subjects or complements of the verb.[6] There is very often a pause following a switch topic,

---

[6] Vallduví (1993:54–65) uses the term 'link' to refer to switch topics; a link must be sentence-initial and functions as the "address pointer" telling the addressee to "go to an existing address," that is, to select an entity in the current discourse as the new topic.

7.2 Information structure

and occasionally an interjection may separate the topic from the rest of the clause (such as *ndo* in example [672]). This indicates that even when the topic is a 'subject' NP, it is often left-dislocated (that is, syntactically outside of the clause core). Where the topic is an 'object' NP which precedes the rest of the clause and there is a coreferential VC in the verb group, it is always left-dislocated (see §7.1.2.2). The rest of the clause provides new information in the form of the predicate and its complement, and is therefore predicate focus, also known as the comment. In the following example, *mtihani* is a left-dislocated switch topic, and the grammatical object is the coreferential class 3 VC -*u*.

(673) *Vino mwanangu watukuzwa,* **mtihani wauhenda vinono.**

'Now my child you have earned praise, **in the exam, you did well.**'

mtihani	wa-**u**-hend-a	vi-nono.
3.exam	2SG.PST-3-do-FV	8-good
[Topic]	[Comment	...]

In example (674), *barabara* 'road' is a switch topic which is implied by the mention of the subject travelling. It is an object, so is left-dislocated with a coreferential VC (verb complement concord), *i*-, on the following verb:

(674) *Phahi, waphiya vyakpwe, akafika ko mbere,*
barabara *ndipho a-ka-i-rich-a*
9.road then 3SG-SEQ-9-leave-FV

'So, he went on his way, he reached (a place) ahead, **the road** then he left **it**'

In all of the preceding examples, the topic has preceded the rest of the clause. Topics do not always occur clause-initially, however; they can be right-dislocated (occurring after the predicate, outside of the clause core). When the topic is also the 'subject' NP, which is usually the case, this results in a superficial VS word order. With VS word order, if S is semantically definite (indicated, for example, by the presence of a demonstrative) it is always a right-dislocated topic. (For a discussion of postverbal subjects which are not right-dislocated topics, see §7.2.5.) Right-dislocation can occur for various reasons, which will be discussed below.

VS order often occurs at the point in a narrative where the chronological sequence of events begins, after the scene has been set. The major participant (the protagonist) is usually introduced in the scene setting and is therefore a topic. However, the position before V is reserved for switch topics, and so if S is lexically encoded it cannot occur before V, and therefore has to occur after V. Since it is definite, it is right-dislocated. The following example illustrates this. The topic is the husband, who is introduced in the first paragraph when the scene is set. In the second paragraph, the husband is a continued topic but because this is the point at which the action begins, he is referred to using a NP (*yuya mlume* 'that man'). Since the position before V is reserved for switch topics, the NP occurs after V:

(675) *Hipho kare, kpwahenda mchetu yekala karya sima, arya nyama bahi. Phahi yuya mlume waamba, "Mkpwazangu karya sima, arya nyama za sokoni za kuhendagula, n'ndaremwa, baha nphiye tsakani nkahege mihambo ili mkpwazangu aphahe nyama."* **Waphiya yuya bwana hiko tsakani** ....

'Long ago, there was a woman who did not eat ugali, she only ate meat. So her husband (lit: that man/husband) said, "My wife doesn't eat ugali, she eats meat from the market which has to be bought, I will become exhausted, it is better I go to the forest to go and set traps so that my wife can get meat." **He went, that man, to the forest** ....'

Wa-phiy-a	**yuya**	**bwana**	hiko	tsaka-ni.
3SG.PST-go-FV	1.DEM2	1a.man	17.DEM3	5.forest-LOC
[Focus ...	[	Topic]	...	Focus]

In example (676), *simba* 'lion' and *mchetu* 'woman' are already topical, and the fact that the woman has been caught in a trap is introduced in a dependent clause, as a complement of *waona* 'he saw'. This important piece of information is repeated using the anterior aspect marker *ka-* and VS word order. The information is not new, but is presented a second time in an independent clause for emphasis. As in the previous example, the position before V is reserved for switch topics, and so the topic *yuya mchetu* 'that woman' is right-dislocated:

(676) *Simba waona yuya mchetu achigbwirwa ni muhambo,* **akagbwirwa ni muhambo yuya mchetu.**

'The lion saw (that) the woman had been caught by a trap, **she had been caught by a trap, that woman.**'

a-ka-gbwir-w-a	ni	mu-hambo	**yuya**	**m-chetu**
3SG-ANT-seize-PAS-FV	by	3-trap	1.DEM2	1-woman
[Focus	...	...]	[Topic	...]

In some cases (for example after an extended period of direct speech) it is desirable to 'reactivate' a topic, that is, to remind the addressee of what the topic is even though it has not changed. Since the position before V is reserved for switch topics, reactivated topics occur after V:

7.2 Information structure

(677) *Yuya bwana warima munda uchifika dza Mazera, na hiku uchifika dza Malindi ela kaguwire hata tsere mwenga. Achidziuza mwakpwe rohoni, "Pho munda nkauhenda mkpwulu na sikaphaha hata tsere mwenga, kpwani nini?" Lakini **achinyamala mutu yuyu**, wala kayagomba na mutu.*

'That man farmed a field reaching to Mazeras, and on the other side reaching Malindi, but he did not harvest even one cob of corn. He asked himself in his heart, "That field I made it big and I didn't get even one cob of corn, whyever not?" But **he remained silent that man**, neither did he speak with anyone.'

a-chi-nyamal-a	***mutu***	***yuyu***
3SG-CONS-be_silent-FV	1.person	1.DEM1_VARIANT
[Focus]	[Topic	...]

Finally, right-dislocated topics can also be objects. In the following example, *mino* 'me' is mentioned for emphasis (the object is already indicated in the verb group by the VC *ni*). From the context it is clear that the man will get meat from his traps, and the lion (who owns the forest) wants to know what he will receive in return. Since the position before V is reserved for switch topics, *mino* is right-dislocated:

(678) *Yuyu mutu achiamba, "Mino mkpwazangu karya sima, arya nyama kpwa nyama, pho nkaona ichikala nndahega mihambo bila ya kukpwambira, si vizuri, baha edze hushibane."*
*Anaambwa ni hiye simba, "**Uchigbwira nyama undaniphani mino?**"*

'That man said, "(As for) me, my wife does not eat ugali, she only eats meat, so I thought if I set traps without telling you, it is not good, it is better we come and talk together."
'He was told by the lion, "**If you catch an animal, what will you give me?**"'

U-chi-gbwir-a	*nyama*	*u-nda-ni-pha=ni*	***mino***
2SG-DEP-catch-FV	1a.animal	2SG-FUT-1SG-give=Q	1SG

7.2.3 Topic-comment articulation and predicate focus

Information about a topic NP is often provided by the predicate (a verb group) and (optionally) its complements, that is, in the form of predicate focus. When predicate focus follows the topic, this is known as topic-comment articulation (that is, a 'comment' is a predicate focus which follows the topic).[7] Statistically,

---

[7] Within topic-comment articulation it is also possible to distinguish between undifferentiated comments, in which all the information contained in the comment is of equal importance, and comments containing one element which is more important than the rest; this important element is known as the "dominant focal element (DFE)" (Heimerdinger 1999:167). Levinsohn (2004:§4, p.5) notes that "[i]n some languages, the identification of a DFE among the constituents of the

this is the most common sentence articulation in Digo, with the exception of clauses where there is no overt lexical topic.

Predicates can also be nonverbal, as in copula sentences, and therefore predicate focus can also be expressed with nonverbal predicates. In so-called 'equational' sentences, in which two noun phrases are juxtaposed, the first functioning as the subject and the second as the (nonverbal) predicate, the order of subject and predicate cannot always be reversed. This is because the first NP is the topic and the second is the focus (since there is no verb, this is a case of predicate focus rather than argument focus). In example (679), *Mimi* 'I' refers to the speaker and is therefore a situational topic, but the information that the speaker is the addressee's father is new in the context of the story from which this example is taken, and so is the focus. In example (680), at this point in the story the addressee knows that he has been given a wife as a reward, but he does not know that the particular woman designated by *hiyu* is the one who will be his wife. The order of the NPs in these examples cannot be reversed.

(679) Mimi   sowe   tu.
      1SG   1a.your_father   only
      [Topic]   [Comment]
      'I am only your father.'

(680) Mche-o   babu   hiyu.
      1.wife-1.2SG.POS   1a.grandfather*   3SG.DEM3   (*term of respect)
      [Topic]   [Comment]
      'Your wife, sir, is this one.'

7.2.4 Identificational articulation and argument focus

Identificational sentences "serve to identify a referent as the missing argument in an open proposition" (Lambrecht 1994:122). The missing element which is identified is expressed using argument focus (that is, the focal element is encoded by a single constituent, or argument). Identificational articulation is also referred to as focus-presupposition sentence articulation because it occurs in contexts where a proposition is already presupposed, such as information questions (Lambrecht and Michaelis 1998). In example (681), the question 'What will the crocodile have to eat?' presupposes the proposition 'The crocodile will have *something* to eat.' The following clause identifies the missing element (the 'something') as *uwe* 'you (SG)' which occurs at the end of the clause:

---

comment can be of great value in explaining variations in constituent order or the position of a prominence-marking particle .... In others, there seems to be little value in identifying a DFE." In Digo, there is no evidence that DFEs are distinguished structurally from the rest of the predicate, and so they will not be discussed further.

(681) *Chakurya-che   chi-nda-kal-a   **uwe.***
7.food-7.3SG.POS   7-FUT-be-FV   2SG
'Its food will be **you**.'

The subject of a clause can be focused through the use of a cleft construction (see §7.3.4.2 and §8.2.2), in which the focused element is embedded in a relative clause containing the construction *ndi*+referential marker (see §8.1.2.1). In the following example, the fact that there is a leader is presupposed (the section of the book from which the sentence comes is headed *Ulongozi* 'Leadership'); the sentence serves to identify the leader:

(682) *Hangu   jadi,   **m-lume   ndi=ye**   a-kala-ye   chilongozi.*
since   9.custom   1-man   COP=3SG.REF   3SG-be-3SG.REL   7.leader
'According to custom, **it was a man who** was leader.'

In example (683), the hearers/readers of the story already know that there is a particular bird which magically lays money, but the woman in the story does not know this. The sentence expresses the fact that the bird which the woman has just slaughtered is that same bird which lays money:

(683) *Yuya   m-chetu   wa-m-gbwir-a   a-chi-m-tsindz-a,*
1.DEM2   1-woman   3SG.PST-3SG-seize-FV   3SG-CONS-3SG-slaughter-FV

*kumbavi   **iye   ndi=ye**   kala   a-nya-ye   pesa.*
EXCLAM   3SG   COP=3SG.REF   PST   3SG-lay-3SG.REL   10.money
'That woman seized it and slaughtered it, (but) good heavens **that was the one which** laid money.'

7.2.5 Presentational articulation and sentence focus

Presentational articulation is so called because it is a way of presenting an entity for the first time without giving information about an existing topic or a presupposed proposition. Presentational articulation in Digo often involves locative inversion (see §7.5) in which the SC on the verb is from a locative noun class:

(684) *Hipho kare   **ku**-a-kal-a   na   a-sichana   a-iri ...*
long ago   17-PST-be-FV   COM   2-girls   2-two
'Long ago there were two girls ...'

Since there is no topic, presentational sentences exhibit sentence focus. Sentence focus also includes 'event-reporting' sentences. Presentational sentences and event-reporting sentences are often syntactically similar, if not identical, and both can be subsumed under the more general category of 'thetic sentences'. The characteristic of a thetic sentence is that it "introduces a new element into the discourse without linking this element either to an already established topic or to some presupposed proposition" (Lambrecht 1994:144). Following Sasse (1987), the terms 'entity-central' and 'event-central' thetic sentences are sometimes used to refer to presentational sentences and event-reporting sentences, respectively.

Sentence focus in Digo can be expressed by positioning subjects after the verb group. Postverbal subjects can be distinguished from right-dislocated topics because nontopic subject NPs are bare and indefinite, and there is no pause between the verb group and the subject. In the following example, although cats have been mentioned, the particular cats which are slaughtered have not been previously identified and so the right-dislocated NP is not a topic. This is a case of an event-reporting sentence:

(685) *Wamuamba Sulutani, "Mkpwongo nkamuona mino, ela niphahira minyau sabaa." Yo minyau hipho pha Sulutani ni minji hata taina kazi, ichiphahikana kare.* **Ichitsindzwa minyau sabaa** *ichihendwa hirizi, ...*

'He said to the Sultan, "The patient I have seen her, but give me seven cats." The cats there at the Sultan's place were very many, and they were easily obtained. **Seven cats were slaughtered** and they were made (into) charms, ...'

I-chi-tsindz-w-a	minyau	sabaa
4-CONS-slaughter-PAS-FV	4.cats	seven

'They were slaughtered seven cats'

Sentence focus can be structurally identical to topic-comment articulation where there is a bare lexical subject NP, and sentence focus and predicate focus can also be structurally identical where there is no lexical subject NP. In such cases, context alone indicates which kind of focus is intended. The following passage contains three thetic sentences, each of which is expressed using a different kind of sentence focus: first with a bare lexical subject NP and SV word order; second with a bare lexical subject NP and VS word order; and third with no subject NP.

(686) *Phahi waphiya hata kaya, akafika kaya, waamba, "Nataka nyumba ishirini za simiti."* **Nyumba zadzengbwa** *chilimwenga ni hicho chuma, ela adzengao taaonekana. Anaamba, "Nataka magunia mia mbiri ga vyakurya."* **Gachizembuka magunia mia mbiri**, *achiaamba, "Nataka ng'ombe kumi."* **Zichizembuka**, *na n'cho chuma.*

'So he went home, he arrived home, he said, "I want twenty houses of cement." **Houses were built** at once by that iron, but those who built were not visible. He says, "I want two hundred sacks of food." **Two hundred sacks appeared (lit: They appeared two hundred sacks)**, and he said, "I want ten cows." **They appeared**, and it was (because of) that iron.'

7.2 Information structure

In example (686), *Nyumba zadzengbwa* 'Houses were built' has the usual SV word order; although the NP *nyumba* was previously mentioned in direct discourse, the houses themselves did not yet exist at that time, so the previous sentence does not provide information about actual houses. In other words, in the second sentence, the bare lexical subject NP *nyumba* is not a topic. Rather, this is an example of an event-centred thetic sentence expressed using sentence focus.

Gachizembuka magunia mia mbiri 'They appeared two hundred sacks' differs in that the emphasis is not on the event but on the entity. Although the sacks of food are mentioned in the previous clause (in direct speech) they do not as yet exist and so this is an entity-centred thetic sentence. It states the existence of the sacks and introduces them into the story using right-dislocation of the subject (VS word order). The fact that the NP is bare (no demonstrative, etc.) and semantically indefinite indicates that this is not a right-dislocated topic (see above).

Finally, *Zichizembuka* 'They appeared' referring to *ng'ombe* 'cows' contains no lexical subject and so could express either predicate focus or sentence focus. The fact that this clause introduces the cows into the story, suggests that this should be viewed as sentence focus.

7.2.6 The focus marker *che*

The focus marker *che* (discussed briefly in §6.2.4) can (optionally) precede the part of a clause which expresses either predicate focus or sentence focus (no examples of *che* preceding argument focus have been recorded). If a predicate is preceded by a topic, *che* intervenes between the topic and the predicate, and there is a notable pause after the topic, indicative of left-dislocation:

(687) *Ndipho naye anatambukira gara achigoambirwa phara usiku, akagagbwira kare. Mana **hara atu achiomuambira, che sio atu, che ni shetani**.*

'The he remembered what he had been told that night, and he understood immediately. For **those people who had told him, *che* they were not people, *che* they were demons**.'

hara	*atu*	*a-chi-o-mu-ambir-a,*	*che*	*sio*	*atu,*
2.DEM2	2.people	2-CONS-2.REL-3SG-tell-FV	FOC	NEG.COP	2.people
[Topic	...	...]		[Predicate Focus]	

che	*ni*	*shetani*
FOC	COP	10.demons
[Predicate Focus]		

In the majority of occurrences in the corpus of nontranslated texts, the topic expression is one of the independent personal pronouns, with metarepresentational forms of the first and second person (see §3.3.2) predominating. In the following example from the end of the story about a woman who only ate meat, *che* occurs four times, each time following an independent pronoun:

(688) *"Mino nakurehera nyama chila siku, sambi kura tsakani **we che ukalungani**?"*
Anaamba, *"**Mino** hata nkedza nyuma mlume wangu, **che náona gaga maini kuna mchetu kuko ahewaye**. Sambi **mino che nákulunga-lunga** edze nikutane na hiye mchetu nipigane naye, anipige nimpige. **Mino che náriwa ni wivu**, kumbavi mahumbo gariwa ni simba."*

'"Me I brought you meat every day, now there in the forest **you *che* what were you looking for**?"'

'She says, "Me even I came behind my husband, ***che* I thought those livers there was a woman there who was given (them)**. Now me *che* I followed you so that I could meet this woman and fight with her, she hitting me and I hitting her. **Me *che* I was eaten up by jealousy**, yet the innards were eaten by the lion."'

a.	we	che	u-ka-lung-a=ni		
	2SG	FOC	2SG-HOD-search=Q		
	[Topic]		[Predicate Focus]		
b.	Mino ...	che	ná-on-a	gaga	ma-ini ...
	1SG	FOC	1SG.PST-see-FV	6.DEM1_VARIANT	6-liver
	[Topic]		[Predicate Focus		...]
c.	mino	che	ná-ku-lung-a-lung-a		
	1SG	FOC	1SG.PST-2SG-follow-FV-follow-FV		
	[Topic]		[Predicate Focus]		
d.	Mino	che	ná-ri-w-a	ni	wivu
	1SG	FOC	1SG.PST-eat-PAS-FV	by	14.jealousy
	[Topic]		[Predicate Focus	...	...]

The focus marker *che* can also emphasize predicate focus within a conditional clause (in the following example, indicated by *kala* 'if'), as well as in subordinate clauses (for example, following *mana* 'for'):

(689) *Simba anaamba, "We bwana, usinicheleweshe phano, **mino kala che ni m'baya**, **che sikuiha, mana che kumanya** kala nyama akagbwirwa nyumazo.*

'Lion says, "You sir, do not delay me here, **me, if *che* I were bad, *che* I would not call you, for *che* you do not know** that an animal has been caught behind you."'

mino	kala	che	ni	m'-baya,	che	si-ku-ih-a	mana
1SG	if	FOC	COP	1-bad	FOC	1SG.NEG-2SG-call-FV	for

che	ku-many-a
FOC	2SG.NEG-know-FV

7.2 Information structure 243

Finally, *che* can emphasize parenthetical clauses (for example *taphana mboga* 'there was no sauce' embedded within the topic-comment structure *mino ... nkamtsindza* 'me ... I slaughtered it' in the following example):

(690) *Nyama hiyu ni ye ariye mo chumbani, mino **che taphana mboga** nkamtsindza.*

'This meat/animal is the (bird) which was in the room, me, **che there was no sauce**, and I slaughtered it.'

mino	che	ta-pha=na	mboga	n-ka-m-tsindz-a.
1SG	FOC	COP-16=COM	9.sauce	1SG-SEQ-3SG-slaughter-FV
		[Sentence	Focus]	
[Topic]				[Predicate Focus]

7.2.7 Text

To end this section, part of a narrative text is presented, with every clause described in terms of information structure.

1.	point of departure	sentence focus	(presentational articulation)
	Hipho kare,	*kpwahenda mutu na mchewe,*	
	Long ago,	there was a person and his wife	

2.	predicate focus	(*mutu na mchewe* in 1. functions as topic)
	achivyala mwana wao.	
	they bore their child.	

3.	predicate focus	(continued topic so no lexical topic expression)
	Achirima tsulu mwenga	
	They farmed one termite mound	

4.	implied topic (left-dislocated object)	predicate focus	(elaboration)
	vyakuryavye	*taavimala*	*hata kala ni miaka mihahu.*
	its food	they did not finish it	even after three years.

5.	switch topic	predicate focus	(speech acts as complement)
	Yuya m-lume	*achiamba,*	
	That man	said	

6.	situational topic	point of departure	predicate focus
	"*Mino*	*rivyo nchirima tsula*	*n'naphaha,*
	"Me	when I farmed a termite mound	I was getting

7.		predicate focus	(elaboration)
	phahi	ndarima dza phapha na ko Mwamtsola,	ili niphahe vitu vinji vyanjina niguze nigule ng'ombe."
	so	I will farm from here to Mwamtsola,	so that I can get many other things to sell and buy a cow."

8.	topic[8]	predicate focus	
	Yuya bwana	warima munda uchifika dza Mazera, na hiku uchifika dza Malindi	
	That man	he farmed a field reaching from Mazeras to Malindi	

9.		predicate focus
	ela	kaguwire hata tsere mwenga.
	but	he did not peel even a single maize cob.

10.	predicate focus (speech acts as complement)	(continued topic)
	Achidziuza mwakpwe rohoni,	
	He asked himself in his heart	

11.	switch topic	predicate focus
	"Pho munda	nkauhenda mkpwulu
	"That field	I have made it big

12.		predicate focus	(elaboration)
	na	sikaphaha hata tsere mwenga,	kpwani nini?"
	and	I have not got even a single maize cob,	but why?"

13.		predicate focus	continued topic[9]	(from before speech)
	Lakini	achinyamala	mutu yuyu,	
	But	he stayed silent	that person,	

14.		predicate focus
	wala	kayagomba na mutu.
	neither	did he speak with anyone.

15.	point of departure	switch topic	predicate focus
	Halafu	hura munda	achiuenjereza zaidi
	Then	that field	he increased it even more

---

[8] Readers may have noticed that the topic has not in fact changed; there has been some direct speech since the last mention of the man, but no other topic has been introduced. The most likely explanation for repeating *Yuya bwana* before the verb, in the position reserved for switch topics, is that a significant amount of time has passed between the events in lines 7 and 8, and the speaker wishes to indicate that line 8 starts a new 'thematic unit', hence the man is treated as if he were a new topic.

[9] The situation here is different from that in line 8. Here in line 13, *mutu yuyu* occurs after the verb as a right-dislocated continued topic, indicating that line 13 is a continuation of thematic unit which was begun in line 8.

16.		predicate focus	(continued topic, no lexical topic expression)
	ela	achikosa vivyo.
	but	he failed none the less.

7.3 Relative clauses

7.3.1 Introduction

A relative clause (RC) is a clause which is embedded within a noun phrase and which serves to identify or provide information about the referent of the head noun (if there is one). All RCs with an overt head noun are postnominal in Digo; that is, the relative clause follows the head noun if there is one. In discussing relative clauses in Digo, I will use the following terminology:

Head: the noun phrase which is modified by the relative clause; syntactically it occurs outside of the relative clause. In the examples, the head will always be underlined. As will be seen, an overt head is optional.
Relative clause (RC): this is the clause which modifies the head noun. In the examples the relative clause will always be enclosed in square brackets (in both the Digo example and the following free translation).
Relative concord: the morpheme within the RC which is coreferential with the head, showing noun class agreement with the head noun. In the examples, the relative concord will always be highlighted using bold type.
Relativizer: this is the element which introduces the RC in much the same way that a complementizer introduces a complement clause. As will be seen, not all RCs contain a relativizer. A relative concord is suffixed to the relativizer if the relativizer is present.

In this section, I will discuss RCs in Digo from three perspectives. First, in §7.3.2, I will focus on the RC itself, distinguishing three structurally distinct kinds of RC. Then in §7.3.3, I will consider RCs from the perspective of the grammatical role of the head, using the NP accessibility hierarchy of Keenan and Comrie (1977). In §7.3.4, I will describe the function of RCs in Digo in terms of the restrictive/nonrestrictive distinction and the use of RCs in cleft constructions, including questions. Finally, in §7.3.5, I will provide examples of phonological variation with noun class 2. RCs containing copulas are discussed separately in §8.1.5.

7.3.2 Types of relative clause

There are three RC constructions in Digo: (1) those without a relativizer which are inflected for tense/aspect, (2) those without a relativizer which are not inflected for tense/aspect, and (3) those with a relativizer. In all three constructions, the relative concord for first and second person head nouns is that of noun class 1 (for singular heads) and 2 (for plural heads); example (691) illustrates class 1 agreement with a 2SG head, and example (692) illustrates class 2 agreement with a 2PL head:

(691) <u>uwe</u>   ndi=<u>we</u>   [ni-ku-voy-a-**ye**]
     2SG   COP=2SG.REF 1SG-2SG-pray-FV-1.REL
     'you are the one [to whom I pray]' (lit: 'you it is you [to whom I pray]')

(692) <u>Mwimwi</u> [ambao mnakula] ni dzulu yenu kumanyirira mifugo yenu.
     'You [who are growing up] it is up to you to know about your animals.'

     <u>Mwimwi</u>   [amba-**o** m-na-kul-a]
     2PL   REL-2.REL 2PL-CONT-grow-FV

After the three constructions have been discussed, this subsection will conclude with a description of constructions involving sequences of RCs.

7.3.2.1 Inflected relative clauses

In inflected RCs, the relative concord occurs between the TAM/negative marker and the verb stem (and before the verb complement concord if there is one). The TAM markers which can occur in inflected RCs are the following (see chapter 5 for details):

    na-   continuous aspect marker (which also occurs in matrix clauses)
    ri-   relative past tense
    ndi-   relative future tense
    chi-   relative anterior aspect marker
    si-   negative

No examples of headless inflected RCs (that is, inflected RCs without an overt head noun) have been recorded.

With the relative past tense (see §5.2.3.1), the SC and TAM marker are often omitted when the subject is relativized. In the following relative clauses, the subject of the RC agrees with the head noun and the tense is past, but whilst this information is overtly encoded in (693) through the SC and the TAM marker respectively, in (694) this information must be inferred.

(693) <u>m-chetu</u>   [a-ri-**ye**-fwerer-w-a   ni   m-lume]
     1-woman   3SG-PST-1.REL-bereave-PAS-FV by 1-man
     'a/the woman [who was bereaved of her husband]'

(694) <u>yuya</u>   <u>m-chetu</u>   [**ye**-zik-w-a   dzana]
     1.DEM2 1-woman   1.REL-bury-PAS-FV yesterday
     'that woman [who was buried yesterday]' (same as a-ri-ye-zik-w-a)

7.3 Relative clauses

When an argument other than the subject is relativized, the SC and TAM marker are included far more frequently and the VC (verb complement marker) is optional. In the following object relative clauses, the class 14 VC *u-* is present in *ariouimba* in example (695) but the class 6 VC *ga-* does not occur in *hurigobisha* in example (696):

(695) <u>wira</u>   wenye   [*a-ri-o-u-imb-a*]
      14.song   14.ASS   3SG-PST-14.REL-14-sing-FV
      'the song itself [which he sang]'

(696) <u>gara</u>   [*hu-ri-go-bish-a*   *dzuzi*]
      6.DEM2   1PL-PST-6.REL-discuss-FV   day_before_yesterday
      'those (matters) [which we discussed two days ago]'

It is possible for the SC and TAM to be omitted when a nonsubject is relativized, but this situation occurs far less frequently than when the subject is relativized:

(697) <u>hiye</u>   ndi=<u>ye</u>   [***ye****-ku-ambir-a-ni*]
      1.DEM3   COP=1.REF   1.REL-2-tell-FV-PL
      'that is he [about whom I told you/who I told you about]'

Equivalent to:

<u>hiye</u>   ndi=<u>ye</u>   [*ni-ri-**ye**-ku-ambir-a-ni*]
1.DEM3   COP=1.REF   1SG-PST-1.REL-2-tell-FV-PL

(698) <u>Mutu</u>   [***ye****-gany-a*   *na=ye*   *mkahe*],
      1.person   1.REL-share-FV   COM=1.REF   3.bread
      ndi=<u>ye</u>   [***ye****-ni-galuk-ir-a*].
      COP=1.REF   1.REL-1SG-turn-APPL-FV
      'The person [with whom I shared bread], is he [who has turned against me].'

Equivalent to:

<u>Mutu</u>   [*ni-ri-**ye**-gany-a*   *na=ye*   *mkahe*],
1.person   1SG-PST-1.REL-share-FV   COM=1.REF   3.bread
ndi=<u>ye</u>   [*a-ri-**ye**-ni-galuk-ir-a*].
COP=1.REF   3SG-PST-1.REL-1SG-turn-APPL-FV

The relative future TAM marker *ndi-* (see §5.2.3.2) only occurs with an overt 2nd person plural subject concord marker (example [699]), although this is optional (example [700]); for all other persons and noun classes, the SC is obligatorily omitted. However, the TAM marker itself cannot be omitted:

(699) si   mwimwi   [m-ndi-o-gomb-a]
      NEG.COP   2PL   2PL-FUT-2.REL-speak-FV
      'it is not you(pl) [who will speak]'

(700) wakati   [ndi-pho-kal-a   m-tumiya]
      14.time   FUT-16.REL-become-FV   1-old_person
      'the time [when you will become an old man]'

The relative anterior aspect marker *chi-* (see §5.3.1.5) usually occurs with an overt SC, but when the subject is relativized, this can be omitted (obligatorily when the subject is 3SG). Unlike the relative past tense, however, but like the relative future tense, the relative anterior TAM marker itself cannot be omitted:

(701) gara   [ga-chi-go-gomb-w-a]
      6.DEM2   6-ANT-6.REL-speak-PAS-FV
      'those (words) [which have been spoken]'

(702) rira   [chi-ro-angamik-a]
      5.DEM2   ANT-5.REL-be_lost-FV
      'that [which has been lost]' (equivalent to *ri-chi-ro-angamik-a*)

Negative inflected relative clauses

None of the TAM markers which occur in inflected RCs can co-occur with a negative marker. However, the negative marker *si-* can occur in the 'slot' otherwise occupied by a TAM marker. This construction usually expresses negation in relation to nonspecific or present time, as in example (703), but it can be used in past time contexts, as in example (704):

(703) maingu   [ga-si-go-reh-a   mvula]
      6.clouds 6-NEG-6.REL-bring-FV   9.rain
      'clouds [which do not bring rain]'

(704) Mana   kare   sisi   hw-a-kal-a   a-jinga,
      for   long_ago   1PL   1PL-PST-be-FV   2-fools
      [a-si-o-sikir-a   na   a-ri-o-cheng-w-a].
      3PL-NEG-2.REL-hear-FV   COM   3PL-PST-2.REL-deceive-PAS-FV
      'For long ago we were fools, [who did not listen and who were deceived].'

More often, to express a negative relative with past time reference a construction containing the *amba-* relativizer plus a relative concord followed by a negative past tense verb form is used. Alternatively, the relative past tense

7.3 Relative clauses

form of the auxiliary verb *kala* 'be' can be followed by a general negative verb form, as in (705):

(705) *hipho kare ku-a-hend-a m-chetu [ye-kal-a ka-ry-a sima].*
long_ago 17-PST-do-FV 1-woman 3SG.REL-be-FV 3SG.NEG-eat-FV 9.maize_meal
'long ago there was a woman [who did not eat maize meal]'

With the negative marker *si-*, the SC can be omitted with relativized subjects. The negative cannot co-occur with an overt TAM marker, and so when the SC is omitted, only the negative marker remains:

(706) *chakurya [si-**cho**-banang-ik-a]*
7.food NEG-7.REL-destroy-STAT-FV
'food [which does not go bad]'

With relativized nonsubjects, the SC is obligatory (note that the VC is optional— *chi-* refers to *chochosi* in example (707), but in (708) there is no verb complement concord (VC) *ga-* coreferential with *mambo*):

(707) *chochosi [a-si-**cho**-chi-many-a]*
7.whatever 3SG-NEG-7.REL-7-know-FV
'whatever [he does not know]'

(708) *mambo [a-si-**go**-elew-a]*
6.matters 3SG-NEG-6.REL-understand-FV
'matters [which she does not understand]'

7.3.2.2 Uninflected relative clauses

In uninflected RCs there is no TAM marker in the verb group and the relative concord occurs in the postfinal slot (after the final vowel; see §4.1.10.2). Because it is not inflected for tense/aspect, this construction can only be used when the time reference is either coreferential with the current context or 'universal', as in example (709):

(709) *Unga hinyo nkutiwa lungoni na nkutsungbwa, na* **unga** *[uphahikanao] ndio [ujitwao jora].*

'That flour is put into a winnowing basket and sifted, and **the flour [which is obtained] is [what is used to cook jora].**'

unga [u-phah-ikan-a-o] ndi=o [u-jit-w-a-o] jora
14.flour 14-get-STAT-FV-14.REL COP=14.REF 14-cook-PAS-FV-14.REL 9.jora[10]

---

[10] A staple similar to maize meal but made from dried and powdered cassava.

Uninflected RCs can occur without an overt head noun (that is, they can be headless):

(710) *[Aphiyaye ukalani] achiuya ni auye na nyama phano.*
'[The one who goes hunting] when he returns he should bring meat.'

[*A-phiy-a-**ye*** *ukala-ni*]
3SG-go-FV-1.REL 14.hunting-LOC

As with inflected RCs, the verb complement concord (VC) is optional when the head is a complement of the verb; in (711) *zi-* is the VC referring to *koma zosi*, but in (712) there is no VC *chi-* referring to *chitabu*:

(711) <u>*koma*</u>   <u>*z-osi*</u>   [*ni-**zi**-many-a-**zo*** na *ni-si-**zo**-**zi**-many-a*]
10.spirits 10-all 1SG-10-know-FV-10.REL COM 1SG-NEG-10.REL-10-know-FV
'all the ancestral spirits [which I know and those which I don't know]'

(712) *chitabu* [*a-som-a-**cho***]
7.book 3SG-read-FV-7.REL
'the book [which she reads]'

7.3.2.3 Relative clauses with the amba- relativizer

In RCs with a relativizer, the relative concord is suffixed to the relativizer *amba-* which occurs at the beginning of the RC. The relative clauses which follow an *amba-* relativizer do not differ structurally from main clauses, and can contain any tense or aspect; the following examples illustrate RCs with the future tense (713), habitual aspect (714), and the past anterior complex construction (715).

(713) <u>*chakurya-cho*</u> [*amba-**cho*** *u-nda-ry-a*]
7.food-7.2SG.POS REL-7.REL 2SG-FUT-eat-FV
'your food [which you will eat]'

(714) *Jora ni* <u>*chakurya*</u> [*amba-**cho*** *nku-r-ik-a sana*].
jora COP 7.food REL-7.REL HAB-eat-STAT-FV DEG
'Jora is food [which is very good to eat].'

7.3 Relative clauses

(715) Hira   Jumane   [amba-**yo**   kala   a-ka-amb-w-a   a-phiy-e]
9.DEM2 Wednesday REL-9.REL PST   3SG-ANT-tell-PAS-FV 3SG-go-SUB
ka-phih[11]-ire,   a-chi-phiy-a   Alamisi.
3SG.NEG-go-PFV 3SG-CONS-go-FV Thursday

'That Wednesday [on which he had been told to go], he did not go, he went on Thursday.'

As with inflected and uninflected RCs, the VC is optional with the *amba-* relativizer; in (716), *undachirya* with the VC *chi-* is also grammatical:

(716) chakurya-cho   [amba-**cho**   u-nda-ry-a]
7.food-7.2SG.POS REL-7.REL   2SG-FUT-eat-FV

'your food [which you will eat]'

The *amba-* relativizer can introduce headless RCs:

(717) [Amba-**ye**   ka-taki   ku-rim-a]   na=a-si-ry-e
REL-1.REL 3SG.NEG-want INF-farm-FV EMPH=3SG-NEG-eat-SUBJ

'[Whoever does not want to farm], let him not eat.'

Material such as the adverbial phrase *mara nyinji* 'many times' can intervene between the *amba-* relativizer and the predicate (in this case, the copula *ni*):

(718) Alimu a <u>atu hinya</u> [ambao mara nyinji ni anache] ni avyere.

'The teachers of these people, [who often are children], are older people.'

atu   hinya   [amba-o   mara   nyinji   ni   anache]
2.people 2.DEM1   REL-2.REL 10.times 10.many   COP   2.children

At the start of stories when a major participant is introduced, a past tense RC involving the copula *kala* is sometimes found where in other contexts *amba* would be expected. (See §8.1.5.2 for details of RCs with *kala*.)

(719) Hipho kare, kpwahenda <u>mutu</u> [yekala kaziye ni kutema mihi na kutsanga kuni].

'Long ago, there was a man [whose work was to fell trees and split firewood].' (lit: 'who was his work was to ...')

mutu   [**ye**-kala   kazi-ye   ni   ku-tem-a   mihi...]
1.person 1.REL-PST.COP 9.work-9.3SG.POS COP   INF-fell-FV 4.trees

instead of:

mutu   [amba-**ye**   kazi-ye   ni   ku-tem-a   mihi...]
1.person REL-1.REL   9.work-9.3SG.POS COP INF-fell-FV 4.trees

---

[11] Note the irregular negative perfective form of the verb *phiya*; the root *phih-* is the historically older form from which *phiy-* developed (see sec. 4.2.4).

7.3.2.4 Relative clauses in sequence

When a head is modified by more than one clause, only the first has the formal properties of a RC; the other clauses use one of the dependent tense forms (the consecutive *chi-* following the relative past tense or the sequential *ka-* otherwise) and do not contain a relative concord marker. (Example (720) lacks an overt TAM marker, but this can only be an underlying past as only the relative past tense marker can be omitted together with the SC.)

(720) Makopa ni *manga* [*ye*-guwi-w-a na
 makopa COP 1a.cassava 1.REL-peel-PAS-FV COM
 a-*chi*-anik-w-a na dzuwa hadi a-*chi*-um-a].
 1-CONS-leave_out-PAS-FV COM 5.sun until 1-CONS-dry-FV

 'Makopa is cassava [which has been peeled and left out in the sun until it dries].'

(721) Takuna [afwa*ye* akauya wala akasikirwa anaimba], phahi koma dza koma.

 'There is not (any person) [who dies and returns nor is heard singing], that is madness, total madness.'

 Ta-ku=na [a-fwa-*ye* a-*ka*-uy-a wala a-*ka*-sikir-w-a a-na-imb-a]
 NEG-15=COM 3SG-die-1.REL 3SG-SEQ-return-FV nor 3SG-SEQ-hear-PAS-FV 3SG-CONT-sing-FV

7.3.3 Relativized heads and the NP accessibility hierarchy

According to the NP accessibility hierarchy of Keenan and Comrie (1977), a language may have a primary relativization strategy which may be restricted in terms of the grammatical role of the head noun. Grammatical roles are arranged in the implicational scale, such that if a head noun with a given grammatical role can be relativized using the primary relativization strategy, any head noun with a grammatical role to the left of it can also be relativized using the same strategy:

SU > DO > IO > OBL > GEN (possessor)[12]

The most restricted relative clause constructions are those in which the relative concord occurs on the verb (inflected and uninflected RCs). These will be treated as a single type and termed *internal relative constructions*. RCs formed using the *amba-* relativizer, which will be termed *external relative constructions* for the purpose of comparison, have a wider distribution. This suggests that

---

[12]There is a final grammatical role in the hierarchy: OCOMP (object of comparison), e.g. 'The house [which the giant is bigger than].' There are no examples of this construction in the corpus and it will not be discussed.

7.3 Relative clauses

internal relative constructions represent the 'primary' relativization strategy in terms of the accessibility hierarchy. The remainder of this section will deal with object, oblique, and genitive (possessor) relativization.

7.3.3.1 Object relativization

Digo has primary and secondary objects, rather than direct and indirect objects; that is, recipients behave like patients in that both can occur immediately after the verb and may have a coreferential VC, whereas the theme (the object undergoing a change of location or ownership) does not have these properties (see §7.1.3 for a discussion). Primary and secondary object relative clauses are discussed together because both exhibit the same properties as far as relativization is concerned in Digo. For example, there is no morphosyntactic difference between the complements of the verb *laga* 'promise' in the following two examples. The complement in example (722) is the recipient, a role associated with primary objects, and the complement in example (723) is the theme, a role associated with secondary objects; however, both immediately precede the relative clause and are marked on the verb by a relative concord.

(722) aho   ndi=o   [a-ri-o-a-lag-a   ku-a-ph-a   nguma]
3PL   COP=2.REF   3SG-PST-2.REL-3PL-promise-FV   INF-3PL-give-FV   9.honour
'they are those [to whom he promised to give honour]'

(723) u-vyazi-o   [n-ri-o-ku-lag-a]
14-offspring-14.2SG.POS   1SG-PST-2.REL-2SG-promise-FV
'your offspring [whom I promised you]'

When the subject of an internal object relative clause is expressed lexically, it obligatorily occurs immediately after the verb:

(724) ta-m-many-a   siku   [ndi-yo-uy-a   bwana   wenu]
NEG-2PL-know-FV   9.day   FUT-9.REL-return-FV   1a.master   1.2PL.POS
'you(pl) do not know the day [when your master will return]'

*ta-m-many-a   siku   [bwana   wenu   ndi-yo-uy-a]
NEG-2PL-know-FV   9.day   1a.master   1.2PL.POS   FUT-9.REL-return-FV

When the subject of an external object relative clause is expressed lexically, it usually occurs before the verb (a lexical subject can occur in a postverbal position within a relative clause if the discourse structure of the text requires it):

(725) mambo   [amba-**go**   Mlungu   wa-ga-hend-a].
      6.things   REL-6.REL   1a.God   3SG.PST-6-do-FV
      'the things [which God did].'

7.3.3.2 Oblique relativization

The OBL (oblique) role includes beneficiary, goal and source, location, instrument, manner, and accompaniment. Both internal and external relativization strategies can be used to relativize all oblique roles. Examples of relativization of the different kinds of obliques are provided below.

7.3.3.2.1 Beneficiary

Example (726) illustrates internal relativization of a beneficiary using an inflected RC (the 1SG SC *a-* and the relative past tense marker *ri-* are not overtly marked in this example).

(726) Hiye chiswere [**ye**henderwa vilinje achiphozwa] ka ana zaidi ya miaka arubaini.

'That lame man [to/for whom the miracle was done and who was healed] was over forty years old.'

Hiye   chiswere   [**ye**-hend-er-w-a   vilinje   a-chi-phoz-w-a]
1.DEM3   7.lame_man   1.REL-do-APPL-PAS-FV   8.miracles   3SG-CONS-heal-PAS-FV

Example (727) illustrates external relativization of a beneficiary using the *amba-* relativizer.

(727) Dzambo hiro andahewa hara [ambao aikirwa kare].

'This thing will be given to those [for whom it was prepared in advance].'

hara   [amba-**o**   a-ik-ir-w-a   kare].
2.DEM2   REL-2.REL   3PL-put-APPL-PAS-FV   ANT

7.3.3.2.2 Source, goal, and location

Source, goal, and location (which are not always distinguished morphosyntactically in Digo) can be relativized internally and externally. Example (728) illustrates a headless RC with an internally relativized source and goal using relative concords of the locative noun class 17.

(728) Huchihendani hivyo hundamanya [huri**ko**la na huna**ko**phiyani].

'If we all do this we will know [where we come from and where we are going].'

[hu-ri-**ko**-l-a   na   hu-na-**ko**-phiy-a-ni].
1PL-PST-17.REL-come_from-FV   COM   1PL-CONT-17.REL-go_to-FV-PL

7.3 Relative clauses

The following two examples illustrate relativized locations using the locative noun class 16; (729) uses internal relativization and (730) uses external relativization. Note that, as with object relative clauses, a lexical subject occurs after the verb in an internal relative construction and before the verb in an external relative construction:

(729) chaa-ni   [a-ri-**pho**-zik-w-a   yuya   m-sichana]
      7.enclosure-LOC 3PL-PST-16.REL-bury-PAS-FV 1.DEM2   1-girl
      'the enclosure [in which they buried that young girl]'

(730) "Rome" ni phahali [amba**pho** mtumiya akasagala na anae a chilume kubisha ng'andzi zao].
      'A "rome" was a place [in which an elder sat with his sons to have their discussions].'

      phahali   [amba-**pho**   m-tumiya   a-ka-sagal-a ...]
      16.place REL-16.REL   1-old_person   3SG-ANT-sit-FV

Location is not only expressed by means of the three locative noun classes; where a noun refers intrinsically to a location (such as *tsi* 'country') the relative concord can agree with the inherent noun class of the noun:

(731) tsi   [**yo**-sagal-a   ise]
      9.country   9.REL-live-FV   1.our_father
      'the country [in which our father lived]'

7.3.3.2.3 Instrument

The following example illustrates inflected and uninflected RCs in which the instrument has been internally relativized.

(732) Chipimo   [m-pim-ir-a-**cho**]   aya-wenu],
      7.measure   2PL-measure-APPL-FV-7.REL   2.fellows-2.2PL.POS
      ndi=cho   [ndi-**cho**-pim-ir-w-a   mwimwi].
      COP=7.REF   FUT-7.REL-measure-APPL-PAS-FV   2PL
      'The measure [with which you measure your fellow], this is (the measure) [with/by which you will be measured].'

7.3.3.2.4 Manner

Noun class 8 is used in Digo to create "manner deictics," such as the demonstrative form *vira* which refers in the examples below to the manner of speaking as well as to the content of the speech. Example (733) illustrates internal relativization of manner using an inflected RC. Note that the lexical subject *msemo* 'saying' occurs before the verb; this is in contrast to the position of lexical subjects in internal object and location relative constructions.

(733) Kama <u>vira</u> msemo [*urivyoamba*], "Mchiya na mwanawe, tajiri na maliye."
       'As the saying goes, "A poor man and his child, a rich man and his wealth."'

<u>vira</u>   msemo   [*u-ri-**vyo**-amb-a*]
8.DEM2   4.saying   4-PST-8.REL-say-FV

lit: '<u>how/thus</u> the saying [**how** it was said]'

Example (734) illustrates external relativization using the *amba-* relativizer:

(734) <u>vira</u>   [*amba-**vyo**   na-ku-amb-ir-a*]
       8.DEM2   REL-8.REL   1SG.CONT-2SG-say-APPL-FV
       'how/what I tell you'

7.3.3.2.5 Accompaniment

In independent clauses, accompaniments (noun phrases which refer to entities which accompany the entity referred to by the grammatical subject of the clause) occur outside of the clause core and are preceded by the comitative particle *na*. When an accompaniment is relativized, a referential marker of the same noun class is cliticized to *na*. In the following examples, which illustrate internal and external relativization strategies respectively, the comitative particle and cliticized referential marker have been underlined. For each relative clause, the corresponding independent clause has been provided for comparison.

(735) <u>ayangu</u>   [*n-ri-o-phiy-a*   <u>na=o</u>]
       2.fellows.2.1SG.POS   1SG-PST-2.REL-go-FV   COM=2.REF
       'my companions [with whom I went]' or 'my companions [whom I went with]'

       ná-phiy-a   *na*   *ayangu*
       1SG.PST-go-FV   COM   2.fellows.2.1SG.POS
       'I went with my companions'

(736) <u>atu</u>   osi   [*amba-o*   *u-na-safiri*   <u>na=o</u>]
       2.people   2.all   REL-2.REL   2SG-CONT-travel   COM=2.REF
       'all the people [with whom you are travelling]'

       u-na-safiri   *na*   *atu*   *osi*
       2SG-CONT-travel   COM   2.people   2.all
       'you are travelling with all the people'

7.3 Relative clauses

Idiomatic uses of accompaniments can also be relativized in the same ways. In the examples below, being afraid is expressed as being with fear, and being ashamed of something is expressed as seeing shame with something.

(737) <u>wasiwasi-we</u>   [a-ri-o-kal-a   <u>na=o</u>]
      14.fear-14.3SG.POS   3SG-PST-14.REL-be-FV   COM=14.REF

'what he was afraid of' (lit: 'his fear [which he was with it]')

(738) <u>mambo</u>   [amba-**go**   sambi   m-na-on-a   haya   <u>na=go</u>]
      6.things   REL-6.REL   now   2PL-CONT-see-FV   9.shame   COM=6.REF

'the things of which you are now ashamed' (lit: 'the things [which now you see shame with them]')

7.3.3.3 Genitive (possessor) relativization

Genitive possession in Digo uses a resumptive pronoun strategy where alienable possession is concerned. That is, when relativizing a possessor in Digo, the head (i.e. the possessor) must be referred to separately within the RC either by means of a coreferential NP or by means of a coreferential possessive construction. In example (739) the head noun phrase is repeated within the RC preceded by the associative particle *ga* as part of the noun phrase *madzi ga chisima hichi* 'water of this well'.

(739) *Iye wahurichira <u>chisima hichi</u> [amba-**cho** iye mwenye, anae na mifugoye, osi anwa madzi ga <u>chisima hichi</u>].*

'He left to us this well [whose water he himself, his children and his flocks, all drank].' (lit: '... this well [which he himself, his children and his flocks, all drank the water of this well].')

chisima	hichi	[amba-**cho**	...	osi	a-nw-a
7.well	7.DEM1	REL-7.REL		2.all	3PL.PST-drink-FV

madzi	ga	chisima	hichi].
6.water	6.ASS	7.well	7.DEM1

In example (740), the 3SG possessive suffix *-vye* is coreferential with the head noun *mutu* 'person' as well as agreeing with the noun class of the possessed items *virahu* 'shoes'.

(740) lakini   a-redz-a   <u>mutu</u>   [amba-**ye**   mimi
      but   3SG-CONT.come-FV   1.person   REL-1.REL   1SG

      si-fwah-a   hata   ku-vul-a   <u>virahu-**vye**</u>]
      1SG.NEG-be_worthy-FV   even   INF-remove-FV   8.shoes-8.3SG.POS

'but a person is coming whose shoes I am not worthy to remove' (lit: '... a person [whom I am not even worthy to remove his shoes].')

Genitive relativization occurs most frequently with external relativization, which is illustrated in the examples above, but internal relativization is also possible, as the following example illustrates.

(741) mutu   hiye   [m-na-**ye**-gomb-a   habari-ze]
      1.person 1.DEM3   2PL-CONT-1.REL-speak-FV   10.news-10.3SG.POS
      'that person [about whom you speak]' (lit: 'this person [whom you speak his news]')

In cases of inalienable possession, the possessor behaves like an object and no resumptive pronoun is required:

(742) Hiye   ni   Johana   [n-ri-**ye**-m-kat-a   chitswa],   a-ka-fufuk-a.
      1.DEM3 COP   NAME   1SG-PST-1.REL-3SG-cut-FV   7.head   3SG-ANT-resurrect-FV
      'That is John [whose head I cut off], come back to life.' (lit: '... John [whom I cut him the head] ...')

7.3.4 Functions of relative clauses

In this subsection, some of the functions of RCs in Digo are described. First, RCs may either identify a referent or provide information about an already identifed referent; these functions are known as restrictive and nonrestrictive respectively and are discussed in §7.3.4.1. Second, RCs occur in cleft constructions either for emphasis or to maintain topic-comment word order (for example, in questions); these functions are discussed in §7.3.4.2.

7.3.4.1 *Restrictive and nonrestrictive relative clauses*

Restrictive RCs help to identify the intended referent by specifying or restricting the set of individuals referred to by the head. Nonrestrictive (or descriptive) RCs provide information about the intended referent, which is assumed to be already identifiable. Both restrictive and nonrestrictive RCs are found in the Digo corpus of nontranslated texts, but nonrestrictive RCs are more common. There is no formal indication of whether a RC is to be interpreted as restrictive or nonrestrictive; instead the context determines the intended interpretation.

In example (743), two individuals are mentioned and a relative clause is used to identify the intended referent of the final clause; that is, the RC is restrictive.

(743) Wa-enderer-a   ku-mu-ph-a   vitu,   a-chi-hew-a
      3SG.PST-continue-FV INF-3SG-give-FV   8.things   3SG-CONS-be_given-FV
      vitu,   chisha   yuya   [a-lavy-a-ye   vitu]   wa-dzi-uz-a ...
      8.things   then   3SG.DEM2 3SG-offer-FV-1.REL   8.things 3SG.PST-REF-ask-FV
      'He continued to give things, and he was given things, then the one [who was giving things] asked himself ...'

In example (744), the referents which are modified by RCs are both already uniquely identifiable, one because it is referred to by a proper name and the other because it is the first referent's mother (and a person only has one mother). The relative clauses can therefore only be interpreted as nonrestrictive (or descriptive).

(744) Mwenehu   ni   uwe   Mwalugundzu Lui
      my_brother   COP   2SG   PROPER NAME
      [u-ri-ye-sal-a   ndani-ni   mwa   mayo,
      2SG-PST-1.REL-remain-FV   inside-LOC   18.ASS   1a.mother
      [amba-ye   wa-fw-a   mwaka   dzana]].
      REL-1.REL   3SG.PST-die-FV   3.year   yesterday
      'My brother it is you Mwalungundzu Lui [who is the only remaining child of your mother [who died last year]].'

Example (744) also illustrates that it is possible for one RC to be embedded within another. No cases of multiple embedding (i.e. involving more than two RCs) have been recorded.

7.3.4.2 Cleft constructions

Cleft constructions are formed when a RC is preceded by a copula construction consisting of the copula *ndi* (negative: *si*) plus a referential marker. They are typically used to express identificational articulation (that is, focus-presupposition sentence articulation) in which the head of the RC is the focused element (see §7.2.4 and §8.2.2), as in the following examples.

(745) hiro   ndi=ro   [ro-m-phah-a   mutu   wa   kani].
      5.DEM3   COP=5.REF   5.REL-3SG-get-FV   1.person   1.ASS   stubborn
      'that is [what happened to the stubborn man].' (lit: 'that it is [that happened to the stubborn man].') (Presupposed: something happened to the stubborn man.)

(746) Iye   ndi=ye   [a-ri-ye-hend-a   mambo   higo].
      3SG   COP=1.REF   3SG-PST-1.REL-do-FV   6.things   6.DEM3
      'It was she who did those things.' (lit: 'She it was she [who did those things].') (Presupposed: someone did those things.)

(747) M-chetu   yuno   si=ye   [ye-ni-vyal-a]   mimi?
      1-woman   1.DEM4   NEG.COP=1.REF   1.REL-1SG-bear-FV   1SG

'Is this not the woman who gave birth to me?' (lit: 'This woman is it not she [who gave birth to me]?') (Presupposed: someone gave birth to me.)

In example (748), the theme of the passage is the work done by children before the advent of schools, and this is explicitly mentioned in the relative clause *kazi ihendwayo ni anache* 'work which was done by young children'. This is identified with *kurisa* through the referential predicator *ndiyo*.

(748) *Siku hizo mwana kala achifikisa miaka mitsano hadi miaka kumi kala kuweza kumhuma cheteni, ela kala anaweza kurisa. Pho kare kala takuna sukuli, ela* **kurisa kala ndiyo kazi [ihendwayo ni anache].**

'In those days when a child reached between five and ten years of age you couldn't send him to the market, but he could herd. Long ago there weren't any schools, but **herding was the work [which was done by young children].**'

ku-ris-a   kala   ndi=yo   kazi   [i-hend-w-a-yo   ni   anache].
INF-herd-FV   PST   COP=9.REF   9.work   9-do-PAS-FV-9.REL   COP   2.children

In *wh*-questions, Digo obligatorily exhibits the order topic-comment rather than Subject-Verb. Since *wh*-question words are inherently focal (that is, they refer to new information) they cannot occur clause-initially. To avoid violating this constraint, *wh*-question words which correspond to the subject are preceded by a copula and the comment clause is 'demoted' to a relative clause:

(749) Ni   a=ni   [ye-ku-hend-a   m-tawala   w-ehu   na   m-kanyi]?
      COP   1=Q   1.REL-2SG-make-FV   1-ruler   1-1PL.POS COM   1-judge

'Who made you our ruler and judge?' (lit: 'It is who [who made you our ruler and judge]?')

*Ani akuhenda mtawala wehu na mkanyi?

7.3.5 Phonological variation

Occasionally, the relative concord and referential marker for class 2 take the form *nyo* which occurs in demonstratives of type 3 (see §3.4.2.3). At present it is unclear what influences the use of this form over the regular relative concord *-o*. The following examples illustrate this variant form:

(750) Kondo iriphogbwa makabila gosi garigokala hipho gatsamukana kuphiya kpwatu tafwauti-tafwauti, ela <u>Muhuruma</u> ndi<u>o</u> [**nyo**baki nyuma].

'When war flared up (lit: seized) all of the tribes which were there scattered to go to their various locations, but the Muhuruma were those [who remained behind.]'

ela	<u>Muhuruma</u>	ndi=<u>o</u>	[**nyo**-baki	nyuma].
but	PROPER_NAME	COP=2.REF	2.REL-remain	behind

(751) kaya hino yaandzwa ni achina Boza na achina Ngala, ndi<u>o</u> [**nyo**kala enye a kaya hino].

'this shrine was founded by the Boza clan and the Ngala clan, and it was they [who became the owners of this shrine].'

ndi=<u>o</u>	[**nyo**-kal-a	enye	a	kaya	hino].
COP=2.REF	2.REL-become-FV	2.owners	2.ASS	9.shrine	9.DEM4

(752)
Achina	Gandi	kala	ndi=**nyo**	Achina	Manji.
PL	NAME	PST	COP=2.REF	PL	NAME

'The Gandi clan were in fact the Manji clan.'

7.4 Complex sentences

This section describes complex sentences resulting from two important processes: clause chaining and complementation. Both clause chaining and complementation involve two or more clauses which occur in sequence, and in which the second and subsequent clauses are syntactically dependent on the first clause, as only the first clause is inflected. In clause chaining the syntactically dependent clauses are semantically independent of the first clause (they are semantically coordinate with the first clause) whilst complement clauses are semantically as well as syntactically dependent on the first clause (they are semantically subordinate).

7.4.1 Clause chaining

'Clause chaining' refers to constructions in which only one verb in a series of clauses is fully inflected. In Digo, if the first verb in a series of clauses is fully inflected the following verbs may either lack full inflection (i.e. they may take the infinitive prefix or be in the subjunctive mood) or if they are inflected the TAM marker is a semantically dependent form such as the consecutive or sequential (see §5.2.2.1 and §5.2.2.2). Since the use of inflected forms has been dealt with in chapter 5, this section will focus exclusively on clause chaining involving infinitive and subjunctive verb forms.

7.4.1.1 Clause chaining with infinitive verb forms

The infinitive (formed with the prefix *ku-*) has various uses. *Ku-* functions in many ways like a noun class concord, and in fact is given the number 15 in the set of noun class concords (see §3.1); infinitive verb forms also occur in certain complement clauses (see §7.4.2). In this section we will consider only the use of the infinitive within a series of independent clauses, in which case it is usually preceded by the comitative marker *na* (see §6.1.1 for a discussion of *na*).

The clauses which are 'chained' together using the infinitive form of the second and subsequent verbs are conceptually linked in some way, but the precise nature of the connection between them is not indicated by the infinitive (or the combination of the comitative marker *na* plus the infinitive form of the verb), rather it must be inferred from the context. The following examples illustrate various relations between clauses in a clause-chaining relationship involving the infinitive.

The infinitive can be used when two verbs are used to represent what is conceptually a single action; in example (753) the imperative verb form *zidi* 'increase' is linked by the comitative particle *na* with the infinitive verb form *kuvoya* 'to pray' to express the notion 'continue to pray':

(753) Pore kpwa vira ukafika hipha mzima, usitiye wasiwasi, uwe **zidi na kuvoya** nasi hundakuvoyera.

'Sorry, for how you arrived here alive, do not be worried, you **continue to pray** and we will also pray for you.'

zidi	na	**ku**-voy-a
increase	COM	INF-pray-FV

An infinitive verb form can be used when the event it describes is a consequence of a previously mentioned event; note that in example (754) there is no comitative marker *na* preceding the infinitive:

(754) Kondo iriphogbwa makabila gosi garigokala hipho **gatsamukana kuphiya kpwatu tafwauti-tafwauti**, ela Muhuruma ndio nyobaki nyuma.

'When war broke out all the tribes that were there **scattered and went their various ways**, except the Muhuruma who remained behind.'

ga-tsamuk-an-a	ku-phiy-a	kpwatu	tafwauti-tafwauti
6.PST-disperse-RECIP-FV	INF-go-FV	17.place	different-different

Where there is no cause-consequence relationship, events may nonetheless occur in sequence; in such cases, either the consecutive tense marker *chi* (following an initial verb in the past tense) or the sequential tense marker *ka* (following any other verb form) may be used for the verbs which describe the second and subsequent events. Alternatively, an infinitive verb form may be used for the final event in a sequence, indicating a closer relationship between the events than if either *chi* or *ka* were used. The infinitive is appropriate in the following

7.4 Complex sentences

examples because the event described by the previous verb in the sequence serves as a preparation for, if not actually a direct cause of, the event described by the infinitive verb form. Thus, picking up one's walking stick and shirt is a prelude to starting on a journey; placing a baby on its mother's back enables the mother to carry the baby wherever she goes; and washing a pot prepares it to be filled with water. Note that in the final example, which is taken from a procedural text (an instruction manual) describing how to make a particular kind of food, there are two preparatory events—taking the pot, and washing it—which are expressed using verbs with the continuous aspect marker *na-*; only the culminating event— filling the pot with water—is described using an infinitive verb form.

(755) Saa sita **wahala fimboye na chifulanache na kugbwira yo barabara** anaphiya pharatu Rikoni akaendze phahali aoge madzi ga bahari.

'At 12 o'clock **he picked up his stick and his vest and took the road** going right to Likoni to find a place to bathe in the sea water.'

wa-hal-a	fimbo-ye		na	chi-fulana-che
3SG.PST-take-FV	9.staff-9.3SG.POS		COM	7-shirt-7.3SG.POS

na	**ku**-gbwir-a	yo	barabara
COM	INF-seize-FV	9.DEM3_VAR	9.road

(756) Ka achivyalwa anamala siku tahu tu tovu ichikatika **anaerekpwa kare mongoni na kuphiya na nine** kpwahali kokosi hata kama ni mndani.

'After it was born it [the baby] would stay [inside] for around 3 days until the umbilical cord had dropped off [and then] **it would immediately be put on its mother's back and go with its mother** wherever [she went], even if [she went] to the fields.'

a-na-erek-w-a	kare	mongo-ni	na	**ku**-phiy-a	na	nine
3SG-CONT-carry-PAS-FV	ANT	9.back-LOC	COM	INF-go-FV	COM	1a.mother

(757) nyungu **inahalwa inatsukutswa na kutiwa madzi** chiasi cha hura unga.

'a water pot **is taken, washed and filled with water** according to the amount of flour.'

i-na-hal-w-a	i-na-tsukuts-w-a	na	**ku**-ti-w-a	madzi
9-CONT-take-PAS-FV	9-CONT-wash-PAS-FV	COM	INF-put_in-PAS-FV	6.water

Infinitive verb forms are also used to indicate separate actions which might— but need not—be sequential, so long as they are conceptually linked in some way, such as eating and drinking, which are conventionally linked:

(758) *kula kaya sino hwakpwedza phamwenga, huchifika phatu enye hunaoya, chisha* **hunarya mikahe yehu na kunwa madzi.**

'from home we came together, when we reach a place we rest, then **we eat our bread and drink water.**'

hu-na-ry-a	*mi-kahe*	*y-ehu*	*na*	***ku**-nw-a*	*madzi*
1PL-CONT-eat-FV	4-bread	4-1PL.POS	COM	INF-drink-FV	6.water

In the following example, an infinitive verb form is used to describe an action (leaving space for the doors) which is performed in the process of performing another action (tying sticks around the whole house), and which, in fact, could not be performed unless this other action took place. The infinitive is appropriate here, as in the previous examples, because the two events are closely linked conceptually.

(759) | *U-chi-mal-a* | *ku-tiy-a* | *vyatsi,* | *u-na-fung-a* | *fwiho* | *ku-zunguluk-a* |
|---|---|---|---|---|---|
| 2SG-DEP-finish-FV | INF-put_in-FV | 8.poles | 2SG-CONT-tie-FV | 10.sticks | INF-surround-FV |

nyumba	*yosi*	*na*	***ku**-ik-a*	*nafasi*	*ya*	*mi-ryango.*
9.house	9.all	COM	INF-place-FV	9.space	9.ASS	4-doors

'When you finish putting in the upright poles, you tie the sticks around the whole house **leaving** space for the doors.'

Two verbs may be linked conceptually by virtue of expressing similar meanings. When two closely related verb forms are used to describe what is essentially the same event or situation, the second may be in the infinitive and the resulting construction is one which exhibits parallelism.

(760) | *Phahi* | *hara* | *kal-a* | *a=na* | *vyakurya* | *vi-nji* | *kala* |
|---|---|---|---|---|---|---|
| so | 2.DEM2 | [3PL-PST-2.REL-]be-FV | 3PL=COM | 8.food | 8-much | PST |

a-chi-ogoph-e-w-a	*na*	***ku**-heshim-i-w-a*	*sana.*
3PL-IMPFV-respect-APPL-PAS-FV	COM	INF-honour-APPL-PAS-FV	DEG

'So those who had a lot of food were respected and **honoured** very much.'

(761) *Mwana ambaye kala ana umuhimu ni mwana mlume. Hiye* **kala achirerwa na kumanyirirwa vinono** *hadi wakati wa kupata dzumbare.*

'The child who was [most] important was a boy. He **would be raised and cared for well** until the time came [for him] to get his 'bachelor house'.'

kala	*a-chi-rer-w-a*	*na*	***ku**-manyirir-w-a*	*vi-nono*
PST	3SG-CONS-raise-PAS-FV	COM	INF-care_for-PAS-FV	8-good

Finally, a verb may be repeated for emphasis, once with a finite verb form and once with the *ku-* infinitive prefix, in either order. (These constructions are not

7.4 Complex sentences

strictly cases of clause chaining, as conceptually only one event is described and only one verb is involved.) In the following passage from the conclusion of a folk tale, the infinitive form *kuricha* 'to stop' precedes the finite form *tachiricha* 'it doesn't stop', whereas the infinitive form *kusaga* 'grinding' follows the finite *chinasaga* 'it is grinding' which is being treated as a nominal as it is preceded by the demonstrative *cho*:

(762) ... *meli yaandza kuweka mana chira chuma ka chinasaga magunia ga munyu. Chinasaga cho chuma **kuricha tachiricha**, wala kamanya agombe nacho viphi hata chiriche. Uchigomba manaye chinaricha, kugomba manaye **cho chinasaga kusaga**.*

'... the ship began to tilt because that iron was grinding sacks of salt. It was grinding that iron [and] it didn't stop (lit: **to stop it doesn't stop**), nor did he know how to speak to it so that it would stop. If you say the correct words (lit: speak its meaning) it stops, (if) you don't say the correct words that grinding grinds (lit: **that it is grinding to grind**).'

Chi-na-sag-a	*cho*	*chuma*	***ku**-rich-a*	*ta-chi-rich-a ...*
7-CONT-grind-FV	7.DEM3_VAR	7.iron	INF-stop-FV	NEG-7-stop-FV

ku-gomb-a	*mana-ye*	*cho*	*chi-na-sag-a*	***ku**-sag-a.*
2SG.NEG-speak-FV	9.meaning-9.3SG.POS	7.DEM3_VAR	7-CONT-grind-FV	INF-grind-FV

7.4.1.2 Clause chaining with subjunctive verb forms

In addition to being used in certain complement clauses (see §7.4.2) and to express desires and commands (see §4.1.9.2), subjunctive verb forms (with the subjunctive suffix *-e*) occur in clause chaining to express purpose. In this use, a subjunctive form may be preceded by the connective *ili* 'in order to, so that' but need not be.

(763) *Ariphomuona, mwanache wa chichetu wazama, **ili amgute-gute na ahakikishe** kala kpweli akafwa hebu ni handzo.*

'When she saw him, the girl child bent over, **in order to touch him and make sure** that truly it was a lie that he had died.'

ili	*a-m-gut-e-gut-e*	*na*	*a-hakikish-e*
in_order	3SG-3SG-touch-SUB-touch-SUB	COM	3SG-ensure-SUB

It is usual to use the subjunctive with purpose clauses, but infinitive verb forms are also possible, albeit rare; the following example contains two pairs of verb forms which have been 'chained': two subjunctive verb forms ('open for him' and 'to save him'), and a subjunctive and an infinitive verb form ('close' and 'to keep').

(764) Anaphomuona, hiyu mutu ariye dzulu ya uringo kala akatiya likululu, ili hara ario mura ndani **amuvugurire miryango myawao amtivye**, chisha **afunge miryango kpwa haraka ili kuika usalama wa fuko.**

'When he saw him, the person who was on top of the watchtower would shout loudly, so that those who were there inside would **open the gates for their fellow to save him**, then **close the gates quickly in order to keep the stockade safe.**'

a-mu-vugur-ir-*e*	mi-ryango	mya-wao	a-m-tivy-*e* ...
3PL-3SG-open-APPL-SUB	4-gates	1.fellow-1.3PL.POS	3PL-3SG-save-SUB

a-fung-*e*	mi-ryango	kpwa haraka	ili	**ku**-ik-a	usalama
3PL-close-FV	4-gates	quickly	in_order	INF-place-FV	14.safety

7.4.2 Complement clauses

Complement clauses are clauses which function as the complement of verbs such as 'persuade', 'appear', 'promise', and 'threaten' (which I shall call 'the verb in the matrix clause'). Complement clauses in Digo can contain either nonfinite or finite verb forms, with the nonfinite verb forms being either infinitive (with the *ku-* prefix) or subjunctive (with the subjunctive suffix *-e*). The choice of which kind of complement clause to use depends on the verb in the matrix clause and whether the subject of this verb is the same as or different from the subject of the verb in the embedded clause. Unless there is an understood complementizer, the following general rule applies:

If the subject of the verb in the complement clause is the same as the subject of the verb in the matrix clause, an infinitive verb form must be used in the complement clause; if the subject of the verb in the complement clause is different from the subject of the verb in the matrix clause, a subjunctive verb form must be used in the complement clause.

This can be illustrated with the verbs *kubali* 'agree' and *kata shauri* 'decide' which can occur with both same-subject complement clauses and different-subject complement clauses. The first three examples illustrate the use of the *ku-* infinitive with same-subject complement clauses:

(765) | Ta-pha-na | a-ri-ye-kubali | **ku**-tsupir-a | njira | hiyo. |
|---|---|---|---|---|
| NEG-16-COM | 3SG-PST-1.REL-agree | INF-pass-FV | 9.way | 9.DEM3 |

'There was no one who was willing (who agreed) to pass that way.'

(766) | Mino | na-uy-a | kaya, | mino | si-nda-kubali | **ku**-phiy-a. |
|---|---|---|---|---|---|
| 1SG | 1SG.CONT-return-FV | 9.home | 1SG | 1SG.NEG-FUT-agree | INF-go-FV |

'As for me I am returning home, for my part I will not agree to go.'

(767) Wa-kat-a shauri **ku**-baki kuko.
3SG.PST-cut-FV 5.advice INF-remain 17.DEM3_VARIANT
'He decided to remain there.'

The following examples illustrate the use of the subjunctive -e with different-subject complement clauses:

(768) ka-nge-kubali nyumba-ye i-vundz-w-**e**
3SG.NEG-COND-agree 9.house-9.3SG.POS 9-break-PAS-SUB
'he would not allow his house to be broken into'

(769) Ni-kubali ni-lol-**e** mifugo-yo rero.
1SG(VC)-agree 1SG(SC)-look-SUB 4.flocks-4.2SG.POS today
'Allow me to look at your flock today.' (logical subject of the matrix clause verb is 2SG.)

(770) Anji a-kat-a shauri atu a-enderer-**e** na charo.
2.many 3PL-cut-FV 5.advice 2.people 3PL-continue-SUB COM 7.journey
'Many decided we (lit: people) should continue with the journey.'

These complement clause constructions must be distinguished from constructions such as the following. In example (771), the complement of *kubali* is a tensed relative clause (containing the dependent tense marker *chi-*). In example (772), the second clause is not a complement of *kubali*, rather the complement of *kubali* is indicated by the 1SG verb complement (object) marker *ni-*. In both of these examples, an appropriate English translation of *kubali* is 'accept', which is not the case in the examples above.

(771) Na-kubali m-**chi**-vyo-amb-a.
1SG.CONT-agree 2PL-CONS-8.REL-say-FV
'I agree to/with what you have said.' *or* 'I accept what you have said.'

(772) Labuda a-nda-**ni**-kubali a-ku-samehe-ni dambi zenu.
perhaps 3SG-FUT-1SG-agree 3SG-2PL-forgive.SUB-PL 10.sins 10.2PL.POS
'Perhaps he will accept me and forgive your sins.'

The following examples illustrate complement clauses with various verbs. (A preceding ? indicates that the sentence is borderline grammatical or unnatural sounding, and * indicates that the sentence is ungrammatical.) When the verb in the matrix clause is *tisha* 'threaten' or *laga* or *ahidi* 'promise' and the subject of the verb in the embedded clause is the same, either an infinitive complement clause or a finite complement clause must be used:

(773) Sauli wa-zidi ku-tish-a **ku**-olag-a a-fuasi
Saul 3SG.PST-continue INF-threaten-FV INF-kill-FV 2-followers
a Jesu.
2.ASS Jesus
'Saul continued to threaten to kill the followers of Jesus.'

(774) Wa-lag-a **ku**-mu-ph-a pesa.
3SG.PST-promise-FV INF-3SG-give-FV 10.pesa
'He promised to give him money.'
*Wa-lag-a a-mu-ph-**e** pesa.
3SG.PST-promise-FV 3SG-3SG-give-SUB 10.pesa (subjunctive: -e)

(775) Wa-lag-a a-**nda**-mu-ph-a pesa.
3SG.PST-promise-FV 3SG-FUT-3SG-give-FV 10.pesa (finite: nda- future)
'He promised he would give him money.'

The previous example is accepted only if it is understood as having an elided complementizer *(ku)kala*:

(776) Wa-lag-a **kala** a-nda-mu-ph-a pesa.
3SG.PST-promise-FV COMP 3SG-FUT-3SG-give-FV 10.pesa
'He promised that he would give him money.'

If the subject of the verb in the complement clause is different from the subject of the verb in the matrix clause, the complementizer *(ku)kala* must be used:

(777) Na-ku-ahidi **kala** vivi rero hu-nda-kal-a h-osi Peponi.
1SG.CONT-2SG-promise COMP now today 1PL-FUT-be-FV 1PL-all Paradise
'I promise you that this very day we will both be in Paradise.'

When the verb in the matrix clause is *ambira* 'tell', *lagiza* 'order, command', *bembeleza* 'persuade, beg, urge', *onya* 'warn', or *himiza* 'encourage, urge' and the subject of the verb in the complement clause is different from that of the matrix clause, the subjunctive is usually used:

(778) A-ri-pho-mal-a wa-ambir-a aya-e
3SG-PST-16.REL-finish-FV 3SG.PST-tell-FV 2.fellows-2.3SG.POS
a-andz-**e** charo cha ku-uy-a ku-ao.
3PL-begin-SUB 7.journey 7.ASS INF-return-FV 17-3PL.POS
'When he had finished he told his companions to begin the journey back home.'

7.4 Complex sentences

(779) a-chi-a-lagiz-a   a-kany-e   chila phahali mura nyumba-ni.
      3SG-CONS-3PL-order-FV 3PL-excrete-SUB each 16.place 18.DEM2 9.house-LOC
      'and she ordered them to excrete everywhere inside the house.'

(780) Yuya   mutu   wa-m-bembelez-a   a-kal-e   mbere
      1.DEM2 1.person   3SG.PST-3SG-urge-FV 3SG-be-SUB ahead
      na   aya-e   lakini   a-chi-rem-a.
      COM   2.fellows-2.3SG.POS but   3SG-CONS-refuse-FV
      'That man urged him to go ahead with his companions but he refused.'

(781) Chisha a-chi-a-ony-a   a-si-mu-ambir-e   mutu   yeyesi
      then   3SG-CONS-3PL-warn-FV   3PL-NEG-3SG-tell-SUB   1.person 1.any
      ku-m-husu.
      INF-3SG-concern
      'Then he warned them not to tell any person about him.'

In addition to the subjunctive, infinitival complement clauses (although hardly ever attested in the available data) were judged grammatical, except in negative clauses where they were judged ungrammatical:

(782) Wa-a-bembelez-a   a-ry-e   chakurya.
      3SG.PST-3PL-urge-FV   3PL-eat-SUB 7.food   (subjunctive: -e)
      'He begged them to eat food.'

      ? Wa-a-bembelez-a   **ku**-ry-a chakurya.
      3SG.PST-3PL-urge-FV   INF-eat-FV 7.food   (infinitive: ku-)

(783) Fundz-a mambo   higa   g-osi na w-a-himiz-e
      teach-FV 6.things 6.DEM1 6-all COM 2SG-3PL-encourage-SUB
      atu   a-ga-phoker-e.
      2.people 3PL-6-receive-SUB (subjunctive: -e)
      'Teach all these things and encourage people to receive them.'

(784) Fundz-a mambo   higa   g-osi na w-a-himiz-e
      teach-FV 6.things 6.DEM1 6-all COM 2SG-3PL-encourage-SUB
      atu   **ku**-ga-phoker-a.
      2.people INF-6-receive-FV (infinitive: ku-)
      'Teach all these things and encourage people to receive them.'

(785) Hwa-m-bembelez-a   Paulo a-**si**-phiy-e   Jerusalemu.
      1PL.PST-3SG-urge-FV   Paul   3SG-NEG-go-SUB   Jerusalem
      'We begged Paul (that) he not go to Jerusalem.' (subjunctive: -e)

*Hwa-m-bembelez-a   Paulo **kusa**-phiy-a   Jerusalemu.
1PL.PST-3SG-urge-FV   Paul   NEG.INF-go-FV   Jerusalem
(negative infinitive: *kusa-*)

Usually, as we have seen, when the subject of the complement clause is the same as the subject of the matrix clause, an infinitive verb form is used in the complement clause. However, when the verb in the matrix clause is *onekana* 'appear, seem', the complement clause usually contains a finite verb form, and the *ku-* infinitive is only marginally acceptable (a subjunctive is still ungrammatical, as we would expect).

(786) Hata   i-chi-kal-a   hu-nda-onekan-a   hu-**ka**-shind-w-a
      even   9-DEP-be-FV   1PL-FUT-seem-FV   1PL-ANT-defeat-PAS-FV

      hu-nda-vumirir-a.
      1PL-FUT-persevere-FV   (finite: *ka-* anterior)

      'Even if we will be seen to have been defeated, we will persevere.'

      ? ... **ku**-shind-w-a   ...
             INF-defeat-PAS-FV   (nonfinite: *ku-*)

      * ... hu-shind-w-**e**   ...
            1PL-defeat-PAS-SUB   (subjunctive: *-e*)

When *onekana* occurs with a nonverbal complement, there is no overt copula (787), in contrast to *kubali* 'agree, accept' (788):

(787) Sisi   hu-na-onekan-a   a-zuzu.
      1PL   1PL-CONT-seem-FV   2-fools   (no overt copula)

      'We appear (to be) fools.'

      ?Sisi hu-na-onekan-a   **hu**   a-zuzu.
       1PL   1PL-CONT-seem-FV   1PL   2-fools   (1PL copula: *hu*)

      *Sisi hu-na-onekan-a   **ni**   a-zuzu.
       1PL   1PL-CONT-seem-FV   COP   2-fools   (generic copula: *ni*)

(788) Kalapho m-na-kubali   **m'**=vipofu,   ta-m-nge-kal-a
      if   2PL-CONT-agree   2PL=8.blind_people   NEG-2PL-COND-be-FV

      na   hukumu.
      COM   9.judgment

      'If you accepted that you are blind, you would not be under judgment.'
      (2PL copula: *mu*)

Another exception to the rule that an infinitive complement clause is used with same-subject complement clauses occurs where the matrix clause involves a verb of movement. In this case, the complement clause can contain *ka-* + *-e* (movement to a location plus subjunctive; see §5.5.1.3) in place of an infinitive or a regular subjunctive. The resulting construction can be interpreted similarly to a simple clause with the *ya* (future + movement) movement gram (§5.5.1.2) as the following example illustrates:

(789) "*Ela **unaphiya ukaoge** hiko Mambasa madzi ga pwani kuno dzana atu alala na ndzala na vino andasinda nayo, na we **uyaoga**, dzitswaro hiwe.*"

"'But **you were going to bathe** there in Mombasa at the seaside while yesterday people slept with hunger and now they will spend the day likewise, whilst you, **you are going to bathe**, you big head.'"

u-na-phiy-a   u-ka-og-e ...
2SG-CONT-go-FV   2SG-IT-bathe-SUB

u-ya-og-a
2SG-FUT.IT-bathe-FV

Summary

Matrix and complement clause have the same subject:

Matrix clause verb	Form of complement clause verb
ahidi 'promise'	*ku-* infinitive
laga 'promise'	*ku-* infinitive
tisha 'threaten'	*ku-* infinitive
onekana 'appear, seem'	finite verb
phiya 'go'	*ka-* + *-e* movement to + subjunctive

Matrix and complement clause have different subjects:

Matrix clause verb	Form of complement clause verb
ambira 'tell'	*-e* subjunctive
bembeleza 'persuade, beg, urge'	*-e* subjunctive (or *ku-* infinitive)
himiza 'encourage, urge'	*-e* subjunctive (or *ku-* infinitive)
lagiza 'order, command'	*-e* subjunctive (or *ku-* infinitive)
onya 'warn'	*-e* subjunctive

7.5 Locative inversion—parameters of variation

In locative inversion, the subject concord (SC) on the verb agrees with one of the locative classes (16 *pha-*, 17 *ku-*, and 18 *mu-*) whilst the logical or thematic subject is a noun phrase from another class which follows the verb. The presence of a locative which agrees with the SC is optional, and the locative, if present, may occur after both the verb and the logical subject NP or before the verb. These three possibilities are illustrated below.

(790) **Ku-a-tsap-a**   a-jema.
      17-PST-pass-FV   2-tapper
      'There passed palm wine tappers.' [No overt locative]

(791) Halafu   **mwa-tuluk-a**   nyoka   [**mo**   kuni-ni].
      then   18.PST-emerge-FV   9.snake 18.DEM3_VAR firewood-LOC
      'Then there emerged a snake [from within the firewood].'
      [Postverbal locative]

(792) [**Pho**   **muho-ni**]   **pha-tuluk-a**   ng'ombe   sabaa.
      16.DEM3_VAR river-LOC   16.PST-emerge-FV   10.cows   seven
      '[From the river] there emerged seven fat cows.'
      [Preverbal locative]

In the last example (which comes from the Digo translation of Genesis 41:2), it is clear that although the SC *pha-* (SC *pha-* + past tense *a-*) on the verb *tuluka* 'emerge' agrees with *muhoni* 'in/from the river', it is not the river that emerges from the cows but the cows that emerge from the river. That the cows are the logical or thematic subject of the verb can be seen clearly by the continuation of this example (provided below), in which the SC on the second verb *andza* 'begin' is class 10, agreeing with *ng'ombe* 'cows'. In the second sentence, which parallels the first, the grammatical subject is *ng'ombe* throughout and the SC on the verb *tuluka* 'emerge' is *za-* (SC *zi-* + past tense *a-*); the fact that this sentence does not exhibit locative inversion may reflect the fact that cows (as a generic concept) have already been introduced into the narrative (see discussion immediately below).

(793) Pho   muho-ni   **pha**-tuluk-a   **ng'ombe**   sabaa
      16.DEM3_VAR 3.river-LOC 16.PST-emerge-FV   10.cows   seven

      za   kunon-a,   **zi**-chi-andz-a   kuris-a   pho
      10.ASS   INF-be_fat-FV 10-CONS-begin-FV   INF-feed-FV 16.DEM3_VAR

      kanda-kanda ya   muho.   Halafu   **za**-tuluk-a   **ng'ombe**
      beside   9.ASS   3.river then   10.PST-come_out-FV   10.cows

      z-anjina   sabaa;   hizi   kala   zi-ka-ond-a   hata
      10-other   seven   10.DEM1   COP.PST   10-ANT-become_thin-FV   until

      zi-na-tish-a ...
      10-CONT-scare-FV

      'From the river there emerged seven fat cows, and they began to feed there beside it. Then seven other cows emerged; these were frighteningly thin (lit: these had become thin until they were scary) ...'

7.5 Locative inversion—parameters of variation

The most common use of locative inversion in the corpus of nontranslated Digo texts is to introduce major participants into a narrative, a function known as 'presentational articulation' (see §7.2.5). Most traditional stories begin with presentational articulation, usually with the copula construction *kala na* 'be with', but occasionally with other verbs. The locative SC can agree either with class 16 or with class 17 with no marked preference for one over the other (but not with class 18 unless a coreferential location has been previously specified). The locative SC can occur either affixed to an inflected form of *kala* as in (794), affixed to the comitative particle *na* as in (795), or affixed to both as in (796). When a locative SC is affixed to *na* rather than to an inflected form of *kala*, this is not actually a case of locative inversion, but it is illustrated here for comparison and because these three constructions seem to be used interchangeably. (For further details of existential predicate constructions, see §8.2.5.)

(794) *Chisha **pha**-chi-kala na mjeni   phapho   pha-o   lalo-ni.*
      then   16-CONS-COP COM 1.stranger 16.DEM3 _VARIANT 16-3PL.POS village-LOC
      'Now there was a stranger there at their place.'

(795) *Lakini kahi   ya   hara atu   kala   **pha**-na m-mwenga*
      But   among 9.ASS 2.DEM2 2.people PST.COP 16-COM   1-one
      amba-ye   kala   a-na   kani.
      REL-1.REL PST.COP 3SG-COM 9.stubbornness
      'But among those people there was one who was stubborn.'

(796) *Pha-gbwir-an-a-pho   na   mlungu   a-chi-kala   ta-a-na*
      16.PST-seize-RECIP-FV-16.REL   COM 3.heaven 3PL-CONS-COP 3PL-NEG-COM
      *njira ya   ku-tsup-ir-a   na   **pha**-chi-kala **pha**-na atu*
      9.way 9.ASS INF-pass-APPL-FV   COM 16-CONS-COP   16-COM   2.people
      anji   amba-o   kala   kala   a-na-tak-a   ku-tsup-a   piya.
      2.many REL-2.REL PST.COP PST.COP 3PL-CONT-want-FV INF-pass-FV also
      'Where it [a stone] had joined heaven they had no way of passing, and there were many people who also wanted to get past.'

Other verbs can also be used for presentational focus, as illustrated in the following examples. In example (797), the verb *henda* is glossed as 'do', which is its usual translation, but in presentational constructions it lacks a complement and indicates existence rather than action. (Usually, when a story begins by introducing a man and his wife and stating that they gave birth to a child, it is the child who is the protagonist in the story and not his or her parents, who may not even be mentioned again.)

(797) Hipho kare, **ku-a**-hend-a mutu na mchewe, a-chi-vyal-a
long ago 17-PST-do-FV 1.person COM 1.his_wife 3PL-CONS-bear-FV
mwana wa-o.
1.child 1-3PL.POS

'Long ago, there lived (lit: there did) a man and his wife, and they had a son.'

(798) Pho-fik-a usiku m-kulu **pha**-kpwedz-a nyama wa
16.REL-arrive-FV 14.night 14-big 16.PST-come-FV 1a.animal 1.ASS
mapha pho phondze, paaa, a-na-ng'al-a dza taa.
6.wings 16.DEM3_VAR 16.outside IDIO 1-CONT-shine-FV like 9.lamp

'When night had completely fallen <u>there came</u> a bird outside, whoosh, shining like a lamp.'

In all of the examples so far, the locative SC precedes either a past or a consecutive tense marker, reflecting the fact that locative inversion is typically found in past time contexts in the data. However, there is no grammatical restriction on the tenses with which locative inversion may occur; the following example illustrates locative inversion with a future tense marker.

(799) Na Jumamosi **pha-nda**-zembuk-a magunia kumi ga mtele.
COM Saturday 16-FUT-appear-FV 6.sack ten 6.ASS 9.rice

'And on Saturday ten sacks of rice will appear.'

Finally, one further example is provided below to illustrate that the logical subject (the nonlocative NP) need not be an animate, or even a physical, entity.

(800) N'pha-huphu pho kaya tse, hata
COP:16-empty 16.DEM3_VAR 5.home completely even

pha-ka-uy-a **ndzala** dza pho kare.
16-ANT-return-FV hunger like 16.DEM3_VAR old

'It's totally hopeless at home, even **hunger has returned** (lit: there has returned hunger] like before.'

7.5.1 Parameters of variation

Many Bantu languages exhibit locative inversion (henceforth LI), but there is considerable cross-linguistic variation. According to Marten (2006:102), "variation exists with respect to the function of locative subject markers, and to the thematic restrictions on predicates which can be used in locative inversion." In all Bantu languages with LI, it seems that the following features are found:

7.5 Locative inversion—parameters of variation

1. The locative NP is the grammatical subject and the discourse topic.
2. The postverbal NP is the logical subject and cannot be omitted or separated from the verb.
3. The postverbal NP is presentationally focused.
4. There can be no verb complement concord ('object marker') on the verb.

There is variation between Bantu languages in the following ways (Marten 2006:106):

1. Some languages allow only one locative class in LI (e.g. Tswana cl.17), whereas others allow two locative classes (e.g. Chaga cl.17 and 18) and others allow all three locative classes (e.g. Chewa, Herero cl.16, 17 and 18).
2. In the absence of a full locative NP some languages allow a locative reading (e.g. Chaga, Chewa, Herero, Shona) whilst others only allow a presentational focus reading (e.g. Tswana, Sotho).
3. Some languages restrict LI to unaccusative predicates and passivized transitives and ditransitives (e.g. Chewa), others to all predicates except unergatives and active transitives and ditransitives (e.g. Shona), others to all predicates except active transitives and ditransitives (e.g. Sotho, Tswana) and others to all predicates except active ditransitives (Herero).

Each of these parameters of variation will be discussed in more detail below in relation to Digo.

7.5.1.1 Permitted locative classes

Digo allows LI with all three locative classes, as has already been illustrated. Class 16 and 17 SCs may occur with or without an explicit locative, but for a class 18 SC to occur, there must be a previously mentioned locative NP to which it refers. This locative NP must be explicitly mentioned rather than inferred from the context, although it need not occur in the same clause as the SC with which it agrees, and it need not be inherently in noun class 18, as the following example from the Digo translation of Revelation 9:2 illustrates. In this example, the locative NP is *kuzimu* 'hades' which is in class 9, but the class 18 SC *mwa-* can occur because *kuzimu* describes an interior location.

(801) A-ri-pho-vugul-a   hira   kuzimu,   **mwa**-tuluk-a   dzi-mosi ...
      3S-PST-16.REL-open-FV 5.DEM2   9.hades   18.PST-emerge-FV   5-smoke
      'When he opened hades, thick smoke emerged ...'

7.5.1.2 Interpretation

When there is no overt locative with which the SC agrees, some Bantu languages (e.g. Tswana, Sotho) only allow a presentational focus (or 'expletive') reading; that is, the clause exhibiting LI serves to introduce a participant or entity into the narration. Other languages (e.g. Chaga, Chewa, Herero, Shona) allow the SC to refer to a specific, known location even when there is no overt locative. Furthermore, in some of those languages which allow a locative reading, one locative class is specialized for use in presentational contexts; that is, one of the locative classes has undergone grammaticalization in the form of loss of locative information. In Shona this is class 17 and in Herero this is class 16 (Marten 2006:117).

As already noted, Digo only allows LI without an overt locative with classes 16 and 17; for a SC of class 18 to occur, there must be a coreferential locative NP. Usually, when LI occurs without an overt locative NP, it has a presentational function, as in the examples discussed in the introductory section. Occasionally, however, such constructions serve not only presentationally, to introduce participants, but also locatively, to specify a location. Example (802), with the class 16 SC, not only introduces the old woman (who becomes a minor participant in the story) but also indicates that she passed by the place where the major participants (the subject of the verb *aza*) were located (in an evil spirit's house in which the major participants were being held captive).

(802) Wakati   a-na-az-a,   **pha**-tsup-a   chi-chetu   cha   kare.
      14.time 3PL-CONT-wish-FV   16.PST-pass-FV   7-woman   7.ASS old
      'While they were wishing (not to be eaten), an old old woman passed by.'

The next example gives an even clearer indication that LI is being used not only to introduce participants into a story but also to specify the location at which subsequent events take place. The SC in this case is class 17, and it is clear that, even though there is no overt locative NP, the specific location to which the people come is the well into which the major participant in the story had been pushed the day before.

(803) Ku-ka-ch-a,   **ku-a-kpwedz-a**   atu   a-na-tak-a   ku-hek-a
      17-ANT-dawn-FV   17-PST-come-FV   2.people   2-CONT-want-FV INF-draw-FV
      madzi,   a-ri-pho-tsungurir-a   a-on-a   mutu.
      6.water   3PL-PST-16.REL-look_inside-FV 3PL-PST-see-FV   1.person
      'Early in the morning people came (to the well) wanting to draw water; when they looked inside (the well) they saw a person.'

From this, it can be concluded that, although the most common function of LI without an overt locative NP in Digo is presentational, a locative reading, in which the locative SC indicates a specific location, is also possible. Furthermore, the possibility of a presentational focus reading and a locative reading has been noted with both class 16 and class 17 SCs. Thus Digo conforms to the correlation observed by Demuth and Mmusi (1997, cited in Marten 2006:116) that languages which allow more than one locative SC in LI always allow a locative interpretation in the absence of an overt locative NP.

7.5.1.3 Permitted predicates

Demuth and Mmusi (1997) and Marten (2006) distinguish four types of predicate:

1. Unaccusatives are expressed by intransitive verbs in which the logical subject of the verb is affected; that is, the only permitted thematic role (apart from <location> which is present in all four types of predicate) is <theme>. Examples include 'be', 'come', and 'sit'.
2. Unergatives are expressed by intransitive verbs in which the logical subject of the verb is the agent, hence the only permitted thematic role (apart from <location>) is <agent>. Examples include 'sing' and 'plough'.
3. Transitives are expressed by verbs which have both <agent> and <theme> as permitted thematic roles (that is, the subject of the verb acts on the object of the verb in some way). Passivized transitives resemble unaccusatives in that the highest thematic role is <theme>.
4. Ditransitives are expressed by verbs which have <agent>, <theme>, and <patient> as permitted thematic roles. Passivized ditransitives also resemble unaccusatives in that the highest thematic role is <theme>, with <patient> also expressed.

Some languages restrict LI to unaccusative predicates and some passives (e.g. Chewa), others to unaccusatives and all passives (e.g. Shona), others to all predicates except transitives and ditransitives (e.g. Sotho, Tswana) and others to all predicates except ditransitives (Herero). There is thus an implicational hierarchy among these types of predicate: if a language allows unergatives to participate in LI, then it is to be expected that it will allow unaccusatives and passivized transitives also; if a language allows transitive predicates, then it will allow unergatives also; and if a language allows ditransitive predicates, then it will allow all the other types of predicate. This implicational hierarchy holds for Digo, but the types of permitted predicate are also affected by the presence or absence of a coreferential locative. Only unaccusatives, passivized transitives, and unergatives were found in the corpus of Digo texts, with very few unergatives. Transitives were elicited and were accepted as grammatical, but only with an overt coreferential locative. Ditransitives proved impossible to elicit, and when presented to Digo speakers were accepted as grammatical only with difficulty, so are not discussed further here.

7.5.1.3.1 *Unaccusatives and passivized transitives*

All of the examples of LI in Digo cited above involve unaccusative predicates. Unaccusative predicates in Digo also include a number of stative verbs, such as *patikana* 'be available', *tsembuka/zembuka* 'appear', *tsoloka* 'arrive', and *fwa* 'die'.

Passivized transitives are illustrated in the following examples. The first involves the future tense of the passivized transitive predicate *henda kazi* 'do work', and the second involves a passivized transitive within a relative clause. The wider context for both examples is provided.

(804) Anaambwa, "Uchitaka nyumba za mabamba zindadzengbwa ni hichi chuma, uchitaka vitu undaviphaha, go maduka gandaphahikana hipho, ni hichi chuma, uwe kuna uchiya tsona na **phandahendwa kazi hipho phako ni hicho chuma**."

'He was told, "If you want beautiful houses they will be built by this iron, if you want things you will get them, shops will be provided right here by this iron; you are no longer poor and **the work will be done at your place by this iron**."'

pha-nda-hend-w-a	kazi	hipho	phako	ni	hicho	chuma
16-FUT-do-PAS-FV	9.work	16.DEM3	16.POS.2SG	COP	7.DEM3	7.iron

(805) Achiphiya ko aphiyako hata anauya **phatu pharatu ambapho phatsolwa chidziwe** phakagbwirana na mlungu.

'They went where they were going until they returned to **the same place where the small stone had been picked up** and it had (grown and) joined with heaven.'

phatu	pharatu	amba-pho	**pha**-tsol-w-a	chi-dziwe
16.place	16.DEM2_VARIANT	REL-16.REL	16.PST-pick_up-PAS-FV	7-stone

7.5.1.3.2 Unergatives

LI can occur with unergative predicates in Digo, although less frequently than with unaccusatives and passivized transitives. (The following example is the only one contained in a corpus of nontranslated narrative texts.) An overt locative NP is optional.

(806) Yuya bwana waiha, "We mchina-tsakaee, we mwenye mchina-tsakaee." **Kuaihika mutu kuko tsini**, anaambwa, "Ndzoo."

'That man called, "Hey, you owner of the forest, hey you owner of the forest." **Someone replied from below**, and he was told, "Come here."'

Ku-a-ihik-a	mutu	kuko	tsini,
17-PST-reply-FV	1.person	17.DEM3_VARIANT	below

7.5.1.3.3 Transitives

No examples of LI with transitives were found in the Digo corpus of nontranslated or translated texts. However, the following examples were either elicited or accepted as grammatical when presented to native speakers. Transitive predicates are only possible if there is an overt locative with which the locative SC agrees:

7.5 Locative inversion—parameters of variation

(807) **Muho-ni** **pha**-na-hek-a   atu   madzi.
river-LOC   16-CONT-draw-FV   2.people   6.water
'People are drawing water at/from the river.'

***Pha**-na-hek-a   atu   madzi.

Some unergative predicates can be made into transitives by the addition of a verb complement, and in these cases too LI is possible so long as a locative is present:

(808) **Tsaka-ni**   **ku**-na-imb-a   atu.
forest-LOC   17-CONT-sing-FV   2.people
'People are singing in the forest.' (Unergative)

(809) **Tsaka-ni**   **ku**-na-imb-a   atu   mawira.
forest-LOC   17-CONT-sing-FV   2.people   6.song
'People are singing songs in the forest.'
(Transitive: verb complement = *mawira*)

Class 18 is also possible with transitive predicates, as in the final example.

(810) **Mo**   **chumba-ni**   **mu**-na-andik-a   mutu   baruwa.
18.DEM3_VAR   room-LOC   18-CONT-write-FV   1.person   9.letter
'Someone is writing a letter in the room.'

8

Being and Having

Being and having are dealt with together beacause of the similarities in the way these notions are expressed in Digo. For example, to have something in Digo is to be with it, and one way to express that an entity is in a place is to say that the place is with that entity. Within the notion of 'being', as opposed to 'having', a distinction can made between comparative constructions and other constructions, collectively referred to as copula constructions. In this chapter I will first briefly describe the various forms used in Digo copula constructions and then illustrate the use of these forms for particular functions. Following this, I will describe comparative constructions, which can be thought of as the expression of how an entity is with respect to some characteristic compared with another entity (or in the case of sufficiency and excess, compared with an understood norm). I will then describe possessive constructions in Digo, and conclude with a passage from a narrative text which illustrates various of the constructions discussed in this section.

8.1 Copula constructions: Forms

In Digo, copula constructions are constructions in which the predicate (the part of the clause which gives information about the subject) is the element which follows the copula rather than the copula itself. I also include here constructions with no overt copula. A form of the verb 'be' (*kala*) is used in tensed copula constructions, but otherwise all copula constructions are verbless. Copula constructions in Digo can be classified using purely formal criteria into (1) invariable constructions, (2) constructions which indicate the noun class or person/number of the subject, and (3) constructions which inflect for subject and tense. Different constructions are used in relative clauses, and these will be dealt with separately.

8.1.1 Invariable constructions

Occasionally nominal predicates ('X is Y' where X and Y are both noun phrases) are expressed simply by juxtaposition of X and Y, as in the following examples; in example (812), a vocative expression *babu* intervenes between the nominal arguments.

(811) **Mimi** sowe tu.
 1SG 1a.your_father only
 'I am only your father.'

(812) **Mche-o** babu **hiyu**.
 1.wife-1.2SG.POS 1a.grandfather* 1.DEM1 (*term of respect)
 'This, sir, is your wife.' (lit: 'Your wife grandfather this.')

Adjectival predicates can also be formed through juxtaposition:

(813) *Maruwa-ge mereru.*
 6.flower-6.3SG.POS 6.white
 'Its flowers are white.'

The most frequent strategy for both nominal and adjectival predicates involves the copula *ni* (sometimes abbreviated to *n'* and cliticized to the following word):

(814) Mutu hiyu ***ni*** daktari.
 1.person 1.DEM1 COP 1a.doctor
 'The person is a doctor.'

(815) Chitabu ***n'***=chi-kulu.
 7.book COP=7-big
 'The book is big.'

The time reference of a clause containing *ni* is determined by the context or is indicated elsewhere in the utterance. In the following example, all the material in square brackets serves to indicate past time reference which is 'inherited' by the tenseless possessive and copula constructions (in bold):

8.1 Copula constructions: Forms

(816) [Hipho kare kpwahenda mutu na mchewe achivyala ana airi alume. Phahi yuya mutu na mchewe, asagala, achisagala lakini achikala] yuya mwana wao mmwenga **kana** chitu, **ni mchiya** na mmwenga **ni tajiri sana**.

'[Long ago there was a man and his wife and they had two sons. So that man and his wife, they stayed, and they stayed but he was] one of their sons **did not have** a thing, **he was poor**, and the other (lit: and one) **was very rich**.'

yuya	mwana	wao	m-mwenga	**ka=na**	chitu,
1.DEM2	1.child	1.3PL.POS	1-one	3SG.NEG=COM	7.thing

ni	**m-chiya**	na	m-mwenga	**ni**	tajiri	sana.
COP	1-poor	COM	1-one	COP	wealthy	DEG

For explicit past time reference, tense is indicated by the past tense auxiliary *kala* or the hodiernal past tense auxiliary *che* preceding the copula. For other time references an inflected form of *kala* (now functioning as the verb 'be') is used without *ni*.

(817) *Dzuwa ni kali rero.*   'The sun is hot today.'
Dzana dzuwa kala ni kali.   'Yesterday the sun was hot.'
Ligundzu dzuwa che ni kali.   'This morning the sun was hot.'
Muhondo dzuwa rindakala kali.   'Tomorrow the sun will be hot.'

The negative counterpart of *ni* without explicit time reference (i.e. without *kala* or *che*) is *si*+referential marker (see §4.1.10.2) or *si* alone. (The negative form with explicit past time reference is described in §8.1.2.1.)

(818)
Hu=na	nyumba	ya	mutsi,	ndi-yo-meny-a	ela	**si=yo**
1PL=COM	9.house	9.ASS	3.day	FUT-9.REL-enter-FV	but	NEG.COP=9.REF

hino,	hino	ni	ya	usiku.
9.DEM4	9.DEM4	COP	9.ASS	14.night

'We have a house for the day, which we will go into, but **it is not** this, this is for the night.'

(819)
Mino	**si**	dza	atu	anjina
1SG	NEG.COP	like	2.people	2.other

'**I am not** like other people.'

Invariable predicate constructions can be used without an overt subject (note that the English free translation requires either a subject pronoun or a 'dummy' subject 'it'):

(820)
"Yuno	m-chetu	**si=ye**	mche-o	wee?"
1.DEM4	1-woman	NEG.COP=1.REF	1.wife-1.2SG.POS	2SG

A-na-amb-a,	"**Ni**	mkpwazangu."
3SG-CONT-say-FV	COP	1.wife-1.1SG.POS

'"That woman, **is she not** your wife?" He said, "[She] **is my wife**."'

(821) *"Uwe dzana wahenda ngata vino ndipho henda uganga." Yuya bwana anaamba,* **"Kala ni uganga,** *mino námala dzana, sina vyanjina tsona."*

"'Yesterday you applied first aid, now (you should) administer proper treatment." That man said, "**It was proper treatment**, I finished yesterday, I don't have any more [to do]."'

kala	**ni**	u-ganga
PST	COP	14-healing

8.1.2 Constructions indicating noun class or person/number

8.1.2.1 ndi/si + *referential marker*

In the construction *ndi*+referential marker, the form of the referential marker used with persons may be derived from, or otherwise related to, the final syllable of the free personal pronouns. The exception is the 1st person plural for which the class 2 relative concord marker is used. The 3rd person singular and plural pronoun suffixes are identical to the referential markers of noun classes 1 and 2. The free personal pronouns and their respective *ndi*+referential marker copula constructions may co-occur as follows: *mimi ndimi* 'I am', *sisi ndio* 'we are', *uwe ndiwe* 'you (SG) 'are', *mwimwi ndimwi* you (PL) 'are', *iye ndiye* 's/he is', *aho ndio* 'they are'. The 'metarepresentational' free personal pronouns may also occur in this construction:

(822) Mino ndi=mi mu-andishi.
1SG COP=1SG.REF 1-writer
'I am the writer.'

A free personal pronoun need not always precede the *ndi*+referential marker copula construction:

(823) u-many-e ana-o, mana **ndi=o** ngao-yo
2SG-know-SUB 2.children-2.3SG.POS for COP=3PL.REF 9.shield-9.3SG.POS
na a-zik-i-o a machero.
COM 3PL-bury-APPL-3PL.REL 2.ASS tomorrow
'know your children, because **they are** your shield and the ones who will bury you in the future.'

The forms of the *ndi*+referential marker construction for a selection of other noun classes are provided below:

(824) a. *Kulungu* **ndiye** *wangu.* 'The antelope is mine' (cl.1)
b. *Mwanga* **ndio** *uhendao vitu vionekane.* 'Light is what makes things visible.' (cl.3)
c. *Hiri* **ndiro** *lagizo mrirosikira.* 'This is the command which you heard.' (cl.5)

d. *Higo **ndigo** mafundzo ga Shariya.* 'These are the teachings of the Law.' (cl.6)
e. ***Ndiyo** mana sedzere.* 'This is the reason I did not come.' (cl.9)

For explicit past time reference, tense is indicated by *kala* (or *che* for the hodiernal past tense) preceding the copula. This construction is very rare in comparison with *ni* preceded by *kala* or *che* and is used for emphasis. When *kala* occurs without any overt inflection it encodes the past tense; otherwise tense is indicated by the inflection on *kala* (see 8.1.2.3 for further details).

(825) *Waphiya hiku na hiku dza viratu dzinare,*
 kala **ndi=ye** *Njira Nyinji.*
 PST COP=1SG.REF 10.paths 10.many (used as proper name)
 'He went here and there just like his name, he really was Many Paths.'

(826) *na=we u-nda-kal-a* **ndi=we** *dziwe ra msingi*
 COM=2SG 2SG-FUT-be-FV COP=2SG.REF 5.stone 5.ASS 3.foundation
 'and you will be/become the foundation stone'

The negative counterpart of *ndi* is *si*; the subject marker is the bound personal pronoun for all persons and numbers, including the 1st person plural: *si+swi* (swi < swiswi), although *sio* is also occasionally found with the 1st person plural.

(827) a. *Mino **simi** mtumwa.* 'I am not a slave.'
 b. ***Siswi** atu a handzo.* 'We are not liars (lit: people of falsehood).'
 c. *Sisi **sio** makachero.* 'We are not spies.'
 d. ***Siwe** mutu wa handzo.* 'You are not a liar.'
 e. ***Simwi** ajeni tsona.* 'You are not strangers any longer.'
 f. ***Siye** mchina dambi.* 'He is not a sinner.'
 g. *Ana **sio** akpwe.* 'The children are not his.'

The forms of the *si+*referential marker construction for a selection of other noun classes are provided below:

(828) a. *Kuzira **siro** dzambo nono.* 'To hate is not a good thing.' (cl.5)
 b. *Mang'ondzi **sigo** gakpwe.* 'The sheep are not his.' (cl.6)
 c. ***Sicho** chitu cha mana.* 'It is not an important thing.' (cl.7)
 d. *Hiyo **siyo** sababu ndzuri.* 'This is not a good reason.' (cl.9)
 e. *Ukongo hinyo **sio** wa kumurya.* 'This sickness is not fatal (lit: of eating him).' (cl.14)

For explicit past time reference, tense is indicated by *kala* (or *che* for the hodiernal past tense) preceding the copula:

(829) a. *Mtsanga **kala** sio munji.* 'The soil was not deep (lit: much).'
      b. *Dzana dzuwa **kala** siro kali.* 'The sun was not hot yesterday.'

(830) a. *Rero ligundzu mayo wangu **che siye** mkpwongo.* 'This morning my mother wasn't ill.'
      b. *Rero ligundzu chironda **che sicho** chikulu.* 'This morning the wound was not big.'

This construction also functions as the negative counterpart of the invariable form *ni*, as in example (831). Note that here, the time reference is the general past (the narrator is recounting fictional events as if they occurred in the distant past) and the form *che* here is the homophonous focus marker (see §7.2.6 for a discussion).

(831) Mana   hara   atu   a-chi-o-mu-amb-ir-a,
      for   2.DEM2 2.people   3PL-ANT-2.REL-3SG-speak-APPL-FV

      che   **si**=o   atu   che   **ni**   shetani.
      FOC   NEG.COP=3PL.REF   2.people   FOC   COP   10.demons

      'For those people who had spoken to him, they were not people, they were spirits.'

8.1.2.2 Subject concord used as a copula

The subject concord of the noun being described can occur without an accompanying verb when the predicate is nonverbal. In negative clauses, the subject concord is prefixed by the appropriate negative prefix (see §4.1.1.1). Whilst these negative forms are fairly common with persons (especially 1st and 2nd person) they are extremely rare with other noun classes (instead the invariable negative copula *si* is used).

The subject concords are strictly speaking clitics (which can be affixed to phrases), and occasionally written forms such as *tahuphamwenga* 'we are not together' are seen.[1] However, in order to avoid creating orthographic words with a capital letter in the middle, e.g. *tamuAdigo* 'you are not Digos', the subject concords are usually written as separate words, whether preceding nouns, relational expressions (*phamwenga* 'together', *jiza=ni* 'darkness=LOC', etc.), or adjectives (*moho* 'hot', *tayari* 'ready', etc.), e.g. *tahu phamwenga* 'we are not together', *tamu Adigo* 'you are not Digos'. Note that the forms of the 1st person singular (*ni* and *si*) are the same as the invariable forms described above. Examples of other persons and noun classes are provided below:

(832) a. ***Hu** anji.*   'We are many.'
      b. ***Tahu** achache.* 'We are not few.'
      c. ***U** mjeni.*   'You are a stranger/guest.'

---

[1] As is the case in the orthographies of some other Bantu languages, such as Lucazi (Fleisch 2000:199): *njiciheve* 'I am a fool', *uciheve* 'you are a fool', *tuviheve* 'we are fools', *muviheve* 'you are fools'.

8.1 Copula constructions: Forms

- d. **Tamu** atu a handzo. — 'You are not liars.'
- e. **Mu** atu anono. — 'You are good people.'
- f. **A** sawa na aphuye. — 'He was the same (size) as his uncle.' (3sg/cl.1)
- g. Mwanache **a** sukuli. — 'The child is at school.' (3sg/cl.1)
- h. **Ka** kure. — 'He is not far away.' (3sg/cl.1)
- i. Anache **a** sukuli. — 'The children are at school.' (3pl/cl.2)
- j. Mikahe **i** mfukoni. — 'The loaves are in the bag.' (cl.3)
- k. Kabati dzikulu **ri** tele pesa. — 'The large cupboard was full of money.' (cl.5)
- l. Gara ambago **taga** wazi-wazi. — 'Those [words] that are not clear.' (cl.6)
- m. Chitabu **chi** tayari. — 'The book is ready.' (cl.7)
- n. Kahawa **i** moho. — 'The coffee is hot.' (cl.9)
- o. Wakati **u** phephi. — 'The time is near.' (cl.14)

In the 3rd person singular, an alternative form *yu*, perhaps borrowed from Swahili, is occasionally found:

(833) a. **Yu** moyo. — 'He is alive.'
 b. **Yu** phamwenga nasi. — 'He is with us.'

For explicit past time reference, the past tense auxiliary *kala*, or the reduced form *ka*, is used before the subject concord, following the pattern of the invariable form *ni*. Past time negative clauses are formed using *si*+subject marker (see §8.1.2.1).

(834) a. Dzuwa **kala ri** phephi na kutswa. — 'The sun was almost setting.'
 b. Anjina enu **kala mu** dza vivyo. — 'Some of you were like that.'
 c. Mizi **ka i** dzulu-dzulu. — 'The roots were shallow.'

8.1.2.3 Constructions which inflect for subject and tense

The form *kala*, which we have seen functioning as a past tense auxiliary (8.1.2.2.), can also function as a finite predicate inflecting for subject and tense. This construction can be used both as a copula and as a predicate meaning 'become', and the intended meaning must be determined according to the context of use. The following examples illustrate respectively past and future tense, and conditional forms of *kala*.

(835) **Hwa-kal-a** ma-adui.
 1pl.pst-be-fv 6-enemies
 '**We were/became** enemies.'

(836) Hiye ndi-ye-lagul-a yuno na=ye **a-nda-kal-a** tajiri sana.
 1.dem3 fut-1.rel-heal-fv 1.dem4 com=3sg 3sg-fut-be-fv rich deg
 'He who heals, this one also **will become** very rich.'

(837) *Kpwa mfwano, kala chigulu chingeamba, "Mino simi mkpwono, kpwa hivyo simi seemu ya mwiri," hata hivyo hicho chigulu **chingekala bado ni seemu ya mwiri**. Naro sikiro kala ringeamba, "Mino simi dzitso, kpwa hivyo simi seemu ya mwiri," hata hivyo hiro sikiro **ringekala bado ni seemu ya mwiri**.*

'For example, if a foot said/were to say, "I am not a hand, therefore I am not a part of the body," even so this foot **would still be a part of the body**. And likewise if an ear said/were to say, "I am not an eye, therefore I am not a part of the body," even so this ear **would still be a part of the body**.' (1 Corinthians 12:15–16[2])

chi-**nge**-kal-a	bado	ni	seemu	ya	mwiri.
7-COND-be-FV	still	COP	9.part	9.ASS	3.body

Note the use of *kala* in the protasis (the 'if-clause' of the conditional); this is a contraction of *ichikala* 'if it is (the case that)' (see §5.4.2). Note also the combination of *kala* and *ni* in the apodosis (the consequence clause) where *kala* and *ni* jointly function as a copula.

8.1.3 Aspectual copulas

Digo has two aspectual copulas, the persistive aspect marker *chere*, meaning 'still' and the negative inceptive aspect marker *dzangbwe*, meaning 'yet' (always in a negative polarity context). These are identical in form and meaning to the aspectual markers *chere* and *dzangbwe* (see §5.3.2.3 and §5.3.2.2) except that they are not prefixed to a verb. When it functions as part of a copula construction, *chere* is prefixed by a subject concord and followed by a nonverbal predicate, such as *moyo* 'alive':

(838) *a-chere moyo*
3SG-PERS 3.heart
's/he is still alive'

Temporal reference with the persistive (other than when the time reference is present or universal) is indicated by *kala*:

(839) *Hiro likumundi ra atu **kala ri-chere** phapho.*
5.DEM2 5.crowd 5.ASS 2.people PST 5-PERS 16.DEM3_VARIANT
'That huge crowd of people **was still** there.' (past)

(840) *na=si **ndi-o-kal-a hu-chere** moyo ...*
COM=1PL FUT-2.REL-be-FV 1PL-PERS 3.heart
'and we who **will still be/remain** alive ...' (future)

---

[2]This is the only example of a conditional copula construction in the corpus of translated and nontranslated texts.

When *dzangbwe* functions as a copula it is prefixed by a subject concord and (almost always) a negative prefix and occurs clause finally (i.e. not prefixed to a verb stem or followed by any other predicate):

(841) Wakati   w-angu   **ta-u-dzangbwe.**
      14.time   14-1SG.POS   NEG-14-INC
      'My time is not yet.' (i.e. 'My time has not yet come.')

8.1.4 Hypothetical clauses (if X had been Y)/(if X were Y)

The invariable copula forms *ni* and *si* can follow the conditional marker *ichikala* 'if it be' or its contracted form *kala*, which is homophonous with the past tense auxiliary.

(842) Kala   ni   nabii,   a-nge-many-a
      if   COP   1a.prophet   3SG-COND-know-FV
      'if he were a prophet, he would know'

(843) Kala   si   hivyo ...
      if   NEG.COP   8.DEM3
      'If it were not so ...' (implied, 'but it is so')

(844) "... mino **kala che ni m'baya**, che sikuiha, mana che kumanya kala nyama akagbwirwa nyumazo ..."

"'... me **if I were bad**, then I would not have called you, for you did not realize that an animal had been caught behind you [i.e. after you had left] ...'"

kala   che   ni   m'-baya
if   FOC   COP   1-bad

8.1.5 Copula constructions in relative clauses

Let us first make clear what we are **not** concerned with in this section. A relative clause may itself function as a predicate, as in the following examples:

(845) Mwimwi   si=mwi   m-ri-o-ni-tsambul-a
      2PL   NEG=2PL   2PL-REL.PST-2.REL-1SG-choose-FV
      'It was not you who chose me.' Or 'You were not the ones who chose me.'

The constructions with which we will be concerned in this section are ones in which the relative clause itself consists of a subject, a copula, and a predicate. In example (846), the relative clause *mriokala nami* functions as a predicate (following the copula *ndimwi*) but also contains a predicate (*nami*) following the *kala* (here functioning as the copula verb 'be' with the relative past tense *ri-*). The predicates have been enclosed in square brackets and the copulas have been highlighted to illustrate the embedding relation between them.

(846) Mwimwi **ndi=mwi** [m-ri-o-**kal**-a   [na=mi]]
      2PL   COP=2PL   2PL-PST-2.REL-be-FV   COM=1SG
      'You are [the ones who were [with me]]'

It is the 'innermost' copula construction that will be dealt with in the rest of this section. The 'outermost' copula construction is an example of identificational articulation (see §7.2.4 and §7.3.4.2), and is dealt with in §8.2.2.

There are three kinds of relative clause which function as copula constructions: uninflected constructions which contain the copulas *ri* (in affirmative clauses) and *si* (in negative clauses); constructions which inflect for tense containing the copula verb *kala*; and a construction involving the *amba* relativizer plus a regular copula. Following the convention adopted in §7.3, in each of the examples in this section, the relative clause is enclosed in square brackets, the head noun phrase is underlined, and the relative concord marker is highlighted in bold type.

8.1.5.1 sc – **ri** – *rel*/sc – **si** – *rel*

This construction is identical to that involving uninflected relative clauses with verbal predicates, except that the existential copula *ri* takes the place of the verb in affirmative clauses and the negative existential copula *si* takes the place of the verb in negative clauses. Because it is not inflected for tense/aspect, this construction can only be used when the time reference is either coreferential with the current context or 'universal'. This should not be confused with the use of *ri* as a past tense marker in relative clauses (*iye ndiye ariyehenda mambo higo* 'it was she who did those things'), although historically the two forms almost certainly share a common origin.

(847) hiyu   mutu   [a-**ri**-ye   hipha   dzulu   ya   muhi]
      1.DEM1 1.person 3SG-COP-1.REL   16.DEM1   top   9.ASS   3.tree
      'this man who is up here in the tree'

(848) mutu   [a-**si**-ye   M-digo]
      1.person 3SG-NEG.COP-1.REL 1-Digo
      'a person/anyone who is not a Digo'

(849) mwimwi m-osi   [**m-ri**-o   hipha]
      2PL   2PL-all   2PL-COP-2.REL   here
      'all you who are here'

(850) mbuzi   [i-**ri**-yo   na   mimba]
      9.goat 9-COP-9.REL   COM   3.pregnancy
      'a pregnant goat'

8.1 Copula constructions: Forms

(851) <u>vyo</u>　　　[i-ri-**vyo**　　kulu]
　　　8.DEM3_VAR　9-COP-8.REL　big
　　　'how big it is' (lit: 'how how it is big'; it = *meli* 'ship' cl.9)

8.1.5.2 Finite forms with kala

Another way to express copula relative clauses involves finite forms of the copula verb *kala* 'be'. For example, when *kala* is prefixed with the relative future tense marker *ndi-* plus a relative noun class marker, the clause receives a future time interpretation:

(852) Na=<u>si</u>　　[ndi-o-kal-a　　hu-chere　moyo] ...
　　　COM=1PL　　FUT-2.REL-be-FV　1PL-PERS　3.heart
　　　'And we who will remain alive ...'

In past tense relative clauses, the SC and the relative past tense marker *ri-* are often omitted (e.g. *ariyekala* > *yekala*; see §5.2.3.1 for details). As a result, when *kala* is prefixed with a relative marker alone, it must be interpreted as the copula verb with an elided past tense rather than as a past tense auxiliary (see §8.1.1 and §8.1.2):

(853) Phahi　hi<u>vyo</u>　ndi=vyo　　safari　　　y-angu　　ya　　kpwandza
　　　so　　　8.DEM3　COP=8.REF　9.journey　9-1SG.POS　9.ASS　first

　　　ya　　　Nairobi　　　　[**vyo**-kal-a]　　(short form of　**i-ri-vyo**-kal-a).
　　　9.ASS　PLACE_NAME　8.REL-be-FV　　　　　　　　　　　9-PST-8.REL-be-FV
　　　'So this was how my first journey to Nairobi was.'

(854) Yuya myawe wamuuza **yuya yekala mchina-mikahe** anaambwa, "We kpwani ndiwe ani?"
　　　'His companion asked **the one who was the owner of the bread**, "Who are you?"'

　　　<u>yuya</u>　　[**ye**-kal-a　　mchina-mikahe]　　(short form of　**a-ri-ye**-kal-a)
　　　1.DEM2　　1.REL-be-FV　1.owner-bread　　　　　　　　　　　　3SG-PST-1.REL-be-FV

The copula verb *kala* can also occur with the negative marker *si*, which in the absence of a tense or aspect marker can receive a conditional interpretation:

(855) Sisi　　[hu-**si**-pho-kal-a　　a-aminifu] ...
　　　1PL　　1PL-NEG-16.REL-be-FV　2-faithful
　　　'As for us if we are not faithful ...'

8.1.5.3 Amba *plus copula*

This construction functions in the same way as the *amba-* relative construction with verbal predicates (§7.3.2.3); the nonverbal predicate may be any of the forms already listed. The following examples illustrate some of the possibilities.

Amba plus invariable copula *ni* (856a) and copula verb *kala* (856b):

(856) a. *Ku=na* <u>atu</u> [*amba-o ni a mwisho*]
17=COM 2.people REL-2.REL COP 2.ASS last

b. [*amba-o a-nda-kal-a a mwandzo*].
REL-2.REL 3PL-FUT-be-FV 2.ASS first

'There are people who are last who will be first.'

Note that the entire noun phrase *atu ambao ni a mwisho* 'people who are last' in (856a) functions as the head of the RC in (856b), not just the noun *atu* 'people'.

Amba plus invariable negative copula *si*+referential marker:

(857) *Atu* [*amba-o si=o A-digo*].
2.people REL-2.REL NEG=3PL 2-Digos

'People who are not Digos.'

(858) *Mwimwi* [*amba-o si=mwi A-digo*].
2PL REL-2.REL NEG=2PL 2-Digos

'You who are not Digos.'

8.2 Copula constructions: Functions

Copula constructions in Digo can be classified using functional criteria in various ways. In this section, I have chosen to divide them as follows: (1) nominal predicates which identify an entity or describe an entity as an example of a particular class, (2) focus predicates which highlight new information, (3) adjectival predicates which describe a characteristic of an entity, (4) locative predicates which establish the location of an entity whose existence is already supposed, and (5) existential predicates which establish the existence of an entity. Since the forms of the various copula constructions have been described in detail above, I do not provide a morpheme-by-morpheme gloss of every example in this section.

8.2.1 Nominal predicates

Nominal predicates (X is Y) may be referential (identifying): 'Lion is the owner of the forest' or descriptive (nonreferential): 'The lion is an animal.' In addition, the predicate may be a possessive noun phrase, in which case it may be referential: 'Giraffes are my favourite animals' or descriptive: 'You are my guest.'

8.2.1.1 Referential predicates

Occasionally nominal predicates are expressed simply by juxtaposition of X and Y. This strategy is rare, and seems to be restricted to predicate nominals used as introductions (see §7.2.2 for further discussion), as in the following example (see also examples [811] and [812]).

(859) Bwana   Sulutani   **m-ganga**   **hiyu.**
      1a.lord   Sultan   1-healer   1.DEM1
      'Lord Sultan, this is the healer.' (lit: 'healer this.')

The invariable copula *ni* and the construction *ndi*+referential marker are far more common than juxtaposition; *ni* is the most frequently found form in all nominal predicates (see examples in §8.1.1) but for contrast and/or emphasis *ndi*+referential marker is used. In the following examples, in addition to the *ndi*+referential marker copula construction, emphasis on the subject is also indicated by the use of the independent pronouns *uwe* 'you', *we* 'you' (short form), the emphatic interrogative *kpwani*, and *mino* 'I' (metarepresentational pronoun—see §3.3.2 and §3.4.3.1.4):

(860) *"Mimi mwenye n'naphiya hiko kuna mudzi wanjina mkpwulu ela **uwe** phapha **ndiwe liwali**."*

"'I myself am going away to where there is another large town, but here **you will be governor**.'"

(861) *"**We kpwani ndiwe ani?**" Achiamba "**Mino ndimi Nia Mwenga**."*

"'**Well who are you?**" He said, "**I am Nia Mwenga**.'"

One feature of referential predicates is that they are 'equational', which means that the subject and the predicate can, in principle, be reversed. However, in Digo the clause-initial position (the preverbal position with verbal predicates) is the position in which the topic occurs, regardless of its grammatical role (see §7.2.2 for discussion). The subject and the predicate in the above juxtaposed examples cannot be reversed since the predicate contains new information and therefore cannot be a topic. In example (860), *uwe* refers to the addressee and is therefore inherently topical, but the information that the addressee is to be the governor is new; in the second example the name *Nia Mwenga* is new information and so cannot occur in clause-initial position. This is also illustrated in example (862). In the first sentence, it is already assumed that the forest has an owner, but the fact that the speaker is that owner is new information; in the second sentence a standard introduction is used with the inherently topical speaker being mentioned by name before the predicate:

(862) *"We bwana unataka mwenye mchina-tsaka, mwenye mchina-tsaka **ni mimi**. Simba **ndimi mwenye** ..."*

"'You sir you want the owner of the forest, the actual owner of the forest **is me**. (I) Lion **I am the owner** ...'"

8.2.1.2 Descriptive (nominal) predicates

The invariable forms *ni* and *si* (§8.1.1), the constructions *ndi*+referential marker and *si*+referential marker (§8.1.2.1), and the subject concord alone (§8.1.2.2) can all be used with descriptive predicates:

(863) a. *Mino **ni** mimi mutu.*   'I **am** just a person.' (lit: 'I am me person.')
     b. *Mimi **si** hiye mumgodzaye.*   'I **am not** he for whom you are waiting.'

(864) *Mdigo **siye** mutu bii.*

'A Digo **is not** a person at all.'

(865) *Ichikala **u mwanadamu** masikirogo nagasikize vinono*

'If **you are a human being**, let your ears hear clearly'

(866) *We bwana **u mjeni**, na atu a kure **ndimwi aganga**.*

'You sir **are a stranger**, and (you) people from afar **you are great healers**.'

[Note: *atu a kure* is not the grammatical subject of *ndimwi*, which is 2nd person plural agreeing with an understood *mwimwi* 'you.PL'.]

8.2.1.3 Possessive predicates

Predicates which take the form of possessive noun phrases are formed like other descriptive nominal predicates:

(867) Mafuha   **ni**   **g-angu**   ná-ga-lavy-a   mw-enye.
       6.oil   COP   6-1SG.POS   1SG.PST-6-give-FV   1-EMPH

'The oil **was mine** I gave it away myself.'

(868) uwe   **u**   **m-jeni**   **w-angu**   na=mi   **ndi=mi**   **mwenyezi-o**.
       2SG   2SG.SC   1-guest   1-1SG.POS   COM=1SG.REF   COP=1SG.REF   1.host-2SG.POS

'**you are my guest** and **I am your host**.'

8.2.2 Focus predicates

Focus predicates highlight the new information in the sentence (the part which is 'in focus') as opposed to other elements which are assumed to be known.

They indicate identificational articulation (see §7.2.4 and §7.3.4.2) expressed through focus-presupposition sentence articulation (Lambrecht 1994:122). The new information is the subject of the sentence, which is followed by the *ndi*+referential marker construction and an existential relative construction. In the following examples, the presupposed information is 'something is in the trap' and 'something was placed here' respectively, and the new information (the focal element) is the identity of that something.

(869) ... *mbona ye mchetu **ndiye ariye phapha** na ye kulungu kapho?*

'... why is it the woman **who is there** [in the trap] and the antelope is not there?'

ndi=ye   a-ri-ye   phapha
COP=3SG.REF   3SG-PST.COP-3SG.REL 16.DEM3_VARIANT

(870) *ye maiti nchiyemuona na fisi **ndiye achiyeikpwa hipha**!*

'the corpse which I saw with the hyena **is the one which was placed here**!'

ndi=ye   a-chi-ye-ikpw-a   hipha
COP=3SG.REF   3SG-CONS-3SG.REL-place.PAS-FV 16.DEM1

8.2.3 Adjectival predicates

The invariable copula *ni* (or the invariable negative copula *si*) are used to describe permanent or inherent characteristics or states:

(871) *yuya mwana wao mmwenga kana chitu **ni mchiya** na mmwenga **ni tajiri sana**.*

'one of their sons did not have a thing, **he was poor/a poor person**, and (the other) one **was very rich**.'

(872) *Yo minyau hipho pha Sulutani **ni minji**.*

'The cats there at the Sultan's place **were many**.'

When an explicit time reference is included in a description, an inflected form of the copula verb *kala* 'be' or the past tense auxiliary *kala* (or hodiernal past auxiliary *che*) plus the invariable copula *ni* are used:

(873) *Hiye ndiyelagula yuno naye **andakala tajiri sana**.*

'He who heals her (lit: that one) also **will become very rich**.'

(874) *Jumane siyaphaha nafasi, mana mchetu wangu **kala ni mkpwongo**.*

'I didn't have an opportunity on Tuesday, because my wife **was sick**.'

When describing a currently existing temporary state rather than an inherent characteristic or a temporary state in the past or future, the subject concord of the noun being described must be used. However, the subject concord can also be used for other descriptive predicates (such as *u mwanadamu* 'you are a human being' in §8.2.1.2).

(875) a. *Kahawa i tayari.*   'The coffee is ready.'
      b. *Chitabu chi tayari.*   'The book is ready.'
      c. *Hu tayari.*   'We are ready.'

Persistent states can be expressed using the persistive form *chere* (see §8.1.3) which in other constructions functions as an aspect marker (§5.3.2.3):

(876) ndugu-ye   Mwiya   m-dide   **a-chere**   **m-zima**
      9.brother-9.3SG.POS   NAME   1-small   3SG-PERS   1-whole
      'his brother Mwiya the younger **is still alive**'

8.2.4 Locative predicates

Locative predicates are used when the emphasis is on the location of an entity, the existence of which is presupposed (i.e. not in question). Typically, locative predicates can be used to ask or respond to 'where' questions. If the time reference is the present, locative predicates can be formed using the subject concord followed by the location word or by the question word *kuphi* 'where'.

(877) *Mwanache a kuphi?*   *A sukuli.*
      'Where is the child?'   'She is at school.' (cl.1)

(878) *Anyama a kuphi?*   *A vuweni.*
      'Where are the animals?'   'They are in the bush.' (cl.2)

(879) *Chungbwa ri kuphi?*   *Ri mezani.*
      'Where is the orange?'   'It is on the table.' (cl.5)

(880) *Mayayi ga kuphi?*   *Ga mfukoni.*
      'Where are the eggs?'   'They are in the bag.' (cl.6)

(881) *Nazi i kuphi?*   *I mnazini.*
      'Where is the coconut?'   'It is on the palm tree.' (cl.9)

(882) *Nazi zi kuphi?*   *Zi dukani.*
      'Where are the coconuts?'   'They are in the shop.' (cl.10)

In the 3rd person singular an alternative form *yu*, probably borrowed from Swahili, is occasionally found: *Yu phaphi?* 'Where is he?'

The negative forms of the subject concords also function to indicate where something is not located:

(883) *Mlungu ka kure naswi.*   'God is not far from us.'

Locative demonstratives can follow the located noun without any overt copula:

(884) a. *Hiyu hipha.* 'He is here.'
b. *Hiye hiko.* 'She is there.'

When the time reference is other than the present, a variety of forms are possible, including the subject concord (as above), the invariable copula *ni*, and finite forms of the copula verb *kala*. In the following examples, the copula plus the location have been highlighted:

(885) *"Nkaambwa mlunguni **ni phapha**."*

"I was told heaven **was here**."

(886) *Siku mwenga yuya Mwiya mvyere **ariphokala hiko marisani** ...*

'One day Mwiya the elder **when he was there at the pasture** ...'

In relative clauses, the referential marker of one of the locative noun classes can be used to indicate location in conjunction with the relative copula *ri*. A locative referential marker (*mo* in the following example) is required whether or not the location is independently represented:

(887) *Nyama   hiyu   ni   ye   **a-ri-ye=mo**   chumba-ni ...*
1a.animal 1.DEM1 COP 1.DEM3_VAR 3SG-COP-3SG.REL=18.REF room-LOC

"This animal is that **which was inside the room** ..."

The locative referential marker can occur when there is no relative clause. In example (888), the class 17 referential marker *ko* follows the copula *ri*, although this is not a relative clause but a tenseless locative predicate. In example (889), the class 16 referential marker *pho* occurs as a clitic on the 3SG negative subject concord. By way of contrast, example (890) illustrates the use of a reduced form of the class 17 demonstrative *hiko* which is not cliticized to anything:

(888) *Si-m-many-a   a-ri=ko.*
1SG.NEG-3SG-know-FV 3SG-COP=17.REF

'I do not know where he is.'

(889) *Kulungu   ka=pho.*
1a.antelope 3SG.NEG=16.REF

'The antelope is not there.'

(890) *Yuya   Njira Nyinji   kala   a   ko   nyuma-ze*
1.DEM2 PROPER NAME PST 3SG.SC 17.DEM3_VAR 10.behind-10.3SG.POS

'That Njira Nyinji was **there behind him**'

Locations can also function as the focal element (i.e. new information) in an identificational expression (see §7.2.3). In this use, the location is the subject of the sentence, and is followed by the *ndi*+referential marker construction and an existential relative construction in which the relative concord marker is that of the locative noun class of the subject. The located noun phrase is preceded by the comitative marker *na* (indicating association with a person or thing):

(891) *Pharatu   ndi=pho   pha-ri-pho   na   ye   mlungu.*
      16.DEM2_VARIANT COP=3SG.REF 16-COP-16.REL   COM 1.DEM3_VAR 1a.god
      'There is the place where the god is.'

8.2.5 Existential predicates

The function of existential predicates is to establish the existence of an entity.

8.2.5.1 *Existential predicates expressing location*

Existential predicates expressing location differ from locative predicates in that the emphasis is on the existence of the entity rather than its location. They are not appropriate as responses to 'where' questions in which the existence of the subject is presupposed. When the time reference is the present, existential predicates expressing location are most often formed from one of the locative noun class prefixes plus the comitative predicate *na*: *kuna/phana/muna* 'there is'/'there are':

(892) a. *Kuna magari mane barabarani.*   'There are four cars on the road.'

Compare with the locative predicate construction:

b. *Magari mane ga barabarani.*   'Four cars are on the road.'

With temporal reference other than the present there are two ways in which existential location can be expressed. One strategy is to use the past tense auxiliary *kala* (or the short form *ka*) or the hodiernal past auxiliary *che* followed by one of the locative noun class prefixes plus the comitative marker *na*:

(893) *Phara kaya **ka phana** tabu.*

   'There at home **there was** trouble.'

(894) *Himo ndani **kala muna** nyama wa mapha mwereru tse-tse-tse.*

   'There inside [the room] **there was** a completely white bird.' (lit: 'animal of wings white completely')

(895) *Rero ligundzu **che kuna** magari matsano barabarani.*

   'This morning **there were** five cars on the road.' (hodiernal past)

The other strategy to is to prefix the subject concord of one of the locative noun classes to the verb *kala* followed immediately by the comitative marker *na* (indicating association with a person or thing) and the located entity:

(896) *Dzana **kpwakala na** magari sita barabarani.*

   'Yesterday **there were** six cars on the road.' (past)

8.2 Copula constructions: Functions 299

(897) Muhondo **kundakala na** magari manji sana barabarani.
'Tomorrow **there will be** very many cars on the road.' (future)

The difference between existential predicates expressing location and locative predicates proper is illustrated in the following example taken from a first person narrative text. In the first clause, the focus is on the existence of the lions rather than on their precise location and the class 17 subject concord *ku* plus comitative marker *na* is used; in the second clause, the emphasis shifts to the location of the lions and the class 1 subject concord *a* is used instead:

(898) Na   ná-many-a   **ku=na**   simba   anjina   phephi
     COM 1SG.PST-know-FV   17=COM   2a.lions 2.other   near
     lakini si-manyir-e   a   u-pande   gani.
     but   1SG.NEG-know-FV   3PL.SC   14-side   which[3]

'And I knew that there were other lions nearby (existential) but I did not know in which direction they were.' (locative)

8.2.5.2 Existential predicates expressing existence only

In Digo, as in most Bantu languages, the preverbal position is reserved for sentence topics; that is, elements that are already established in a discourse. (In §7.2 it was shown that the preverbal position in Digo is reserved for switch topics.) If it is necessary to state the existence of an entity, then the existence of that entity is probably not assumed and hence the expression which refers to the entity is not a sentence topic.[4] For this reason, expressions referring to entities whose existence is being asserted typically occur in a postverbal position. The subject concord of the preceding verb is one of the locative noun classes, even if the precise location of the entity in question is not known or is not at issue. Class 17 is usually found in affirmative clauses and class 16 is usually found in negative clauses, although this is not a hard and fast rule. When introducing new major participants in a narrative, two constructions are typically used: *kpwakala na* (lit: 'there was with') and *kpwahenda* (lit: 'there did'); note that the comitative particle *na* is used with *kpwakala* but not with *kpwahenda*:

(899) Hipho kare,   ku-a-kala   na   mutu   m-mwenga ...
     long ago   17-PST-COP   COM   1.person   1-one
     'Long ago, there was a man ...'

---

[3] This is not the class 6 form but an invariable question word borrowed from Swahili.
[4] The same is true for question words such as *ani* 'who'. If the identity of an entity is in question, it cannot be a topic, and so the question word cannot occur in the preverbal position. Instead, the question word is the focus of the sentence and occurs in a focus-presupposition construction (see §7.2.4).

(900) pha-chi-kala   na   mjeni   phapho   pha-o   lalo-ni.
      16-CONS-COP   COM   1.stranger   16.DEM3_VARIANT   16-3PL.POS   dwelling-LOC
      'there was a stranger there at their place.'

(901) **Kundakala na phuto rero** mana mlungu u kundu na maingu manji.

   '**There will be storms today** for the sky is red with many clouds.'

   Ku-nda-kala   na   phuto   rero
   17-FUT-COP   COM   10.storm   today

(902) Hipho kare,   ku-a-hend-a   mutu   na   mche-we.
      long ago   17-PST-do-FV   1.person COM   1.wife-1.3SG.POS
      'Long ago, there was a man and his wife.'

Negative existential predicates are often formed by prefixing a locative noun class prefix (usually class 16) to the comitative marker *na* followed by the referent of the entity whose existence is being denied. When the time reference is not the present, this construction is preceded by a tensed form of the verb *kala*, the past tense auxiliary *kala*, or the hodiernal past copula *che* as appropriate.

(903) Ta-pha=na   hata   nyumba.
      NEG-16=COM   even   9.house
      'There is not even a house.'

(904) Kpwa vira **kala taphana cha kumzuwiya wala kugbwira**, waphiya kuphiya hadi ndani.

   'Since **there was nothing to prevent him or hold him back**, he went right inside.'

   kala   ta-pha=na   cha   ku-m-zuwiy-a   wala   ku-gbwir-a
   PST   NEG-16=COM   7.ASS   INF-1-prevent-FV   nor   INF-hold-FV

When the existence of an entity which has already been established in a discourse is being confirmed or denied, the referential marker of one of the locative noun classes is used. In example (905), the class 17 referential marker *ko* is cliticized to the negative form of the 3PL subject concord; in example (906), which contains three affirmative relative clauses, *ko* is cliticized to a copula construction:

(905) Ta-a=ko.
      NEG-3PL=17.REF
      'They are no more.'

(906) ye-kal-a=ko,   a-ri-ye=ko,   na
 3SG.REL-be-FV=17.REF   3SG-COP-3SG.REL=17.REF   COM
 ndi-ye-kal-a=ko
 FUT-3SG.REL-be-FV=17.REF

 'he who was, who is, and who will be'

8.3 Comparative constructions

Comparisons in Digo are expressed through a variety of verbal and nonverbal predicates. The classification adopted in this section derives from Schadeberg (2006), which in turn draws on Sacleux (1909) among others. However, I have not included 'inferiority'—X is less (Y) than Z—since there is no construction that corresponds to this in Digo. Instead, either an antonym is used or one of the other comparative constructions is negated:

(907) Ta-i-zidi   laki   mwenga.
 NEG-9-exceed   9.hundred_thousand   9.one

 'It does not exceed one hundred thousand.' (i.e. 'It is less than one hundred thousand.')

(908) Mbona   dzana   na   rero   **ta-m-ya-hend-a**   chiasi   cha
 why   yesterday   COM   today   NEG-2PL-NEG.PST-do-FV   7.amount 7.ASS
 ma-tofali   dza   phara   mwandzo
 6-bricks   as   16.DEM2   first

 'Why yesterday and today **did you not make the (same) amount of bricks** as you did at first?' (i.e. 'Why did you make fewer bricks than at first?')

8.3.1 Superiority

The superiority comparison—X is more (Y) than Z—can be expressed using various constructions in Digo.

8.3.1.1 *Selective comparatives*

The selective comparative presents the two entities to be compared and then attributes a property to one of these:

(909) Mombasa   na   Nairobi,   Mombasa   ni   phephi.
 Mombasa   COM   Nairobi   Mombasa   COP   near

 '(Out of) Mombasa and Nairobi, Mombasa is near(er).'

8.3.1.2 Locative comparatives

The locative comparative uses the expression *kuriko* which is a fossilized form of the class 17 relative copula (*ku-ri-ko*). It still functions as a locative expression (see example [910]) but also indicates comparison, either alone, as in (911), or in conjunction with the degree word *zaidi* 'more', as in (912):

(910) *Sambi, yuya Nia Mwenga wauka, lakini* **kuriko na myawe** *kamanya n'kuphi wala n'kuphi.*

'Now that Nia Mwenga left, but **where his companion was** he had not the faintest idea.'

ku-ri-ko	na	mya-we
17-COP-17.REL	COM	1.fellow-1.3SG.POS

(911) Kundi mwenga ri-nda-kala na **nguvu** **kuriko** r-anjina.
5.group 5.one 5-FUT-COP COM 9.strength COMP 5-other
'One group will have (more) **strength than** the other.'

(912) A-lavy-a-ye nku-jali-w-a zaidi **kuriko** a-phoker-a-ye.
3SG-give-FV-3SG.REL HAB-bless-PAS-FV more COMP 3SG-receive-FV-3SG.REL
'He who gives is blessed **more than** he who receives.'

Kuriko can also express the notion of preference:

(913) Baha ni-ku-loz-e uwe **kuriko** mutu wanjina.
better 1SG-2SG-marry.CAUS-SUB 2SG COMP 1.person 1.another
'It is better I give (my daughter) in marriage to you (rather) **than** another person.'

8.3.1.3 Degree comparatives

Superiority can be expressed using the degree word *zaidi* 'more' followed by the class 9 form of the associative marker *ya* (or followed by *kuriko* as illustrated above), and by the degree word *baha* 'better, improved' followed by *kuriko* when the object of comparison is overtly mentioned.

(914) A-lume kala a-ka-lól-a **zaidi ya** m-chetu m-mwenga.
2-men PST 3PL-ANT-marry-FV more 9.ASS 1-woman 1-one
'Men used to marry **more than** one woman.'

(915) **Ni baha** ni-uy-e kaya.
COP better 1SG-return-SUB 9.home
'**It is better** that I return home.'

8.3 Comparative constructions

(916) Ndoa   mbaya   **ni**   **baha**   **kuriko**   ugungu   m-nono.
      9.marriage 9.bad   COP   better   COMP   14.singleness   14-good
      'A bad marriage **is better than** good singleness.'

8.3.1.4 Verbal comparatives

Comparisons of superiority can be expressed through verb forms, of which the verbs *zidi* 'increase' (from the same root as *zaidi*), *shinda* 'defeat, surpass', and *tsupa* 'pass' are the most common:

(917) Ukongo   u-ka-m-**zidi**.
      14.illness 14-ANT-3SG-increase
      'He has got worse.' (lit: 'Illness has increased to him.')

(918) A-ka-**zidi**-w-a   ni   ukongo.
      3SG-ANT-increase-PAS-FV   COP   14.illness
      'He has got worse.' (lit: 'He has been increased by illness.')

(919) Kala   ta-ku=na   a-ri-ye   m-kulu   ku-m-**shind**-a.
      PST   NEG-17=COM   3SG-COP-1.REL   1-great   INF-3SG-defeat-FV
      'There was nobody who was greater than he.'

(920) Nyani   ni   m-kulu   ku-**tsup**-a   chima   na   tumbiri.
      baboon   COP   1-big   INF-pass-FV   vervet   COM   Sykes
      'The baboon is bigger than the vervet monkey and the Sykes monkey.'

8.3.2 Equality

Comparisons of equality—X is (not) as Y as Z, or X is (not) like/the same as Z—are expressed primarily using *sawa* 'same' plus the comitative particle *na* or *kama* 'like, as':

(921) Yuyatu mwanache, siyo mwanache ndipho, **a sawa na aphu-ye**.
      'That child, he was no longer a child, he was **the same as his uncle**.'

      a   sawa   na   aphu-ye.
      3SG   same   COM   1a.uncle-1.3SG.POS

(922) ri-na-ng'al-a   kama   bafuta.
      5-CONT-shine-FV   like   9.linen
      'shining like linen (i.e. very white).'

Kama is also used for general comparisons:

(923) Anache   a-na-tal-w-a   kama   chitu   muhimu.
      2.children   3PL-CONT-count-PAS-FV as   7.thing important
      'Children are counted as something important.'

8.3.3 Sufficiency

To express 'X is (Y) enough' the verb *tosha* 'suffice' is used, either as a finite verb or, more frequently, in the nonfinite form preceded by the associative particle *-a* with the appropriate noun class concord. In both constructions, *tosha* may be followed by a complement and be preceded by a verb complement (object) marker:

(924) Mbao   hizi   zi-na-tosh-a   u-refu.
      10.planks 10.DEM1   10-CONT-suffice-FV 14-long
      'These planks are long enough.' (lit: 'These planks suffice length')

(925) chakurya cha   ku-tosh-a
      7.food   7.ASS INF-suffice-FV
      'enough food' (lit: 'food of sufficing')

(926) chakurya cha   ku-ku-tosh-a   na   atu-o
      7.food   7.ASS INF-2SG-suffice-FV   COM 2.people-2.2SG.POS
      'enough food for you and your people'

(927) chakurya cha   ku-tosh-a   nyumba-ye
      7.food   7.ASS INF-suffice-FV   9.house-9.3SG.POS
      'enough food for his household'

8.3.4 Superlative

To express the notion 'X is the most Y' either *kushinda -osi* 'defeating all' or *kutsupa -osi* 'passing all' can follow the Y element.

(928) Lakini edz-a-ye   kula mlungu-ni   ni   m-kulu ku-shind-a   osi.
      but   come-FV-1.REL   from 3.heaven-LOC   COP 1-big   INF-defeat-FV   2.all
      'But he who comes from heaven is greater than them all.'

Superlatives can also be expressed by using a focus predicate, as in the following examples:

(929) Ndi=yo   meli   i-ri-yo   kulu.
      COP=9.REF   9.ship   9-COP-9.REL   9.big
      'This ship is the biggest.' (lit: 'It is the ship which is big.')

(930) Meli   hino   ndi=yo   kulu.
     9.ship 9.DEM4   COP=9.REF   9.big
     'This ship is the biggest.' (lit: 'This ship it is big.')

8.3.5 Excessive

To express 'X is very/extremely/too Y' Digo uses degree adverbs (see §6.4.1.2), ideophones (see §6.4.2), the augmentative noun class prefix (e.g. *dzi-nyama dzi-kulu* 'a very large animal, a huge beast'), or reduplication of the Y element (exemplified below):

(931) mihi   mi-kulu   mi-kulu
     4.tree   4-big   4-big
     'very large trees'

Another means of expressing the superlative is through the verb phrases *kutsupa chiasi* 'passing amount' and *kutsupa mphaka* 'passing limit':

(932) Ta-hu-nda-dzikary-a   ku-tsup-a   chiasi.
     NEG-1PL-FUT-boast-FV   INF-pass-FV   7.amount
     'We will not boast more than is proper.'

(933) Digbwa   ri   ngbwadu   ku-tsup-a   mphaka.
     5.vinegar   5SC   sour   INF-pass-FV   3.limit
     'The vinegar is extremely sour.'

Intensifiers can also modify verb phrases:

(934) U-si-lung-e   kamare   mambo   higa.
     2SG-NEG-follow-SUB   INTENS   6.matters   6.DEM1
     'Do not follow these things at all.'

(935) U-si-lung-e   sana   mambo   higa.
     2SG-NEG-follow-SUB   INTENS   6.matters   6.DEM1
     'Do not follow these things very much.'

8.3.6 Completive

To express 'X is completely Y' Digo uses the intensifier *kabisa* 'completely' which may be reduplicated as in line 8 in the narrative text in §8.5:

(936) tabiya   nyi-phya   kabisa
     9.character   9-new   INTENS
     'a completely new character'

8.4 'Having' or 'being with'

In common with other Bantu languages, Digo does not have a fully inflecting verb 'have'. Instead, the comitative particle *na* functions as a predicate, as either a bound or a free morpheme. Note that some relations which in English are expressed with the verb 'be', such as 'be hungry' and 'be certain' are in Digo expressed with *na* followed by a noun: *Nina ndzala* 'I am hungry' (lit: 'I have hunger'); *sina hakika* 'I am not certain' (lit: 'I do not have certainty'). This use of *na* has already been illustrated in the description of existential predicates expressing location (§8.2.5.1).

8.4.1 'Having' in simple declarative clauses

'To have (not)' in the present is expressed with the comitative marker *na* preceded by the subject concord and (where applicable) the negative prefix. The comitative marker functions syntactically as a clitic in this construction, and semantically as a predicator.

(937) a. *Ni=na chitabu.* b. *Si=na chitabu.*
   1SG=COM 7.book   1SG.NEG=COM 7.book
   'I have a book.'   'I do not have a book.'

(938) a. *Chitabu chi=na ma-neno ma-nji.*
   7.book 7=COM 6-words 6-many
   'The book has many words.'

  b. *Chitabu ta-chi=na ma-neno ma-nji.*
    7.book NEG-7=COM 6-words 6-many
    'The book does not have many words.'

If the object is known, it can be expressed by the referential marker which is suffixed to *na*:

(939) *Chitabu, ni=na=cho.*
   7.book 1SG=COM=7.REF
   'The book, I have it.'

In the affirmative, the past tense is formed from the inflected form of the copula verb *kala* plus the comitative predicate *na* which is a free morpheme in this construction:

(940) a. *Dzana nákala na chitabu.* 'Yesterday I had a book.'
  b. *Chitabu chakala na maneno manji.* 'The book had many words.'
  c. *Dzana duka rakala na matunda.* 'Yesterday the shop had fruit.'

8.4 'Having' or 'being with'

In the negative, the (uninflected) past tense auxiliary *kala* precedes the negative construction described above (sc+neg=*na*):

(941) a. *Dzana kala sina homa kali.*
'Yesterday I didn't have a high fever.'

b. *Dzana duka kala tarina matunda.*
'Yesterday the shop didn't have fruit.'

c. *Dzana kala tamuna kazi nyinji.*
'Yesterday you (pl) didn't have much work.'

The affirmative form of the hodiernal past is formed by preceding the sc=*na* construction with the hodiernal past auxiliary *che*. (The 1st person singular form *nina* may be reduced to *na* in rapid speech):

(942) a. *Ligundzu che na homa kali.*
'This morning I had a high fever.'

b. *Ligundzu duka che rina matunda.*
'This morning the shop had fruit.'

c. *We, che una ndzala.*
'You were hungry (earlier today).'

The negative form of the hodiernal past is formed with *che* and the corresponding negative construction:

(943) a. *Ligundzu che sina homa kali.*
'This morning I did not have a high fever.'

b. *Che kuna ndzala.*
'You weren't hungry.'

c. *Rero che tahuna masomo manji.*
'Today we did not have many lessons.'

Affirmative and negative forms of other tenses consist of the inflected form of the copula verb *kala* plus the comitative predicate *na*, which is a free morpheme in this construction. The following examples illustrate the affirmative and negative forms of 'have' in the future tense:

(944) a. *Muhondo n'ndakala na chitabu.*
'Tomorrow I will have a book.'

b. *Duka rindakala na matunda tsona.*
'The shop will have fruit again.'

c. *Tahundakala na masomo manji.*
'We will not have many lessons.'

Other aspects and compound tenses with *na* are formed in the same way; the following examples contain the persistive aspect marker *chere*:

(945) U-na-tambukir-a   hino   kofiya?   **N'-chere**   **na=yo.**
2SG-CONT-remember-FV   9.DEM4   9.hat   1SG-PERS   COM=9.REF
'Do you remember that hat? I still have it.'

(946) A-ri-pho-kala   **a-chere na**   siku   mwenga   ku-fik-a   kpwa-o ...
3PL-PST-16.REL-COP   3PL-PERS COM   9.day   9.one   INF-arrive-FV   17-3PL.POS
'When they were still one day from home ...' (lit: 'When they were still with one day to arrive at their place ...')

8.4.2 'Having' in relative clauses

In relative clauses formed with the *amba* relative construction, the form of 'have' in the clause following *amba* is the same as in simple declarative clauses (described in §8.4.1):

(947) Mwiya wavyalwa ni ise tajiri, na
      amba-ye   kala   a=na   ng'ombe   nyinji   sana.
      REL-1.REL PST.COP   1=COM   10.cows   10.many   DEG
'Mwiya was born with a rich father, who had very many cattle.'

(948) yuya   wanjina   amba-ye   a-nda-kala   a=na=cho
      1.DEM2   1.other   REL-1.REL 1-FUT-COP   1=COM=7.REF
'that other person who will have it'

In relative clauses formed with the affirmative copula *ri* or the negative copula *si*, the comitative predicate *na* occurs as a free morpheme; there is no subject concord prefixed to it:

(949) **Ariye na nguwo mbiri,** naamuphe myawe mwenga **asiye na nguwo.**

'Whoever has two garments, let him give his fellow one **who does not have clothes.'**

A-ri-ye   na   nguwo   mbiri,   ...   a-si-ye   na   nguwo
1-COP-1.REL   COM   10.clothes   10.two   ...   1-NEG.COP-1.REL   COM   10.clothes

If a relative construction with *ri* is followed by the comitative predicate in its bound form (preceded by a subject concord) then *ri* is the relative past tense and not a copula, and the whole clause will have a past time interpretation. Compare the following examples. Example (950) begins with *ariye* followed by *na* as a free morpheme and ends with the *amba* relative construction followed by *na* prefixed by a negative subject concord. This is interpreted as having a present or universal time reference, and therefore *ri* in this example is a copula. In example (951), *ariye* is followed by *na* suffixed to a negative subject concord. This clause is interpreted as having past time reference and therefore *ri* is the relative past tense; this is confirmed by the use of the past tense auxiliary *kala* in the complex tense construction *kala achiihwa* 'used to be called' in the following clause.

(950) **Ariye na chakurya** *naamganyire myawe* **ambaye kana**.

'He who has food let him share with his fellow who does not have (food).'

a-ri-ye   na   chakurya   ...   amba-ye   ka=na
1-COP-1.REL COM   7.food   ...   REL-1REL NEG.1=COM

(951) **Mutu ariye kana nguvu** *za kuweza kuphaha mimba au kuvyala, mchetu kala achiihwa tasa na mlume mgbwumba.*

'A person who did not have the ability to get pregnant or to have children, the woman used to be called barren and the man sterile.'

Mutu   a-ri-ye   ka=na   nguvu
1.person   1-PST-1.REL   NEG.1=COM   10.strength

8.5 Examples from a narrative text

The following extract from a nontranslated first-person narrative illustrates various of the forms described above. The numbers refer to sentences in the text, and indicate where material has been omitted (for example, sentences 3–7 have not been included as they did not contain any copula, comparative or possessive constructions). Only clauses involving nonverbal predicates have been glossed.

1a   *Chisa ambacho n'ndachisemurira hivi sambi,*

   The story which I will tell you now

1b   ni   chisa   amba-cho   cha-ni-phah-a   miaka   minji   yo-tsup-a
     COP   7.story REL-7.REL 7.PST-1SG-get-FV   4.years   4.many   4.REL-pass-FV

   is a story which happened to me many years ago

1c   na   n'=chisa   amba-cho   n'=cha   kpweli.
     COM   COP=7.story   REL-7.REL   COP=7.ASS   true

   and it is a story which is true.

2	*Kala*	*ni*	*mwaka*	*wa*	*1969 mwezi wa phiri tarehe kumi na tahu.*			
	PST	COP	3.year	3.ASS	1969 month of second date ten and three			

It was in the year 1969 on the 13th of February.

8	*Siku*	*hizo*	*baba*	*a-chere*	*na*	*nguvu-ze*	*kabisa kabisa.*
	10.days	10.DEM3	1a.father	3SG-PERS	COM	10.strength- 10.3SG.POS	complete

In those days my father still had his full strength.

12a   *Dzuwa taridzangbwedunga sawa sawa, taridzangbwetuluka sawa sawa,*

       The sun was not yet shining through, it had not yet come out fully,

12b	*ku-chere*	*chimiri-miri.*
	17-PERS	7.half_light

it was still only half light.

13a   *Nchipanda mwango,*

13b	*mwango*	*hinyo*	*siku*	*hizo*	*u=na*	*mihi*	*mi-kulu*	*mi-kulu.*
	3.hill	3.DEM3	10.days	10.DEM3	3=COM	4.trees	4-big	4-big

I climbed the hill, that hill in those days had very large trees on it.

14a	*Ni*	*tsaka*	*ra*	*ku-tish-a*	*na*
	COP	5.forest	5.ASS	INF-frighten-FV	COM

14b	*mara*	*nyinji*	*kala*	*ku=na*	*ma-tsui.*
	10.times	10.many	PST	17=COM	6-leopards

It was a frightening forest and many times there were leopards there.

15a   *Phahi wakati nátsupa mura njirani nálola hiku na hiku,*

       So as I passed there on the way I looked about me here and there,

15b   *mara násikira dza chitu chikagbwa, mara*

       sometimes it sounded as if something had fallen down, sometimes

15c	*ná-sikira*	*avi*	*ku=na*	*nyama*	*anapanda-panda*	*hivi.*
	1SG.PST-hear	as_if	17=COM	1a.animal	climbing_around	8.DEM1

it sounded like there was an animal climbing around.

16a	*Lakini*	*ná-fikiri*	*kala*	*ni*	*chima,*
	but	1SG.PST-think	PST	COP	7.vervet (also generic monkey)

But I thought it was a monkey,

16b   *na mara nyinji chima taahenda rorosi.*

       and usually monkeys do not do any harm.

8.5 Examples from a narrative text

18a   *Nchituluka tsaka rira, photuluka námanya*

18b   *ta-ku=na   ma-tatizo   gogosi.*
       NEG-17=COM   6-problems   6.at_all

       I came out of that forest (and) when I came out I knew (that) there were no problems at all.

20c   *... dza hivi náona dzi-nyama dzi-kulu sana.*

       at that moment I saw a very large animal.

21a   *Rangi-ye   ni   kama   amba-yo   i   kundukundu   si   kundukundu*
       9.colour-9.3SG.POS   COP   like   REL-9.REL   9SC reddish   NEG reddish

       Its colour was some kind of reddish hue

21b   *lakini   kala   ni   nyama ambaye námuona hipho chitambo,*
       but   PST   COP   1a.animal

       but it was an animal which I saw there for a while,

21c   *námuona chiphephi lakini nyama hiye hasa   kala   n'=simba.*
                                                     PST   COP=1a.lion

       I saw it close up and that animal was definitely a lion.

Appendix A

Sample Texts

The following four texts (two narratives, one hortatory text, and one expository text) are presented as follows:

Line 1: vernacular text written orthographically
Line 2: vernacular text, morpheme-by-morpheme
Line 3: corresponding glosses for the morphemes
End of each sentence: free translation.

A.1 Narrative text 1

The following text was spoken on tape by Ali Madzi Nyembwe and transcribed by Rodgers Maneno. It was published in 2002 as part of Digo Language Story Book 2, *Nia Mwenga Anaphaha Uliwali*, arranged and revised by Rodgers Maneno, Joseph Mwalonya, and Juma Mwayani and published in Nairobi by BTL.

Title Mhegi wa Mihambo

M-hegi   wa   Mi-hambo
1-setter 1.ass 4-trap

The Setter of Traps

Paragraph 1

1a **Hipho kare, kpwakala na mutu mmwenga**
    Hipho   kare,   ku-a-kal-a   na   mutu   m-mwenga
    16.DEM3 long_ago   17-PST-be-FV   COM   1.person   1-one

1b **kaziye ichikala ni kuhega mihambo.**
    kazi-ye   i-chi-kal-a   ni   ku-heg-a   mi-hambo.
    9.work-9.3SG.POS   9-CONS-be-FV   COP   INF-set-FV 4-traps

    Long ago, there was one man (and) his work was to set traps.

2a **Wahega mihambo achihega mihambo,**
    Wa-heg-a   mi-hambo   a-chi-heg-a   mi-hambo,
    3SG.PST-set-FV   4-traps   3SG-CONS-set-FV   4-traps

2b **siku zanjina anagbwira.**
    siku   z-anjina   a-na-gbwir-a.
    10.days   10-some/other   3SG-CONT-catch-FV

    He set traps and he set traps, and some days he caught (something).

3   **Siku mwenga, mutu hiyu wagbwira kulungu.**
    Siku   mwenga,   mutu   hiyu   wa-gbwir-a   kulungu.
    9.day   9.one   1.person   1.DEM1   3SG.PST-catch-FV   1a.antelope

    One day this person caught an antelope.

4a **Kumbavi kuku kaya kala kukafwa mchetu,**
    Kumbavi   kuku   kaya   kala   ku-ka-fw-a   m-chetu,
    EXCLAM   17.DEM1   9.home   PST.COP   17-SEQ-die-FV   1-woman

4b **achizikpwa, akazikpwa hiye mchetu,**
    a-chi-zik-w-a,   a-ka-zik-w-a   hiye   m-chetu,
    3SG-CONS-bury-PAS-FV   3SG-SEQ-bury-PAS-FV   1.DEM3   1-woman

4c **fisi rakpwendamfukula mura dibwani,**
    fisi   ra-kpwenda-m-fukul-a   mura   dibwa-ni,
    5.hyena   5.PST-ITIVE-3SG-dig_up-FV   18.DEM2   5.pit-LOC

4d **richimguruta kuphiya naye.**
    ri-chi-m-gurut-a   ku-phiy-a   na=ye.
    5-CONS-3SG-drag-FV   INF-go-FV   COM=3SG.REF

    However, there at home a woman had died, she was buried, and having been buried, that woman, a hyena came and dug her up from in the pit, and it dragged her to go with her.

A.1 Narrative text 1

5a **Yuyu bwana ambaye ni mhegi wa mihambo**
Yuyu   bwana   amba-ye   ni   m-hegi   wa   mi-hambo
1.DEM1   1a.man   REL-1.REL COP   1-setter 1.ASS 4-trap

5b **naye achiguruta kulunguwe,**
na=ye   a-chi-gurut-a   kulungu-we,
COM=3SG.REF   3SG-CONS-drag-FV   1a.antelope-1.3SG.POS

5c **ko mbere achendakutana na fisi**
ko   mbere   a-ch-enda-kutan-a   na   fisi
17.DEM3 ahead   3SG-CONS-ITIVE-meet-FV   COM   5.hyena

5d **rinaguruta yuya mchetu.**
ri-na-gurut-a   yuya   m-chetu.
5-CONT-drag-FV   1.DEM2   1-woman

This man who was a setter of traps he also dragged his antelope, and there ahead he went and met with the hyena dragging that woman.

6a **Fisi rajibu hiyu mutu rinamuamba,**
Fisi   ra-jibu   hiyu   mutu   ri-na-mu-amb-a,
5.hyena   5.PST-answer   1.DEM1   1.person   5-CONT-3SG-say-FV

6b **"O mzigoo na wangu mzuri ni uphi?"**
"O   m-zigo-o   na   w-angu   m-zuri   ni   u-phi?"
EXCLAM   3-burden-3.2SG.POS   COM   3-1SG.POS   3-good   COP   3-Q

The hyena answered this person telling him, "Oh, your burden and mine, which is good?"

7a **Yuya mwanadamu waamba, "Yosi yosi tapha mui,**
Yuya   mwanadamu   wa-amb-a,   "Yosi   yosi   ta-pha   mu-i,
1.DEM2   1.human   3SG.PST-say-FV   4.all   4.all   NEG-16   3-evil

7b **we amba kpwako ni mzuri**
we   amba   ku-ako   ni   m-zuri
2SG   DM   17-2SG.POS   COP   3-good

7c **nami wangu kpwangu ni mzuri,**
na=mi   w-angu   ku-angu   ni   m-zuri,
COM=1SG.REF   3-1SG.POS   17-1SG.POS   COP   1-good

7d **kulungu n'naphiya naye."**
kulungu   n'-na-phiy-a   na=ye."
1a.antelope   1SG-CONT-go-FV   COM=3SG

That human said, "Neither are evil, say yours is good and also mine is good for me, the antelope, I am going with it."

8a **Fisi anaamba, "Uchifika kaya**
  Fisi   a-na-amb-a,   "U-chi-fik-a   kaya
  5.hyena   3SG-CONT-say-FV   2SG-DEP-arrive-FV   9.home

8b **usiphiye uchamuambira mcheo**
  u-si-phiy-e   u-cha-mu-ambir-a   m-che-o
  2SG-NEG-go-SUB   2SG-DIST-3SG-tell-FV   1-wife-2SG.POS

8c **kukala yuya mchetu yezikpwa dzana**
  kukala   yuya   m-chetu   ye-zik-w-a   dzana
  COMP   1.DEM2   1-woman   3SG.REL-bury-PAS-FV   yesterday

8d **nkamuona na fisi, usiseme tse-tse-tse.**
  n-ka-mu-on-a   na   fisi,   u-si-sem-e   tse-tse-tse.
  1SG-HOD-3SG-see-FV   COM   5.hyena   2SG-NEG-report_badly-SUB   IDEO

The hyena says, "When you arrive home don't go and tell your wife that that woman who was buried yesterday, you have seen her with a hyena, don't give a bad report at all."

9a **Hala kulunguo uphiye vyako**
  Hal-a   kulungu-o   u-phiy-e   vy-ako
  take-FV   1a.antelope-2SG.POS 2SG-go-SUB   8-2SG.POS

9b **nami n'nahala maiti wangu**
  na=mi   n'-na-hal-a   maiti   w-angu
  COM=1SG   1SG-CONT-take-FV   1a.corpse   1-1SG.POS

9c **n'phiye vyangu kpwangu mapangoni."**
  n'-phiy-e   vy-angu   ku-angu   ma-pango-ni."
  1SG-go-SUB   8-1SG.POS   17-1SG.POS   6-cave-LOC

Take your antelope and go (on) your way and I will take my corpse and go (on) my way to my place in the caves."

Paragraph 2

10a **Yuya mwanadamu akakala anaphiya vyakpwe,**
  Yuya   mwanadamu   a-ka-kal-a   a-na-phiy-a   vy-akpwe,
  1.DEM2   1.human   3SG-SEQ-be-FV   3SG-CONT-go-FV   8-3SG.POS

10b **ku nyuma fisi wampima yuya mutu,**
  ku   nyuma   fisi   wa-m-pim-a   yuya   mutu,
  17.DEM1   behind   5.hyena   3SG.PST-3SG-measure-FV   1.DEM2   1.person

10c **achiamba, "N'lazima akamuambire mchewe**
  a-chi-amb-a,   "N'=lazima   a-ka-mu-ambir-e   mche-we
  3SG-CONS-say-FV   COP=necessity   3SG-ITIVE-3SG-tell-SUB   1.wife-1.3SG.POS

A.1 Narrative text 1

10d **yuya, mana Mdigo siye mutu bii."**
yuya,   mana   M-digo   si=ye   mutu   bii."
1.DEM2   for   1-digo   NEG=3SG.REF   1.person   IDEO

That human was going (on) his way, there behind the hyena judged that person, saying, "It is inevitable (that) he will go and tell his wife that one, for a Digo isn't a person at all."

Paragraph 3

11a **Phahi yuya mutu wakpwedza hata kaya,**
Phahi   yuya   mutu   wa-kpwedz-a   hata   kaya,
so   1.DEM2 1.person   3SG.PST-come-FV   until   9.home

11b **anafika hipho kaya wamuamba mchewe,**
a-na-fik-a   hipho   kaya   wa-mu-amb-a   mche-we,
3SG-CONT-arrive-FV   16.DEM3 9.home   3SG.PST-3SG-tell-FV   1.wife-1.3SG.POS

11c **"We mkpwazangu,**
"We   m-kaz-angu,
2SG   1-wife-1.1SG.POS

11d **yuya ning'anya mino nkamuona na fisi**
yuya   ning'anya   mino   n-ka-mu-on-a   na   fisi
1.DEM2   9.so_and_so   1SG   1SG-HOD-3SG-see-FV   COM   5.hyena

11e **anagurutwa kuphiya ko mapangoni."**
a-na-gurut-w-a   ku-phiy-a   ko   ma-pango-ni."
3SG-CONT-drag-PAS-FV   INF-go-FV   17.DEM3   6-cave-LOC

So that person went all the way home, arriving there at home he said to his wife, "You my wife, that so-and-so, me I have seen her with a hyena being dragged towards the caves."

12 **Kumbavi fisi ro ri pho ndzingo kare rinasikira.**
Kumbavi   fisi   ro   ri   pho   ndzingo   kare
EXCLAM   5.hyena   5.DEM3   5SC   16.DEM3   9.behind_house   already
ri-na-sikir-a.
5-CONT-listen-FV

Now that hyena was already there behind the house listening.

13 **Ramanya andaphiya akaseme na mchewe.**
Ra-many-a   a-nda-phiy-a   a-ka-sem-e   na   mche-we.
5.PST-know-FV   3SG-FUT-go-FV   3SG-ITIVE-report_badly-SUB   COM   1.wife-1.3SG.POS

It knew he would go and give a bad report to his wife.

14a **Yuya mwanadamu achimuamba mchewe,**
　　Yuya　　mwanadamu　　a-chi-mu-amb-a　　mche-we,
　　1.DEM2　　1.human　　3SG-CONS-3SG-tell-FV　　1.wife-1.3SG.POS

14b **"Mkpwazangu, tiya madzi buruni, uhale manga**
　　"M-kaz-angu,　　tiy-a　　madzi　　buru-ni,　　u-hal-e　　manga
　　1-wife-1SG.POS　　put_in-FV　　6.water　　5.gourd-LOC　　2SG-take-SUB　　1a.cassava

14c **huphiye vyehu kura kpwehu ndalani**
　　hu-phiy-e　　vy-ehu　　kura　　ku-ehu　　ndala-ni
　　1PL-go-SUB　　8-1PL.POS　　17.DEM2　　17-1PL.POS　　9.camp-LOC

14d **hukayule kulungu wehu**
　　hu-ka-yul-e　　kulungu　　w-ehu
　　1PL-ITIVE-skin-SUB　　1a.antelope　　1-1PL.POS

14e **hukayule kulungu wehu hurye na hiyu manga."**
　　hu-ry-e　　na　　hiyu　　manga."
　　1PL-eat-SUB　　COM　　1.DEM1　　1a.cassava

That man said to his wife, "My wife, put water in a gourd, take some cassava (and) let us go (on) our way there to our camp (and) let us skin our antelope and eat (it) with this cassava."

Paragraph 4

15a **Phahi, fisi rauka fuli**
　　Phahi,　　fisi　　ra-uk-a　　fuli
　　so　　5.hyena　　5.PST-return-FV　　quickly

15b **richendahala yuya kulungu**
　　ri-ch-enda-hal-a　　yuya　　kulungu
　　5-CONS-ITIVE-take-FV　　1.DEM2　　1a.antelope

15c **richiricha yuya maiti pharatu.**
　　ri-chi-rich-a　　yuya　　maiti　　pharatu.
　　5-CONS-leave-FV　　1.DEM2　　1a.corpse　　16.DEM2_VAR[1]

So, the hyena went and took that antelope and left that corpse right there.

16a **Kikiri kikiri ya madzi kuhekpwa**
　　Kikiri　　kikiri　　ya　　madzi　　ku-hek-w-a
　　IDEO　　IDEO　　9.ASS　　6.water　　INF-draw-PAS-FV

---

[1] Both long and short variant forms of demonstratives are glossed as VAR in this appendix.

A.1 Narrative text 1

16b hata kuganya miyo yao, ndipho "Haya huphiye."
  hata   ku-gany-a   miyo   y-ao,   ndipho   "Haya   hu-phiy-e,"
  until   INF-share-FV 4.bowls 4-3PL.POS then   okay   1PL-go-SUB

  Glug glug of water being drawn until sharing their bowls, then, "Okay let's go."

17a Anafika hipho kulungu taphana
  A-na-fik-a   hipho   kulungu   ta-pha=na
  3PL-CONT-arrive-FV   16.DEM3   1a.antelope   NEG-16=COM

17b ariyepho ni yuyatu maiti.
  a-ri-ye=pho   ni   yuyatu   maiti.
  3SG-COP-3SG.REL=16.REF   COP   1.DEM2_VAR   1a.corpse

  They arrive there and there is no antelope, what is there is that very same corpse.

18a Yuyu mchetu ndipho anauza,
  Yuyu   m-chetu   ndipho   a-na-uz-a,
  1.DEM1   1-woman   then   3SG-CONT-ask-FV

18b "Amba we ukaamba kala
  "Amba   we   u-ka-amb-a   kala
  DM   2SG   2SG-HOD-say-FV   COMP

18c yuno maiti ukamuona na fisi,
  yuno   maiti   u-ka-mu-on-a   na   fisi,
  1.DEM4   1a.corpse   2SG-HOD-3SG-see-FV   COM   5.hyena

18d nawe ukagbwira kulungu,
  na=we   u-ka-gbwir-a   kulungu,
  COM=2SG   2SG-HOD-catch-FV   1a.antelope

18e mbona ye mchetu ndiye ariye phapha
  mbona   ye   m-chetu   ndi=ye   a-ri-ye   phapha
  why   1.DEM3_VAR   1-woman   COP=1.REF   3SG-COP-3SG.REL   16.DEM1

18f na ye kulungu kapho?"
  na   ye   kulungu   ka=pho?"
  COM   1.DEM3_VAR   1a.antelope   3SG.NEG=16.REF

  Then the woman asked, "Say, you said that that corpse you saw it with a hyena, whereas you had caught an antelope, (so) why is it that woman that is here and the antelope isn't?"

Paragraph 5

19 **Yuya mutu waangalala sana mwakpwe rohoni,**
Yuya   mutu   wa-angalal-a   sana   mw-akpwe   roho-ni,
1.DEM2 1.person 3SG.PST-wonder-FV DEG   18-3SG.POS   9.heart-LOC
That person wondered greatly in his heart,

20a **"Nimuambedze yuno mkpwazangu, na**
"Ni-mu-amb-e=dze   yuno   m-kaz-angu,   na
1SG-3SG-say-SUB=Q   1.DEM4   1-wife-1.1SG.POS   COM

20b **mino che n'namanya kala kulungu ndiye wangu**
mino   che   n'-na-many-a   kala   kulungu   ndi=ye   w-angu
1SG   FOC   1SG-CONT-know-FV   COMP 1a.antelope   COP=1.REF   1-1SG.POS

20c **na ndiye chemreha hipha**
na   ndi=ye   che-m-reh-a   hipha
COM   COP=1.REF   3SG.ANT.1.REL-3SG-bring-FV   16.DEM1

20d **nkamuika hipha ndalani,**
n-ka-mu-ik-a   hipha   ndala-ni,
1SG-HOD-3SG-place-FV   16.DEM1   9.camp-LOC

20e **nkalunga mkpwazangu, ela vino kulungu kapho,**
n-ka-lung-a   m-kaz-angu,   ela   vino   kulungu   ka=pho,
1SG-SEQ-fetch-FV   1-wife-1.1SG.POS   but   now   1a.antelope   3SG.NEG=16.REF

20f **ye maiti nchiyemuona na fisi**
ye   maiti   n-chi-ye-mu-on-a   na   fisi
1.DEM3_VAR   1a.corpse   1SG-ANT-1.REL-3SG-see-FV   COM   5.hyena

20g **ndiye achiyeikpwa hipha!**
ndi=ye   a-chi-ye-ik-w-a   hipha!
COP=1.REF   3SG-ANT-1.REL-place-PAS-FV   16.DEM1

"What should I say to that wife of mine, and me I knew that the antelope was mine and I am he who brought it here and I placed it here at the camp, (then) I fetched my wife, but now the antelope isn't here, the corpse which I saw with the hyena that is what has been placed here!"

21a **Yu kulungu akahalwa ni yuyu fisi,**
Yu   kulungu   a-ka-hal-w-a   ni   yuyu   fisi,
1.DEM1_VAR   1a.antelope   3SG-HOD-take-PAS-FV   by   1.DEM1_VARIANT   5.hyena

A.1 Narrative text 1

21b lakini taphana neno."
lakini ta-pha=na neno."
but NEG-16=COM 5.word

The antelope has been taken by the hyena, but what can I say?" (lit: but there is no word.)

Paragraph 6

22a Auya kaya na mchewe, akauya kaya,
A-uy-a kaya na mche-we, a-ka-uy-a kaya,
3PL.PST-return-FV 9.home COM 1.wife-1.3SG.POS 3SG-SEQ-return-FV 9.home

22b yuya mlume wauka achendalunga-lunga
yuya m-lume wa-uk-a a-ch-enda-lunga-lung-a
1.DEM2 1-man 3SG.PST-leave-FV 3SG-CONS-ITIVE-follow-FV

22c hura mguruto wa kulungu hata pangani,
hura mguruto wa kulungu hata panga-ni,
3.DEM2 3.track 3.ASS 1a.antelope until 5.cave-LOC

22d akamenya pangani na fisi.
a-ka-meny-a panga-ni na fisi.
3SGG-SEQ-enter-FV 5.cave-LOC COM 5.hyena

He returned home with his wife, on returning home, that man left and went and followed the track of the antelope to a cave, it had entered the cave with the hyena.

23a Yuya mutu achiamba,
Yuya mutu a-chi-amb-a,
1.DEM2 1.person 3SG-CONS-say-FV

23b "Rivyo rino fisi rikamenya pangani phano,
"Ri=vyo rino fisi ri-ka-meny-a panga-ni phano,
(3SG-)COP=8.REF 5.DEM4 5.hyena 5-HOD-enter-FV 5.cave-LOC 16.DEM4

23c mino usiku nredza nrilatse."
mino usiku n-redz-a n-ri-lats-e."
1SG 14.night 1SG-come.CONT-FV 1SG-5-shoot-SUB

That person said, "Since that hyena has entered this cave, me tonight I am coming to shoot it."

24a Wauya kaya yuya mutu,
Wa-uy-a kaya yuya mutu,
3SG.PST-return-FV 9.home 1.DEM2 1.person

24b akafika phara kaya
a-ka-fik-a   phara   kaya
3SG-ANT-arrive-FV 16.DEM2   9.home

24c wasagala ye hata saa mbiri,
wa-sagal-a   ye   hata   saa   mb-iri,
3SG.PST-stay-FV 1.DEM3_VAR until 10.hour 10.two

24d achiuka achiphiya kuratu pangani.
a-chi-uk-a   a-chi-phiy-a   kuratu   panga-ni.
3SG-CONS-leave-FV   3SG-CONS-go-FV   17.DEM2_VAR   5.cave-LOC

He returned home that person, he arrived there at home (and) he stayed until eight o'clock, (then) he left and went (back) there to the cave.

25a Ariphofika hipho, wakpwera dzulu ya muhi
A-ri-pho-fik-a   hipho,   wa-kpwer-a   dzulu ya   mu-hi
3SG-PST-16.REL-arrive-FV   16.DEM3   3SG.PST-climb-FV   up   9.ASS 3-tree

25b kulola pharatu phatulukirapho fisi.
ku-lol-a   pharatu   pha-tuluk-ir-a=pho   fisi.
INF-see-FV   16.DEM2_VAR   16.PST-emerge-APPL-FV=16.REF   5.hyena

When he arrived there, he climbed up a tree to see that place from where the hyena would emerge.

Paragraph 7

26a Phahi wakala hipho hata zinapiga saa nne,
Phahi   wa-kal-a   hipho   hata   zi-na-pig-a   saa   n-ne,
so   3SG.PST-be-FV   16.DEM3   until   10-CONT-hit-FV   10.hour   10-four

26b ratuluka fisi, rina chitswa dza cha mutu,
ra-tuluk-a   fisi,   ri=na   chitswa   dza   cha   mutu,
5.PST-emerge-FV 5.hyena 5=COM   7.head   like   7.ASS   1.person

26c rinang'ala kama bafuta, rinaamba,
ri-na-ng'al-a   kama   bafuta,   ri-na-amb-a,
5-CONT-shine-FV   like   9.linen   5-CONT-say-FV

26d "Tulukani anangu edze nkulagizeni."
"Tuluk-a-ni   anangu   edz-e   n-ku-lagiz-e-ni."
emerge-FV-PL   2.child.2.1SG.POS come-SUB   1SG-2PL-instruct-SUB-PL

So he remained there until it was ten o'clock, a hyena emerged, it had a head like (that) of a person, it was shining like linen, it was saying, "Come out my children come (so that) I may instruct you."

A.1 Narrative text 1

27a Akatuluka raandza kulagiza, rinaamba,
  A-ka-tuluk-a   ra-andz-a   ku-lagiz-a,   ri-na-amb-a,
  3SG-ANT-emerge-FV 5.ANT-begin-FV INF-instruct-FV 5-CONT-say-FV

27b "We, phiya hipho, phana mbuzi zikaangamika,
  "We, phiy-a   hipho, pha=na mbuzi   zi-ka-angam-ik-a,
  2SG go-FV   16.DEM3 16=COM 10.goat 10-HOD-lose-STAT-FV

27c ukahale mbiri wedze nazo.
  u-ka-hal-e   mb-iri w-edz-e   na=zo.
  2SG-ITIVE-take-SUB 2-two 2SG-come-SUB COM=10.REF

When they emerged it began to instruct, saying, "You, go there, there are goats (which) have got lost, go and take two (and) come (back) with them.

28a Na uwe nawe phiya phana mutu na mchewe
  Na uwe na=we   phiy-a pha=na mutu   na   mche-we
  COM 2SG COM=2SG go-FV 16=COM 1.person COM 1.wife-1.3SG.POS

28b akaphiya ngomani, ukahale kuku wedze nao.
  a-ka-phiy-a ngoma-ni, u-ka-hal-e   kuku   w-edz-e   na=o.
  3PL-HOD-go=FV 9.dance-LOC 2SG-IT-take-SUB 2a.chicken 2SG-come-SUB COM=3PL

And you also go, there are a person and his wife they have gone to a dance, go and take chickens (and) come (back) with them.

29a Uwe nawe, phiya kpwa yuya fulani
  Uwe na=we,   phiy-a ku-a   yuya   fulani
  2SG COM=2SG go-FV 17-ASS 1.DEM2 1a.so_and_so

29b akaricha mbuzize mo nyumbani, lume na chetu,
  a-ka-rich-a   mbuzi-ze   mo   nyumba-ni, lume   na   chetu,
  3SG-HOD-leave-FV 10.goat-10.3SG.POS 18.REF 9.house-LOC 5.male COM 5.female

29c ukahale yo ndenje wedze nayo,
  u-ka-hal-e   yo   ndenje   w-edz-e   na=yo,
  2SG-ITIVE-take-SUB 9.REF 9.billy_goat 2SG-come-SUB COM=9.REF

29d mana ye mchetu akaphiya ngomani.
  mana ye   m-chetu   a-ka-phiy-a   ngoma-ni.
  for   1.DEM3_VAR 1-woman 3SG-HOD-go-FV 9.dance-LOC

You also, go to (the place of) that so-and-so, she has left her goats in the house, male and female, go and take the billy goat and come with it, for that woman has gone to a dance.

30a Upesi sana uchendahala hiyo mbuzi
  Upesi   sana u-ch-enda-hal-a   hiyo   mbuzi
  quickly DEG   2SG-DEP-ITIVE-take-FV   9.DEM3 9.goat

30b edze uhale hiyu mutu
     edz-e   u-hal-e   hiyu   mutu
     come-SUB 2SG-take-SUB 1.DEM1 1.person

30c ariye hipha dzulu ya muhi.
     a-ri-ye   hipha   dzulu ya   mu-hi.
     3SG-COP-1.REL 16.DEM1 up   9.ASS 3-tree

Very quickly when you go and take that goat come and take this person who is here up the tree.

31a Hiyu mutu ye hata akachimbira
     Hiyu   mutu   ye   hata   a-ka-chimbir-a
     1.DEM1 1.person 1.DEM3_VAR even 3SG-POT-flee-FV

31b n'kazi ya bure,
     n'=kazi   ya   bure,
     COP=9.work 9.ASS pointless

31c andafwa vivyo, edze hipha pangani.
     a-nda-fw-a   vivyo,   edz-e   hipha   panga-ni.
     3SG-FUT-die-FV 8.DEM3_VAR come-SUB 16.DEM1 5.cave-LOC

This person, even if he flees it will be pointless, he will die come what may (lit: he will die thus), come here to the cave.

32 Haya phiyani, mino namenya nyumbani."
    Haya   phiy-a-ni,   mino na-meny-a   nyumba-ni."
    okay   go-FV-PL   1SG   1SG.CONT-enter-FV 9.house-LOC

Okay go, (as for) me I am going into the house."

Paragraph 8

33a Phahi, fisi ramenya mwakpwe pangani,
     Phahi, fisi   ra-meny-a   mw-akpwe   panga-ni,
     so   5.hyena 5.PST-enter-FV 18-3SG.POS 5.cave-LOC

33b rikamenya pangani fisi, ye chelagizwa
     ri-ka-meny-a   panga-ni   fisi,   ye   che-lagiz-w-a
     5-ANT-enter-FV 5.cave-LOC 5.hyena 1.DEM3_VAR 3SG.ANT.1.REL-instruct-PAS-FV

33c chila mutu akahumwa akaphiya.
     chila   mutu   a-ka-hum-w-a   a-ka-phiy-a.
     each   1.person 3SG-SEQ-send-PAS-FV 3SG-SEQ-go-FV

So, the hyena entered its cave, on entering the cave, the one who had been instructed each person was sent and went.

A.1 Narrative text 1

34a Yuya bwana phara dzulu akamaka, anadziuza ndipho,
Yuya bwana phara dzulu a-ka-mak-a, a-na-dzi-uz-a
1.DEM2 1a.man 16.DEM2 up 3SG-ANT-wonder-FV 3SG-CONT-REFL-ask-FV

34b ndipho, "Pho mino nchichelewa phapha
ndipho, "Pho mino n-chi-chelew-a phapha
then 16.DEM3_VAR 1SG 1SG-DEP-delay-FV 16.DEM1

34c sindakpwedza nkahalwa ni yuyu chehumwa?"
si-nda-kpwedz-a n-ka-hal-w-a ni yuyu che-hum-w-a?"
1SG.NEG-FUT-come-FV 1SG-POT-take-PAS-FV COP 1.DEM1_ 3SG.ANT.1REL-send-PAS-FV
                                                    VARIANT

That man up there in the tree was amazed, then he was asking himself, "Then (as for) me if I delay here will I not come and be taken by that one who was sent?"

35a Watserera, achigbwira na vuweni
Wa-tserer-a, a-chi-gbwir-a na vuwe-ni
3SG.PST-descend-FV 3SG-CONS-seize-FV COM 9.savanna-LOC

35b asionane na yuya achiyehumwa hata kaya.
a-si-on-an-e na yuya a-chi-ye-hum-w-a hata kaya.
3SG-NEG-see-RECIP-SUB COM 1.DEM2 3SG-ANT-1.REL-send-PAS-FV until 9.home

He descended, (and) he went through (lit: caught with) the savanna so that he would not be seen by that one who had been sent, until (he reached) home.

36a Wamaka, "Aa, mbavi gano mafisi gahendalagizwa
Wa-mak-a, "Aa, mbavi gano ma-fisi ga-henda-lagiz-w-a
3SG.PST-wonder-FV EXCLAM EXCLAM 6.DEM4 6-hyenas 6.PST-EMPH-instruct-PAS-FV

36b gachikala ganaphiya gakatsume!
ga-chi-kal-a ga-na-phiy-a ga-ka-tsum-e!
6-CONS-be-FV 6-CONT-go-FV 6-ITIVE-gather-SUB

He wondered, "Ah, really those hyenas were actually instructed (and) they were going to gather!

37a Simanyire mino, na nkaambwa hata nkachimbira
Si-many-ire mino, na n-ka-amb-w-a hata n-ka-chimbir-a
1SG.NEG-know-PFV 1SG COM 1SG-HOD-say-PAS-FV until 1SG-POT-flee-FV

37b n'ndadziyuga bure, mino n'ndafwa
n'-nda-dzi-yug-a bure, mino n'-nda-fw-a
1SG-FUT-REFL-disturb-FV pointlessly 1SG 1SG-FUT-die-FV

37c **edze n'halwe ni fisi vivyo.**
  edz-e   n'-hal-w-e   ni   fisi   vivyo.
  come-SUB   1SG-take-PAS-SUB   COP   5.hyena   8.DEM3_VAR

(As for) me I didn't know, and I was told that even if I fled I would be putting myself out for nothing, me I would die (and) come (and) be taken by the hyena thus.

38a **Phahi nkachimbira, nkalumwa ni chitswa**
  Phahi   n-ka-chimbir-a,   n-ka-lum-w-a   ni   chitswa
  so   1SG-POT-flee-FV   1SG-POT-hurt-PAS-FV   COP   7.head

38b **manyani ni miwewe hiyoo."**
  manya-ni   ni   miwewe   hiyoo."
  know-PL   COP   4.fear   4.DEM3 (lengthened for emphasis)

So if I flee, I will get a headache and for sure this is my fear."

Paragraph 9

39a **Siku ya nne ya tsano,**
  Siku   ya   n-ne   ya   tsano,
  9.day   9.ASS   9-four   9.ASS   9.five

39b **yuya mutu walumwa n'chitswa,**
  yuya   mutu   wa-lum-w-a   n'=chitswa,
  1.DEM2   1.person   3SG.PST-hurt-PAS-FV   COP=7.head

39c **achifwa na achedzahalwa ni mafisi**
  a-chi-fw-a   na   a-ch-edza-hal-w-a   ni   ma-fisi
  3SG-CONS-die-FV   COM   3SG-CONS-VENT-take-PAS-FV   COP   6-hyenas

39d **achendabebenwa ko matsakani.**
  a-ch-enda-beben-w-a   ko   ma-tsaka-ni.
  3SG-CONS-ITIVE-crunch-PAS-FV   17.DEM3_VAR   6-forest-LOC

On the fourth or fifth day, that person got a headache, (then) he died and came and was taken by hyenas (and) he was crunched up there in the forest.

Paragraph 10

40 **Hadisi na ngano ikasira na hipho.**
  Hadisi   na   ngano   i-ka-sir-a   na   hipho.
  9.story   COM   9.fable   9-SEQ-end-FV   COM   16.DEM3

The story and fable ends here.

A.2 Narrative text 2

The following text was spoken on tape by Oda Zani and transcribed by Rodgers Maneno. It has not previously been published.

Title   Mwiya Anatiwa Dibwani ni Mkaza Ise

    Mwiya   a-na-ti-w-a   dibwa-ni   ni   mkaza   ise
    name   3SG-CONT-put_in-PASS-FV   5.pit-LOC   by   1.wife   1a.father
    Mwiya is put in a pit by his father's wife

Paragraph 1

1a   **Zamani za kare kpwakala na mvulana mmwenga**
      Zamani za kare,   ku-a-kal-a   na   m-vulana   m-mwenga
      Long_ago   17-PST-be-FV   COM   1-young_man   1-one

1b   **yeihwa Mwiya.**
      ye-ih-w-a   Mwiya.
      3SG.REL.PST-call-PASS-FV   NAME
      Long ago, there was one boy who was called Mwiya.

2a   **Mwiya wavyalwa ni ise tajiri,**
      Mwiya   wa-vyal-w-a   ni   ise   tajiri,
      name   3SG.PST-born-PASS-FV COM   1a.father wealthy

2b   **na ambaye kala ana ng'ombe nyinji sana,**
      na   amba-ye   kala   a=na   ng'ombe   nyinji   sana,
      COM   REL-1.REL PST   2SG=COM   10.cows   10.many   DEG

2c   **na kala achirima kpwakpwe mindani**
      na   kala   a-chi-rim-a   ku-akpwe   mi-nda-ni
      COM   PST   3SG-DEP-farm-FV   17-3SG.POS   4-field-LOC

2d   **kala achitsenga vyakurya vinji, matsere, muhama,**
      na   a-chi-tseng-a   vyakurya   vi-nji,   matsere,   muhama,
      PST   3SG-IMPFV-harvest-FV   8.food   8-many   6.maize   3.millet

2e   **ngano, mphunga na vyakurya vyanjina vinji.**
      ngano,   mphunga   na   vyakurya   vy-anjina   vi-nji.
      9.wheat   3.rice   COM   8.food   8-others   8-many

    Mwiya was born to a wealthy father, who had very many cows, and who when he farmed in his fields used to harvest a lot of food, maize, millet, wheat, rice and lots of other food.

3a Kama vyokala desturi ya atu hipho kare,
Kama vyo-kal-a desturi ya atu hipho kare,
as 8.REL.PST-be-FV 9.custom 9.ASS 2.people 16.DEM3 long_ago

3b mutu ka achikala tajiri,
mutu ka a-chi-kal-a tajiri,
1.person PST 3SG-DEP-be-FV wealthy

3c ka n'lazima alóle achetu anji.
ka n'=lazima a-lól-e a-chetu a-nji.
PST COP=necessary 3SG-marry-SUB 2-women 2-many

As was the custom of people long ago, if a person was rich, he had to marry many wives.

4a Phahi, mzee Mwazewe, ambaye kala ni ise wa Mwiya,
Phahi m-zee Mwazewe, amba-ye kala ni ise wa Mwiya
so 1-elder NAME REL-1.REL PST COP 1a.father 1.ASS NAME

4b naye piya walóla mchetu wa phiri.
na=ye piya wa-lól-a m-chetu wa phiri.
COM=3SG also 3SG.PST-marry-FV 1-woman 2.ASS second

So elder Mwaziwe, who was the father of Mwiya, he also married a second wife.

Paragraph 2

5a Huya mchetu ariphogbwira mimba,
Huya m-chetu a-ri-pho-gbwir-a mimba,
1.DEM2_VARIANT 1-woman 3SG-PST-16.REL-catch-FV 9.womb

5b wavyala mwana wa chilume,
wa-vyal-a mwana wa chi-lume,
3SG.PST-bear-FV 1.child 1.ASS 7-male

5c achimuiha Mwiya.
a-chi-mu-ih-a Mwiya.
3SG-CON-3SG-call-FV name

That woman, when she became pregnant she gave birth to a son and she called him Mwiya.

6a Hiye mchetu mvyere ariphoona mchetu
Hiye m-chetu m-vyere a-ri-pho-on-a m-chetu
1.DEM3 1-woman 1-elder 3SG-PST-16.REL-see-FV 1-woman

A.2 Narrative text 2

6b myawe naye akavyala mwana wa chilume,
mya.we   na=ye   a-ka-vyal-a   mwana   wa   chi-lume,
1.fellow.1.3SG.POS COM=3SG.REF 3SG.PST-bear-FV 1.child 1.ASS 7-male

6c wamanya hira mali indaganywa, kpwa hivyo
wa-many-a   hira   mali   i-nda-gany-w-a,   kpwa hivyo
3SG.PST-know-FV 9.DEM2 9.wealth 9-FUT-divide-PASS-FV therefore

6d achiona baha amuolage yuya mchetu mdide
a-chi-on-a   baha   a-mu-olag-e   yuya   m-chetu   m-dide
3SG-CONS-see-FV better 3SG-3SG-kill-FV 1.DEM2 1-woman 1-younger

6e phamwenga na hiye mwanawe na utsai.
phamwenga na   hiye   mwana-we   na   utsai.
together   COM 1.DEM3 1.child-1.3SG.POS COM 14.witchcraft

That senior wife, when she saw that her cowife had also given birth to a son, she realized that the inheritance would be divided, therefore she decided to kill that junior wife together with her son by witchcraft.

Paragraph 3

7a Juma na chisiku yuya mchetu mdide
Juma   na   chi-siku   yuya   m-chetu   m-dide
9.week COM 7-DAY   1.DEM2 1-woman   1-younger

7b wafwa gafula na ukongo mbaya sana.
wa-fw-a   gafula   na   u-kongo   m-baya   sana.
3SG.PST-die-FV suddenly COM 14-illness 14-bad   DEG

After a week and a bit that junior wife died suddenly from a very bad illness.

8a Yuya mchetu mvyere kala achijita chakurya
Yuya   m-chetu   m-vyere   kala   a-chi-jit-a   chakurya
1.DEM2 1-woman   1-elder   PST   3SG-IMPF-cook-FV 7.food

8b anamupha mwanawe bahi,
a-na-mu-ph-a   mwana-we   bahi,
3SG-CONT-3SG-give-FV   1.child-1.3SG.POS   only

8c na yuya mwana wa kufwererwa,
na   yuya   mwana   wa   ku-fw-erer-w-a,
COM   1.DEM2 1.child   1.ASS   INF-die-APPL-PASS-FV

8d **kala achimtsuphira makanda ga palawanda.**
 kala a-chi-m-tsuph-ir-a   ma-kanda   ga   palawanda.
 PST   3SG-IMPFV-throw-APPL-FV   6-skins   6.ASS 10.vegetable

That senior wife used to cook food giving to her own child only, and that child of the deceased, she used to throw him *palawanda* skins.

9a **Wakati ayae kala anarya chakurya**
 Wakati   aya-e   kala   a-na-ry-a   chakurya
 14.time 2.fellows-2.3SG.POS PST 3SG-CONT-eat-FV   7.food

9b **yuya mwana mgayi kala achiimba wira huno:**
 yuya   mwana   m-gayi   kala   a-chi-imb-a   wira   huno:
 1.DEM2 1.child 1-poor   PST 3SG-IMPFV-sing-FV   14.song   14.DEM4

While his fellows were eating food that poor child used to sing this song:

10a **"Palawanda ndizo mchizorya, palawanda.**
 Palawanda   ndi=zo   m-chi-zo-ry-a,   palawanda
 10.vegetables COP=10.REF 2PL-ANT-10.REL-eat-FV   10.vegetables

10b **Kutsatsa makanda mryangoni.**
 Ku-tsats-a   ma-kanda   m-ryango-ni.
 INF-collect-FV   6-skins   3-door-LOC

10c **Mayo dzana waologbwa."**
 Mayo   dzana   wa-olag-w-a.
 1a.mother yesterday   3SG.PST-kill-PASS-FV

"*Palawanda* is what you have eaten, *palawanda*. Collecting the skins at the door. My mother was killed a short while ago."

Paragraph 4

11a **Yuya mwana kala nkuhenderana mazuma**
 Yuya   mwana   kala   nku-hend-er-an-a   ma-zuma
 1.DEM2 1.child PST   HAB-do-APPL-RECIP-FV   6-turns

11b **ga kurisa mbuzi na ng'ombe zao**
 ga   ku-ris-a   mbuzi   na   ng'ombe   z-ao
 6.ASS INF-graze-FV 10.goats COM 10.cows   10-10.3PL.POS

11c **na nduguye, Mwiya mvyere.**
 na   ndugu-ye   Mwiya   m-vyere.
 COM 9.brother-9.3SG.POS NAME   1-elder

That child used to take turns grazing their goats and cows with his brother, Mwiya senior.

A.2 Narrative text 2

12a **Iriphofika zumare,**
I-ri-pho-fik-a zuma-re,
9-PST-16.REL-arrive-FV 5.turn-5.3SG.POS

12b **yuya nine mvyere wamlunga hiko weruni**
yuya nine m-vyere wa-m-lung-a hiko weru-ni
1.DEM2 1a.mother 1-elder 3SG.PST-3SG-follow-FV 17.DEM3 11.bush-LOC

12c **achendamuologa chiwanga ndani ya dibwa.**
a-ch-enda-mu-olag-a chiwanga ndani ya dibwa.
3SG-CONS-IT-3SG-kill-FV secretly inside 9.ASS 5.pit

When his turn came, that senior mother followed him into the bush and went and killed him secretly in a pit.

13a **Phofika dziloni,**
(i-ri-)pho-fik-a dziloni,
(9-PST-)16.REL-arrive-FV evening

13b **mbuzi na ng'ombe zauya macheye.**
mbuzi na ng'ombe za-uy-a macheye.
10.goats COM 10.cows 10.PST-return-FV alone

When evening came, the goats and cows returned on their own.

14a **Ariphoona hivyo, apiga mbiru**
A-ri-pho-on-a hivyo, a-pig-a mbiru
3PL-PST-16.REL-see-FV 8.DEM3 3PL.PST-hit-FV 9.horn

14b **achiiha atu osi hipho laloni**
a-chi-ih-a atu osi hipho lalo-ni.
3PL-CONS-call-FV 2.people 2.all 16.DEM3 9.area-LOC

14c **na achendamuendza hiko weruni.**
na a-ch-enda-mu-endz-a hiko weru-ni.
COM 3PL-CONS-IT-3SG-search-FV 17.DEM3 11.bush-LOC

When they saw this, they blew a horn and called all the people from that area and they went to search for him in the bush.

15a **Lakini Mwiya, taamuonere,**
Lakini Mwiya, ta-a-mu-on-ere,
but NAME NEG-3PL-3SG-see-PFV

15b **mwishowe achiusa hanga.**
mwisho-we a-chi-us-a hanga.
3.end-3.3SG.POS 3PL-CONS-remove-FV 9.funeral

But Mwiya, they didn't find him, and finally they held a funeral.

Paragraph 5

16a **Siku mwenga, yuya Mwiya mvyere**
Siku   mwenga   yuya   Mwiya   m-vyere
9.day   9.one   1.DEM2   NAME   1-elder

16b **ariphokala hiko marisani,**
a-ri-pho-kal-a   hiko   marisa-ni,
3SG.PST-16.REL-be-FV   17.DEM3   6.grazing-LOC

16c **wasikira sauti ndani ya dibwa kummanyisa**
wa-sikir-a   sauti   ndani   ya   dibwa   ku-m-many-is-a
3SG.PST-hear-FV   9.voice   inside   9.ASS   5.pit   INF-3SG-know-CAUS-FV

16d **kukala nduguye Mwiya mdide achere mzima.**
kukala   ndugu-ye   Mwiya   m-dide   a-chere   m-zima.
COMP   9.brother-9.3SG.POS   NAME   1-younger   3SG-PERS   1-alive

One day, when Mwiya senior was at the grazing place, he heard a voice inside a pit telling him that his brother Mwiya junior was still alive.

17a **Wira wenye ariouimba**
Wira   w-enye   a-ri-o-u-imb-a
14.song   14-ASS   3SG-PST-14.REL-14-sing-FV

17b **kala ni huno wa kusononeka:**
kala   ni   huno   wa   ku-sononek-a:
PST   COP   14.DEM4   14.ASS   INF-sorrow-FV

The actual song which he sang was this sorrowful one:

18a **"Mwiyaa, Mwiyaa, bombo Mwiyaa. (repeated once)**
Mwiyaa,   Mwiyaa,   bombo   Mwiyaa.
NAME   NAME   EXCL   NAME

18b **Yuno mayo ndiye mui bombo Mwiyaa." (repeated once)**
Yuno   mayo   ndi=ye   mu-i   bombo   Mwiyaa.
1.DEM4   1a.mother   COP=1.REF   1-evil   EXCL   NAME

"Mwiyaa, Mwiyaa, *bombo* Mwiyaa. Your mother is evil *bombo* Mwiyaa."

Paragraph 6

19a **Yuya Mwiya mvyere ariphosikira hivyo**
Yuya   Mwiya   m-vyere   a-ri-pho-sikir-a   hivyo
1.DEM2   NAME   1-elder   3SG-PST-16.REL-hear-FV   8.DEM3

A.2 Narrative text 2

19b **wakpwendamuambira ise kukala**
wa-kpwenda-mu-ambir-a ise kukala
3SG.PST-ITIVE-3SG-tell-FV 1a.father COMP

19c **kumbavi Mwiya kafwere ni mzima.**
kumbavi Mwiya ka-fw-ere ni m-zima.
EXCLAM NAME 3SG.NEG-die-PFV COP 1-alive

When Mwiya senior heard this he went and told his father that incredibly Mwiya had not died (but) was alive.

20 **"Nkamsikira anaimba dibwani ko marisani."**
N-ka-m-sikir-a a-na-imb-a dibwa-ni ko marisa-ni.
1SG-HOD-3SG-hear-FV 3SG-CONT-sing-FV 5.pit-LOC 17.DEM3_VAR 6.grazing-LOC

"I heard him singing in a pit there at the grazing place."

21a **Nine achiamba, "Uwe mwana unaanga,**
Nine a-chi-amb-a, "Uwe mwana u-na-ang-a,
1a.mother 3SG-CONS-say-FV you child 2SG-CONT-babble-FV

21b **tsona u vyoni!**
tsona u vyoni!
ADD 2SG abnormal

21c **Takuna afwaye akauya,**
Ta-ku=na a-fw-a-ye a-ka-uy-a,
NEG-17=COM 3SG-die-FV-1.REL 3SG-SEQ-return-FV

21d **wala akasikirwa anaimba,**
wala a-ka-sikir-w-a a-na-imb-a,
nor 3SG-SEQ-hear-PASS-FV 3SG-CONT-sing-FV

21e **phahi koma dza koma."**
phahi koma dza koma.
so madness like madness

His mother said, "You child are talking nonsense, and you are abnormal! No one who dies has returned (to life), nor has been heard singing, that is madness total madness."

22a **Yuya mwana na isengbwa achinyamala**
Yuya mwana na ise-ngbwa a-chi-nyamal-a
1.DEM2 1.child COM 1a.father-POSS 3PL-CONS-keep_silent-FV

22b **wala taayagomba chitu.**
wala ta-a-ya-gomb-a chitu.
nor NEG-3PL-PST-speak-FV 7.thing

That child and his father kept quiet, they didn't say a word.

Paragraph 7

23a **Ligundzu ra phiri,**
Ligundzu　　ra　　phiri,
5.morning　5.ASS　second

23b **yuya Mwiya ariphokala anaphiya marisani,**
yuya　　Mwiya　a-ri-pho-kal-a　　　　　　a-na-phiy-a　　　　marisa-ni,
1.DEM2　NAME　3SG-PST-16.REL-be-FV　3SG-CONT-go-FV　6.grazing-LOC

23c **ise wamlunga-lunga chisiri.**
ise　　　　　wa-m-lunga-lung-a　　　chisiri.
1a.father　3SG.PST-3SG-follow-FV　secretly

The following morning, when that Mwiya was going to the grazing place, his father followed him secretly.

24a **Chisha ariphokala a kure chidide na yuya mwanawe,**
Chisha　a-ri-pho-kal-a　　　　　　a　　kure　chidide　　na　　yuya　　mwana-we,
then　　3SG-PST-16.REL-be-FV　3SG　far　7_little　COM　1.DEM2　1.child-1.3SG.POS

24b **wasikira sauti za atu airi anaimba mazuma,**
wa-sikir-a　　　　　sauti　　　za　　　atu　　　　a-iri　　a-na-imb-a　　　　ma-zuma,
3SG.PST-hear-FV　10.voices　10.ASS　2.people　2-two　3PL-CONT-sing-FV　6-turns

24c **mmwenga a dibwani na wanjina a kondze.**
m-mwenga　a　　　dibwa-ni　　na　　wanjina　　a　　　kondze.
1-one　　　　3SG　5.pit-LOC　COM　1.other　　3SG　outside

Then when he was a little way from his child, he heard the voices of two people singing in turn, one in the pit and the other outside it.

Paragraph 8

25a **Isengbwa ariphosikira hivyo,**
Ise-ngbwa　　　　a-ri-pho-sikir-a　　　　　　hivyo,
1a.father-POS　3SG-PST-16.REL-hear-FV　8.DEM3

25b **waphiya mairo mpaka phara phokala phaimire mwanawe.**
wa-phiy-a　　　　mairo　mpaka　phara　　　pho-kal-a　　　　　　pha-im-ire　　　　mwana-we.
3SG.PST-go-FV　fast　　until　　16.DEM2　16.REL-be-FV　16.PST-stand-PFV　1.child-1.3SG.POS

When his father heard this, he ran to where his son was standing.

26 Ariphofika hipho, yuya mwana wazidi kuimba.
    A-ri-pho-fik-a   hipho, yuya   mwana wa-zidi   ku-imb-a.
    3SG-PST-16.REL-arrive-FV 16.DEM3 1.DEM2 1.child 3SG.PST-increase INF-sing-FV
    When he reached there, that child sang even more.

27a Kala anaimba mazuma,
    Kala   a-na-imb-a   ma-zuma,
    PST   3SG-CONT-sing-FV   6-turns

27b kuphokezana na yuya ariyekala dibwani,
    ku-phokez-an-a   na   yuya   a-ri-ye-kal-a   dibwa-ni,
    INF-pay-RECIP-FV   COM   1.DEM2 3SG-PST-1.REL-be-FV   5.pit-LOC

27c ili ammanyise ise kala gara arigogomba dzana
    ili a-m-many-is-e   kala   gara   a-ri-go-gomb-a   dzana
    so   3SG-3SG-know-CAUS-SUB COMP   6.DEM2 3SG-PST-6.REL-speak-FV yesterday

27d ni ga kpweli.
    ni   ga   kpweli.
    COP   6.ASS true   (Class 6 *gara* ... refers to implicit *maneno* 'words'.)

    He was singing in turns, exchanging with the one who was in the pit, in order to show his father that what he said the day before was true.

28a Naye yuya mzee wakatika mairo kaya
    Na=ye   yuya   m-zee   wa-katik-a   mairo   kaya
    COM=1.REF   1.DEM2 1-elder 3SG.PST-cut-FV   fast   5.home

28b kpwendaiha ayae phamwenga na mchewe,
    ku-enda-ih-a   aya-e   phamwenga   na   mche-we,
    INF-ITIVE-call-FV   2.fellows-2.3SG.POS together   COM   1.wife-1.3SG.POS

28c edze alole garigo hiko dibwani
    edze   a-lol-e   ga-ri=go   hiko   dibwa-ni
    come-SUB   3PL-see-SUB 6-COP=6.REF   17.DEM3   5.pit-LOC

28d ichikala ni kpweli.
    i-chi-kal-a   ni   kpweli.
    9-DEP-be-FV   COP   true

    And that old man ran quickly home to go and tell his fellows and his wife, so they should come and see if the things (happening) there in the pit were true.

Paragraph 9

29a Hinyo atu ariphofika hipho, atezeka sana
Hinyo   atu   a-ri-pho-fik-a   hipho,   a-tezek-a   sana
2.DEM3 2.people   3PL-PST-16.REL-arrive-FV   16.DEM3 3PL.PST-wonder-FV   DEG

29b mana asikira sauti za atu airi,
mana   a-sikir-a   sauti   za   atu   a-iri,
for   3PL.PST-hear-FV   10.voices   10.ASS   2.people   2-two

29c mmwenga a kondze na wanjina a dibwani.
m-mwenga   a   kondze   na   wanjina   a   dibwa-ni.
1-one   3SG   outside   COM   1.other   3SG   5.pit-LOC

When those people arrived there, they were astonished because they heard the voices of two people, one outside and the other in the pit.

30a Hiye mchetu ariyemtiya yuya mwanache dibwani,
Hiye   m-chetu   a-ri-ye-m-tiy-a   yuya   mwanache   dibwa-ni,
1.DEM3 1-woman   3SG-PST-1.REL-3SG-put_in-FV   1.DEM2   1.child   5.pit-LOC

30b wagbwirwa ni mchecheta achigbwa.
wa-gbwir-w-a   ni   mchecheta   a-chi-gbw-a.
3SG.PST-seize-PAS-FV   COP   3.panic   3SG-CONS-fall-FV

That woman who had put the child in the pit, she was seized by panic and fell down.

31a Ndipho atu achimanya kukala
Ndipho   atu   a-chi-many-a   kukala
then   2.people   3PL-CONS-know-FV   COMP

31b iye ndiye ariyehenda mambo higo.
iye   ndi=ye   a-ri-ye-hend-a   mambo   higo.
3SG   COP=1.REF   3SG-PST-1.REL-do-FV   6.things   6.DEM3

Then people knew that it was her who did these things.

Paragraph 10

32a Hinyo atu ariokala akedza phara
Hinyo   atu   a-ri-o-kal-a   a-k-edz-a   phara
2.DEM3   2.people   3PL-PST-2.REL-be-FV   3PL-ANT-come-FV   16.DEM2

32b amfukula yuya mwanache mura dibwani
a-m-fukul-a   yuya   mwanache   mura   dibwa-ni
3PL.PST-3SG-unearth-FV   1.DEM2   1.child   18.DEM2   5.pit-LOC

A.2 Narrative text 2

32c **na achimtuluza mzima achiphiya naye kaya.**
na a-chi-m-tuluz-a m-zima a-chi-phiy-a na=ye kaya.
COM 3PL-CONS-3SG-remove-FV 1-alive 3PL-CONS-go-FV COM=1.REF 9.home

Those people who had come there, they unearthed the child from inside the pit and got him out alive and took him home with them.

33a **Atu ariphofika kaya,**
Atu a-ri-pho-fik-a kaya,
2.people 3PL-PST-16.REL-arrive-FV 9.home

33b **yuya mwanache waeleza**
yuya mwanache wa-elez-a
1.DEM2 1.child 3SG.PST-explain-FV

33c **vira arivyotiwa mura dibwani**
vira a-ri-vyo-ti-w-a mura dibwa-ni
8.DEM2 3SG-PST-8.REL-put_in-PAS-FV 18.DEM2 5.pit-LOC

33d **ni hiye nine mvyere.**
ni hiye nine m-vyere.
COP 1.DEM3 1a.mother 1-senior

When the people arrived home, that child explained how he was put into the pit by that senior wife (lit: his senior mother).

Paragraph 11

34a **Phahi hiye mchetu adabuye, wazolwa phara kaya,**
Phahi hiye m-chetu adabu-ye wa-zol-w-a phara kaya,
so 1.DEM3 1-woman 9.punishment-3SG.POS 3SG.PST-chase-PAS-FV 16.DEM2 9.home
     9.3SG.POS

34b **na yuya mzee achilóla mchetu wanjina**
na yuya m-zee a-chi-lól-a m-chetu wanjina
COM 1.DEM2 1-elder 3SG-CONS-marry-FV 1-woman 1.other

34c **achisagala na anae osi vinono.**
a-chi-sagal-a na ana-e osi vinono.
3PL-CONS-stay-FV COM 2.children-2.3SG.POS 2.all 8.good

So that woman her punishment, she was chased away from her home, and that old man married another woman and they lived happily with both of his children.

Paragraph 12

35 **Hadisi na ngano ichisira na hipho.**
    Hadisi   na   ngano   i-chi-sir-a   na   hipho.
    9.story   COM   9.fable   9-CONS-end-FV COM   16.DEM3
    The story and fable ends here.

A.3 Hortatory text

The following text was produced by Hamisi Kulola, Headmaster of Ziwani Primary School, in January 1999. It has not previously been published.

Farewell advice to a son going to study abroad

Father:

1a "**Mwanangu mwanangu ni uwe, mwanangu mlume,**
    "Mwanangu   mwanangu   ni   uwe, mwanangu   m-lume,
    1.child.1.1SG.POS   1.child.1.1SG.POS   COP   2SG   1.child.1.1SG.POS   1-male

1b **mwanangu uwe ndiwe nyota yangu ya nyumba hino.**
    mwanangu   uwe   ndi=we   nyota   y-angu   ya   nyumba   hino.
    1.child.1SG.1.POS   2SG   COP=2SG   9.star   9-1SG.POS 9.ASS   9.house   9.DEM4
    My child, my child it is you, my son, my child, you are my star of this house.

2   **Mwanangu uwe ndiwe ngao yangu.**
    Mwanangu   uwe   ndi=we   ngao   y-angu.
    1.child.1.1SG.POS   2SG   COP=2SG   9.shield   9-1SG.POS
    My child, you are my shield.

3a **Nyumba hino taindakala na mwangaza sana**
    Nyumba   hino   ta-i-nda-kal-a   na   mwangaza   sana
    9.house   9.DEM4   NEG-9-FUT-be-FV   COM   1.light   DEG

3b **na Mlungu ni uwe.**
    na   Mlungu   ni   uwe.
    COM   God   COP   2SG
    This house will not have light if it does not have God it is you.

4a **Nyumba hino taindakala na urindzi**
    Nyumba   hino   ta-i-nda-kal-a   na   urindzi
    9.house   9.DEM4   NEG-9-FUT-be-FV   COM   14.protection

A.3 Hortatory text

4b **hata chila mmwenga anyendekaye**
hata   chila   m-mwenga   a-nyendek-a-ye
even   each   1-one   3SG-visit-FV-1.REL

4c **aiogophe ni uwe, mwanangu.**
a-i-ogoph-e   ni   uwe,   mwanangu.
3SG-9-respect-SUB   COP   2SG   1.child.1.1SG.POS

This house will not have protection since what everyone who comes by respects is you, my child.

5a **Vino mwanangu watukuzwa,**
Vino   mwanangu   wa-tukuz-w-a,
8.DEM4   1.child.1.1SG.POS   3SG.PST-praise-PAS-FV

5b **mtihani wauhenda vinono,**
m-tihani   wa-u-hend-a   vi-nono,
3-examination   3SG.PST-3-do-FV   8-good

5c **hata vino unaphiya ukasome kondze.**
hata   vino   u-na-phiy-a   u-ka-som-e   kondze.
even   8.DEM4   2SG-CONT-go-FV   2SG-ITIVE-study-SUB   17.outside

Now my child you have earned praise, in the exams you did well, so (well) now you are leaving to go and study abroad.

6a **Mwanangu ni razi nawe, ni razi nawe,**
Mwanangu   ni   razi   na=we,   ni   razi   na=we,
1.child.1.1SG.POS   COP   9.blessing   COM=2SG   COP   9.blessing   COM=2SG

6b **hangu phapha nigombapho hata kuko ndikophiya.**
hangu phapha   ni-gomb-a=pho   hata   kuko   ndi-ko-phiy-a.
since   16.DEM1_VAR   1SG-speak-FV=16.REF   until   17.DEM3_VAR   FUT-17.REL-go-FV

My child blessings be with you, blessings be with you from here where I am speaking to the place you will go.

7 **Ni razi kabisa. Eh navoya nguvu.**
Ni   razi   kabisa.   Eh   na-voy-a   nguvu.
COP   9.blessing   completely   EXCLAM   1SG.CONT-pray-FV   9.strength

It is a complete blessing. Eh, I pray for strength.

8a **Kala n'chijana dza vivyo uwe mwanangu nami**
Kala   n'=chi-jana   dza vivyo   uwe   mwanangu   na=mi
if   COP=7-youth   like   8.DEM3_VAR   2SG   1.child.1.1SG.POS   COM=1SG

8b **nkaamba masomo gano ...**
n-ka-amb-a   ma-somo   gano ...
1SG-ANT-say-FV   6-studies   6.DEM4

8c mbona mino ela he! utumiya.

mbona	mino	ela	he!	u-tumiya.
EXCLAM	1SG	but	EXCLAM	14-old_age

If I were a youth like you, my child, I also would have said (I will go for) these studies but me, hey! old age.

9 Waambwa ujana ni mosi uchiphiya tauuya.

Wa-amb-w-a	u-jana	ni	mosi	u-chi-phiy-a	ta-u-uy-a.
2SG.PST-say-PAS-FV	14-youth	COP	9.smoke	14-DEP-go-FV	NEG-14-return-FV

You were told youth is like smoke, once gone it does not return.

10 Mwanangu nakuvoyera uzima. Kasome.

Mwanangu	na-ku-voy-er-a	u-zima.	Ka-som-e.
1.child.1.1SG.POS	1SG.CONT-pray-APPL-FV	14-whole	ITIVE-study-SUB

My child I pray you have health. Go and study!

11a Atu nkpwambwa, "Aphiyaye ukalani

Atu	nku-amb-w-a,	"A-phiy-a-ye	u-kala-ni
2.people	HAB-say-PAS-FV	3SG-go-FV-1.REL	14-hunting-LOC

11b achiuya ni auye na nyama phano."

a-chi-uy-a	ni	a-uy-e	na	nyama	phano."
3SG-DEP-return-FV	COP	3SG-return-SUB	COM	9.meat	16.DEM4

People are told, "The one who goes hunting when he returns he should bring meat there."

12a Uwe unaphiya chisomoni,

Uwe	u-na-phiy-a	chisomo-ni,
2SG	2SG-CONT-go-FV	7.study-LOC

12b chisomo ni kama kpwamba unaphiya ukalani,

chisomo	ni	kama	kpwamba	u-na-phiy-a	u-kala-ni,
7.study	COP	like	COMP	2SG-CONT-go-FV	14-hunting-LOC

12c na ni uuye na nyama.

na	ni	u-uy-e	na	nyama.
COM	COP	2SG-return-SUB	COM	9.meat

You are going to study, studying is like going hunting, and you should return with meat.

13a Uchedza mwnanangu uchinikuta ni mzima,

U-ch-edz-a	mwnanangu	u-chi-ni-kut-a	ni	m-zima,
2SG-DEP-come-FV	1.child.1.1SG.POS	2SG-DEP-1SG-meet-FV	COP	1-whole

A.3 Hortatory text

13b nchikuguza, "Tandzi baba?"
n-chi-ku-guz-a,   "Tandzi   baba?"
1SG-DEP-2SG-ask-FV   9.trap   1a.father

13c uambe, "Ni nyama mwanangu."
u-amb-e,   "Ni   nyama   mwanangu."
2SG-say-SUB   COP   9.meat   1.child.1.1SG.POS

When you come (back), my child, and meet me and I am well, when I ask you, "What have you trapped, father?" you are to say, "I have meat, my child."

14a Aha ukanikuta náphiya kare mbere za haki,
Aha   u-ka-ni-kut-a   ná-phiy-a   kare   mbere   za   haki,
EXCLAM   2SG-POT-1SG-meet-FV   1SG.PST-go-FV   COMPL   ahead   10.ASS 9.right

14b kisha ni salama nduguzo za phapha.
kisha   ni   salama   ndugu-zo   za   phapha.
then   COP   9.peace   10.sibling-10.2SG.POS   10.ASS   16.DEM1_VAR

But if you find I have already passed on before my time, then that is fine, your brothers and sisters are there.

15 Navoya mwanangu salama salimini.
Na-voy-a   mwanangu   salama   salimini.
1SG.CONT-pray-FV   1.child.1.1SG.POS   safely   safely

I pray my child that you will be safe and sound.
(*salama salimini* is a borrowed Swahili idiom)

16a Ukakale mwasaga nguluwe,
U-ka-kal-e   mwasaga   nguluwe,
2SG-ITIVE-be-SUB   1.trampler   9.pig

16b kazi ndiyokala ukailunga
kazi   ndi-yo-kal-a   u-ka-i-lung-a
9.work   FUT-9.REL-be-FV   2SG-SEQ-9-follow-FV

16c kuko ukale ndiyo ndiyohenda.
kuko   u-kal-e   ndi=yo   ndi-yo-hend-a.
17.DEM3_VAR   2SG-be-SUB   COP=9.REF   FUT-9.REL-do-FV

May you trample like a pig, the work for which you are going there let that be the one which you will do.

17a Mwanangu nakpwamba, uwe unaphiya ujenini,
Mwanangu   na-ku-amb-a,   uwe   u-na-phiy-a   u-jeni-ni,
1.child.1.1SG.POS   1SG.CONT-2SG-say-FV   2SG   2SG-CONT-go-FV   14-foreign-LOC

17b **kumanya mutu nao hiko taakumanya.**
ku-many-a   mutu   na=o   hiko   ta-a-ku-many-a.
2SG.NEG-know-FV 1.person COM=3PL.REF 17.DEM3 NEG-3PL-2SG-know-FV

My child, I tell you, you are going abroad, you do not know anyone and no one there knows you.

18a **Wasiya wangu ni kukala,**
Wasiya   w-angu   ni   ku-kal-a,
14.advice   14-1SG.POS   COP   INF-be-FV

18b **mdide naakale msenao,**
m-dide   na=a-kal-e   m-sena-o,
1-small   EMPH=3SG-be-SUB   1-friend-1.2SG.POS

18c **mvyere naakale msenao.**
m-vyere   na=a-kal-e   m-sena-o.
1-old   EMPH=3SG-be-SUB   1-friend-1.2SG.POS

My advice is that the young should be your friend and the old should be your friend.

19 **Ulimi hinyu taudzenga, kaziye ni kubomola.**
U-limi   hinyu   ta-u-dzeng-a,   kazi-ye   ni   ku-bomol-a.
14-tongue   14.DEM1   NEG-14-build-FV 9.work-9.3SG.POS COP   INF-destroy-FV

The tongue does not build, its work is to destroy.

20 **Mkpwono mrefu taudzenga, kaziye ni kubomola.**
M-kono   m-refu   ta-u-dzeng-a,   kazi-ye   ni   ku-bomol-a.
3-hand   3-long   NEG-3-buid-FV   9.work-9.3SG.POS COP   INF-destroy-FV

Stealing (lit: long hand) does not build, its work is to destroy.

21 **Na zinaa mwanangu yala!**
Na   zinaa   mwanangu   yal-a!
COM   9.adultery   1.child.1.1SG.POS   forget-FV

And adultery, my child, avoid (it)!

22a **Yala zinaa mwanangu ichikala unanisikira**
Yal-a   zinaa   mwanangu   i-chi-kal-a   u-na-ni-sikir-a
forget-FV   9.adultery   1.child.1.1SG.POS   9-DEP-be-FV   2SG-CONT-1SG-listen-FV

22b **vira ambavyo nakpwambira. Yala zinaa! Yala zinaa!**
vira   amba-vyo   na-ku-ambir-a.   Yal-a   zinaa!
8.DEM2   REL-8.REL   1SG.CONT-2SG-tell-FV   forget-FV   9.adultery

Avoid adultery, my child, listen very carefully to what I say. Avoid adultery!

A.3 Hortatory text

23 **Zinaa ndiyo ichiyotiya vumbi dunia nzima.**
Zinaa   ndi=yo   i-chi-yo-tiy-a   vumbi   dunia   n-zima.
9.adultery   COP=9.REF   9-ANT-9.REL-put_in-FV   5.dust   9.earth   9-whole
It is adultery that has made the whole world dirty.

24 **Atu anafwa, atu anafwa kama mvula.**
Atu   a-na-fw-a,   atu   a-na-fw-a   kama   mvula.
2.people   3PL-CONT-die-FV   2.people   3PL-CONT-die-FV   like   9.rain
People are dying, people are dying like rain.

25a **Na indakala makosa sana mwanangu uphiye hiko,**
Na   i-nda-kal-a   ma-kosa   sana   mwanangu   u-phiy-e   hiko,
COM   9-FUT-be-FV   6-mistake   DEG   1.child.1.1SG.POS   2SG-go-FV   17.DEM3

25b **ela, eh, siomba.**
ela,   eh,   si-omb-a.
but   EXCLAM   1SG.NEG-pray-FV
And it would be a very big mistake, my child, should you go that way, but eh!, I pray not.

26a **Na ni vii hivyo taviombwa,**
Na   ni   v-ii   hivyo   ta-vi-omb-w-a,
COM   COP   8-bad   8.DEM3   NEG-8-pray-PAS-FV

26b **kalole rako mwanangu.**
ka-lol-e   r-ako   mwanangu.
ITIVE-look-SUB   5-2SG.POS   1.child.1.1SG.POS
And those are bad things for which no one asks, (so) go and look to your own things, my child.

27a **Mtswano wa charo ni ukale uchedza kula hiko**
Mtswano   wa   charo   ni   u-kal-e   u-ch-edz-a   kula   hiko
3.sweetness   3.ASS   7.journey   COP   2SG-be-FV   2SG-DEP-come-FV   from   17.DEM3

27b **ukale ukadzifunganya na umanyikane ukapatani.**
u-kal-e   u-ka-dzi-fungany-a   na   u-many-ik-an-e   u-ka-pat-a=ni.
2SG-be-SUB   2SG-ANT-REFL-pack-FV   COM   2SG-know-STAT-RECIP-SUB   2SG-ANT-get-FV=Q
The sweetness of the journey is that when you return from there you will have gained things (lit: packed yourself) and it will be known what you have got.

28 **Ndivyo virivyo.**
Ndi=vyo   vi-ri-vyo.
COP=8.REF   8-COP-8.REL
That's how it is.

29 **Pho navoya Mlungu mwanangu salama salimini.**
    Pho   na-voy-a   Mlungu mwanangu   salama salimini.
    16.DEM3_VAR 1SG.CONT-pray-FV God   1.child.1.1SG.POS safely safely
    So I pray to God my child (that you will be kept) safe and sound.

30a **Kahale chisomo cha sawa sawa,**
    Ka-hal-e   chi-somo   cha   sawa   sawa,
    ITIVE-take-SUB 7-study   7.ASS same   same

30b **na uwedze kaya salama.**
    na   u-edz-e   kaya   salama.
    COM 2SG-come-SUB 9.home safely
    Go and get a good education, and return home safely.

31 **Hivyo hivyo mwanangu.**
    Hivyo   hivyo   mwanangu.
    8.DEM3   8.DEM3   1.child.1.1SG.POS
    That's how it is my child.

32a **Haya nine wa anache, ndzoo,**
    Haya   nine   wa   anache,   ndzoo,
    EXCLAM 1a.mother 1.ASS 2.children come (IMPERATIVE)

32b **ulagane na mwana,**
    u-lag-an-e   na   mwana,
    2SG-say_goodbye-RECIP-SUB COM 1.child

32c **mana mwana anaphiya vyakpwe na ichiajaliwa**
    mana mwana   a-na-phiy-a   vy-akpwe   na   i-chi-a-jali-w-a
    for   1.child   3SG-CONT-go-FV 8-3SG.POS COM 9-DEP-3PL-bless-PAS-FV

32d **charo chindakala muhondo juma mosi."**
    charo   chi-nda-kal-a   muhondo   juma   mosi."
    7.journey 7-FUT-be-FV   tomorrow   9.day   9.one

    "So mother of my children, come, say goodbye to your son, for your son is going away and God willing his journey will be tomorrow, Saturday."

Mother:

33 **"Haya mino edze nigombe gaphi vyo?"**
    "Haya   mino edz-e   ni-gomb-e   ga=phi   vyo?"
    EXCLAM   1SG   come-SUB   1SG-speak-SUB   6=Q   8.DEM3_VAR
    "So what sort of thing could I come and say?"

A.3 Hortatory text

Father:

34a "Lagana naye tumvoyere Mlungu
  "Lag-an-a   na=ye   tu-m-voy-er-e   Mlungu
  say_goodbye-RECIP-FV   COM=3SG.REF   1PL-3SG-pray-APPL-SUB   God

34b aphiye salama, aedze hipha salama."
  a-phiy-e   salama,   a-edz-e   hipha   salama."
  3SG-go-SUB   safely   3SG-come-SUB 16.DEM1   safely

"Say goodbye to him let us pray to God that he will go safely, and come here safely."

Mother:

35a "Mino che naamba uchikala undaphiya hiko,
  "Mino   che   na-amb-a   u-chi-kal-a   u-nda-phiy-a   hiko,
  1SG   FOC   1SG.CONT-say-FV   2SG-DEP-be-FV   2SG-FUT-go-FV   17.DEM3

35b ukalole rako, mwanangu.
  u-ka-lol-e   r-ako,   mwanangu.
  2SG-ITIVE-see-SUB   5-2SG.POS   1.child.1.1SG.POS

"I say this, when you go there, you look out for yourself, my child.

36 Dunia ya sambi siyo.
  Dunia   ya   sambi   si=yo.
  9.earth   9.ASS   now   NEG=9.REF

37 Gangu ni gago."
  G-angu   ni   gago."
  6-1SG.POS   COP   6.DEM3_VAR

Today's world is not (good). That is what I have to say."

A.4 Expository text

The following text comes from Garashi et al. (2007:13ff.).

Uvyazi (Birth)

Paragraph 1

1a **Anache anatalwa kama chitu muhimu**
   Anache   a-na-tal-w-a   kama   chitu   muhimu
   2.children 2PL-CONT-count-PAS-FV as   7.thing   important

1b **katika maisha ga mwanadamu.**
   katika   maisha   ga   mwanadamu.
   in   6.life   6.ASS   1.human

   Children are considered a very important aspect of a person's life.

2a **Mutu ariyekala kana nguvu za**
   Mutu   a-ri-ye-kal-a   ka=na   nguvu   za
   1.person   3SG-PST-1.REL-be-FV   3SG.NEG=COM   10.strength 10.ASS

2b **kuweza kuphaha mimba au kuvyala,**
   ku-wez-a   ku-phah-a   mimba   au   ku-vyal-a,
   INF-be_able-FV   INF-get-FV   9.womb   or   INF-birth-FV

2c **kala achiihwa tasa na mlume mgbwumba.**
   kala   a-chi-ih-w-a   tasa   na   m-lume   m-gumba.
   PST   3PL-IMPFV-call-PAS-FV   barren   COM   1-male   1-infertile

   Anyone who was unable to get pregnant or to give birth, was called 'tasa' (barren woman) and a man 'mgbwumba' (infertile man).

3a **Kama vira msemo urivyoamba,**
   Kama   vira   msemo   u-ri-vyo-amb-a,
   as   how   3.saying   3-PST-8.REL-say-FV

3b **"Mchiya na mwanawe, tajiri na maliye."**
   M-chiya   na   mwana-we,   tajiri   na   mali-ye.
   1-poor   COM   1.child-1.3SG.POS rich_person   COM   9.wealth-9.3SG.POS

   As the saying goes, "A poor man and his child, a rich person and his wealth."

Paragraph 2

4a **Achetu ariokosa uvyazi**
   A-chetu   a-ri-o-kos-a   u-vyazi
   2-women   3PL-PST-2.REL-fail-FV   14-pregnancy

A.4 Expository text

4b kala achihenderwa uganga
    kala   a-chi-hend-er-w-a   u-ganga
    PST   3PL-IMPFV-do-APPL-PAS-FV   14-medicine

4c ili aweze kuvyala,
    ili   a-wez-e   ku-vyal-a
    so_that   3PL-be_able-SUB   INF-birth-FV

4d kama kuphungbwa na kuvwikpwa marero.
    kama   ku-phung-w-a   na   ku-vwik-w-a   ma-rero.
    like   INF-exorcise-PAS-FV   COM   INF-dress-PAS-FV   6-charms

If a woman failed to get pregnant she was given traditional medicine in order that she would be able to give birth, such as '*kuphungbwa*', (performing a traditional dance to appease evil spirits) and being dressed in '*marero*'.

5a Marero ni pingu zinazovwalwa chitswani,
    Ma-rero   ni   pingu   zi-na-zo-vyal-w-a   chitswa-ni,
    6-charms   COP   10.charms   10-CONT-10.REL-wear-PAS-FV   7.head-LOC

5b mikononi, singoni na pambavuni,
    mi-kono-ni,   singo-ni   na   pambavu-ni,
    4-arms-LOC   9.neck-LOC   COM   9.chest-LOC

5c ambapho piya kala vichiihwa visingu.
    amba-pho   piya   kala   vi-chi-ih-w-a   vi-singu.
    REL-16.REL   also   PST   8-IMPFV-call-PAS-FV   8-headbands

Marero are charms which are worn on the forehead, arms, neck and chest, and which are also called '*visingu*' (headbands).

6a Chisha kala achihewa mwana wa ndonga na
    Chisha   a-chi-hew-a   mwana   wa   ndonga   na
    then   3SG-CONS-give.PAS-FV   1.child   1.ASS   9.gourd   COM

6b malagulo ganjinage.
    ma-lagulo   ganjina-ge.
    6-treatments   6.others-6.3SG.POS

Then she* would be given a little '*ndonga*' (bottle gourd used to store medicine) and other treatments.
(*It is unclear whether the reference is singular or plural at this point.)

7a Achiphaha mimba, anatsimbirwa mihi kama
    A-chi-phah-a   mimba,   a-na-tsimb-ir-w-a   mihi   kama
    3SG-DEP-get-FV   9.womb   3SG-CONT-dig-APPL-PAS-FV   4.plants   like

7b mbokpwe, mchinjiri, chidori na muhumba.
 mbokpwe, mchinjiri, chidori na muhumba.
 3.PLANT_NAME 3.PLANT_NAME 7.PLANT_NAME COM 3.PLANT_NAME

If she then got pregnant roots would be dug up for her from trees such as 'mbokpwe' (*Annona senegalensis*—wild custard apple), 'mchinjiri' (*Dichrostachys cinerea*—sickle bush), 'chidori' (*Harrisonia abyssinica*) and 'muhumba' (*Cassia occidentalis*—stinking weed/wild coffee).

8a Mizi hino kala nkukatwa-katwa
 Mizi hino kala nku-kat-w-a-kat-w-a
 4.roots 4.DEM4 PST HAB-cut-PAS-FV-cut-PAS-FV

8b na chisha ikajitwa,
 na chisha i-ka-jit-w-a,
 COM then 4-SEQ-cook-PAS-FV

8c ikaokohwa dabwa-dabwa hadi ikagaluka rangi.
 i-ka-okoh-w-a dabwa-dabwa hadi i-ka-galuk-a rangi.
 4-SEQ-boil-PAS-FV thoroughly until 4-SEQ-change-FV 9.colour

These roots would be cut up and then cooked, they were boiled thoroughly until they changed colour.

9 Halafuye akahewa hino dawa akanwa.
 Halafu-ye a-ka-hew-a hino dawa a-ka-nw-a.
 9.after-9.3SG.POS 3SG-SEQ-give.PAS-FV 9.DEM4 9.medicine 3SG-SEQ-drink-FV

Afterwards the woman would be given this medicine to drink.

10a Piya mayo kala achirangbwa
 Piya mayo kala a-chi-rang-w-a
 also 1a.mother PST 3SG-IMPFV-massage-PAS-FV

10b ili mwana asagikpweto asedze akachingama.
 ili mwana a-sag-ik-w-e=to a-sedze a-ka-chingam-a.
 so_that 1.child 3SG-stay-STAT-PAS-SUB=WELL 3SG-lest 3SG-POT-cross-FV

Then the woman would be massaged so that the baby would be in a good position and would not 'cross' (so that the baby would not be side-on).

Paragraph 3

11a Siku ya utsungu, kala kuna dawa za mizi
 Siku ya utsungu kala ku=na dawa za mizi
 9.day 9.ASS 14.pain PST 17=COM 10.medicine 10.ASS 4.roots

A.4 Expository text

11b **ambazo kala zikafungbwa dzulu ya dari.**
amba-zo   kala   zi-ka-fung-w-a   dzulu   ya   dari.
REL-10.REL   PST   10-ANT-tie-PAS-FV   up   9.ASS 9.ceiling

When the woman went into labour there was a medicine made from roots which would be tied up on the ceiling.

12a **Dawa hizi kala nkufungbwa**
Dawa   hizi   kala   nku-fung-w-a
10.medicine   10.DEM1   PST   HAB-tie-PAS-FV

12b **kama hiha ra kuni.**
kama   hiha   ra   kuni.
like   5.bundle   5.ASS   9.firewood

This medicine was tied up like a bundle of firewood.

13 **Mazumunige kala kuzuwiya mruwo.**
Mazumuni-ge   kala   ni   ku-zuwiy-a   mruwo.
6.purpose-6.3SG.POS PST   COP   INF-prevent-FV   3.haemorrhage

Its purpose was to prevent heavy bleeding.

14a **Utsungu kala uchizidi,**
Utsungu   kala   u-chi-zidi,
14.pain   PST   14-IMPFV-increase

14b **dawa zira kala zikakatwa zikagbwa photsi.**
dawa   zira   kala   zi-ka-kat-w-a   zi-ka-gbw-a   photsi.
10.medicine   10.DEM2   PST   10-ANT-cut-PAS-FV   10-SEQ-fall-FV 16.floor

As the labour progressed, these medicinal roots were cut down so that they fell to the floor.

15a **Piya kala kuna mizi yanjina ya kuzidisha**
Piya   kala   ku=na   mizi   y-anjina   ya   ku-zid-ish-a
also   PST   17=COM   4.roots   4.others   4.ASS   INF-increase-CAUS-FV

15b **utsungu ambayo kala nkuafunwa,**
utsungu   amba-yo   kala   nku-afun-w-a
14.pain   REL-4REL   PST   HAB-chew-PAS-FV

15c **na yanjina ikakunwa-kunwa halafu ikajitwa**
na   y-anjina   i-ka-kun-w-a-kun-w-a   halafu   i-ka-jit-w-a
COM   4.others   4-POT-grate-PAS-FV-grate-PAS-FV   after   4-SEQ-cook-PAS-FV

15d **chisha akahewa akainwa**
chisha   a-ka-hew-a   a-ka-i-nw-a
then   3SG-SEQ-give.PAS-FV 3SG-SEQ-4-drink-FV

15e ili izidishe utsungu.
    ili   i-zid-ish-e   utsungu.
    so_that   4-increase-CAUS-SUB   14.pain

There were also other roots which were to increase the contractions and which were chewed, and others which were grated and boiled and then given as a drink in order to increase the contractions.

16 Mwana naye kala nkutuluka kutoka ndanini.
    Mwana   na=ye   kala   nku-tuluk-a   ndani-ni.
    1.child   COM=3SG.REF   PST   HAB-come_out-FV   9.abdomen-LOC

Then the baby would be born.

Paragraph 4

17a Mwana anaphovyalwa, ninengbwa
    Mwana   a-na-pho-vyal-w-a,   nine-ngbwa
    1.child   3SG-CONT-16.REL-birth-PAS-FV   1a.mother-POS

17b kala akarangbwa ama akaminywa ndani
    kala   a-ka-rang-w-a   ama   a-ka-miny-w-a   ndani
    PST   3SG-ANT-massage-PAS-FV   or   3SG-ANT-squeeze-PAS-FV   9.abdomen

17c hadi dzadzo rikatuluka.
    hadi   dzadzo   ri-ka-tuluk-a.
    until   5.placenta   5-ANT-come_out-FV

When the child had been delivered the mother would be massaged or squeezed on her abdomen until the placenta was delivered.

18a Ichikala bado dzadzo rinareha tabu
    I-chi-kal-a   bado   dzadzo   ri-na-reh-a   tabu
    9-DEP=be-FV   not_yet   5.placenta   5-CONT-bring-FV   9.trouble

18b kutulukakpwe, phahi akunga kala nkuhumira
    ku-tuluk-a-ku-e   phahi   a-kunga   kala   nku-humir-a
    INF-come_out-FV-15-3SG.POS   so   2-midwives   PST   HAB-use-FV

18c ushanga ama mikono ikatiywa mromoni
    ushanga   ama   mi-kono   i-ka-tiy-w-a   mromo-ni
    14.beads   or   4-hands   4-POT-put_in-PAS-FV   3.mouth-LOC

A.4 Expository text

18d ili aoke dzadzo riweze kugbwa photsi.
ili   a-ok-e   dzadzo   ri-wez-e   ku-gbw-a   photsi.
so_that 3SG-retch-SUB 5.placenta 5-be_able-SUB INF-fall-FV 16.floor

If the placenta was delayed in coming out, then the midwives would put beads or their hands in her mouth in order to make the mother retch and so expel the placenta.

19a Badaye mwana kala akakatwa muhanga
Badaye   mwana   kala   a-ka-kat-w-a   mu-hanga
afterwards 1.child PST 3SG-ANT-cut-PAS-FV 3-umbilical_cord

19b na chirumu cha maso.
na   chi-rumu   cha   maso.
COM 7-knife   7.ASS 6.sharp_blade

Afterwards the umbilical cord would be cut with a small, sharp knife.

20a Ichikala piya dzadzo rikachelewa kutuluka,
I-chi-kal-a   piya   dzadzo   ri-ka-chelew-a   ku-tuluk-a,
9-DEP=be-FV also   5.placenta 5-ANT-delay-FV INF-come_out-FV

20b muhanga nkukatwa vivyo hivyo,
mu-hanga   nku-kat-w-a   vivyo   hivyo,
3-umbilical_cord HAB-cut-PAS-FV 8.DEM3_VAR 8.DEM3

20c lakini mvyazi nkufungbwa dziwe
lakini   m-vyazi   nku-fung-w-a   dziwe
but   1-parent HAB-tie-PAS-FV 5.stone

20d pho mwisho wa muhanga.
pho   mwisho   wa   mu-hanga.
16.DEM3_VAR 3.end   3.ASS 3-umbilical_cord

If the placenta had still failed to deliver, the cord would still be cut, but the mother would have a stone tied to the end of the cord.

21a Dziwe hiri kala ni ra kuzuwiya dzadzo
Dziwe   hiri   kala   ni   ra   ku-zuwiy-a   dzadzo
5.stone 5.DEM1 PST COP 5.ASS INF-prevent-FV 5.placenta

21b risiuye ndani.
ri-si-ny-e   ndani.
5-NEG-discharge-SUB inside

This stone was to prevent the placenta returning inside (the mother).

22 **Hinyu muhanga kala nkufungbwa wuuzi wa ukonje.**
Hinyu   mu-hanga   kala   nku-fung-w-a   wu-uzi   wa   u-konje.
3.DEM1   3-umbilical_cord   PST   HAB-tie-PAS-FV 14-thread   14.ASS 14-sisal

The umbilical cord was tied with a thread of sisal.

23a **Wuuzi hinyu kala ni wa kuzuwiya**
Wu-uzi   hinyu   kala   ni   wa   ku-zuwiy-a
14-thread   14.DEM1   PST   COP   14.ASS INF-prevent-FV

23b **milatso isimwagike.**
mi-latso   i-si-mwag-ik-e
4-blood   4-NEG-spill-STAT-SUB

This string was to prevent the cord from continuing to bleed.

24a **Halafu mwana kala nkutsulwa na mitsanga,**
Halafu   mwana   kala   nku-tsul-w-a   na   mi-tsanga
after   1.child   PST   HAB-wash-PAS-FV   COM   4-sand

24b **badala ya sabuni,**
badala   ya   sabuni
instead   9.ASS   9.soap

24c **chisha akapakpwa mafuha ga nyono mwiri mzima.**
chisha   a-ka-pak-w-a   mafuha   ga   nyono   mwiri   m-zima.
then   3SG-SEQ-smear-PAS-FV   6.oil   6.ASS   9.castor   3.body   3-whole

Then the baby would be rubbed down with sand instead of soap, then it would be massaged with castor oil all over its body.

25a **Mwishoni akaphanguswa na demu safi ili**
Mwisho-ni   a-ka-phangus-w-a   na   demu   safi   ili
3.end-LOC   3SG-SEQ-wipe-PAS-FV   COM   5.rag   clean   so_that

25b **auswe uchafu ulao ndanini.**
a-us-w-e   u-chafu   u-l-a-o   ndani-ni.
3SG-remove-PAS-SUB   14-dirt   14-come_from-FV-14.REL   9.abdomen-LOC

Finally it would be wiped with a clean rag to remove the remaining birth fluids.

Appendix B

Wordlist and Botanical Names

B.1 SIL Comparative African Wordlist

This wordlist is based on the SIL Comparative African Wordlist[1] comprising 1,700 words. Some words have been omitted because no Digo equivalent exists or because the Digo equivalent is not known. The items in this wordlist are arranged semantically under twelve main headings as follows:

1. Man's physical being
2. Man's nonphysical being
3. Persons
4. Personal interaction
5. Human civilisation
6. Animals
7. Plants
8. Environment
9. Events and actions
10. Quality
11. Quantity
12. Grammatical items

A trilingual dictionary has been published separately (Mwalonya et al. 2012).

---

[1] The SIL Comparative Wordlist was compiled by Keith Snider and James Roberts (in English and French), and was originally published in the *Journal of West African Languages* 31(2):73–122. The wordlist has been reproduced in SIL Electronic Working Papers 2006-005 (http://www.sil.org/resources/publications/entry/7882). Further details and resources, including spreadsheet templates, database templates and instructions for collection and submission of collected wordlists can be found at http://www.comparalex.org/.

1 Man's physical being

1.1 Body parts

| 0001 | body | mwiri, ungo |
| 0002 | skin (of man) | chingo, ngozi |

1.1.1 Head

0003	head	chitswa
0004	forehead	komo, chikomo, chilangu, chirangbwi cha uso
0005	face	uso, sura
0006	eye	dzitso
0007	eyebrow	kumbi, nyusi
0008	eyelid	luswi, nyuswi
0009	eyelash	luswi, nyuswi, kophe
0010	pupil (of eye)	mboni (ya dzitso)
0011	nose	pula, pura
0012	bridge (of nose)	mgongo wa pula
0013	ear	sikiro
0014	cheek	ndzeya, funda, ndzalipo
0015	mouth	mlomo, mromo, kanwa
0016	lip	domo
0017	tongue	lilimi, rurimi, lilaka, ruraka
0018	tooth	dzino
0019	molar tooth	dzino ra jego, shine
0020	palate	lilaka-laka
0021	jaw	jego
0022	chin	cheru
0023	neck	singo
0024	nape of neck	msipha
0025	throat	bombolibo, bomboribo, umiro
0026	voice box, larynx, Adam's apple	kororo
0027	hair (of head)	nyere
0028	beard	cheru, dzendze
0029	hair (of body)	laika
0030	tuft, lock (of hair)	linyere

1.1.2 Trunk

0031	shoulder	fuzi, bega
0032	shoulder blade	-
0033	chest	laga, chifuwa
0034	breast	nyaho, linyaho, runyaho
0035	side (of body)	lavu

B.1 SIL Comparative African Wordlist

0036	waist	chibiru, gbwidi, chunu
0037	navel	tovu, bungo
0038	umbilical cord	tovu, muhanga
0039	abdomen (external)	ndani
0040	stomach (internal)	ndani, tumbo
0041	womb	tumbo
0042	back	mongo, ungo
0043	small of back	-
0044	buttock	hako, tako
0045	anus	mkpwundu
0046	penis	mbolo, mzunga
0047	testicle	chende, ngoko
0048	vagina	njini
0049	clitoris	chilembo, chirembe, chilebe-lebe, chinyadolo

1.1.3 Limbs

0050	arm	mkpwono
0051	armpit	kpwapha
0052	upper arm	-
0053	elbow	chisuku-suku
0054	forearm	-
0055	wrist	chitengu cha mkpwono
0056	hand	chigandzo
0057	fist	konde, ngumi
0058	palm (of hand)	fumba
0059	finger	chala, chara
0060	thumb	dzala gumbe
0061	knuckle	ngoto
0062	fingernail	kombe, likombe
0063	leg	chigulu
0064	hip	nyonga, chibiru
0065	thigh	chiga, nyonga
0066	knee	vwindi, goti, goyo
0067	shin	mlundi
0068	calf of leg	tsafu
0069	ankle	nguyu
0070	foot	gulu
0071	heel	chisigino, chijimbe, jimbe, pazi
0072	sole	ruwayo, layo
0073	toe	chala, chara

1.1.4 Internal parts and products

0074	bone	msoza, mfupha
0075	bone marrow	-
0076	skeleton	misoza, mifupha
0077	skull	bebe ra chitswa, zekeya ra chitswa
0078	breastbone	-
0079	spine, backbone	mongomongo
0080	rib	mbavu, lavu, chibavu
0081	brain	bongo, wuongo
0082	heart	moyo
0083	liver	ini
0084	kidney	rendu, figo
0085	lung	pafu
0086	intestines	uhumbo, mahumbo, ndei
0087	bladder	chibofu, chikodzo, chibuko
0088	gall bladder	chihumbo utsungu
0089	muscle	mshipa
0090	tendon	mshipa, kano
0091	vein	mshipa, likano
0092	breath	pumuzi
0093	saliva	mahe, luhe
0094	phlegm	-
0095	nasal mucus, snot	mamira, tsololo
0096	earwax	papa wa sikiro
0097	tears (n)	matsozi
0098	blood	mlatso, damu
0099	bile, gall	nyongo
0100	semen	shahawa
0101	urine	mkodzo
0102	excrement, faeces	mavi

1.2 Body processes, functions

0103	blink	gbwinya
0104	wink (eye)	fwinya dzitso, tsupha nuswi
0105	blow nose	mika mamira
0106	breathe	soha, phuma, tweta, vuta pumuzi
0107	yawn	piga myayu
0108	snore	ngorota, piga myono
0109	pant	vumahika
0110	blow (with mouth)	vuma vuvurira, fufurira
0111	spit (v)	tsitsa (mahe), teha, twa
0112	cough (v)	kolola
0113	belch	beha, boha

B.1 SIL Comparative African Wordlist

0114	hiccough (n)	tsetsevu, chitsetsevu
0115	sneeze (v)	piga myasa
0116	groan (with pain)	hula, piga migumi
0117	grunt (from effort)	koroma
0118	palpitate (of heart)	phatsuka, guguta
0119	urinate	kodzola, tabawala (piga tsi, mwaga madzi)
0120	break wind, fart	pufula, shuha
0121	defecate	nya
0122	shiver, tremble	kakama
0123	perspire, sweat	hoka, rurumuka
0124	bleed	ruwa
0125	coagulate, clot	tuma
0126	(be) dizzy	chizunguzungu, chisundzi
0127	faint	zimiya, angamiza ngoro, fwa pungire
0128	sleep (v)	lala
0129	dream (n)	ndoso
0130	wake up (intr)	lamuka, vumbuluka

1.2.1 Senses

0131	see	ona, tundza
0132	notice (v)	ona
0133	look at, watch	ona, lola, lolera, rorera
0134	hear	sikira, sikiza
0135	listen	sikira, sikiza, simila, phundza
0136	smell (v)	nusa
0137	feel (passive)	ona, sikira
0138	touch, feel (active)	guta, phaphasa
0139	taste	tata

1.2.2 Ingestion

0140	eat	rya
0141	bite (v)	ng'ata, gadula
0142	crunch	bebena, gogoda
0143	chew	bebena, afuna
0144	gnaw	tsuna, guguna
0145	swallow	miza
0146	choke	kpwarwa
0147	lick	lamba
0148	suck	fyondza, amwa, mumunya, nyudza
0149	drink	nwa

1.3 Body movement

0150	sit	sagala
0151	rise up (intr)	unuka, zuka
0152	lie down	ambalala, lala
0153	turn round (intr)	galuka
0154	walk	nyendeka, weha
0155	step (v)	vyoga (=step on)
0156	stumble	kpwala
0157	limp	gutsira, gumwira, vuhira, tsetsera
0158	crawl	ambala
0159	run	zola, diganya, mairo (adjective)
0160	swim	ojorera, tula
0161	jump (v)	tina, uruka
0162	kick	tsupha lago, piga teke
0163	stamp (with foot)	piga mawala
0164	trample	vyoga-vyoga
0165	wave (hand as a greeting) (v)	tsuph(iran)a mikono
0166	indicate, point (as with the finger)	oloha, lekeza
0167	clap (hands)	piga makofi
0168	slap (v)	waguza, tiya/piga/zaba kofi

1.4 Body states and conditions

1.4.1 Body positions

0169	stand	ima
0170	straddle	panula vigulu
0171	lean against (intr)	jejemera, gandamira
0172	bend down, stoop	bong'ola, bumama
0173	bow (as in greeting)	zama
0174	(be) seated	segere, sagala
0175	squat	tatama
0176	kneel	chita vwindi/goyo
0177	(be) lying down	lala

1.4.2 Body conditions

0178	(be) hot (of person)	(kala) na dzoho
0179	(be) hungry, hunger (v)	(kala) na ndzala/kusikira ndzala
0180	(be) sated	mvuna, shiba
0181	(be) thirsty, thirst (v)	(kala) na chiru
0182	(be) drunk	lewa
0183	(be) tired	remwa, korwa
0184	(be) sleepy	kuka

B.1 SIL Comparative African Wordlist

0185	rest	oya, pumzika
0186	(be) awake, alert	(kala) matso, chonjo

1.5 Irregular conditions

0187	wrinkle (on skin)	mkpwetse (wrinkled person)
0188	pimple	chiiwe
0189	hump (of hunchback)	nundu

1.5.1 Abnormal qualities (adjectival)

0190	(be) bald	-a chiparangato, chiphala
0191	(be) blind	(kala) chipofu, pofuka
0192	(be) myopic, (be) shortsighted	-
0193	(be) thin	(kala) -embamba, kala chinyembe-nyembe
0194	(be) impotent	(kala) -tasa

1.5.2 Handicapped people

0195	barren woman	mgumba (also refers to infertile man), tasa
0196	blind person	chipofu
0197	deaf (mute) person	masito
0198	hunchback	chinundu
0199	cripple (n)	chiswere
0200	dwarf	mbilichimo, chindururu
0201	giant	dzitu
0202	stupid person	mzuzu, pomboo
0203	senile person	mkpwetee
0204	mad person	mutu wa koma

1.6 Health and disease

0205	(be) healthy, (be) well	(kala) zima
0206	(be) sick, (be) ill	(kala) -kongo
0207	hurt oneself	lumiza, rumira
0208	heal (tr), cure (v)	phoza
0209	medicine	dawa, muhaso
0210	get well, recover	phola
0211	revive	vuvumuka

1.6.1 Abnormalities

0212	abcess	mtochi
0213	swelling	maduru-duru, mavirivindza
0214	tumour	tezi
0215	bruise (n)	(ruwira = be bruised)
0216	burn (n)	magandza
0217	goiter	tezi
0218	hernia (umbilical)	ngiri, mshipa wa ngiri

0219	ulcer (leg)	chironda
0220	wound, sore	chironda
0221	pus	ufira, usaha
0222	scar	magandza
0223	intestinal worm	mnyololo

1.6.2 Diseases, malaise

0224	illness, disease	ukongo
0225	elephantiasis	hende
0226	ringworm	bato, mwalidago, mashilingi
0227	leprosy	mahana
0228	malaria (fever)	homa
0229	fever (not malaria)	homa
0230	pain (n)	mwimbo, maumivu
0231	give pain, hurt	luma, lumiza
0232	throb (with pain)	lumwa
0233	vomit (v)	haphika
0234	stomachache, upset stomach	lumwa n'ndani, vimbirwa
0235	headache	lumwa n'chitswa
0236	diarrhoea	fyokpwa, lifyoka
0237	scabies (the itch)	uphere

1.6.3 Life and death

0238	life	maisha, uzima
0239	(be) alive	(kala) hai, -zima, moyo (idiom)
0240	menstrual period	siku za mwezini
0241	(be) pregnant	(kala) na mimba
0242	miscarriage	voromosa (v)
0243	labour (n), birth pains	utsungu wa kuvyala
0244	bear (child), give birth	vyala, dzivugula
0245	(be) born	vyalwa
0246	(be) young	(kala) mdide
0247	grow up	kula
0248	(be) old (not young)	(kala) mtumiya, mkpwota, mkpwetee
0249	die	fwa
0250	death	chifo, mauti
0251	(be) dead	mfwadzi (n)

2 Man's nonphysical being

2.1 Know, believe, teach

0252	think	ona, fikiri
0253	believe	amini
0254	hope (v)	tumaini, kuluphira

B.1 SIL Comparative African Wordlist

0255	know (something or someone)	manya, bara
0256	knowledge	maarifwa, ujuzi
0257	wisdom	maarifwa, ujuzi, ikima
0258	(be) wise	kala na ikima
0259	(be) intelligent	werevu, achili (n)
0260	(be) stupid	(kala) -zuzu
0261	(be) confused	tatizika achili
0262	learn	dzifundza, dzibaza, soma
0263	teach	fundza, baza, somesha
0264	show	elekeza, onyesa
0265	remember	tambukira
0266	forget	yala, raya

2.2 Emotions

0267	(be) happy, (be) joyful	furahi, hererwa, (kala) na raha
0268	rejoice	furahia
0269	laugh	tseka
0270	smile	tsekera
0271	(be) sad	sikitika
0272	cry, weep	rira, yengesa
0273	sorrow (n)	sonono, huzuni, majondzi, mkunguru
0274	shame (n)	haya, waibu
0275	pity (n)	huruma, mbazi
0276	fear (n)	hofu, wuoga, chiwewe
0277	frighten	ogofya, ondosa, tishira
0278	startle, surprise	shangaza
0279	(be) angry	tsukirwa, reya
0280	calm (oneself)	tuwa, hurira
0281	(be) proud	(kuhenda) nundu, shobo, ngulu, dzivuna, dzinyumbula
0282	respect (v)	ishimu, heshimu
0283	honour (v)	ishimu
0284	love (v)	mendza
0285	hate (v)	zira, tsukira
0286	despise, disdain	mena, kpwinya, bera, ipha kogo

2.3 Human will

0287	want, desire (v)	taka, londa, ronda, kala na hamu
0288	decide	kata shauri, amuwa
0289	choose (tr), pick (tr)	tsambula, tsola
0290	hesitate	ima-ima
0291	abstain	richana
0292	allow, permit	ruhusu, baliya
0293	forbid	kahaza, kahala

0294	prevent	zuwiya, ziza, phila-phila, remeza, chichisa
0295	plan (n)	mradi, mpango
0296	try	jeza, jaribu
0297	succeed	fwaulu
0298	fail	bwaga, tsupha (idiomatic)
0299	pretend	dzihenda

2.4 Human character

0300	(be) kind	(kala) mpole, adzo-adzo
0301	(be) generous	(kala) na moyo mnono
0302	(be) selfish	(kala) uchoyo, choyo
0303	(be) honest	(kala) muaminifu
0304	(be) corrupt	(kala) mbaya, muovu
0305	(be) wicked	(kala) mui
0306	(be) fierce	(kala) siru, kali
0307	(be) jealous	(kala) na wivu
0308	(be) shy	(ona) haya
0309	(be) courageous, (be) brave	(dina) chilume
0310	coward	(kala) muoga
0311	(be) curious	(kala) mdadisi
0312	(be) eager, (be) zealous	(kala) na hamu
0313	(be) lazy	(kala) mvivu, itsi-itsi
0314	(be) patient	vumirira
0315	(be) impatient	(kala) wa more
0316	(be) restless, (be) unsettled	tsuga-tsuga, hangaika
0317	(be) stubborn	likani, likakado, ubishi
0318	reputation	sifwa

2.5 Difficulty

0319	hardship, distress	ngerye
0320	(be) difficult	(kala) -gumu
0321	suffer	gaya
0322	obstruct	zuwiya, remeza
0323	stumbling block, obstruction	chizuwizi
0324	danger	hatari
0325	problem, trouble	shida, neno, tatizo

3 Persons

0326	human being, person	mutu, binadamu
0327	self	nafsi
0328	man (male)	mlume, mwanalume
0329	woman	mchetu, mwanachetu

B.1 SIL Comparative African Wordlist

| 0330 | white man | mzungu |

3.1 Stages of life

0331	foetus	mimba
0332	baby	mwana, mwana mtsanga (mjeni - idiomatic use)
0333	twin	patsa
0334	child	mwana, mwanache
0335	boy	mvulana, mwanache wa chilume
0336	girl	msichana, mwanache wa chichetu
0337	adult	ndzigamba (adult man), mutu mvyere
0338	young man	barobaro, kijana, mvuka, muhana
0339	virgin	chigoli, mwanamwali
0340	old person	mzehe, mtumiya, mkpwota, mkpwetee

3.2 Blood relations

0341	relative (by blood)	m'bari, mchina (must be joined to family/clan in mention e.g mchina-ngome)
0342	ancestor	mkare
0343	grandparent	tsawe, wawa
0344	father	baba, ise
0345	mother	mayo, nine
0346	brother (elder/younger)	kaka
0347	sister (elder/younger)	dada
0348	father's brother (uncle)	baba mvyere, baba mdide
0349	mother's brother (uncle)	aphu
0350	mother's sister (aunt)	mayo mvyere, mayo mdide
0351	father's sister (aunt)	shangazi
0352	cousin	mkpwoi (only born to shangazi/aphu, others are brother/sister)
0353	firstborn	mvugula sandzu, mwana wa mbere
0354	descendant	chivyazi
0355	son	mwana mlume
0356	daughter	mwana mchetu
0357	grandchild	mdzukulu
0358	nephew	muwa
0359	name	dzina
0360	namesake	somu

3.3 Marriage relations

0361	in-law, relative by marriage	shemegi
0362	husband	mlume, mwanalume (unlawful husband)
0363	wife (my)	mchetu wangu, mkpwazangu
0364	fellow-wife, cowife	wawa, mchetu myangu

0365	father-in-law	baba vyala, mtsedza
0366	mother-in-law	mayo vyala, mtsedza
0367	brother-in-law	mlamu
0368	sister-in-law	mlamu, wifi
0369	son-in-law	mtsedza
0370	daughter-in-law	mkpwaza mwana
0371	widow	gungu
0372	widower	-
0373	orphan	mwanachiya
0374	fiancé (betrothed boyfriend)	mchumba
0375	fiancée (betrothed girlfriend)	mwari
0376	bastard, illegitimate child	mwana wa vuweni

3.4 Relations, extended and social

0377	tribe, ethnic group	kabila
0378	clan	ukoo, fuko (matrilineal), mbari (patrilineal)
0379	family	jamaa
0380	friend	msena
0381	neighbour	jirani
0382	acquaintance	myao
0383	host	mwenyezi
0384	guest, visitor	mjeni
0386	enemy	adui, mgala
0387	traitor	mguza myawe
0388	thief	mwivi
0389	guide (n)	muonyesa njira
0390	messenger	mjumbe
0391	crowd	kundi, dida ra atu, umati
0392	chief, headman	mkpwulu, mbaha
0393	elder	mzee, mutumiya
0394	master	bwana, tajiri
0395	slave	mtumwa, mgbwulwa, muhunde

3.5 Professions

0396	farmer	mkurima
0397	fisherman	mvuvi, mgala-gala na pwa
0398	hunter	muindza, mkala
0399	blacksmith	mpiga fuawi
0400	potter	muumba nyungu
0401	weaver	msuka jamvi, kaphu
0402	butcher (n)	mtsindzadzi
0403	trader	mchuuzi
0404	(domestic) servant	mtumishi, muhumwa
0405	beggar	mvoyi

0406	soldier	mwanajeshi, asikari
0407	prostitution	ukabaa, umalaya, ushoga, uhanisi, udiya
0408	midwife	mkunga, mvyalusadzi
0409	medicine man, traditional healer	mgbwanga
0410	fetish priest	mtabiri
0411	sorcerer (male)	mtsai
0412	witch (female)	mtsai
0413	fortune-teller, diviner	mpiga mburuga

4 Personal interaction

4.1 Association of persons

0414	meet, encounter	kuta
0415	accompany	sindikiza
0416	(be) together	(kala) phamwenga, (kala) aro
0417	assemble, meet together	kutana
0418	invite	alika
0419	(be) alone	macheyo
0420	abandon	uka, richa
0421	flee, run away from	chimbira
0422	drive away	zoresa
0423	avoid	hepa, phisa, tsega-tsega
0424	(be) same	sawa, sawa-sawa
0425	(be) different	tafwauti, mbali-mbali
0426	resemble	fanana, igana
0427	imitate	iga, igiza
0428	admire	fwahirwa
0429	befit, suit	ajira

4.2 Speech, language

0430	language	luga, chiryomo
0431	word	neno
0432	meaning (n)	mana
0433	say	amba
0434	voice	sauti, kauli
0435	speak, talk	nena, gomba
0436	whisper (v)	nong'oneza
0437	shout (v), cry out	chema, kota likululu
0438	chat (v)	bisha, semurira
0439	mumble	afuna maneno
0440	stutter	babaika, sita
0441	(be) eloquent	manya kugomba
0442	(be) silent	hurira, gbwi, zii

4.2.1 Greeting

0443	greet (v)	lamusa, jambosa, phozera
0444	call (someone)	iha
0445	say goodbye, take leave of	laga

4.2.2 Information and questions

0446	announce	tangaza, piga mbiru
0447	announcement	matangazo
0448	news	habari
0449	explain	semurira, eleza
0450	advise	shauri
0451	gossip (v)	sengenya, vumisa, tsengerera
0452	lie (n) (falsehood)	katira, tsindzira, ziga
0453	ask, request	voya, uza
0454	plead, implore	lalama, lalamira
0455	request (n)	voyo
0456	answer, reply(v)	jibu, lavukiza, vumikiza
0457	thank	shukuru

4.2.3 Promise

0458	promise (n)	chilagane, ahadi
0459	oath	chirapho
0460	swear	lapha

4.2.4 Strife and praise

0461	insult (v)	gombera, laphiza
0462	insult (n)	kashifa, lisengenyo
0463	slander (v)	tsuna, tsererenga, singizira, ochera ngulu
0464	threaten	tishira, ogofya
0465	argue	heha, gomba, lumbana
0466	argument	mvwehano, lumbano
0467	grumble, complain	nung'unika, rurumika, reya
0468	contradict	rema, kosana
0469	accuse	laumu, shitaki
0470	deny	tsamalala, kana,
0471	admit (to a wrong)	kubali kosa
0472	agree	lagana, kubali, elewana, phahana
0473	agreement	makubaliano, maelewano
0474	persuade	chenga-chenga, rai
0475	praise (n)	sifwa, togo
0476	bless, praise (someone)	lika, togola
0477	congratulate	togoresa
0478	boast, brag	dzivuna, dzikarya

B.1 SIL Comparative African Wordlist

4.2.5 Discourse genres

0479	tell, recount (story)	ambira, semurira
0480	story (tale)	ngano, hadisi, chisa
0481	proverb	fumbo, msemo
0482	speech, discourse	mazungumzo, hotuba
0483	account (report) (n)	lavya isabu

4.3 Interpersonal contact

0484	embrace, hug (v)	kumbatira
0485	caress (v)	phaphasa, nyegeza (intended towards sex)
0486	kiss (v)	donera, busu
0487	copulate, have sexual intercourse	ombana, lalana, kpwerana
0488	nurse, suckle (baby) (tr)	amwisa
0489	tickle (v)	tseketsa
0490	spank (child)	chapa
0491	whip	Verbs: phuphuta, chapa, kota milawa Nouns: chikoto, mlawa, mwendze

4.4 Help and care

0492	help	terya, saidiya
0493	protect, defend	rinda, kanira, tetea
0494	look after	rinda, roroma
0495	bring up (a child)	rera, tundza

4.5 Dominion and control

0496	rule over, dominate	tawala
0497	order (someone to do something)	lagiza
0498	command (n)	lagizo, shariya
0499	duty, obligation	wajibu
0500	send (someone to do something)	huma
0501	serve	humikira
0502	lead, guide (v)	longoza, tanguliya
0503	follow	lunga-lunga
0504	obey	sikiza, tii

4.6 Conflict and resolution

0505	please, satisfy	hamira, fwahira, tosheleza
0506	annoy, disturb	reyeza, sinya, chokoza
0507	deceive	chenga, pasha
0508	quarrel	heha
0509	fight	pigana, bwagana
0510	stab	dunga rumu
0511	kill, murder	olaga
0512	take revenge	riphiza

0513	resolve, settle (dispute)	elewana, sikizana, phahana
0514	intercede, mediate	kanya
0515	compromise	kubaliana
0516	appease, pacify	rizisha

4.7 Crime and justice

0517	steal	iya
0518	rape	ondzorera, gbwavukira
0519	judge (v)	amula, hukumu
0520	law	shariya
0521	(be) fair, just	(henda) irivyo haki
0522	(be) guilty	hatia
0523	(be) innocent	(kala) bila kosa
0524	punish	toza makosa, tiya adabu
0525	penalty, punishment	hukumu

5 Human civilisation

5.1 Settlement

0526	dwell, inhabit	sagala, ishi
0527	inhabitant, resident	mwenyezi, chivyarira
0528	bush dweller	mnyika
0529	move away, migrate	tsama
0530	country, ethnic area	tsi
0531	frontier (of ethnic area)	mphaka
0532	town, city	mudzi
0533	village	chidzidzi, lalo, mtaa
0534	camp, encampment	kambi
0535	market (n)	chete, soko

5.2 Clothing and adornment of body

5.2.1 Clothing

0536	article of clothing, clothes	nguwo
0537	wear clothes	vwala
0538	dress (v)	vwala, vwisa
0539	undress	vula
0540	(be) naked	chihuphu, chitsaha
0541	hat	kofiya
0542	shirt	shati
0543	trousers	suruwale
0544	loincloth	shuka
0545	robe (man's gown)	kandzu
0546	cloth worn by a woman	leso, gora, sidiriya

B.1 SIL Comparative African Wordlist

0547	baby sling	mkambe
0548	shoe, sandal	chirahu

5.2.2 Adornment and accessories

0549	bead	tsalu
0550	string, thread (beads) (v)	uzi, uzi wa tsalu
0551	bracelet	dzango
0552	necklace	useja, mkufu
0553	ankle ring, bangle	chikuku
0554	ring (finger)	pete
0555	earring	chipuli
0556	pierce (ears)	dunga, kobola
0557	labret, lip plug, lip disk	-
0558	plait, braid (hair)	songa, suka (nyere)
0559	(facial) incision(s), tattoo(s)	ndembo
0560	cane, walking stick	bakora, mgbwufu, ndata, mseche

5.2.3 Care for body

0561	bathe, wash oneself	oga
0562	apply (ointment), besmear	siriga, kirita
0563	wipe off (excreta)	phangusa
0564	cut (hair)	dirya, kata (nyere)
0565	shave (v)	nyola
0566	razor	wembe
0567	comb (n)	shanuwo, chitsana
0568	tooth stick, toothbrush	msuwaki

5.3 Food and drink

5.3.1 Food

0569	food	chakurya
0570	meat	nyama
0571	fat	mafuha
0572	oil	mafuha
0573	soup, broth	mtsuzi
0574	pap, mushy food	muswa, uji, wari
0575	bread	mkpwahe
0576	crust (n)	ukoko
0577	flour	unga
0578	salt	munyu
0579	breakfast	chai (literally: 'tea'), fungula (v)
0580	evening meal	chakurya cha dziloni/usiku
0581	feast	karamu, nyambura

0582	leftovers	mwiku (food that remained overnight), mseto (made from rice and beans/green grams), masaza, makombo
0583	spoil (food) (intr)	vunda
0584	mould (n)	koga

5.3.2 Drink

0585	milk (n)	maziya
0586	curdled milk	maziya ga mtindi
0587	alcohol (general)	uchi
0588	beer (traditional)	uchi
0589	mead, honey beer	-
0590	palm wine	uchi wa mnazi

5.4 Food preparation

5.4.1 Kitchen preparation

0591	prepare (food to cook)	tayarisha
0592	cut (tr)	kata
0593	cut open (fruit)	dokola, nengula, bambandzula
0594	slice	checha, chera
0595	peel (v)	gandula, guwa, yula, fula
0596	mix (v)	koroga, burunga
0597	stir	fwidza, vuga, koroga, burunga
0598	strain (food) (v)	tsudza
0599	pound	phonda, hwa, bunduga, bunda
0600	grind	saga
0601	knead	kanda
0602	pluck (feathers)	fwatsula, mwafula

5.4.2 Cooking

0603	cook (v)	jita, biya
0604	roast	ocha, wada
0605	fry	kalanga
0606	bake (in ashes)	ocha
0607	(be) smoked	fukiza
0608	boil (water), bubble up	chemusha, okoha, tserusa
0609	ferment (alcohol)	jema

5.5 Domestic utensils and containment

5.5.1 Kitchen utensils

0610	cooking pot (earthenware)	chidzungu, dzungu
0611	metal pot	sufuriya
0612	pot (for water)	nyungu, chigbwashe

B.1 SIL Comparative African Wordlist

0613	ladle	liphazi, liphinga
0614	cooking stone	figa, dziko
0615	grinding stone	lala
0616	upper grinding stone	-
0617	lower grinding stone	-
0618	pestle, pounding stick	mutsi
0619	mortar, pounding pot	chinu

5.5.2 Eating utensils

0620	plate	sahani, siniya
0621	bowl	liga, bakuli, dzaya
0622	cup	chikombe, mboko
0623	spoon (traditional)	ndzele, mwiko

5.5.3 Containers and containment

0624	bag	mfuko, mkoba
0625	box	sanduku
0626	basket	kaphu
0627	bucket, pail	ndoo, ngaito
0628	calabash	ndzele
0629	bottle	tupa
0630	stopper, plug	fwiniko
0631	handle	mphini
0632	pour	kupula, mwaga
0633	spill (liquid) (tr)	mwagika
0634	take out (from container)	tsomoza, tuluza, futsula
0635	fill	odzaza
0636	(be) full	(kala) tele
0637	(be) empty	(kala) huphu, tuphu
0638	(be) open	(kala) ereru, wazi, laza
0639	open (tr)	vugula
0640	close, shut (tr)	sindika
0641	stop up	fundira, ziba
0642	cover (v)	fwinika, bwiningiza
0643	uncover	fwenula, phenula
0644	store (up)	rundika, ika
0645	bundle (n)	bunda, hiha
0646	heap (n)	chifungu, ndulu, tsumbi
0647	heap up	henda ndulu, henda tsumbi
0648	wrap up	linga-linga
0649	unwrap	vugula
0650	pack (v)	funganya
0651	strap (n)	lugbwe
0652	string (n)	kamba, lugbwe

0653	rope	kamba
0654	knot	fundo
0655	fasten, bind (load)	ngirita, ndzirita
0656	tie (knot)	funga, piga fundo
0657	untie	vugula
0658	tighten (tr)	lingita, dina
0659	(be) tight	bana
0660	loosen	rejeza
0661	(be) loose, slack	rejera, (kala) reje-reje

5.6 Habitation

5.6.1 Parts of a house

0662	compound, house	muhala, nyumba
0663	hut	banda, chibanda
0664	wall	ukuta
0665	door, doorway cover	mryango, luvwi
0666	doorway	ryango
0667	window	dirisha
0668	roof	chombo
0669	beam, rafter	mgamba, phalu
0670	floor	sakafu
0671	room	chumba, chipaa
0672	bedroom	chumba
0673	kitchen	dzikoni
0674	entrance hut	-
0675	courtyard	muhala
0676	fence (n)	lichigo, uchigo
0677	fence in (v)	zungulusira lichigo
0678	granary	dungu, chitsaga
0679	well (n)	chisima
0680	bathing place	riko, uwa
0681	latrine, toilet	choo, chikopesa
0682	garbage dump	dzala
0683	garden	busitani, chunga, munda
0684	shelter (n)	chibanda

5.6.2 Construction

0685	build	dzenga, kandika
0686	mark out, peg out (ground)	-
0687	mud block	tofali
0688	thatch (n)	makuti
0689	plaster (n)	-
0690	lime, whitewash	chokaa

B.1 SIL Comparative African Wordlist

0691	paint (n)	(paka) rangi
0692	ladder	ngazi

5.6.3 Furniture

0693	chair	chihi
0694	stool	chihi
0695	wickerwork	-
0696	bed	chitanda, litsaga, mwakisu, tandara
0697	mat	jamvi, mcheka, tandiko
0698	lamp, torch	taa, makalanga, chimwindi
0699	fan (n)	chiphephero, banka
0700	bell	kengele
0701	ring (bell) (v)	piga kengele

5.7 Professions and work

0702	act, do	henda
0703	work (n)	kazi
0704	mend, repair	tengeza

5.7.1 Smithing

0705	forge (n)	sana (v), fula chuma (v)
0706	hammer	gongomeha, nyundo
0707	anvil	-
0708	bellows	-

5.7.2 Pottery

0709	lump (clay, mud)	ulongo, dongo
0710	mould (pottery)	finyanga
0711	potter's kiln	dzocho

5.7.3 Wood work

0712	wood	muhi, mbao
0713	cut down (tree)	bwaga (muhi)
0714	log	gogo, chigogo
0715	hollow out (log)	-
0716	axe	mbadzo, shoka, tezo
0717	chop into pieces	rengeta, tsanga-tsanga
0718	saw (n)	msumeno
0719	saw (wood) (v)	keresa, rekesa
0720	plank (n)	mbao
0721	knot (in wood)	-
0722	splinter, sliver (n)	chibao
0723	chisel (n)	tindo, patasi
0724	nail (n)	msumari

5.7.4 Tailoring and weaving

0725	sew	shona
0726	needle	sumba, sindano
0727	thread (n)	uzi
0728	hem (n)	msiso, mkungo, pindo
0729	pocket	bindo
0730	(be) torn	ahuka, kpwanyuka
0731	weave	suka
0732	cloth	tambara, chitambara

5.7.5 Domestic work

0733	rag	demu
0734	broom	liphyero
0735	sweep	phyera
0736	polish	siriga
0737	wash (clothes, utensils)	fula (clothes), suwa (utensils)
0738	draw water	heka
0739	fetch (firewood)	reha (bring), endza (look for)
0740	dig	tsimba, tiga
0741	rubbish	chifusi, iyi

5.8 Agriculture

5.8.1 Cultivation

0742	cultivate, farm (v)	rima
0743	field	munda
0744	boundary (of field)	mphaka
0745	fertile soil	mtsanga
0746	(be) barren (of land)	chitsapi
0747	clear (land for planting)	safisha (lit: 'clean')
0748	sow, plant	phanda
0749	transplant	-
0750	weed (v)	buruga, burugira
0751	hoe (v)	rima
0752	hoe (n)	jembe
0753	big hoe	jembe-mbadzo
0754	sickle	butu
0755	machete, cutlass	phanga

5.8.2 Harvest

0756	harvest season	mavuno
0757	harvest (maize) (v)	vuna
0758	harvest, dig up (yams)	fuka
0759	pick, pluck (fruit)	ngobola, tsenga (nazi - coconut)

0760	harvest, collect (honey from hive)	runa
0761	threshing-floor	lungo ('winnowing basket')
0762	thresh, beat (grain)	banda
0763	winnow (n)	siya, pheha
0764	winnow, throw in air (grain) (v)	pheha, phepheheka
0765	shell (groundnuts) (v)	guwa
0766	husk (corn) (v)	phukusa, hwa, fula (nazi - coconut)

5.8.3 Animal husbandry

0767	domesticate, tame	fuga
0768	herd (cattle, sheep) (n)	guphuphu
0769	herd, tend (cattle, sheep) (v)	tindizha
0770	cattle pen	chaa, chitindizho
0771	tether (sheep, goats) (v)	funga
0772	feed (animals)	risa
0773	milk (cows, goats) (v)	kama
0774	castrate	tula

5.9 Hunting and fishing

5.9.1 Hunting

0775	hunt (v)	indza, ongola
0776	stalk (v)	nyapa
0777	chase (v)	zoresa, bandikira, bagaza
0778	track (animal) (n)	gurufu, msindzi ('trail'), mwanya ('path through a thicket')
0779	footprint (human)	nyayo
0780	bow (hunting)	uha
0781	arrow	hondza
0782	poison (on arrow)	sumu
0783	head of arrow	chigumba
0784	quiver (n)	ryaka
0785	lance (spear) (n)	mkuki, fumo
0786	knife	rumu
0787	throwing stick (n), throwing knife	-
0788	club, cudgel	rungu, chirungu
0789	hunting net	chimia
0790	birdlime (adhesive to catch birds)	sokota
0791	trap (n)	muhego, muhambo
0792	set (trap)	hega, fyusa
0793	trap (animal) (v)	gbwira
0794	evade	chimbira
0795	escape	girigiza
0796	wound (animal)	lumiza

0797	slaughter, kill (animal for butchering)	tsindza
0798	skin (animal) (v)	yula

5.9.2 Fishing

0799	fish (v)	vuwa, lowa, kokohera
0800	fish dam	mtsara
0801	fish trap	uzio, mbgwono, tole
0802	fishing net	chimiya
0803	fishing line	msiphi
0804	fishhook	chiloo
0805	bait	chambo

5.10 Possessions and commerce

5.10.1 Possessions

0806	have, possess	kala na
0807	need (v)	taka, hitaji
0808	get, obtain	phaha
0809	give	pha, lavya
0810	return (tr), give back	uyiza
0811	belongings	mwiyo, milki
0812	owner	mwenye, mchina
0813	rich man	tajiri
0814	poor man	mchiya, mgayi
0815	(be) rich	(kala) tajiri
0816	(be) poor	(kala) mchiya, mgayi

5.10.2 Money exchange, finances

0817	money	pesa
0818	cowrie shell	kola
0819	barter, exchange (of goods)	mali kpwa mali
0820	buy	gula
0821	sell	guza
0822	(be) scarce	haba
0823	(be) expensive	gali
0824	(be) inexpensive	rahisi
0825	price	bei
0826	haggle, negotiate a price	pigana bei
0827	payment	ripho, maripho
0828	pay (for goods, services, etc.)	ripha, riphira
0829	gift	zawadi
0830	hire (v)	kodisha
0831	beg (for money)	voya

0832	borrow	aphasa, kopa
0833	lend	aphasa, kopa
0834	debt	deni
0835	offer (v)	lavya
0836	accept, receive	kubali, phokera
0837	refuse	rema
0838	tax (n)	kodi
0839	tribute	tuzo
0840	inheritance	urisi, ufwa
0841	inherit	risi, hala ufwa

5.11 Travel and transportation

0842	journey, trip (n)	charo, safari
0843	travel, go on a trip (v)	safiri
0844	traveller	msafiri
0845	wander	weha-weha, yeya, tanga, zunguluka
0846	(be) lost	angamika, yaya
0847	path, road	njira
0848	fork (in path), bifurcation,	panda
0849	crossroads, intersection	maganiko
0850	cross (river)	tsapika
0851	canoe	ngarawa, mtumbwi
0852	paddle (n)	kafi, kasiya
0853	paddle (v)	piga kafi
0854	bale out (canoe, boat)	-
0855	capsize	tabwika, didimiya
0856	bring	reha
0857	take (away), carry away	tsukula
0858	send (something to someone)	phirika
0859	carry (in arms)	tsukula
0860	carry (child) on back	ereka
0861	carry on head	dzihika
0862	headpad	kaha
0863	load, burden (n)	mzigo
0864	load (v)	unula, bandika mzigo
0865	unload	hula/usa/tsereza mzigo

5.12 War

0866	war	kondo, viha
0867	peace	amani, msitarehe
0868	army	jeshi
0869	spy (n)	kachero
0870	spy (v), spy on	peleleza
0871	sword	mufyu, upanga

0872	gun	bunduchi
0873	shield (n)	ngao
0874	conquer, defeat	shinda
0875	(be) defeated	shindwa
0876	prisoner, captive	mfungbwa, busu, mateka
0877	plunder (a town)	hala nyara

5.13 Arts and leisure

5.13.1 Music and dance

0878	music	-
0879	song	wira
0880	sing	imba, vwina
0881	hum (v)	vuma
0882	whistle (v)	piga milozi
0883	dance (n)	ngoma
0884	dance (v)	vwina, fwiha, fwinya

5.13.2 Musical instruments

0885	big(gest) drum	mchirima
0886	small(est) drum	chapuwo
0887	talking drum	ganda
0888	hour glass drum	patswe
0889	flute	chivoti, mwarutu
0890	harp (stringed instrument)	ngephephe
0891	balafon	-
0892	horn (musical instrument)	ngoli
0893	shell (musical instrument)	buru (gourd)
0894	rattle (musical instrument)	kayamba
0895	play instrument	piga ...
0896	blow (horn)	piga ...

5.13.3 Arts

0897	draw (picture)	chora
0898	decorate	pamba
0899	carve	tsonga

5.13.4 Leisure

0900	play (child) (intr)	vumba
0901	game	mchezo
0902	tobacco pipe	bombolibo
0903	pipe-stem	-
0904	tobacco	tumbaku

5.14 Religion and the supernatural

0905	awe, reverence (for God)	ucha (n), cha (v)

5.14.1 Supernatural beings

0906	God (supreme being)	Mlungu
0907	god (lesser), fetish (spirit)	shetani, foro, dzuni
0908	demon, evil spirit	pepho, nyagu
0909	ghost (visible apparition)	mwanga, koma, zimu
0910	soul, spirit (of living person)	nafsi, roho
0911	spirit (of dead person) (invisible)	koma, mzimu

5.14.2 Religion and witchcraft

0912	pray	voya
0913	blessing	razi, baraka, majaliwa
0914	divine, prophesy (v)	tabiri
0915	prophecy (n)	unabii, mlamulo, mburuga
0916	vision (supernatural)	ruwiya, njozi
0917	omen	chigulu chii (bad omen)
0918	witchcraft	utsai
0919	bewitch, cast spell	loga, anga
0920	curse (v)	lani, apiza, piga bako
0921	curse (n)	bako, lana
0922	poison (n)	sumu
0923	poison (a person) (v)	tiira sumu
0924	amulet, charm, fetish	fingo, pingu, hirizi
0925	protect by charm	kaga, risa kago
0926	mask (n)	chinyagu
0927	(be) taboo	miko, mvi, mzizo, mviga
0928	exorcise	sindika pepho
0929	sacrifice	asa, piga sadaka
0930	pour libation	lavya sadaka
0931	dwelling place of the dead (spiritual)	kuzimu

5.15 Ceremonies

0932	tradition, custom	kasi, jadi, mzizo, mviga, desturi
0933	feast (n)	karamu
0934	naming ceremony (baby)	-
0935	circumcision (male)	tsatsa
0936	excision (female)	-
0937	initiation (male)	deka, tiya tsatsani
0938	initiation (female)	-

5.15.1 Marriage

0932	tradition, custom	kasi, jadi, mzizo, mviga, desturi
0933	feast (n)	karamu
0934	naming ceremony (baby)	-
0935	circumcision (male)	tsatsa
0936	excision (female)	-
0937	initiation (male)	deka, tiya tsatsani
0938	initiation (female)	-
0946	polygamy	-
0947	adultery	uzinifu, uzindzi, uzembe zinaa, zini (v.)
0948	divorce (v)	ata

5.15.2 Funeral

0949	funeral (at occasion of death)	hanga
0950	mourning	hanga, chiriro
0951	wail, ululate (at funeral) (v)	rira, piga njere-jere
0952	condole, comfort (v)	fariji
0953	corpse	maiti, lufu, mwiri
0954	bury	zika
0955	grave	mbira
0956	cemetery	vikura

6 Animals

0957	animal	nyama

6.1 Domestic animals

6.1.1 Bovines

0958	ox (general term), bovine	ng'ombe
0959	bull	ndzau
0960	cow (female)	ng'ombe, goma
0961	heifer	mtamba, ndama
0962	steer	ndewa
0963	calf	ndama
0964	herd (of cattle)	guphuphu

6.1.2 Ovines and caprines

0965	goat	mbuzi
0966	he-goat, billy goat	ndenje, ndila
0967	she-goat, nanny goat	goma, mvarika
0968	kid	chibuzi, mvarika
0969	sheep	ng'ondzi
0970	ram	turume

B.1 SIL Comparative African Wordlist

0971	ewe	mwati
0972	lamb	mwana-ng'ondzi, mwati
0973	flock (of sheep, goats)	guphuphu

6.1.3 Poultry

0974	chicken	kuku
0975	rooster (cock)	dzogolo, (porwa, mruru)
0976	hen	kolo
0977	chick	chifinye, muhehera
0978	turkey	kolekole
0979	guinea fowl	kanga
0980	duck	bata

6.1.4 Beasts of burden

0981	camel	ngamia
0982	horse	farasi
0983	stallion	-
0984	mare (female horse)	-
0985	colt	mwana-farasi
0986	donkey	punda

6.1.5 Other

0987	pig	nguluwe (wild pig)
0988	boar (male pig)	-
0989	sow (female pig)	-
0990	piglet	mwana-nguluwe
0991	dog	diya
0992	pup	mwana-diya
0993	cat	mnyau
0994	kitten	chinyau

6.2 Mammals

0995	elephant	ndzovu
0996	hippopotamus	chiboko
0997	buffalo	nyahi
0998	rhinoceros	chifwaru, chifaru
0999	giraffe	twiga
1000	warthog	gbwase
1001	monkey	chima, tumbiri
1002	baboon	nyani, nguli
1003	hyena	fisi
1004	jackal	bawa, diya mbewa, bakaya, kala
1005	antelope	kulungu
1006	zebra	punda miliya

1007	anteater, aardvark, antbear	godzo
1008	pangolin, scaly anteater	-

6.2.1 Rodents

1009	mouse	panya
1010	rat	panya, kotso
1011	cane rat, cutting grass, grass cutter	tsanje, ndezi
1012	palm rat	jule
1013	shrew	-
1014	mole	fuko
1015	mongoose	kala konje
1016	hare	tsungula
1017	squirrel	tuhe, chituhe
1018	porcupine	nungu
1019	bat	nundu
1020	fruit bat	nundu ndema

6.2.2 Cats

1021	wild cat	mnyau tsaka, chororo
1022	civet cat	mondzo, fungo
1023	genet	chikanu
1024	leopard	tsui
1025	lion	simba, marara

6.2.3 Mammal parts

1026	hide (of animal)	chingo
1027	fur	nyoya
1028	horn	liphembe, lipembe
1029	hump (of cow)	nundu
1030	udder	chiwele
1031	tail	mchira, mwingo
1032	hoof	kpwatsa
1033	mane	madzere
1034	elephant's trunk	mroi
1035	elephant's tusk	pembe ya ndzovu
1036	den, lair, hole	fuko, mwamdifwitso

6.2.4 Mammal actions

1037	bark (as dog) (v)	pheka
1038	bare, show (teeth)	-
1039	growl	vumira
1040	ruminate, chew cud	tserura

6.3 Birds

1041	bird	nyama wa mapha
1042	crow	kurabu, kunguru
1043	dove	njiya manga, gugu, puji
1044	weaver-bird	tsongo
1045	parrot	kpwendzi
1046	partridge	-
1047	cattle egret	-
1048	heron	manjera
1049	kingfisher	membe, tilili
1050	hornbill	pholophondo
1051	pelican	manjera
1052	stork (marabou)	manjera
1053	ostrich	mbuni
1054	owl	chimburu, mtiti, vumatiti
1055	eagle	kozi, pungu, sanganira
1056	hawk	mweko
1057	vulture	nderi

6.3.1 Bird parts and things

1058	feather	nyoya, linyoya, loya
1059	wing	apha
1060	beak, bill	mlomo
1061	crest (of bird)	-
1062	comb (of rooster)	remba
1063	crop (of bird)	-
1064	gizzard	tambo
1065	claw	kombe
1066	egg	yayi, tumbi
1067	eggshell	-
1068	yolk (of egg)	chiini
1069	nest	fuko
1070	flock (of birds)	guphuphu

6.3.2 Bird actions

1071	fly (v)	uruka
1072	dive	-
1073	soar	-
1074	land (v), alight	dulama
1075	perch	sagala
1076	flap the wings	piga mapha
1077	cackle (as of chicken)	hehera, kokoreka
1078	crow (as a rooster) (v)	ika, hika

1079	peck (tr)	-
1080	lay (eggs)	bwaga
1081	incubate, set (on eggs)	sagarira
1082	hatch	kokota

6.4 Fish

1083	fish	samaki, ng'onda
1084	catfish	lungulungu
1085	mudfish (lives in the mud during dry season)	fumi
1086	eel	mkunga

6.4.1 Fish parts

1087	fish bone	msoza, mfupha
1088	fish-scale	mamba
1089	gill	makairwa
1090	fin	pezi

6.4.2 Shellfish and mollusks

1091	crab	tande
1092	shrimp	dura
1093	clam	gandamira
1094	snail	kola

6.5 Reptiles

1095	snake	nyoka
1096	spitting cobra	fwira
1097	puff adder	bafwe
1098	python	tsahu
1099	green mamba	liga-lakanga
1100	lizard	(no generic term for 'lizard')
1101	agama lizard (red-headed)	valavala
1102	chameleon	lumbwi
1103	gecko	mjusi kafiri
1104	monitor lizard	mbulu, mbulu kenge
1105	crocodile	mamba
1106	frog	gula
1107	toad	gula
1108	tortoise (land)	kobe
1109	turtle (water)	kasa

6.5.1 Reptile parts

1110	fang (of snake)	dzino
1111	venom (of snake)	sumu
1112	shell (of turtle)	bebe

6.5.2	Reptile actions	
1113	slither (snake)	hereza
1114	bite (snake)	hondza, bata, ng'ata
1115	crawl (lizard)	ambala
1116	hiss	-

6.6 Insects

1117	insect	mdudu
1118	flea	dadada, tawatawa
1119	louse	tsaha
1120	bedbug	kunguni
1121	maggot (in rotten meat)	bulu
1122	cockroach	kombamwiko
1123	ant	phepha, kolokolo, pambo, tsungutsungu (varieties – no generic term)
1124	army ant, soldier ant	tsalafu
1125	flying ant	tswa
1126	termite	lutswa, bamama
1127	spider	dzwidzwidzwi
1128	tarantula	-
1129	scorpion	chisuse
1130	dung beetle	chidundu
1131	jigger	fundza, ngondo, mganda, mau, mubanda
1132	grasshopper	bandzi, barare, chibarare
1133	cricket	nyendze, chenene
1134	locust	ndzije
1135	praying mantis	dungudungu
1136	leech	-
1137	caterpillar	kpwanya, kunyale
1138	centipede	munjemunje
1139	millipede	gongolo
1140	earthworm	mango

6.6.1 Flying insects

1141	fly (n)	indzi
1142	mosquito	imbu
1143	bee	bung'o, nyuchi
1144	mud wasp	muvwi
1145	dragonfly	mwamvuvu
1146	butterfly	popho-popho, popho
1147	moth	-

6.6.2 Insect things

1148	antenna	-
1149	sting (v)	shuhira
1150	stinger	-
1151	spider's web	utando
1152	cocoon	-
1153	termite hill	chitsulu
1154	beehive	mwato, mzinga
1155	beeswax, bee-bread	-
1156	honey	asali
1157	swarm (n)	dzendze, bumba

7 Plants

7.1 Types of plants (see Supplement: Botanical names)

7.1.1 Trees

1160	mahogany tree	mbambakofi (Afzelia quanzensis)
1161	teak tree	mvure
1162	baobab tree	muuyu (Adonsonia digitata)
1163	silk-cotton tree, kapok tree	msufi (Ceiba pentandra)
1164	shea-butter tree, shea-nut tree	-
1165	fig tree	mtini, mkpwuyu, mdiryo
1164	shea-butter tree, shea-nut tree	-
1165	fig tree	mtini, mkpwuyu, mdiryo
1166	thorn tree	chigundigundi (Acacia nilotica), chikpwata (Acacia senegalensis), mongololi (Acacia depranolobium)
1167	tamarind tree	mkpwadzu
1168	oil palm	mtsikitsi (Elaeis guineensis)
1169	coconut palm	mnazi (Cocos nucifera)
1170	raffia palm	mlala, mvaale (Raphia ruffia)
1171	date palm	mwambangona (Balanites aegyptica), mtende, uchindu (Phoenix reclinata)
1172	bush	tsatsa, chidzihi

7.1.2 Grasses

1173	grass	linyasi, lifusi
1174	bamboo	mwanzi
1175	reed	gugu, mridza
1176	weeds	kpwekpwe, mbondo

7.2 Plant parts

1177	leaf	kodza, likodza
1178	branch (of tree)	panda
1179	trunk (of tree)	kolo, gogo
1180	bark (of tree)	gopha
1181	sap	ukaka
1182	stump	gutu
1183	root	muzi
1184	bulb, tuber	-
1185	stem, stalk (of maize, millet, etc.)	kolo, mgoti, mlita, buwa
1186	silk, hair (of maize)	-
1187	blade (of grass)	linyasi
1188	flower	ruwa
1189	bud	makodza (n – also leaf), tsephula (v)
1190	shoot (new plant)	mtsatsa
1191	vine	mzabibu
1192	tendril	-
1193	thorn	mwiya
1194	palm branch, frond	mkpwuti, kuti
1195	midrib of palm-frond	m'bati
1196	palm needle	ndifu

7.3 Plant products

7.3.1 Plant product parts

1197	juice	madzi
1198	stone, pit	tembe, mbeyu
1199	regime (of bananas)	humba
1200	corn cob	tsere
1201	kernel (of corn, maize)	chitsa
1202	seed	tembe, mbeyu
1203	skin (of fruit)	gada
1204	shell (of groundnut)	-
1205	corn husk (n)	guguta
1206	chaff	maphephe, suya

7.3.2 Fruits

1207	fruit	tunda
1208	banana	izu, ndizi
1209	plantain	izu, ndizi
1210	lemon	limau, kapu
1211	orange	chungbwa
1212	grapefruit	-

1213	pawpaw, papaya	papali	
1214	pineapple	nanasi	
1215	guava	pera	
1216	avocado	ovakado	
1217	fig	kuyu	
1218	date	tende	

7.3.3 Vegetables

1219	tomato	nyanya
1220	onion	chitunguu
1221	garlic	chitunguu saumu
1222	pepper (green)	pilipili hoho
1223	red pepper, hot pepper	mwatsaka
1224	okra	benda
1225	egg-plant	bunguliya
1226	mushroom	woga

7.3.4 Tubers

1227	cassava, manioc	manga
1228	cocoyam, taro	-
1229	yam	-
1230	sweet potato	muyogbwe
1231	potato	chiazi

7.3.5 Cereals

1232	maize, corn	matsere, pemba
1233	millet (rainy season)	mhama
1234	sorghum (dry season)	-
1235	guinea corn	-
1236	rice	mphunga, mtsele

7.3.6 Other plant products

1237	groundnut, peanut	tendegbwa, ndzugu
1238	sesame seed	ufuha
1239	cola nut	-
1240	palm nut	-
1241	sugar cane	muwa
1242	coffee	kahawa
1243	rubber	mpira
1244	cotton	pamba

7.4 Plant processes

1245	grow (of plants)	meza
1246	sprout (v)	tondomera, tsephula
1247	(be) ripe	(kala) -ivu

1248	ripen, become ripe	ivwa
1249	(be) unripe	(kala) -itsi
1250	(be) rotten	(kala) -ovu
1251	(be) shrivelled, (be) wrinkled (fruit)	mkpwetse (n. e.g. overdry cashew nut)
1252	wither (plant)	nyala, finyalala
1253	blight (n)	-

8 Environment

8.1 Nature

8.1.1 Areas, region

1254	world	dunia, ulimwengu
1255	place	phahali, kpwatu
1256	desert	jangbwa
1257	grassland	vuwe, herera
1258	forest	tsaka
1259	open place, clearing	weruni
1260	bush country, rural area	mitaa, mindani

8.1.2 Physical features

1261	ground, land	tsi
1262	mountain	mwango
1263	summit, highest point	chirere
1264	cliff	mavoromoko
1265	valley	dzeha, mweha, dete, vwasi
1266	ditch	mfumbi, mtaru
1267	pit	dimbwi, dibwa
1268	hole	tundu, kobo
1269	crevice	mwanya
1270	cave	pango

8.1.3 Natural things (minerals, etc.)

1271	rock (large)	jabali, mwamba
1272	stone (small)	dziwe, mwamba
1273	gravel	mtsanga wa mawe
1274	sand	difwiri, mtsanga
1275	dust	vumbi
1276	dirt, soil	mtsanga
1277	clay	ulongo, dongo, gandika
1278	mud	ulongo, matope
1279	iron	chuma
1280	gold	zahabu

1281	silver	feza
1282	copper	shaba
1283	rust (n)	kanga, ng'andu, kutu

8.1.4 Water-related

1284	water	madzi
1285	ocean, sea	bahari
1286	lake	ziya
1287	pool	mtsara
1288	waterhole	mtsara
1289	marsh	dimbwi, gugu
1290	spring	pula
1291	waterfall	poromoko
1292	brook, stream	riko
1293	river	muho
1294	current (river, stream)	mtsirizi (n. any flow of liquid), jera (v. 'flow'), kukusa (v. 'be fast flowing')
1295	riverbed (dry), wadi	swena (v. 'dry up')
1296	river bank	ng'ambo
1297	ford (n)	chivuko
1298	bridge	mdandando, daraja
1299	island	chisiwa
1300	beach	langbwa, ufuwo
1301	wave	imbi
1302	bubble	-
1303	foam	povu, fulo
1304	slime (organic)	-

8.1.5 Fire-related

1305	fire	moho
1306	flame	jimbi
1307	spark	tsetse
1308	smoke	mosi
1309	fireplace	dziko
1310	firewood	kuni
1311	charcoal	makala
1312	ashes	ivu

8.1.6 Sky

1313	sky	mlungu
1314	air (breathed)	hewa
1315	cloud	ingu
1316	rainbow	lukore, chisichi cha mvula
1317	sun	dzuwa

1318	moon	mwezi
1319	full moon	yenga (v) (mwezi unayenga)
1320	new moon	mwezi mtsanga
1321	eclipse (moon)	golowa (v)
1322	star	nyenyezi, nyota
1323	Pleiades	chirimira
1324	Big Dipper, Plough, Great Bear	chisuse, chizimba, gurufu, ndata
1325	Orion	chivungo (Orion's belt)
1326	shooting star, meteor	-

8.1.7 Other

1327	noise, sound (n)	kururu, hoyo, likululu, lichemi
1328	rustle (leaves) (v)	
1329	squeak (wheel) (v)	gbenye-gbenye (idiophone)

8.2 Weather

1330	wind (n)	upepo, phuto
1331	harmattan	kusi
1332	storm	kusi
1333	thunder	chiguru-guru
1334	lightning	umeme, limeme, rumu
1335	rain	mvula
1336	drizzle	churu-churu (adv)
1337	hail	mvula ya mawe
1338	dew	manena
1339	flood (n)	furiko
1340	dry up, evaporate	mumbu
1341	drought, famine	-, ndzala

8.2.1 Seasons

1342	season	majira, msimu, likarare (onset of season)
1343	rainy season	mwaka
1344	dry season	kazikazi
1345	hot weather	dzoho
1346	cold weather	umande

8.2.2 Ambient conditions

1347	light	mwanga, mwangaza
1348	sunshine	(dzuwa)
1349	moonlight	(mwezi)
1350	shadow	chivuri-vuri, pepho
1351	darkness	giza, jiza, chilungu-lungu

8.3 Time

1352	time	wakati, mara, minga, endzi
1353	now	samba, vivi, vino, punde-punde
1354	before	kabla
1355	after	bada ya
1356	early	mapema
1357	late	kaa (v), chelewa (v)
1358	once	(mara mwenga)
1359	again	tsona, chisha
1360	sometimes	mara zanjina
1361	often	mara nyinji
1362	usually	kpwa kawaida
1363	always	siku zosi, wakati wosi
1364	never	dzangbwe
1365	spend time, pass time	sinda, derwa
1366	wait	godza

8.3.1 Time periods

1367	day	siku
1368	month	mwezi
1369	year	mwaka
1370	today	rero
1371	yesterday	dzana
1372	day before yesterday	dzuzi
1373	tomorrow	muhondo, machero
1374	day after tomorrow	kusinda muhondo
1375	olden times	zamani, hipho kare

8.3.2 Times of the day

1376	dawn (before sunrise)	pepho za kucha, chiti
1377	sunrise	limbiti-mbiti, chidani-dani, ligandzi-gandzi
1378	morning	ligundzu, rugundzu
1379	noon	namutsi, mutsi
1380	afternoon	dzuwa ra kutswa, dziloni
1381	sunset	dzuwa richitswa
1382	dusk, twilight (after sunset)	jiza rinaanda
1383	daytime	mutsi, namutsi
1384	night	usiku

8.4 Space and objects

1385	thing	chitu, utu
1386	piece	chisiku

B.1 SIL Comparative African Wordlist

1387	top	chirere
1388	bottom	kotsi
1389	front (of something)	mbere
1390	back (of something)	nyuma
1391	side (of something)	uphande, kanza
1392	middle	kahi-kahi
1393	edge (n)	mkungo, mchechemo, msiso
1394	point (n)	lombo, tsa, atsa, lutsa
1395	bump (n), protuberance	mungu
1396	spot (n)	dowa, bara, chibara

9   Events and actions

9.1   Movement (mostly intransitive)

1397	move (intr)	ambala, tsama ('move home')
1398	movement	-
1399	come	edza
1400	go	phiya
1401	approach (v)	lunga, sengera
1402	arrive	fika, loka, tsoloka
1403	remain, stay	sala, bara, baki
1404	leave (place)	uka
1405	return, go back	uya
1406	go round, detour	zunguluka
1407	enter, go in	injira, menya, phenya
1408	come (or go) out, exit (v)	tuluka, turuka
1409	ascend, go up	ambuka
1410	descend, go down	ara, tserera
1411	fall (intr)	gbwa
1412	swing (v), go back and forth	liya-liya
1413	slide	hereza
1414	roll	pingilika, petuka
1415	spread (disease, fire)	enea, gota, goteza
1416	burst	palika, humbuka, ahuka
1417	disappear	yaya, yoyoma
1418	speed (n)	kasi
1419	(be) fast	mairo, upesi
1420	(be) slow	pore-pore
1421	hasten, hurry	harakisha (vt), henda wanbgwi (vi), kukala na more (vi. hurrying because of strong

9.2 Actions, events affecting matter

9.2.1 General

1422	take	hala, tsukula
1423	snatch, seize	vwatula, nyang'anyira
1424	catch (object in air)	nyaka, gbwira
1425	pick up	tsola
1426	hold	gbwira
1427	raise, lift	unula
1428	lower (tr)	hula
1429	drop (tr)	tsopoza, bwaga
1430	throw	tsupha, urusa
1431	shoot (v)	latsa
1432	knock down, knock over	gbwaga
1433	turn over (tr)	pendula, pekula
1434	pull	vuta, tsomola, vweha
1435	drag	buruta
1436	push	sukuma
1437	steer (v)	lekeza
1438	overtake, pass (tr)	tsapa
1439	surround	zunguluka, zangira, linga-linga
1440	twist	songolosa
1441	fold (v)	kundza
1442	coil (rope) (v)	kuba
1443	hang up	delesa
1444	spread out (maize) (tr)	eneza, goteza
1445	stretch	ntulula, golosa, nyoosha

9.2.2 Percussion

1446	hit, strike	piga, banda
1447	beat	banda
1448	bump (v), knock against	bakula
1449	rub	siriga, suguwa, kirita, fikitsa
1450	scrape (v)	kpwaruta, kuna
1451	scratch (v)	fwaruta, gbwarura
1452	pierce	dunga, kobola, chita
1453	tear (tr)	kpwanyula, ahula
1454	strip off (bark)	yula
1455	shake (tr)	suka, zuguza
1456	squeeze	gandamiza, minya
1457	crush (tr)	bumbundisa, hopeza

9.2.3 Creation and destruction

B.1 SIL Comparative African Wordlist

1458	create, make	unda, umba
1459	alter, change (tr)	galuza
1460	break (tr)	vundza, bonda
1461	destroy, spoil	bananga, angamiza, bomola
1462	(be) ruined, (be) spoiled	banangika, banandzika

9.2.4 Association of things

1463	join, put together	gbwizanya, unga
1464	accumulate	rundika, tsadzira
1465	gather	kusanya, tsola-tsola, tundiza
1466	divide, separate (tr)	ganya, tanya
1467	scatter (tr)	gota
1468	throw away, get rid of	bwaga

9.2.5 Placement

1469	put, place, set	ika, bandika, tiya
1470	leave (something somewhere)	richa
1471	keep, save	ika
1472	hide (tr)	fwitsa, sitiri
1473	lose (tr)	angamiza, yaza
1474	look for	endza, rorera, lorera
1475	find	ona, phaha

9.2.6 Action of wind

1476	blow (of wind) (v)	vuma
1477	blow down	sawa
1478	blow away (intr)	phepheruka
1479	fan (v)	vuvurira

9.2.7 Action with liquids

1480	flow	jera
1481	drip	twena, doda, tona
1482	leak (v)	vudza, omboka
1483	sprinkle	nyunyiza, timvya, nyunyiriza
1484	smear (tr)	paka
1485	dip	vwika
1486	soak	lweka
1487	wring out	minda
1488	dry out (clothes)	anika
1489	float	engelela, elea
1490	sink (v)	tabwika, dodomera, didimiya
1491	drown (intr)	hoha

9.2.8 Action of light

1480	flow	jera

1481	drip	twena, doda, tona
1482	leak (v)	vudza, omboka
1483	sprinkle	nyunyiza, timvya, nyunyiriza

9.2.9 Action of heat, fire

1496	light (fire) (v)	kuta
1497	quench, extinguish	zimya
1498	burn (intr), blaze	aka, phya, tsoma (burn fiercely)
1499	melt (intr)	tsatsamuka, yeyuka, bubudzika
1500	singe	ocha, phya

9.3 Aspect

1501	begin	andza
1502	beginning	chandzo
1503	continue, resume	enderera, dina
1504	end (n)	mwisho
1505	cease, stop	richa, ima
1506	finish, complete (v)	mala, marigiza

10 Quality

10.1 Dimension, shape

1507	(be) big	-kulu, -baha
1508	enlarge	kutula
1509	(be) small	(kala) -dide, -phutsu
1510	diminish	onda, phunguka
1511	(be) high	(kala) dzulu
1512	(be) low	(kala) tsini-tsini
1513	(be) long	(kala) -re, -ire, -refu
1514	lengthen	lungiza
1515	(be) short	(kala) -fupi
1516	shorten	fupisha
1517	(be) fat, (be) thick	nona (v), (kala) -ziho
1518	(be) thin	(kala) -embamba
1519	(be) wide	(kala) -pana
1520	widen	kutula
1521	(be) narrow	(kala) -embamba
1522	(be) deep	(kala) chilindi
1523	deepen	tiga ('dig deep')
1524	(be) shallow	(kala) dzulu-dzulu
1525	(be) flat	(kala) sambarare, sambamba
1526	flatten	laza
1527	(be) hollow	(kala) -huphu
1528	swell (intr)	futuka

B.1 SIL Comparative African Wordlist

1529	(be) round	(kala) -a mviringo
1530	(be) straight	goloka (v), nyooka (v), (kala) chocho, twaa
1531	straighten	golosa, golola, nyoosha
1532	(be) crooked	phongoloka, songoloka
1533	bend, crook, curve (n)	mlingo
1534	(be) heavy	remera, (kala) -ziho
1535	weight	chipimo
1536	(be) light (not heavy)	phepheya

10.2 Feel

1537	(be) sharp	-kali, rya
1538	sharpen (knife)	nola, tiya maso, tiya makali
1539	sharpen, bring to point (arrow)	nola, tiya maso, tiya makali
1540	(be) blunt, dull	fwa
1541	(be) rough	maugu-maugu, karaza
1542	(be) smooth	laini, sirisiri
1543	make smooth	lainisha
1544	(be) hard	(kala) -ifu, -gumu
1546	(be) soft	(kala) -embamba
1547	soften	-
1548	(be) dry	(kala) kavu, -ifu
1549	(be) wet	lwama, zizima
1550	(be) slippery	(kala na) likosi (n), (kala na) uhereza (n)
1551	(be) sticky	nyumbuka
1552	(be) hot (objects)	(kala) dzoho
1553	(be) cold (objects)	zizima, ngota, (kala) zii

10.3 Colour

1555	(be) white	(kala) -ereru, tse-tse-tse
1556	(be) black	(kala) -iru, pi-pi-pi
1557	(be) red	do, do-do-do, (kala) kundu
1558	(be) blue	(kala) -a buluu
1559	(be) green	(kala na) rangi ya linyasi liitsi
1560	(be) brown	(kala na) rangi ya kawiya, rangi ya dongo
1561	(be) yellow	(kala na) rangi ya mandano
1562	(be) dark (colour)	pi-pi-pi, (kala na) rangi ya ini
1562	(be) dark (colour)	pi-pi-pi, (kala na) rangi ya ini

10.4 Taste and smell

1564	taste (n)	mtswano
1565	(be) sweet	(kala) mtswano, hama
1566	(be) sour	(kala) ngbwadu
1567	(be) bitter	(kala) utsungu
1568	odour, smell (n)	harufu

1569	stink, smell (bad)	lovu, kungu, mruche

10.5 Ability

1570	(be) able (to)	weza, turya
1571	(be) strong (physically)	(kala) imara, -ifu, a mkpwotse
1572	strength	imara, nguvu, mkpwotse
1573	(be) weak	(kala) -nyonje
1574	(be) great, (be) powerful	(kala) -enyezi
1575	splendour, glory	nguma

10.6 Value

1576	(be) good	-dzo, -ema, -nono, -zuri
1577	(be) bad	-baya, -i
1578	right, (be) correct	sawa-sawa
1579	truth	ukpweli
1580	(be) perfect	(kala) -kamilifu
1581	(be) wrong	kosa, koseka
1582	(be) beautiful	(kala) -zuri, -nono
1583	(be) ugly	kusahama
1584	(be) clean	(kala) -safi
1585	(be) dirty	(kala) -chafu, tsama
1586	(be) important	(kala) muhimu, -kulu
1587	(be) amusing, funny	(kala) -a kutsekpwa, (kala) na chitseko

10.7 Maturity

1588	(be) new	(kala) -phya
1589	(be) old (not new)	(kala) -a kare

11 Quantity

11.1 Cardinal numbers

1590	one (1)	-mwenga
1591	two (2)	mbiri, -iri
1592	three (3)	tahu, -hahu
1593	four (4)	nne, -ne
1594	five (5)	-tsano
1595	six (6)	sita, -andahu
1596	seven (7)	sabaa, fungahe
1597	eight (8)	-nane
1598	nine (9)	tisiya, chenda
1599	ten (10)	kumi, mrongo
1600	eleven (11)	kumi na mwenga
1601	twelve (12)	kumi na mbiri
1602	thirteen (13)	kumi na tahu

1603	fourteen (14)	kumi na nne
1604	fifteen (15)	kumi na tsano
1605	sixteen (16)	kumi na sita
1606	seventeen (17)	kumi na sabaa
1607	eighteen (18)	kumi na nane
1608	nineteen (19)	kumi na tisiya
1609	twenty (20)	ishirini
1610	twenty-one (21)	ishirini na mwenga
1611	twenty-two (22)	ishirini na mbiri
1612	thirty (30)	salasini
1613	forty (40)	arubaini
1614	fifty (50)	hamsini
1615	sixty (60)	sitini
1616	seventy (70)	sabini
1617	eighty (80)	samanini
1618	ninety (90)	tisini
1619	hundred (100)	gana, mia
1620	two hundred (200)	magana mairi, mia mbiri
1621	five hundred (500)	magana matsano, mia tsano
1622	thousand (1000)	chikwi, elufu

11.2 Ordinal numbers

1623	(be) first	(kala) -a kpwandza, mwandzo
1624	(be) second	(kala) -a phiri
1625	(be) third	(kala) -a hahu
1626	(be) last	(kala) -a mwisho

11.3 Order

1627	add	zidisha, enjereza, dzarigiza
1628	subtract, take away	raphiya
1629	increase (intr)	enjereza
1630	decrease (intr)	phungula
1631	count (v)	tala, isabu, olanga
1632	arrange	panga, tunga
1633	(be) equal	(kala) sawa-sawa, vira-vira, viratu

11.4 Relative quantity

1634	(be) abundant	tosha
1635	enough	bahi, -a kutosha
1636	lack (v)	kosa
1637	(be) used up	sira

11.5 Quantifiers and negation

1638	all	-osi

1639	many	-nji
1640	few	-chache
1641	half	nusu
1642	whole	-osi
1643	everybody	atu osi, chila mutu, chila mmwenga
1644	everything	chila chitu, vitu vyosi
1645	everywhere	phosi
1646	nobody	-
1647	nothing	-

12 Grammatical items

12.1 Pronouns (See chapter 3)

1648	I	mino, mimi
1649	you (masc., sing.)	uwe
1650	he (human)	iye
1651	we (incl.)	sino, sisi, swi, swiswi
1652	you (pl.)	mwino, mwimwi
1653	they (human)	hinyo, aho

12.2 Relationals (See chapter 6)

1654	here	hipha, phapha, hiku, kuku, himu, mumu
1655	there	hipho, phapho, pho, kuko, hiku, himo
1656	far	kure
1657	near	phephi
1658	north	kazikazini
1659	south	kusini, mwakani
1660	east	mashariki, mlairo wa dzuwa
1661	west	mtswerero wa dzuwa
1662	up	dzulu
1663	down	photsi, tsini
1664	forward (direction)	chimbere-mbere
1665	backward (direction)	chinyume-nyume
1666	right (direction)	kuririra, kulume
1667	left (direction)	kuchetu, kumotso, kushoto
1668	over, above	dzulu ya
1669	under, below	tsini ya
1670	in front of, before	mbere ya/za
1671	behind	nyuma ya
1672	beside	kanda ya, kanda-kanda ya
1673	inside	ndani
1674	outside	kondze
1675	between	kahi-kahi
1676	towards	uphande wa, hadi (reaching)

1677	away from	kanda
1678	with	na

12.3 Demonstratives, articles (See chapter 3)

1679	this (man)	hiyu, yuyu, hiye, yuno
1680	that (man)	yuya, hiye
1681	some (men)	-anjina
1682	other (men)	-anjina

12.4 Question words (See chapter 6)

1683	who?	ani? yuphi?
1684	what?	nini? ni?
1685	which (one)?	-ani? –phi?
1686	where?	kuphi? –phi?
1687	when?	rini?
1688	why?	mbona? kpwa utu wani? kpwani? kpwadze?
1689	how?	jinsi? viphi?
1690	how many?	-ngaphi?

12.5 Conjunctions, adverbials, etc. (See chapter 6)

1691	and	na
1692	if	kama, ichikala, kala
1693	because	mana, chisa ni, kpwa sababu
1694	perhaps	labuda, mendzere, medzerepho, chahi
1695	really, truly	kpweli
1696	well (adv)	sawa-sawa, =to
1697	poorly	vyongo-vyongo
1698	only	bahi, tu
1699	yes	hee, oho, sawa, ehe, naam
1700	no	la, a'a (exclamation)

B.2 Botanical names

This list of 113 botanical names was originally published (without the English names) in Nicolle 2002a.[2]

Botanical	Digo	English
Abrus precatorius	Mwamsusumbika	Crab's eyes, coral pea (*Papilionaceae*)
Acacia drepanolobium	Mongololi	Whistling thorn, black/ant-galled acacia
Acacia nilotica	Chigundigundi	Egyptian mimosa, Egyptian thorn, Scented pod acacia
Acacia senegal	Chikpwata	Three-thorned acacia, Sudan gum arabic
Adansonia digitata	Muuyu	Baobab
Aerva lanata	Chivwa	(*Amaranthaceae*)
Afzelia quanzensis	Mbambakofi	Lucky-bean tree, pod mahogany, mahogany tree
Agathisanthemum bojeri	Chivuma nyuchi	(*Rubiaceae*)
Allophylus alnifolius	Mvudzakondo	(*Sapindaceae*)
Amaranthus dubius, Amaranthus graecizans	Chiswenya	Amaranth
Anacardium occidentale	M'bibo	Cashewnut tree
Ananas sativus	Ananasi	Pineapple
Annona senegalensis	M'bokpwe	Wild custard apple, wild soursop
Antidesma venosum	Chikuro, Mdzengatsongo	(*Euphorbiaceae*)
Artabotrys sp., Annona uncinata	Mumbu	(*Annonaceae*)
Artocarpus heterophyllus	Mfenesi	Jackfruit
Asystasia gangetica	Futswe, Futsure, Talakushe	(*Acanthaceae*)
Averrhoa bilimbi	Mbirimbi	(*Oxalidaceae*)
Azadirachta indica	Mkilifi, Mwarobaini	Margosa tree, neem tree
Balanites aegyptiaca	Mwambangoma	Desert date
Bauhinia thonningii	Mtseketse	Camel foot
Blighia unijuguta	Mpwakapwaka	(Lychee family)
Borassus aethiopum	Muvumu	Borassus palm, deleb plant, African fan palm, palmyra palm
Bridelia sp.	Mtsani	Bridelia

---

[2] If the English entry is blank, this means that the English name is either not known or does not exist. If the English entry contains a term in parenthesis, this is the botanical name of a family or sub-family. If the English entry contains both a common English name and a botanical (sub-)family name in parenthesis, this indicates that the English name can be applied to various members of the (sub-)family and not just the specific species designated by the Digo name.

B.2 Botanical names

Cajanus cajun	Mbalazi	Pigeon pea
Canthium glaucum	Myundzu	
Capsicum frutescens	Mwatsaka	Chili pepper
Carica papaya	Mpapali	Papaya, pawpaw
Carissa edulis	Mtambuu	Simple-spined carissa, Carissa
Cassia occidentalis	Muhumba	Stinking weed, wild coffee
Catha edulis	Mvumo	Khat, Abyssinia tea
Catunaregum nilotica	Mdzongodzongo	
Ceiba pentandra	Msufi	Kapok tree
Clerodendrum capitatum	Mbavumbavu	
Coccinia sp.	Mbodoki	Ivy gourd, scarlet gourd
Cocos nucifera	Mnazi	Coconut palm
Coffee arabica	Mkahawa	Coffee tree
Commelina sp.	Dzadza	(*Commelinaceae*)
Commiphora africana	Chibambara	Poison-grub commiphora
Corchorus olitorius	Mlenda, Mrenda, Mwatsaka wa bara	Jute, bush okra, Jew's mallow
Crotalaria sp.	Mkelekele wa nyika	Crotalaria
Cyphostemma adenocaulis	Mwenjeri	(*Ampelidaceae*)
Dalbergia melanoxylon	Mphingo	African blackwood, African ebony
Desmodium velutinum	Chibalazi Mlungu	
Dichrostachys cinerea	Mchinjiri	Sickle bush
Diospyros mespiliformis	Mbara, Mkulu	Jackal berry tree
Dolichos lablab	Mpupu	Lablab
Elaeis guineensis	Mtsikitsi	Wild oil palm, Guinea oil palm
Euclea divinorum	Mdaa	Euclea, diamond-leaved euclea
Fernandoa magnifica	Mulanga	(*Bignoniaceae*)
Flacourtia indica	Mnyondoiya	Governor's plum, Indian plum
Flueggea virosa	Mkpwamba	(*Euphorbiaceae*)
Garcinia livingstonei	Chisambwe, Mfungatsandzu	
Grewia bicolor, Grewia tembensis	Mkone	(*Tiliaceae*)
Harrisonia abyssinica	Chidori	(*Simaroubaceae/ Balanitaceae*)
Harungana madagascariensis	Mbonobono	(*Guttiferae/ Hyperaceae*)
Hoslundia opposita	Mtserere	(*Labiatae*)
Hyphaene compressa	Mkoma	Doum palm
Hyphaene coriacea	Mkoma mlume	Coastal doum palm
Hyphaene paravula	Mkoma muke	Doum palm
Jasmimum sp.	Mtundahofu	(*Oleaceae*)
Keetia zanzibarica	Mnyundzu	

404 — Appendix B: Wordlist and Botanical Names

Lablab purpureus	Mpupu	Hyacinth bean, bonavist bean, lablab bean
Landolphia kirkii	Libugu, Mpira	Rubber vine, Zanzibar rubber tree
Lantana camara	Njasasa	Lantana, Curse of India
Launaea cornuta	Mtsunga	
Lawsonia inermis	Muhina	Henna, Zanzibar bark
Ludwiga jussiaeoides	Murindaziya	
Mangifera indica	Mwembe	Mango tree
Manihot esculenta	Manga	Cassava, manioc
Manilkara sansibarensis	Mung'ambo	(*Sapotaceae*)
Manilkara sulcata	Mndzezi, Mtsedzi	(*Sapotaceae*)
Nymphaea nouchali	Toro	Water lily
Ocimum basilicum	Chivumbasi rahani	Mosquito bush, basil
Ormocarpum sp.	Chitadzi	Caterpillar pod
Ozoroa insignis	Msalasanga	Tropical resin tree
Pandanus sp.	Mkpwadi	Screw pine, walking pine
Phaseolus mungo	Podzo	Mung, green gram
Phoenix reclinata	Uchindu	Wild date palm, Senegal date
Piliostigma thonningii	Mtseketse	Camel foot
Psidium guajava	Mpera	Guava
Raphia ruffia	Mvaale	Raffia palm
Rhizophora mucronata	Mkpwoko	Mangrove
Rhus natalensis, Rhus vulgaris	Mgbwanyahi	Kwa Zulu Natal rhus (*Anacardiaceae*)
Ricinus communis	Mwono	Castor-oil plant
Salvadora persica	Msuwaki	Tooth brush bush, mustard tree
Sanseviera sp.	Konje	(*Agavaceae*)
Sarcostemma viminale	Utundi	(*Asclepiadaceae*)
Sclerocarya birrea, caffra	Mng'ongo	Morula, cider tree
Senecio syringifolius	Reza	(Sunflower family/ *Compositae*)
Sesamum calycinum	Mrenda	Sesame (*Pedaliaceae*)
Sesamum orientale	Ufuha	Sesame, baniseed, sesamum
Sesbania bispinoza	Murindaziya	(*Papilionaceae*)
Solanum sp.	Mtungudza	Black nightshade, wonderberry
Sorghum bicolor	Mhama	Sorghum, Guinea corn
Sorindeia usambarensis	Mkunguma	(*Anacardiaceae*)
Sphaeranthus kirkii	Chivumbani	
Sterculia triphaca	Mugoza	(*Sterculiaceae*)
Strychnos cocculoides (madagascariensis, spinoza)	Muhonga	Elephant orange, monkey orange, spiny monkey ball, corky bark
Synsepalum brevipes	Msami	

B.2 Botanical names

Syzygium cordatum (*Eugenia cordata*), *Syzygium guineense*	Muziahi	Waterberry, water pea (*Myrtaceae*)
Tamarindus indica	Mkpwadzu	Tamarind
Terminalia catappa	Mukungu	Indian almond, tropical almond
Thespia danis	Muhowe	(*Malvaceae*)
Uvaria acuminata	Mudzala, Mumbweni	(*Annonaceae*)
Vangueria infausta	Mviru	False medler, wild medlar
Vernonia cinerea	Chikuse, Chiphatsa	(*Compositae*)
Vigna subterranea	Tendegbwa mawe	Bambarra groundnut, Madagascar groundnut, baffin pea
Vigna unguiculata	Kunde, mtsafwe	Cowpea
Vitex mombassae	Mfundukoma	(*Verbenaceae*)
Ximenia americana	Mtundukula	Wild plum, sour plum, tallow nut
Zanthoxylum chalybeum	Mdungu	Knobwood
Ziziphus mauritiana	Mkunazi	Indian plum, Jujube tree, Chinese date
Ziziphus mucronata (*Ziziphus mitis*)	Mgorodo, Mugugune	Buffalo thorn

Appendix C

The Relationship Between Digo and Swahili

Swahili—both the standard variety taught in Kenyan and Tanzanian schools and used in the local and national media of both countries, and the Kimvita variety spoken in Mombasa town—has exerted a considerable influence on Digo. Swahili is the national and official language of both Tanzania and Kenya[1] and most Digo speakers are also proficient in Swahili.

In Chigato village, where the author lived with his family for four years, proficiency in Swahili was observed to begin at an early age. Most young children were addressed in Swahili by their parents and other adults, and Swahili was used for most peer group interaction up to the age of around seven years old. Although young children had a passive understanding of Digo, since this was the usual language spoken between adults and older children in the home, young children were generally more proficient in Swahili than in Digo. Parents said that they addressed the young children in Swahili to ensure that they would do well at school, where the language of instruction is Swahili even in the youngest classes. However, by the age of ten or eleven, most children had become proficient speakers of Digo and were habitually addressed in Digo by their elders. It appeared that between the ages of seven and ten, most Digo children were allowed to join groups of older children and play beyond the confines of their home compound and immediate neighbours. The older children mainly used Digo among themselves, and the younger members of the groups also started speaking Digo within the group. Digo became, for them, a badge of identity, and the use of Digo in conversation with adults seemed to be a sign that they were beginning to be accepted into adult society.

---

[1] In Kenya, Swahili is an official language of the country alongside English.

There is little evidence of any shift from Digo to Swahili in an absolute sense, but exposure to Swahili from an early age and the dominance of Swahili in many social domains inevitably has some effect on how people speak Digo. This is noticeable in the vocabulary and grammar of Digo, and to a lesser extent in pronunciation. In the following sections I will briefly address these three areas.

C.1 Swahili influence on Digo vocabulary

The extent of borrowing from Swahili is not as great as has been previously supposed. For example, Hinnebusch (1999:182) lists eleven 'core' (i.e. basic) words in Digo which have been borrowed from Swahili, together with the corresponding words used in other Mijikenda languages (excluding Digo), claiming that the Swahili loan words have replaced the Mijikenda words in Digo. These are listed in table C.1 (spelling has been adapted from the original).

Table C.1. Swahili loans in Digo listed in Hinnebusch (1999) with attested Digo forms

Swahili loan	Gloss	Other Mijikenda	Mwalonya et al. (2012) entry
-baya	bad	-ii	-baya (bad); -i (bad, evil)
-ema	good[a]	-dzo	-ema; -dzo (also -nono and -zuri)
-fupi	short	-fuhi/-futi	-fupi
-refu	long	-re	both occur
-zee	old[b]	-tumia	mzee (old person); mtumiya (a)[c] (old person); utumiya (old age)
damu	blood	milatso	damu (-); mlatso (mi)
mfupha	bone	musoza	mfupha (mi); msoza (mi)
mguru (mi)	leg[d]	gulu (ma or vi)	chigulu (vi); chiguru (ma); gulu (ma)
nyota	star	nyenyezi	both occur
yai	egg	iji/tumbi	yayi (ma); tumbi (ma)
pika	cook	gita/jita	jita; biya; vuga (but not pika)

[a] The adjectives -ema and -zee only occur in restricted contexts: -ema is more frequent in Tanzanian than in Kenyan Digo but is one of four almost synonymous terms in common usage (-zuri is also of Swahili origin).
[b] -zee and -tumiya can only refer to humans, the usual term for 'old' being -a kare.
[c] Forms in parentheses indicate the plural form of nouns.
[d] The various words for 'leg (of a person)' are all in noun classes 5/6 or 7/8 whereas the supposed Swahili loan word is in class 3.

However, as the final column shows, out of the eleven illustrative Mijikenda forms supposedly replaced by Swahili loan words in Digo, ten are in fact listed in the Digo-English-Swahili dictionary of Mwalonya et al. (2012) (only -fuhi/-futi does not occur). In nine of the eleven rows, both the 'Swahili' and 'Mijikenda' forms were listed in Mwalonya et al. (2012) either as synonyms or near synonyms. Certain dialects and individual speakers typically show a preference for one word over another (for example, speakers nearer the coast tend to use more words of Swahili origin than speakers from further inland), but most speakers know—and many will use—both words.

C.2 Possible Swahili influence on Digo grammar

I will briefly describe ongoing changes affecting the use of demonstratives and the noun class system, both of which are tending to make Digo more similar to Swahili and which may reflect the influence of Swahili on speakers of Digo.

C.2.1 Demonstratives

Digo has more demonstrative forms than Swahili; each Swahili noun has three potential demonstrative forms, whereas each Digo noun has four basic demonstrative forms (or 'series'), three of which have variants, plus short forms of some of these.[2] The class 1 demonstratives in Swahili and Digo are listed in table C.2.

Table C.2. Swahili and Digo demonstratives

Swahili	Digo
huyu proximal	*hiyu* proximal
	yuyu proximal, variant form
	yu proximal short variant form
huyo nonproximal or 'anaphoric'	*hiye* nonproximal
	ye nonproximal, variant form
yule distal	*yuya/huya* distal
	yuyatu distal variant form
n/a	*yuno* 'metarepresentational'

It is usually only older speakers who know how to use all or most of the Digo demonstratives. For example, one very old man from a village near Kwale used each of the demonstratives listed here (apart from *huya*) in a single story. In contrast, stories told by younger speakers (aged between 30 and 50) usually contained only 3 or 4 of these demonstratives, and never all of them. This suggests that younger speakers of Digo may have control of a restricted subset of demonstratives. If this is the case, and if these younger speakers do not develop competency in the full range of demonstrative forms later in life, then it is likely that the range of demonstratives in Digo will become reduced resulting in a simpler system of demonstratives, similar to that used in Swahili.

---

[2] See §3.4 for a detailed discussion of Digo demonstratives.

C.2.2 Noun class system

The noun classes of Digo and Swahili are identical, except for some singular-plural pairings and the fact that Digo has both noun class 11, distinguished by the prefix *li-*,[3] and noun class 14, distinguished by the prefix *u-*, whereas in Swahili noun class 11 has been merged into noun class 14. There is some evidence that noun class 11 may be in the process of being absorbed into noun class 14 in Digo also.

First, in some words either the *li-* (class 11) prefix or the *u-* (class 14) prefix can be used with no change of meaning, e.g. *lichigo* and *uchigo* (both mean 'fence'). Second, there is considerable free variation in the plural forms of class 11 nouns. Most plural forms of nouns in class 11 are class 10 nouns which characteristically either have no prefix or have a prefix beginning with a homorganic nasal:

liga 'clay bowl' cl.11	*mbiga* 'clay bowls' cl.10
linyasi 'blade of grass' cl.11	*nyasi* 'grass' cl.10

When the first sound after the *li-* prefix is [β] (represented orthographically as /ph/), the class 10 plural form usually begins with *p*, but there is some variation:

liphazi 'ladle' cl.11	*pazi* 'ladles' cl.10
liphyero 'broom' cl.11	*pyero* or *phyero* 'brooms' cl.10

However, other words in class 11 are made plural by adding the noun class 6 prefix *ma-*, and the class 11 *li-* prefix is sometimes retained. This includes some words which can also take class 10 plurals:

liphungo 'twig, cutting' cl.11	*maphungo* 'twigs, cuttings' cl.6
liphazi 'ladle' cl.11	*maliphazi* 'ladles' cl.6
	or *pazi* 'ladles' cl.10

The fact that Digo speakers' use of noun class 11 has become so variable suggests that it no longer constitutes a distinct, stable category and may be close to being lost from the language. In particular, the fact that the *li-* prefix is retained in some class 6 plurals indicates that it is being treated as part of the noun stem rather than as a noun class prefix[4] in some contexts by some speakers. When there is no longer any agreement on how to use these kinds of nouns, their distinctive forms may well stop being used and words currently in noun class 11 will come to function in either class 5/6, class 9/10 or class 14. The result would be a noun class system almost identical to that in Swahili.

---

[3] This is not the prefix for class 5, as in some Bantu languages. In Digo, the prefix for class 5 is *dz-/Ø*.
[4] Singular forms of plural nouns in noun class 6 are usually in noun class 5, which for most words does not have a noun class prefix.

C.3 Possible Swahili influence on Digo pronunciation

Most Bantu languages exhibit lexical and grammatical tone, but Swahili (along with some other languages of Guthrie's Zone G) is a stress-accent language (Clark 1988) in which the penultimate syllable of each word receives a nontonal accent in the form of relatively higher pitch.[5] Digo also has stress on the penultimate syllable of words (realized as increased length sometimes accompanied by increased amplitude and higher than normal pitch), but this need not be due to the influence of Swahili, as many Bantu languages have stress-accent (usually on the penult), often in combination with tonal properties (Downing 2004). However, the functional load of tone in Digo is low, in the sense that there are very few lexical or grammatical distinctions which are dependent on tone. As noted in chapter 2, the Digo orthography only marks tone in a few very specific cases, and comprehension is not adversely affected by the lack of tone marking. It is possible that the loss of tonal distinctions in Digo is, at least in part, due to the influence of (nontonal) Swahili. That said, the prosody of Digo (in laymen's terms, the Digo accent) is quite distinct from that of Swahili.

---

[5]The term 'pitch-accent' is sometimes used to describe the use of pitch to give prominence to a syllable, or to describe languages in which only one syllable in any given word can be tone-bearing. I have avoided using the term here because there is no widely accepted definition of what pitch-accent is; Hyman (2006) argues that pitch-accent languages exhibit a range of systems which share some of the properties of tone-accent and stress-accent systems to differing degrees without there being a single pitch-accent prototype.

Appendix D

Publications on Digo Language and Culture

(These publications relate specifically to the language and culture of the Digo people but are not listed in References and are not cited in the text.)

Bible Translation and Literacy. 2007. *Chilagane Chiphya* [The New Testament in the Digo language of Kenya]. Nairobi: Bible Translation and Literacy.
Boerma, Ties. 1989. Maternal and child health in an ethnomedical perspective: Traditional and modern medicine in Kwale. Ms. UNICEF.
Dammann, Ernst. 1960a. Ein Nachtrag zur Geschichte der Digo [An addendum to the history of the Digo]. *Afrika und Übersee* 44:37–40.
Dammann, Ernst. 1960b. Schwangerschaft, Geburt und Aufzucht der Kleinkinder bei den Digo [Pregnancy, birth, and rearing of infants among the Digo]. *Afrika und Übersee* 44:93–109.
Eisemon, Thomas O., and Ali Wasi. 1987. Koranic schooling and its transformation in coastal Kenya. *International Journal of Educational Development* 7:89–98.
Gerlach, Luther P. 1963. Traders on bicycle: A study of entrepreneurship and culture change among the Digo and Duruma in Kenya. *Sociologus* 13:32–49.
Gerlach, Luther P. 1965a. Nutrition in its sociocultural matrix: Food getting and using along the east African coast. In David Brockensha (ed.), *Ecology and economic development in tropical Africa*, 245–268. Berkeley: Institute of International Studies, University of California.
Gerlach, Luther P. 1965b. Nyika. *Encyclopedia Britannica* XVI:809–810.
Gomm, Roger. 1972. Harlots and bachelors: Marital instability among the coastal Digo of Kenya. *Man* 7:95–113.

Gomm, Roger. 1975. Bargaining from weakness: Spirit possession on the south Kenya coast. *Man* 10.4:530-543.

Kayamba, H. M. T. 1947. Notes on the Wadigo. *Tanganyika Notes and Records* 23:80-96.

Lundeby, Erling Andreas. 1993. The Digo of the south Kenyan coast: Description and annotated bibliography. MTh thesis. Fuller Theological Seminary, Pasadena.

Mutoro, Henry W. 1987. An archeological study of the Mijikenda 'Kaya' settlements on hinterland Kenya coast. PhD dissertation. University of California at Los Angeles.

Nicolle, Steve. 2001. A comparative study of ethnobotanical taxonomies: KiSwahili and ChiDigo. *Notes on Anthropology* 5.1:33-43.

Nicolle, Steve. 2002. Anaphora and focus in Digo. In A. Branco, T. McEnery, and R. Mitkov (eds.), *Proceedings of the 4th Discourse Anaphora and Anaphora Resolution Colloquium (DAARC 2002)*, 141-146. Lisbon: Edições Colibri.

Nicolle, Steve. 2004. The relevance of ethnobotanical studies to linguistic vitality: The case of plant use and classification among the Digo of Kenya. *University of Nairobi Occasional Papers in Linguistics* 2:86-103.

Nicolle, Steve. 2012. Semantic-pragmatic change in Bantu –no demonstrative forms. *Africana Linguistica* 18:193-233.

Nicolle, Steve. 2014. Discourse functions of demonstratives in eastern Bantu narrative texts. *Studies in African Linguistics* 43(2):113-132. https://journals.flvc.org/sal/article/view/107265.

Nicolle, Steve. 2015a. Digo narrative discourse. *SIL Language and Culture Documentation and Description 26*. https://www.sil.org/resources/archives/61297.

Nicolle, Steve. 2015b. Variation in the expression of information structure in eastern Bantu languages. In Doris L. Payne, Sara Pacchiarotti, and Mokaya Bosire (eds.), *Diversity in African languages: Selected papers from the 46th Annual Conference on African Linguistics*, 377-394. Berlin: Language Science Press. https://langsci-press.org/catalog/book/121.

Patel, L. R. 1965. Notes on the law of succession in three Kenya coastal tribes: Wadigo, Waduruma and Wagiriama. *East African Law Journal* 1:184-190.

Sperling, David C. 1970. Some aspects of Islamization in East Africa with particular reference to the Digo in southern Kenya. Paper no. 10. Nairobi: Department of History, University of Nairobi.

Sperling, David C. 1985. Islamization in the coastal region of Kenya to the end of the nineteenth century. In Bethwell A. Ogot (ed.), *Kenya in the 19th Century*, 33-82. Nairobi: Bookwise and Anyange Press.

Sperling, David C. 1988. The growth of Islam among the Mijikenda of the Kenya coast, 1826-1933. PhD dissertation. School of Oriental and African Studies, University of London.

Sperling, David C. 1993. Rural *madrasas* of the southern Kenya coast, 1971-92. In Louis Brenner (ed.), *Muslim Identity and Social Change in Sub-Saharan Africa*, 198-209. London: Hurst and Company.

Zani, Z. M. S. 1954. A comparative note on the possessive in Chi-Digo. *Journal of the East Africa Swahili Committee* 24:58-59.

References

Amidu, Assibi A. 2001. *Argument and predicate relations in Kiswahili*. Köln: Rüdiger Köppe.
Andrews, Avery. 2007. The major functions of the noun phrase. In Shopen, 132–223.
Bastin, Yvonne, and Thilo C. Schadeberg, eds. 2003. Bantu lexical reconstructions 3. Accessed 21 June 2011. http://www.metafro.be/blr.
Bearth, Thomas. 2003. Syntax. In Nurse and Philippson (2003), 121–142.
Beidelman, T. O. 1967. *The matrilineal peoples of Eastern Tanzania*. Ethnographic Survey of Africa: East Central Africa, Part XVI. London: International African Institute.
Bentley, Mayrene, and Andrew Kulemeka. 2001. *Chichewa*. München: Lincom Europa.
Besha, Ruth Mfumbwa. 1989. *A study of tense and aspect in Shambala*. Berlin: Reimer.
Bergman, Jeanne L. 1988. Symbol, spirit, and social organization: A comparative study of Islam and indigenous religion among two Mijikenda peoples. Paper No. 182 presented at the Institute of African Studies, University of Nairobi, 18 February 1988.
Botne, Robert. 1999. Future and distal -*ka*-'s: Proto-Bantu or nascent form(s)? In Hombert and Hyman, 473–515.
Bourdin, Philippe. 1992. Constance et inconstances de la déicticité: La resémantisation des marqueurs andatifs et ventifs. In M-A. Morel and L. Danon-Boileau (eds.), *La deixis: Colloque en Sorbonne 8-9 juin 1990*, 287–307. Paris: Presses Universitaires de France.
Bourdin, Philippe. 2000. À propos des 'futurs' ventifs et itifs: Remarques sur un paradoxe. *Verbum* 22:293–311.
Bresnan, Joan, and Jonni M. Kanerva. 1989. Locative inversion in Chichewa: A case study of factorization in grammar. *Linguistic Inquiry* 20:1–50.

Bybee, Joan. 1985. *Morphology: A study of the relation between meaning and form.* Typological Studies in Language 9. Amsterdam: John Benjamins.

Cammenga, Jelle. 2004. *Igikuria phonology and morphology: A Bantu language of south-west Kenya and north-west Tanzania.* Köln: Rüdiger Köppe.

Clark, Mary. 1988. An accentual analysis of the Zulu noun. In H. van der Hulst and N. Smith (eds.), *Autosegmental studies on pitch accent,* 51–79. Dordrecht: Foris.

Cole, Desmond T. 1955. *An introduction to Tswana grammar.* Cape Town: Longman.

Comrie, Bernard. 1985. *Tense.* Cambridge: Cambridge University Press.

Costello, John R. 2003. The evolution of prepositions in Mayan and Indo-European: A case of reducing ambiguity. In Mary Ruth Wise, Thomas N. Headland, and Ruth M. Brend (eds.), *Language and life: Essays in memory of Kenneth L. Pike,* 483–511. Dallas: SIL International and University of Texas at Arlington.

Croft, William. 1990. A conceptual framework for grammatical categories (or, a taxonomy of propositional acts). *Journal of Semantics* 7:245–279.

Croft, William. 2001. *Radical construction grammar: Syntactic theory in typological perspective.* Oxford: Oxford University Press.

Crystal, David. 1991. *A dictionary of linguistics and phonetics.* Third edition. Oxford: Blackwell.

Dammann, Ernst. 1938. Erzählungen eines Digo zur Geschichte seines Stammes [Tales of a Digo about the history of his tribe]. *Zeitschrift für Eingeborenen Sprachen* 29:293–311.

Dammann, Ernst. 1944. Zur Geschichte der Digo [On the history of the Digo]. *Zeitschrift für Eingeborenen Sprachen* 34:53–69.

Dancygier, Barbara, and Eve Sweetser. 2005. *Mental spaces in grammar: Conditional constructions.* Cambridge Studies in Linguistics 108. Cambridge: Cambridge University Press.

Daniel, Michael, and Edith Moravcsik. 2013. The associative plural. In Matthew S. Dryer and Martin Haspelmath (eds.), *The world atlas of language structures online.* Leipzig: Max Planck Institute for Evolutionary Anthropology. Accessed 18 August 2021. http://wals.info/chapter/36.

de Groot, Martien. 1988a. Description of the Digo verb system. Appendix 6 to the Progress Report 1988 of the Research Project "Bible Translation and Literacy in the Digo Language." Nairobi: Bible Translation and Literacy.

de Groot, Martien. 1988b. Habitual aspect in Digo. Ms. Nairobi: Bible Translation and Literacy.

Demuth, Katherine, and Sheila Mmusi. 1997. Presentational focus and thematic structure in comparative Bantu. *Journal of African Languages and Linguistics* 18:1–19.

Devos, Maud. 2008. *A grammar of Makwe (Palma, Mozambique).* München: Lincom Europa.

Dimmendaal, Gerrit J. 1983. *The Turkana language.* Dordrecht: Foris.

Dixon, R. M. W. 1991. *A new approach to English grammar, on semantic principles.* Oxford: Clarendon Press.

Doke, Clement M. (1930) 1990. *Textbook of Zulu grammar.* Cape Town: Maskew Miller Longman.
Doke, Clement M. 1931. *A comparative study in Shona phonetics.* Johannesburg: University of the Witwatersrand Press.
Doke, Clement M. 1935. *Bantu linguistic terminology.* London: Longman, Green & Co.
Downing, Laura J. 2004. What African languages tell us about accent typology. *ZAS Papers in Linguistics* 37:101–136.
Dryer, Matthew S. 1997a. Are grammatical relations universal? In Joan Bybee, John Haiman, and Sandra A. Thompson (eds.), *Essays on language function and language type,* 115–143. Amsterdam: John Benjamins.
Dryer, Matthew S. 1997b. On the six-way word order typology. *Studies in Language* 21:69–103.
Dryer, Matthew S. 2007a. Clause types. In Shopen, 224–275.
Dryer, Matthew S. 2007b. Word order. In Shopen, 61–131.
Elderkin, Edward D. 2003. Herero. In Nurse and Philippson (2003), 581–608.
Erteschik-Shir, Nomi. 2007. *Information structure: The syntax-discourse interface.* Oxford: Oxford University Press.
Fauconnier, Gilles. 1994. *Mental spaces: Aspects of meaning construction in natural language.* Second edition. Cambridge, MA: Cambridge University Press. First edition 1985. Cambridge, MA: MIT Press.
Fleisch, Axel. 2000. *Lucazi grammar: A morphosemantic analysis.* Köln: Rüdiger Köppe.
Fleisch, Axel. 2005. Agent phrases in Bantu passives. In F. K. Erhard Voeltz (ed.), *Studies in African linguistic typology,* 93–111. Amsterdam: John Benjamins.
Floor, Sebastian. 2002. The -ki- tense-aspects in Mwani. *Afrikanistische Arbeitspapiere* 70:141–166.
Foley, William A., and Robert D. Van Valin, Jr. 1984. *Functional syntax and universal grammar.* Cambridge: Cambridge University Press.
Garashi, Maliki, Joseph Mwalonya, and Alison Nicolle, eds. 2007. *Utamaduni wa Mdigo* [Digo culture]. Nairobi: Bible Translation and Literacy.
Gerlach, Luther P. 1961. The social organization of the Digo of Kenya. PhD dissertation. University of London.
Gillette, Cynthia. 1978. A test of the concept of backwardness: A case study of Digo society in Kenya. PhD dissertation. Cornell University.
Givón, Talmy. 1970. *An outline of the grammatical structure of Central Bantu languages: A field manual.* Los Angeles: UCLA.
Güldemann, Tom. 2002. When 'say' is not say: The functional versatility of the Bantu quotative marker *ti* with special reference to Shona. In Tom Güldemann and Manfred von Roncador (eds.), *Reported discourse: A meeting ground for different linguistic domains,* 253–287. Amsterdam: John Benjamins.
Güldemann, Tom. 2003. Grammaticalization. In Nurse and Philippson (2003), 182–194.

Gundel, Jeanette. K. 1988. Universals of topic-comment structure. In Michael Hammond, Edith A. Moravcsik, and Jessica Werth (eds.), *Studies in syntactic typology*, 209–239. Amsterdam: John Benjamins.

Guthrie, Malcolm. 1967–1971. *Comparative Bantu: An introduction to the comparative linguistics and prehistory of the Bantu languages*, 4 vols. Farnborough: Gregg International.

Harjula, Lotta. 2004. *The Ha language of Tanzania*. Köln: Rüdiger Köppe.

Heimerdinger, Jean-Marie. 1999. Topic, focus and foreground in Ancient Hebrew narratives. *Journal for the Study of the Old Testament: Supplement Series 295*.

Heine, Bernd, Ulrike Claudi, and Friederike Hünnemeyer. 1991. *Grammaticalization: A conceptual framework*. Second edition. Chicago: University of Chicago Press.

Heine, Bernd, Tom Güldemann, Christa Kilian-Hatz, Donald A. Lessau, Heinz Roberg, Mathias Schladt, and Thomas Stolz, eds. 1993. *Conceptual shift. A lexicon of grammaticalization processes in African languages*. Afrikanistische Arbeitspapiere, 34–35. Köln: Institut fur Afrikanistik.

Heine, Bernd, and Tania Kuteva. 2002. *World lexicon of grammaticalization*. Cambridge: Cambridge University Press.

Hewson, John, Derek Nurse, and Henry Muzale. 2000. Chronogenetic staging of tense in Ruhaya. *Studies in African Linguistics* 29:33–56.

Hinnebusch, Thomas J. 1973. Prefixes, sound change, and sub-grouping in the coastal Kenyan Bantu languages. PhD dissertation. UCLA.

Hinnebusch, Thomas J. 1999. Contact and lexicostatistics in comparative Bantu studies. In Hombert and Hyman, 173–205.

Hollis, A. C. 1900. Notes on the history of Vumba, East Africa. *Journal of the Anthropological Institute* 30:275–297.

Hombert, Jean-Marie, and Larry M. Hyman, eds. 1999. *Bantu historical linguistics: Theoretical and empirical perspectives*. Stanford, CA: CSLI Publications.

Hopper, Paul J. 1982. Aspect between discourse and grammar. In Paul J. Hopper (ed.), *Tense-aspect: Between semantics and pragmatics*, 3–18. Amsterdam: John Benjamins.

Hyman, Larry M. 1999. The historical interpretation of vowel harmony in Bantu. In Hombert and Hyman, 235–295.

Hyman, Larry M. 2006. Word-prosodic typology. *Phonology* 23:225–257.

Keenan, Edward and Bernard Comrie. 1977. Noun phrase accessibility and universal grammar. *Linguistic Inquiry* 8:63–99. Reprinted in Keenan, Edward L. 1987. *Universal grammar: 15 essays*, 3–46. London: Croom Helm.

Kimenyi, Alexandre. 1980. *A relational grammar of Kinyarwanda*. Berkeley: University of California Press.

Kipacha, Ahmadi. 2006. The impact of the morphological alternation of subject markers on tense/aspect: The case of Swahili. *ZAS Papers in Linguistics* 43:81–96.

Kisseberth, Charles W. 1984. Digo tonology. In George N. Clements and J. Goldsmith (eds.), *Autosegmental studies in Bantu tone*, 105–182. Dordrecht: Foris.

Kozinskij, Isaak Š. 1988. Resultative: Results and discussion. In Vladimir P. Nedjalkov (ed.), *Typology of resultative constructions*, 497–525. Amsterdam: John Benjamins.

Lambert, H. E. 1957. *Ki-Vumba: A dialect of the southern Kenya coast*. Studies in Swahili dialects II. Kampala: East African Swahili committee.

Lambrecht, Knud. 1994. *Information structure and sentence form*. Cambridge Studies in Linguistics 71. Cambridge: Cambridge University Press.

Lambrecht, Knud, and Laura A. Michaelis. 1998. On sentence accent in information questions. In Jean-Pierre Koenig (ed.), *Discourse and cognition: Bridging the gap*, 387–402. Stanford: CSLI.

Levinsohn, Stephen H. 2000. *Discourse features of New Testament Greek: A coursebook on the information structure of New Testament Greek*. Second edition. Dallas: SIL International.

Levinsohn, Stephen H. 2002. Towards a typology of additives. *Afrikanistische Arbeitspapiere* 69:171–188.

Levinsohn, Stephen H. 2004. Self-instruction materials on narrative discourse analysis. Ms. Dallas: SIL International.

Lewis, M. Paul, ed. 2009. *Ethnologue: Languages of the world*. Sixteenth edition. Dallas: SIL International. Online version: http://www.ethnologue.com/.

Lichtenberk, F. 1991. On the gradualness of grammaticalization. In Elizabeth Closs Traugott and Bernd Heine (eds.), *Approaches to grammaticalization*. Vol. I, 37–80. Amsterdam: John Benjamins.

Longacre, Robert E. 1990. *Storyline concerns and word order typology in East and West Africa*. Studies in African Linguistics, Supplement 10. Los Angeles: University of California.

Maganga, Clement. 1990. A study of the morphophonology of Standard Swahili, Kipemba, Kitumbatu and Kimakunduchi. PhD dissertation. University of Dar es Salaam.

Maho, Jouni. 2003. A classification of the Bantu languages: An update of Guthrie's referential system. In Nurse and Philippson (2003), 639–651.

Marten, Lutz. 2006. Locative inversion in Otjiherero: More on morphosyntactic variation in Bantu. *ZAS Papers in Linguistics* 43:97–122.

Marten, Lutz, Nancy C. Kula, and Nhlanhla Thwala. 2007. Parameters of morphosyntactic variation in Bantu. *Transactions of the Philological Society* 105:253–338.

Mchombo, Sam. 2004. *The syntax of Chichewa*. Cambridge: Cambridge University Press.

Meeussen, Achilles Emile. 1967. Bantu grammatical reconstructions. *Annalen van het Koninklijk Museum voor Midden-Afrika* 61:79–121.

Miller, George A. and Philip Johnson-Laird. 1976. *Language and perception*. Cambridge: Cambridge University Press.

Möhlig, Wilhelm J. G. 1992. Language death and the origin of strata: Two case studies of Swahili dialects. In Matthias Brenzinger (ed.), *Language death: Factual and theoretical explanations with special reference to East Africa*, 157–179. Berlin: Mouton de Gruyter.

Morimoto, Yukiko. 2006. Agreement properties and word order in comparative Bantu. *ZAS Papers in Linguistics* 43:161–187.

Mous, Maarten. 2003. *The making of a mixed language: The case of Ma'a/Mbugu.* Amsterdam: John Benjamins.

Mous, Maarten. 2004. *A grammatical sketch of Mbugwe: Bantu F34, Tanzania.* Köln: Rüdiger Köppe.

Mwalonya, Joseph, Alison Nicolle, Steve Nicolle, and Juma Zimbu, comps. 2012. *Mgombato: Digo-Swahili-English dictionary.* Second edition. Köln: Rüdiger Köppe Verlag.

Nedjalkov, Vladimir P., ed. 1988. *Typology of resultative constructions.* Amsterdam: John Benjamins.

Nicolle, Steve. 2000. Markers of general interpretive use in Amharic and Swahili. In Gisle Andersen and Thorstein Fretheim (eds.), *Pragmatic markers and propositional attitude.* Pragmatics and Beyond New Series 79, 173–188. Amsterdam: John Benjamins.

Nicolle, Steve. 2002a. *Mihi ihumirwayo ni Adigo.* [Plants used by the Digo people: A Digo ethnobotany]. Kwale, Kenya: Digo Language and Literacy Project.

Nicolle, Steve. 2002b. The grammaticalisation of movement verbs in Digo and English. *Révue de Sémantique et Pragmatique* 11:47–68.

Nicolle, Steve. 2003. Distal aspects in Bantu languages. In Katarzyna Jaszczolt and Ken Turner (eds.), *Meaning through language contrast.* Vol. 2. Pragmatics and Beyond New Series 100, 3–22. Amsterdam: John Benjamins.

Nicolle, Steve. 2006. Review of The making of a mixed language: The case of Ma'a/Mbugu, by M. Mous. *Journal of African Languages and Linguistics* 27:99–105.

Nicolle, Steve. 2007a. The grammaticalization of tense markers: A pragmatic reanalysis. *Cahiers Chronos* 17, 47–65.

Nicolle, Steve. 2007b. Metarepresentational demonstratives in Digo. In Randi Alice Nilsen, Nana Aba Appiah Amfo, and Kaja Borthen (eds.), *Interpreting utterances: Pragmatics and its interfaces. Essays in honour of Thorstein Fretheim,* 127–146. Oslo: Novus.

Nicolle, Steve. 2007c. Textual functions of Chidigo demonstratives. *SOAS Working Papers in Linguistics* 15:159–171.

Nicolle, Steve. 2012. Diachrony and grammaticalization. In Robert I. Binnick (ed.), *The Oxford handbook of tense and aspect,* 370–397. Oxford: Oxford University Press.

Nurse, Derek. 1982. Segeju and Daisu: A case study of evidence from oral tradition and comparative linguistics. *History in Africa* 9:175–208.

Nurse, Derek. 1999. Towards a historical classification of East African Bantu languages. In Hombert and Hyman, 1–41.

Nurse, Derek. 2000. *Inheritance, contact, and change in two East African languages.* Köln: Rüdiger Köppe.

Nurse, Derek. 2008. *Tense and aspect in Bantu.* Oxford: Oxford University Press.

Nurse, Derek, and Thomas Hinnebusch. 1993. *Swahili and Sabaki: A linguistic history.* UC Publications in Linguistics 121. Berkeley: University of California Press.

Nurse, Derek, and Gérard Philippson, eds. 2003. *The Bantu languages.* London: Routledge.

Nurse, Derek, and Gérard Philippson. 2006. Common tense-aspect markers in Bantu. *Journal of African Languages and Linguistics* 27:153–194.

Nurse, Derek, and Martin Walsh. 1992. Chifundi and Vumba: Partial shift, no death. In Matthias Brenzinger (ed.), *Language death: Factual and theoretical explorations with special reference to East Africa,* 181–212. Berlin: Mouton de Gruyter.

Nyembwe, Ali Madzi, and Rodgers Maneno. 2002. *Nia Mwenga anaphaha uliwali* [Folk stories and proverbs]. Kwale, Kenya: Digo Language and Literacy Project.

Paluku, André Mbula. 1998. *Description grammatical du Kitalinga: Langue Bantu du nord-est du Zaïre.* München: Lincom Europa.

Prince, Ellen. 1981. Topicalization, focus-movement, and Yiddish-movement: A pragmatic differentiation. *Proceedings of the Seventh Annual Meeting of the Berkeley Linguistics Society.* BLS 7, 249–264.

Pullum, Geoffrey K., and William A. Ladusaw. 1996. *Phonetic symbol guide.* Second edition. Chicago: University of Chicago Press.

Riedel, Kristina. 2002. The tense-aspect system of KiNungwi. Ms. Department of the Languages and Cultures of Africa, SOAS.

Riedel, Kristina. 2006. Demonstrative noun orders and DP internal focus. Paper presented at Bantu Grammar: Description and Theory, SOAS, 20–22 April 2006.

Rose, Sarah, Christa Beaudoin-Lietz, and Derek Nurse. 2002. *A glossary of terms for Bantu verbal categories.* München: Lincom Europa.

Rugemalira, Josephat M. 2002. *Orunyambo: Runyambo-Kiswahili-English lexicon.* Dar es Salaam: University of Dar es Salaam.

Sacleux, Ch. 1909. *Grammaire des dialectes Swahilis.* Paris.

Sasse, Hans-Jürgen. 1987. The thetic/categorical distinction revisited. *Language* 25:511–580.

Schadeberg, Thilo C. 1977. Der Kohortativ 'Dual' und plural in den Bantusprachen. In W. Voigt (ed.), *Deutscher Orientalistentag vom 28. September bis 4 Oktober 1975 in Freiburg im Breisgau: Vorträge. Zeitschrift der Deutschen Morgenländischen Gesellschaft Supplementa,* 1502–1507.

Schadeberg, Thilo C. 2003. Derivation. In Nurse and Philippson (2003), 71–89.

Schadeberg, Thilo C. 2006. Expressing comparison in Swahili: Description and typology. Paper presented at Bantu Grammar: Description and Theory, SOAS, 20–22 April 2006.

Schultze-Berndt, Eva. 2006. Taking a closer look at function verbs: Lexicon, grammar, or both? In Felix K. Ameka, Alan Dench, and Nicholas Evans (eds.), *Catching language: The standing challenge of grammar writing,* 359–391. Berlin: Mouton de Gruyter.

Shopen, Timothy, ed. 2007. *Language typology and syntactic description.* Vol. III, *Grammatical categories and the lexicon.* Second edition. Cambridge: Cambridge University Press.

Sirya, Stephen T., J. Muramba, Stephen Nzomo, A. Mtawali, and R. P. Margetts. 1993. *The verbal morphology of Kigiryama*. Nairobi: Bible Translation and Literacy.

Snider, Keith L., and James S. Roberts. 2006. *SIL comparative African wordlist (SILCAWL)*. SIL Electronic Working Papers 2006-005. https://www.sil.org/resources/publications/entry/7882.

Spear, Thomas. 1978. *The Kaya complex: A history of the Mijikenda peoples of the Kenya coast to 1900*. Nairobi: Kenya Literature Bureau.

Spear, Thomas. 1981. *Traditions of origin and their interpretation: The Mijikenda of Kenya*. Athens, OH: Ohio University Center for International Studies.

Talmy, Leonard. 1985. Lexicalization patterns: Semantic structure in lexical forms. In Shopen, 57–149.

Thornell, Christina. 1997. *The Sango language and its lexicon*. Traveaux de l'Institut de Linguistique de Lund 32. Lund, Sweden: Lund University Press.

Thwala, Nhlanhla. 2006. Parameters of variation and complement licensing in Bantu. *ZAS Papers in Linguistics* 43:209–232.

Torrend, J. 1891. *A comparative grammar of the South-African Bantu languages*. London: Kegan Paul, Trench, Trübner & Co.

Vallduví, Enric. 1993. *The informational component*. IRCS Report No. IRCS-93-98. Philadelphia: University of Pennsylvania Institute for Research in Cognitive Science.

Van Otterloo, Karen, and Roger Van Otterloo. 2008. *The Kifuliiru language*. Dallas: SIL International.

Van Valin, Robert D., Jr. 2005. *Exploring the syntax-semantics interface*. Cambridge: Cambridge University Press.

Volk, Erez. 2007. High, low and in between: Giryama tonology. MA thesis. Tel Aviv University.

Volk, Erez. 2008. Tone in Mijikenda. Paper presented at Colloquium on African Languages and Linguistics 38, Leiden, 25–27 August 2008.

Volk, Erez. 2011. Mijikenda tonology. PhD dissertation. Tel Aviv University.

Wald, Benji. 1976. Comparative notes on past tenses in Kenyan Northeast Bantu languages. *Studies in African Linguistics*, Supplement 6, 267–281.

Walsh, Martin T. 1986. The northern (Likoni-Diani) dialect of Digo: A revision of Hinnebusch's word list. Ms. Fort Jesus Museum Library, Mombasa.

Walsh, Martin. T. 1990. The Degere: Forgotten hunter-gatherers of the East African coast. *Cambridge Anthropology* 14:68–81.

Walsh, Martin T. 1992. Mijikenda origins: A review of the evidence. *Transafrican Journal of History* 21:1–18.

Walsh, Martin T. 1992/1993. The Vuna and the Degere: Remnants and outcasts among the Duruma and Digo of Kenya and Tanzania. *Bulletin of the International Committee on Urgent Anthropological and Ethnological Research* 34/35:133–147.

Walsh, Martin T. 2006. A click in Digo and its historical interpretation. *Azania* 41:158–166.

Walsh, Martin T. 2014. The Segeju complex? Linguistic evidence for the precolonial making of the Mijikenda. In Rebecca Gearhart and Linda L. Giles (eds.), *The role of the Mijikenda and their neighbors in re-centering Kenya coastal history and society*, 25–51. Trenton, NJ: Africa World Press.

Whiteley, W. H. 1968. *Some problems of transitivity in Swahili.* London: School of Oriental and African Studies.

Whiteley, W. H., and J. D. Mganga. 1969. Focus and entailment: Further problems of transitivity in Swahili. *African Language Review* 8:108–125.

Willis, Justin. 1993. *Mombasa, Swahili, and the making of the Mijikenda.* Oxford: Clarendon Press.

Yourgrau, Palle, ed. 1990. *Demonstratives.* Oxford: Oxford University Press.

Zimmermann, Wolfgang, and Paaro Hasheela. 1998. *Oshikwanyama grammar.* Windhoek: Gamsberg Macmillan.

Author Index

Amidu, Assibi A. 89, 106n, 117, 118, 184, 224n
Andrews, Avery 232

Bastin, Y. 152n
Bearth, Thomas 96n, 194
Beidelman, T. O. 5
Bentley, Mayrene 49n
Bergman, Jeanne L. 4
Besha, Ruth Mfumbwa 87, 89
Botne, Robert 168
Bourdin, Philippe 164n
Bresnan, Joan 193
Bybee, Joan 171

Cammenga, Jelle 49n, 50, 55, 157
Clark, Mary 411
Cole, Desmond T. 56
Comrie, Bernard 154n, 245, 252
Costello, John R. 183n
Croft, William 5, 6
Crystal, David 14n

Dammann, Ernst 2
Dancygier, Barbara 160n
Daniel, Michael 19n
De Groot, Martien 2, 142, 147, 162
Demuth, Katherine 276
Devos, Maud 57n
Dimmendaal, Gerrit J. 164n
Dixon, R. M. W. 124
Doke, Clement M. 56, 57n, 217
Downing, Laura J. 411
Dryer, Matthew S. 5, 225, 228

Elderkin, Edward D. 184
Erteschik-Shir, Nomi 232

Fauconnier, Gilles 160n
Fleisch, Axel 1n, 16, 40n, 47, 55, 57n, 119n, 180n, 195, 286n
Floor, Sebastian 145n, 159n
Foley, William A. 171, 227

Garashi, Maliki 346
Gerlach, L. P. 5
Gillette, Cynthia 5
Givón, Talmy 57n
Gundel, Jeanette. K. 232
Guthrie, Malcolm 1, 27n, 142, 411
Güldemann, Tom 57, 115n, 156, 184

Harjula, Lotta 57n
Hasheela, Paaro 56
Heimerdinger, Jean-Marie 237n
Heine, Bernd 153, 164 180
Hewson, John 134, 152, 156n, 181
Hinnebusch, Thomas J. 1, 2, 3, 166n, 408
Hollis, A. C. 5
Hopper, Paul J. 149, 179n
Hyman, Larry M. 101n, 411n

Johnson-Laird, P. 164n, 188n

Kanerva, Jonni M. 193
Keenan, Edward 245, 252
Kimenyi, Alexandre 194
Kipacha, Ahmadi 135n, 166n
Kisseberth, Charles W. 15, 16
Kozinskij, Isaak Š. 154n
Kulemeka, Andrew 49n
Kuteva, Tania 153

Ladusaw, William A. 14n
Lambert, H. E. 2
Lambrecht, Knud 231, 238, 240, 295
Levinsohn, Stephen H. 202, 206, 208, 210, 212, 237n
Lewis, M. Paul 1n
Lichtenberk, F. 177
Longacre, Robert E. 136

Maganga, C. 166n
Maho, Jouni 1
Maneno, Rodgers 6, 313, 327
Marten, Lutz 5, 99n, 274, 276
Mchombo, Sam 110n, 225
Meeussen, Achilles Emile 101n, 164n
Mganga, J. D. 106n, 224n
Michaelis, Laura A. 238
Miller, G. A. 164n, 188n
Mmusi, S. 276
Möhlig, Wilhelm J. G. 2
Moravcsik, Edith 19n
Morimoto, Yukiko 91
Mous, Maarten 89, 152n, 156n
Muzale, Henry 134
Mwalonya, Joseph 3n, 6, 41n, 313, 353, 408
Mwayani, Juma 313

Nedjalkov, Vladimir P. 130n
Nicolle, Alison 57n, 81n
Nicolle, Steve 5, 57n, 68n, 73, 165, 180, 189n, 197, 402
Nurse, Derek 1, 2, 3, 4n, 89, 134, 166n, 177n, 178, 180

Paluku, André Mbula 48
Philippson, Gérard 1n, 177n
Prince, Ellen 232
Pullum, Geoffrey K. 14n

Riedel, Kristina 81, 135n
Roberts, James S. 353n
Rose, Sarah 129, 130, 143, 159, 164, 166n
Rugemalira, Josephat M. 152n

Sacleux, Ch. 301
Sasse, Hans-Jürgen 240
Schadeberg, Thilo C. 27n, 115, 152n, 184, 193, 301

Schultze-Berndt, Eva 124, 126, 127
Sirya, S. T. 177, 178
Snider, Keith L. 353n
Spear, Thomas 2, 5
Sweetser, Eve 160n

Talmy, Leonard 188n
Thornell, Christina 188n
Thwala, Nhlanhla 95, 106n, 224n
Torrend, J. 57n

Vallduví, E. 231, 234n
Van Otterloo, Karen 156

Van Otterloo, Roger 156
Van Valin, Robert D., Jr. 130n, 171, 227
Volk, Erez 15, 16, 133n

Wald, Benji 177
Walsh, Martin T. 2, 3, 4
Whiteley, W. H. 106n, 224n
Willis, Justin 4

Yourgrau, Palle 56

Zimmermann, Wolfgang 56

Language Index

Arabic 41, 113

Bantu 1, 5, 6, 15, 18, 21, 23, 57, 87, 91, 95, 115, 177, 189, 193, 274, 275, 299, 306
Bemba 96n

Chaga 96n, 275, 276
Chewa 96n, 110n, 165n, 193, 275, 276, 277
Chichewa. *See* Chewa
Chinondo 2
Chonyi 1, 2, 177
Cokwe 16

Daiso 4n, 89
Degere 3
Duruma 1, 2, 3, 5, 39, 90, 142, 153n, 176, 177

Fuliiru 156n

Ganda 195
Gĩkũyũ 81, 123
Giryama 1, 2, 12, 39, 133n, 153n, 177, 178
Greek 212

Haya 96n, 134, 195
Herero 96n, 275, 276, 277

Igikuria. *See* Kuria
Ila 195

Jibana 1, 2

Kambe 1, 2
Kauma 1, 2

Kikuyu. *See* Gĩkũyũ
Kitalinga 48
Kuria 50, 157

Lega 166n
Lozi 96n
Luba 195
Lucazi 1n, 16, 40n, 119n, 179n, 286n

Ma'a. *See* Mbugu
Makhuwa 81, 165n
Makunduchi. *See* Swahili
Mayan 183n
Mbugu 152n, 156
Mbugwe 89, 152n
Mijikenda 1–5, 15, 123, 135n, 152n, 177, 408
Mwani 145n, 159n

Nguni languages 5, 80
Nungwi. *See* Swahili
Nyakyusa 193

Pare 5, 80
Pokomo 4, 178
Proto-Bantu 101, 114, 151, 156, 180
Pungu 3

Rabai 1, 2
Rangi 5, 80
Ribe 1, 2
Ruhaya. *See* Haya
Runyambo 96n, 152n
Russian 179n
Rwanda 96n, 194

Sabaki 1, 123, 145n, 159n
Segeju 1, 3, 4, 5

Setswana. *See* Tswana
Shambala 5, 80, 89
Shona 123, 156, 195, 275, 276, 277
Shungwaya 4, 5
Sotho 195, 275, 277
Swahili 1n, 2, 3, 4, 5, 7, 12, 16, 20, 21, 29, 33n, 39, 41, 48, 57, 78, 81, 89, 96n, 104, 105, 112, 113, 119n, 123, 124, 140, 152n, 156, 157n, 165n, 178, 184, 195, 197, 287, 296, 299n, 341, 407–411
Swahili, Makunduchi dialect 166n
Swahili, Nungwi dialect 135n
Swahili, Vumba dialect 166n
Swati 96n

Tembo 166n
Thagicu (Thagicũ) 3, 4n
Tiwi 3
Tonga 195
Tiwi 3
Ts'imba (Tsimba) 2, 3
Tswana 96n, 195, 275, 277
Tsw'aka (Chwaka, Chw'aka, Tswaka) 2, 3

Ungu (Lungu) 2

Venda 195
Vumba. *See* Swahili

Waata 3

Xhosa 96n, 110n, 166n, 195

Yanzi 166n

Zulu 166n, 195

Subject Index

accompaniment 186, 230, 233, 254, 256
additive. *See under* relational expression
address, forms of 33, 114, 161n, 282
adjectival predicate 282, 292, 295–296
adjective 21, 25, 26, 34, 35, 40, 56, 103, 104, 124, 126n, 214, 286
  lexical 29–30, 40–44, 46, 50
  phrasal 29–30, 40–44, 46–47, 50, 189
adjectives 408
adverb 28, 36, 42, 43, 204, 206, 213–217, 219, 305
adverbial 28, 73–75, 78–79, 130–131, 141–142, 148, 152, 183–184, 196–197, 200, 204, 251
agent 24, 28, 52, 91, 102–103, 106, 108, 115, 158, 170, 184, 186, 195–196, 209–213, 228, 277
agreement 17, 19–23, 39, 43, 109, 214–215, 224, 245–246
  role-based 91
  salience-based 91
allative. *See* movement: itive
andative. *See* movement: itive
animacy 19–20, 26, 48, 96–97, 195, 274

anterior. *See under* aspect
applicative 101, 106–108, 110–111, 184
aspect
  anterior 93, 131, 141, 142, 146–149, 150, 151, 155, 159, 164, 172–175, 177, 179–180, 236, 250, 270
  completive 131, 141–142, 152, 153, 305
  continuous 90, 92, 121, 131, 134, 138, 141–142, 163, 171–175, 246, 263
  emphatic 46, 94, 127n, 130n, 131, 157, 169
  general negative 93, 131, 143, 144, 160
  generic 93, 131, 141, 143
  habitual 93, 131, 137, 141–143, 172, 178, 250
  imperfective 93, 131, 141, 145, 172
  inceptive 92, 131, 142, 154, 156, 288
  negative perfective 100, 114, 123, 131, 141, 151, 157, 163, 251n
  perfective 111, 129, 151, 157
  persistive 93, 131, 141, 156, 164, 288, 296, 308
  relative anterior 93, 131, 138, 141, 144–146, 248

resultative 114, 121, 131, 141, 149–151, 157, 175
simultaneous 78, 93, 131, 141, 150
associative 19n, 28
-a 12, 16, 20, 22, 30–31, 34, 37, 40, 45, 54, 184, 188–189, 204, 215, 304
-enye 45, 47, 194
augmentative 20, 21, 25, 26, 305
auxiliary. *See under* verb

beneficiary 97, 106–107, 184, 254

causative 29, 101–105, 110–111, 114, 124
cause-consequence 262
class. *See* noun class
classifier 30, 31, 56
clause
  chaining 200, 223, 261–265
  complement 113, 223, 225, 236, 253, 261, 265–270
  core 224, 227, 230, 233, 235, 256
  dependent 92, 159–160, 163, 202, 223, 236, 261
  ditransitive 228
  intransitive 106n, 224–226
  matrix 113, 138, 140, 246, 266–271
  nucleus 171, 214
  relative 45, 85, 92–93, 95, 98, 107, 116–117, 119n, 129, 131, 132, 137, 138, 140–141, 144–145, 155, 156, 157, 174–175, 178, 229, 239, 245, 247–248, 250–253, 255–258, 260, 267–289, 290–292, 297, 300, 308
  transitive 102, 106–107, 126, 143, 225–228, 275 277–278
cleft construction 239, 245, 258–259
clitic 10, 53, 55, 88–89, 114–117, 118–120, 185–186, 196–197, 207, 231, 282, 286, 297, 306
colour 44, 217, 220, 397
comitative. *See under* relational expression

comparison 233, 252n, 285, 302–303
complement clause. *See under* clause
complementizer 162, 225, 245, 266–268
complex tense. *See under* tense
compounding 28–29
concord. *See* agreement
conditional 92, 93, 129–131, 158, 161–163, 171, 174, 178, 242, 287, 289, 291
conjoined NPs 23, 81
conjunction. *See* relational expression
consecutive. *See under* tense
constituent order 224–240, 258, 260
continuous (*see* aspect, continuous)
copula 48, 54, 116–117, 119, 139, 145, 155, 156, 162, 164, 172, 176, 195, 198, 200, 229, 230, 238, 259, 260, 270, 273, 281–300, 306–307
  invariable 281–283, 292–293, 295, 297
  negative 48, 155, 176, 308
  referential marker 117, 283–285, 292–293, 295, 297, 300
  relative 118, 156, 251, 308
  subject concord 286–289

degree 215–216, 219, 302, 305
demonstrative 5, 14, 27, 30–31, 47–48, 55–85, 118, 185–186, 190, 193–194, 226, 234, 235, 255, 265, 296, 297, 401, 409
  distal 57–58, 61, 63, 70, 72, 75
  metarepresentational 58, 61, 67, 72–74, 78, 80, 409
  nonproximal 57–58, 61, 65, 70–71, 73, 76, 193, 409
  order of 5, 31, 56, 80–85
  proximal 57–58, 61, 69, 73, 75
denominalization 29
dependent clause. *See under* clause
dependent marker. *See under* status marker
descriptive predicate 294–295

diachrony. *See* grammaticalization
dialect 2, 3, 16, 78, 93, 122, 150, 408
diminutive 20, 25–26
discourse marker. *See under* relational expression
distal. *See under* movement
dual 91, 115

emphasis 49, 53, 55n, 66, 67, 72, 73, 78, 82, 88–89, 120, 153, 160, 194, 213, 216, 218, 236–237, 241, 242, 258, 264, 285, 293, 296, 298–299, 336. *See also under* aspect
emphatic. *See under* aspect
evidential 129
existential predicate 176, 273, 292 298–300

final vowel 16, 24, 28, 29, 59, 88, 99, 100, 102, 111–113, 144, 161
focus 223, 229, 230, 275–276, 299
  argument 238
  marker 142, 176, 198, 231, 241–242, 286
  predicate 235, 237, 243–244, 292, 294, 304. *See also* identificational articulation
  sentence 231–232, 234–236, 239–243, 259
fronting. *See* left-dislocation; topicalization
future. *See under* tense

gender. *See* noun class
generic. *See under* aspect
goal 97, 106, 189, 254
grammaticalization 91, 94, 179, 276

habitual. *See under* aspect
hodiernal past. *See under* tense
hortatory text 208, 211, 338

identificational articulation 232, 238, 259, 290, 295
ideophone 44, 126, 213, 217–118, 220, 305
imperative 87, 91, 111, 115, 121, 160, 162, 168–170, 176, 228, 262
imperfective. *See under* aspect
inceptive. *See under* aspect
infinitive 18, 21, 24, 40, 45–46, 91, 94, 111, 121, 137, 138, 150, 155, 157, 169–170, 177, 178, 179, 189, 261–270
instrument 24, 87, 95–96, 106–109, 183, 187, 195, 204, 230, 233, 254, 255
interrogative. *See* question
itive. *See under* movement

juxtaposition 238, 282, 293

kinship term 19, 31–33

labialization 12
language change. *See* grammaticalization
left-dislocation 84, 220, 227, 233, 235, 241
location 21, 60, 61–68, 72–73, 87, 95, 97, 106–108, 116–117, 130, 164, 166–170, 183–185, 187–189, 191–194, 230, 233, 253, 254–255, 271, 273, 275–276, 286–299. *See also* spatial deixis
locative 21, 27, 46, 60–68, 80, 85, 91n, 96–97, 99, 107, 109, 110n, 118, 184, 185–186, 189–191, 193–194, 212, 224–225, 254, 292, 296–300, 302
locative inversion 223, 225, 239, 271–274

manner 28, 56–57, 61, 116, 119, 217, 230, 233, 254, 255
manner deixis 57, 74–79, 255

matrilineality 5
modality 129–130, 197
mood 129–130, 261
morphophonological process 17–18, 23
movement 87–88, 92, 129–130, 132, 137, 164–166, 168–171, 175, 184, 271, 358, 393
  distal 92, 132, 164–166, 172
  future + itive 132, 166, 271
  itive 94, 123, 129, 132, 155, 157, 164–165, 168–169, 176
  itive + subjunctive 93, 113, 132, 168, 176
  ventive 94, 129, 132, 151, 155, 157, 164–165, 170

narrative text 57, 60–61, 65, 69–73, 79–82, 142, 166, 169, 180n, 187, 208, 212, 235, 243, 273, 299, 309, 313, 327
negation 87, 88–89, 92–94, 107, 112, 114, 118, 121–123, 129, 130, 131n, 133, 136, 138–139, 141, 143, 144, 150, 154–155, 158, 160–163, 174, 176–180, 217, 246, 248, 259, 269, 283, 285–288, 290–292, 295–297, 299, 300, 306–307, 309. *See also* aspect: general negative; aspect: negative perfective; tense: negative past
neuter. *See* stative
New Testament 6, 165, 172, 177
nominalization 23–28
noun class 12, 17–28, 30, 31, 36, 39–40, 42–43, 48, 53, 55–61, 67, 71, 73–74, 80–81, 84–85, 88, 90, 91n, 93, 96, 97. 99, 107, 116, 118, 140, 142, 143, 144, 191, 193–194, 207, 233, 225, 239, 245–247, 254, 255, 257, 271, 273, 275, 276, 281, 284–285, 297–298, 300, 305, 408, 410
numeral 21, 29–30, 34, 36, 39–41, 50

object 16, 21, 47, 49, 87, 95, 96–99, 102, 106, 109, 116, 124, 209, 224–228, 233, 235, 237, 247, 253, 258, 277, 306
object marker. *See* verb complement concord
oblique 47, 49, 109, 170, 185–187, 195, 214, 225, 230, 233, 253–254
onomatopoeic 213, 217, 220

participant 57, 208–211
  introduction of 70, 79, 236, 251, 273, 276, 299
  major 69–71, 74, 82, 187, 235, 251, 273, 276, 299
  minor 70–71, 79
  reference 49, 73, 79
passive 87, 93, 96, 100, 101, 107, 109–111, 123, 143, 158, 170, 184, 195, 275, 277
past. *See under* tense
patient 24, 28, 97, 102, 109, 211, 228, 253, 277
perfect. *See* aspect: anterior
perfective. *See under* aspect
persistive. *See under* aspect
polar question. *See* question: polar
possession 20, 22, 29–35, 40, 47, 52, 54, 56, 67, 85, 116, 156, 188, 190, 191, 194, 228, 252, 257, 281–282, 293, 294, 309
postfinal 91, 95, 96, 114–116, 119–120, 249
postposing. *See* right-dislocation
potential. *See under* status marker
preposition 6, 104, 183–185. *See also* relational expression
prepositional. *See* applicative
present. *See* aspect: continuous
presentational articulation 232, 239, 273
procedural text 83, 263
pronoun 47–56
  exclusive 49–52
  independent 47–51, 57, 89, 185–186, 194, 207, 241, 293

Subject Index 435

interrogative 19, 40n, 47, 53, 55
metarepresentational 48, 80, 241, 293
resumptive 227, 257
vocative 53
purpose 79, 108, 113, 265

qualificative 17, 27, 29–47, 56, 213–214, 217
quantifier 22, 25, 29–31, 34–38, 40–43, 45, 47, 50, 54, 399
question 20, 53, 67, 155, 245, 258
 content (wh-) (informational) 55, 56, 72, 74, 115, 119, 198, 213, 238, 260, 296, 298, 299n, 401
 polar 229

reason 108, 230
recipient 106–107, 228, 253
reciprocal 101, 108–110, 186
reduplication 35, 42, 53, 59, 100, 106, 213, 215–220, 305
referential marker 10, 37, 48, 59n, 116, 118, 185–186, 200, 207, 239, 256, 259–260, 283–285, 292–293, 295, 297, 300, 306
referential predicate 49, 293
reflexive 49n, 96–97, 101
relational expression 50, 62–63, 104, 183–195, 213–215, 286
 additive 48, 117, 185, 202, 206–212
 comitative 10, 48, 89, 109, 117, 184–185, 191–192, 195, 204, 207, 212, 256, 262, 273, 298–299, 303, 306–307, 308
 discourse marker 196–200
 logical 200
relative. See clause, relative
 marker 22, 30–31, 34–35, 59n, 75, 77, 95, 114–119, 132, 141, 246, 247, 252, 260, 284, 291,297
relative tense. See under tense
reversive 101

right-dislocation 220, 224–225, 227, 232, 235, 237, 240–241, 244n
Role and Reference Grammar 130n, 171

sentence adverbial 131, 141, 152, 196, 200, 214
sequential 92, 94, 131, 136–138, 147, 164, 176–180, 252, 261–262
simultaneous. See under aspect
spatial deixis 56–57, 61, 79. See also location
spirantization 24, 101
static 101
stative (also called neuter) 101–102, 110, 145n, 148, 206, 277
status marker 92, 158, 171
 complex 162
 conditional 130–131, 162
 dependent 130–131, 159–160
 potential 130–131, 158, 177–178
subject 21, 47, 87, 91, 96–97, 102, 106, 108, 109, 113, 136–137, 138, 195, 209, 211, 224, 246–249, 253, 255–256, 260, 266–268, 270, 274, 376–277, 281, 283, 285, 293–294, 297–298
subject concord 16, 34, 49, 53, 55, 88, 90–91, 93, 119, 132, 133n, 139, 140–141, 144, 171, 189, 224–226, 228, 232, 234, 139, 246, 271, 286, 291, 294–298, 300, 306, 308
subjunctive 88–91, 93, 111–113, 115, 121, 132, 158, 160–162, 168–170, 178, 261, 265–266, 268–269, 271
subordinate clause. See clause: dependent
syllabic nasal 12, 99, 143
tail-head linkage 72
tense 87–88, 92, 93, 95, 112, 116–118, 121, 129–132, 133–141, 166, 171, 178, 274, 281–283, 285, 287, 290, 297, 300, 307

complex 135, 142, 174, 309
consecutive 136, 252, 262
future 121, 123, 135, 173
hodiernal past 121, 133, 175–177, 179–180, 283
negative past 112, 133, 248
present 121–122, 134, 178
relative future 140, 246, 291
relative past 107n, 139, 246, 248, 252, 291, 309
remote past 90, 93, 133
sequential 137–138, 147, 173, 177–179, 262
thetic sentence 239–240
time deixis 67, 74–75, 79
tone 15–16, 91, 93, 133, 142, 145n, 177n, 217, 411
topic 84, 91, 96, 223–228, 231–237, 239, 241–242, 275, 293, 299
topic-comment articulation 232, 235, 237, 240, 243, 258, 260
topicalization 97, 99, 117n, 118n, 228

ventive. *See under* movement
verb 17, 21, 24–25, 29, 45, 87–127, 129–181, 195, 225–228, 261–265, 271, 275, 277, 281, 290
    auxiliary 93, 123, 129, 131, 141, 151, 157, 171, 173–174, 249, 283, 287, 289, 295, 298, 300, 307, 309
    borrowed 104, 112–113, 408
    defective 121–122, 199
    irregular 112, 121, 123, 251n
    light 124–127
    monosyllabic 90–91, 99, 105, 106
    root 24, 87–88, 96, 99–100, 103, 104–105, 111, 121, 123, 155, 156–157, 161, 217, 251n
    stem 15–16, 24, 88, 93, 100, 102, 106, 111, 114, 121, 132, 217, 246
verb complement concord 49, 95, 102, 132, 186, 230, 235, 246, 247, 250, 267, 275, 304
vocative. *See* address, forms of
vowel height harmony 100, 102–103, 106, 114, 156

wh-question. *See* pronoun: interrogative; question, content (wh-) (informational)
word order, basic. *See* constituent order

SIL International® Publications
Publications in Linguistics Series
ISSN 1040-0850

153. **The geometry and features of tone**, second edition, by Keith L. Snider, 2020, 198 pp., ISBN 978-1-55671-414-6.
152. **Kankanaey: A role and reference grammar analysis**, by Janet L. Allen, 2014, 402 pp., ISBN 978-1-55671-296-8.
151. **Understanding biblical Hebrew verb forms: Distribution and function across genres**, by Robert E. Longacre and Andrew C. Bowling, 2015, 642 pp., ISBN 978-1-55671-278-4.
150. **Sudanese Arabic – English, English – Sudanese Arabic: A concise dictionary**, by Rianne Tamis and Janet L. Persson, 2013, 415 pp., ISBN: 978-1-55671-272-2.
149. **A grammar of Digo: A Bantu language of Kenya and Tanzania**, by Steve Nicolle. 2013, 462 pp., ISBN: 978-1-55671-281-4.
148. **A grammar of Bora with special attention to tone**, by Wesley Thiesin and David Weber. 2012, 555 pp., ISBN 978-1-55671-301-9.
147. **The Kifuliiru language, Volume 2: A descriptive grammar**, by Roger Van Otterloo, 2011, 612 pp., ISBN 978-1-55671-270-8.
146. **The Kifuliiru language, Volume 1: Phonology, tone, and morphological derivation**, by Karen Van Otterloo, 2011, 512 pp., ISBN 978-1-55671-261-6.
145. **Language death in Mesmes**, by Michael B. Ahland, 2010, 155 pp., ISBN 978-1-55671-227-2.
144. **The phonology of two central Chadic languages**, by Tony Smith and Richard Gravina, 2010, 267 pp., ISBN 978-155671-231-9.

SIL International® Publications
7500 W. Camp Wisdom Road
Dallas, TX 75236-5629 USA

General inquiry: publications_intl@sil.org
Pending order inquiry: sales@sil.org
publications.sil.org

Steve Nicolle earned a DPhil in Linguistics from the University of York in 1996 and has been involved in linguistic research and translation with SIL since 1999, working as translation advisor with the Digo Language and Literacy Project in Kenya (1999–2007), linguistics coordinator for SIL Africa Area (2008–2011), and head of the Department of Linguistics and Translation at Africa International University in Nairobi (2012–2013). Throughout this time he worked with various translation teams in Africa as a linguistics consultant and translation consultant. He is currently an SIL International senior linguistics consultant and director of the MA in Linguistics and Translation at the Canada Institute of Linguistics, Trinity Western University, in British Columbia. Bantu languages and discourse analysis are his primary areas of research and writing.

Academic website
sil.org/biography/steve-nicolle

Works by this author in SIL Language & Culture Archives
sil.org/resources/search/contributor/nicolle-steve

Works by this author in Google Scholar
scholar.google.com/citations?hl=en&user=TLB7J7EAAAAJ

www.ingramcontent.com/pod-product-compliance
Lightning Source LLC
Chambersburg PA
CBHW050524300426
44113CB00012B/1953